国家出版基金项目
NATIONAL PUBLICATION FOUNDATION

# 大中华文库

# LIBRARY
# OF CHINESE CLASSICS

大中华文库

汉英对照

# Library of Chinese Classics
## Chinese-English

# 晏子春秋

# THE SPRING AND AUTUMN ANNALS OF MASTER YAN (Ⅰ)

［以色列］欧永福　导言、注释、翻译

张　飘　刘　喆　今译

INTRODUCED, COMMENTED AND TRANSLATED BY Yoav Ariel

MODERN CHINESE TEXT BY Zhang Piao and Liu Zhe

中国人民大学出版社

China Renmin University Press

本书古文选自《晏子春秋逐字索引》，由商务印书馆（香港）有限公司
授权使用

ISBN 978-7-300-26113-3
© China Renmin University Press, 2018


Publisher:
China Renmin University Press
31 Zhongguancun Street, 100080 Beijing, China
Homepage: www.crup.com.cn


Printed in the People's Republic of China

# 总　序

杨牧之

　　《大中华文库》终于出版了。我们为之高兴，为之鼓舞，但也倍感压力。

　　当此之际，我们愿将郁积在我们心底的话，向读者倾诉。

一

　　中华民族有着悠久的历史和灿烂的文化，系统、准确地将中华民族的文化经典翻译成外文，编辑出版，介绍给全世界，是几代中国人的愿望。早在几十年前，西方一位学者翻译《红楼梦》，将书名译成《一个红楼上的梦》，将林黛玉译为"黑色的玉"。我们一方面对外国学者将中国的名著介绍到世界上去表示由衷的感谢，一方面为祖国的名著还不被完全认识，甚而受到曲解，而感到深深的遗憾。还有西方学者翻译《金瓶梅》，专门摘选其中自然主义描述最为突出的篇章加以译介。一时间，西方学者好像发现了奇迹，掀起了《金瓶梅》热，说中国是"性开放的源头"，公开地在报刊上鼓吹中国要"发扬开放之传统"。还有许多资深、友善的汉学家译介中国古代的哲学著作，在把中华民族文化介绍给全世界的工作方面作出了重大贡献，但或囿于理解有误，或缘于对中国文字认识的局限，质量上乘的并不多，常常是隔靴搔痒，说不到点子上。大哲学家黑格尔曾经说过：中国有最完备的国史。但他认为中国古代没有真正意义上的哲学，还处在哲学史前状态。这么了不起的哲学家竟然作出这样大失水准的评论，何其不幸。正如任何哲学家都要受时间、地点、条件的制约一样，黑格尔也离不开这一规律。当时他也只能从上述水平的汉学家译过去的文字去分析、理解，所以，黑格尔先生对中国古代社会的认识水平是什么状态，也就不难想象了。

中国离不开世界，世界也缺少不了中国。中国文化摄取外域的新成分，丰富了自己，又以自己的新成就输送给别人，贡献于世界。从公元 5 世纪开始到公元 15 世纪，大约有一千年，中国走在世界的前列。在这一千多年的时间里，她的光辉照耀全世界。人类要前进，怎么能不全面认识中国，怎么能不认真研究中国的历史呢？

## 二

中华民族是伟大的，曾经辉煌过，蓝天、白云、阳光灿烂，和平而兴旺；也有过黑暗的、想起来就让人战栗的日子，但中华民族从来是充满理想，不断追求，不断学习，渴望和平与友谊的。

中国古代伟大的思想家孔子曾经说过："三人行，必有我师焉。择其善者而从之，其不善者而改之。"孔子的话就是要人们向别人学习。这段话正是概括了整个中华民族与人交往的原则。人与人之间交往如此，在与周边的国家交往中也是如此。

秦始皇第一个统一了中国，可惜在位只有十几年，来不及做更多的事情。汉朝继秦而继续强大，便开始走出去，了解自己周边的世界。公元前138年，汉武帝派张骞出使西域。他带着一万头牛羊，总值一万万钱的金帛货物，作为礼物，开始西行，最远到过"安息"（即波斯）。公元73年，班超又率36人出使西域。36个人按今天的话说，也只有一个排，显然是为了拜访未曾见过面的邻居，是去交朋友。到了西域，班超派遣甘英作为使者继续西行，往更远处的大秦国（即罗马）去访问，"乃抵条支而历安息，临西海以望大秦"（《后汉书·西域传》）。"条支"在"安息"以西，即今天的伊拉克、叙利亚一带，"西海"应是今天的地中海。也就是说甘英已经到达地中海边上，与罗马帝国隔海相望，"临大海欲渡"，却被人劝阻而未成行，这在历史上留下了遗恨。可以想见班超、甘英沟通友谊的无比勇气和强烈愿望。接下来是唐代的玄奘，历经千难万险，到"西天"印度取经，带回了南亚国家的古老文化。归国后，他把带回的佛教经典组织人翻译，到后来很多经典印度失传了，但中国却保存完好，以至于今天，没有玄奘的《大唐西域记》，印度人很难编写印度古代史。明代郑和"七下西洋"，把中华文化传到东南亚一带。鸦片战争以后，一代又一代先进的中国人，为了振兴中华，又前赴后继，向西方国家学习先进的科学思想和文明成果。这中间有我们的领导人朱德、周恩来、邓小平；有许许多多大科学家、文学家、艺术家，如郭沫若、李四光、钱学森、冼星海、徐悲鸿等。他们的追求、奋斗，他们的博大胸怀、兼收并蓄的精神，为人类社会增添了光彩。

中国文化的形成和发展过程，就是一个以众为师、以各国人民为师，不断学习和创造的过程。中华民族曾经向周边国家和民族学习过许多东西，假如没有这些学习，中华民族绝不可能创造出昔日的辉煌。回顾历史，我们怎么能够不对伟大的古埃及文明、古希腊文明、古印度文明满怀深深的感激？怎么能够不对伟大的欧洲文明、非洲文明、美洲文明、澳洲文明，以及中国周围的亚洲文明充满温情与敬意？

中华民族为人类社会曾作出过独特的贡献。在 15 世纪以前，中国的科学技术一直处于世界遥遥领先的地位。英国科学家李约瑟说："中国在公元 3 世纪到 13 世纪之间，保持着一个西方所望尘莫及的科学知识水平。"美国耶鲁大学教授、《大国的兴衰》的作者保罗·肯尼迪坦言："在近代以前时期的所有文明中，没有一个国家的文明比中国更发达，更先进。"

世界各国的有识之士千里迢迢来中国观光、学习。在这个过程中，中国唐朝的长安城渐渐发展成为国际大都市。西方的波斯、东罗马，东亚的高丽、新罗、百济，南亚的南天竺、北天竺，频繁前来。外国的王侯、留学生及在长安供职的外国官员、商贾、乐工和舞士，总有几十个国家，几万人之多。日本派出"遣唐使"更是一批接一批。传为美谈的日本人阿倍仲麻吕（晁衡）在长安留学的故事，很能说明外国人与中国的交往。晁衡学成仕于唐朝，前后历时五十余年。晁衡与中国的知识分子结下了深厚的友情。他归国时，传说在海中遇难身亡。大诗人李白作诗哭悼："日本晁卿辞帝都，征帆一片远蓬壶。明月不归沉碧海，白云愁色满苍梧。"晁衡遇险是误传，但由此可见中外学者之间在中国长安交往的情谊。

后来，不断有外国人到中国来探寻秘密，所见所闻，常常让他们目瞪口呆。《希腊纪事》（希腊人波桑尼阿著）记载公元 2 世纪时，希腊人在中国的见闻。书中写道："赛里斯人用小米和青芦喂一种类似蜘蛛的昆虫，喂到第五年，虫肚子胀裂开，便从里面取出丝来。"从这段对中国古代养蚕技术的描述，可见当时欧洲人与中国人的差距。公元9世纪中叶，阿拉伯人来到中国。一位阿拉伯作家在他所著的《中国印度闻见录》中记载了曾旅居中国的阿拉伯商人的见闻：

——一天，一个外商去拜见驻守广州的中国官吏。会见时，外商总盯着官吏的胸部，官吏很奇怪，便问："你好像总盯着我的胸，这是怎么回事？"那位外商回答说："透过你穿的丝绸衣服，我隐约看到你胸口上长着一个黑痣，这是什么丝绸，我感到十分惊奇。"官吏听后，失声大笑，伸出胳膊，说："请你数数吧，看我穿了几件衣服？"那商人数过，竟然穿了五件之多，黑痣正是透过这五层丝绸衣服显现出来的。外商惊得目瞪口呆，官吏说："我穿的丝绸还不算是最好的，总督穿的要更精美。"

——书中关于茶（他们叫干草叶子）的记载，可见阿拉伯国家当时还没有喝茶的习惯。书中记述："中国国王本人的收入主要靠盐税和泡开水喝的一种干草税。在各个城市里，这种干草叶售价都很高，中国人称这种草叶叫'茶'，这种干草叶比苜蓿的叶子还多，也略比它香，稍有苦味，用开水冲喝，治百病。"

——他们对中国的医疗条件十分羡慕，书中记载道："中国人医疗条件很好，穷人可以从国库中得到药费。"还说："城市里，很多地方立一石碑，高10肘，上面刻有各种疾病和药物，写明某种病用某种药医治。"

——关于当时中国的京城，书中作了生动的描述：中国的京城很大，人口众多，一条宽阔的长街把全城分为两半，大街右边的东区，住着皇帝、宰相、禁军及皇家的总管、奴婢。在这个区域，沿街开凿了小河，流水潺潺；路旁，葱茏的树木整然有序，一幢幢宅邸鳞次栉比。大街左边的西区，住着庶民和商人。这里有货栈和商店，每当清晨，人们可以看到，皇室的总管、宫廷的仆役，或骑马或步行，到这里来采购。

此后的史籍对西人来华的记载，渐渐多了起来。13世纪意大利旅行家马可·波罗，尽管有人对他是否真的到过中国持怀疑态度，但他留下一部记述元代事件的《马可·波罗游记》却是确凿无疑的。这部游记中的一些关于当时中国的描述使得西方人认为是"天方夜谭"。总之，从中西文化交流史来说，这以前的时期还是一个想象和臆测的时代，相互之间充满了好奇与幻想。

从16世纪末开始，由于航海技术的发展，东西方航路的开通，随着一批批传教士来华，中国与西方开始了直接的交流。沟通中西的使命在意大利传教士利玛窦那里有了充分的体现。利玛窦于1582年来华，1610年病逝于北京，在华二十余年。除了传教以外，做了两件具有历史象征意义的事，一是1594年前后在韶州用拉丁文翻译《四书》，并作了注释；二是与明代学者徐光启合作，用中文翻译了《几何原本》。

西方传教士对《四书》等中国经典的粗略翻译，以及杜赫德的《中华帝国志》等书对中国的介绍，在西方读者的眼前展现了一个异域文明，在当时及稍后一段时期引起了一场"中国热"，许多西方大思想家的眼光都曾注目于中国文化。有的推崇中华文明，如莱布尼兹、伏尔泰、魁奈等，有的对中华文明持批评态度，如孟德斯鸠、黑格尔等。莱布尼兹认识到中国文化的某些思想与他的观念相近，如周易的卦象与他发明的二进制相契合，对中国文化给予了热情的礼赞；黑格尔则从他整个哲学体系的推演出发，认为中国没有真正意义上的哲学，还处在哲学史前的状态。但是，不论是推崇还是批评，是吸纳还是排斥，中西文化的交流产生了巨大的影响。随着先进的中国科学技术的西传，特别是中国的造纸、火药、印刷术和指南针四大发明的问世，大大改变了世界的面貌。马克思说："中国的火药把骑士阶层炸得粉碎，指南针打开了世界市场并建立了殖民地，而印刷术则变成了新教的工具，变成对精神发展创造必要前提的最强大的杠杆。"英国的哲学家培根说：中国的四大发明"改变了全世界的面貌和一切事物的状态"。

三

大千世界，潮起潮落。云散云聚，万象更新。中国古代产生了无数伟大的科学家：祖冲之、李时珍、孙思邈、张衡、沈括、毕昇……产生了无数科技成果：《齐民要术》、《九章算术》、《伤寒杂病论》、《本草纲目》……以及保存至今的世界奇迹：浑天仪、地动仪、都江堰、敦煌石窟、大运河、万里长城……但从15世纪下半叶起，风水似乎从东方转到了西方，落后的欧洲只经过400年便成为世界瞩目的文明中心。英国的牛顿、波兰的哥白尼、德国的伦琴、法国的居里、德国的爱因斯坦、意大利的伽利略、俄国的门捷列夫、美国的费米和爱迪生……光芒四射，令人敬仰。

中华民族开始思考了。潮起潮落究竟是什么原因？中国人发明的火药，传到欧洲，转眼之间反成为欧洲列强轰击中国大门的炮弹，又是因为什么？

鸦片战争终于催醒了中国人沉睡的迷梦，最先"睁眼看世界"的一代精英林则徐、魏源迈出了威武雄壮的一步。曾国藩、李鸿章搞起了洋务运动。中国的知识分子喊出"民主与科学"的口号。中国是落后了，中国的志士仁人在苦苦探索。但落后中饱含着变革的动力，探索中孕育着崛起的希望。"向科学进军"，中华民族终于又迎来了科学的春天。

今天，世界毕竟来到了21世纪的门槛。分散隔绝的世界，逐渐变成联系为一体的世界。现在，全球一体化趋势日益明显，人类历史也就在愈来愈大的程度上成为全世界的历史。当今，任何一种文化的发展都离不开对其他优秀文化的汲取，都以其他优秀文化的发展为前提。在近现代，西方文化汲取中国文化，不仅是中国文化的传播，更是西方文化自身的创新和发展；正如中国文化对西方文化的汲取一样，既是西方文化在中国的传播，同时也是中国文化在近代的转型和发展。地球上所有的人类文化，都是我们共同的宝贵遗产。既然我们生活的各个大陆，在地球史上曾经是连成一气的"泛大陆"，或者说是一个完整的"地球村"，那么，我们同样可以在这个以知识和学习为特征的网络时代，走上相互学习、共同发展的大路，建设和开拓我们人类崭新的"地球村"。

西学仍在东渐，中学也将西传。各国人民的优秀文化正日益迅速地为中国文化所汲取，而无论西方和东方，也都需要从中国文化中汲取养分。正是基于这一认识，我们组织出版汉英对照版《大中华文库》，全面系统地翻译介绍中国传统文化典籍。我们试图通过《大中华文库》，向全世界展示，中华民族五千年的追求、五千年的梦想，正在新的历史时期重放光芒。中国人民就像火后的凤凰，万众一心，迎接新世纪文明的太阳。

1999年8月　北京

# FOREWORD TO THE
# *LIBRARY OF CHINESE CLASSICS*

## Yang Muzhi

The publication of the *Library of Chinese Classics* is a matter of great satisfaction to all of us who have been involved in the production of this monumental work. At the same time, we feel a weighty sense of responsibility, and take this opportunity to explain to our readers the motivation for undertaking this cross-century task.

## 1

The Chinese nation has a long history and a glorious culture, and it has been the aspiration of several generations of Chinese scholars to translate, edit and publish the whole corpus of the Chinese literary classics so that the nation's greatest cultural achievements can be introduced to people all over the world. There have been many translations of the Chinese classics done by foreign scholars. A few dozen years ago, a Western scholar translated the title of *A Dream of Red Mansions* into "A Dream of Red Chambers" and Lin Daiyu, the heroine in the novel, into "Black Jade." But while their endeavours have been laudable, the results of their labours have been less than satisfactory. Lack of knowledge of Chinese culture and an inadequate grasp of the Chinese written language have led the translators into many errors. As a consequence, not only are Chinese classical writings widely misunderstood in the rest of the world, in some cases their content has actually been distorted. At one time, there was a "*Jin Ping Mei* craze" among Western scholars, who thought that they had uncovered a miraculous phenomenon, and published theories claiming that China was the "fountainhead of eroticism," and that a Chinese "tradition of permissiveness" was about to be laid bare. This distorted view came about due to the translators of the *Jin Ping Mei (The Golden Lotus)* putting one-sided stress on the raw elements in that novel, to the neglect of its overall literary value. Meanwhile, there have been many distinguished and well-intentioned Sinologists who have attempted to make the culture of the Chinese nation more widely known by translating works of ancient Chinese philosophy. However, the quality of such work, in many cases, is unsatisfactory, often missing the point entirely. The great philosopher Hegel considered that ancient China had no philosophy in the real sense of the word, being stuck in philosophical "prehistory." For such an eminent authority to make such a colossal error of judgment is truly regrettable. But, of course, Hegel was just as subject to the constraints of time, space and other objective conditions as anyone else, and since he had to rely for his knowledge of Chinese philosophy on inadequate translations it is not difficult to imagine why he went so far off the mark.

China cannot be separated from the rest of the world; and the rest of the world cannot ignore China. Throughout its history, Chinese civilization has enriched itself by absorbing new elements from the outside world, and in turn has contributed to the progress of world civilization as a whole by transmitting to other peoples its own cultural achievements. From the 5th to the 15th centuries, China marched in the front ranks of world civilization. If mankind wishes to advance, how can it afford to ignore China? How can it afford not to make a thoroughgoing study of its history?

## 2

Despite the ups and downs in their fortunes, the Chinese people have always been idealistic, and have never ceased to forge ahead and learn from others, eager to strengthen ties of peace and friendship.

The great ancient Chinese philosopher Confucius once said, "Wherever three persons come together, one of them will surely be able to teach me something. I will pick out his good points and emulate them; his bad points I will reform." Confucius meant by this that we should always be ready to learn from others. This maxim encapsulates the principle the Chinese people have always followed in their dealings with other peoples, not only on an individual basis but also at the level of state-to-state relations.

After generations of internecine strife, China was unified by Emperor

Qin Shi Huang (the First Emperor of the Qin Dynasty) in 221 BC The Han Dynasty, which succeeded that of the short-lived Qin, waxed powerful, and for the first time brought China into contact with the outside world. In 138 BC, Emperor Wu dispatched Zhang Qian to the western regions, i.e. Central Asia. Zhang, who traveled as far as what is now Iran, took with him as presents for the rulers he visited on the way 10,000 head of sheep and cattle, as well as gold and silks worth a fabulous amount. In 73 AD, Ban Chao headed a 36-man legation to the western regions. These were missions of friendship to visit neighbours the Chinese people had never met before and to learn from them. Ban Chao sent Gan Ying to explore further toward the west. According to the "Western Regions Section" in the *History of Later Han*, Gan Ying traveled across the territories of present-day Iraq and Syria, and reached the Mediterranean Sea, an expedition which brought him within the confines of the Roman Empire. Later, during the Tang Dynasty, the monk Xuan Zang made a journey fraught with danger to reach India and seek the knowledge of that land. Upon his return, he organized a team of scholars to translate the Buddhist scriptures, which he had brought back with him. As a result, many of these scriptural classics which were later lost in India have been preserved in China. In fact, it would have been difficult for the people of India to reconstruct their own ancient history if it had not been for Xuan Zang's *A Record of a Journey to the West in the Time of the Great Tang Dynasty*. In the Ming Dynasty, Zheng He transmitted Chinese culture to Southeast Asia during his seven voyages. Following the Opium Wars in the mid-19th century, progressive Chinese, generation after generation, went to study the advanced scientific thought and cultural achievements of the Western countries. Their aim was to revive the fortunes of their own country. Among them were people who were later to become leaders of China, including Zhu De, Zhou Enlai and Deng Xiaoping. In addition, there were people who were to become leading scientists, literary figures and artists, such as Guo Moruo, Li Siguang, Qian Xuesen, Xian Xinghai and Xu Beihong. Their spirit of ambition, their struggles and their breadth of vision were an inspiration not only to the Chinese people but to people all over the world.

Indeed, it is true that if the Chinese people had not learned many things from the surrounding countries they would never have been able to produce the splendid achievements of former days. When we look back upon history, how can we not feel profoundly grateful for the legacies of the civilizations of ancient Egypt, Greece and India? How can we not feel fondness and respect for the cultures of Europe, Africa, America and Oceania?

The Chinese nation, in turn, has made unique contributions to the community of mankind. Prior to the 15th century, China led the world in science and technology. The British scientist Joseph Needham once said, "From the third century AD to the 13th century AD China was far ahead of the West in the level of its scientific knowledge." Paul Kennedy, of Yale University in the U.S., author of *The Rise and Fall of the Great Powers*, said, "Of all the civilizations of the pre-modern period, none was as well-developed or as progressive as that of China."

Foreigners who came to China were often astonished at what they saw and heard. The Greek geographer Pausanias in the second century AD gave the first account in the West of the technique of silk production in China: "The Chinese feed a spider-like insect with millet and reeds. After five years the insect's stomach splits open, and silk is extracted therefrom." From this extract, we can see that the Europeans at that time did not know the art of silk manufacture. In the middle of the 9th century AD, an Arabian writer includes the following anecdote in his *Account of China and India*:

"One day, an Arabian merchant called upon the military governor of Guangzhou. Throughout the meeting, the visitor could not keep his eyes off the governor's chest. Noticing this, the latter asked the Arab merchant what he was staring at. The merchant replied, 'Through the silk robe you are wearing, I can faintly see a black mole on your chest. Your robe must be made out of very fine silk indeed!' The governor burst out laughing, and holding out his sleeve invited the merchant to count how many garments he was wearing. The merchant did so, and discovered that the governor was actually wearing five silk robes, one on top of the other, and they were made of such fine material that a tiny mole could be seen through them all! Moreover, the governor explained that the robes he was wearing were not made of the finest silk at all; silk of the highest grade was reserved for the garments worn by the provincial governor."

The references to tea in this book (the author calls it "dried grass") reveal that the custom of drinking tea was unknown in the Arab countries at that time: "The king of China's revenue comes mainly from taxes on salt and the dry leaves of a kind of grass which is drunk after boiled water is poured on it. This dried grass is sold at a high price in every city in the country. The Chinese call it 'cha.' The bush is like alfalfa, except that it bears more leaves, which are also more fragrant than alfalfa. It has a slightly bitter taste, and when it is infused in boiling water it is said to have medicinal properties."

Foreign visitors showed especial admiration for Chinese medicine. One wrote, "China has very good medical conditions. Poor people are given money to buy medicines by the government."

In this period, when Chinese culture was in full bloom, scholars flocked from all over the world to China for sightseeing and for study. Chang'an, the capital of the Tang Dynasty was host to visitors from as far away as the Byzantine Empire, not to mention the neighboring countries of Asia. Chang'an, at that time the world's greatest metropolis, was packed with thousands of foreign dignitaries, students, diplomats, merchants, artisans and entertainers. Japan especially sent contingent after contingent of envoys to the Tang court. Worthy of note are the accounts of life in Chang'an written by Abeno Nakamaro, a Japanese scholar who studied in China and had close friendships with ministers of the Tang court and many Chinese scholars in a period of over 50 years. The description throws light on the exchanges between Chinese and foreigners in this period. When Abeno was supposedly lost at sea on his way back home, the leading poet of the time, Li Bai, wrote a eulogy for him.

The following centuries saw a steady increase in the accounts of China written by Western visitors. The Italian Marco Polo described conditions in China during the Yuan Dynasty in his *Travels*. However, until advances in the science of navigation led to the opening of east-west shipping routes at the beginning of the 16th century Sino-Western cultural exchanges were coloured by fantasy and conjecture. Concrete progress was made when a contingent of religious missionaries, men well versed in Western science and technology, made their way to China, ushering in an era of direct contacts between China and the West. The experience of this era was embodied in the career of the Italian Jesuit Matteo Ricci. Arriving in China in 1582, Ricci died in Beijing in 1610. Apart from his missionary work, Ricci accomplished two historically symbolic tasks — one was the translation into Latin of the "Four Books," together with annotations, in 1594; the other was the translation into Chinese of Euclid's *Elements*.

The rough translations of the "Four Books" and other Chinese classical works by Western missionaries, and the publication of Père du Halde's *Description Geographique, Historique, Chronologique, Politique, et Physique de l'Empire de la Chine* revealed an exotic culture to Western readers, and sparked a "China fever," during which the eyes of many Western intellectuals were fixed on China. Some of these intellectuals, including Leibniz, held China in high esteem; others, such as Hegel, nursed a critical attitude toward Chinese culture. Leibniz considered that some aspects of Chinese thought were close to his own views, such as the philosophy of the *Book of Changes* and his own binary system. Hegel, on the other hand, as mentioned above, considered that China had developed no proper philosophy of its own. Nevertheless, no matter whether the reaction was one of admiration, criticism, acceptance or rejection, Sino-Western exchanges were of great significance. The transmission of advanced Chinese science and technology to the West, especially the Chinese inventions of paper-making, gunpowder, printing and the compass, greatly changed the face of the whole world. Karl Marx said, "Chinese gunpowder blew the feudal class of knights to smithereens; the compass opened up world markets and built colonies; and printing became an implement of Protestantism and the most powerful lever and necessary precondition for intellectual development and creation." The English philosopher Roger Bacon said that China's four great inventions had "changed the face of the whole world and the state of affairs of everything."

**3**

Ancient China gave birth to a large number of eminent scientists, such as Zu Chongzhi, Li Shizhen, Sun Simiao, Zhang Heng, Shen Kuo and Bi Sheng. They produced numerous treatises on scientific subjects, including *The Manual of Important Arts for the People's Welfare, Nine Chapters on the Art of Mathematics, Treatise on Febrile Disease Caused by Cold* and *Compendium of Materia Medica*. Their accomplishments included ones whose influence has been felt right down to modern times, such as the armillary sphere, seismograph, Dujiangyan water conservancy project, Dunhuang Grottoes, Grand Canal and Great Wall. But from the latter part of the 15th century, and for the next 400 years, Europe gradually became the cultural centre upon which the world's eyes were fixed. The world's most outstanding scientists then were England's Isaac Newton, Poland's Copernicus, France's Marie Curie, Germany's Rontgen and Einstein, Italy's Galileo, Russia's Mendelev and America's Edison.

The Chinese people then began to think: What is the cause of the rise and fall of nations? Moreover, how did it happen that gunpowder, invented in China and transmitted to the West, in no time at all made Europe powerful enough to batter down the gates of China herself?

It took the Opium War to wake China from its reverie. The first generation to make the bold step of "turning our eyes once again to the rest of the world" was represented by Lin Zexu and Wei Yuan. Zeng Guofan and Li Hongzhang started the Westernization Movement, and later intellectuals raised the slogan of "Democracy and Science." Noble-minded patriots, realizing that China had fallen behind in the race for modernization, set out on a painful quest. But in backwardness lay the motivation for change, and the quest produced the embryo of a towering hope, and the Chinese people finally gathered under a banner proclaiming a "March Toward Science."

On the threshold of the 21st century, the world is moving in the direction of becoming an integrated entity. This trend is becoming clearer by the day. In fact, the history of the various peoples of the world is also becoming the history of mankind as a whole. Today, it is impossible for any nation's culture to develop without absorbing the excellent aspects of the cultures of other peoples. When Western culture absorbs aspects of Chinese culture, this is not just because it has come into contact with Chinese culture, but also because of the active creativity and development of Western culture itself; and vice versa. The various cultures of the world's peoples are a precious heritage which we all share. Mankind no longer lives on different continents, but on one big continent, or in a "global village." And so, in this era characterized by an all-encompassing network of knowledge and information we should learn from each other and march in step along the highway of development to construct a brand-new "global village."

Western learning is still being transmitted to the East, and vice versa. China is accelerating its pace of absorption of the best parts of the cultures of other countries, and there is no doubt that both the West and the East need the nourishment of Chinese culture. Based on this recognition, we have edited and published the *Library of Chinese Classics* in a Chinese-English format as an introduction to the corpus of traditional Chinese culture in a comprehensive and systematic translation. Through this collection, our aim is to reveal to the world the aspirations and dreams of the Chinese people over the past 5,000 years and the splendour of the new historical era in China. Like a phoenix rising from the ashes, the Chinese people in unison are welcoming the cultural sunrise of the new century.

*August 1999 Beijing*

# 引 言

历史中的晏子形象与《晏子》文本

## （Ⅰ）待时而举：从公元前 6 世纪到公元前 3 世纪的晏子形象

首先出现在历史中的，当然是晏婴这个人。在他去世多年以后，出现了"晏子"——《晏子春秋》中的同名主人公。作为公元前 6 世纪生活于齐国的一个历史人物，有关于他的生平的可靠史料非常稀少并且难以考证。尽管如此，从公元前 5 世纪到公元前 4 世纪，晏婴的个人特征逐渐合并汇聚成一个独特的形象。最初，晏婴只是在《论语》中被简单提及，《论语·公冶长》中记载：子曰："晏平仲善与人交，久而敬之。"接着，晏婴在《左传》中首先作为历史人物登场。《左传》中记载了晏婴的几个故事，这些故事主要发生在公元前 6 世纪下半叶齐国公室衰微、田氏即将取而代之这一历史背景之下。所有这些故事集中在一起塑造出一个极具吸引力的形象，作为齐国的大臣，晏婴善于巧妙进谏，同时，在侍奉三位不称职的君主的时候，他坚持原则、不畏权势。

接着，在公元前 4 世纪下半叶，晏子的形象开始在文学中产生影响，其形象毁誉参半。稷下学宫的成员之一淳于髡（生活于公元前 340 年左右），在向齐威王（公元前 378 年—前 320 年）进谏时曾经充满赞美地称引晏婴。然而，孟子（公元前 372 年—前 289 年）的弟子，来自齐国的公孙丑，坚持将孟子与管仲和晏子比较的时候，却使孟子觉得受到冒犯。孟子傲慢地回应弟子的提问，否认管仲和晏子作为两位伟大的齐国大臣的重要性，他把他们看作是严格受限于他们所处的时代与地位的两位普通官员。稍后于孟子，在荀子（公元前 310 年—前 235 年，一说公元前 314 年—前 217 年）的著作中，同样也记录了对待晏子和管仲的轻蔑态度。《荀子·大略》中云："子谓子家驹续然大夫，不如晏子；晏子功用之臣也，不如子产；子产惠人也，不如管仲；

管仲之为人，力功不力义，力知不力仁，野人也，不可以为天子大夫。"管仲尚是"野人"而"不可以为天子大夫"，晏婴的成就还不如管仲，那么他对待晏婴的态度就可想而知了。

## （Ⅱ）粉墨登场：从公元前3世纪到公元前2世纪的晏子形象

在公元前300年到公元前200年之间，晏子的形象逐渐发生了变化。无论是在包含有晏婴形象的故事中，还是在冠上他的名字的文献记载里，晏婴都变成一个越来越中心化的人物。直到公元前3世纪中期，晏婴的所作所为，无论是被赞许还是被批评，一直被文本中他所处的历史环境所遮蔽，晏婴的形象超越了自我言说所展现的个性特征，服务于更广泛的目的。然而在公元前250年左右，在叙述中处于边缘地位的晏子形象逐渐占据了中心位置。随后，晏婴这一人物被广泛引用并受到越来越多的关注。他的形象也越来越复杂——有时候具有示范意义，有时候又暧昧不清——并且最终形成一系列极具特色的轶事，这些轶事不仅聚焦于他的所作所为，同时也关涉到他具有独特思维模式的个性特征。这些主角化的变化反映在当时三部重要的著作中：《墨子》、《吕氏春秋》和《韩非子》。

在《墨子》的第三十九篇《非儒》中，晏子不再是一个附属的人物，而是成为墨家学派中"非儒"的一名主将。他被描绘为齐君的密友与顾问，他对于儒家的世界观和过于现实的做法的一系列敌对观点促成了齐君站在墨家立场上反对儒家。晏子的态度非常激烈；他不仅谴责孔子本身是一个谋逆者甚至是一个凶手，还批判儒家的核心价值，指出儒家的鼓吹者是一群进行无用表演的人。从此以后，晏子不仅成为一个墨家学者，而且变成了一位反对孔子和儒家学派的领头人，晏子的这一身份在其他一些文献和注释中同样也有所反映。

在《吕氏春秋》中，晏子作为一个道德高尚的、善于自省的、无畏的独特模范而发挥作用。书中有三段记载，描写了晏子在绝望和生命受到威胁的情况下的举动。在第一段记载中，晏子的仁慈与道德使得他人愿意为他牺牲自己的生命。在第二段记载中，他的仁慈的行为描画出他极为可贵的自省与自律的能力，一个完美主义者可以从他的全部行为中意识到其中所蕴含的意义。在第三段记载中，当晏子面对迫在眉睫的死亡威胁的时候，他所展现出的伟大的真正的勇气足以作为典范。

在《韩非子》中有三段非常尖锐地批评了晏子对君主关切的问题所做的分析、他仁慈的救济主张以及他有关于严刑与缓刑的心理上的考虑。看起来《韩非子》似乎把晏子当作是一种具有威胁性的世界观的体现，从法家的立场上看，必须对其进行挑战与批驳。因而，晏子在文本中受到激烈的哲学批判，甚至他的一些论点从某种程度上被看作是"不忠诚"的体现。这三段中的第一段记载抨击了晏子著名的节俭与节制的特点。文章不仅论证了这两种价值的无意义，因为他们在某种程度上导致大臣们对获得成功缺乏动力，更宣称孔子曾经专门批评过晏子。第二段记载则认为晏子对于官僚系统和百姓的仁慈与慷慨反映出他缺乏摆脱困境的能力，从而会使他的君主面临更加严重的灾难。最后，在第三段中则抨击了晏子的缓刑主张，认为晏子自己也不相信自己的论点。对于《韩非子》来说，晏子的宽缓态度表明晏子并未清楚地了解治理的意义。

## （Ⅲ）独奏者：汉代前期的晏子形象与《晏子》文本

### （Ⅲ-1）《淮南子》中的"晏子谏"

所有这些文本的例子表明在公元前200年左右，晏子的形象不仅在相关的叙述中扮演着越来越重要的角色，而且很有可能促成了某些独特文本的形成，这些文本仅关注晏子的历史，有些甚至把他的名字作为标题。公元前139年，晏子形象的演进变得非常明显。在这一年，汉宗室刘安向汉武帝进献了一部百科全书式的哲学著作《淮南子》。《淮南子》第21篇《要略》，目的在于总结分析之前二十篇的内容，最后又通过回顾和解释那些在过去扮演着重要角色的杰出人物之所以开创新说的原因为全书的结束。《要略》中说：

> 齐景公内好声色，外好狗马，猎射亡归，好色无辨。作为路寝之台，族铸大钟，撞之庭下，郊雉皆响，一朝用三千钟赣，梁丘据、子家哙导于左右，故晏子之谏生焉。

首先，《淮南子》在这里交代了"晏子之谏"这一文本之所以产生的背景。其次，晏子对齐景公的"谏"，不仅仅是今传本《晏子春秋》的核心内容，而且还是刘向（公元前 77 年—前 6 年）整理的《晏子》的前两章的标题。最后，《淮南子》所列举引起晏子之"谏"的齐景公的乱政，与今传本《晏子春秋》中近一半的内容相符合。我们据此或许可以得出这样的认识，在公元前 139 年左右，存在着一部题名与"晏子"相关的书，这部书的内容与今传本《晏子春秋》的部分内容非常接近。实际上，大约五十年之后，晏子已经被看作是一位直言敢谏、充满勇气的大臣，并且他还成为当时流行于世的《晏子春秋》的作者。晏子的形象，最终被司马迁（约公元前 145 年—前 86 年）《史记》中那些令人难以忘怀的传记记载所定型。

### （III—2）《史记》中的晏子形象与《晏子春秋》

晏子的传记记载于《史记》的第六十二卷，司马迁把管仲的传记放在晏子之前写在同一章《管晏列传》中。在晏子的传记中，前两段专门叙述晏子，而后面两段则是将管仲和晏子放在一起讨论。在《史记》卷三十二《齐太公世家》中，也记载了来自《左传》的有关于管仲和晏子的很多传记资料。读者应该注意到，《齐太公世家》中有关于管子的内容，被概括进了《管晏列传》，而有关于晏子的内容则没有被司马迁记录到《管晏列传》中。另外我也希望读者在开始阅读《管晏列传》之前，先关注一下司马迁在《管晏列传》的结尾所做的总结。司马迁在其中表达了自己对于晏子极深的敬意，他说："假令晏子而在，余虽为之执鞭，所忻慕焉。"

司马迁对于晏子的敬意，在整篇《列传》中得到彻底的体现，也影响到其内容的选择。司马迁在叙述完管仲的事迹之后说："管仲卒，齐国遵其政，常强于诸侯。后百余年而有晏子焉。"司马迁用这句话将管仲和晏子联系在一起，使二者的传记构成了一个完整的历史序列。虽然管仲与晏子在历史上所发挥的作用不可同日而语，但是读者却不得不对二人做出比较：管仲，一位杰出的政治家，建立了齐国的霸业、塑造了齐国一百年的历史；而晏子，一位杰出的谏臣，却无法挽救齐国公室被取代的命运。在晏子传记的开头，司马迁写道：

> 晏平仲婴者，莱之夷维人也。事齐灵公、庄公、景公，以节俭力行重于齐。既相齐，食不重肉，妾不衣帛。其在朝，君语及之，即危言；语不及之，即危行。国有道，即顺命；无道，即衡命。以此三世显名于诸侯。

读完晏子传记的第一部分，再回想管仲的传记，读者可以看到管仲在齐国历史上的重要时刻发挥着关键作用，并塑造了齐国后来的历史。然而，在晏子的生平中却没有类似的叙述。晏子传记的开头部分，仅仅是简单地介绍了晏子的名字、籍贯以及侍奉的君主。读者从中看不出晏子对于齐国历史有任何贡献，这里既没有涉及任何重要的历史事件，也没有可以让人留下深刻印象的人生事业。相反，这些记述倒是比较详细地描述了晏子的个性和道德行为的特点，仿佛他是一部缺少故事主线的书中的主人公。因此，当读者读完晏子传记的开头部分，会觉得晏子在齐国历史的地位远逊于管仲。此外，除去粗疏的大背景，读者对于晏子生平的主要事迹几乎毫无线索。这也就是说，晏子之所以在当时出名，是因为他节俭、勇毅、正直、诚实与大胆等个性特征，而这也成为吸引后人注意的主要原因。

从这一点上来看，读者会对司马迁将二者合并为一个列传的做法感到困惑。然而，根据列传最后的总结，读者或许可以多少理解这一令人费解的处理方法。司马迁对晏子的为人推崇备至，他竭力缩小管仲与晏子这两位齐国大臣在历史影响力上的巨大差距。为了达到这一目的，司马迁将管仲的历史成就与晏子的高尚德行相并列，从而避免了对二者历史作用的直接比较。

晏子传记的第二个部分包含了有关于晏子的两个故事，这两个故事也出现在今传本的《晏子春秋》中。第一个故事相当于《晏子春秋》

21

第五卷第 24 篇"晏子之晋睹齐累越石父解左骖赎之与归"的简写。这个故事讲述晏子用自己的一匹马赎回了贤人越石父，之后晏子用一般性的礼节对待他，这引起了越石父的不满与抗议，晏子立刻忏悔自己的过失并且待之如上宾。第二个故事则与《晏子春秋》第五卷第 25 篇"晏子之御感妻言而自抑损晏子荐以为大夫"完全相同。在这段故事中，晏子的车夫为晏子驾车时得意扬扬，车夫的妻子看到后要求与他离婚，并且说，晏子身不满六尺，相齐国，名显诸侯，然而态度谦卑，而你身长八尺，为人驾车，反而志得意满。这番话令车夫悔过，并从此改变了自己的态度，晏子觉察到车夫的变化，便推荐他担任了齐国的大夫。

这两个故事非常微妙地提出一个隐含的问题：一个人的真正身份到底由什么构成？从这一角度来看，这两段故事既可以从哲学的层面来分析，也可以从心理学层面来讨论。而在这两段故事中，除了暗示晏子是一个小个子之外，再无有关于他生活的任何其他信息。看起来，这两段故事同样也是通过描述晏子的美德来向读者展现晏子两方面的人格特点：他不遗余力地解救处于困境中的人，并且他善于自省从而有能力调整自己在复杂情况中的态度；另外，他有一种巨大的超越表象和探寻内在品质的能力。

司马迁在晏子的传记中记录了这两个故事，到底想要表达什么呢？有鉴于他在列传最后的总结中对晏子所表达的"忻慕"之情，相比于对管仲的记载，关于晏子的记载无论在字数上还是在内容上都显得比较单薄。

在列传的最后部分，司马迁说："吾读管氏《牧民》、《山高》、《乘马》、《轻重》、《九府》及《晏子春秋》，详哉其言之也。既见其著书，欲观其行事，故次其传。至其书，世多有之，是以不论，论其轶事。"

这段话在晏子文本的历史上是非常重要的一段记载。司马迁非常明确地指出他曾经读过管仲的五篇论述以及《晏子春秋》这部书。

司马迁表示《晏子春秋》为晏子所作。他同时还指出，这部书写得很详细，在当时很流行。司马迁的这段话充分证明在大约公元前100 年左右，《晏子春秋》已经被看作是有关于晏子的真实传记。《史记》中将其题名为"晏子春秋"，并且这个名字多次出现在汉代学者的记述中，"春秋"本来是史书的名字，既然这部书题名为"春秋"，也证明其书写了有关于晏子的历史。

最后，司马迁对管仲和晏子分别做出评价。对于管子，司马迁含蓄地表达出严厉的批评态度：

> 管仲世所谓贤臣，然孔子小之。岂以为周道衰微，桓公既贤，而不勉之至王，乃称霸哉？语曰"将顺其美，匡救其恶，故上下能相亲也"。岂管仲之谓乎？

所谓"孔子小之"，是指《论语》中记载孔子曾经说过"管仲之器小哉"。司马迁通过引用孔子的观点，将之前所记载的管子的所有成就进行了贬损。相反，对于晏子，司马迁却表达出强烈的赞美以及将其看作是个人偶像的崇敬：

> 方晏子伏庄公尸哭之，成礼然后去，岂所谓"见义不为无勇"者邪？至其谏说，犯君之颜，此所谓"进思尽忠，退思补过"者哉！假令晏子而在，余虽为之执鞭，所忻慕焉。

《管晏列传》至此结束，司马迁在最后表达出自己渴望侍奉晏子的崇敬之情，这使读者反思这部《列传》中的两位主人公，到底哪一位才是齐国更加杰出的人物。司马迁在《史记》中非常聪明地将二人联系到一起，而他的目的也很快达到，《史记》成书后不久，晏子已经成为与管子相并列并且在此基础上去评价和衡量的重要人物。

公元前 1 世纪，晏子的形象继续在汉代学者的著述中留下痕迹。桓宽在《盐铁论》中不止一次提到晏子，晏子不仅作为历史人物被提及，他说过的话也被当作是引用的对象。更重要的是，在公元前 1 世纪末，刘向整理校订出一部书题名为"晏子"并且为该书写了一篇前言，晏子的形象在这部书中更加令人难以忘怀。

### (III-3) 刘向整理的《晏子》

公元前 26 年，汉成帝（公元前 33 年—前 7 年在位）命令刘向校理群书。作为结果，刘向搜集了超过八百个有关于晏子的生平以及其生活时代的故事，并且努力将它们编联成一个由 215 章组成的整体，

23

这215章展现出比较明显的主题，大致按照年代顺序排列，最终形成了晏子独特的个人形象。这是一个身材矮小但是具有强烈使命感的杰出人物形象；是一个节俭与慷慨双重性格的缩影；一位心理操纵与喜剧表演的大师；一位具有渊博的知识、语用推理能力并且强烈反对盲目崇拜超自然现象的杰出学者；一位试图挽救无可救药的君主、像希绪弗斯一样努力的勇气与道德的模范；一位与管仲比肩、与孔子竞争的人物。然而更重要的是，刘向所整理的这215章内容，是中国古代有关于晏子这个独特的人物形象的第一本文学传记，描画了这位“社稷之臣”，这位没有门生的大师，这位生活中真正的英雄的一生。刘向几乎为他所整理的所有图书都写有“叙录”，“叙录”中的内容包括本书的内容简介、版本来源、作者生平以及对于本书的意义和真实性的讨论等等。在刘向的《晏子叙录》中，同样也涉及了这些内容。《晏子叙录》中先列举了《晏子》八篇的内容。前六篇被称作“内篇”，并分别题名为“谏上”“谏下”“问上”“问下”“杂上”“杂下”。第七篇和第八篇被称作“外篇”。第七篇题名为“重而异者”，第八篇题名为“不合经术者”。在列举了《晏子》八篇之后，刘向交代了校订《晏子》的各种版本及来源。之后，他比较清楚简洁地记录了晏子的生平事迹。最后，他对《晏子》这部书做出评价，对不同部分的真实性做出说明。刘向在《晏子叙录》中说：

> 护左都水使者光禄大夫臣向言：所校中书《晏子》十一篇，臣向谨与长社尉臣参校雠。太史书五篇、臣向书一篇、参书十三篇，凡中外书三十篇，为八百三十八章，除复重二十二篇六百三十八章，定著八篇二百一十五章。外书无有三十六章，中书无有七十一章。中外皆有以相定。中书以“夭”为“芳”、又为“备”、“先”为“牛”、“章”为“长”，如此类者多，谨颇略椾。皆已定。以杀青。书可缮写。
>
> 晏子名婴，谥平仲，莱人。莱者，今东莱地也。晏子博闻强记，通于古今。事齐灵公、庄公、景公。以节俭力行、尽忠极谏道齐。国君得以正行，百姓得以附亲。不用则退耕于野，用则必不诎义。不可胁以邪。白刃虽交胸，终不受崔杼之劫。谏齐君，悬

而至，顺而刻。及使诸侯，莫能诎其辞。其博通如此。盖次管仲。内能亲亲，外能厚贤。居相国之位，受万钟之禄，故亲戚待其禄而衣食五百余家，处士待而举火者亦甚众。晏子衣苴布之衣，麋鹿之裘，驾敝车疲马，尽以禄给亲戚朋友。齐人以此重之。晏子盖短。

其书六篇，皆忠谏其君。文章可观，义理可法，皆合六经之义。又有复重，文辞颇异，不敢遗失，复列以为一篇。又有颇不合经术，似非晏子言，疑后世辩士所为者，故亦不敢失，复以为一篇。凡八篇，其六篇可常置旁御观。谨第录。臣向昧死上。"

显然，《叙录》中的第一部分是刘向根据自己校理《晏子》时的实际经验所写。只有他才可以真正告诉未来的读者，《晏子》的定本是如何形成的。在第三部分，同样也展现出刘向是本书的直接整理者，他认为前六章是关于晏子言语的真实记录，而后两章的真实性值得怀疑，尽管如此，刘向依然审慎地将其附录在书末。在记录晏子生平的第二部分，如果读者与《史记》中的晏子传记相比较就会发现，刘向像司马迁一样表达出对晏子的崇敬之情。然而，尽管司马迁说他曾经读过《晏子春秋》，但是他在写作晏子传记的时候依然非常小心地避免直接从中选取材料来组织晏子的传记；相反，刘向却从自己所编订的《晏子》中借用了大量材料来构成自己对晏子生平的描述。

从此以后，晏子的历史形象主要被刘向所整理的《晏子》以及其《晏子叙录》所确定，而其他文献中所记录的晏子在历史的记忆中则越来越模糊。

## （Ⅳ）流传中逐渐定型——从东汉到唐代《晏子》与《晏子春秋》的演变

刘向去世以后到唐代，晏子的文本，或者题名为《晏子》，或者题名为《晏子春秋》，在流传过程中被以下的15部著作所列举、引用或者评价：

25

据张守节《史记正义》中的记载，刘歆曾经在《七略》中儒家著作的部分记录有"《晏子春秋》七篇"。

班固（公元 32 年—92 年）《汉书·艺文志》著录有"《晏子》八篇"。

王充（公元 27 年—100 年）在《论衡》中称"管仲、晏婴，功书并作"，并且屡次称引晏子所说的话，这些话几乎都见于今传本《晏子春秋》。

应劭（大约死于公元 204 年左右）《风俗通义》引用了今传本《晏子春秋·内篇·杂下》"景公病水瘖与日斗晏子教占瞢者以对"章并直接表明引自《晏子春秋》。

在王肃（公元 195 年—256 年）年轻时写的《孔丛子》中，曾提到"晏子之书亦曰春秋"，王肃在书中还猛烈批评了把晏子看作是反对儒家的墨家信徒的观点。

刘勰（公元 465 年—522 年）在《文心雕龙·诸子》中说道："管、晏属篇，事核而言练。"

郦道元（死于公元 527 年）在《水经注》中提到"刘向叙《晏子春秋》"，并称引了今传本《晏子春秋·谏下》"景公养勇士三人无君之义晏子谏"章的内容。

虞世南（公元 558 年—638 年）在唐朝建立之前编辑的类书《北堂书钞》中多次称引《晏子》与《晏子春秋》，所有的内容均见于今传本《晏子春秋》。

欧阳询（公元 557 年—641 年）在公元 622 年至 624 年之间编成的类书《艺文类聚》中也多次称引《晏子》和《晏子春秋》的内容，所有的内容亦均见于今传本《晏子春秋》。

魏征（公元 580 年—643 年）在公元 631 年编成的《群书治要》中，包含了 38 条称引自《晏子》的内容，这些内容也全部见于今传本《晏子春秋》。这 38 条引用均比较完整，有 7 千余字，相当于今传本《晏子春秋》百分之十七的内容。魏征在书中将这 38 条引用重新排列，尽管它们都被标明为来自内篇六篇的相应篇章，但是实际上其中也包括了现在属于外篇两篇的内容。

同样有魏征参与撰写的《隋书·经籍志》子部儒家类中著录有"《晏子春秋》七卷"，作者被标为"齐大夫晏婴"。《隋书·经籍志》是从汉代到唐代唯一保留下来的完整的书目著作，其中还保存了现在已经失传的唐代之前的一些书目——如阮孝绪（公元 479 年—549 年）《七录》——的内容与特点。

在唐代的正史，如后晋刘昫（公元 887 年—946 年）所编撰的《旧唐书》以及宋代学者欧阳修（公元 1007 年—1072 年）和宋祁（公元 998 年—1061 年）编撰的《新唐书》中，《晏子春秋》均著录于儒家类，七卷，作者为晏婴。

李善（死于公元 689 年）在《文选注》中引用《晏子春秋》40 次。所有的引用均见于今传本《晏子春秋》的八篇中。

徐坚（公元 649 年—729 年）所编撰的类书《初学记》中，多次引用《晏子》与《晏子春秋》的内容。所有的引用也都见于今传本《晏子春秋》。

马总（死于公元 823 年）的《意林》中引用了 16 条题名为《晏子》的内容，这部《晏子》共八篇，所有的内容均见于今传本《晏子春秋》。

总而言之，在这一时期：

1. 著录、称引、流传的晏子文本有两个题名:《晏子》和《晏子春秋》。

2. 刘向的《晏子叙录》广泛流传并且直接被引用。

3. 晏子文本中"内篇"六篇的标题在当时已经存在并且被引用。

4. 晏婴被看作是晏子文本的作者。

5. 晏子文本被归类为儒家文献。

6. 晏子文本的文学意义被高度赞扬。

7. 大量的晏子文本出现在类书或类似的书中。

8. 晏子文本的"外篇"两篇有时被合并为一篇。偶尔地还有将外篇内容归类到内篇的情况。因此，我们有理由推测，外篇的内容在分卷或分篇时，它们的归属比较灵活多变。

## （Ⅴ）身份突变：柳宗元（公元 773 年—819 年）对《晏子春秋》墨家性质的论辩

公元 8 世纪末，晏子文本被高度重视并且稳步流传的进程被打断。

那曾经被看作是晏子所作，冠以刘向的《叙录》，在各主要书目中被归类为儒家文献，在各种著述中被广泛引用并被当作历史典故的晏子文本，其身分认同在柳宗元的质疑后迅速瓦解。柳宗元在《辩晏子春秋》中说：

> 司马迁读《晏子春秋》高之，而莫知其所以为书。或曰：晏子为之，而人接焉。或曰：晏子之后为之。皆非也。吾疑其墨子之徒有齐人者为之。墨好俭，晏子以俭名于世，故墨子之徒尊著其事，以增高为己术者。且其旨多尚同、兼爱、非乐、节用、非厚葬久丧者，是皆出墨子。又非孔子，好言鬼事，非儒、明鬼，又出墨子。其言问枣及古冶子等，尤怪诞。又往往言墨子闻其道而称之，此甚显白者。

柳宗元总结了墨家学说的特点，并且指出《晏子春秋》的内容与墨家学说非常接近。柳宗元接着说：

> 自刘向、歆、班彪、固父子，皆录之儒家中。甚矣，数子之不详也！盖非齐人不能具其事，非墨子之徒其言不若是。后之录诸子书宜列之墨家。非晏子为墨也，为是书者墨之道也。

柳宗元将晏子文本看作是冒名晏婴的墨家弟子的著作，并且切断了其与并非墨家的历史人物晏婴的关联，这一结论貌似公允，实际却极具颠覆性。而且，柳宗元还否定了晏子文本为晏子后人所创作的可能性，这就相当于将该书看作是一部"伪书"了。柳宗元的论辩的结果，推翻了对晏子文本原来的认识，使其成为齐国墨家暗中宣扬自己主张的工具。

总之，刘向已经指出，在他所整理出的《晏子》八篇中，包含有一些后世创作的并非晏子所作的内容。接着，王肃在《孔丛子》中竭力辩驳晏子并非反对儒家，尽管在《晏子春秋》中有一些墨家的观点。然而柳宗元直言不讳的批评彻底改变了《晏子春秋》的流传轨迹，从此之后，有关于这部书的真实性、成书时间、作者以及其中的哲学观点都成为争论的焦点，而后世所有相关的争论无不回应着柳宗元破除古代文本偶像的观点与精神。

# （Ⅵ）混乱的著录：宋代的《晏子春秋》

到了宋代，《晏子春秋》的流传出现了两条不同的线索：一条是在类书的引用中，似乎晏子的文本依然稳定；另一条则在各种书目的著录中，著录中的晏子文本似乎并不稳定。

## （Ⅵ－1）宋代类书中的《晏子春秋》

当我们检查宋代类书中直接或间接引用的《晏子春秋》的时候，我们似乎可以得出这样的印象，在这 300 多年的历史中，《晏子春秋》似乎只有一个版本，而且这个版本非常稳定，被反复引用。

我统计了 122 条直接引用的晏子文本，从中可以看出晏子文本的流行趋势以及其在宋代作为古代典故所具有的稳定性。

| 类书 | 编者 | 直接标明从《晏子春秋》中引用的数量 |
| --- | --- | --- |
| 《太平御览》 | 李昉（公元 925 年—996 年） | 86 |
| 《事类赋注》 | 吴淑（公元 947 年—1002 年） | 11 |
| 《记纂渊海》 | 潘自牧（生活于约 1195 年） | 10 |
| 《玉海》 | 王应麟（公元 1223 年—1296 年） | 15 |

如果我们将宋代类书中所引用的《晏子春秋》的内容与唐代类书和各种选集中所引用的《晏子春秋》的内容合并成一个综合数据库，我们根据两个时代的重复引用率可以看出《晏子春秋》的文本从唐初到宋末稳定流传的线索。在这个数据库中有一条内容特别值得注意，那就是今传本《晏子春秋》的最后一条内容（第 215 条），这条内容不仅首先在两部唐代类书《群书治要》（公元 631 年）和《意林》（约 823 年）中被直接引用，而且随后又在宋代的类书《太平御览》（公元 938 年）、最后在明代的类书《天中记》（公元 1569 年）中被引用。而这一条内容甚至还有更古老的源头，在银雀山汉简本《晏子》中第 624 至 630 简上，我们也发现了相同的内容。这七根竹简，从银雀山 1 号墓（公元前 140 年）穿越到唐、宋、明时期的类书中，最后又出现在今传

本《晏子春秋》各种各样的印本中，我们因而可以认为《晏子春秋》的整个文本具有超越时代的稳定形态。

### （Ⅵ-2）宋代书目中的《晏子春秋》

从公元 1 世纪到隋唐时期，晏子的文本在流传过程中往往被题名为《晏子》或者《晏子春秋》，或者是 8 篇，或者 7 篇，或者是 7 卷。在此时期，晏子文本的作者一直被认定为晏婴本人，除了柳宗元（公元 773 年—819 年），他认为晏子的文本是齐国墨家学派的作品。到了宋代，很多记载列出的晏子的文本变成了 12 卷。宋代的一些学者认为汉代出现的八篇的晏子文本已经失传，一些主要的书目拒绝承认晏婴为晏子文本的作者。

最早记录 12 卷本《晏子春秋》的，大概是王尧臣（公元 1001 年—1056 年）。他在《崇文总目》儒家类中记录有《晏子春秋》12 卷，并且指出汉代八篇的晏子文本已经亡佚，同时，王尧臣还认为将晏子文本的作者看作晏婴是错误的，实际上这一个文本应该是后人所作。

在王尧臣之后，晁公武（公元 1105 年—1180 年）在他的《郡斋读书志》中也记录了 12 卷的《晏子春秋》。晁公武大段引述柳宗元的观点，并且将《晏子春秋》归类到"墨家类"著作中。

之后，陈振孙（约 1211 年—1249 年）在《直斋书录解题》中也著录了《晏子春秋》12 卷，陈振孙依然将其归类为"儒家类"著作，并且说："《晏子春秋》十二卷，齐大夫平仲晏婴撰。《汉志》八篇，但曰《晏子》。《隋》《唐》七卷，始号《晏子春秋》。今卷数不同，未知果本书否？"

南宋末年，王应麟（公元 1223 年—1296 年）在《汉书艺文志考证》中亦采用了柳宗元的观点，认为此书实乃墨家学派的著作，王应麟还指出晏子的文本之所以从八篇变为七卷乃至十二卷，是因为"后人采婴行事为书，故卷颇多于前《志》"。

清末，刘师培（公元 1884 年—1919 年）也曾经对《晏子春秋》从八篇变为七卷再到十二卷的过程有比较详细的讨论。他在《晏子春秋篇目考》中说："隋唐《志》皆七卷，盖合《杂》上下二篇为一。"

至于宋代出现的 12 卷本，他认为是将七卷本中除"外篇"上下二篇之外的五篇各分为二篇，这十卷内容与"外篇"两篇共同构成了 12 卷本的《晏子春秋》。

相比于刘师培的推论，一百多年前的《四库提要》对《晏子春秋》卷数的说明似乎更为严谨。《四库提要》中说："《汉志》《隋志》皆作八篇，至陈氏、晁氏《书目》乃皆作十二卷，盖篇帙已多有更改矣。"在这短短的几句话中，四库馆臣承认历来书目著录上的差异，并且将其看作是文本流传过程中技术上的必然现象，无须过分解读。这一总结，将所有不确定性归结为文本流传的漫长历史。四库馆臣在这一问题的处理上比刘师培强作解人的做法更为可取。

# （Ⅶ）印本流传：从宋代到清代的《晏子春秋》

### （Ⅶ-1）《晏子春秋》的早期印本：元刻本与明活字本

我们首先必须指出，《晏子春秋》的木刻本应当在宋代就已经出现。然而，宋刻本既无明确记载亦无实物留存，因此相关讨论均属推测。而我们现在能够找到明确记载的两部最早的印本《晏子春秋》分别是：

（1）江苏常熟张金吾（公元 1787 年—1829 年）《爱日精庐藏书志》著录有元刻本《晏子春秋》八卷，并云："凡内篇六卷，外篇二卷，合八卷。卷首有吴岫印记、刘向序。"元刻本今亦不传，相关记载亦可参见吴寿旸（公元 1771 年—1835）《拜经楼藏书题跋》。

（2）浙江仁和丁松生（公元 1832 年—1899 年）八千卷楼藏明活字本。这一版本亦八篇，书前有刘向的叙录，每篇前有本篇的目录。这一版本在 20 世纪被影印，收录入《四部丛刊初编》，然后成为"先秦两汉古籍逐字索引丛刊"史部第四种《晏子春秋逐字索引》所依据的底本。

### （Ⅶ-2）《晏子春秋》的后期版本：1780 年《四库全书》本与1788 年孙星衍的《晏子春秋音义》

四库馆臣将《晏子春秋》归入史部"传记类"，如此分类，避免了正面回答《晏子春秋》到底是属于儒家学说还是墨家学说的各种疑问。根据《四库提要》的记录,《四库全书》所录《晏子春秋》为"明李氏绵眇阁刻本",这一版本不像明活字本一样有目录和叙录,《晏子春秋提要》列在书前被当作序言。该提要浓缩了从汉代到宋代千余年的目录记载历史,将《晏子春秋》与唐代魏征的《谏录》和李绛的《论事集》并列。提要还指出,《晏子春秋》的编辑者姓名佚失,题名"晏婴"乃"依托也",书中又有后人窜入内容,已非原本。针对这部书到底是儒家著作还是墨家著作的问题,提要认为,《吕氏春秋·仲春纪·当染篇》中记载鲁惠公时留止周桓王使者史角,史角的后人居住鲁国,墨子曾经从史角的后人问学,晏婴生活的时代稍早于墨子,自然也有可能先闻其说,因此书中有近似于墨家学说的内容并不奇怪。提要最后还讨论了晏子文本《晏子》与《晏子春秋》"二名兼行"的问题以及之所以选择"明李氏绵眇阁刻本"的原因。

孙星衍校订的七卷本《晏子春秋》包括了晏子八篇的内容。通过篇卷混编,孙星衍希望能够解决著录中汉代八篇与隋唐七卷的文本差异问题。孙星衍的校本,依据两个明代版本,这两个明代版本既无前言亦无目录,孙星衍将刘向的叙录放在书前,还加上自己的一篇序言。书后,附录两卷考证内容,题名为"音义",是孙星衍据《艺文类聚》、《初学记》、《太平御览》以及《文选》注等文献对《晏子春秋》的异文和部分内容所作的研究和分析。孙星衍在《晏子春秋》校本的序言中作出如下结论:

1. 根据文本内部的证据和书目中的记载,流传下来的晏子文本绝非伪书。

2. 流传下来的晏子文本成书于战国时期,材料来源于齐国的史书,由晏子的宾客在他死后搜集成书。

3. 明代的某些刊本变乱次序、删改内容,讹谬甚矣。

4. 晏子文本的内六篇符合六经之义,属于儒家内容。

5.《玉海》引《崇文总目》著录《晏子春秋》十四卷,认为是后人采晏婴故事成书,因此导致卷数增多。《玉海》的说法不足信。

6. 柳宗元等人认为晏子文本的内容为墨家学派的作品,属于不学无术的无知之论。

7. 古人书外篇多为依托，刘向也已经怀疑晏子文本的外篇为后世辩士所为，外篇之依托不足以损害内篇记录晏子言行之真实。

### （Ⅶ－3）晚清民国时的《晏子春秋》

晚清民国时期，对于《晏子春秋》的文本研究并没有更多突破。此时比较著名的研究者是梁启超（公元 1873 年—1929 年）和刘师培（公元 1884 年—1919 年）。梁启超对于《晏子春秋》文本的看法，实际上整合了过去两千年来中国学者的各种意见。梁启超提出了一个大胆的推测，他认为《汉书·艺文志》中所著录的《晏子》，不仅即是司马迁在《史记》中所提到的《晏子春秋》，而且很可能与刘安在《淮南子》中所提到的"晏子之谏"为同一文本。接着，梁启超遵循柳宗元的观点，认为《晏子春秋》是齐国的晏子宾客所作，他同时还强调，按照四库馆臣的意见，这些齐国的晏子宾客并不知道墨子（这样就使得《晏子春秋》中即使有一些类似于墨家的思想，但是也与墨子没有关联）。梁启超最后总结说，《晏子春秋》以"晏子"为书名是比较晚的事情，这部书的实际成书时代可能从战国时期一直延续到汉代初年。对于流传下来的晏子文本，梁启超怀疑其不一定与司马迁和刘安所提到的文本相一致，但是他同时论证，流传下来的晏子文本很可能就是刘向所编辑整理的本子，而不太可能是后世的作品。

清代末年，在上海出现了最早的西方人对《晏子春秋》的评价。英国传教士伟烈亚力（Alexander Wylie）在 1867 年按照《四库全书》的分类编成了《中国文献录》，他在其中的传记类也列举了《晏子春秋》，并且介绍这本书完成于公元前若干世纪，这是一本有关于晏婴的个人传记，而晏婴是墨子的知名门徒。

总而言之：清末民初，有关于《晏子春秋》的真实性与思想特征等决定性问题依然悬而未决。持续进行的有关于《晏子春秋》文本的学术研究需要一个更广阔的研究者和读者圈子，以便能够创造出一个可以包容新观点从而解决围绕着文本的众多不确定问题的空间。实际上，这个更广阔的圈子在 20 世纪出现了，对于《晏子春秋》的研究已经大大扩展到西方世界。

## （Ⅷ）考古发现与数字人文：《晏子春秋》研究在 20 世纪和 21 世纪的拓展

### （Ⅷ－1）1923 年至 1972 年的《晏子春秋》

1972 年，在银雀山发现的 102 枚"晏子"竹简及残片，震惊了学术界，对《晏子春秋》的文本研究造成了巨大的影响。在此之前，不少中外学者努力使《晏子春秋》更容易为研究中国哲学的学生所利用，并且在其作者、时代以及真实性等方面都提出了一些新的意见。这些学者包括：德国汉学家伏尔克（Alfred Forke, 1867—1944）；法国汉学家马伯乐（Henri Maspero, 1883—1945）；美国华裔学者高克毅（George Kao, 1912—2008）；美国学者吴克（Richard L. Walker, 1922—2003）；美国学者伯顿·沃森（Burton Watson, 1925—2017）。而中国学者则包括：张纯一（1871—1955）；吴则虞（1913—1977）；王更生（1928—2010）。

1923 年，伏尔克（Alfred Forke）在西方学界发表了具有开创性的关于《晏子春秋》的论文，至今依然有重要的影响。伏尔克坚决主张《晏子春秋》是一部真实的古代文献，产生于公元前 5 世纪。他认为，《晏子春秋》的主角晏子，之所以将他的一生致力于服务他的君主和人民，是因为一系列的实用主义的价值观。对于伏尔克来说，晏子是一位政治家，而不是在抽象的知识与艰深的学习世界中开拓道路的儒家理论家。在伏尔克眼中，晏子也达不到管仲那样伟大的政治家的地位，然而，作为一个"角色"，晏子明显比管仲更出色。伏尔克的论文由多部分组成，其中包括从不同文献中搜集并重新编排的完整的晏子生平传记，有关于晏子文本历史的详细讨论，对于不同主题如伦理、节俭、人际关系、君民关系等所作的长篇的哲学分析。颇具突破意义的是，伏尔克提出，相比较于孔子和墨子的宗教信仰，晏子文本中所表现出来的对于某种"自然宗教"的支持显示出晏子思想更具理性主义的特征。最后，伏尔克在文章中表达出一个相当有见地的意见，他认为《晏子春秋》第八篇开头的几条猛烈抨击孔子和儒家学说的内容应该也是真实可信的。

1927 年，马伯乐（Henri Maspero）在《古代中国》（*La Chine antique*）中讨论《晏子春秋》的内容还不到两页，然而这两页内容却包含了对晏子整个文本的精彩描述。马伯乐认为《晏子春秋》成书于公元前 4 世纪中叶，相比于同时代的其他文本，《晏子春秋》是一部历史浪漫主义的作品，也就是说，作者将真实的历史事件与自己的想象混合在一起从而创作了这样一部作品。马伯乐是第一位指出晏子文本中除了倾向墨家、反对儒家之外同时还反对管子的学者，但他也认为《晏子春秋》中的哲学思想无聊乏味。然而就文学风格而言，马伯乐赞赏文本中很多场景的生动描写。在有关于书目的大段注释中，他厘清了从汉代到唐代原本《晏子春秋》的不同的流传线索，即使其在宋代和元代屡被改编，但是原本《晏子春秋》文本中的大部分内容依然被保留在今传本中，马伯乐的这一分析极具说服力。

1946 年，高克毅（George Kao）在《中国智慧与幽默》（*Chinese Wit & Humor*）的选集中收录了《晏子春秋》中十二段相对较长的内容的英文翻译。在选集中，高克毅不仅向西方读者介绍了机智的晏子，而且在智慧角度上，将晏子看作是与孔子、孟子、庄子、列子和韩非子相并列的不朽形象。

1952 年，吴克（Richard L. Walker）有关于《晏子春秋》的极具分量的分析研究探索了中国学者长期争论的很多复杂问题，从而将《晏子春秋》介绍到英语世界的学术圈中。时至今日，对于那些希望研究像《晏子春秋》这样的文本的人来说，吴克的论文依然如同一个路标值得重视。吴克最主要的目标是提升始终徘徊在主流研究之外的《晏子春秋》的地位，并且检查伏尔克 1923 年的论文在发表二十五年之后如何经受时间的考验。为了达到这一目的，吴克建议将"晏子春秋"这一比较古典而庄严的书名改换成比较平易近人的书名，如"晏子说""晏子格言"等。同时，他根据文本中所展现出来的晏子的特点，将其仅仅定性为善于"通过语言技巧摆脱困境"的人。至此，读者对吴克的真正意图困惑不解。显然，人们不明白如何通过贬低书名以及将主人公贬低为只会耍嘴皮子的人来提升其地位。而实际上，在他的论文的开场白以及所有的介绍性的评论与结论中，吴克始终瞄准着他的真正目标：有关伏尔克的 1923 年的论文中，他在文章开始阶段，先是表达了几句对于伏尔克在文本历史以及相关学术领域所做大量工作的赞美之词，接着便开始批评伏尔克对于文本的过度的哲学解读，并且列举了其在汉学研究方法论上的缺陷，吴克用多少有些蔑视的态度说："因此，虽然我们可能会同意伏尔克教授关于《晏子春秋》成书于更早时代的结论，但是并非因为他给出的理由。"接着，吴克批判性地考察了《晏子春秋》成书时的政治背景，以记载了类似内容的其他文献为参考，从语法上分析了《晏子春秋》的语言习惯，并且对多层次文本中包括什么和没包括什么进行了出色的评估，从而得出以下结论：

> 《晏子春秋》是一个真实的古代文本，它很可能产生于《左传》成书之前。《晏子春秋》的成书时代大约是晏子死后两到三代人的时候，当时晏子的故事已经成为传奇，而且晏子死去不久，否则不可能的虚构故事就会进入文本或者文本将会在思想上和形制上逐渐定型。如此看来，这大约发生在公元前 400 年之前的某一个时间段。

1962 年，伯顿·沃森（Burton Watson）在《早期中国文学》（*Early Chinese Literature*）中有关于《晏子春秋》的一篇很短但是非常精彩的章节。这一章节为理解和探索晏子文本，特别是在心理学层面上，指明了新的方向。伯顿·沃森在他对早期中国文学的考察中，将《晏子春秋》归类于"哲学"部分，并且将其主人公晏子描绘为一个提倡节俭并且因为他无可躲避的唠叨而使得他放纵的君主生活痛苦的严厉墨家。对于两千年来所形成的一个直言敢谏的崇高榜样，伯顿·沃森提出了一个新的理解，而在这一理解中，伯顿·沃森站在了自我放纵的齐君这边。他的新思路颠覆了千年以来《晏子春秋》文本崇高的道德核心，将其转变为一出现代戏剧，同时邀请观众对其自由解读。此外，沃森将这部戏剧的未来读者吸引到一幅既不能进步也不能突破的静止世界的画像前。这个世界和《晏子春秋》中的主要角色在他们原本的位置上固定不动，实际上，按照沃森所描述的："几乎总是齐君承认他的愚蠢并且承诺改革，而在接下来的故事中，我们发现他不停地重蹈覆辙、故技重施。"毫无疑问，沃森对于《晏子春秋》的观点使这部书充满戈多式的荒诞——主人公啥事也没干。

从 1930 年到 1962 年,中国大陆出现了两部《晏子春秋》的注释本,这为读者提供了极大的方便。

1936 年,张纯一出版了《晏子春秋校注》,这是一部内容极其丰富和详细的注本。张纯一首先向读者提到孙星衍 1788 年对《晏子春秋》所做的工作,然后他仔细比较了其他经典文献中的类似内容,对《晏子春秋》的各种异文作出细致的梳理与考证。

1962 年,一部应当被看作是最全面详细的《晏子春秋》注本出版,这就是吴则虞的《晏子春秋集释》。在这部书中,吴则虞对于《晏子春秋》本身的各种有价值的资料以及其成书和流传的各种线索做了百科全书式的搜集与整理工作。两千年来,对于《晏子春秋》文本的每一条引用、每一条注释几乎都被吴则虞搜罗殆尽。吴则虞不仅对每一个难以理解的问题都给出了自己的意见,这些意见广征博引、极具启发,同时他还附录了大量的参考文献供读者了解整个学术史的发展。在前言中,吴则虞提出五条意见论证《晏子春秋》的作者是类似于淳于越那样的来自齐国的学者,在秦统一天下后所作。其中前三条意见属于文本之外的外部证据,说服力不大。但是第四条和第五条意见则为讨论《晏子春秋》的作者提供了一个新的思考维度。在这两条意见中,吴则虞指出淳于越所提出的"师古长久"与《晏子春秋》中的"毋变尔俗""重变古常"的思想相一致,而《晏子春秋》中的谏议,带有托古讽今的意味,又与李斯所说的"各以其学议之"的"议"相一致,因此吴则虞认为《晏子春秋》的成书,"极有可能就是淳于越之类的齐人,在秦国编写的"。可惜,吴则虞可以用来比较的淳于越与晏子的材料数量太少,导致他的结论很难成为定论。尽管如此,这些有关于文章体裁的争论应该已经激起汉学界足够兴趣,促使汉学家建立一个相似文体的数据库,搜集各种线索的马赛克,它们或许会给我们指出一个方向,从此我们可以辨认出创造《晏子春秋》文本原型的那只"隐形的手"。总而言之,吴则虞作为一个注释者、目录学家和一个文本比较研究的创新者,其所取得的成果有目共睹,今后任何有关于《晏子春秋》的研究都必须以他的著作作为出发点。

1966 年，台湾师范大学王更生完成了他的博士论文《晏子春秋研究》。这是王更生研究《晏子春秋》的第一个贡献，随后，他又出版了两部《晏子春秋》的白话翻译以及很多其他优秀的成果，这使他成为《晏子春秋》研究领域的专家。在其博士论文以及之后其编辑的《晏子春秋》读本中，王更生将已经出现在吴则虞书中的那些传统中国学者所关注的作者、真实性以及成书年代等问题做了简明扼要的总结。在他编辑的《晏子春秋》读本中，包括有完整详细的编年体的晏子传记，还有从诸如形而上学、精神、生死、伦理、政治哲学、财政、外交、自我修养、文学体裁、语法和修辞等各种角度对《晏子春秋》文本所作的分析与描述。

毫无疑问，在 1972 年之前的数十年间，无论是对于中国读者还是西方读者来说，《晏子春秋》都变得越来越容易接近和阅读。这不能不归功于众多学者在注释、翻译以及研究方面持续不断的努力。然而，1972 年银雀山竹简的发现，迫使具有漫长历史的《晏子春秋》文献研究不得不面对这 102 根竹简重新评价已有的各种结论。

### （Ⅷ-2）银雀山汉墓竹简

1972 年，在山东临沂东南的银雀山，发现了两座汉代墓葬，出土 4 942 枚竹简和大量残片。这两座墓葬的埋葬时间大概是公元前 140 年至 134 年和公元前 118 年，但是竹简的书写年代应当更早。银雀山汉简整理小组的成员将银雀山 1 号墓出土的 4 942 枚竹简分成两组。第一组竹简所记录的内容见于传世文献，而第二组竹简所记录的内容则早已佚失。在第一组竹简中，有 102 枚竹简组成了一个连续的序列（编号 528—630），其中包括 16 段比较清楚的文本，这些文本包含了今传本《晏子春秋》八篇中每一篇的部分内容。值得注意的是，这 102 枚竹简共有 2 970 个字，这相当于今传本《晏子春秋》7.2% 的内容。

此外，1972 年至 1977 年，在甘肃破城子、河北定县、安徽阜阳的考古发现中，都发现了《晏子》文本的一些残片，这些残片的时代大约是公元前 179 年至公元前 49 年。可惜，所有这些残片都太过残破，以至于没有办法复原出哪怕是一段完整的内容。

总之，在银雀山汉简与今传本《晏子春秋》间，存在着惊人的相似文本。根据 1972 年至 1977 年其他考古挖掘中所发现的类似《晏子》文本的残片，以及《淮南子》中所提到的"晏子之谏"，我们推测在大约公元前 200 年或者更早，有若干种竹简本《晏子》在知识阶层广泛流传。据此，我们可以得出一个更加令人兴奋的假设，那就是《晏子》文本的原型很可能在更早的时候就已经开始形成。

### (Ⅷ－3) 淳于髡（约生活于公元前 340 年）、滑稽与稷下学宫

1936 年，罗焌（公元 1874 年—1932 年）在研究过《晏子春秋》的学术史后得出了一个崭新的、惊人的结论。他认为:《晏子春秋》中所记录的故事和谏言，与齐国的淳于髡、楚国的优孟和秦国的优旃的事迹非常近似。很明显，这个想法太过唐突而且毫无根据。然而，它给我们提供了一个新的视角，它剥去了晏子文本中独特的历史和哲学身份，将其主角晏子从一个渊博的学者和政治家替换为一位修辞大师或者一名俳优。

四十年后，在 1976 年，王更生也提出了一个类似的观点。王更生指出，在晏子的文本中多次出现了没有意义的调笑段落，这暗示着作者或许是像淳于髡一样的俳优，晏子的文本反映出齐国稷下学宫中辩士的特点。

1986 年，"淳于髡假设"被吕斌再次强调。吕斌提出五条证据来论证淳于髡的言行和生平与《晏子春秋》中的内容有密切的联系，因此或许淳于髡即《晏子春秋》的作者。特别是，他指出淳于髡的劝谏就是建立在对晏子的崇拜的基础上；他可以直接进入齐国档案馆并从中获取有关于晏婴的材料；他就像晏子一样并不严格属于哪一学派；而且在整部《晏子春秋》中到处都展现出他的主张与滑稽风格。最后，吕斌把"淳于髡假设"又推进一步，他指出，无论是淳于髡还是晏子，都被描述成极为矮小的人。这一身材上惊人的相似，与其他证据一起，构成了吕斌的假说，一位与淳于髡生平非常近似的作者将自己的个人经验、哲学思想以及身体特征投射到他所编写的文本上，这一文本借用了历史上的名人晏子的名字，《晏子春秋》就此诞生了。

　　渐渐地，"淳于髡假设"成为《晏子春秋》作者问题上一个重要的意见。1998 年，陶梅生在《新译晏子春秋》中提出淳于髡的追随者编写了《晏子春秋》的看法。2000 年，林心欣在她的硕士论文《晏子春秋研究》中讨论了将《晏子春秋》归类为"儒家"、"墨家"和"传记类"的各种问题，她提出应将其归类为"俳优"，并进而讨论了淳于髡与《晏子春秋》的作者之间的关系。2005 年，赵逵夫在论文《〈晏子春秋〉为齐人淳于髡编成考》中提出了八条证据论证《晏子春秋》为淳于髡所编。赵逵夫的意见重复了吕斌在 1986 年所作《淳于髡著〈晏子春秋〉考》一文中的观点并且更加详细地论证了这一假说，他指出身材矮小的淳于髡编写了《晏子春秋》这样一部有关于身材矮小的晏子的故事集，通过这部书，淳于髡为自己赢得尊重。2011 年，Andrew Meyer 发表了一篇具有启发意义的综合性的论文，在论文中，他令人信服地指出《晏子春秋》是在田齐（公元前 379 年—221 年）统治者支持下所创作的，无论是《管子》还是《晏子春秋》，它们最初被编成的目的是让齐国的知识阶层将自己当作"齐国学派"，而非"儒家"或者"墨家"。

　　如今，在汉学研究领域以及相关的互联网上，《晏子春秋》为淳于髡或者其追随者所编的意见越来越成为一种共识。Andrew Meyer 的论文所讨论的内容以及深入的分析为未来的汉学研究铺平了道路，也许今后可以将他的观点与其他学者对稷下学宫、淳于髡的生平和中国古代俳优传统的研究结合在一起得出更进一步的结论。到那个时候，《晏子春秋》最初是由谁创作或者编写的，我们或许会得到一个确定的答复。

### （Ⅷ−4）近年来《晏子春秋》的研究以及未来数码人文和计算机思维时代的《晏子春秋》研究

　　自从 1974 年以后银雀山汉简整理出版，《晏子春秋》变成了新的汉学研究领域的焦点。许多学者分享他们的见解与专业知识，探索与《晏子春秋》相关的文本考察方面与历史问题方面研究的新路径。在这些学者中，值得注意的是 Rainer Holzer，他在 1983 年将《晏子春秋》内六篇翻译成德语，他在译文中加入一篇研究性的导言、详细的文本考证和许多宝贵的注释。1993 年，Stephen Durrant 在 Michael Loewe

的《早期中国文献书目指南》中为《晏子春秋》的文本和历史贡献了一份精练的学术提要，从而为研究《晏子春秋》的学生提供了极其宝贵的帮助。在中国，除了众多白话翻译和注释之外，从1974年到2010年，有不少于280篇与《晏子春秋》相关的学术论文在学术期刊上发表。此外，从1995年到2010年，在不同的大学和学院有30篇相关学位论文提交。

如此看来，除非在未来的考古挖掘中再次发现新的有关于晏子的竹简或相关文献，《晏子春秋》最初成书问题的研究将很难在过去研究的基础上再有突破。未来对于《晏子春秋》起源的研究，恐怕需要依靠最近被数码人文学学者发展出来的计算和统计工具进行。在谷歌搜索引擎中，输入"晏子春秋"，大约会看到400 000条结果。网站，比如中国古代文献数据库（CHANT）、中文文献计划（Ctext）、台湾汉学数字典藏资源等等，提供了数以百万计的可搜索字符，保存了浩瀚如海洋的中文文献，无论古代还是现代，无论是经典还是非经典，也无论是广泛流传还是极其罕见。文本挖掘方法一定能够分析这些数以百万计字符的大型数据库，并提出首次出现某些名称、词汇或成语的时间以及之后它们被如何使用等各种建议，从而使研究人员能够成功地回答有关文本形成时间的问题。而且，某些网站如DID-ACTE和费正清中心已经开始支持主要依靠计量文献学（stylometric analysis）和数据提取的汉学研究新技术。事实上，计量文献学程序可以学习某位作者的写作模式，并计算出这位作者写出一个作者身份不明的已知文本的可能性，从而解决关于某些特定文本的作者问题。根据最近的报道，来自得克萨斯大学奥斯汀分校的两位研究人员，用程序学习了某位作者的54个戏剧作品的模式，并计算出该作者撰写出一个已知文本的可能性，而这一已知文本在之前被看作是他人的作品。他们的测量分析确定了《将错就错》（*Double Falsehood*）这部从前被看作是莎士比亚学者刘易斯·西奥博尔德（Lewis Theobald，1688—1744）的作品，实际上是威廉·莎士比亚本人的作品。这一发现，震动了莎士比亚学界，也为我们提供了充分的理由去想象，在不久的将来在《晏子春秋》研究领域很可能也会发生类似的颠覆现象。

（欧永福　文，吴洋　译）

# Introduction

## The Yanzi Figure and the *Yanzi* Text in History

### ( Ⅰ ) Waiting in the Wings: The Yanzi Figure From the 6th through the 3rd Century BCE

First came Yan Ying[1] 晏婴 — the person. Years later, after he had long passed away,[2] came Yanzi 晏子 — the eponymous protagonist of *The Spring and Autumn Annals of Master Yan* 晏子春秋. Reliable evidence about the life and times of Yan Ying as a historical figure who lived in Qi 齐 during the 6th century BCE is scarce and cannot be accurately assessed.[3] Through the fifth and fourth centuries BCE his identity, nevertheless, gradually coalesced into a distinctive portrait. Initially, Yan Ying was briefly mentioned in the *Analects* 论语, in which he was succinctly praised by

---

1   Following the first line of Yanzi's biography in the *Shiji* 史记 (*Shiji*, 2134), Sima Zhen's (fl. 730) 司马贞, the author of the *Shiji suoyin* 史记索隐, points out that Yanzi's personal name was "Ying" (婴), posthumous name "Ping" (平), and courtesy name "Zhong" (仲). According to Liu Xiang 刘向 (79–8 BCE), "Ping Zhong 平仲" was his posthumous name. See, Section (III-3). On the basis of his posthumous name "Ping 平," he is often referred to as Yan Pingzhong 晏平仲.

2   Yan Ying is traditionally believed to have lived from 589 to 500 BCE. While the *Shiji* 史记, 1505, gives the year of Yanzi's death (500 BCE), his birth year remains uncertain and disputed. For a detailed discussion of the sources for these dates, see Wang Gengsheng 王更生, *Yanzi chunqiu yanjiu* 晏子春秋研究. Wenshi 文史, Taibei (1976): 18-34.

3   It would be, nevertheless, unreasonable to cast doubt on the traditional view of the historicity of Yan Ying who lived in this period. See the observation Richard L. Walker made decades ago in his "Some Notes on the *Yen-tzu ch'un-ch'iu*." *Journal of the American Oriental Society* 73.3 (1953): 156.

Confucius as a person who excelled at social relationships.[1] Next, he made his debut as an historical figure in the *Zuozhuan* 左传.[2] This text contains several anecdotes about him, centering on the pivotal events of the waning of the ruling house in Qi and the rise of the Tian 田 clan to supremacy during the second half of the sixth century BCE. These anecdotes, taken together, form an appealing personal portrait of Yan Ying as a minister who both delivered eloquent remonstrations and played a principled and courageous role in the service of three failing rulers.[3]

---

[1] *Analects* 论语, 5.17/10/21. For alternative datings of the *Analects*, see Michael Hunter. *Confucius beyond the Analects*. Studies in the History of Chinese Texts. Leiden and Boston: Brill, 2017; John Makeham, "The Formation of *Lunyu* as a Book." *Monumenta Serica* 44 (1996); Tae Hyun Kim and Mark Csikszentmihalyi, "History and Formation of the Analects," in Amy Olberding, ed., *Dao Companion to the Analects*. Dao Companions to Chinese Philosophy 4. Dordrecht, Netherlands: Springer, (2013): 21-36.

[2] *Zuozhuan* 左传, A9.1/226-B10.32/406, passim. For a reconstruction of Yanzi's biography elicited from the *Zuozhuan* and other traditional sources, see Zheng Qiao 郑樵 (1104–1162), *Tongzhi* 通志, 卷九二, *Siku Quanshu* 四库全书, 15A8-24B7; http://ctext.org/library.pl?if=en&file=10374&page=30 (2006-2017); Wang Gengsheng, ibid., 9-18; Alfred Forke, "Yen Ying, Staatsmann und Philosoph, und das Yen-tse tsch'untch'iu." *Asia Major* (first series) Introductory Volume (*Hirth Anniversary Volume*) (1923): 107-124; Rainer Holzer, *Yen-tzu und das Yen-tzu ch'un-ch'iu*. Peter Lang, Frankfurt, (1983): 2-7.

[3] The three dukes whom Yanzi served were Duke Ling 灵 (r. 581-554 BCE), Duke Zhuang 庄 (r. 553–548 BCE), and Duke Jing 景 (r. 547–490 BCE). For a vivid portrait of Yan Ying from the Spring and Autumn period (722–453 BCE) based on several anecdotes of the *Zuozhuan*, see Yuri Pines, "From Teachers to Subjects: Ministers Speaking to the Rulers, from Yan Ying 晏婴 to Li Si 李斯," in Garrett P. S. Olberding, ed. *Facing the Monarch: Modes of Advice in the Early Chinese Court*, Harvard East Asian Monographs 359, Cambridge, Mass., and London (2013): 70-80. For a literary-poetic analysis of two dialogues in the *Zuozhuan* — one between Yan Ying and Shuxiang 叔向, and another between Yan Ying and Duke Jing 景公 — see Wai-yee Li, *The Readability of the Past in Early Chinese Historiography*. Harvard East Asian Monographs 253. Cambridge, Mass., (2007): 349-355. However, (见下页)

Subsequently, during the second half of the fourth century BCE, the presence of Yanzi's figure in the literature began to make a mark, as he received both praise and critique. Chunyu Kun 淳于髡 (c. 340 BCE), a member of the Jixia 稷下 patronage community,[1] cited him with admiration in the remonstrations he delivered to Duke Wei of Qi 齐威王 (c. 378–320 BCE).[2] Mencius 孟子 (c. 372–c. 289 BCE), on the other hand, was offended when his disciple, Gongsun Chou 公孙丑 from Qi, persisted in weighing the abilities of his master Mencius against those of Guan Zhong 管仲[3] and Yanzi.[4] Mencius responded to the notion condescendingly by denying the importance of both Guan Zhong and Yanzi as two great ministers in Qi, characterizing them instead as two state functionaries whose

---

(接上页) regarding the historicity of the portrait of Yan Ying in the *Zuozhuan*, we should also note with caution Pines' remark about the ongoing "heated dispute" regarding the "several datings" of the *Zuozhuan*. See Yuri Pines, "Rethinking the Origins of Chinese Historiography: The *Zuo Zhuan* Revisited" *Journal of Chinese Studies*, The Chinese University of Hong Kong, 49 (2009): 429-442. See also the "Introduction," in Stephen Durrant, *et al.*, trs. *Zuo Tradition* / Zuozhuan 左传: *Commentary on the "Spring and Autumn Annals"*. 3 vols. Classics of Chinese Thought. Seattle: University of Washington Press, 2016; Barry B. Blakeley, "On the Authenticity and Nature of the *Zuo zhuan* Revisited." *Early China* 29 (2004): 217-67.

1   I borrow the term "the Jixia patronage community" from Andrew Meyer, "'The Altars of the Soil and Grain are Closer than Kin' 社稷戚于亲: The Qi 齐 Model of Intellectual Participation and the Jixia 稷下 Patronage Community." *Early China* 33-34 (2010-11): 37-99.

2   *Shiji*, 2347.

3   Guan Zhong (c. 720–645 BCE) or Guanzi 管子 is the famous seventh-century prominent minister in the State of Qi who effectively served Duke Huan 桓公 (d. 643 BCE) and was chief instrumental in making him the first Overlord (霸) in the Spring and Autumn Period. The philosophical collection entitled *Guanzi* 管子 is traditionally ascribed to him.

4   For Andrew Meyer's penetrating analysis of the rivalry between Mencius, representing the "textual ideal," and Yanzi, representing "social reality," see Andrew Meyer, ibid., 86-95.

value was strictly limited to their own immediate time and place.[1] The same dismissive attitude towards Yanzi and Guan Zhong was recorded a bit later in the preserved philosophical writings of Xunzi 荀子 (ca. 310–235 BCE; alt. ca. 314–ca. 217 BCE). A certain "Master," points that both Yan Ying and Guan Zhong are presented as ministers of major accomplishments; he then indicates that the accomplishments of Guan Zhong were superior to those of Yan Ying; finally, he concludes the section by calling Guan Zhong "a rustic boor" who did not properly fulfill the post of minister to his ruler, the Son of Heaven.[2] By implication, what is one to think of Yan Ying, whose achievements were claimed to be inferior to those of Guan Zhong?

### ( ‖ ) Center Stage: The Yanzi Figure from the 3rd through the 2nd Century BCE

Between the years 300 BCE and 200 BCE the Yanzi figure gradually underwent a change. His character evolved into a more central figure, both in narrated episodes in which he played a role, and in textual records that bore his name. Until the middle of the third century BCE his deeds, admired or dismissed, were always overshadowed by the general historical circumstances that framed his place in the text, and his character served a broader purpose than the limited scope of his pronouncements. However, around 250 BCE, the Yanzi figure moved from the periphery to occupy center stage in the narrated episodes. In the following years, his figure became a source for full references and attracted increasing critical attention.

---

1 *Mencius* 孟子, 3.1/14/6-15. Notably, however, *Mencius* 2.4/9/9-17 contains also a favorable reference to Yanzi in a poetic form concerning the remarkable persuasive power of Yanzi to bring about a fundamental change in Duke Jing's attitude towards his people.

2 *Xunzi* 荀子, 27/131/16-17. It is not clear who the "Master" is; it can be either Confucius or Xunzi.

The *Xunzi* also contains an episode (27/134/1-4) in which Yanzi bids farewell to Zengzi 曾子 with some wise words.

His image became more complex — sometimes exemplary, sometimes dubious — and eventually gave rise to a body of characteristic anecdotes that focused not only on his public deeds but also on his personality as an individual with a unique thought process. This shift towards the center is reflected in the following three major texts of the era: In *Mozi* 墨子;[1] *Lüshi chunqiu* 吕氏春秋,[2] and *Hanfeizi* 韩非子.[3]

In *Mozi*'s 墨子 chapter thirty-nine, "Against the Confucians" 非儒, Yanzi no longer plays a subsidiary character role, but rather emerges as a dominant figure on the "anti-Confucian," Mohist stage. He is portrayed as a close confidant and advisor to the Duke of Qi, whose Mohist agenda against the Confucians elicits from Yanzi a series of hostile views against the Confucians' worldview and excessive practices.[4] His attitude is harsh; he not only denounces Confucius personally as a rebellious and even murderous figure, but also strips Confucianism of its core values, presenting its advocates as practitioners of useless showmanship. From this point in the text onwards, the Yanzi figure becomes identified in several other texts and references as well, not only as a Mohist but also as a torchbearer against

---

1 For a discussion of the dating of *Mozi*'s Chapter 39 to the late Warring States Period, see Sixin Ding, "A Study on the Dating of the *Mozi* Dialogues and the Mohist View of Ghosts and Spirits." *Contemporary Chinese Thought,* vol. 42/4 (2011): 51-53; Carine Defoort and Nicolas Standaert, eds. *The* Mozi *as an Evolving Text: Different Voices in Early Chinese Thought.* Studies in the History of Chinese Texts 4. Leiden and Boston: Brill (2013): 5; John Knoblock and Jeffrey Riegel, trs. *Mozi* 墨子: *A Study and Translation of the Ethical and Political Writings*. China Research Monograph 68. Berkeley: Institute of East Asian Studies, University of California (2013): 40.

2 The *Lüshi chunqiu* compiled in 239 BCE by a group of scholars retained by Lü Buwei, aimed to explore all the knowledge of the world in one monumental encyclopedia.

3 Han Fei 韩非 (ca. 280–233 BCE) was the name of a multifaceted Chinese philosopher who, with several other philosophers and statesmen, developed the main doctrines of Legalism (*Fajia* 法家) in the end of the Warring States period.

4 *Mozi* 墨子, 9.7/65/24-66/14.

Confucius and Confucians alike.[1]

In the *Lüshi chunqiu* 吕氏春秋, the Yanzi figure functions authentically as a unique paradigm of a moral, self-critical, and courageous individual. The text contains three episodes that portray him acting in desperate and life-threatening situations. In the first, his benevolence and moral authenticity is so exemplary and inspirational for others that those he encounters devotedly sacrifice their lives for him.[2] In the second, his act of benevolence demonstrates his rare ability to be self-critical and self-demanding — a perfectionist's awareness of the implications of the entire scope of his actions and conduct.[3] In the third, he is presented as a model of great authentic courage, as he faces imminent execution.[4]

The *Hanfeizi* 韩非子 contains three sections on Yanzi pointedly directed against his reasoning regarding governmental concerns, against his humane approach to relief efforts, and against his psychological considerations in regard to harsh and lenient punishments. It seems as if the *Hanfeizi* considered the Yanzi figure a threatening embodiment of a world view that had to be challenged and refuted on Legalist grounds. The Yanzi figure is therefore met in the text with sharp philosophical criticism, and at one point he is even branded "insincere," with respect to his own argument. The first among these three sections attacks Yanzi's famous traits of frugality and abstemiousness. The text not only argues against the

47

---

1  E.g., *Kongcongzi* 孔丛子, 6.1/60/5-62/28 where Kung Fu 孔鲋 (子鱼), an eighth generation descendant of Confucius who went to great lengths to refute a set of Mohist claims that Yanzi was an anti-Confucian who criticized Confucius on the basis of a Mohist agenda. See also Zhang Zhan's 张湛 (fl. ca. 370 CE) commentary on the *Liezi* 列子 (冲虚真经), *SBCK*, 7/2B14; Liu Zongyuan 柳宗元 (773–819), *Bian Yanzi chunqiu* 辩晏子春秋, http://ctext.org/wiki.pl?if=gb&chapter=493447 (2006–2017): No. 16.

2  *Lüshi chunqiu*, 12.2/59/1-14.

3  Ibid., 16.2/91/19-26.

4  Ibid., 20.3/130/27-29.

senselessness of these two values, insofar as they can result in a complete lack of motivation amongst ministers to succeed, but also claims that Confucius himself had previously voiced this particular criticism against Yanzi.[1] The second section claims that Yanzi's humane and generous approach towards officialdom and the people shows that he lacked the ability to remove troubles and thereby exposed his ruler to grave disaster.[2] Finally, in the third episode, the text attacks Yanzi's lenient approach to punishment, claiming that Yanzi himself did not believe his own argument. For the *Hanfeizi*, Yanzi's lenient approach shows that Yanzi failed to understand clearly the meaning of governance.[3]

### (Ⅲ) The Soloist: The Yanzi Figure and the *Yanzi* Text during the Former Han

### (Ⅲ-1) The *Remonstrations of Yanzi* 晏子谏 in the *Huainanzi* 淮南子

All these textual examples suggest that around 200 BCE, the Yanzi figure not only played a more central role in narrated episodes that bear his name, but also most likely constituted the inspiration for several distinctive texts that focused entirely on his legacy — some of which included his name in the title. In 139 BCE, this stage in the evolution of the Yanzi figure became evident. In that year, the imperial kinsman Liu An 刘安 presented to Emperor Wu 武帝 an encyclopedic philosophical text known as the *Huainanzi*. The text's twenty-first chapter, entitled "An Overview of the Essentials 要略,"[4] aims to summarize and analyze the entire preceding twenty chapters and concludes by reviewing and explaining the genesis of important texts written by significant advisors and thinkers who played an

---

1  *Hanfeizi*, 33/90/19-23.

2  Ibid., 34/97/20-24; 34/98/22-99/9.

3  Ibid., 37/117/26-118/4.

4  *Huainanzi*, 21/223/19-228/31.

influential role in the past. The text reads:

Duke Jing of Qi

enjoyed music and sex while inside his palace

and enjoyed dogs and horses while outside his palace.[1]

When hunting and shooting, he would forget to return home.[2]

When enjoying sex, he did so indiscriminately.[3]

He built a terrace over the Road Bedchamber[4]

and cast a grand bell.

When it was struck in the audience hall,

the sound [was so thunderous that] all the pheasants outside the city

walls cried out.[5]

In a single morning [i.e., one court session] he distributed three thousand bushels of grain as largesse.[6] Liangqiu Ju and Zijia Kuai[7] led him about from the left and the right. Therefore, *The Remonstrations of Yanzi* 晏子谏 were born.[8]

To sum up: First, the *Huainanzi* discusses the circumstances that

---

1   See, e.g., *YZCQ*, Item – 1.5 [5]; Item – 1.25 [25].

2   See, e.g., *YZCQ*, Item – 1.23 [23].

3   See, e.g., *YZCQ*, Item – 3.5 [55]; Item – 4.2 [82].

4   See, e.g., *YZCQ*, Item – 2.7 [32].

5   See, e.g., *YZCQ*, Item – 8.9 [206]. According to Item 8.9 [206] in the received version, the huge bell indeed emitted a thunderous sound; however, the received version does not mention pheasants crying out outside the city walls when the bell was struck. In view of the "missing pheasants" from the received version of the *YZCQ*, Rainer Holzer raised doubts regarding the affiliation between the text referred by the *Huainanzi* as *The Remonstration of Yanzi* and the received version. See Holzer's comment, ibid. 9.

6   See, e.g., *YZCQ*, Item – 4.1 [81].

7   See, e.g., *YZCQ*, Item – 1.12 [12].

8   *Huainanzi*, 21/228/13-14. Except for two minor changes, the translation is adapted from John S. Major, *et al.*, trs. *The Huainanzi: A Guide to the Theory and Practice of Government in Early Han China*. Translations from the Asian Classics. New York: Columbia University Press (2010): 865.

gave rise to a text that it refers to as *The Remonstrations of Yanzi*; second, "remonstrations" voiced by Yanzi against Duke Jing are not only one of the core subjects of the entire bulk of the received version of the *YZCQ* but also the title name that Liu Xiang 刘向 (77–6 BCE) gave to the first two chapters of his definitive text of *Yanzi*;[1] third, the *Huainanzi*'s description of the seven circumstances that gave rise to this *The Remonstrations of Yanzi* match their corresponding items in four of the eight chapters of the received version of the *YZCQ*. We may thus conclude with relative confidence that around 139 BCE a text existed whose title identified it with Yanzi and whose contents shared a great similarity to the received version of the *YZCQ*. And indeed, some fifty years later, this stage of textual development was clearly defined when Yanzi's legacy was sealed as an outspoken and courageous minister and as the author of a popular, circulating text, entitled *The Spring and Autumn Annals of Master Yan* 晏子春秋. This legacy was secured among other unforgettable biographical narratives in Sima Qian's (c. 145 – c. 86 BCE) *Shiji* 史记.

### (Ⅲ-2) The Yanzi figure and the *YZCQ* in the *Shiji*

Yanzi's biography appears in chapter 62 of the *Shiji*, following that of Guan Zhong, which constitutes the first part of the Chapter.[2] It consists of four parts: the first two deal exclusively with Yanzi, while the third and fourth focus on him and Guan Zhong together. A number of biographical

---

1   For Liu Xiang's definitive text of *Yanzi*, see, Section (Ⅲ-3).

2   *Shiji*, 2131–2137. Translated in William H. Nienhauser, Jr. Ed. *The Grand Scribe's Records. Memoirs of Pre-Han China*. Bloomington and Indianapolis: Indiana University Press (1994): vol. 7, 14-17. For Nienhauser's analysis of the biographies of Guan Zhong and Yan Ying in the *Shiji*, see "The Implied Reader and Translation: The *Shih Chi* as Example," in Eugene Eoyang and Lin Yao-fu eds. *Translating Chinese Literature*. Indiana University Press, Bloomington, (1995): 15-40. See also Nienhauser's "Sima Qian and the *Shiji*," in Andrew Feldherr and Grant Hardy, *The Oxford History of Historical Writing*. New York, Oxford University Press, vol.1, (2011): 472.

sketches of both Yanzi and Guan Zhong, mostly drawn from the *Zuozhuan*, are scattered throughout the preceding chapter 32 of the *Shiji*.[1] Readers should note, however, that Sima Qian does not include in chapter 62 any of those biographical sketches previously related to Yanzi — only those of Guan Zhong's are recapitulated in the latter's biography. They should also note at the outset the concluding line of Yanzi's biography, before commencing to read this piece regularly from beginning to end. In this line, Sima Qian expresses his own profound admiration for Yanzi's personality in the following emotive statement:

If Yanzi were still alive, though I were only holding the whip for him, I would be pleased and longing to serve him.[2]

Now, as the readers return to the opening lines of the biography, they may notice that this concluding statement of admiration actually resonates throughout the entire memoir, shaping its choices regarding contents. Sima Qian first weaves the two memoirs together by establishing an historical link between Guan Zhong and Yanzi with the following words:

After Guan Zhong died, the state of Qi followed his governmental policies and Qi was regularly stronger than the other feudal states. Over one-hundred years later, Yanzi was there.[3]

*51*

Both the convergence and divergence between the biographies of Guan Zhong and Yanzi are thus established, bringing together chapter 62 as one historical unit. Readers are now compelled to examine and evaluate from a comparative perspective two figures of unequal historical magnitude: Guan

1  *Shiji*, 1477–1513. Translated in William H. Nienhauser, Jr. Ed. *The Grand Scribe's Records. The Hereditary Houses of Pre-Han China, Part I.* Bloomington and Indianapolis: Indiana University Press (2006): vol. V.1, 31-130.

2  *Shiji*, 2137.

3  *Shiji*, 2134. Except for a few changes, this translation of Yanzi's biography is adapted from William H. Nienhauser, Jr., *Memoirs, ibid.* For the calculation of over a hundred years' gap between Guan Zhong and Yanzi, see *Memoirs*, ibid., p. 14, n. 39.

Zhong, a minister whose brilliant policies are now pronounced to have shaped over 100 momentous years in Qi history; and Yanzi, a brilliant and outspoken minister, but a complete failure in saving the ruling house of Qi from its eventual demise. The first part of Yanzi's biography reads:[1]

> Yan Pingzhong 晏平仲, Ying 婴, was a native of Yiwei 夷维 in Lai 莱.[2] He served Duke Ling 灵 (r. 581–554), Duke Zhuang 庄 (r. 553–548), and Duke Jing 景 (r. 547–490) and because of his frugality[3] and vigor, he was esteemed in Qi. Even after he became Prime Minister of Qi, he did not have two servings of meat, and his concubines did not wear silk. At court, if the Duke addressed him, he would speak audaciously; if the Duke did not address him, he would act audaciously.[4] If the Way prevailed in the country, he would follow orders. If it did not, he would weigh the consequences of the orders. For these reasons, he was renowned among the princes in his service during three reigns.[5]

After reading this first part of Yanzi's biography bearing in mind the preceding biography of Guan Zhong, readers see that Guan Zhong is presented in chapter 62 as a remarkable figure who helped shape the history of Qi and who was personally involved in major turning points of its history. However, no similar narration is provided in the presentation of Yanzi's life. The first part of Yanzi's biography contains only a succinct record of names,

---

1 *Shiji*, 2134.

2 For a discussion of the location of Yiwei in Lai — Donglai 东莱, see *Memoirs*, ibid., p. 14. n. 40.

3 Notably, this particular reference to Yanzi's frugality is one of the rare cases that indicates a direct textual affiliation between the biography of Yanzi in the *Shiji* and the *YZCQ*. References to Yanzi's lifelong "frugality" with one term "俭" appear in several Han texts; however, the *Shiji* uses here the compound expression "节俭," which appears in connection to Yanzi only in the *YZCQ*, (2.14/15/27; 4.14/34/27) and not in any other pre-Han or Han texts.

4 Cf. *Analects*, 14.3/37/10.

5 *Shiji*, 2134.

place of residence, rank, and an approximate count of the years he spent in his official service to three dukes. Readers are offered no information regarding any major historical achievement of Yanzi in Qi; the text describes neither any important incidents nor any significant developments in his personal life by which readers might form a judgment. In contrast, the text itself does provide judgment in the form of a detailed list of observations regarding Yanzi's traits, virtuous conduct, and personality, as if he were a protagonist in a book whose story-line was somehow missing. Thus, after finishing reading the first part of Yanzi's biography, readers might well conclude that Yanzi played a much lesser role in the history of Qi than did Guan Zhong. Moreover, except for general background, readers receive no substantial information about the actual events and major developments of Yanzi's life. That said, they would most likely be attracted to his personality as a protagonist whose frugality, vigor, courage, honesty, integrity, and audacity were evident throughout his life, having made him eminently famous among the people of his time.

At this point, readers may find themselves perplexed by Sima Qian's selection of different types of biographical data for the two parts of the chapter. However, in light of the concluding line, they may resolve this discrepancy in view of Sima Qian's admiration of Yanzi's personality and his attempt to minimize the significant gap between the historical impacts of these two ministers on the fate of Qi. Sima Qian achieved this by posing Guan Zhong's historical achievements against Yanzi's finest virtues, thereby avoiding a direct comparison between the former, whose historical significance was great, and the latter, who bore almost no historical status but instead was a unique individual with rare qualities.

The second part of the biography[1] consists of two consecutive

---

1  *Shiji*, 2135.

episodes about Yanzi, which appear in the received text of the *YZCQ*.[1] The first among the two narrates in concise form an episode strikingly similar to Item 5.24 [134]. It tells the story of Yanzi's ransoming a certain Yue Shifu from captivity by selling one of his four horses, but failing, afterwards, to treat Yue Shifu with the proper respect. The ransomed prisoner reacts in protest against Yanzi's neglect of the proper rites, which brings Yanzi to immediately repent and treat him as an honored guest. The second episode is identical, word for word, with Item 5.25 [135]. It narrates the episode of the wife of Yanzi's eight-foot tall charioteer who is seeking to divorce her husband on the grounds that he drives Yanzi's chariot in a pompous manner. Yanzi, she argues, is not even six-feet tall[2] and acts modestly, even though he is a renowned prime minister. Her argument brings the charioteer to immediately repent and change his manner driving and Yanzi, who notices the change, recommends him for a high governmental post.

The two episodes are subtle, focusing on one implicit question: what does authentic identity consist of? In that regard, the two episodes can be analyzed from both philosophical and psychological perspectives. However, regarding Yanzi's biography, they contain no information about his life except for giving indirectly the detail that he was a person of diminutive stature. It seems that this part of Yanzi's biography again merely illustrates his set of virtues by narrating two accounts that lead the readers to realize two aspects of Yanzi's character: that he spared no effort to save a fellow

---

1 *YZCQ*, Items 5.24 [134]; 5.25 [135], 47/18-48/14. In the third part of the biography, however, Sima Qian specifically states that these two items were just "neglected stories" that were not selected from the text of *The Spring and Autumn Annals of Master Yan* that he read.

2 Since the ancient Chinese foot, *chi* 尺, is said to be about 23 centimeters, according to the narrated episode in Yanzi's biography in the *Shiji* and Item 5.25 [135], Yanzi's height would be less than 138 centimeters and his eight-feet charioteer would be184 centimeters. According to Item 7.1 [171], however, Yanzi's height was no more than five *chi* (115 centimeters).

person from a life-threatening predicament; that he was self-critical and thus able to change attitude in a complex personal situation; and that he had a profound ability to go beyond the outward appearances and fathom the inner reality of the people who surrounded him.

What was Sima Qian in incorporating these two episodes into Yanzi's biography? Again, in light of the "admiring" concluding epilogue, and given that Guan Zhong's biography in chapter 62 consists of 525 words while Yanzi's (at this point) consists of only 75, it appears that Sima Qian needed to lengthen Yanzi's biography in order to create a more balanced proportion between his discussions of Yanzi and Guan Zhong.

The third part of the biography[1] is mainly a literary assessment focusing on the respective writings of Guan Zhong and Yanzi. It reads:

"I have read through Mr. Guan Zhong's [1] 'Shepherding the People,'[2] 'Mountains on High,' [3] 'Chariots and Horses,' [4] 'Light and Heavy,' and [5] 'Nine Bureaus'[2] as well as the [6] *Spring and Autumn Annals of Master Yan.*' Their words are expressed with such detail that having seen the books they wrote I wanted to examine their actions and therefore have attached their biographies. As for their books, many people today have copies of them and therefore I have not selected from them but instead have selected some neglected stories."[3]

The third part of the biography entails a major stage in the history of the Yanzi's text. Sima Qian clearly states that he read five titles attributed

55

---

1 *Shiji*, 2136.

2 For a discussion of these five titles, some of which appear in the received text of *Guanzi*, see Allyn W. Rickett, tr. *Guanzi: Political, Economic, and Philosophical Essays from Early China*. Princeton Library of Asian Translations, Princeton (1985): vol. 1, p 6, n. 12-16.

3 These "neglected stories" (轶事) are most probably mentioned here in reference to the two episodes previously recounted in the second part of Yanzi's biography. They cannot be related to the major events narrated in Guan Zhong's biography, which do not fall into the category of "neglected stories."

to Guan Zhong as well as an additional sixth text, entitled *The Spring and Autumn Annals of Master Yan* 晏子春秋 attributed to Yanzi. He also states that these texts were finely written and very popular in his time. This statement provides solid evidence that by around 100 BCE, Yanzi's text had assumed its textual identity as an authentic biography. Further confirmation for this status is offered by its metonymic title (春秋)[1] given in the *Shiji*, and also by its broad circulation in the Han intellectual milieu.[2]

The last, fourth part of chapter 62 is the epilogue of the two combined

---

1  Later the editors of the *Siku Quanshu* would comment that like the *YZCQ*, some other texts, such as *Lüshi chunqiu*, were not arranged in strict chronological order by years and months and nevertheless bore in their title the metonymy *Chunqiu* 春秋. ("Spring and Autumn").

2  Notably, the present third part of the biography might be somewhat garbled. The title *The Spring and Autumn Annals of Master Yan* 晏子春秋, which appears at this point in the received text of the *Shiji*, as the sixth in a series of titles of Guan Zhong, was not included in the text of the *Shiji* that Liu Xiang quoted from in his Preface to the *Guanzi*. The latter reads: "His Honor the Grand Scribe said: 'I have read through Mr. Guan Zhong's [1] "Shepherding the People," [2] "Mountains on High," [3] "Chariots and Horses," [4] "Light and Heavy," and [5] "Nine Bureaus." His words are expressed with such detail.'" (*SBCK*, 1B12-2A1). Indeed, *The Spring and Autumn Annals of Master Yan* 晏子春秋 was not included as the sixth title in the text of the *Shiji* that Liu Xiang quoted from. In addition, the fact that Liu Xiang himself, about 75 years later, entitled his collated text of Yanzi "*Yanzi* 晏子" and not "*Yanzi chunqiu* 晏子春秋" might show that he was not aware of the latter title, although he was quite familiar with the biography of Yanzi in the *Shiji*, as his Preface to his *Yanzi* 晏子 indicates. See, in the present Section (III-3). Since the next reference to Yanzi's text as *The Spring and Autumn Annals of Master Yan* 晏子春秋 occurred about 300 years later, in Ying Shao's 应劭 (d. ca. 204 CE) *Fengsu tongyi* 风俗通义 (9.2/65/19) and the *Kongcongzi* 孔丛子 (5.3/58/13), the title, *The Spring and Autumn Annals of Master Yan* 晏子春秋 in the received text of the *Shiji* may have been a later insertion. It is quite possible, on the other hand, that the quoted passage from Liu Xiang's text of the *Shiji*, in his Preface to the *Guanzi*, was incomplete and that the parallel passage in the receive text of the *Shiji* is the text that genuinely records the complete set of the six texts that Sima Qian read, including *The Spring and Autumn Annals of Master Yan* 晏子春秋.

biographies of Guan Zhong and Yanzi.[1] Sima Qian presents the hidden tension between the historical memories of the two Qi ministers that he combined in chapter 62 to its culmination by issuing an implied harsh judgment against Guan Zhong:

Guan Zhong was what the world refers to as a worthy official, but Confucius belittled him. Could it be because he considered the Way of the Zhou to be in decline and [because] Duke Huan was worthy, yet Guan Zhong did not exhort him to become king, but rather proclaimed himself Overlord?

With these words, all of Guan Zhong's previously narrated achievements as a figure who shaped the history of Qi are reduced to mediocrity, with the metaphor Confucius had coined about him: "Guan Zhong was a vessel of small capacity" 管仲之器小哉.[2] As for Yanzi, however, Sima Qian brings the epilogue to its end with words of strong praise that show his great admiration for him as a personal idol:

"When Yanzi fell down upon the corpse of Duke Zhuang, he would not leave until he completed his ritual duties for his lord.[3] Could we say that he was 'one who regards seeing what was right but not doing it as cowardice'?[4] When it came to remonstrating, he was not afraid to brave his ruler's displeasure, and he was one whom we might refer to as 'exhausting his utmost in how to be loyal as he advances, and in how to correct his ruler's faults as he withdraws.'[5] If Yanzi were still alive, though I were only

57

---

1  Ibid., 2137.

2  Cf. *Analects*, 3.22/6/18.

3  Cf. Item 5.2 [112]; *Zuozhuan*, B9.25/283/12; *Shiji*, 1502. For a refined analysis of the episode that narrates the reaction of Yanzi to Cui Zhu's assassination of Duke Zhuang, see Wai-yee Li, *The Readability of the Past in Early Chinese Historiography*. Harvard East Asian Monographs 253. Cambridge, Mass., (2007): 322-326.

4  Cf. ibid., 2.24/4/21.

5  Cf. *Zuozhuan*, B7.12.5/176/7; *Xiaojing* 孝经, 17/4/18.

holding the whip for him, I would be pleased and longing to serve him."[1]

These final words with which Sima Qian imagines himself playing the role of Yanzi's old driver during the dangerous time surrounding the assassination of Duke Zhuang[2] conclude Chapter 62 of the *Shiji*. Sima Qian expresses his longing to serve Yanzi and admiration for him, leaving the reader to reflect upon the two memoirs and ponder who among their two heroes ascended to a greater dominance in the history of Qi. However, the link between the two memoirs has been cleverly achieved and, indeed, in the years immediately following the composition of the *Shiji*, Guan Zhong and Yanzi were referred to jointly and evaluated in comparative judgment as equals.[3]

The Yanzi figure continued to make a mark in the Han intellectual sphere during the first century BCE. The *Yantie lun* 盐铁论 by Huan Kuan 桓宽 (fl. 81–60 BCE) refers to him several times not only as a historical personage[4] but also as the source of a quoted text.[5] Moreover, toward the end of the century, his figure took on unforgettable proportions in a definitive text that Liu Xiang collated, prefaced, and entitled "*Yanzi*."

58

### (Ⅲ-3) The Formation of Liu Xiang's *Yanzi*

In 26 BCE, Emperor Cheng 成帝 (r. 33–7 BCE) ordered Liu Xiang 刘向, the great Han bibliographer, to collect and collate canonical scriptures, traditional narratives, and philosophical and literary works

---

1 This admiring statement, whereby Sima Qian assumes the role of Yanzi's driver, is made in reference to Yanzi's chariot driver during the time before and after the assassination of Duke Zhuang. See, Items 5.2 [112]; 5.3 [113].

2 See Items 5.2 [112]; 5.3 [113].

3 See Liu Xiang Preface to the *Yanzi* text where Yanzi is said to be the equal of Guan Zhong. See also, *Lunheng* 论衡, 82/357/12-13: "Guan Zhong and Yan Ying were both successful statesmen and writers."

4 *Yantie lun* 盐铁论, 5.4/ 32/8; 6.2/44/20; 7.1/50/20-23.

5 Ibid., 5.5/32/32.

of diverse kinds from all over the empire, along with those stored in the repositories of the palace.[1] Subsequently, Liu Xiang collected over eight hundred anecdotes that focused on the life and time of Yanzi and with much effort turned them into a set of 215 glued items which exhibit an apparent thematic and faint chronological order, that form the definitive text from which Yanzi's distinctive personal legacy was fashioned. This was a legacy of an exceptional personality of self-defined vocation and of diminutive body stature; an epitome of thriftiness and generosity alike; a master of psychological manipulation and comic, theatrical gestures; a profound scholar of vast knowledge and pragmatic reasoning, and a strong advocate against slavishly following the supernatural; a moral authority and courageous role model for the people of his era, who made Sisyphean efforts to lead the absurdly corrupt rulers he served towards just rulership; an equal to Guan Zhong and a match — even a rival — to Confucius.[2] Above all, however, the definitive text of 215 items that Liu Xiang produced

---

1  For several excellent discussions and references to Liu Xiang's bibliographical enterprises, see Anne Behnke Kinney, tr. *Exemplary Women of Early China: The Lienü zhuan of Liu Xiang*. New York: Columbia University Press: (2014): xv-xvii; Bret Hinsch, "The Composition of *Lienüzhuan*: Was Liu Xiang the Author or Editor?" *Asia Major* (third series) 20.1 (2007): 1-23; David R. Knechtges and Taiping Chang eds. *Ancient and Early Medieval Chinese Literature*. Leiden: Brill (2010): vol. 1, 560-565; Haun Saussy, "The Unreliable Anthologies: Liu Xiang and Liu Xin in Historical perspective." AAS Annual Meeting, Chicago, March 1997; Michael Loewe, *Biographical Dictionary of the Qin, Former Han and Xin Periods (221 BC–AD 24)*. Handbuch der Orientalistik IV.16. Leiden: Brill (2000): 372-375; Piet Van Der Loon. "On the Transmission of the *Kuan-tzu*." *T'oung Pao* 41 (1952): 358-93; Deng Junjie 邓骏捷, *Liu xiang xiao shu kao lun* 刘向校书考论. Ren min chu ban she, Beijing, 2012.

2  For an excellent discussion entitled "The 'anti-Confucius' of Qi: The *Yanzi chunqiu* and the Defense of the Qi Model," see Andrew Meyer, "'The Altars of the Soil and Grain are Closer than Kin' 社稷戚于亲: The Qi 齐 Model of Intellectual Participation and the Jixia 稷下 Patronage Community." *Early China* 33-34 (2010-11): 59-66.

was the first literary biography in ancient China that focused exclusively on one leading protagonist — Yanzi — a rare individual, a minister of the Altars of Soil and Grain;[1] a master without a disciple, who was a true hero of his life.[2] For almost each of his collated works, Liu Xiang presented a memorial to the Emperor consisting of a table of contents; an account of the textual material that was used in forming the collated text; a short narrative of the life, time, and works of the eponymous author; and a discussion of the value, authenticity, and authorship of the presented text.[3] Liu Xiang's report on *Yanzi* 晏子,[4] follows the exact same pattern: It opens with a table of contents which consists of eight *pian*. The first six are named "Inner Chapters" (内篇) and are respectively entitled "Remonstrations" 1 and 2 (谏上下), "Queries" 1 and 2 (问上下), and "Miscellany" 1 and 2 (杂上下). The seventh and eighth *pian* are designated "Outer chapters" (外篇) and are respectively entitled "Repetition cum Difference" (重而异者) and "Incompatible with Classical Learning" (不合经术者).[5] After the table of

---

1 *She* 社 was the spirit of the five colors of soil; *Ji* 稷 was the spirit of the five major grains. The altars of these two spirits (*Sheji* 社稷) were located at the center of each capital of the various territorial domains in ancient China and were used as a common political symbol for the state or the nation. Regarding the concept of "loyalty to the altars," see Yuri Pines, "Friends or Foes: Changing Concepts of Ruler-Minister Relations and the Notion of Loyalty in Pre-Imperial China." *Monumenta Serica* 50 (2002): 35-74.

2 Paraphrasing Charles Dickens' opening of *David Copperfield*: "Whether I shall turn out to be the hero of my own life, or whether that station will be held by anyone else, these pages must show." For different, more reserved analyses of the narrative license of the *YZCQ*, see Burton Watson, *Early Chinese Literature*. New York: Columbia University Press (1962): 185; Brian Moloughney, "History and Biography in Modern China" (PhD diss., Australian National University1994): 12-13. See also Henri Maspero, *La Chine antique*. Presses Universitaires de France - PUF; Édition: Nouv. Éd, Paris (1985): 486-7.

3 See Piet Van Der Loon, ibid., 360.

4 Liu Xiang's report on *Yanzi* is included as a "Preface" in many early and later editions of the *YZCQ*.

5 *SBCK*, 1A2-9.

contents, it opens with the project he set himself to accomplish, in which he recounts the main points surrounding the process involved in collating the different texts of *Yanzi*, and acknowledges the people who, under his editorial leadership, contributed to bringing the definitive text into existence. In the second part, he draws a lucid biographical sketch documenting recurring themes in Yanzi's legacy. Finally, in the third and last part of his report, he critically evaluates the literary and philosophical value of *Yanzi*, providing some answers regarding the authenticity and the authorship of the text and justifying his bold editorial decision to include anti-canonical items in the text. The Report reads:

The Commissioner of Water Management of the Eastern Part of the Metropolitan Area and Counsellor of the Palace, Your Servant [Liu] Xiang says: The royal copies of *Yanzi* 晏子, which Your Servant has collated, consisted of eleven *pian* 篇. Together with [Fu] Can 富参,[1] the Commandant of Changshe 长社, Your Servant has carefully collated and compared them with the five-*pian* text used by the Grand Astrologer, with Your Servant's own one-*pian* text, and with the thirteen-*pian* text used by [Fu] Can. The entire corpus of royal copies and private copies of *Yanzi* formed a set of thirty *pian*, comprising 838 items 章. I discarded twenty-two *pian* that duplicate the same material comprising 638 items, and established a definitive text of eight *pian* comprised of 215 items. Thirty-six items in the definitive text were absent from the private copies, while seventy-one items were absent from the royal copies. The royal and private copies were incorporated into the definitive text after comparing each of the variants and fixing the text on this basis. The royal copies had the character *yao* 夭 for *fang* 芳; the character *you* 又 for *bei* 备; the character *xian* 先 for *niu* 牛; and the character *zhang* 章 for *zhang* 长—and many other occurrences of this kind.[2] I have combined and pruned them with great care and after

---

1   For a discussion of the identity of Fu Can, see Piet Van Der Loon, ibid., p. 361, n. 2.

2   For a detailed analysis of the interchangeability of these characters, see *JS*, 51.

having transcribed everything into the definitive text, I inscribed it on dried bamboo slips cured over fire so that fine copies may be made from them.

Yanzi's personal name was Ying, his posthumous name Ping-zhong 平仲. He was a native of Lai — today's Donglai 东莱. He was a person of broad learning and retentive memory, and possessed a thorough understanding of ancient and modern learning. He served Dukes Ling, Zhuang, and Jing of Qi, and carried out his activities with parsimony.[1] He exhibited supreme loyalty and remonstrated relentlessly in leading the state of Qi. On the strength of his efforts, these rulers were able to rectify their conduct and the people were able to keep their family together. When he was not in government service, he retired and plowed in the countryside; when he was in government office, he never violated his principles. He could not be intimidated by evil; even when a naked blade was placed upon his chest, he did not relent to Cui Zhu's 崔杼 intimidation. He presented his remonstrations to the dukes of Qi; his words were elusive but telling, rhetorically pleasing but cutting. When he served as an envoy to the state sovereigns, no one could contravene his arguments. Such was the extent of his broad knowledge and thorough understanding. He was virtually equal to Guan Zhong 管仲. Within his family, he treated his relatives with proper affection; towards others, he treated the worthy generously. He served in the position of Prime Minister and received an emolument of ten-thousand *zhong* 钟.[2] Therefore, there were more than five hundred family members and relatives that depended upon his emolument in order to buy clothing and food, and the number of scholar-recluses who depended upon

1  Duke Zhuang was invested as the ruler of Qi by the powerful Cui Zhu 崔杼, who later murdered him for having an extra-marital affair with his wife. For a detailed description of Duke Zhuang's assassination and for an exposition of Yanzi's moral dilemma over serving the new ruler of Qi, Duke Jing 景公, who was also enthroned by Cui Zhu, see *YZCQ*, Item 5.3 [113]; *Zuozhuan*, B9.25.2/282.

2  *Zhong* 钟, a measure of grain in the state of Qi, consisted of six-hundred and forty liters.

his emolument in order to receive their daily bread was great. Yanzi wore coarse clothing and covered himself in deer pelts; he drove a worn out nag and a broken down chariot. He exhausted his entire emolument on family, relatives, and friends. Because of all this, the people of Qi treated him with honor. Apparently, Yanzi was a person of diminutive height.

All the text's first six *pian* are loyal remonstrations presented to his rulers; their literary style is remarkable, their moral principles can serve as paradigms, and all of them accord with the principles of the Six Classics. In addition to these six *pian,* there were duplicate items of somewhat different words and phrases that I dared not omit but rather rearranged them into one additional *pian.* There were also items that were somewhat not in accord with the learning of the Classics. They do not seem to be the words of Yanzi. I suspect that they were the product of masters of rhetoric of a later age. Once more, I did not dare omit them and have arranged them in one *pian.* Altogether the text consists of eight *pian*; the first six should always be available at your majesty's side for your royal perusal. I have carefully arranged the text according to its proper sequence. Your Servant, [Liu] Xiang, hereby presents them to your Majesty, at the risk of my own life. [1]

Certainly, the first part of Liu Xiang's Preface is exclusively based on a body of various pericopae laid before him as the chief editor, and collator of the text. Only he could authentically tell future readers how the process of producing the definitive text of *Yanzi* had evolved. His personal involvement with this process is also reflected in the third and last part of the Preface, in which he expresses not only his scholarly views regarding the value of the text but also his misgivings about setting off the items of the six "Inner Chapters" — which he thought authentically recorded Yanzi's own words — from the spurious items cited by masters of rhetoric of later times, in the eighth, "Outer Chapter," that he decided to retain. As for the second,

---

1  *SBCK*, 1B1-2B7.

biographical part of the Preface — readers who examine it in comparison to the biography of Yanzi in the *Shiji* will notice that Liu Xiang shares with Sima Qian the same admiration for Yanzi. Nevertheless, while Sima Qian was very careful not to draw extremely from the text that he, according to his own statement, had carefully read — *The Spring and Autumn Annals of Master Yan,*[1] Liu Xiang borrowed heavily from his collated *Yanzi* in drawing up his version of Yanzi's biography.[2]

From that moment onward, the historical legacy of Yanzi has been primarily represented and judged by the text (and preface) that Liu Xiang produced and introduced to his peers. Almost all other recorded echoes of Yanzi that have been found to date in other texts have been dimmed within the historical recollection.

### (Ⅳ) Taking Hold in the Process of Transmission: The *Yanzi* and the YZCQ from the Later Han through the Tang

After the death of Liu Xiang (d. 8 BCE), from the first century CE through the Tang, Yanzi's text, entitled either *Yanzi* or *YZCQ*, was listed, quoted and evaluated in the following 15 stages in its textual transmission:

It was probably listed under the title *YZCQ* in the section devoted to Confucian writings in Liu Xin's 刘歆 (d. CE 23) bibliographical catalogue —

---

1 For a rare case in which Sima Qian borrows a term directly from one of Yanzi's texts, see n. 42, above. Moreover, Sima Qian's reference to Yanzi's conduct in the events surrounding the assassination of Duke Zhuang is recorded in both the *YZCQ* the *Zuozhuan*. See above, n. 60.

2 Liu Xiang biographical portrait of Yanzi derives the basic facts about the time and places in which Yanzi lived from the biography of Yanzi in the *Shiji*. However, all other personal references in this portrait, such as to Yanzi's emolument of ten-thousand *zhong*; to his support of more than five hundred family members, relatives, and scholar-recluses; to his coarse clothing; and to his driving a worn out nag and broken down chariot, do not appear in any other source and therefore are most probably drawn entirely from Liu Xiang's collated text.

*Qilue* 七略 (*Seven Summaries*), as a text of 7 *pian*.[1]

It was listed under the title "*Yanzi*" in the section devoted to Confucian writings in Ban Gu's 班固 (32–92 CE) bibliographical chapter of the *Hanshu* 汉书 — *Yiwenzhi*'s 艺文志 (*Treatise on Literature*), as a text of 8 *pian*.[2]

The *Lunheng* 论衡, by Wang Chong 王充 (27–100 CE), referred to both Yanzi and Guan Zhong as "successful writers;"[3] it also quoted various statements pronounced by the Yanzi figure, almost all of which appear in parallel in the received text of the *YZCQ*.

The *Fengsu tongyi* 风俗通义, by Ying Shao 应劭 (d. ca. 204 CE), quoted the entire item 6.6 [146] of the *YZCQ*, identifying it as drawn from the *YZCQ*.[4]

The *Kongcongzi* 孔丛子, a work written by Wang Su (195–256 CE) in his youth,[5] noted that the title *Chunqiu* 春秋 was included in the title of the "Book of Yanzi."[6] It also strongly attacked the notion that Yanzi was an

---

1    See Zhang Shoujie's 张守节 (fl. 725–735), *Shiji zhengyi* 史记正义, *Shiji*, 2136. Years later, Liu Shipei 刘师培 (1884–1919), claimed that Zhang Shoujie was mistaken in replacing "eight" (八) *pian* with "seven" (七) *pian*, and in replacing the title of Ruan Xiaoxu's (479–549) lost catalogue *Qilu* 七录 with Liu Xin's *Qilue* 七略. See "Yanzi chunqiu pianmu kao" 晏子春秋篇目考 in his *Zuoan ji* 左盦集, VII2A; http://ctext.org/library.pl?if=gb&file=81813&page=4 (2006-2017).
    Liu Xin's *Qilue* was based on the previous work of his father Liu Xiang — *Bielu* 别录 (*Separate Records*). Both the *Bielu* and the *Qilue* were lost at the end of the Tang dynasty.

2    *Hanshu*, 1724. Ban Gu's *Yiwenzhi* 艺文志 (*Treatise on Literature*) preserved selected and abridged extracts from Liu Xing's *Qilue*.

3    *Lunheng*, 82/357/12-13.

4    *Fengsu tongyi*, 9.2/65/19.

5    For a discussion of the authenticity, date, and authorship of the *Kongcongzi*, see Yoav Ariel, *K'ung-ts'ung-tzu: The K'ung Family Master's Anthology*. Princeton Library of Asian Translations. Princeton, (1989) 56-69.

6    *Kongcongzi*, 5.3/58/13.

anti-Confucian who subscribed to Mohist views.[1]

Liu Xie 刘勰 (465–522) stated in his *The Literary Mind and the Carving of Dragons* 文心雕龙 that Yanzi's and Guan Zhong's writings are characterized by clarity in their factual accounts through their refined language style.[2]

The *Shuijing zhu* 水经注, by Li Daoyuan 郦道元 (d. 527), quoted a section from Item 2.24 [49] of the *YZCQ*, specifying Liu Xiang's prefaced text of the *YZCQ* as the source of the citation.[3]

The Tang encyclopedia (类书), *Beitang shuchao* 北堂书钞, completed by Yu Shinan 虞世南 (558–638) before 618, quotes the *Yanzi* and the *YZCQ* dozens of times,[4] all of which appear throughout the eight *pian* of the received text of the *YZCQ*.[5]

The Tang encyclopedia, *Yiwen leiju* 艺文类聚, completed by Ouyang Xun 欧阳询 (557–641) between the years 622 and 624, quoted the *Yanzi* and the *YZCQ* dozens of times, all of which appear scattered throughout the eight *pian* of the received text of the *YZCQ*.[6]

The *Qunshu zhiyao* 群书治要, an anthology of canonical and early historical statecraft, completed in 631 by Wei Zheng 魏征 (580–643), contains, listed under the authorship of Yan Ying, a collection of 38 full

---

1   Ibid., 6.1/60/5-62/28.

2   *Wenxin diaolong* 文心雕龙, *SBCK*, 6A9.

3   *Shuijing zhu* 水经注, 4.1 河水; *SBCK*, 35B3.

4   All the similar determinations that will follow were arrived at by digitally comparing and locating parallels between the received text of the *YZCQ* and the encyclopedic compilations or anthologies under consideration in http://ctext.org (2006–2017).

5   Of these instances, the *YZCQ* is explicitly cited in Bei-tang shu-chao ten times. Some of the quoted items in the Tang encyclopedias cite the *YZCQ* for their textual source, but many others are introduced with "晏子曰" ("Yanzi said"), without direct reference to the *YZCQ* as the specified source. All these quotations, however, appear in the received text of the *YZCQ*.

6   Of these instances, the *YZCQ* is explicitly cited 11 times.

items entitled *Yanzi*,[1] all of which appear throughout the eight *pian* of the received text of the *YZCQ*.[2] These 38 intact items consisted of 7,047 characters, which amount to no less than 17% of the entire bulk of 41,324 characters of the received text. The items are rearranged, sometimes in slightly different sequence, to form a *Yanzi* anthology of six parts. Although they are titled identically as the six "Inner Chapters" of Liu Xiang's *Yanzi*: "Remonstrations," (1 and 2), "Queries" (1 and 2), and "Miscellany" (1 and 2), they also include several items from the 7th and the 8th "Outer Chapters" of the text as well.

The bibliographical monograph of the *Suishu Jingji zhi* 隋书经籍志 from 656 listed the *YZCQ* in the section devoted to Confucian writings as a seven-*juan* 卷 text, authored by Yan Ying.[3] This bibliographical monograph is the only one compiled between the Han and the Tang, which is still preserved intact, and includes features from several now lost pre-Tang catalogues including Ruan Xiaoxu's 阮孝绪 (479–549) *Qilu* 七录.

The official dynastic history of Tang, the *Jiu Tangshu* 旧唐书 by Liu Xu 刘昫 (887–946), was later recompiled by the Song scholars Ouyang Xiu 欧阳修 (1007–1072) and Song Qi 宋祁 (998–1061) as *Xin Tangshu* 新唐书. The two "histories" listed the *YZCQ* in the section devoted to Confucian writings as a seven-*juan* 卷 text, authored by Yan Ying.[4]

The Li Shan 李善 (d. 689) commentary to the *Wen Xuan* 文选注 quoted the *YZCQ* about 40 times. All these references appear in the eight *pian* of the received text of the *YZCQ*.

67

---

1 The *Qunshu zhiyao* also contains in its section of the *Shiji* a full quotation from Yanzi's biography, which refers to Yanzi's text not as *Yanzi* but as *YZCQ*. See, http://ctext.org/text.pl?node=278855&if=en [3] (2006-2017).

2 See, http://ctext.org/text.pl?node=278901&if=en (2006-2017).

3 *Suishu*, 34, 997. According to the *Siku quanshu tiyao* (*YZCQ*) 四库全书提要 (晏子春秋), 2A6, the *Suishu Jingji zhi* listed the *YZCQ* as an "eight [*pian*]" text, not "seven [*pian*]."

4 *Jiu Tangshu*, 2023; *Xin Tangshu*, 1509.

The Tang encyclopedia *Chuxueji* 初学记 by Xu Jian 徐坚 (659–729) quoted the *Yanzi* and the *YZCQ* dozens of times, all of which appear throughout the received text of the *YZCQ*.[1]

The philosophical anthology Yilin 意林, authored by Ma Zong 马总 (d. 823), listed the text under the title *Yanzi*, as an eight-*pian* text, comprising 16 items, all of which appear in the received text of the *YZCQ*.[2]

To sum up, during the period under discussion:

1. The *Yanzi* text was listed, recognized, and transmitted under two titles: *Yanzi* and *YZCQ*.

2. Liu Xiang's prefaced *Yanzi* was circulated and directly referred to as a source of citation.

3. All the text's Inner Chapters' titles were known and referred to by their names.

4. Yan Ying was ascribed with the authorship of the text.

5. The text was classified as a Confucian text.

6. The literary value of the text was highly appreciated.

7. A considerable part of the text appeared in encyclopedias and compendia alike.

8. The text's two Outer Chapters were sometimes reduced to one "Outer Chapter." Occasionally, in the reduction of these two chapters, items from them were scattered under the names of the six "Inner Chapters." Thus, we may reasonably assume that the outer chapters' text subdivision to either *pian* or *juan* was somewhat flexible.

## (Ⅴ) Identity Mutation: Liu Zongyuan's 柳宗元 (773–819) Mohist View of the *YZCQ*

This stable transmission of a highly regarded text, ascribed to its

---

1  Of these instances, the *YZCQ* is explicitly cited 9 times.

2  See *Yilin* 意林, 卷 1, 1/5B1; http://ctext.org/library.pl?if=en&file=33691&page=32 (2006–2017).

ancient author and bearing a preface by its historical imperial collator, was suddenly disrupted. The fixed status that the text enjoyed until the end of the eighth century — its repeated listings in all dynastic bibliographies and major catalogues alike as a Confucian text, as well as the extensive quotations as a source of traditional lore in the most celebrated encyclopedias — ended rapidly. It was the great poet and statesman of the Late Tang, Liu Zongyuan, whose short essay "Discussing *YZCQ*" placed the exalted status of the text into doubt. His essay reads:

Sima Qian read the *YZCQ* and highly valued it, but he did not know how this text came to be. Some say: "Yanzi wrote it and others carried it forward." Others say: "It was written by the descendants of Yanzi." All of them are wrong. I suspect that it was someone among the followers of Mozi in Qi who wrote it. Mozi loved frugality and Yanzi was famous for this trait in his generation. Therefore, the followers of Mozi wrote his deeds with great respect in order to promote their own methods.

At this point, Liu Zongyuan summarizes basic features in Mohist philosophical agendas, concluding that the *YZCQ* shares basic traits with them.[1] He then continues:

69

---

1　Liu Zongyuan's list of the Mohist's dominant features, which he claims the *YZCQ* shares, is problematic. While the six "Inner Chapters" of the *YZCQ* bear notable Mohist features such as "Moderate Consumption" (节用) and an enthusiastic attitude in favor of friendly and humane interaction among people (an attitude Liu Zongyuan might have incorrectly, in my opinion, interpreted as the famous Mohist trait of "Impartial Love — 兼爱"), his reference to the "condemnation of Confucius" (非孔子) and "condemnation of Confucianism" (非儒) as Mohist features are prevalent only in the eighth *pian*, the outer-heretical chapter of the received text. As for the Mohist trait of fondness for discussing the affairs of the ghosts (好言鬼事) — ghosts do not play any part in the entire text and there is not a single passage that speaks to "condemnation of music" (非乐). Yanzi indeed expresses in Item 1.6 [6] his revulsion of popular music, but only because he is piously inclined, as he himself proclaims, only to the music of antiquity. Furthermore, in Item 2.22 [47], Yanzi pronounces his objection to the lavish burial (非厚葬) Duke Jing is about to give (见下页)

Ever since Liu Xiang and Liu Xin, Ban Biao (3–54) and Ban Gu, fathers and sons all classified the text among Confucian works. It is extremely regrettable that all these scholars did not examine it more closely. Had the author not been a man from Qi, he could not have recounted Yanzi's deeds; had the author not been a follower of Mozi, he could not have rendered it the way he did. Henceforth, when classifying the text amongst philosophical books, it should be classified Mohist. It is not that Yanzi was a Mohist, but those who wrote the book were followers of the way of Mohism.[1]

This concluding line is a bombshell in disguise — it disassociates the historical, "non-Mohist" Yan Ying from the Mohist-oriented text that bears his name. Furthermore, given the previous statement that Yanzi's descendants likewise did not author the text, it implies that the text was not authentic. The upshot of this contention is that it did not represent authentically what it presumes to represent but serves as a vehicle to advance a hidden agenda of some Mohists from Qi to promote their own ideas.

To summarize: Liu Xiang had stated previously that the 8th *pian* of the *Yanzi,* which he created, contained problematic material that did not reflect the words of Yanzi but was probably the product of masters of rhetoric of a later age. Subsequently, the young Wang Su made a stupendous effort throughout the whole 18th chapter of the *Kongcongzi* to persuade his readers that Yanzi was not an anti-Confucian who subscribed to Mohist

---

(接上页) Liangqiu Ju; yet his objection is not to lavish burials, but rather to the lavish burial of a manipulative minister such as Liangqiu Ju. Liu Zongyuan may have come to realize the possible weakness of his "Mohist" argument and therefore sealed the argument by pointing out a true textual fact that garners for the *YZCQ* a Mohist flavor. On two different occasions in the text, Mozi himself proclaims consecutively his exaltation of Yanzi's Way (道). See Items 3.5 [55]; 5.5 [115].

1　辩晏子春秋, in 增广注释音辩唐柳先生集, *SBCK*, http://ctext.org/library. pl?if=gb&file=78042&page=126 (2006-2017).

views identical to those he himself pronounced in the 8th *pian* of the *YZCQ*. But it was rather Liu Zongyuan's blunt and unsparing criticism that changed the course of the entire text of *YZCQ*'s trajectory — its authenticity, date, authorship, and philosophical vision henceforth always would be subject to debate[1] — and almost each of these debates will always echo Liu Zongyuan's iconoclastic views of the text, at least in spirit.

## (Ⅵ) A Bibliographical Confusion: The *YZCQ* during the Song

The transmission of the *YZCQ* during the Song splits into two inconsistent lines of transmission: the encyclopedic, which manifests the impression of a stable transmission of the text; and the bibliographical, which seems to undermine this impression.

### (Ⅵ-1) The *YZCQ* in Song encyclopedias

The incorporation of many direct and indirect quotations from the *YZCQ* into the major encyclopedic compilations of the Song establishes an image of stable transmission of a single text over a period of 300 consecutive years throughout the Song.[2] The following list of 122

71

---

1  This debate has spanned a thousand years. Scholars like Chao Gongwu 晁公武 (1105–1180) and Zhang Xuecheng 章学诚 (1738–1801) adapted Liu Zongyuan's "Mohist" view of the text (*JS*, 605); but others, like Sun Xingyan 孙星衍 (1753–1818), rejected it completely. Much later, Zhang Chunyi 张纯一, in his preface to his commentary edition of the *YZCQ* of 1930, suggested that the text was made of mixed material—60–70% Mohist, and 30–40% Confucian. See his Preface in *Yanzi chunqiu jiaozhu* 晏子春秋校註 in the *Xinbian Zhuzi jicheng* 新编诸子集成 series, Vol. 6. Taibei, Shijie shuju 台北, 世界书局 (1972): 1. http://ctext.org/library.pl?if=gb&file=94142&page=513 (2006–2017).

2  All of the following Song encyclopedia quotations appear in the received text of the *YZCQ*. However, as is the case with the Tang encyclopedias, some of the quoted items in the Song encyclopedias cite the *YZCQ* as their textual source, but many others are introduced with "晏子曰" ("Yanzi said"), without direct reference to the *YZCQ* as the specified source.

directly quoted items demonstrates the scope of the text's popularity and its unchanging transmission-status as a source of ancient lore during the Song:

| Encyclopedia | Compiler | Quoted items directly referring to the *YZCQ* |
|---|---|---|
| *Taiping yulan* 太平御览 | Li Fang 李昉 (925–996) | 86 items |
| *Shilei fu zhu* 事类赋注 | Wu Shu 吴淑 (947–1002) | 11 items |
| *Jizuan yuanhai* 记纂渊海 | Pan Zimu 潘自牧 (ca. 1195) | 10 items |
| *Yuhai* 玉海 | Wang Yinglin 王应麟 (1223–1296) | 15 items |

When all the Song encyclopedia quotations of the *YZCQ* are digitally assembled to form an integrated database together with all the *YZCQ* quotations that appear in the Tang encyclopedias and anthologies, the appearance of identical items repeatedly quoted from the two eras suggests a continuous line of stable transmission of the *YZCQ* text that starches from the early Tang to the end of the Song.[1] One specific item in this database, however, deserves a privileged status in evaluating the transmission of the text. The last, 215th item in the received text of the *YZCQ* is not only first

---

1   See, e.g., Item 1.25/10/27 [25] in the received text, which appears in parallel and is referred to directly to the *YZCQ* in both the Tang anthology *Qunshu zhiyao*, 群书治要, 卷三十三, 晏子, 杂上, and, almost 600 years later, in the Song encyclopedia *Jizuan yuanhai* 记纂渊海 (卷四十八). See http://ctext.org/text.pl?node=417989&if=en [5] (2006-2017), and http://ctext.org/wiki.pl?if=gb&chapter=433368 [90] (2006-2017), respectively.

directly quoted in two Tang anthologies, *Qun shu zhi yao* (631) and *Yi-lin* (ca. 823), but is then subsequently quoted in the Song encyclopedia *Taiping yulan* (938), and finally is quoted in the Ming encyclopedia *Tian zhong ji* 天中记 (1569). However, this passage can also be traced back to its ancient origin as bamboo strips no. 624-630, which comprises the sixteenth item in the Yinqueshan *Yanzi*.[1] The stages that these seven bamboo strips have traversed in their journey from Tomb #1 in Yinqueshan (140 BCE), through the Tang anthologies and the Song and Ming encyclopedias, up to the formation of the received text from the various printed editions, can therefore be specified, and can enhance the impression of the stable transmission of the entire text of the *YZCQ* throughout the ages.[2]

### (VI-2) The *YZCQ* in Song catalogues and bibliographical lists

From the 1st century CE through the Sui and the Tang, the *Yanzi* text was persistently transmitted under the titles *Yanzi* or *YZCQ* as either

73

---

1   For a discussion of the discovery of 102 *Yanzi* bamboo strips and fragments, excavated in 1972 at Yinqueshan, see, Section (VIII-2).

2   See *YZCQ*, 8.18a/75/3-7 [215]; *Yinqueshan Han mu zhujian* (*yi*), [释文; 注释], 104-105; 群书治要, 卷 三十三, 晏子, 杂下, http://ctext.org/text.pl?node=417998&if=en [4] (2006-2017); 意林, 卷一, 晏子八卷, http://ctext.org/text.pl?node=566572&if=en [16] (2006-2017); 太平御览, 鳞介部七, 鱼上, http://ctext.org/text.pl?node=409716&if=en [44] (2006-2017); and *Tian-zhong ji* 天中记, 卷二十七, http://ctext.org/wiki.pl?if=en&chapter=73792[6] (2006-2017). For a full discussion of the Yinqueshan Han bamboo strips 银雀山汉墓竹简, see, Section (VIII-2). The fact that all sixteen items of the Yinqueshan Han bamboo strips, from ca. 140 BCE, comprise 7.2% of the entire received text of *YZCQ*, reflects conclusively on the text's authentic stable transmission from the Han onwards up to the present. However, the fact that at least one of these items can be traced to its various transmitted Tang, Song and Ming stages throughout the ages gives the impression of this authentic transmission of the *YZCQ* text more weight.

an 8 *pian, 7 pian* or 7 *juan* text. Throughout this period, all ascribed the authorship of the text to Yan Ying himself, except for Liu Zongyuan (773–819), who argued in his "Mohist" essay that the text was a product of a follower of Mozi from Qi.[1] In the Song, however, many sources began to list the text as a 12 *juan* one.[2] Some scholars argued that Yanzi's 8 *pian* text of the Han was no longer extant, and several major bibliographers denied to Yan Ying the authorship of the text.[3]

Wang Yaochen 王尧臣 (1001–1056) was probably the first to record in his catalogue, *Chongwen zongmu* 崇文总目, a 12 *juan* text of the *YZCQ*. He placed the text in the section devoted to Confucian writings, stated that the 8 *pian* text of the Han was no longer extant, and determined that it would be wrong to ascribe the authorship of the text to Yan Ying because, as he argued, the text was written by later authors.[4]

Following Wang Yaochen, Chao Gongwu 晁公武 1105–1180 also listed the *YZCQ* as a 12 *juan* text in his private library catalogue *Junzhai dushu zhi* 郡斋读书志. However, he incorporated a large quotation from Liu Zongyuan's "Mohist" essay, explicitly adapted Liu's argument, and

---

1 See, Section (V).

2 The *Songshi Yiwenzhi* 宋史艺文志 (*Songshi*, 5171), compiled after the Song by Tuotuo 脱脱 (1313–1355), situates the *YZCQ* in the section devoted to Confucian writings also as a 12 *juan* text.

3 An exception to this Song attitude can be found in the Song encyclopedia *Cefu Yuangui* 冊府元龟 (1013), which identifies "Yan Ying, the Prime Minster of Qi" as the author of the *YZCQ*. Nevertheless, the encyclopedia does not refer to the number of the *pian* or *juan* in the text, while almost all other entries for texts offer specified number of either *pian* or *juan*. This absence gives the impression that the compiler of the encyclopedia, Wang Qinruo 王钦若 (962–1025), may have been aware of the conflicting information regarding the number of *pian* or *juan,* and sought to avoid the problem altogether by ignoring it completely. See *Cefu Yuangui*, 卷八百五十四, http://ctext.org/wiki.pl?if=en&chapter=64829 [5] (2006-2017).

4 *Chongwen zongmu* 崇文总目, http://ctext.org/wiki.pl?if=en&chapter=415282 [72] (2006-2017).

placed the text in the section devoted to Mohist writings.[1]

Somewhat later, Chen Zhensun 陈振孙 (fl. 1211–1249) added in his *Zhizhai shulu jieti* 直斋书录解题 a detailed reference to the *YZCQ,* in which he tried to incorporate all possible bibliographical worlds. He placed the text back in its traditional section devoted to Confucian writings and then made the following comment:

*YZCQ* in 12 *juan.* Written by Yan Ying Ping Zhong, a High Officer from Qi. The *Hanshu* states that the text consists of 8 *pian* but the reference is to a text entitled *Yanzi.* In the Sui and Tang, the text was listed as 7 *juan* text and began to be entitled *YZCQ.*[2] Now the number of *juan* differs so I do not know if this text is indeed the original text or not.[3]

At the end of the Song era, Wang Yinglin 王应麟 (1223–1296), commenting on the section devoted to Confucian writings in the *Hanshu Yiwenzhi*, adapted Liu Zongyuan's "Mohist" view of the text. He also proffered an awkward explanation concerning the discrepancy regarding whether the text involves 8 *pian* or 12 *juan.* He followed Wang Yaochen's argument according to which later authors compiled the text and thereby arrived at the conclusion that later textual accretion of material altered the

75

---

1   *Junzhai dushu zhi* 郡斋读书志, 卷十一道家类法家类墨家类纵横家类 [95; 96]; http://ctext.org/wiki.pl?if=gb&chapter=564340 [95; 96] (2006-2017). The entry's inclusion of the directly referred long quotation from Liu Zongyuan's "Mohist" essay pronounced some 300 years earlier testifies to the formative status of Liu Zongyuan's essay in the history of the *YZCQ* text.

2   Obviously, Chen Zhensun was not very familiar with the biography of Yanzi in the *Shiji*, in which Sima Qian explicitly states that he read a text entitled *YZCQ*. See, Section (III-2).

3   *Zhizhai shulu jieti*, 卷九, 儒家类, http://ctext.org/wiki.pl?if=gb&chapter=811528# 儒家类 (2006-2017).

inner division of the text from 8 *pian* to 12 *juan*.[1]

It is worth noting that, as late as the end of the Qing, Liu Shipei 刘师培 (1884–1919) added another convoluted explanation in order to deal with the conflicting bibliographical references to the text of the *YZCQ* as either 8 *pian* or 7 or 12 *juan* text. He suggested that during the Sui and the Tang, the two "Miscellany" (杂) chapters (*pian* 5 and 6) were combined to form one *juan* and that afterwards, in the Song, the first 5 *juan* of this "new" 7 *juan* edition were divided into two *juan*, forming a set of 10 *juan* that together with the "Outer" 2 *juan* (which remained intact) gave rise to the 12 *juan* edition of the *YZCQ*.[2]

It seems, however, that the elegant way in which the editors of *Siku quanshu* (1782) dealt with this puzzle of divergent bibliographical references, approximately 100 years before Liu Shipei, should have resolved this confusion. Toward the end of the "Synopsis" (提要) of their textual version of the *YZCQ,* they added the following short section in which they discussed the bibliographical discrepancies of the text:

The *Hanzhi* [*Hanshu Yiwenzhi*] and the *Suizhi* [*Suishu Jingjizhi*] listed the text as an 8 *pian* text. Then, in the bibliographies of Chen Zhensun and Chao Gongwu it was listed as a 12 *juan* text. It turned out that by then, the

---

1 *Han Yiwenzhi kaozheng* 汉艺文志考证, 卷五, http://ctext.org/wiki.pl?if=en&chapter=556508 [5; 6] (2006-2017). See also, Wang Yinglin's *Yuhai*, 玉海, 卷四十一. http://ctext.org/wiki.pl?if=gb&chapter=933116&remap=gb [11; 12] (2006-2017). About 500 years later, Sun Xingyan 孙星衍 (1753–1818), in his introduction to his commentary edition of the *YZCQ*, argued that in the Song *YZCQ text*, each of the 7 *juan* was split into two, forming a 14 *juan* text. He argued that the *Yuhai* reference to the *YZCQ* as a 12 *juan* text was an error and characterized Wang Yinglin's explanation of the discrepancies in the number of *juan* of the text as "preposterous" (妄言). See, *Yanzi Chunqiu* 晏子春秋, *Sibu beiyao*, Shanghai, Zhonghua shuju (1989): Vol. 53, 1A5; 1B15.

2 See "Yanzi chunqiu pianmu kao" 晏子春秋篇目考 in his *Zuoan ji* 左盦集, VII2A-B; http://ctext.org/library.pl?if=gb&file=81813&page=4 (2006-2017).

arrangements of the text's chapters have already been considerably altered.[1]

In these few short lines, the *Siku Quanshu*'s editors first acknowledge the existence of the bibliographical discrepancies recorded from the Han throughout the Song. They then suggest the obvious. Namely, they claimed that these discrepancies were the result of the considerable changes in the arrangement of chapters that the text had undergone over the decades; that is, that all these discrepancies were purely technical in nature, and nothing more. Simply stated, the entire uncertainty boils down to the confusion surrounding the transmission and editing of the text over the years.

## (Ⅶ) In Print: The *YZCQ* from Song through Qing

### (Ⅶ-1) Early Editions of the *YZCQ*: The Yuan woodblock and the Ming movable type editions

It is entirely reasonable to infer that a woodblock edition of the *YZCQ* already existed in the Song; however, evidence to that effect is quite paltry, almost nonexistent. Therefore, any such assumptions remain a matter of conjecture.[2] In any event, two of the notably earliest woodblock and

77

---

1   *Siku quanshu tiyao* (*YZCQ*) 四库全书提要 (晏子春秋), 2A7-8.

2   The Li family Mianmiaoge woodblock edition of the Ming 明李氏绵眇阁刻本, in Feng Mengzhen's 冯梦桢 (1546–1605) *Xian Qin zhuzi hebian* 先秦诸子合编, was said to be based on a Song woodblock edition, according to one of its two added postscripts (*JS*, 43). In contrast, however, the catalogue of Ju Yong 瞿镛 (1794–1846) records it as based on a Yuan woodblock edition. See, http://ctext.org/library.pl?if=gb&file=29296&page=6 (2006-2017). Furthermore, Wu Zeyu 吴则虞 (1913–1977), in his critical discussion of the Li Family edition of the late Ming (*JS*, ibid.) points out that the fact that the last item of the received version (*YZCQ*, 8.18 [215]) is missing from this edition indicates that it could not have been produced in the Song. Notably, moreover, the Li Family edition of the late Ming was the edition upon which the editors of the *Siku quanshu* 四库全书 choose to base their edition, but their "Synopsis" refers to neither the Song nor the Yuan editions, upon which their choice of this late Ming edition was based. See, http://ctext.org/library.pl?if=gb&file=62378&page=3(2006-2017).

moveable type editions of the *YZCQ* whose existence has been verified are:

(1) A woodblock edition stored in the family collection of Zhang Jinwu's 张金吾 (1787–1829) in Zhao-wen 昭文 — today's Changshu City (常熟) in Jiangsu Province (江苏).[1] It was comprised of 8 *pian* and included a table of contents for each chapter and explanatory headings that were inserted at the beginning of all 215 items of the text.[2]

(2) A movable type edition produced in the Ming, and preserved in Ding Songsheng's 丁松生 (1832–1899) Library of 8,000 *juan* of Movable Type Editions in Renhe County (仁和) in Zhejiang Province (浙江省).[3]

This edition also consisted of 8 *pian* and included a table of contents for each chapter and explanatory headings that were inserted at the beginning of all the 215 items of the text. Years later, this Ming movable type edition was reproduced in the 20th century in the *SBCK* series and then became the text on which the text of the *YZCQ ICS Ancient Chinese Text Concordance Series* was based.[4]

### (Ⅶ-2) Later editions of the *YZCQ*: The Siku Quanshu edition of 1780 and Sun Xingyan's commentary edition of 1788

The *Siku Quanshu* editors classified the *YZCQ* in the sub-category of

---

1 昭文张氏所藏元刻本.

2 This Yuan woodblock edition is no longer extant. For a detailed description of it, see Wu Shouyang's 吴寿旸 (1771–1835), *Bai jing lou cangshu tiba ji* 拜经楼藏书题跋, http://ctext.org/wiki.pl?if=gb&chapter=105945#晏子春秋 (2006-2017).

3 仁和丁松生八千卷楼藏明活字本.

4 For an encyclopedic list arranged in chronological order of extant and no longer extant editions, commentaries, and other major referential works regarding the *YZCQ*, see Yan Lingfeng 严灵峰, Zhou Qin Han Wei zhuzi zhijian shumu 周秦汉魏诸子知见书目, Taibei, 正中书局 (1975–1977): vol. 3, 1-29. For a similar list and discussion, see Wang Gengsheng 王更生, *Xinbian Yanzi chunqiu* 新篇晏子春秋, Taibei, 台湾古籍 (2001): 745-774. See also Lin Xinxin's 林欣心 discussion of major printed editions of the *YZCQ* in, *Yanzi chunqiu yanjiu* 晏子春秋研究 (MA Thesis, Sun Yat-Sen University, 2000): 12-17.

"Biographical Works" (传记) in the "History Branch" of their monumental collection of texts. In doing so, they avoided the need to determine whether the *YZCQ* comprised a Confucian or a Mohist text.[1] Their textual version, as previously noted, was based on the Li family Mianmiaoge woodblock edition of the late Ming and therefore included neither a table of contents nor item headings, as did the late Ming movable type edition that was based on the Yuan woodblock edition. Their Synopsis (提要), which is printed as a preface to the text, begins by condensing into a few lines over 1,000 years of bibliographical history, from the late Han through the Song. They then characterize the contents of the text as similar to those of two famous Tang admonishment texts,[2] and then render their judgment concerning the text's authorship problem. They hold that the name of the text's compiler was missing from the original text and that therefore Yan Ying was named as its author in order to give the text credibility. The editors then point to an absurd item that could not have possibly been included in the original text.[3] They continue to present the historical debate between those scholars who considered the *YZCQ* a Confucian text and those who thought the text was Mohist. They conclude that Yan Ying, the person, lived a bit before Mozi, at the time the wandering scholar Shi Jue (史角), whose disciples

---

1  Stephen Durrant, however, has argued that this "biographical" classification gave rise to a new problem because the term "Biography" should not be applied strictly to a text such as the *YZCQ*. See his "Yen tzu ch'un ch'iu" in Michael Loewe, ed. *Early Chinese Texts: A Bibliographical Guide*. Early China Special Monograph Series 2. Berkeley (1993): 487.

2  The two Tang texts are Wei Zheng's 魏征 *Jianlu* 谏录 and Li Jiang's 李绛 (764–830) 论事集 *Lunshiji*.

3  The Synopsis refers here to Item 8.12 [209] in the received version. This item carries explicit homosexual implications and was therefore absent from several editions, including from the *Siku quanshu* version. However, not only did this "homosexual" item remained intact in the received version, but it was also anthologized in Mark Stevenson and Cuncun Wu, eds., *Homoeroticism in Imperial China: A Sourcebook*. Routledge, New York (2013): 10.

eventually became Mozi's teachers, was staying in Lu,[1] so Yan Ying might have known him and been introduced to "Mohist" ideas even before Mozi himself. The Synopsis then refers to the fact that the text was listed under two titles — *Yanzi* and *YZCQ* — and determines that the use of the title *YZCQ* was appropriate because some texts such as *Lüshi chunqiu* and others were not chronologically arranged by years and months and nevertheless bore in their title the metonymy *Chunqiu* 春秋 ("spring and autumn"). The Synopsis ends by presenting the divergent bibliographical references to the text and explains their editorial choice for the adapted Ming edition.

Sun Xingyan's 7-*juan* commentary edition contained 8 *pian*.[2] By interweaving *pian* and *juan,* Sun Xingyan managed to resolve the historical problem of the bibliographical discrepancy that arose from the bibliographical references to the Han 8-*pian* text and the Tang 7-*juan* text. His edition, which was based on two Ming editions, included neither a table of contents nor any item headings. He appended a long set of philological notes, entitled *Yinyi* 音义,[3] of textual variations and clarifications, many of which were based on extracts from major encyclopedias such as *Yiwen leiju, Chuxue ji,* and *Taiping yulan,* as well as from the commentary to the literary anthology *Wen Xuan.* His edition included Liu Xiang's Preface to the text, as well as his own Preface,[4] in which he made the following important statements:

1. Based on internal textual and external bibliographical evidence — the text could not possibly have been considered a forgery.[5]

---

1   See, *Lüshi chunqiu*, 2/4/10/10.

2   See, *Yanzi Chunqiu* 晏子春秋, *Sibu beiyao* 四部备要, Beijing 北京, Zhonghua shuju 中华书局, (1989): Vol. 53, 3-49.

3   Ibid., 51A-88B. The *Sibu beiyao* edition also appends an additional set of notes to the *YZCQ* by Huang Yizhou 黄以周 (1828–99), see ibid., 91A-121A.

4   Ibid., 1A-2A.

5   These decisive anti-forgery arguments that Sun Xingyan incorporated throughout his Preface were made in response, *inter alia,* to Qing scholars such as Wu Dexuan 吴德旋 (1767–1840) and Guan Tong 管同 (1780–1831), who believed that the *YZCQ* was a forgery of the Six Dynasties period (220–589 CE) or even later. See, *JS*, 630-631.

2. The text was created during the Warring States period after Yanzi's death by the hands of guest retainers who collected stories about his deeds and activities from the official annals of the state of Qi.[1]

3. The censorship performed by some Ming publishers against the anti-Confucian items that appear in the last Outer Chapter of the text is unjustified.

4. The textual material in the six Inner Chapters of the text justifies its traditional inclusion under the section devoted to Confucian writings.

5. The explanation provided in the *Yuhai* for the discrepancies in the number of *juan* in the text is "preposterous."

6. Scholars, such as Liu Zongyuan, who considered the *YZCQ* a Mohist text, are ignorant and lacking in understanding.[2]

7. The material contained in the last Outer Chapter of the text in no way harms the "great Way" of Confucianism. Liu Xiang likewise referred to the last Outer Chapter of the *YZCQ* as containing inauthentic material written by later people, and that in contrast to the authentic "inner chapters," half of all ancient textual "outer chapters" always served as a platform for inauthentic writers seeking credibility.

## (Ⅶ-3) The *YZCQ* during last decades of the Qing

During the last several decades of the Qing, the continuing textual scholarship on the *YZCQ* did not register any major breakthrough providing new insights into the text. Notable during this period is the celebrated late Qing and early Republican scholar Liang Qichao 梁启超 (1873–1929), who, together with scholars such as the aforementioned Liu Shipei 刘师

---

1 These state annals of Qi are mentioned in *Mozi*, 8.3/52/14.

2 Sun Xingyan's use of such harsh rhetoric against Liu Zongyuan because of Liu's "Mohist" theory, was later approved and reinforced by Liu Shipei (1884–1919). See his "Yanzi fei Mojia bian" 晏子非墨家辨, in his *Zuoan ji* 左盦集, VII1A; http://ctext.org/library.pl?if=gb&file=81813&page=2 (2006-2017).

培 (1884–1919), focused on the central questions related to the *YZCQ*. Liang's view of the text is a composite of many of the previous insights that Chinese scholarship had produced over the preceding two millennia.[1] Liang first offered the daring bibliographical observation according to which the *Yanzi* text listed in the *Hanshu* was not only the same text to which Sima Qian referred in the *Shiji*,[2] but probably the same text Liu An referenced in his *Huainanzi*; that is, the *Remonstrations of Yanzi*.[3] He then followed Liu Zongyuan's view that the *YZCQ* was written by followers of Yanzi in Qi but nevertheless simultaneously stressed, in light of the *Siku Quanshu* editors' perspective, that these followers from Qi did not know Mozi (alluding to the fact that although the *YZCQ* might have a Mohist flavor, it had nothing to do with Mozi the person). Liang concluded his short piece by stating that the *YZCQ* acquired the celebrated name of "Yanzi" in its title only in later times, and that the actual date of its composition might be stretched beyond the Warring States period into the beginning of the Han dynasty. As for the received version, Liang expressed doubts as to whether the version is identical to the text referred to by Sima Qian and Liu An, but simultaneously averred that the received version is most probably the same text Liu Xiang compiled and is thus by no means a later product.

Towards the end of the Qing, one of the earliest scholarly references to the *YZCQ* in a Western language appeared in Shanghai. The British missionary Alexander Wylie in 1867 followed the *Siku Quanshu* classification and listed the text in the section devoted to biographical works of his *Notes on Chinese Literature*. He then added a short comment saying that the *YZCQ* was written some centuries before the Christian era and that

---

1   See *JS*, 632.

2   See Section (III-2).

3   See Section (III-1).

it was "a personal narrative" of Yan Ying, "a reputed disciple of" Mozi.[1]

In summary: at the end of the Qing and during the early Republic years, the decisive questions about the authenticity and philosophical characteristic of the *YZCQ* remained suspended in air — the ongoing textual scholarship of the *YZCQ* was in need of a broader circle of contributors and committed readers of the text in order to create a space in which new alternative voices could cope with the unsettled questions surrounding the text. Indeed, as it turned out, during the 20th century, the *YZCQ*'s scholarly circles of committed readers and contributors did expand significantly — westwards.

## (VII) An Archeological Breakthrough and Digital Humanities: Expanded Accessibility to the *YZCQ* during the 20th Century and into the 21st

### (VII-1) The *YZCQ* from 1923 to 1972

The discovery of 102 "Yanzi" bamboo strips and fragments, excavated at Yinqueshan in 1972, shook up the long history of textual scholarship of the *YZCQ*.[2] Prior to that, during the first seven decades of the 20th century, several Western and Chinese scholars made the *YZCQ* more accessible to students of Chinese philosophy and provided new perspectives regarding the problem of the text's authorship, date, and authenticity. These scholars include Alfred Forke (1867–1944); Henri Maspero (1883–1945); George Kao (1912–2008); Richard L. Walker (1922–2003); and Burton Watson (1925–2017). In China the most prominent *YZCQ* scholars were, among others, Zhang Chunyi 张纯一 (1871–1955); Wu Zeyu 吴则虞 (1913–1977); and Wang Gengsheng 王更生 (1928–2010).

83

---

1  See, Alexander Wylie, *Notes on Chinese Literature*. Shanghai: Presbyterian Mission Press, 1867, rpt., Taipei: Bookcase Shop Limited (1970): 34.

2  See, Section (VIII-2).

Alfred Forke's pioneering 1923 essay on the *YZCQ* still resonates to this day with important insights.[1] Forke argued that the *YZCQ* was an authentic — that is, an ancient — text, which he dated to the fifth century BCE.[2] He claimed that the text's chief protagonist, Yanzi, dedicated his life to the service of his ruler and his people based on a set of pragmatic values. For Forke, Yanzi was a politician and not a pathbreaking theoretician immersed as Confucians had been — in his view — in a world of abstract knowledge and profound learning. Nor was he, in Forke's eyes, a great statesman of Guan Zhong's caliber; however, as a "charakter," Forke argued, Yanzi outstripped the latter. Forke's essay was comprised of several parts including a fully reconstructed biography of Yanzi drawn from various traditional sources; a detailed discussion of the history of the text; and a lengthy analysis of the text's philosophy regarding topics such as ethics, thrifty, human relationships, and the interaction between the ruler and the people. Notable among these points is Forke's groundbreaking analysis of the text's advocacy of a kind of "natural religion" that makes it "ganz rationalistisch" in comparison to Confucius' and Mozi's religious beliefs. Finally, the essay presented an insightful examination of the authenticity of the first few items of the eighth chapter of the *YZCQ*, which contain aggressive attacks on Confucius and Confucianism.

---

1  Alfred Forke, "Yen Ying, Staatsmann und Philosoph, und das Yen-tse tsch'un-tch'iu."*Asia Major* (first series) Introductory Volume (*Hirth Anniversary Volume*) (1923): 101-144. Forke abridged this article in his *Geschichte der Alten Chinesischen Philosophie*. Hamburg: L. Friederichsen and Co. (1927), Rep., Cram, De Gruyter & CO (1964): 82-92. For two critical reviews of Forke's essay, see Paul Pelliot, "Un nouveau périodique oriental: *Asia Major*," *T'oung Pao* 22, (1923): 354-5; Richard L. Walker, "Some Notes on the *Yen-tzu ch'un-ch'iu*." *Journal of the American Oriental Society* 73.3 (1953): 156-8.

2  A year earlier, the great modern Chinese scholar and reformer Hu Shi 胡适 "rejected" (in his own words) the *YZCQ* from his book on the grounds of the text's "doubtful authenticity." See his *The Development of the Logical Method in Ancient China*. The Oriental Book Company, Shanghai (1922): "Preface," 1.

Henri Maspero's 1927 discussion of the *YZCQ* in his *La Chine antique* was less than two pages long; yet it comprised a masterful characterization of the entire text.[1] Maspero dated the *YZCQ* to the middle of the fourth century BCE and identified it, among other texts of that era, as a "historical romance"; that is, as a text whose writer mixed genuine historical facts with his own imagination. Maspero was the first to observe that the text exhibits in addition to its Mohist inclination a contrarian attitude not only towards Confucius but also towards the *Guanzi*. He nevertheless maintained that the *YZCQ*'s philosophical ideas, for all their intellectual value, were uninteresting and banal. Regarding literary style, however, Maspero expressed his admiration for the liveliness with which many of the scenes were staged. His long bibliographical note[2] in which he traced references to the authentic *YZCQ* in various sources from Han through the Tang — that is, references to the text before it underwent editorial changes during the Song and Yuan — still serves as a persuasive argument that a great part of the original *YZCQ* text was authentically transmitted through the received version.

George Kao's 1946 anthology *Chinese Wit & Humor*[3] included English translation of twelve relatively long items of the *YZCQ*. The anthology not only introduced the witty Yanzi to the Western reader but also granted Yanzi equal footing, as far as "wit" was concerned, with such monumental figures in Chinese history as Confucius, Mencius, Zhuangzi, Liezi and Hanfeizi.

---

1   Henri Maspero, *La Chine antique*. Presses Universitaires de France - PUF; Édition: Nouv. Éd, Paris (1985): 486-7.

2   Ibid., 486.

3   George Kao, *Chinese Wit & Humor*. Coward-McCann, Inc. New York (1946): 37-46. For further discussions of the *YZCQ*'s strong elements of humor, see Christoph Harbsmeier, "Humor in Ancient Chinese Philosophy." *Philosophy East and West,* 39.3 (1989): 295-6; David R. Knechtges, "Wit, Humor, and Satire in Early Chinese Literature (to A.D.220)." *Monumenta Serica* 29 (1970-71): 88.

Richard Walker's 1952 weighty sinological analysis of the *YZCQ* introduced the text to academic circles in the English-speaking world and explored many of the text's complexities long discussed by Chinese scholars.[1] To this day, Walker's essay still provides a roadmap that sinologists should take into account when constructing their own critical studies of a text such as the *YZCQ*. Walker's primary goal was to elevate the status of the *YZCQ*, "which has remained outside the pale of the extensive research," and to see how Forke's 1923 essay "stood the test of time" 25 years after it was published. In doing so, Walker suggests to replace the dignified title "*Annals of the Philosopher Yen*" with a more casual title such as "*Speeches*" or *Aphorisms*" of Yanzi. At the same time, he characterizes Yanzi's ability as it emerges from the text as merely "to extricate himself from ticklish situations by verbal gymnastics." Thus, the reader is left perplexed as to the essayist Walker's real intention. Obviously, one cannot elevate a long-ignored text like the *YZCQ* to the status of the most celebrated text of ancient China by deflating its title and by characterizing its protagonist as proficient in nothing more than the mediocre art of "verbal gymnastics." And indeed, as the opening statements of the essay and all its introductory comments conclude, Walker actually aims at the heart of his real target: Forke's 1923 essay. He begins by recording a few agreeable words concerning Forke's "great amount of spadework" on the history of the text and its surrounding scholarship, and then launches an attack on Forke's philosophical over-reading of the text and on his sinological methodology by listing flaws, culminating in the following somewhat disparaging statement: "Thus, while we may agree with Professor Forke on

---

1   Richard Walker, "Some Notes on the *Yen-tzu ch'un-ch'iu*." *Journal of the American Oriental Society* 73.3 (1953): 156-163. Walker's PhD dissertation which he completed at Yale (1950) was entitled, "The Multi-State System of Ancient China." It was published under the same title in 1953 by Shoe String Press, Hamden CT. For his view of Yanzi's achievements as a minister in Qi, see ibid., p. 69-71; 77-78."

an early date for the *YTCC* [*YZCQ*], it is not alone for the reasons which he gives".[1] Walker then critically examines the political milieu surrounding the composition of the text, grammatically analyzes the language of the text in comparison to other texts that exhibits similar contents, and brilliantly evaluates what is included and what is "not included" in the multi-layer text to reach the following conclusion:

The *YTCC* [*YZCQ*] is an authentic text most probably pre-dating the *Tso-chuan* [*Zuozhuan*]. A likely date of composition is sometime two or three generations after the death of Yen-tzu [Yanzi] when stories about him had become legendary, and not so long after his death for impossible fabrications to have entered in or for the text to have been formalized, philosophically or institutionally. This would probably place it some time before 400 B.C.[2]

In 1962, Burton Watson's excellent short subchapter on the *YZCQ* paved new directions for understanding and exploring the text, especially on psychological levels.[3] Watson placed the *YZCQ* in the "Philosophy" section of his survey of early Chinese literature and portrayed its chief protagonist, Yanzi, as a dour Mohist who advocated frugality and made the life of his indulgent ruler very difficult as a result of his "ubiquitous carpings." Offering a fresh perspective on a story that for almost two millennia was championed as a rare example of a minister of great integrity who delivered honest remonstrations against his self-indulgent ruler, Watson took the Duke's "side." Watson's new approach contravened the pious moralizing the text had as its core for millennia, and transformed it into a modern theatrical drama that the audience is invited to interpret freely. Furthermore, Watson drew the attention of future readers of this drama to its portrait of

87

---

1 Richard Walker, "Some Notes on the *Yen-tzu ch'un-ch'iu*." *Journal of the American Oriental Society* 73.3 (1953): 159.

2 Ibid., p. 162.

3 Burton Watson, *Early Chinese Literature*. New York: Columbia University Press (1962): 183-6.

a static world that allows neither progress nor breakthroughs. The world and the main protagonists of the *YZCQ* remain unmoved from their original positions; indeed, in Watson's words: "Almost invariably the Duke admits his folly and agrees to reform. Yet in the following anecdote we find him back at his old mischief." No doubt, Watson's view of the *YZCQ* gave the text a flare of Godot absurdity — "Nothing to be done."[1]

Between 1930 and 1962, two new annotated editions appeared in China that made the *YZCQ* much more accessible to potential readers everywhere. In 1936, Zhang Chunyi 张纯一 published an annotated edition entitled: *Yanzi chunqiu jiaozhu* 晏子春秋校注 (preface, 1930).[2] This extremely rich and detailed commentary dealt with the textual difficulties of the text by first referring the reader to Sun Xingyan's commentary of 1788 and then by making extensive comparative references to commentaries dealing with similar textual difficulties in other classical texts.

Then, in 1962, what still ought to be regarded as the most comprehensive edition of the *YZCQ*, was published in China. Wu Zeyu's 吴则虞 *Yanzi chunqiu jishi* 晏子春秋集释[3] offered an encyclopedic work containing everything worth knowing about the text itself and the surrounding circumstances of its composition and transmission. Nearly all of significance that had been stated about the text — every quote and every interpretation over a period of almost two millennia — can be found in Wu Zeyu's edition. Not only is his own commentary instructive and altogether enlightening regarding almost every textually difficult passage — to which he attached

---

1   See Samuel Beckett, *Waiting for Godot*. Grove Press, New York (1982): 2.

2   *Yanzi chunqiu jiaozhu* 晏子春秋校注 in the *Xinbian Zhuzi jicheng* 新编诸子集成 series, Vol. 6. Taibei, Shijie shuju 台北, 世界书局, 1972. http://ctext.org/library.pl?if=gb&file=94142&page=513 (2006-2017).

3   Wu Ze-yu's 吴则虞, *Yanzi chunqiu jishi* 晏子春秋集释, 2 vols. Beijing, Zhonghua shuju 中华书局, 1962. A revised, extended edition was published in 2011 under the title (*Zeng ding ben*) *Yanzi chunqiu jishi* (增订本) 晏子春秋集释. Beijing tushuguan chubanshe, 北京图书馆出版社, 2011.

a myriad of textual references from many other commentaries[1] — but he also provided appendices that gave the reader an extensive array of references to historical scholarship that had accumulated throughout the ages.[2] In his "Preface"[3] he developed a five-point argument in which he traced the authorship of the text to such Academicians as Chunyu Yue 淳于越 (ca. 214 BCE) from Qi, who relocated to Qin 秦 and served the First Emperor after the unification of China.[4] The first three of Wu Zeyu's five arguments were contextually external and therefore did not carry much weight; however, his fourth and fifth arguments provided a new dimension for the discussion of the authorship of the text. They pointed to some striking value-based ideas and stylistic similarities between Chunyu Yue's recorded remonstrations and those pronounced by Yanzi in the *YZCQ*. Unfortunately, the number of items in this list of compared similarities presented by Wu Zeyu was too small to derive a definitive conclusion that Chunyu Yue was behind the compilation of the text. Nevertheless, until now, these stylistic arguments should stir enough sinological interest to prompt the formation of a digital database of such similarities, a mosaic of "clues," which could point at the direction of the identity of the "hands" which weaved the proto-text of the *YZCQ*. To conclude, Wu Zeyu's monumental achievement as commentator, as bibliographer and as innovator of textual

89

---

1   *JS*, 1-523.

2   *JS*, 525-657.

3   The "Preface" appears in *JS*, 21-23, preceding p. 1 of the beginning of vol. 1 of the commentary.

4   Wu Zeyu was very cautious not to attribute the authorship of the *YZCQ* directly to Chunyu Yue as the single person who compiled the text. He nevertheless pronounced his verdict on the authorship in such an ambiguous way (淳于越之类的齐人, 在齐国编写的) that scholars interpreted Wu Zeyu's position as saying that he considered Chunyu Yue to be the final compiler of the text. See e.g., Masayuki Sato, *The Confucian Quest for Order: The Origin and Formation of the Political Thought of Xun Zi*. Sinica Leidensia 58. Leiden, Brill: (2003): 211, n. 79.

comparative research, is such that any future study of the *YZCQ* will have to regard his edition as the proper point of departure.

In 1966, Wang Gengsheng 王更生 completed his PhD dissertation "Yanzi chunqiu yanjiu 晏子春秋研究" ("Research on the *YZCQ*") at the Taiwan National Normal University.[1] This was his first contribution to the study of *YZCQ*, which was subsequently followed by several other excellent works and two *baihua* translations[2] of the text, which garnered for him a central place in the historical scholarly study of *YZCQ*. The dissertation and its subsequently revised book edition constitute a concise summary of material that had already appeared in Wu Zeyu's work of traditional Chinese scholarship concerning the authorship, authenticity, and date of composition of the *YZCQ*. The revised book also included a fully detailed biography and chronology of Yanzi's life, as well as a thorough exposition and analysis of the text's views on both philosophical and linguistic matters such as metaphysics, the spirits, life and death, ethics, political philosophy, finance, diplomatic affairs, self-cultivation, literary style, syntax, and the use of analogies.

Indeed, during the several decades prior to 1972, the *YZCQ* became much more accessible to readers and scholars in China and in the West alike. It was due to the continuous scholarly efforts in the study, commentary and partial translation of the text. In 1972, however, the discovery of bamboo strip fragments excavated at Yinqueshan forced the long history of textual scholarship of the *YZCQ* to reevaluate its own convictions in light of 102 bamboo strips.

---

1  The dissertation was published later under the same title. See Wang Gengsheng Wang 王更生, in *Yanzi chunqiu yanjiu* 晏子春秋研究. Wenshi 文史, Taibei, 1976.

2  Wang Gengsheng 王更生, *Yanzi chunqiu jinzhu jinyi* 晏子春秋今注今译. Taiwan shang wu yin shu guan 台湾商务印书馆, 1987; *Xinbian Yanzi chunqiu* 新编晏子春秋. Taiwan guji chuban 台湾古籍出版, Taibei 台北, 2001.

**(Ⅶ-2) The *Yanzi* Text in the Yinqueshan Han bamboo strips 银雀山 汉墓竹简**[1]

In 1972, in the course of a construction project, 4,942 bamboo strips and fragments were excavated at Tomb #1 and Tomb #2 at the Yinqueshan 银雀山, a small hill southeast of the city of Linyi 临沂 in Shandong Province, located, by some estimates, within the southern reaches of the state of Qi. The period of burial for both tombs has been dated to approximately 140/134 BCE and 118 BCE, but the 21,728 characters[2] written in Clerical Script (隶) on the 4,942 unearthed bamboo strips were probably written somewhat earlier.[3] Members of The Committee for the Reconstruction of Yinqueshan Han Dynasty Bamboo Strips divided the 4942 bamboo strips excavated at Tomb #1 into two groups. The first group consisted of bamboo strips that bore textual material comparable to extant traditional texts, and the second group consisted of textual materials that

---

1  For the discovery of the Yinqueshan bamboo strips of *Yanzi* 银雀山竹简, 晏子, see *Wen wu* 文物 (1974-6): 17-19, 37; Pian Yuqian 骈宇骞, *Yinqueshan zhujian Yanzi chunqiu jiaoshi* 银雀山竹简 晏子春秋校释, Wenjuan, Taibei, (2000) 10-19. See also *Yinqueshan Han mu zhujian (yi)* 银雀山汉墓竹简 (壹). Wenwu chubanshe, Beijing, 1985; Wu Jiulong 吴九龙, *Yinqueshan Han jian shiwen* 银雀山汉简释文. Wenwu chubanshe, Beijing 1985; "Background to the Excavation at Yinqueshan," in D. C. Lau and Roger T. Ames, *Sun Bin: The Art of Warfare. A Translation of the Classic Chinese Work of Philosophy and Strategy*. SUNY Series in Chinese Philosophy and Culture. Albany (2003) 187-196.

2  For the numbers and distribution of the characters of the various texts written on the Yinqueshan Han Bamboo Strips excavated from Tomb #1, see "A Computerized Database of Excavated Wood/Bamboo and Silk Scripts of China (Jianbo)," CHANT (Chinese Ancient Texts Database), last modified 2005, http://www.chant.org/jianbo1/stat.aspx.

3  The *terminus post quem* of the Yinqueshan Han Bamboo Strips cannot be dated much earlier than approximately 200 BCE because all the characters on the strips from Tomb # 1 belong to an early period in the standardization of the clerical script; this script had become the standard style after the unification of Chinese states under the state of Qin in 221 BCE.

otherwise have been lost. Within the first group, 102 strips arranged in a continuous sequence (numbers 528-630) formed sixteen distinct textual sets, which comprise at least one item from each and every one of the eight *pian* of the received version of *YZCQ*, corresponding in content and phraseology, with very similar strings of wording. Notably, the 102 Yinqueshan Bamboo Strips of *Yanzi* consisted of 2,970 characters, which amount to no less than 7.2% of the entire bulk of 41,324 characters of the received text.[1]

Two tables are presented below. Table 1 demonstrates the nearly exact textual correspondence between the first set of the *Yanzi* bamboo strips (No. 528-531) and the corresponding Item 3 in the received version of the *YZCQ*. Table 2 lists all the 102 Bamboo Strips, grouped in sixteen sets arranged in continuous order, alongside their corresponding items and chapter numbers in the parallel Items in the received version of the *YZCQ*.

*Table 1: Textual correspondence between the first set of the Yanzi bamboo strips*

*(No. 528-531) and the corresponding Item 3 in the received version of the YZCQ.*

1st row: Yinqueshan zhujian 银雀山汉墓竹简 *Yanzi*[2]

2nd row: Transcribed copy[3]

3rd row: *YZCQ*, Chapter 1.3 [Item 3]

---

1    For the list of all the 41,324 characters that appear in the received version of the *YZCQ*, see D. C. Lau and Chen Fong Ching, *A Concordance to the Yanzi chunqiu*. The Commercial Press, Hong Kong (1993): 427-432.

2    For a reproduced copy the original 102 Yinqueshan *Yanzi* Bamboo strips, see *Yinqueshan Han mu zhujian (yi)* 银雀山汉墓竹简 (壹). Wenwu chubanshe, Beijing (1985): [摹本] 81-89.

3    For a fully edited and annotated transcription of the clerical script text written on the 102 Yinqueshan *Yanzi* Bamboo strips, see ibid., *Yinqueshan Han mu zhujian (yi)* [释文] 87-106.

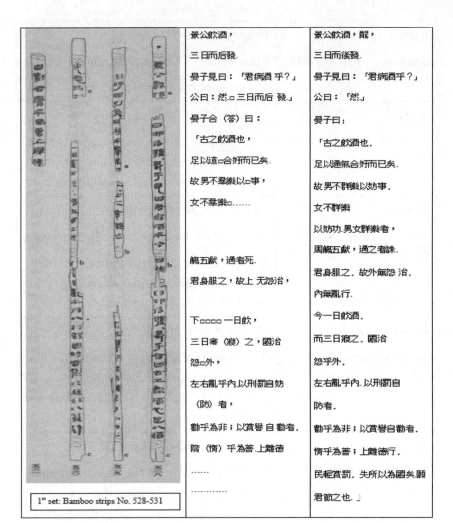

| 景公飲酒， | 景公飲酒，醒， |
| 三日而后發． | 三日而後發． |
| 晏子見曰：「君病酒乎？」 | 晏子見曰：「君病酒乎？」 |
| 公曰：然。口三日而后 發．」 | 公曰：「然」 |
| 晏子合（答）曰： | 晏子曰： |
| 「古之飲酒也， | 「古之飲酒也． |
| 足以道口合姸而已矣． | 足以通氣合姸而已矣． |
| 故男不羣樂以口事， | 故男不羣樂以妨事． |
| 女不羣樂口…… | 女不羣樂 |
| | 以妨功．男女羣樂者， |
| | 周觴五獻，過之者誅． |
| 觴五獻，過者死． | 君身服之．故外無怨 治． |
| 君身服之，故上 无怨治， | 內無亂行． |
| | 今一日飲酒． |
| 下口口口口 一日飲， | 而三日寢之．國治 |
| 三日寑（寢）之，國治 | 怨乎外． |
| 怨口外， | 左右亂乎內．以刑罰自 |
| 左右亂乎內以刑罰自姸 | 防者． |
| （防）者， | |
| 勸乎為非；以賞譽 自 勸者． | 勸乎為非；以賞譽自勸者． |
| 隋（惰）乎為善．上離德 | 惰乎為善；上離德行． |
| …… | 民輕賞罰．失所以為國矣．願 |
| ………… | 君節之也．」 |

1ˢᵗ set: Bamboo strips No. 528-531

*Table 2: The bamboo scripts and their corresponding items and chapter numbers in the parallel items in the received version of the YZCQ*

Yinqueshan zhujian *Yanzi*          *YZCQ*'s Received version

| 1st set | Chapter 1.3/1/31-2/3. [Item 3] |
| Bamboo strips No. 528-531. | Item heading: Duke Jing drank wine, and after a three-day hangover he recovered. Yanzi remonstrated. |

93

| 2nd Set<br>Bamboo strips No. 532-538. | Chapter 1.9/4/9-24. [Item 9]<br>Item heading: Duke Jing loved his concubine and indulged her desires. Yanzi remonstrated. |
|---|---|
| 3rd Set<br>Bamboo strips No. 539-541. | Chapter 1.20/9/3-8. [Item 20]<br>Item heading: Duke Jing wore a robe of white fox fur and did not know that the weather was cold. Yanzi remonstrated. |
| 4th Set<br>Bamboo strips No. 542-551. | Chapter 1.22/9/24-10/6. [Item 22]<br>Item heading: Duke Jing was about to attack Song. He dreamed of two men standing before him with a furious demeanor. Yanzi remonstrated. |
| 5th Set<br>Bamboo strips No. 552-555. | Chapter 2.18/17/12-19. [Item 43]<br>Item heading: Duke Jing ascended the Terrace over the Road Bedchamber but could not reach its top. He was displeased and Yanzi remonstrated. |
| 6th Set<br>Bamboo strips No. 556-560. | Chapter 3.3/22/5-11. [Item 53]<br>Item heading: Duke Jing consulted about attacking Lu. Yanzi replied that it would be preferable to cultivate good government and wait for internal disorder in Lu to arise. |
| 7th Set<br>Bamboo strips No. 561-567. | Chapter 3.10/25/8-16. [Item 60]<br>Item heading: Duke Jing inquired regarding his intention to assign the Invocator and the Ancestral Attendant to seek good fortune. Yanzi replied that the Duke should ask forgiveness for his guilt rather than seek good fortune. |

| | |
|---|---|
| 8th Set<br><br>Bamboo strips No. 568-572. | Chapter 3.17/27/26-30. [Item 67]<br><br>Item heading: Duke Jing asked how a worthy ruler governs his state. Yanzi replied that worthy governance consists of appointing worthy and loving the people. |
| 9th Set<br><br>Bamboo strips No. 573-577. | Chapter 3.18/28/3-9. [Item 68]<br><br>Item heading: Duke Jing asked what moral instruction should be given to the people by an enlightened king. Yanzi replied that the enlightened king first puts righteousness into effect. |
| 10th Set<br><br>Bamboo strips No. 578-584. | Chapter 3.20/28/21-24. [Item 70]<br><br>Item heading: Duke Jing asked what the conduct of a loyal minister should be like. Yanzi replied that a loyal minister does not practice evil in collusion with the ruler. |
| 11th Set<br><br>Bamboo strips No. 585-589. | Chapter 4.22 - 4.23/37/25-38/6. [Items 103; 104]<br><br>Item heading: Shuxiang asked which idea is the loftiest and which conduct is the most generous. Yanzi replied, loving and making the people happy.<br><br>Item heading: Shuxiang asked how thrift, miserliness and covetousness are reflected in conduct. Yanzi replied that thrift is the way of a man of noble character. |

| 12th Set<br><br>Bamboo strips No. 590-597. | Chapter 5.2/40/15-25. [Item 112]<br><br>Item heading: Duke Zhuang paid no heed to Yanzi's advice. Yanzi returned his fief-cities and withdrew from service. Then the calamity of Cui Zhu occurred. |
|---|---|
| 13th Set<br><br>Bamboo strips No. 598-610. | Chapter 6.4/50/29-51/13. [Item 144]<br><br>Item heading: Bochang Qian cast out an owl by exorcism. When the owl was found dead, he sought to prolong the life of Duke Jing. Yanzi realized that this was absurd. |
| 14th Set<br><br>Bamboo strips No. 611-616. | Chapter 7.19/67/14-20. [Item 189]<br><br>Item heading: Gaozi inquired regarding Yanzi's service to Duke Ling, Duke Zhuang, and Duke Jing, and their respect for him. Yanzi replied that he had served them with a single mind. |
| 15th Set<br><br>Bamboo strips No. 617-623. | Chapter 8.1/70/10-19. [Item 198]<br><br>Item heading: Confucius met Duke Jing for an audience. Duke Jing wanted to confer upon him a fief but Yanzi thought this would not be proper. |
| 16th Set<br><br>Bamboo strips No. 624-630. | Chapter 8.18a/75/3-7. [Item 215]<br><br>Item heading: Yanzi passed away. The Duke's entourage flattered the Duke. Xuanzhang remonstrated and Duke Jing granted him fish. |

Furthermore, between 1972 and 1977, other archeological findings such as bits of fragments of the *Yanzi* text dated from 179–49 BCE were excavated at Pochengzi 破城子 in Gansu 甘肃 (1972–1974), Dingxian 定县 in Hebei 河北 (1973), and Fuyang 阜阳 in Anhui 安徽 (1977). All these scripts, however, were too fragmented to allow a reconstruction of even one full coherent passage of the earliest text.[1]

To conclude: Striking textual similarities exist between the sixteen "Yanzi" sets of the 102 Yinqueshan Han Bamboo Strips and their corresponding items in the *YZCQ*'s received version. In light of all the other archeological findings of bits of fragments of the *Yanzi* text that were excavated in China between 1972 and 1977, and the internal textual evidence of the *Huainanzi* (according to which a text identified as *The Remonstrations of Yanzi* was known in 139 BCE, whose contents were notably similar to those of the received version of the *YZCQ*),[2] it would be quite reasonable to establish that around 200 BCE or maybe even earlier, several bamboo strip versions of a certain *Yanzi* text were circulating throughout the intellectual world of the early Han dynasty. And, in light of this conclusion, we may now turn to examine one exciting hypothesis positing the composition of a proto-*Yanzi* text took place at an even earlier date.

97

### (Ⅶ-3) Chunyu Kun 淳于髡 (c. 340 BCE),[3] the "Jesters" 滑稽, and the Jixia 稷下 Patronage Community Connection

In 1936, as Luo Jun 罗焌 (1874–1932) was concluding his survey on

---

1  For an account of these archeological findings, see Pian Yuqian 骈宇骞, ibid., pp. 10-11.

2  See, Section (III-1).

3  Chunyu Kun was an official and envoy, a famous rhetorician and a dwarf jester who, like Yanzi in his time, delivered remonstrations and persuasions to a drunken and debouched duke — in this case Duke Wei of Qi 齐威王 (c. 378–320 BCE ). For an excellent and detailed discussion of Chunyu Kun's activities as a member of the Jixia patronage community, see Giulia Baccini, "The Forest of Laughs (*Xiaolin*): Mapping the Offspring of Self-aware Literature in Ancient China." PhD Diss., Universita Ca'Foscari, Venezia (2011): passim. See also, Oliver Weingarten. "Chunyu Kun: Motifs, Narratives, and Personas in Early Chinese Anecdotal Literature." Journal of the Royal Asiatic Society 27.3 (2017): 501-521.

the historical scholarship of the *YZCQ*,[1] he introduced a, new, staggering idea. Luo proposed his own personal view of the text: that the recorded deeds and remonstrations in the *YZCQ* show great affinity to those recorded about jesters like Chunyu Kun from Qi, Jester Meng 优孟 from Chu, and Jester Zhan 优旃 from Qin.[2] Clearly, this idea was too abrupt and unsubstantiated. Nevertheless, it introduced a new perspective on the long-held view of the text in that it stripped the text of its distinctive historical and philosophical status and replaced the underlying identity of its chief protagonist, Yanzi, from that of a profound scholar-statesman to that of a mere master of rhetoric or jester.[3]

Forty years later, in 1976, Wang Gengsheng tossed a similar idea into the arena of *YZCQ* scholarship. Wang Gengsheng suggested that such nonsense appears several items in the text,[4] indicating that it must have been written by jesters, like Chunyu Kun and his likes, and it must reflect the imprint of the sophists of the Jixia patronage community.[5] Then, in 1986, the "Chunyu Kun hypothesis" was reinforced by Lü Bin 吕斌.[6] Lü presented a five-point argument showing that various elements in Chunyu

---

1  *JS*, 617.

2  For the account in the *Shiji* of these three "Jesters" (滑稽), see *Shiji*, 3197; 3200; 3202 respectively.

3  Luo Jun substantiated his argument by referring his readers to the *Hanshi waizhuan* 韩诗外传, 10.17/76/15, which portrays Yanzi as the greatest master of rhetoric in the world (晏子, 天下之辩士也). Cf. *YZCQ*, Item 6.10 [150], where the King of Chu's entourage portrays Yanzi as a master of the art of rhetoric (习辞者).

4  E.g., items 6.24 [164]; 6.30 [170]; 6.6 [146].

5  Wang Gengsheng 王更生, *Yanzi chunqiu yanjiu*, 72-3. Gao Heng 高亨 suggested even earlier (in 1961) the idea that both the *YZCQ* and the *Guanzi* 管子 were compiled by members of the Jixia patronage community in Qi. See Gao Heng's "Yanzi chunqiu de xiezuo shidai" 晏子春秋的写作时代, in *Wen shi shu lin* 文史述林, Beijing, Zhong hua shu ju, 北京: 中华书局 (1980): 397-398.

6  Lü Bin 吕斌, "Chunyu Kun zhu *Yanzi chunqiu* kao 淳于髡著《晏子春秋》考." *Qilu Xuekan* 齐鲁学刊, (1985; 1): 73-76.

Kun's recorded sayings and life history suggest a strong affiliation with the *YZCQ* and hence an authorial connection. Specifically, he argued that Chunyu Kun's remonstrations were based on admiration for Yanzi;[1] that he had direct access to the Qi archive from which he could derive information concerning Yan Ying; that he, like Yanzi, did not strictly follow any school of philosophy; and that echoes of his ideas and his facetious style resonate throughout the *YZCQ*. Finally, Lü pushed the "Chunyu Kun hypothesis" a step further by pointing out that both Chunyu Kun and Yanzi were portrayed as extremely short people. This striking physical resemblance, Lü argued, in conjunction with all the other evidence, suggests that an author with a biographical profile akin to Chunyu Kun projected his own personal experiences, philosophical ideas, and body image into a text that bore the name of an honored figure — Yanzi — and thus the proto-*YZCQ* was born.[2] Gradually, the "Chunyu Kun hypothesis" became one of the dominant theories of *YZCQ* authorship. Tao Meisheng 陶梅生, in his 1998 *Baihua* translation of the *YZCQ*, raised the possibility that the followers of Chunyu Kun compiled the text.[3] Lin Xinxin 林心欣, in her master's thesis of 2000, after discussing questions of classifying the text as Confucian, or Mohist, or biographical, she added a whole new classification to the *YZCQ* entitled "Jesters" (俳优), in which she discussed

---

1  *Shiji*, 2347.

2  Lü supported his argument regarding the identical diminutive body image of Chunyu Kun and Yanzi by pointing at a possible interchangeability between Item 6.9 [149] in the *YZCQ* and *Xinxu* 新序, 11.24/65/8. In the *YZCQ*, Yanzi is sent on a diplomatic mission to Chu and because of his diminutive stature the people of Chu unsuccessfully attempt to humiliate him. A somewhat parallel episode is found in the *Xinxu*; however, this time the short envoy is Chunyu Kun, who arrives at Chu from Qi and manages to deal with the humiliation the King of Chu rains down upon him for his short height.

3  Tao Meisheng 陶梅生, *Xinyi Yanzi chunqiu* 新译晏子春秋. Taibei Shi, San min shu ju gu fen you xian gong si 台北市, 三民书局股份有限公司 (1998): 30.

the connection between Chunyu Kun and the authorship of the *YZCQ*.[1] Then, in 2005, Zhao Kuifu 赵逵夫 presented an eight-point, detailed and annotated argument largely replicating that of Lü Bin in 1986, in support of the hypothesis that the diminutive Chunyu Kun compiled the *YZCQ*, an account of the diminutive Yanzi, in order to gain respect for himself despite his short stature.[2] Finally, in 2011, Andrew Meyer published a stimulating, comprehensive paper in which he persuasively showed, inter alia, that the *YZCQ* was a product of Qi state patronage of the Tian 田 rulers (379–221 BCE) and that the "proto-*Guanzi* and *YZCQ* served (among other things) as extended pleas to intellectuals to think of themselves not as 'Confucians' or 'Mohists' but as 'Qi-ists.'"[3] The notion that Chunyu Kun or his followers were the compilers of the *YZCQ* became quite commonplace in recent sinological writings, as well as on several internet sites.[4] However, the scope and the in-depth analysis of Meyer's paper paved the way for future sinological research that may bring together his insights with those revealed by other researchers regarding the Jixia patronage community, the life and time of Chunyu Kun, and the jesting tradition in ancient China.

Such research possibly yield a concrete image of the first author or compiler of the proto-*YZCQ*.

---

1 Lin Xinxin 林心欣, *Yanzi chunqiu yanjiu* 晏子春秋研究. National Sun Yat-Sen University, MA Chinese Literature (2000): 41.

2 Zhao Kuifu 赵逵夫, "Yanzi chunqiu wei qiren Chunyu Kun biancheng kao 晏子春秋为齐人淳于髡编成考."*Guangming ribao* 光明日报 (2005; 1; 28).

3 Andrew Meyer, ibid., 66. As noted, already in 1961 Gao Heng claimed that both the Guanzi and the *YZCQ* were the product of the Jixia patronage community in Qi.

4 E.g. Masayuki Sato, ibid., p. 211; Fu Junlian 伏俊琏, "Chunyu Kun jiqi lunbian ti za fu 淳于髡及其论辩体杂赋." ("Chunyu Kun and His Controversial Mixed Fu."). *Qilu xuekan* 齐鲁学刊, (2010; 2) 105-108; Giulia Baccini, ibid., 87, n. 379; https://en.wikipedia.org/wiki/Chunyu_Kun (Last modified on 24 May 2015).

**(Ⅷ-4) The *YZCQ* scholarship in recent years and its future in the age of Digital Humanities and Computational Thinking**

Ever since the Yinqueshan Han Dynasty bamboo strips were reconstructed, analyzed and circulated after 1974, the *YZCQ* became the focus of renewed sinological interest. Many scholars shared their insights and expertise, exploring new avenues to investigate textual aspects and historical issues connected with the study of the *YZCQ*.[1] Notable among these scholars are Rainer Holzer who, in 1983, translated the six Inner Chapters of the *YZCQ* into German, to which he added a learned introduction, detailed textual comments, and many other valuable notes.[2] In 1993, Stephen Durrant contributed an elegant roadmap to the text and its history in Michael Loewe's bibliographical guide on early Chinese texts, thereby creating an invaluable aid for any student of the *YZCQ*.[3] In China,

---

1  In addition to the aforementioned contributions made by Yuri Pines, Wai-yee Li, and Andrew Meyer, see also Masayuki Sato's "The Concept of *Li* in the *Yanzi Chunqiu*" in his *The Confucian Quest for Order: The Origin and Formation of the Political Thought of Xun Zi*. Sinica Leidensia 58. Leiden, Brill, (2003): 211-217; David Schaberg, "Platitude and Persona: *Junzi* Comments in *Zuozhuan* and Beyond," in Helwig Schmidt-Glintzer *et al.*, eds. *Historical Truth, Historical Criticism, and Ideology: Chinese Historiography and Historical Culture from a New Comparative Perspective*. Leiden Studies in Comparative Historiography 1. Leiden and Boston: Brill (2005): 188-192; R. Smart, "How Yanzi Fulfills his Responsibilities as Minister in the Rhetorical Techniques within the *jian* (Remonstrance) of the *Yanzi chun qiu*." MA Thesis, University of Canterbury, 2008; Scott Cook, "The Changing Role of the Minister in the Warring States: Evidence from the *Yanzi chunqiu* 晏子春秋," in Yuri Pines, *et al.*, eds. *Ideology of Power and Power of Ideology in Early China*. Sinica Leidensia 124. Leiden and Boston, Brill (2015): 181-2010.

2  Rainer Holzer, *Yen-tzu und das Yen-tzu ch'un-ch'iu*. Würzburger Sino-Japonica 10. Frankfurt and Berne, Peter Lang, 1983.

3  Stephen Durrant, "Yen tzu ch'un ch'iu," In Michael Loewe, ed. *Early Chinese Texts: A Bibliographical Guide*. Early China Special Monograph Series 2. Berkeley (1993): 483-489. See also Shih Hsiang-lin [SHL], "*Yanzi chunqiu*," in David Knechtges and Taiping Chang eds. *Ancient and Early Medieval Chinese Literature: A Reference Guide*. Leiden [Netherlands], Brill, Boston (2010-2014): 1868-1873.

in addition to the appearance of dozens of new *baihua* annotated translations of the text, no less than 280 scholarly articles have been published about the *YZCQ* in academic journals between 1974 and 2010. Moreover, 30 theses and dissertations have been presented at various Chinese universities and colleges between 1995 and 2010. [1]

It seems, however, that unless a "new" set of bamboo strips of *Yanzi* or any other relevant text [2] is uncovered from some future archaeological site, the study of the birth of the proto-text of the *YZCQ* may have exhausted itself and cannot proceed beyond the achievements of the scholarly work of the past decades. Future study of the origins of the *YZCQ* must therefore be conducted "algorithmically" with tools recently developed by scholars of Digital Humanities. At present the title "晏子春秋" yields a massive approximately 400,000 results in Google search. [3] Websites such as the Chinese Ancient Texts Database (CHANT); the Chinese Text Project (Ctext), the Digital Resources of Sinology of the Academia Sinica, and many others, provide millions upon millions of searchable characters representing the vast ocean of Chinese texts from ancient times to the present, including canonic, marginal, broadly circulated, and rare texts. Text mining methods will definitely enable analysis of the big database of these millions of characters and suggest when certain names, words or idioms appear for the first time, and how they are utilized afterwards, allowing researchers to

---

1   For a detailed list of all of these items, see the recently published massive reference guide on the history of research on the *YZCQ* by Liu Wenbin 刘文斌, *Yanzichunqiu yanjiu shi* 晏子春秋研究史. Renmin wenxue chubanshe 人民文学出版社, Beijing (2015): 228-247.

2   For an example, some traditional sources quote Chunyu Kun as having authored a text entitled *Wangduji* 王度记. The text is long lost, surviving in a miniscule number of passages. A conceivable future archeological discovery of the text may finally settle the case of the true authorial connection between Chunyu Kun and the *YZCQ*.

3   For the sake of comparison, title "孟子" yields at present about 1,880,000 hits in Google search.

successfully answer questions concerning the time of composition of texts.[1] Furthermore, websites like Harvard's China Biographical Database Project (CBDB) and Fairbank Center's Digital China already bear potential for an academic undertaking in which stylometric analysis and data extraction techniques play a major sinological role. Indeed, stylometric programs will learn the patterns of a certain author and calculate the probability that this author wrote a given text whose authorship is yet unknown, thereby solving questions regarding the authorship of particular documents. As recently reported,[2] two researchers from the University of Texas at Austin learned the patterns of 54 dramatic works of a certain author and calculated the probability that this author wrote a given text previously attributed to someone else. Their stylometric analysis identified *Double Falsehood*, a play previously attributed to the Shakespearean scholar Lewis Theobald (1688–1744), as being the work of William Shakespeare himself. This discovery, which has shaken the Shakespearean scholarly community, provides every reason to imagine that a similar disruption in the near future is possible in the world of scholarship of the *YZCQ*.

---

1   I have engaged in such internet-based database analysis in the present study by conducting queries on the combined database of Tang-Song-Ming encyclopedias, and the *Yanzi* Text in the Yinqueshan Han Bamboo Strips, in order to establish a line of stable transmission of the *YZCQ* text that stretches from the early Han through the Tang, Song, until the end of the Ming. See above p. 29, n.87; p. 36.

2   See Melissa Healy, "Study finds a disputed Shakespeare play bears the master's mark." *The LA Times*, April 10, 2015.

# 译文注解、简称和其他相关内容说明

1. 在本书中《晏子春秋》的书名简称为"YZCQ"。

2. 本书每一段英文翻译之前都列有《晏子春秋》简体字原文，原文依据的是先秦两汉古籍逐字索引丛刊史部第四种《晏子春秋逐字索引》，刘殿爵、陈方正主编，香港商务印书馆1993年11月第一版。该索引可以在线浏览和检索，请搜索汉达文库，网址链接：http://www.cuhk.edu.hk/ics/rccat/en/database.html

3. 先秦两汉古籍逐字索引丛刊史部第四种《晏子春秋逐字索引》所依据的底本是《四部丛刊》本（此后简称SBCK）《晏子春秋》，该版本又是依据"仁和丁松生八千卷楼藏明活字本"影印。《晏子春秋逐字索引》中列出了不同版本《晏子春秋》和其他古籍中引用的《晏子春秋》的异文。在《晏子春秋逐字索引》中，圆括号"（）"中的内容代表衍文，应当删除；方括号"[ ]"中的内容代表脱文，应该增补。因此，如果表示应该将"X"删除，将"Y"增补，那么在文中会表示成（X）[Y]。在我的译文中，如果对《晏子春秋逐字索引》的文本有不同意见从而有所改变，我会在注解中特别注明，并将它们的文献依据注在括号中。

105

4. 在本书中，如果采用《晏子春秋逐字索引》注解中所做的校勘，我会在译文的注解中简称为"YZCQ-ICS"并附录页码注解号码，例如"YZCQ-ICS, 9, n.2"的意思是请参见《晏子春秋逐字索引》第9页注2.

5. 吴则虞《晏子春秋集释》（北京：中华书局1962年版）在本书中简称为"JS"，并且在后面附录原书的页码和注解编号：比如"JS, 100/8"，指《晏子春秋集释》第100页注8。《晏子春秋集释》的增订本（北京：国家图书馆出版社2011年版）则不做简称。

6. 除特别注明之外，本书所用先秦两汉文献均依据刘殿爵、陈方正主编的由香港商务印书馆1992年以来出版的"先秦两汉古籍逐字索引丛刊"。本书在引用时，会在书名后面附录卷数、页码、行数：比

如 "Mozi 墨子，8.3/54/25"，指 "先秦两汉古籍逐字索引丛刊" 《墨子逐字索引》，第8卷第3节，第54页，第25行。

7. 本书所涉及的基本历史，依据中华书局1959年至1974年陆续出版的《二十四史》点校本。

8. 本书中所引用的网络内容，会在注解中附录完整链接并注明该内容的上传公布时间。

9. 本书用右箭头(→)来表示文本的修订，如：飾 → 飭，指 "飾" 应当作 "飭"。同时在后面附录《晏子春秋逐字索引》的页码以及注解编号。

10. 本书用双向箭头(↔)表示《晏子春秋》中的某一部分与其他文献中的相关内容类似或者关系密切。

（欧永福　文，吴洋　译）

# Notes on symbols, abbreviations and other conventions

1. The *Yanzi chunqiu* 晏子春秋 (*The Spring and Autumn Annals of Master Yan*) is abbreviated throughout as *YZCQ*.

2. The translation follows the incorporated text, in simplified Chinese, of the *ICS Ancient Chinese Text Concordance Series*: *A Concordance to the Yanzichunqiu*, edited by D. C. Lau and Chen Fong Ching, (Commercial Press, Hong Kong, 1993). The digital version text of this concordance, in traditional Chinese, is searchable and browsable online at CHANT Database 汉达文库, http://www.cuhk.edu.hk/ics/rccat/en/database.html (2016).

3. The incorporated *ICS* text version is adapted from the *Sibu congkan* 四部丛刊 edition (hereafter — *SBCK*) which is based on a movable type edition produced during the Ming dynasty (仁和丁松生八千卷楼藏明活字本). This text was emended by the editors of the *ICS* Concordance Series in accordance with many parallel texts that appear either in different editions of the *YZCQ* or in other traditional texts, commentaries, and encyclopedias. Parentheses — ( ) — in the *ICS* Concordance Series signify deletions while square brackets — [ ] — signify additions. An emendation of character 'X' to character 'Y' is therefore indicated by (X) [Y]. Deviations from the incorporated *ICS* Concordance Series version in the present translation are specified throughout the footnotes, and their sources are referred to in brackets.

4. Emendations from the footnotes of the printed edition of the *ICS Ancient Chinese Text Concordance Series*: *A Concordance to the Yanzichunqiu* (1993) are abbreviated throughout the translation footnotes as *YZCQ-ICS* followed by page and note number in the form: "*YZCQ-ICS*, 9, n. 2."

5. Wu Zeyu's 吴则虞 monumental collection of textual variants and

commentaries on the *YZCQ*: *Yanzi chunqiu jishi* 晏子春秋集释, 2 vols. (Beijing: Zhonghua, 1962), is abbreviated throughout as — *JS* — followed by page and note number in the form: "*JS*, 100/8." The revised and enlarged edition of the *JS*, (增订本) 晏子春秋集释, Beijing: (2011), is not abbreviated.

6. Unless otherwise noted, references to all early texts are always to the concordances in the *ICS Ancient Chinese Text Concordance Series*, edited by D. C. Lau and Chen Fong Ching (The Commercial Press, Hong Kong, 1992- ). The form of reference is to the text title followed by the chapter, page, and line number, in the form: "*Mozi* 墨子, 8.3/54/25."

7. References to the standard histories are according to the pagination of the *Zhonghua shuju* 中华书局 edition (Beijing: 1959-1974).

8. References to websites which are contained in the endnotes specify the URL in full, followed by date of posting, as follows: http://ctext.org/ library.pl?if=en&file=10374&page=30 (2006-2015).

9. A "Rightwards Arrow" (→) is used to indicate a textual emendation in the form: 飾 → 飭, followed by the *YZCQ-ICS* page and note number.

10. "Left Right Arrow" (↔) is used to indicate parallelism, similarities, or affiliations between the *YZCQ*-item under consideration and other texts, as follows: "Item 1.15 [15] ↔ *Shuoyuan*, 18.11/153/16."

# 目　录

## 内　篇

# Contents

# 内　篇

## The Inner Chapters

# 第一卷　谏上

## 1.1 [1] 庄公矜勇力不顾行（义）晏子谏

齐庄公崇尚勇力不在乎德行，晏子进谏

**【原文】**

庄公奋乎勇力，不顾于行。（义）〔尚〕勇力之士，无忌于国，贵（贱）〔戚〕不荐善，逼迩不引过，故晏子见公。公曰：“古者亦有徒以勇力立于世者乎？”晏子对曰：“婴闻之，轻死以行礼谓之勇，诛暴不避强谓之力。故勇力之立也，以行其礼义也。汤、武用兵而不为逆，并

**【今译】**

齐庄公崇尚勇力，不在乎德行。崇尚勇猛有力的人，在国内肆无忌惮，王室亲族不能进献忠言，亲近之臣也不敢指出（庄公的）过失，于是晏子来见庄公。庄公问道：“古时候也有仅凭勇力便能立于世间的人吗？”晏子回答说：“我听说，为了遵行礼法而不惜性命叫作‘勇’，诛除凶暴而不畏强悍叫作‘力’。所以‘勇’和‘力’的存在，就是为了推行礼义。商汤和周武王发动战争而不被称作叛逆，兼并国家也不被视为贪婪，道理就在于他们的做法符合仁义的要求。诛除凶暴不畏强悍，消灭罪恶不怕（对方）人多，这才是勇猛有力的行为。古

# Chapter One   Remonstrations — Part A

## 1.1 [1] DUKE ZHUANG[1] TOOK PRIDE IN COURAGE AND STRENGTH TO THE EXTENT OF NEGLECTING RIGHTEOUS[2] CONDUCT. YANZI REMONSTRATED.

Duke Zhuang showed great enthusiasm for courage and strength[3] to the extent of neglecting righteous conduct.[4] Tremendously strong and courageous officers stopped at nothing in their dealings in the capital; ministers of ducal blood did not offer good advice, and his intimate courtiers did not point out faults. And so Yanzi went to have an audience with the Duke.

The Duke said: "Surely there were those in ancient times who established their prominence in the world solely on the basis of courage and

---

1  Duke Zhuang of Qi 齐庄公 succeeded Duke Ling 灵公 (r. 581–554 BCE) and reigned in Qi 齐 between 553–548 BCE. He was invested as the ruler of Qi by the powerful Cui Zhu 崔杼, who later assassinated him for having an extra-marital affair with his wife. For a detailed description of Duke Zhuang's assassination and for an exposition of Yanzi's moral dilemma over serving the new ruler of Qi, Duke Jing 景公 (r. 547–490 BCE), who was also enthroned by Cui Zhu, see Item 5.3 [113]; *Zuozhuan*, B9.25.2/282.

2  Retain 义 (*SBCK*, I/5a4) delete 尚 (*JS*, 2/3).

3  According to the *Zuozhuan* 左传, B9.21.8/272/11, Duke Zhuang established a special official rank to honor courageous men. For several interesting discussions of the concept of "courage" in the *Analects* and *Mencius*, see Philip J. Ivanhoe, "Mengzi's Conception of Courage." *Dao* 5.2 (2006): 221-34; Xinyan Jiang, "Confucius's View of Courage." *Journal of Chinese Philosophy,* 39.1 (2012): 44-59; Bryan W. Van Norden, "Mencius on Courage." *Midwest Studies in Philosophy* 21 (1997): 237-56; Lee H. Yearley, *Mencius and Aquinas: Theories of Virtue and Conceptions of Courage*. SUNY Series, Toward a Comparative Philosophy of Religions, Albany, 1990.

4  Retain 义 (*SBCK*, I/5b7-8) delete 尚 (*JS*, 2/3).

【原文】

国而不为贪，仁义之理也。诛暴不避强，替罪不避众，勇力之行也。古之为勇力者，行礼义也；今上无仁义之理，下无替罪诛暴之行，而徒以勇力立于世，则诸侯行之以国危，匹夫行之以家残。昔夏之衰也，

【今译】

时候勇猛有力的人，遵行礼义；现在君主在上不推行仁义的道理，臣民在下也没有消灭罪恶、诛除凶暴的行为，（这时候）如果仅靠勇力立于世间，那么诸侯这样做就会国危，百姓这样做就会家破。昔日夏朝衰败的时候，有推侈、大戏；商朝衰败的时候，有费仲、恶来，（这些人都是）足可行千里，手可撕咬虎的勇力之士，（君主）因为勇力而任用他们，他们就会恃勇而欺凌天下百姓，屠戮无罪之人。推崇尊尚勇力，不顾仁义

strength, were there not?"

Yanzi answered: "I have heard[1] that to carry out the rites with little thought of death is called courage. Punishing the violence undeterred by the powerful is called strength. Therefore, to set up courage and strength depends upon practicing the rites and righteousness. Tang[2] and Wu[3] resorted to arms, and yet they were not considered rebellious; they annexed lands of others to their own territory and yet they were not considered avaricious – all because of their principles of humaneness and righteousness. When punishing the violent, they were undeterred by the powerful; when abolishing criminal behavior, they were undeterred by the mob. Such was their practice of courage and strength.[4] Those among the ancients who were courageous and strong were those who implemented rites and righteousness. But now, superiors lack the principles of humaneness and righteousness and inferiors lack the practice of abolishing criminal behavior and punishing the violent. Regional princes attempting to establish their prominence in the world solely on the basis courage and strength do so at the cost of putting their states in peril, and the high officers[5] do so at the cost of bringing ruin upon their families. In the time of the Xia dynasty's decline, there lived Tui Chi and Da Xi;[6] in the time of the Yin dynasty's decline, there lived Fei Zhong and Wu Lai.[7] Their legs were strong enough to walk for a

5

---

1  吾闻, literally: "I have heard," a rhetorical pattern that in many cases introduces a truism, akin to the expression: "it is well known that."

2  Emperor Cheng Tang 成汤, the first king of the Shang 商 (Yin 殷) dynasty (17th–11th cent. BCE).

3  King Wu 武王 (1169–1116 BCE), the first sovereign of the Zhou 周 dynasty (11th cent.–221 BCE).

4  For an identical view of what constitutes "moral courage," see *Mencius*, 3.2/15/13.

5  匹夫 → 大夫 (*JS*, 3-4/8).

6  Tui Chi 推侈, which also appears as the variant names Tui Duo 推哆 or Tui Yi 推移, and Da Xi 大戏, or 大牺, were in the service of King Jie 桀 of the Xia. See also *Mozi* 墨子, 8.3/54/15.

7  Fei Zhong 费仲 and Wu Lai 恶来 served Zhou Xin 纣辛, the last tyrant of Shang (Yin) dynasty. See *Mozi,* 8.3/54/25.

**【原文】**

有推侈、大戏；殷之衰也，有费仲、恶来，足走千里，手裂兕虎，任之以力，凌轹天下，威戮无罪，崇尚勇力，不顾义理，是以桀、纣以灭，殷、夏以衰。今公自奋乎勇力，不顾乎行，（义）〔尚〕勇力之士，无忌于国，身立威强，行本淫暴，贵戚不荐善，逼迩不引过，反圣王之德，而循灭君之行，用此存者，婴未闻有也。"

**【今译】**

之礼，这就是夏桀灭亡、商纣衰败的道理。现在您奋扬勇力，不在乎德行，崇尚勇猛有力之人，在国内肆无忌惮，（他们）立身朝野威权日盛，行为却荒淫残暴，王室亲族不能进献忠言，亲近之臣也不敢指出（您的）过失，（您）一反圣王的德政而因循亡国之君的行为，靠这种行为保全国家的，我从来没有听说过。"

thousand *li*[1] and their arms could tear apart rhinoceroses and tigers. They were recruited into service because of their strength, but they oppressed the world and massacred the innocent. Because Jie and Zhou[2] prized courage and strength and neglected righteousness and moral principle, they were destroyed, and Yin and Xia declined. And now you, my Lord, show great enthusiasm for courage and strength to the extent of neglecting righteous conduct.[3] Tremendously strong and courageous officers stop at nothing in their dealings in the capital; they establish their prominence through power and strength and act on the basis of excessive violence. Your ministers of ducal blood do not offer good advice, and your intimate courtiers do not point out faults. This behavior contradicts the virtue of the sage-kings and follows a course of action that leads to the downfall of rulers. I have never heard of anyone who survived while conducting himself in this manner."[4]

---

1   A *li* 里 was a unit of linear measure of approximately 0.4 kilometer.

2   Jie 桀 and Zhou 纣 were the last tyrant kings, respectively, of the Xia and Shang dynasties.

3   Retain 义 delete 尚 (*JS*, 2/3).

4   The present Item, which records a philosophical exchange between Duke Zhuang and Yanzi, provides a conceptual and rhetorical framework from which many of the next 215 items of the *YZCQ* emerge. This opening Item seems to have a strong rhetorical affiliation with Mencius' style of argument with King Hui of Liang 梁惠 王 in the first lines of *Mencius* (1.1/1/3-9). However, the conceptual focus in this passage is not on "profit – 利," as in *Mencius*, but rather on "courage and strength." As the item unfolds, Duke Zhuang's great passion for the performance of acts of "courage and strength – 勇力" induces him and his staff to neglect moral conduct and therefore threatens to engulf the whole state of Qi in chaos and the threat of immediate destruction. Hence, Yanzi comes to see the Duke in order to give up the destructive endorsement of these virtues and to replace it with a different, moral dimension. In a nutshell: for Yanzi, "courage and strength" depends upon the practice of "the rites" (*li* 礼) and "righteousness" (*yi* 义), and spring from the principles of "humanness" (*ren* 仁) and "righteousness" as defined by the moral conduct of the ancient sage-kings. Notably, chronologically speaking, this item is close to heretical – it obliquely implies that, at a time before Confucius (551–479 BCE) was born, Yanzi (590–500 BCE) was already urging his contemporaries in the state of Qi to return to the ways of the ancient sage-kings as guiding paradigms, and that he played a significant role in transmitting and iconizing their conceptual design of "humanness," "righteousness," and 'the rites."

# 1.2 [2] 景公饮酒酣愿诸大夫无为礼晏子谏

齐景公饮酒兴起希望诸位大夫不在乎礼法，晏子进谏

**【原文】**

景公饮酒酣，曰："今日愿与诸大夫为乐饮，请无为礼。"晏子蹴然改容曰："君之言过矣！群臣固欲君之无礼也。力多足以胜其长，勇多足以弑君，而礼不使也。禽兽（矣）〔以〕力为政，强者犯弱，故（曰）〔日〕日易主；今君去礼，则是禽兽也。群臣以力为政，强者犯弱，而日易主，君将安立矣！凡人之所以贵于禽兽者，以有礼也；故《诗》曰：'人而无礼，胡不遄死！'礼不可无也。"公湎而不听。少间，公出，

**【今译】**

齐景公和大臣们喝酒喝到高兴的时候说："今天我想和各位大夫开怀畅饮，请不必在乎礼法。"晏子听后脸色一变，道："您这话说得不对。大臣们固然希望君主不拘礼法。力气大的人足以胜过他的长辈，勇猛的人足以弑杀他的君主，但礼法（的存在）使他们不能这样做。禽兽以勇力为政教，强者侵犯弱者，所以每天都在更新首领；现在您抛弃礼法，就是禽兽（的行为）了。（倘若）大臣们以勇力为政教，强者侵犯弱者，每天变换国君，那您将置身何地呢！人之所以比禽兽高贵，就是因为人有礼法；所以《诗经》说：'人而无礼，胡不遄死！'礼法是不可以抛弃的。"齐景公背过身去不听（晏子的话）。过了一会儿，齐景公起身出去，晏子不站起来；景公回来，晏子也不站起来；（景公和群臣）相互举杯的时候晏子先把酒喝掉。景公很生气，脸色变得很难看，按住手瞪着晏子说："以前您教我不能不重视礼法，（现在）

## 1.2 [2] DUKE JING, IN HIS CUPS, WISHED THAT HIS HIGH OFFICERS WOULD DISPENSE WITH THE RITES.[1] YANZI REMONSTRATED.[2]

Duke Jing, in his cups, declared: "Today I wish to enjoy myself drinking in the company of all my high officers. Let us therefore dispense with the rites."[3]

Yanzi squirmed, changed expression, and said: "My Lord, what you say is mistaken. All your ministers, in fact, wish that you dispense with the rites. It would be easy enough for anyone with great strength to subdue his superior; it would be easy enough for anyone with great courage to commit regicide – but the rites prevent such occurrences. Wild beasts gain dominion by means of force; the strong assault the weak, and as a result, their leaders are replaced day after day. If you, my Lord, now dispense with the rites, then this situation will be akin to that of the wild beasts.[4] If all your ministers gain dominion by means of force, if the strong assault the weak and the leader is replaced day after day, how would you, my Lord, keep your position as a leader? It is a general principle that humans' superiority over wild beasts derives from people's possession of the rites. As it says in the *Odes*:

A man without the rites,

---

1   For a detailed discussion of the concept of *Li* 礼 ("the rites") in the *YZCQ*, see Masayuki Sato, *The Confucian Quest for Order: The Origin and Formation of the Political Thought of Xun Zi*. Sinica Leidensia 58. Leiden: Brill (2003): 211-217.

2   Item 1.2 [2] ↔ 7.1 [171]; *Hanshi waizhuan* 韩诗外传, 9.8/66/20; *Xinxu* 新序 6.7/33/30.

3   For a discussion of the use of wine in ritual and the attitudes towards wine-drinking in ancient China, see Mu-chou Poo, "The Use and Abuse of Wine in Ancient China." *Journal of the Economic and Social History of the Orient* 42.2 (1999): 123-51; Roel Sterckx, ed. *Of Tripod and Palate: Food, Politics, and Religion in Traditional China*. New York: Palgrave Macmillan (2005): passim.

4   For a similar gloomy picture of a state completely devoid of rites cf. *Mencius*, 7.1/36/6.

**【原文】**

晏子不起，公入，不起；交举则先饮。公怒，色变，抑手疾视曰："向者夫子之教寡人无礼之不可也，寡人出入不起，交举则先饮，礼也？"晏子避席再拜稽首而请曰："婴敢与君言而忘之乎？臣以致无礼之实也。君若欲无礼，此是已！"公曰："（若）〔善〕。是孤之罪也。夫子就席，寡人闻命矣。"觞三行，遂罢酒。盖是后也，饬法修礼以治国政，而百姓肃也。

大中华文库

**【今译】**

我出入您不起身，共饮时您先我而饮，（这难道是）礼法吗？"晏子站起来离开座席，拜了两拜，叩首（对景公）恭敬地说："我怎么敢把和您说过的话忘记呢？我只是想表达抛弃礼法之后的结果。您如果想抛弃礼法，结果就是这样！"景公说："您说得对，这是我的过失。请您回到座位上，我听您的建议就是了。"酒过三巡，（景公）于是就结束宴饮。从此以后，（景公）整顿法纪、治理国家，百姓也恭敬守礼了。

Why should he not die quickly?[1]

It is impossible to dispense with the rites."

But the Duke steeped himself in wine and paid no heed. Shortly afterwards, when the Duke left the room, Yanzi did not rise to his feet, and when the Duke returned to the room, once again Yanzi did not rise. Then, when they raised their goblets in a toast to each other, Yanzi was the first to drink.

The Duke was furious; he changed color, pressed his hands against the table, stared fiercely at Yanzi, and said: "A while ago you, Master, taught me that it would not be right for people to dispense with the rites. Nevertheless, when I left the room and when I reentered it, you did not rise. When we raised our goblets in a toast to each other, you were the first one to drink. Are these proper rites?"

Yanzi withdrew from his mat and bowed twice with his forehead touching the ground and addressed the Duke, saying: "Do you, my Lord, think that I would presume to forget what has been said during this audience? I merely wanted to show you what it would actually be like without the rites. If you, my Lord, wish to dispense with the rites, then this is how things would be."

The Duke said: "Well said; it is my fault. Return to your mat, Master, and I will receive your instruction."

Three more rounds of drinking took place, and then no more drinks were served. From that day onwards, the Duke restored law and cultivated rites, thereby putting the governance of his state in order. And the people were reverential.[2]

11

---

1  *Shijing* 诗经, 52/24/9.

2  This is the first of several consecutive items that deal with the devastating consequences of Duke Jing's excessive drinking, amusements, and pleasure-seeking in general. It is also the first among many similar instances described in the text – instances in which Yanzi, through the use of his practical wisdom involving psychological manipulation, theatrical gestures, wily arguments, and even blunt cheating, causes Duke Jing and the others who disagree to lose their arguments and fail to realize their intentions.

## 1.3 [3] 景公饮酒醒三日而后发晏子谏

齐景公饮酒醉卧三天后才起，晏子进谏

### 【原文】

景公饮酒醒，三日后而发。晏子见曰："君病酒乎？"公曰："然。"晏子曰："古之饮酒也，足以通气合好而已矣。故男不群乐以妨事，女不群乐以妨功。男女群乐者，周觞五献，过之者诛。君身服之，故外无怨治，内无乱行。今一日饮酒，而三日寝之，国治怨乎外，左右乱乎内。以刑罚自防者，劝乎为非；以赏誉自劝者，惰乎为善；上离德行，民轻赏罚，失所以为国矣。愿君节之也！"

### 【今译】

齐景公喝醉了酒，三天后才起来。晏子（听说后）拜见景公说："您醉酒了吗？"景公说："是的。"晏子说："古时候的人喝酒，能够疏通气血友善关系就停止了。所以男人们不在一起饮酒作乐以免影响做事，女人们也不在一起饮酒作乐以免影响女工。男女在一起饮酒作乐时，相互敬酒不能超过五次，超过了就会受到责罚。君主以身作则，所以朝廷之外没有积压不理的政务，朝廷之内没有混乱不法的行为。现在您一天喝醉了酒，就睡了三天，外有积压不理的政务，内有混乱不法的亲随。害怕犯法受罚的人，频繁地为非作歹；希望得到奖赏、荣誉的人，也懒于做善事；君主丧失了德行，百姓不重视赏罚，国家也就失去了立国之本。希望您能节制饮酒！"

## 1.3 [3] DUKE JING DRANK WINE, AND AFTER A THREE-DAY HANGOVER HE RECOVERED. YANZI REMONSTRATED.

Duke Jing drank wine, and after a three-day hangover he recovered.

Yanzi came for an audience with him and said: "Were you suffering from a hangover?"

The Duke said: "Yes."

Yanzi said: "In ancient times, the drinking of wine was sufficient merely to enhance blood circulation and to make people friendly — that and nothing more. Therefore, men did not allow a social gathering for entertainment purposes to hinder their duties, and women did not permit themselves to hinder their tasks. When men and women held large social gatherings for entertainment, five rounds of drinking took place, and those who exceeded this were severely punished. The ruler himself observed this rule, and therefore the governmental policies did not provoke resentment in the country at large and the entourage did not create disorder within the court. But now you drink wine all day long and sleep it off for three days. There is resentment against the governmental policies in the country at large, and your entourage creates disorder within the court. Those who should curb themselves by punishments and are incited to wrongdoing and those who should be self-motivated by rewards and praise are dissuaded from acting well. Superiors depart from virtuous conduct; people belittle rewards and punishments, and the basis for maintaining the state is lost. I wish, my Lord, that you would restrain your drinking."

## 1.4 [4] 景公饮酒七日不纳弦章之言晏子谏

齐景公连续饮酒七日七夜不采纳弦章的谏言，晏子进谏

### 【原文】

景公饮酒，七日七夜不止。弦章谏曰："君（欲）饮酒七日七夜，章愿君废酒也！不然，章赐死。"晏子入见，公曰："章谏吾曰：'愿君之废酒也！不然，章赐死。'如是而听之，则臣为制也；不听，又爱其死。"晏子曰："幸矣，章遇君也！（今）〔令〕章遇桀、纣者，章死久矣！"于是公遂废酒。

大中华文库

### 【今译】

齐景公饮酒，喝了七天七夜还不停止。弦章进谏说："您饮酒已经七天七夜，我希望您停止饮酒！不然的话，就请您将我赐死。"晏子入朝见景公，景公说："弦章向我进谏：'希望您停止饮酒！不然的话，就请您将我赐死。'如果就这样听了他的话，那我就是被臣子管制了；不听，我又舍不得他去死。"晏子说："弦章遇到您，真是他的幸运啊！倘若弦章遇到的是桀、纣那样的暴君，那他早就死了！"于是景公停止了饮酒。

## 1.4 [4] DUKE JING DRANK WINE FOR SEVEN DAYS AND PAID NO ATTENTION TO XIANZHANG'S[1] WORDS. YANZI REMONSTRATED.

Duke Jing drank wine nonstop for seven days and seven nights. Xianzhang remonstrated with him, saying: "My Lord, you have now been drinking wine for seven days and seven nights. I implore you, my Lord, to refrain from drinking. If you do not, I request permission to commit suicide."

Yanzi entered the room for an audience and the Duke said to him: "Zhang remonstrated with me and said that I should refrain from drinking or else he would request permission to commit suicide. If I accept his words, a minister would be exercising control; if I do not accept his words, then I will appear to relish his death."

Yanzi said: "How lucky Zhang has been to interact with you, my Lord. Had he interacted with Jie and Zhou, he would have been long dead."

At that, the Duke refrain from drinking.

15

---

1 An unidentified figure. The *JS*, 12/1, lists several sources such as the *Han Feizi*, *Shuoyuan* 说苑 and *Lüshi chunqiu* 吕氏春秋, in which Xianzhang is named Xianshang 弦商. According to the last item of the *YZCQ* (Item 8.18A [215]), Xianzhang 弦章 carried out Yanzi's moral heritage after Yanzi's death.

# 1.5 [5] 景公饮酒不恤天灾致能歌者晏子谏

齐景公饮酒作乐不抚恤遭受天灾的百姓而罗致能歌善舞的人，晏子进谏

大中华文库

## 【原文】

景公之时，霖雨十有七日。公饮酒，日夜相继。晏子请发粟于民，三请，不见许。公命柏遽巡国，致能歌者。晏子闻之，不说，遂分家粟于氓，致任器于陌，徒行见公曰："〔霖雨〕十有七日矣！（怀宝）〔坏室〕乡有数十，饥氓里有数家，百姓老弱，冻寒不得短褐，饥饿不得糟糠，敝撤无走，四顾无告。而君不恤，日夜饮酒，令国致乐不已，

## 【今译】

齐景公当政的时候，有一年连续下了十七天雨。景公夜以继日地饮酒作乐。晏子请求把府库的粮食分发给受灾的百姓，请求了多次，也没有获得允许。景公命柏遽在全国巡视，网罗善于唱歌的人。晏子听说后，很不高兴，于是就把自己家中的粮食分给百姓，又把装运粮食的器具放在路边，自己步行着去见景公说："（雨已经下了）十七天了！每个乡都有数十家房屋损坏，每个里都有数家饥饿之民，年老体弱的百姓，寒冷中没有粗布短衣可以御寒，饥饿中没有糟糠之食可以充饥，腿脚不便不能行走的人，四处张望也没有诉说苦难的地方。然而国君您不体恤百姓，日夜饮酒作乐，命令全国不停地网罗乐人，用府库的粮食喂马，用牛羊肉喂狗，后宫的姬妾都有充足的粮食和肉。

# 1.5 [5] DUKE JING INDULGED IN WINE WITHOUT TAKING PITY UPON THOSE WHO WERE AFFLICTED BY A HEAVEN-SENT DISASTER. HE ASSEMBLED A GROUP OF TALENTED SINGERS. YANZI REMONSTRATED.

During the time of Duke Jing there was a long, seventeen-day spell of incessant rain, through which the Duke drank wine continuously, day and night. Three times, Yanzi asked that grain be distributed to the people, but his request was denied. At that time the Duke sent Bo Ju[1] on a nationwide tour in search of talented singers. Upon hearing this, Yanzi was displeased and thereupon distributed grain from his own household to the displaced people and abandoned the loading tools along the paths of the fields. [2]

He then walked on foot for an audience with the Duke and said: "It has been raining for seventeen days; there are dozens of ruined houses in every district and several hungry families in every village. The old and weak among the people do not have even short hemp garments to protect them against the cold, nor dregs and bran to fight their hunger. If those whose houses were destroyed seek escape, they have no place to turn, and, though they are looking all over, they find no one to address their complaint to. But you, my Lord, have not been concerned, all this time, with all these and have been occupied in drinking day and night, having issued statewide orders to provide you with music continuously. Your horses eat the grain of the public granaries; your dogs gorge upon fine meats of pastured and grain-fed animals; and the concubines of the three palaces are well provided with

*17*

---

1   An unidentified figure.

2   The grain loading tools used to distribute the food were left abandoned by Yanzi in order to indicate that all his reserves of grain were exhausted.

**【原文】**

马食府粟，狗餍刍豢，三保之妾，俱足（梁）〔梁〕肉。狗马保妾，不已厚乎？民氓百姓，不亦薄乎？故里穷而无告，无乐有上矣；饥饿而无告，无乐有君矣。婴奉数之策，以随百官之吏，民饥饿穷约而无告，使上淫湎失本而不恤，婴之罪大矣。"再拜稽首，请身而去，遂走而出。公从之，兼于涂而不能逮，令趣驾追晏子，其家，不及。粟米尽于氓，任器存于陌，公驱及之康内。公下车从晏子曰："寡人有罪，夫子倍弃不援，寡人不足以有约也，夫子不顾社稷百姓乎？愿夫子之幸存寡人，

**【今译】**

（您）对待狗马姬妾是不是太优厚了呢？对待百姓是不是太薄情了呢？乡里的百姓贫穷无处申诉，就不会喜欢朝廷了；饥饿的百姓无处申诉，也就不会喜欢国君了。我是手捧简策，百官跟随的重臣，让百姓饥饿贫困而无处申诉，让国君沉湎酒色失去民心而不知体恤，我的罪过太大了。"（晏子说完）拜了两拜叩首请求辞职，然后快步走出了宫门。景公赶忙去追，因为道路泥泞没有追上，又命人驾车去追晏子，一直到他家也没有追上。（景公）见晏子家的粮食已经全部分发给了百姓，装运粮食的器具放在路边。景公乘车在大路上追上了晏子，赶忙下车跟在晏子身后说："我犯了大错，以致您抛弃我不愿辅佐我，我没有资

millet and meats. Is this not excessive for dogs, horses, and concubines, and paltry for people in general? It is because of this that the districts and the villages are exhausted,[1] and no authority exists to complain to — subjects lack the comforting presence of a superior. The people are starving and have no one to complain to — they do not enjoy the comforting presence of a ruler.  Holding bamboo counting sticks, I follow the minor officials from the various public offices and learn that the people are starving, suffering hardship and destitution, but have no one to whom to complain. For allowing my superior to be beguiled by drink, leading him to lose his grip and not be concerned with the afflicted — my guilt is great." He bowed twice with his forehead touching the ground, asked to be dismissed from office and quickly ran out from the palace.

The Duke followed him but since the streets were extremely muddy[2] he could not catch up to him. He gave orders to the charioteer to chase after Yanzi to his house, but there, too, he did not catch up to him. The Duke saw that grain had been completely distributed among the displaced people and that the loading tools were abandoned along the paths of the fields.  He then pursued Yanzi and caught up to him at the crossroads.

He stepped down from the chariot, followed Yanzi, and said: "I am guilty, you abandoned me and offer no help. But if I am not worthy to have you defer[3] to me, then will you not be neglecting the altars of soils and grain and the people? I hope to be fortunate enough to have you saving me. Now I would like to propose that the grain and the wealth of Qi be turned over to the people. Your command alone will determine the measures and weights of distribution." Then, in the middle of the road, he made obeisance

---

1   故乡里穷约而无告 → 故里穷而无告 (*JS*, 16/14).

2   兼 → 溓 (*JS*, 17/19).

3   约 → 屈 (*JS* 18/24).

## 【原文】

寡人请奉齐国之粟米财货，委之百姓，多寡轻重，惟夫于之令。"遂拜于途。晏子乃返，命禀巡氓，家有布缕之本而绝食者，使有终月之委；绝本之家，使有期年之食，无委积之氓，与之薪燎，使足以毕霖雨。令柏巡氓，家室不能御者，予之金；巡求氓寡用（财乏）〔乏财〕者（死），三日而毕，后者若不用令之罪。公出舍，损肉撤酒，马不食府粟，

## 【今译】

格让您屈尊，但是您不顾国家和百姓了吗？希望您能留下来继续辅佐我，我愿意把齐国的粮食和财富拿出来赈济百姓，至于多少轻重，全都听您的安排。"于是景公在路上委任晏子处理救灾事宜。于是晏子返回朝廷，命令禀去巡视灾民，（灾民的）家中还有衣物只是断了粮食的，就给他们一个月的粮食；衣食都断了的人家，就给他们一年的粮食，没有柴烧的灾民，就给他们柴草，让他们足以度过霖雨之灾。又命令柏去巡视灾民，（灾民的）房屋不能遮风挡雨的，就给他们钱去修补；巡视中要寻找缺少财物的百姓，限三天内完成，超出时间就按不执行法令治罪。景公也离开后宫，减少肉食，撤去美酒，下令不许再

to Yanzi, and Yanzi then returned and sent Bing[1] on a tour of inspection amongst the displaced people, to give families that had supplies of cloth but lacked food a portion equaling a month's share of grain; and to families that lacked both these resources, a share of food sufficient for a full year. And to displaced people who had nothing stored at all, he gave sufficient firewood to last until the end of rains. He ordered Bo Ju to tour amongst the displaced people and distribute money to families whose roof could not provide shelter. The mission of traveling and locating displaced people who did not have money and materials was to be completed in three days. Whoever was late would be punished as if he had disregarded order. The Duke left the capital and occupied a hut on the outskirts. He ate less meat and abstained from wine. His horses did not eat the grain of the public granaries and his dogs did not eat gruel mixed with meat. The budget for attendants was reduced[2] and gifts were held back from those who were given to drink. After three days, the scribes reported to their superiors that the work was completed: seventeen thousand impoverished households of displaced people had been found, nine-hundred and seventy thousand *zhong*[3] of grain and thirteen thousand carts of firewood had been distributed. Twenty-seven hundred destroyed households had been found and three thousand pieces of gold had been expended. Afterwards, the Duke returned to court and ate a scanty meal while the string instruments of the *qin* and the *se* were not made

---

1   The *JS* (18/32) replaces the personal names of Bing and then of Bo 柏 with the official titles 廩 – Granary Master and 伯 – Earl. This interpretation seems very unlikely at least in the case of Bo, who is mentioned in the beginning of this item by his full name 柏遽.

2   嗛齐 → 减资 (*JS*, 20-22/38).

3   *Zhong* 钟, a measure of grain in the state of Qi, consisted of six-hundred and forty liters.

大
中
华
文
库

**【原文】**

狗不食飦肉，辟拂嗛齐，酒徒减赐。三日，吏告毕上：贫氓万七千家，用粟九十七万钟，薪燎万三千乘；（怀宝）〔坏室〕二千七百家，用金三千。公然后就内退食，琴瑟不张，钟鼓不陈。晏子请左右与可令歌舞足以留思虞者退之，辟拂三千，谢于下陈，人待三，士（侍）〔待〕四，出之关外也。

**【今译】**

用府库的粮食喂马，用肉类养狗，削减近臣的供给，减少酒徒的赏赐。三天期满，巡视的官员完成任务向上汇报：受灾的贫民一万七千家，发放粮食九十七万钟，柴草一万三千车；房屋损坏的百姓两千七百家，资助修补花去三千金。景公听完报告后回到宫中，下令降低饮食标准，不许抚琴弄瑟，敲击钟鼓。晏子请求将近侍和足以使景公留恋歌舞的人遣退，结果三千人被裁汰，姬妾三人，近臣四人，全部被遣出宫外。

taut and the bells and drums were not displayed. Yanzi asked the Duke to dismiss members of the entourage, as well as those who sang and danced so expertly that their presence could entice the Duke with entertainment. Three thousand attendants were dismissed from the lesser palaces. Three concubines and four officers whom the Duke favored were expelled from the palace.[1]

---

1   The "inundated world" of the present items brings to mind a rhetorical device in *Mencius* (*Mencius*, 7.17/38.20). Chunyu Kun 淳于髡 used the gloomy metaphor of a "drowning world—天下溺" to portray the devastation of his time. In that context, he pleaded with Mencius to extend a personal hand to help save the world, which he compared to a "drowning sister-in-law." However, Mencius rejected the analogy, insisting that the world could be helped only by means of the Way. In other words, Mencius argued that the only help he was prepared to give to save the world from drowning was of a "philosophical" kind, meaning that he could rescue the world only by repairing and transforming it into an alternative, utopian reality. In contrast, Yanzi's understanding of the role a philosopher should play in a dystopian society on verge of total ruin is not abstract, like that of Mencius, but rather concrete, like that of Chunyu Kun.

## 1.6 [6] 景公夜听新乐而不朝晏子谏

齐景公夜里听新作之乐而不上朝，晏子进谏

### 【原文】

晏子朝，杜扃望羊待子朝。晏子曰："君奚故不朝？"对曰："君夜发不可以〔朝〕。"晏子曰："何故？"对曰："梁丘据扃入歌人虞，变齐音。"晏子退，命宗祝修礼而拘虞，公闻之而怒曰："何故而拘虞？"

### 【今译】

晏子上朝，杜扃走来走去在朝堂前等待。晏子问："国君为什么不上朝？"杜扃说："国君昨夜兴致很高，彻夜未眠，因此不能上朝。"晏子问道："国君为何兴致很高？"回答说："梁丘据进献了一个叫虞的歌者，他更改了齐国的古音。"晏子离开，命令宗祝根据礼法规定拘捕了虞，齐景公听说后大怒道："为什么要拘捕虞？"晏子说："因为他用新乐迷惑国君。"景公说："诸侯国之间的事务，各级官员的政务，我愿意向您请教。（但我）品味美酒，欣赏音乐这些事，希望您就不要干涉了。音乐，为什么一定要听古音呢？"晏子说："音乐失传了，礼法也就废弃了，礼法废弃了，政事也就荒怠了，政事荒怠了，国家也就离灭亡不远了。国家衰败，我害怕您有违逆政教的行为。过去曾有

# 1.6 [6] DUKE JING LISTENED TO NEW MUSIC DURING THE NIGHT AND COULD NOT CARRY OUT COURT DUTIES. YANZI REMONSTRATED.

When Yanzi went to the court for an audience, Du Jiong[1] was already there waiting for his own audience, gazing into the distance.

Yanzi said: "Why does the Duke not hold court?"

Du Jiong answered: "The Duke was awake all night and therefore he cannot hold court."

Yanzi said: "How did this come about?"

Du Jiong answered: "Liangqiu Ju[2] has brought in the singer Yu, who altered the sound of a traditional Qi melody."

Yanzi retired from the audience hall and ordered the Master of Sacrifices and the Invocator to implement the rules of the rites and to seize Yu.

When the Duke heard this, he was furious and said: "Why did you have Yu arrested?"

Yanzi replied: "Because the new music led you into debauchery, my Lord."

The Duke said: "I wish to consult with you concerning affairs of the regional princes and the affairs of the various governmental offices. However, Master, I do not wish you to meddle with my taste in wine and sweet liquor and the sound of bronze and stone instruments. Why does music always have to be played in accordance with the old fashion?"

Yanzi answered: "When music perishes, the rites follow suit; when the rites perish, the government follows suit; when the government perishes,

---

1   An unidentified figure.

2   Liangqiu Ju 梁丘据 (fl. 530–510 BCE) was a high officer in Qi who exercised corrupt influence on Duke Jing. He appears in eighteen items of the *YZCQ* in which he always plays the role of Yanzi's main adversary.

**【原文】**

晏子曰：“以新乐淫君。”公曰：“诸侯之事，百官之政，寡人愿以请子。酒醴之味，金石之声，愿夫子无与焉。夫乐，何（夫必）〔必夫〕（攻）〔故〕哉？”对曰：“夫乐亡而礼从之，礼亡而政从之，政亡而国从之。国衰，臣惧君之逆政之行。有歌，纣作北里，幽厉之声，顾夫淫以鄙而偕亡。君奚轻变夫故哉？”公曰：“不幸有社稷之业，不择言而出之，请受命矣。”

**【今译】**

这样的歌，（夏桀作东歌南音），商纣作北里之曲，周幽王、厉王作的乐曲，都是淫靡鄙陋之音，他们也和这些乐曲一起灭亡了。您怎么能轻易更改古乐呢？”景公说：“我侥幸拥有国家的基业，口不择言说出了那些话，我愿意接受您的教诲了。”

the state follows suit and declines.[1] I am fearful that you, my Lord, have carried out a perverse policy.[2] The debauched and vulgar character of the composition of the Northern-District Dances, commissioned by Zhou,[3] as well as the music of You and Li,[4] makes it clear why they all perished. How then can you, my Lord, change the music of antiquity so frivolously?"[5]

The Duke said: "It is my misfortune to be responsible for the grand enterprise of the altars of soil and grain. I uttered my words without choosing them correctly. I request to receive your instructions."[6]

---

1  Read: 政亡而国从之衰, omitting 国 before 衰 (*JS*, 25/9).

2  Omit 有歌 (*JS*, 25/10).

3  For the licentious nature of the music composed by Master Juan 师涓 for Zhou, the last tyrant of Shang dynasty, see *Shiji*, 105.

4  Kings Li and You of the Zhou dynasty reigned between the years 893–864 BCE and 781–771 BCE, respectively.

5  The conservative attitude expressed here regarding music sharply contrasts the attitude expressed in *Mencius*, 2.1/7.

6  Notably, Mencius (*Mencius*, 2.1/7/3-32.), during his audience with the King of Qi, expressed his opinion that popular music and the music of antiquity were alike, and that the King's emotional involvement with this "modern" music potentially offers hope to the state of Qi.

## 1.7 [7] 景公燕赏无功而罪有司晏子谏

　　齐景公设宴赏赐无功之人而惩罚不服从命令的官吏，晏子进谏

### 【原文】

　　景公燕赏于国内，万钟者三，千钟者五，令三出，而职计（莫）〔笑〕之（从）。公怒，令免职计，令三出，而士师（莫）〔笑〕之（从）。公不说。晏子见，公谓晏子曰："寡人闻君国者，爱人则能利之，恶人则能疏之。今寡人爱人不能利，恶人不能疏，失君道矣。"晏子曰："婴闻之，君正臣从谓之顺，君僻臣从谓之逆。今君赏谗谀之（民）〔臣〕，而令吏必从，则是使君失其道，臣失其守也。先王之立爱，以

*28*

### 【今译】

　　齐景公在国内设宴赏赐，获万钟粮食赏赐的有三人，获千钟粮食赏赐的有五人，命令发出多次，职计都没有听从。景公大怒，下令罢免职计，命令发出多次，士师也不听从。景公很不高兴。晏子来见景公，景公对晏子说："我听说一个国家的君主，喜爱谁就能给谁好处，厌恶谁就能让谁离开。现在我喜爱谁却不能让他得到好处，厌恶谁又不能让他离开，已经丧失为君之道了。"晏子说："我听说，国君遵行正道臣子依从叫作'顺'，国君行为奸邪臣子依从叫作'逆'。现在您赏赐阿谀奉承的人，还命令官吏必须服从，这就是国君丧失为君之道，臣下玩忽职守了。先王确立所爱，是为了鼓励人们做善事；确立所恶，是为了禁止凶暴不法。以前夏、商、周三代勃兴的时候，对

# 1.7 [7] DURING A BANQUET, DUKE JING REWARDED THOSE LACKING IN MERIT AND PUNISHED AN OFFICE-HOLDER. YANZI REMONSTRATED.

On the occasion of an awards banquet in the capital, Duke Jing sought to reward three men with ten thousand *zhong* of grain each, and five other men with a thousand *zhong* of grain each. The order was issued three times, but the treasurer did not comply with it. The Duke became furious and ordered the treasurer's dismissal. The orders were repeated three times, but the Chief Judge did not comply with the order.

The Duke was displeased, and when Yanzi appeared for an audience, the Duke said to him: "I have heard that he who rules the state has the capacity to grant benefits to those he favors and to alienate those he disfavors. Now, however, I find myself unable to confer benefits upon those I favor and alienate those I disfavor. This means that I have failed with respect to the way of the ruler."

Yanzi responded: "I have heard that if the ruler is correct and the ministers follow suit that is called obedience. If the ruler is aberrant and the ministers follow suit, that is called defiance. But now, if you, my Lord, reward slanderous and flattering ministers and compel your officials to obey; this is what makes you fail with respect to the way of the ruler, and this is what makes ministers fail in maintaining their official responsibilities. The former kings appointed those whom they cherished, in order to encourage excellence, and they removed those whom they did not favor, as preventive measures against political violence. Formerly, when the Three Dynasties prospered,[1] those who were beneficial to the state were cherished and those who were harmful were despised. Therefore, the kings made it clear

---

1  The ancient Three Dynasties: Xia 夏 2205–1766 BCE, Shang 商 or Yin 殷 1766–1123 BCE and Zhou 周 1122–249 BCE.

**【原文】**

劝善也；其（立）〔去〕恶，以禁暴也。昔者三代之兴也，利于国者爱之，害于国者恶之，故明所爱而贤良众，明所恶而邪僻灭，是以天下治平，百姓和集。及其衰也，行安简易，身安逸乐，顺于己者爱之，逆于己者恶之，故明所爱而邪僻繁，明所恶而贤良灭，离散百姓，危覆社稷。君上不度圣王之兴，而下不观惰君之衰，臣惧君之逆政之行，有司不敢争，以覆社稷，危宗庙。"公曰："寡人不知也，请从士师之策。"国内之禄，所收者三也。

**【今译】**

国家有利的人，国君就爱他，对国家有害的人，国君就恨他，所以（国君）表明所爱，贤良的人就变多了，表明所恶；奸邪的人就消失了，因此天下太平无事，百姓安居和睦。到了三代衰败的时候，（国君的）行为安于简单方便，身体安于舒适享乐，顺从自己的人就喜爱，违背自己的人就厌恶，所以（国君）表明所爱，而奸邪的人增多了；表明所恶，而贤良的人消失了，百姓流离失所，国家倾覆衰亡。国君上不考虑圣王兴盛的经验，下不观察昏君衰亡的教训，我担心您倒行逆施，官吏不敢谏争，以致国家倾覆，危及宗庙。"景公说："我不明智啊，就请按照士师的意见办吧。"于是国内发出去的禄米，有很多都被收回来了。

whom they cherished and so the worthy and the good grew in number. They made it clear whom they despised, so the depraved and the deviant were exterminated. Hence, the world was well governed and the people lived in harmony with one another. But when the time came that the Three Dynasties declined, the rulers fell into frivolity and slacking and into indulgence and amusements in their private lives. Those who obeyed them were cherished, but those who disobeyed them were despised. As a result, they made clear what they cherished, and thus the depraved and the devious flourished. They made it clear what they despised, and thus the worthy and the good were exterminated. They drove the people apart and scattered them, and the altars of soils and grain were endangered and destroyed. You, my Lord, did not give thought to the prosperity of the sage-kings, on the one hand, and, on the other, you did not pay heed to the decline of the negligent rulers. I am afraid, my Lord, that in light of your practice of perverse policies, those in office do not presume to contest your policies, and therefore the altars of soil and grain will be destroyed and your ancestral shrine will be endangered."

The Duke said: "I was unwise. I would like to follow the instructions of the Chief Judge."[1]

31

---

1  Omit 国内之禄, 所收者三也 (*JS*, 29/12).

# 1.8 [8] 景公信用谗佞赏罚失中晏子谏

齐景公信赖任用谗佞小人赏罚丧失公平，晏子进谏

## 【原文】

景公信用谗佞，赏无功，罚不辜。晏子谏曰："臣闻明君望圣人而信其教，不闻听谗佞以诛赏。今与左右相说颂也，曰：'比死者勉为乐乎！吾安能为仁而愈黥民耳矣！'故内宠之妾，迫夺于国，外宠之臣，矫夺于鄙，执法之吏，并荷百姓。民愁苦约病，而奸驱尤佚，隐情奄恶，蔽谄其上，故虽有至圣大贤，岂能胜若谗哉！是以忠臣（之）常有灾

## 【今译】

齐景公听信奸佞之臣的谗言，赏赐无功的人，惩罚无罪的人。晏子进谏说："我听说贤明的君主仰慕圣人的德行，信奉他们的教诲，没听说过听信奸佞之臣的谗言来诛杀或赏赐。现在国君和左右的近臣相互取悦称颂，说：'那些快要死去的人尚且尽力寻找快乐，我怎么能为了仁义而过得仅胜于罪犯呢！'所以宫内受宠的姬妾在国都内放肆掠夺，朝堂上受宠的臣子在地方上强行聚敛，执法的官吏，一起苛刻虐待百姓，百姓忧愁苦闷贫病交加，而隐藏的奸佞之人更加猖狂，他们隐瞒真相掩盖罪恶，蒙蔽欺骗国君，所以即使有至圣大贤，也难以胜过这些善于进谗言的奸佞之徒！所以忠诚的臣子常常有灾祸。我听说

# 1.8 [8] DUKE JING ENTRUSTED SLANDERERS AND SYCOPHANTS. HE FAILED TO ACHIEVE THE PROPER BALANCE IN REWARDING AND PUNISHING. YANZI REMONSTRATED.

Duke Jing entrusted slanderers and sycophants. He rewarded those who were lacking in merit and punished the innocent.

Yanzi remonstrated with him, saying: "I have heard that the enlightened ruler looks up to the sages and believes in their moral instructions. I have not heard that he listens to slanderers and sycophants in meting out punishments and rewards. But now you and your entourage take pleasure in singing each other songs of praise: 'With death at hand let us apply all our energy to amusements.[1] There is no way for us to practice humaneness and care for the common people.'[2] Therefore, favored concubines in the palace relentlessly plunder the capital; beyond the palace, favored ministers vigorously plunder the border towns; and the officials who execute the laws lay their yoke[3] on the people. The people grow miserable and sorrowful, poor and sick, while the wicked and the devious[4] enjoy the pinnacle of leisure. The actual state of affairs is obscured and evil is concealed.[5] They hoodwink their superiors, so that even a perfect sage or a great worthy could not possibly stand up to these slanderers. And so, the loyal ministers are often struck by personal disaster. I have heard that in ancient times, if the ruler could ally himself with the officer, he would win him over — if not, he would lose him. If the ruler could ally himself with an officer, he would advance the officer's career — if not, he would hold him back. I request to

*33*

---

1   Cf. Bible, Isaiah 22:13: "Let us eat and drink for tomorrow we shall die."

2   黥 → 黔 (*YZCQ-ICS*, 3, n. 3).

3   荷 → 苛 (*JS*, 31/8).

4   驱 → 匿 (*JS*, 31/10).

5   掩 → 奄 (*JS*, 31/11).

**【原文】**

伤也。臣闻古者之士，可与得之，不可与失之；可与进之，不可与退之。臣请逃之矣。"遂鞭（而马）〔马而〕出。公使韩子休追之，曰："孤不仁，不能顺教，以至此极。夫子休国焉而往，寡人将从而后。"晏子遂鞭马而返。

其仆曰："向之去何速？今之返又何速？"晏子曰："非子之所知也，公之言至矣。"

**【今译】**

古时候做官的人，能与国君相处就辅佐他，不能与国君相处就离开他；国君可以相处，他们就做官；不可以相处，他们就隐退。我请求离开这里了。"于是晏子策马扬鞭离开了朝廷。景公命韩子休追赶晏子，说："我不仁义，不能顺从先王的教诲，因此到了极端昏庸的地步。您丢下国家要到哪里去，我就在后边跟您到哪里去。"晏子于是策马返回。

晏子的仆人问他说："刚刚您离去时怎么那么急？现在返回怎么又这么迅速？"晏子说："这不是你所能理解的，国君的话说的太到位了。"

escape from all this." Thereupon, he whipped his horses and departed.

The Duke ordered Han Zixiu[1] to pursue him, saying: "I am not humane and am incapable of acting in accordance with your instructions. Thus, we have reached this extreme state of affairs. If you, my Master, withdraw from the capital and leave, I will follow right behind you."

Thereupon, Yanzi whipped his horses and turned back. His servant said: "Why did you hastily disappear before, and why do you now just as hastily turn back?"

Yanzi answered: "This is beyond your understanding. The Duke's words were perfect."

35

---

1   An unidentified figure.

## 1.9 [9] 景公爱嬖妾随其所欲晏子谏

齐景公宠爱嬖妾顺从她的欲望，晏子进谏

### 【原文】

翟王子羡臣于景公，以重驾，公观之而不说也。嬖人婴子欲观之，公曰："及晏子寝病也。"居圉中台上以观之，婴子说之，因为之请曰："厚禄之！"公许诺。晏子起病而见公，公曰："翟王子羡之驾，寡人甚说之，请使之示乎？"晏子曰："驾御之事，臣无职焉。"公曰："寡人一乐之，是欲禄之以万钟，其足乎？"对曰："昔卫士东野之驾也，公说之，婴子不说，公曰不说，遂不观。今翟王子羡之驾也，公不说，婴子说，公因说之；为请，公许之，则是妇人为制也。且不乐治人，

### 【今译】

翟王之子羡当了齐景公的臣子，因为用超过礼仪制度规定的马匹数驾车，景公看到后很不高兴。景公的宠妾婴子想看翟王子羡驾车，景公说："等到晏子卧病在床的时候吧。"（等晏子病倒了）二人在养马的园子的高台上观看翟王子羡驾车，婴子很高兴，因而为翟王子羡请求说："请您多多增加他的俸禄吧！"景公答应了。晏子病好之后去见景公，景公说："翟王之子羡驾车，我很喜欢，让他表演给您看看可以吗？"晏子说："驾御车马的事，不是我的职分。"景公说："我喜欢他驾车，想给他万钟的俸禄，足够了吗？"晏子说："从前卫国的东野善于驾车，您喜欢，而婴子不喜欢，您也说不喜欢，就不去观看。现在翟王子羡驾车，您不喜欢，婴子喜欢，您也说喜欢；（婴子）替他求情，您就答应，这是您被妇人挟制了。况且您不热衷

# 1.9 [9] DUKE JING LOVED HIS CONCUBINE AND INDULGED HER DESIRES. YANZI REMONSTRATED.

Xian, the Prince of Di,[1] who was serving Duke Jing as a minister, drove a chariot pulled by twice the usual number of horses.[2] The Duke saw the chariot and was displeased. When the Duke's favorite concubine, Yingzi, expressed her desire to see the chariot, he said: "As long as Yanzi lies ill in bed." Then they took seats on a terrace inside the park and viewed the chariot from there. Yingzi was pleased and she therefore asked the Duke: "Give the Prince a generous emolument!" The Duke agreed.

When Yanzi rose from his sick bed, he went for an audience with the Duke. The Duke said: "I was very pleased with the chariot of Xian, prince of Di.  Shall I ask him to display it for you?"

Yanzi said: "The business of driving a chariot does not pertain to my duties."

The Duke said: "I considered it praiseworthy and took pleasure in it[3] and so I would like to grant him an emolument of ten-thousand *zhong* of grain. Is this enough?"

Yanzi answered: "Formerly, you were pleased with the chariot of Dongye, an officer from Wei, but Yingzi was displeased. For this reason,[4] my Lord, you said that you were displeased with it too, and therefore did not look at it any longer. Just recently you were displeased with the chariot of Xian, Prince of Di, but Yingzi was pleased with it. For this reason, you too are now pleased with it, and you have approved her request. This means that a woman is making the rules. Moreover, you do not enjoy ruling people but you enjoy ruling horses. You do not grant generous emoluments to the

---

1  Di 翟 is identical with *Di* 狄 – i.e., the Di people in the North.

2  I.e., 16 horses, as indicated later in this item.

3  一 → 美 (*JS*, 34/5).

4  曰 → 因 (*YZCQ-ICS*, 4, n. 4).

## 【原文】

而乐治马，不厚禄贤人，而厚禄御夫。昔者先君桓公之地狭于今，修法治，广政教，以霸诸侯。今君一诸侯无能亲也，岁凶年饥，道途死者相望也。君不此忧耻，而惟图耳目之乐，不修先君之功烈，而惟饰驾御之伎，则公不顾民而忘国甚矣。且《诗》曰：'载骖载驷，君子所（诫）〔届〕。'夫驾八，固非制也，今又重此，其为非制也，不滋甚乎？且君苟美乐之，国必众为之，田猎则不便，道行致远则不可，然而用马数倍，此非御下之道也。淫于耳目，不当民务，此圣王之所禁也。

## 【今译】

于处理百姓的事，而热衷于观看车马，不厚待贤良的人，却厚待驾车的车夫。从前先代国君桓公当政时，（齐国的）疆域比现在小，（但桓公）修订法治，推广政教，从而称霸诸侯。现在您没能让一个诸侯亲附齐国。每年都有天灾，每年都有饥民，道路上饿死的人四处可见。您不为此感到担忧和羞耻，反而只追求娱乐消遣，不效法先代君王的功业，只追求装饰车驾的技艺，您也太不顾百姓的死活和国家的兴衰了。况且《诗经》上说：'用三匹或者四匹马驾车，君子来临。'用八匹马驾车，本来就不符合古代的制度规定，现在又加倍如此，这种不守古制的做法，不就更严重了吗？况且您如果以重驾为美而乐于这样做，那么国内必然有很多人效仿，这样既不便于打猎，也不便

worthy, you grant it to a charioteer. In the days of our former ruler, Duke Huan's domain[1] was smaller than it is today. He instituted a system of laws and extended political order and moral cultivation, thereby becoming the overlord of all the regional princes. But now you, my Lord, have failed to cultivate a close relationship with even a single regional prince; it is a year of natural catastrophes and famine, and the roads are covered with corpses staring at each other. Yet you, my Lord, are not worried, nor do you feel shame about this, but you only seek titillation of the eye and ear. You do not promote our former ruler's outstanding accomplishments, but rather are preoccupied only with the skill of charioteering. Hence, you have not paid attention to the people, and you have exceeded in neglecting the interests of the state. As it says in the *Odes*:

> Driving teams of three, teams of four,
>
> The princes are coming.[2]

Driving a chariot of eight horses certainly violates this rule; now, is not doubling this number of horses an even greater violation of that rule? Furthermore, if you, my Lord, really consider this beautiful and enjoy it, then certainly there will be numerous others in the state who will do the same. Hunting will therefore be difficult, and it will be impossible to come from afar via the roads. Under such circumstances, the number of horses needed for your service will be multiplied several times. This is certainly

---

1  Duke Huan (桓公) reigned in Qi between 685 and 643 BCE. He was the first among the regional princes of the Chunqiu period who became a *Ba* 霸 – "Overlord," "Hegemon," or "Lord Protector." For a detailed analysis of *Ba* 霸, see Taeko A. Brooks, "Evolution of the Ba 霸 'Hegemon' Theory;" *Warring States Papers*, 1 (2010): 220-26; John Knoblock, Xunzi: *A Translation and Study of the Complete Works*. Stanford: Stanford University Press, (1990): vol. 2, 140-146; John S. Major, *et al.*, trs. *The Huainanzi: A Guide to the Theory and Practice of Government in Early Han China*. Translations from the Asian Classics. New York: Columbia University Press (2010): 869-870.

2  *Shijing*, 222/109/24.

【原文】

君苟美乐之，诸侯必或效我，君无厚德善政以被诸侯，而易之以僻，此非所以子民、彰名、致远、亲邻国之道也。且贤良废灭，孤寡不振，而听嬖妾以禄御夫以蓄怨，与民为雠之道也。《诗》曰：'哲夫成城，哲妇倾城。'今君不思成城之求，而惟倾城之务，国之亡日至矣。君其图之！"公曰："善。"遂不复观，乃罢归翟王子羡，而疏嬖人婴子。

大中华文库

40

【今译】

于远行，然而使用的马匹却是以前的几倍，这不是统御臣民的方法。只追求声色消遣，不关注国家和百姓的事务，这是贤明的国君所禁止的。您如果喜欢这样做，诸侯中也一定有人效仿，您没有深厚的德行和良好的政策来惠泽诸侯，却代之以违背礼法的邪僻之行，这不是用来爱护百姓、彰显名声、招延远人、亲善邻国的方法。况且贤良之人停置不用，孤寡之人愈加困苦，却听信姬妾之言厚禄车夫来积蓄怨恨，这是和人民结仇的做法。《诗经》上说：'有智谋的男人可以安邦定国，聪慧的女人可以使国家倾覆。'现在您不去考虑兴国安邦，却只做取悦姬妾败坏国家的事，国家灭亡的日子就要到了。请您认真考虑啊！"景公说："好。"于是不再观赏驾车，并遣退了翟王子羡，疏远了爱妾婴子。

the wrong way to hold the reins of power. The sage-kings prohibited indulging in excessive sensual pleasure and not addressing the affairs of the people. If you, my Lord, indeed consider the chariot beautiful and enjoy it, then certainly some among the regional princes will follow our example. My Lord, trying to benefit the regional princes while lacking substantial virtues and good government yourself, and then substituting such virtues for depraved actions is not the way to tend to people as if they were your children, nor the way to earn yourself a glowing reputation, nor the way to make people come from afar to your country, nor the way to promote close ties with the neighboring states. Moreover, the worthy and the good have been abandoned and have perished, widows and orphans have not been supported, yet on advice of your favorite concubine you give a charioteer a generous emolument; so that resentment accumulates. This is the way to make the people your enemies. As it says in the *Odes*:

A clever man rears a city wall;

A clever woman brings it down.[1]

Now you, my Lord, do not apply yourself to promoting[2] the construction of the city wall, but rather are preoccupied only with its destruction. The day of the downfall of your state is at hand. My Lord, give it your careful consideration!"

The Duke said: "Well argued." Thereupon, he did not look at the chariot again. He dismissed Xian, Prince of Di, sending him back home, and distanced himself from his favorite concubine, Yingzi.

41

---

1 *Shijing*, 264/140/31.

2 免 → 勉 (*JS*, 37/21).

大中华文库

# 1.10 [10] 景公敕五子之傅而失言晏子谏

齐景公给五个儿子的师傅下敕命而言语有失，晏子进谏

## 【原文】

景公有男子五人，所使（传）〔傅〕之者，皆有车百乘者也，晏子为一焉。公召其傅曰："勉之！将以而所傅为子。"及晏子，晏子辞曰："君命其臣，据其肩以尽其力，臣敢不勉乎！今有之家，此一国之权臣也，人人以君命命之曰：'将以而所傅为子。'此离树别党，倾国之道也，婴不敢受命，愿君图之！"

## 【今译】

齐景公有五个儿子，被任命教导他们的老师，都是有车百乘的大臣，晏子是其中之一。景公分别召见这些老师说："您要努力把公子教导成才呀！那样我就把您教导的公子立为世子。"轮到晏子的时候，晏子辞谢说："国君任命臣下，让他肩负重任拼尽全力，我怎么敢不尽力而为呢！如今辅佐公子们的大夫，都是有权有势的臣子，（倘若）人人都以国君的命令自命说：'将来要把您教导的公子立为世子。'这是分立不同党派，导致国家灭亡的做法，我不敢接受任命，希望您考虑！"

# 1.10 [10] DUKE JING GAVE ORDERS TO THE TEACHERS OF HIS FIVE SONS AND ERRED IN HIS WORDS. YANZI REMONSTRATED.

Duke Jing had five sons. Those who were commissioned to be their tutors had one hundred chariots each. Yanzi was one of them. The Duke summoned the tutors and said to each: "Do your best, and I will choose the son that you tutor to become my successor."

When Yanzi's turn came, he declined and said: "A ruler gives orders to his ministers to do their utmost, carrying the burden on their shoulders; so how could I, a minister, not presume to do my best? But now, the families that have one hundred chariots[1] are the families of the powerful ministers of the state. If each one of them undertakes your command, my Lord, that says, 'Do your best,[2] and I will choose the son that you tutor to become my successor,' this would result in discord among the heirs and partisan division, leading the way to the overthrow of the state. I do not presume to obey your order and hope that you, my Lord, will give it your careful consideration."

---

1 今有之家 → 今有车百乘之家 (*JS*, 38/4).

2 These two characters — 勉之 ("do your best") — are not present in the original quotation of the command but rather serve as clarification.

# 1.11 [11] 景公欲废嫡子阳生而立荼晏子谏

齐景公打算废掉嫡子阳生而立荼，晏子进谏

## 【原文】

淳于人纳女于景公，生孺子荼，景公爱之。诸臣谋欲废公子阳生而立荼，公以告晏子。晏子曰："不可。夫以贱匹贵，国之害也；置（大）〔子〕立少，乱之本也。夫阳生（而长）〔长而〕国人戴之，君其勿易！夫服位有等，故贱不陵贵；立子有礼，故孽不乱宗。愿君教荼以礼而勿陷于邪，导之以义而勿湛于利。长少行其道，宗孽得其伦。夫

## 【今译】

淳于国送了一个美女给齐景公，生下孺子荼，景公很宠爱他。大臣们谋划打算废掉公子阳生，立荼为世子，景公把这件事告诉了晏子。晏子说："不行。用低贱匹敌高贵，是国家的大害；废太子而立少子，是动乱的本源。阳生年长，百姓们拥戴他，您还是不要更换吧！服饰职位有等级之别，所以地位低的不能欺凌地位高的；册立世子有礼法规定，所以庶子不能扰乱嫡长。希望您用礼法来教导荼，不要让他陷入邪恶；用大义开导他，不要让他沉迷于私利。年长的和年少的各自遵行自己的道义，嫡子和庶子都摆正自己的位置。阳生怎么敢不让荼饱食粱肉美味，欣赏金石之声，怎么敢让他有所忧虑？废掉长子册立少子，不可以用来教育臣民，尊崇庶子轻视嫡子，并不能对您喜爱的（荼）有利。年长年少没有等差，嫡子庶子没有区别，这是祸乱的根源。请您认真考虑！古时候的贤明君主，不是不知道繁复音乐（的

# 1.11 [11] DUKE JING WANTED TO DEPOSE HIS SON, YANG SHENG, AND INSTALL TU AS HIS SUCCESSOR. YANZI REMONSTRATED.[1]

A man from the state of Qunyu[2] gave his daughter as a concubine to Duke Jing and she gave birth to a son[3] named Tu. The Duke loved him and the ministers plotted to depose the crown prince Yang Sheng in favor of Tu. The Duke informed Yanzi about it.

Yanzi said: "It would not be proper. Taking the noble as equal to the lowly is harmful to the state. Setting aside the elder son and installing the younger as a successor is the root of disorder. Yang Sheng is the elder, and the people of the state support him. You, my Lord, should not change this. Clothes and positions have their proper ranks, and therefore the lower do not supersede the higher. There are rites pertaining to the appointment of a son as a successor; therefore, the son of a concubine should not disrupt the family line. I wish that you, my Lord, would teach Tu the rites, so as not to let him fall into perversity, guide him with righteousness and prevent him from sinking into self-interest. When the elder and the younger sons each follow his own proper way, then the wife's son and the concubine's son receive their proper standing. How would Yang Sheng presume not to let Tu appease his hunger with the taste of millet and meat, and delight to the sound of bell and stone, when such conduct would lead to such worries? You cannot instruct those below you by deposing the elder and appointing the younger; you cannot benefit those you love by honoring the concubine's son and degrading the wife's son. If no difference in rank exists between the elder and the younger, and no difference exists between the son of the formal wife and the son of the concubine, then this is the root of fostering

*45*

---

1  Item – 1.11 [11] ↔ *Chunqiu Gongyangzhuan* 春秋公羊传, 12.6.8/153/22.

2  A minor state in the Chunqiu period located in present-day Shandong.

3  Omit *ru* 孺 (*JS*, 40/4).

**【原文】**

阳生敢毋使荼餍（粱）〔粱〕肉之味，玩金石之声，而有患乎？废长立少，不可以教下；尊孽卑宗，不可以利所爱。长少无等，宗孽无别，是设贼树奸之本也。君其图之！古之明君，非不知繁乐也，以为乐淫则哀；非不知立爱也，以〔为〕义失则忧。是故制乐以节，立子以道。若夫恃谗谀以事君者，不足以责信。今君用谗人之谋，听乱夫之言也，废长立少；臣恐后人之有因君之过以资其邪，废少而立长以成其利者。君其图之！"公不听。景公没，田氏杀君荼，立阳生；杀阳生，立简公；杀简公而（耻）〔取〕齐国。

**【今译】**

美妙），（但他们）认为过分沉迷音乐就会哀思；不是不知道册立自己宠爱的人，（但他们）认为丧失礼义就会产生忧患。所以制定音乐要有节制，册立世子要遵礼法。至于那些凭借谗言和阿谀来侍奉国君的人，根本不值得信任。现在您采纳谗谀之人的计谋，听信奸乱之人的言语，废长立少；我怕以后有人因为您的过失而滋生了邪念，通过废少立长来成全自己的利益。请您认真考虑！"景公不听。景公死后，大夫田氏杀掉国君荼，拥立阳生；又杀掉阳生，拥立简公；之后又杀掉简公取代了（姜氏）齐国。

46

the wicked and sowing the seeds of evil. You, my Lord, should give this your careful consideration. It is not that the enlightened rulers of antiquity did not know various pleasures; but rather, they were of the opinion that excessive pleasures result in misery. It is not that they did not know how to install their cherished ones as their successors, but rather, they thought that the loss of righteousness results in troubles. For these reasons, they tempered enjoyment with proper measure and installed sons as successors in accordance with the Way. If people serve you, my Lord, with slanders and flattery, then they are not qualified to be charged with responsibility and trust. But now you, my Lord, make use of the advice of slanderers and you pay heed to the words of those who create disorder, deposing the elder and appointing the younger. I fear that in the future, there will be people who will use your mistakes, my Lord, to support their own perversities. They will depose your younger son and reappoint your elder in order to attain profit for themselves. My Lord, you should give this your careful consideration."

The Duke, however, paid him no heed. After Duke Jing's death, the Tian[1] clan killed Lord Tu and reinstalled Yang Sheng. They then killed Yang Sheng and installed Duke Jian as his successor. They then killed Duke Jian and seized control of the state of Qi.

*47*

---

1 *YZCQ*'s "Tian lineage" (田氏) is identical with the *Zuozhuan*'s "Chen lineage" (陈氏). For a discussion of the interchangeability of these two lineages' names, see Legge, V, 840. See also Item 4.17 [97].

# 1.12 [12] 景公病久不愈欲诛祝史以谢晏子谏

齐景公生病经久不愈打算诛杀祝史来向上帝谢罪，晏子进谏

## 【原文】

景公疥且疟，期年不已。召会谴、梁丘据、晏子而问焉，曰："寡人之病病矣，使史固与祝佗巡山川宗庙，牺牲珪璧，莫不备具，（数其）〔其数〕常多〔于〕先君桓公，桓公一则寡人再。病不已，滋甚，予欲杀二子者以说于上帝，其可乎？"会谴、梁丘据曰："可。"晏子不对。公曰："晏子何如？"晏子曰："君以为祝有益乎？"公曰："然。"晏子免冠曰："若以为有益，则诅亦有损也。君疏辅而远拂，忠臣拥塞，谏

## 【今译】

齐景公生了疥疮又患有疟疾，一年多了还没痊愈。他召见会谴、梁丘据和晏子，问道："我的病越来越严重了，我派史固和祝佗巡行山川宗庙，所用的牺牲和珪璧等祭品，没有一样不齐备的，而且数量还常常多于先君桓公，桓公用一份我就用两份。可是我的病不仅没好，反而更严重了，我想杀了这两个人以取悦上帝，你们觉得可以吗？"会谴和梁丘据都说："可以。"晏子却不回话。景公说："晏子您认为如何？"晏子说："您觉得向神灵祷告对您有好处吗？"景公说："当然。"晏子（摘下帽子）说："如果祷告有益，那么诅咒也就有损害了。您疏

## 1.12 [12] DUKE JING WAS ILL FOR A LONG TIME AND DID NOT RECOVER. HE WANTED TO EXECUTE HIS INVOCATOR AND HIS SCRIBE IN EXPIATION. YANZI REMONSTRATED.[1]

Duke Jing suffered from scabies and intermittent fever for a whole year. He summoned Hui Qian,[2] Liangqiu Ju, and Yanzi and asked them about it: "Since my illness became severe I charged Gu, the Scribe, and Tuo, the Invocator, to tour the temples of the famous mountains and rivers, and the ancestral temple. All the requisite sacrificial animals and the *gui* jade baton and *bi* jade disk for offering were prepared; nothing was missing. I've always provided a greater number of offerings than did my predecessor, Duke Huan—where Duke Huan offered one, I doubled it—and still my illness did not cease but rather worsened greatly. I wish to execute these two in order to make the God on High[3] happy. Would that be advisable?"

Hui Qian and Liangqiu Ju said: "It would." Yanzi did not answer.

1 Item 1.12 [12] ↔ Item 7.7 [177]; *Zuozhuan,* B10.20.6/374/27. For a discussion of the *Zuozhuan's* version, see Yuri Pines, *Foundations of Confucian Thought: Intellectual Life in the Chunqiu Period, 722-453 B.C.E.* Honolulu: University of Hawaii Press (2002): 81-82.

2 An unidentified figure. In the alternative versions, mentioned above, a Qi official by the name of Yi Kuan 裔款 assumes the role of Hui Qian 会谴.

3 Shang-di 上帝 — the God on High or the Supreme Lord of Heaven, one of the most prominent gods of ancient China. For a short analysis and useful references to relevant discussions concerning Shang-di 上帝, see Andrew Plaks, tr. *Ta Hsüeh and Chung Yung (The Highest Order of Cultivation and On the Practice of the Mean).* Harmondsworth, Penguin (2003): 111-112; Mu-chou Poo, *In Search of Personal Welfare: A View of Ancient Chinese Religion.* SUNY Series in Chinese Philosophy and Culture. Albany (1998): 29-30; Julia Jing, *Mysticism and Kingship in China: The Heart of Chinese Wisdom.* Cambridge studies in religious traditions. Cambridge University press, Cambridge: (1997): passim. For a similar case in which a human sacrifice is offered to God on High, see *Mozi*, 4.3/29/10.

**【原文】**

言不出。臣闻之，近臣默，远臣暗，众口铄金。今自聊、（捪）〔摄〕以东，姑、尤以西者，此其人民众矣，百姓之咎怨诽谤，诅君于上帝者多矣。一国诅，两人祝，虽善祝者不能胜也。且夫祝直言情，则谤吾君也；隐匿过，则欺上帝也。上帝神，则不可欺；上帝不神，祝亦无益。愿君察之也。不然，刑无罪，夏、商所以灭也。"公曰："善解予惑，加冠！"命会谴毋治齐国之政，梁丘据毋治宾客之事，兼属之乎

**【今译】**

远辅政的大臣，忠臣有话闷在心里，不敢向您进谏。我听说，近臣沉默，远臣嗫声，众人的言论可以销熔金属。现在从聊、摄以东，姑、尤以西的地方，人口众多，百姓们怨恨指责，向上帝诅咒您的人太多了。一个国家的人诅咒，两个人祷告，即使是精于祷告的人也不能取胜。而且向神灵祷告时诉说实情，就是说您的坏话；隐瞒您的过失，又是欺骗上帝。上帝若是神灵，那就不能欺骗；上帝如果不是神灵，那么即使祷告也没什么帮助。希望您能明察此事。否则，诛杀无罪之人，这就是夏桀、商纣灭亡的原因啊。"景公说："您真是善于解除我的困惑，请您戴上帽子吧！"景公下令命会谴不得再参与齐国的政事，梁丘据不得再管理招待宾客的事，他们的事务都交给晏子处理。晏子推辞，没有得到景公的允许，只好服从命令，接管了会谴和梁丘据的

The Duke said: "Yanzi, what do you think about it?"[1]

Yanzi said:[2] "Do you believe that prayers are beneficial, my Lord?"

The Duke said: "Yes."

Yanzi continued: "If you think that prayers are beneficial, then surely curses are also harmful. If you neglect your aides and distance your reliable advisors, my Lord, then loyal ministers will be blocked and remonstrations will not be issued. I have heard: 'When ministers close at hand are rendered speechless and ministers removed from the throne become mute, the mouths of the masses seethe like molten metal.'[3] Now, numerous people live in the area ranging from the East of Liao and She to the West of Gu and You.[4] Many among the common people reproach, vilify, and curse you to the God on High, my Lord. When an entire state curses you and only two pray for you, then even if they are very good invocators, they will not be able to prevail. Moreover, if the invocators' prayers truthfully describe the state of things, then they will vilify you. If they conceal your mistakes, then they will cheat the God on High, my Lord. If the God on High has numinous force, then he cannot be deceived; but if he has not, then prayer to him is of no benefit. I wish that you would thoroughly consider the matter, my Lord. Otherwise you will execute the innocent, and this was the reason for the downfall of Xia and Shang."

The Duke said: "You are good at dispelling my confusion. I hereby

---

1   The way in which the Duke addresses Yanzi in this item (晏子何如) is somewhat anachronistic. Throughout the entire text, the Duke always addresses Yanzi with the current designation of the period 夫子 or 子 – "Master."

2   *JS*, 45/9, suggests inserting 免冠 into the sentence 晏子曰 so that the newly-formed sentence would read: 晏子免冠曰 ("Yanzi took off his cap saying :").

3   Cf. *Zhanguoce* 战国策, 273/144/17; *Xinxu*, 3.7/16/24.

4   Liao 聊 and She 摄 were two cities on the Western border of Qi. Gu 姑 and You 尤 were two rivers on the Eastern boarder of Qi. Yanzi therefore refers to the population that lives throughout the width of the state of Qi.

**【原文】**

晏子。晏子辞，不得命，受相退，把政，改月而君病悛。公曰："昔吾先君桓公以管子为有功，邑狐与谷，以共宗庙之鲜，赐其忠臣，则是多忠臣者。子今忠臣也，寡人请赐子州款。"辞曰："管子有一美，婴不如也；有一恶，婴不忍为也，其宗庙之养鲜也。"终辞而不受。

**【今译】**

事务，晏子把持政务之后，过了一个月景公的病就好了。景公说："从前我的先祖桓公认为管仲是有功之臣，就把狐、谷两地封给他，以便供应宗庙祭祀所需要的血食，赏赐忠臣，就是嘉奖忠臣。您现在就是忠臣，请允许我把州款这个地方赏赐给您吧。"晏子推辞说："管仲有一美德，我不如他；有一恶行，我也不忍去做，那就是用血食祭祀宗庙。"最终还是推辞没有接受封邑。

endow you with additional official titles.[1] Then he ordered Hui Qian to stop dealing with the business of government in Qi, and Liangqiu Ju to stop dealing with the affairs of guests of the state, and charged Yanzi with both tasks.

Yanzi wanted to refuse, but he was not granted permission to do so. He accepted the position of prime minister and left the audience. He took charge of the affairs of the government, and during the next month the Duke recovered from his illness.

The Duke said: "In the past, my predecessor, Duke Huan, thought that Guanzi[2] was meritorious[3] and enfeoffed him with the cities of Hu and Gu so that he could offer freshly killed game in his ancestors' temple. To grant gifts to a loyal minister is to praise a loyal minister. Now you are my loyal minister; I would like to grant you Zhou-kuan as a fiefdom."

Yanzi declined, saying: "Guanzi had one excellent trait that renders me inferior and one vice that I cannot bear to commit. The latter is his sacrificing of game at the temple of the ancestors."[4]

He ultimately declined and did not accept the enfeoffment.

53

---

1   加冠 may also mean: "You may put on your cap." For this reason the *JS*, 45/9 suggested the alternative wording, which appears in note 68, above: 晏子免冠曰 ("Yanzi took off his cap saying :").

2   Guanzi 管子 is Guan Zhong 管仲, the famous seventh-century Minister of the State of Qi who meritoriously served Duke Huan. The philosophical work entitled *Guanzi* 管子 is traditionally ascribed to him.

3   力 → 功 *JS*, 47/22.

4   *JS*, 47-48/26, regards these seven characters (其宗庙之养鲜也) problematic. It first quotes Sun Xingyan 孙星衍, who stated that the offering of game in the ancestral temple was forbidden and considered a vice by the rites. Wu Zeyu 吴则虞, the compiler of the *JS*, then concludes that all attempts to explain the sentence as an integral part of the *YZCQ* text are doubtful and the seven characters are probably a latter interpolation.

## 1.13 [13] 景公怒封人（祝之）〔之祝〕不逊晏子谏

齐景公因典守封疆的官员祝词出言不逊而发怒，晏子进谏

**【原文】**

景公游于麦丘，问其封人曰：“年几何矣？”对曰：“鄙人之年八十五矣。”公曰：“寿哉！子其祝我。”封人曰：“使君之年长于胡，宜国家。”公曰：“善哉！子其复之。”〔封人〕曰：“使君之嗣寿皆若鄙

**【今译】**

齐景公到麦丘巡游，问当地典守封疆的官员说：“您多大年纪啦？”官员回答说：“我八十五岁了。”景公说：“您高寿啊！请您为我祈祷吧。”官员说：“祝愿您比胡公还要长寿，以利于国家。”景公说：“说得好！请您再次为我祈祷吧。”官员说：“祝愿您的子孙都能像我一样长寿。”景公说：“说得好！请您接着说。”官员说：“祝愿您不要得罪百姓。”景公说：“只有百姓得罪国君才对，哪有国君得罪百姓的呢？”晏子进谏说：“国君您说错了！那些国君疏远的人犯了罪过，亲近的大臣会惩治他们；地位低的人犯了错误，地位高的人会惩治他们；国君

## 1.13 [13] DUKE JING WAS ANGRY OVER AN INSOLENT BLESSING OF A VILLAGER. YANZI REMONSTRATED. [1]

Duke Jing went on a pleasure excursion to Maiqiu[2] and asked a villager:[3] "How old are you?"

He answered: "Your humble servant is eighty-five."

The Duke said: "O, what a long life. Would you bless me?"

The villager said: "May your years increase to a long life that will be good for the state, my Lord."[4]

The Duke said: "Excellent.  Would you bless me again?"

The villager said: "May your descendants, my Lord, all live as many years as your humble servant lived."

The Duke said: "Excellent. Would you bless me again?"

The villager said: "May you, my Lord, not offend the people."

The Duke said: "I grant you that there have been cases where people of low status have offended the ruler. But how can there be a case of a ruler offending the people?"

Yanzi remonstrated: "You are wrong, my Lord. When those who are distant from the ruler commit an offense, they are punished by those who are close to the ruler. When the lowly people commit an offense, the noble punish them. When a ruler offends the people, who will punish him? I

---

1   Item 1.13 [13] ↔ *Hanshi waizhuan*, 10.1/71/; *Xinxu*, 4.18/21/20.

2   Maiqiu 麦丘 is located in present Shandong province in Shanghe district. On the historical maps of China it appears only from the Warring States period (480–221) onwards. It did not exist in the Chunqiu period (722–480). This is the first of several occurrences of the author's artificial topography, which suggests a later provenance for these traditions.

3   封 → 邦 (*JS*, 49/3).

4   *JS*, 49/7, suggests that *hu* 胡 denotes here Duke Hu 胡公, who reigned in Qi between 893–860. In that case, the sentence would translate: "May you, my Lord, live longer than Duke Hu."

**【原文】**

（臣）〔人〕之年。"公曰："善哉！子其复之。"封人曰："使君无得罪于民。"公曰："诚有鄙民得罪于君则可，安有君得罪于民者乎？"晏子谏曰："君过矣！彼疏者有罪，戚者治之；贱者有罪，贵者治之；君得罪于民，谁将治之？敢问：桀、纣，君诛乎？民诛乎？"公曰："寡人固也。"于是赐封人麦丘以为邑。

**【今译】**

得罪了百姓，谁来惩治他呢？请问：夏桀、商纣这样的国君，是被国君诛灭了呢？还是被百姓诛灭了呢？"景公说："是我孤陋寡闻了。"于是把麦丘赐给这位典守封疆的官员作食邑。

presume to ask: Were Jie and Zhou executed by rulers or by the people?"

The Duke said: "I have been obstinate." Thereupon, he granted the city of Maiqiu as a fiefdom to the villager.

# 1.14 [14] 景公欲使楚巫致五帝以明德晏子谏

齐景公打算让楚国巫女招请五帝神灵来表明德行，晏子进谏

## 【原文】

楚巫微（导）〔道〕裔款以见景公，侍坐三日，景公说之。楚巫曰："公，明神（主之）〔之主〕，帝王之君也。公即位〔十〕有七年矣，事未大济者，明神未至也。请致五帝，以明君德。"景公再拜稽首。楚巫曰："请巡国郊以观帝位。"至于牛山而不敢登，曰："五帝之位在于国南，请斋而后登之。"公命百官供斋具于楚巫之所，裔款视事。晏子

## 【今译】

楚国有个叫微的女巫通过裔款来见齐景公，陪伴景公坐谈了三天，景公很欣赏她。楚巫说："您是神灵选定的君主，帝王般的明君。您即位十七年了，功业之所以还没有大的成就，是因为神灵还没有到来。请让我招引五帝之灵，来彰明您的德行。"景公拜了两拜叩头致谢。楚巫又说："请让我到城郊去观测五帝所在的方位。"到了牛山脚下，楚巫不敢上山，说："五帝所在的方位在都城以南，请让我斋戒之后再登山。"景公命令百官准备好斋戒的用具送到楚巫的住所，让裔款负责这件事。晏子听说之后来见景公，说："您让楚巫斋戒祭祀牛山吗？"景公说："是的。招请五帝之灵来彰明我的德行，神灵就会赐福于我，应该会对我有所帮助吧？"晏子说："您说的不对！古时候的圣王，道德

# 1.14 [14] DUKE JING SOUGHT TO HAVE A SHAMAN FROM CHU SUMMON THE FIVE EMPERORS1 IN ORDER TO MAKE HIS VIRTUE SHINE FORTH. YANZI REMONSTRATED.

Through the mediation of Yi Kuan, Wei, a female shaman from Chu,[2] was granted an audience with Duke Jing. For three days she sat in attendance with Duke Jing, who was pleased with her.

The shaman from Chu said: "You, My Duke, are a sovereign with the stature of the bright spirits and a ruler of the caliber of Emperors and Kings.[3] My Lord, seventeen years ago you acceded to your position, but your deeds have not been fully successful because the bright spirits have not descended.[4] I request permission to summon the Five Emperors in order to make your virtue shine forth, my Lord."

The Duke bowed twice, with his forehead touching the ground.

The shaman from Chu continued: "Permit me to make a tour of inspection to the suburbs of the capital in order to identify the place where the Five Emperors are going to reveal themselves."[5]

When the shaman arrived at Mount Niu,[6] she did not dare to ascend

59

---

1  The Five Emperors were the legendary rulers of high antiquity. Different listings of names of these Five Emperors exist. The usual list includes the Yellow Emperor 黄帝, Emperor Zhuan Xu 颛顼 , Emperor Ku 帝喾 and Emperors Yao 尧 and Shun 舜.

2  *Wu* 巫 is a female shaman but in the Chunqiu period, it could also mean a male shaman.

3  I.e., the Five Emperors (see note 78 above) and the Three Kings of antiquity, Yu 禹, Tang 汤 and Wu 武, the founders of the Xia, Shang and Zhou royal dynasties.

4  The *Zuozhuan*, B 3.32.3/65/25, reads 国之将兴, 明神降之 — "When a state is about to prosper, bright spirits descend there to inspect its virtue."

5  The shaman is looking for the proper venue to perform as a medium through which the Five Emperors would reveal themselves.

6  Another example of the author's artificial topography: the present Mount Niu 牛山 (Ox Mountain) is located twenty-five miles south of Linzi 临淄 the historical capital of Qi. It cannot be found on the historical maps of the Chunqiu period (722–480 BCE) but only on the maps of the Warring States period (480–221 BCE) onwards.

## 【原文】

闻而见于公曰："公令楚巫斋牛山乎？"公曰："然。致五帝以明寡人之德，神将降福于寡人，其有所济乎？"晏子曰："君之言过矣。古之王者，德厚足以安世，行广足以容众，诸侯戴之，以为君长；百姓归之，以为父母。是故天地四时和而不失，星辰日月顺而不乱。德厚行广，配天象时，然后为帝王之君，（神明）〔明神〕之主。古者不慢行而繁祭，不轻身而恃巫。今政乱而行僻，而求五帝之明德也？弃贤而用巫，

## 【今译】

高尚足以安定天下，恩泽广布足以包容百姓，诸侯们拥戴他，视其为君主；百姓们归附他，视其为父母。所以一年四季和谐而不失调，日月星辰有序而不混乱。道德高尚、恩泽广布，顺应天意、合乎时令，然后才可以成为帝王般的明君，神灵眷顾的英主。古时候的帝王不放纵行事而频繁地祭祀，不轻视自身而倚靠巫祝。现在政教混乱而且行为不正，能够求来五帝之灵来彰明您的德行吗？抛弃贤良之臣而去重用巫祝，能够求得帝王之业吗？百姓不会随便感激您，福气也不会随便降临到您身上。您的帝王之业，不是很难实现吗？可惜啊！您的地位这么高贵，所说的话却是这么卑微。"景公说："裔款引荐楚巫给我

it, saying: "The site for the Five Emperors to present themselves is south of the capital. I would like to perform a purification ceremony first and then ascend the mountain."

The Duke gave orders to the various officials to prepare the purification utensils at the site indicated by the shaman from Chu. Yi Kuan took charge of the matter.

Yanzi heard of this and went for an audience with the Duke, saying: "Did you order the shaman from Chu to purify herself in order to ascend Mount Niu, My Duke?"

The Duke said: "Yes, she is going to summon the Five Emperors in order to make my virtue shine forth, and then the spirits will shed their blessings upon me. Will that not be helpful?"

Yanzi said: "Your words are wrong. The virtue[1] of the ancient kings was substantial enough to pacify the entire world. Their conduct was broad enough to accommodate the multitude. The regional princes supported them and regarded them as rulers and as superiors; the people gave them their allegiance and regarded them as their own parents. For these reasons, Heaven and Earth and the four seasons were in faultless harmony. Stars, planets, sun, and moon traversed their regular courses without disorder. It was only after their substantial virtue and broad conduct corresponded with the Heaven and accorded with the seasons that they could become rulers of the caliber of Emperors, kings and sovereigns of the stature of the bright spirits. The ancients were not negligent in their conduct, nor did they multiply their sacrifices unduly. They did not belittle themselves by relying on shamans. Now the government is in disorder, conduct is deviant, and you seek the illustrious virtue of the Five Emperors? You discard the worthy, and yet you use a shaman and you want the Five Emperors and the Three Kings to manifest themselves in your presence? The people do not

61

1  得 → 德 (*YZCQ-ICS*, 6, n. 4).

**【原文】**

而求帝王之在身也？夫民不苟德，福不苟降。君之帝王，不亦难乎？惜夫！君位之高，所论之卑也。"公曰："裔款以楚巫命寡人曰：'试尝见而观焉。'寡人见而说之，信其道，行其言。今夫子讥之，请逐楚巫而拘裔款。"晏子曰："楚巫不可出。"公曰："何故？"对曰："楚巫出，诸侯必或受之。今信之以过于内，不知；出以易诸侯于外，不仁。请东楚巫而拘裔款。"公曰："诺。"故曰送楚巫于东，而拘裔款于国也。

**【今译】**

时说：'请您试着见见她、观察她。'我看见她就很欣赏，听信了她的道术，践行她的言论。现在您责问我，请我驱逐楚巫、拘捕裔款。"晏子说："楚巫不能驱逐出齐国。"景公说："为什么？"晏子说："楚巫离开齐国之后，一定会有其他诸侯收留。您因为相信她已经在国内犯下错误，这已经很不明智；再放她离开齐国去危害其他诸侯，这是不仁义。请您放逐楚巫到东海之滨并拘捕裔款。"景公说："好。"因此（景公）就把楚巫放逐到东海之滨，而把裔款拘禁在都城。

acknowledge virtue without good cause; good fortune does not befall upon you without good cause; is it then not difficult, my Lord, to realize your aspirations regarding the Five Emperors and the Three Kings? What a pity! My Lord, your position is noble but your arguments are lowly."

The Duke said: "It was Yi Kuan who directed me, in regard to the Chu shaman, saying: 'Test her and observe the results.' I received the shaman for an audience and was pleased with her. I put faith in her way and followed her words. Now you, my master, have criticized this, and you would have me expel the shaman from Chu and put Yi Kuan into custody."

Yanzi said: "The shaman from Chu should not leave the country."

The Duke said: "Why so?"

Yanzi answered: "If the shaman from Chu is allowed to leave the country, then some regional princes or other is bound to take her in. You, My Duke, trusted her and thereby committed an error within your domain; this is not wise. If you let her leave the country she will, from without, affect the regional princes for the worse; this is inhumane. Please send the shaman from Chu to the East[1] and put Yi Kuan in custody."

The Duke said: "Very well," and then[2] he sent the shaman from Chu to the East and placed Yi Kuan into custody within the capital.

*63*

---

1   Qi was situated in the East; therefore, sending one to the East meant expelling the person almost all the way to the seashore or, in other words, to a place from which there was no exit.

2   Either omit *yue* 曰 or replace it with *qiu* 囚 (*JS*, 54/16).

## 1.15 [15] 景公欲祠灵山河伯以祷雨晏子谏

齐景公打算祭祀灵山河伯来祈祷降雨，晏子进谏

### 【原文】

齐大旱逾时，景公召群臣问曰："天不雨久矣，民且有饥色。吾使人卜（云）〔之〕，崇在高山广水。寡人欲少赋敛以祠灵山，可乎？"群臣莫对。晏子进曰："不可，祠此无益也。夫灵山固以石为身，以草木为发，天久不雨，发将焦，身将热，彼独不欲雨乎？祠之（无）〔何〕

64

### 【今译】

齐国大旱过了农时，齐景公召集群臣问道："上天很久不降雨了，百姓面有饥色。我命人去占卜，说是祸祟（灾祸）在高山大水之间。我想稍微增加一些赋税来祭祀灵山，可以吗？"群臣都默不作声。晏子进谏说："不可以，祭祀灵山没什么帮助。灵山以石头为身体，以草木为头发，上天长时间不下雨，它的头发快要焦枯了，身体快要热坏了，它不是也盼着下雨吗？所以祭祀它没什么帮助。"景公说："不行的话，我打算祭祀河伯，可以吗？"晏子说："不可以。河伯以水为国家，以鱼鳖为百姓，上天长时间不下雨，泉水下降，河流枯竭，它的国家将要衰亡，百姓将要灭绝，它难道不希望下雨吗？祭祀它有什么好处？"

# 1.15 [15] DUKE JING WANTED TO SACRIFICE TO THE NUMINOUS MOUNTAIN<sup>1</sup> AND TO THE LORD OF THE YELLOW RIVER<sup>2</sup> IN ORDER TO PRAY FOR RAIN. YANZI REMONSTRATED.<sup>3</sup>

There was a great drought in Qi for an extended period of time. Duke Jing summoned all his ministers and asked them: "Rain has not fallen from Heaven for a long time, and the people appear to be nearly famished. I had someone divine in the matter and he said that the noxious influence is in the high mountains and the wide waters. I would like to collect a small assessment in order to offer a sacrifice to the Numinous Mountain. Is this permissible?"

Not one of the various ministers answered. Yanzi stepped forward and said: "It would not be proper. There is no advantage in offering this sacrifice. In fact, the Numinous Mountain has stones as its body, and grass and trees as its hair. When rain has not fallen from Heaven for a long time, its hair will be scorched and its body will be seething. How would he alone not wish for rain? What would be the point of offering him a sacrifice?"

Duke Jing said: "If not so, then I wish to sacrifice to the Lord of the Yellow River. Is this permissible?"

Yanzi said: "It would not be proper. There is no advantage in offering it a sacrifice. The Lord of the Yellow River has water as his state and fish and turtles as his people. When rain has not fallen from Heaven for a long time, the level of the springs will recede and all the water will dry up. His

65

---

1  "Numinous Mountain," (灵山), is located twenty miles North-East of Linqu 临朐 district in the present Shandong province.

2  He-bo 河伯 — the God of the Yellow River.

3  Item 1.15 [15] ↔ *Shuoyuan*, 18.11/153/16. For an episode that has the same structure as this item but different protagonists and a different ending, see *Hanshi waizhuan*, 3.8/17/3.

**【原文】**

益。"〔景〕公曰:"不然,吾欲祠河伯,可乎?"晏子曰:"不可。〔夫〕河伯以水为国,以鱼鳖为民,天久不雨,〔水〕泉将下,百川〔将〕竭,国将亡,民将灭矣,彼独不欲雨乎?祠之何益?"景公曰:"今为之奈何?"晏子曰:"君诚避宫殿暴露,与灵山河伯共忧,其幸而雨乎!"于是景公出野(居)暴露,三日,天果大雨,民尽得种时。景公曰:"善哉,晏子之言,可无用乎?其维有德。"

**【今译】**

景公说:"那现在怎么办呢?"晏子说:"如果您能诚心离开宫殿,到野外露宿,和灵山、河伯共同承担忧患,也许就能侥幸下雨!"于是景公离开宫殿露宿于野外,过了三天,果然下了一场大雨,百姓全都得以及时耕种。景公说:"好啊,晏子的话怎能不采纳呢?他是个有德行的人啊。"

country will perish and his people will die. How could he himself not wish for rain? What would be the point of offering the Lord of the Yellow River a sacrifice?"

Duke Jing said: "But what alternatives do I have now?"

Yanzi replied: "My Lord, were you to really leave your palace and expose yourself to the sun, sharing the worries of the Numinous Mountain and the Lord of the Yellow River — isn't it possible that this might be considered a blessing, and rain might fall?"

Thereupon, Duke Jing went out to the open field and exposed himself to the sun. In fact, after three days, Heaven did pour down heavy rain and all the people could sow at the right time.[1] Duke Jing said: "Excellent! How could Yanzi's words not be put to use? He alone has virtue."

---

1  The similarities between the present episode and the story about Honi the Circle Maker from the Babylonian Talmud (BT) tractate *Ta'anit* 19a; 23a is striking. According to the latter story, there was a prolonged drought that the inhabitants of the country were unable to relieve. As a last resort, they turned to Honi. Honi drew a large circle in the ground and placed himself inside it. He called out to God, saying, as a threat, that he would not leave the circle until God would cause rain to fall. Eventually, God obeyed. See also *Mozi*, 4.3/29/10.

## 1.16 [16] 景公贪长有国之乐晏子谏

齐景公贪图长久保有国家的乐趣，晏子进谏

### 【原文】

景公（将）观于淄上，与晏子闲立。公喟然叹曰："呜呼！使国可长保而（傅）〔传〕于子孙，岂不乐哉？"晏子对曰："婴闻明王不徒立，百姓不虚至。今君以政乱国，以行弃民久矣，而（声）欲保之，不亦难乎？婴闻之，能长保国者，能终善者也。诸侯并立，能终善

### 【今译】

齐景公在淄水岸上观赏景色，和晏子站着闲聊。景公长叹一声说："唉！如果能永远保有国家并传给后世子孙，这难道不是一件让人高兴的事吗？"晏子说："我听说贤明的国君不是凭空被拥立的，百姓的归附也不是无缘无故的。现在您的政令祸乱国家，您的行为抛弃百姓已经很久了，却想要要保有国家，这不是很困难吗？我听说能长久保有国家的，是那些能够坚持行善的人。诸侯并立的时候，能够坚持行善的才能成为君长；读书人一起学习的时候，能够坚持行善的才能成为师长。以前您的先祖桓公，当他任用贤良、赞誉有德之人的时候，即

# 1.16 [16] DUKE JING COVETED THE JOY OF POSSESSING THE STATE FOR A LONG TIME. YANZI REMONSTRATED.

Duke Jing was looking at the view from the bank of the Zi River[1] while he was standing idly with Yanzi. The Duke heaved a sigh and said: "Oh, if my state could be protected for a long time and then be passed on to my descendants, would that not be a joy?"

Yanzi answered: "I have heard that the enlightened kings did not ascend the throne without a reason, and the people did not come to them in vain. But now for a long time you, my Lord, have played havoc with the state through your government and by your conduct you have abandoned the people; yet you say[2] you wish to protect the state—is this not difficult? I have heard that he who can protect his state over an extended period is the one who can do good his entire life. Moreover, the regional prince who is able to persist in doing good his entire life becomes the superior among his peers. When officers study together, he who does good his entire life becomes their master. In the past, when our former ruler Duke Huan first employed the worthy and praised the virtuous, even a doomed state might have maintained its existence by relying on him, and an endangered state might have been made safe by looking up to him. For that reason, the people rejoiced at his way of governing, and the entire world highly esteemed his virtue. He traveled to distant places in his campaigns against the violent, and those who labored for him did not complain. He had sway over the entire country between the seas and induced the regional princes

69

---

1   River Zi 淄 appears on the historical maps of the Chunqiu period. It is located in present Shandong province near Mount Tai 泰山.

2   Retain 声 (*SBCK*, I, 19a3).

**【原文】**

者为长；列士并学，能终善者为师。昔先君桓公，其方任贤而赞德之时，亡国恃以存，危国仰以安，是以民乐其政，而世高其德。行远征暴，劳者不疾，驱海内使朝天子，而诸侯不怨。当是时，盛君之行不能进焉。

**【今译】**

将灭亡的国家依靠他而得以保全，动荡不安的国家仰仗他得以安定，因此百姓乐于遵行他的政令，天下人也推崇他的德行。跟着他长途跋涉去征讨凶暴，虽然辛苦但没人抱怨，号召天下诸侯朝见天子，而诸侯们也没有怨言。那时候，他的德行声望已经到达顶峰了。等到他最终德行衰败，懈怠于道德修养而纵情享乐，自己沉迷女色而听信奸邪小人的计谋，所以百姓苦于他的统治，天下也谴责他的行为，因此他死在胡宫不能发丧，尸体生了蛆虫也无人收敛。那时候，夏桀、商纣的下场也不会比他更惨了。《诗经》中说：'事情都有好的开头，却很

to pay court to the Son of Heaven,[1] and they did not complain. During that period, our mighty ruler's virtuous conduct could not have been surpassed. In his final days, however, when the state declined, he neglected virtue and was overcome by pleasure. He became besotted with women, and he plotted matters with Shu Diao.[2] For this reason, the people suffered from his government and the entire world condemned his conduct. Therefore, when he died in the Hu Palace, the burial ceremonies were not performed; even when worms crept out of his corpse, he was still not put into a coffin.[3] During that period, even Jie and Zhou could not have come to a worse end. As it says in the *Odes*:

All are good at first;

But only few succeed to the last.[4]

He who is not able to do good through the end of his days is one who cannot successfully fulfill his role as ruler. But now you, my Lord, rule the people as if they were an enemy; at the sight of someone good, you seem as if you want to escape the heat; you play havoc with the government and you endanger the worthy; you are bound to act contrary to the multitude; you make unrestrained demands on the people and cruelly punish your subjects. I am afraid you will personally suffer the consequences. I am already old

71

1  *Tianzi* 天子 — "Son of Heaven," from the Zhou dynasty on, a standard designation to the supreme sovereign of China. The Son of Heaven was traditionally regarded the mediator between Heaven and the human world and the capital from which he ruled was an *axis mundi,* a pivot about which the four quarters revolved. For a detailed discussion of the title of "The Son of Heaven," see "Son of Heaven: Shamanic Kingship," and "Son of Heaven: Kingship as Cosmic Paradigm" in Julia Jing, ibid, 1-66.

2  Shu Diao 竖刁 was a member of an infamous group of officials who served Duke Huan in his final days. He emasculated himself in order to take charge of the Duke's harem. See *Guanzi*, 11.2/86/1.

3  See *Guanzi*, 10.1/76/1.

4  *Shijing*, 255/131/14.

**【原文】**

及其卒而衰，怠于德而并于乐，身溺于妇侍而谋因〔于〕竖刁，是以民苦其政，而世非其行，故身死于胡宫而不举，虫出而不收。当是时也，桀、纣之卒不能恶焉。《诗》曰：'靡不有初，鲜克有终。'不能终善者，不遂其君。今君临民若寇雠，见善若避热，乱政而危贤，必逆于众，肆欲于民，而（诛虐）〔虐诛〕于下，恐及于身。婴之年老，不能待（于）君使矣，行不能革，则持节以没世耳。"

**【今译】**

少能够善始善终'。不能始终坚持行善，就不能持续保有国君之位。现在您对待百姓如同对待仇敌，见到善行就像躲避火灾，扰乱国家的政务，危害贤良的臣子，一定要违背民意，肆意地掠夺百姓，诛杀臣民，这样恐怕灾祸迟早要落在您自己身上。我已经老了，不能供国君您差遣了，如果您不能改变这些行为，那么我只能保持节操直至死亡了。"

and cannot be expected to continue in my service to you, my Lord, much longer. Unless you are able to radically change your conduct, I will maintain my moral integrity until I die — that and nothing more."

# 1.17 [17] 景公登牛山悲去国而死晏子谏

齐景公登上牛山感慨弃国而死的悲伤，晏子进谏

## 【原文】

景公游于牛山，北临其国城而流涕曰："若何滂滂去此而死乎？"艾孔、梁丘据皆从而泣。晏子独笑于旁，公刷涕而顾晏子曰："寡人今日游悲，孔与据皆从寡人而涕泣，子之独笑，何也？"晏子对曰："使贤者常守之，则太公、桓公将常守之矣；使勇者常守之，则庄公、灵公将常守之矣。数君者将守之，则吾君安得此位而立焉？以其迭处之，迭去之，至于君也，而独为之流涕，是不仁也。不仁之君见一，（谄）〔诌〕谀之臣见二，此臣之所以独窃笑也。"

【今译】

齐景公到牛山巡游，向北望着齐国的都城流着眼泪说："怎么舍得离开这泱泱大国而死去呢？"艾孔、梁丘据都跟着哭了起来。晏子在一旁独自发笑，景公擦干眼泪看着晏子说："我今天（在这里）巡游感觉很悲伤，艾孔和梁丘据都跟着我流眼泪，只有您独自发笑，这是为什么？"晏子说："假如贤明的国君能够常守国君之位，那么太公、桓公就将常守国君之位了。假如英勇的国君能够常守国君之位，那么庄公、灵公就将常守君位了。假如这几位国君能够常守君位，那么您怎么能得到这个位置呢？正因为国君之位不断（有人）得到，不断（有人）失去，这才轮到您啊，您却偏偏为此而流泪，这是不够仁义啊。我见到了一个不仁义的国君和两个谄媚阿谀的臣子，这就是我暗自发笑的原因。"

# 1.17 [17] DUKE JING CLIMBED MOUNT NIU[1] AND WAS SAD ABOUT DEPARTING FROM THE STATE AND DYING. YANZI REMONSTRATED.[2]

Duke Jing went on a pleasure excursion to Mount Niu. He looked northward toward his capital city and burst into copious tears, said: "What can be said of the flood of those who departed this city and died?"

Ai Kong[3] and Liangqiu Ju both followed him and wept. Only Yanzi stood at the Duke's side and laughed.

The Duke wiped his tears away, looked at Yanzi and said: "My touring today was marked by sadness. Kong and Ju both followed me and wept; you alone laughed. Why?"

Yanzi replied: "If the worthy could retain the state forever, then Duke Tai[4] and Duke Huan would have retained it forever. If the courageous could retain the state forever, then Duke Zhuang and Duke Ling would have retained it forever. Yet if these few rulers had retained it, how could you, my Lord, have assumed this position and ascended to the throne? Because of a string of men who occupied the throne and lost it, the position has come down to you, my Lord, and you are the only one who burst into tears over this. This shows a lack of feeling — I saw one ruler who was lack of feeling and two flattering ministers. This is why I alone ventured to laugh."

---

1   Mount Niu 牛山, is situated approximately 21 *li* 里 south of Linzi 临淄, the capital of Qi.

2   Item 1.17 [17] ↔ *Liezi* 列子, 6/37/17.

3   An unidentified figure.

4   Duke Tai's name was Lü Shang 吕尚. He was an advisor of King Wu 武王 (1169–1116 BCE), who enfeoffed him with the state of Qi. He then reigned there between 1122–1078 BCE.

## 1.18 [18] 景公游公阜一日有三过言晏子谏

齐景公到公阜巡游一天之内有三次错误的言辞，晏子进谏

### 【原文】

景公出游于公阜，北面望睹齐国，曰："呜呼！使古而无死，何如？"晏子曰："昔者上帝以人之殁为善，仁者息焉，不仁者伏焉。若使古而无死，丁公、太公将有齐国，桓、襄、文、武将皆相之，君将戴笠衣褐，执铫耨以蹲行畎亩之中，孰暇患死？"公忿然作色，不说。无几何，而梁丘据（御）〔乘〕六马而来，公曰："是谁也？"晏子曰："据也。"公曰："何〔以〕（如）〔知〕〔之〕？"曰："大暑而疾驰，甚

### 【今译】

齐景公到公阜巡游，向北望见了齐国的都城，说："唉！假如自古以来的人都不死去，会是怎样的情景呢？"晏子说："古时候上天的神明认为人的死是一件好事，它让仁义的人得到安息，让不仁义的人消失不见。假如从古至今都没有死人，那么丁公、太公将会一直是齐国的国君，桓公、襄公、文公、武公都将会做齐相，您只能戴着斗笠，穿着粗布衣服，扛着锄头蹲在田亩之间劳作，哪里还会有闲工夫担心死去！"景公气得变了脸色，很不高兴。过了一会儿，梁丘据驾着六匹马的车驾赶来，景公说："那是谁呀？"晏子说："梁丘据。"景公

# 1.18 [18] DUKE JING MADE THREE MISTAKES IN HIS SPEECH DURING A SINGLE DAY WHEN HE WENT ON A PLEASURE EXCURSION TO GONGFU.[1] YANZI REMONSTRATED.[2]

Duke Jing went on a pleasure excursion to Gong-fu. Looking northwards, he saw the capital of Qi and said: "Oh, if from ancient times no death had existed — what would that be like?"

Yanzi said: "In the past, the God on High considered it good that people passed away — the humane find respite in death and the inhumane submit to it. If no death had existed since ancient times, then Duke Ding and Duke Tai would still have the state of Qi, and Dukes Huan, Xiang, Wen and Wu would be its Chief Ministers.[3] You, my Lord, would wear a bamboo hat and a coarse woolen garment and would be going through the fields stooped over hoe and weeder. How much time would you have then to worry about dying?"[4]

The Duke flushed with anger; he was displeased.

After a little while, Liangqiu Ju arrived in a chariot with six horses.

The Duke said: "Who is this?"

Yanzi replied: "It is Ju."

The Duke said: "How do you know that?"

Yanzi replied: "If one drives horses at full gallop during the Greater

77

---

1   An unidentified place.

2   Item 1.18 [18] ↔ Item 7.2 [172]; Item 7.4 [174]; *Zuozhuan*, B10.20.8/375/20; B10.26.11/393/15.

3   Duke Ding succeeded Duke Tai (r. 1122–1078 BCE) and reigned in Qi between 1077–1051 BCE. Duke Xiang reigned in Qi between 697–686 BCE. He preceded Duke Huan (r. 685–643 BCE). Duke Wen reigned in Qi between 815–804 BCE. Duke Wu reigned in Qi between 850–825.

4   Cf. *Hanshi waizhuan*, 10.11/75/4-5.

## 【原文】

者马死，薄者马伤，非据孰敢为之？”公曰：“据与我和者夫！”晏子曰：“此所谓同也。所谓和者，君甘则臣酸，君淡则臣咸。今据也（甘君）〔君甘〕亦甘，所谓同也，安得为和！”公忿然作色，不说。无几何，日暮，公西面望，睹彗星，召伯常骞，使禳去之。晏子曰：“不可！

78

## 【今译】

说：“您是怎么知道的？”晏子说：“这么热的天却让马匹飞奔，严重的话会把马累死，轻的话也会累伤，除了梁丘据谁敢这样做？”景公说：“梁丘据是和我配合得很和谐的人！”晏子说：“这是苟同（不是和谐）。所谓和谐，是指国君说甜而臣子说酸，国君说淡而臣子说咸。现在您说甜梁丘据也说甜，这是苟同，不是和谐！”景公生气的变了脸色，很不高兴。过了一会儿，太阳快要落山了，景公向西眺望看见了彗星，于是召见伯常骞，让他祈禳消灾去除彗星。晏子说：“不可以！这是上

Heat,[1] then at worst, the horses will die and, at best, they would be injured. Who then other than Ju would presume to act so?"

The Duke said: "Ju and I are in harmony with one another — is it not so?"

Yanzi answered: "This is what is called conformity.[2] As for what is called harmony, if the ruler is the sweet then the minister is the sour, and if the ruler is the bland, then the minister is the salt. Now as for Ju: because you, my Lord, are the sweet, he too is sweet. This is called 'conformity'; how can this be called 'harmony'?"

The Duke flushed with anger; he was displeased.

After a little while the sun set. When the Duke looked westward, he saw a broom-comet.[3] He summoned Bochang Qian[4] to exorcise it by sacrifice.[5]

Yanzi said: "You can't do that! This is a Heavenly instruction. Vapor surrounding the sun and moon, untimely wind and rain, and the appearance

---

1  大暑 – "Greater Heat," one of the twenty-four solar periods that lasts throughout the hottest heat waves of the summer.

2  The *Analects*, 13.23/36/21, portrays the man of noble character (*junzi* 君子) as the seeker of "harmony" and the rejecter of "conformity." The petty (*xiaoren* 小人) represents the opposite attitude – he seeks "conformity" and rejects "harmony."

3  *Huixing* 彗星, 'broom stars,' or 'brush stars,' the technical term for comets that 'sweep' through the sky. See David W. Pankenier, *et al. Archaeoastronomy in East Asia: Historical Observational Records of Comets and Meteor Showers from China, Japan, and Korea*. Amherst, N.Y.: Cambria (2008): 6; Joseph Needham, *et al.*, eds. *Science and Civilisation in China*, vol. 3, *Mathematics and the Sciences of the Heavens and the Earth*. Cambridge: Cambridge University Press (1959): 431.

4  Bochang Qian (伯常騫 or 柏常騫), who also appears in items 4.30 [110], 6.4 [144] and 8.9 [209], is an unidentified figure. *Zhuangzi* 庄子, 25/75/21, mentions a Grand Scribe (大史) by the same name. Among other duties, grand scribes used to advise the kings during the Zhou dynasty concerning sacrifices connected with astronomical conditions.

5  Cf. Item 7.6 [176]; *Zuozhuan,* B10.26.10/393/8; *Lunheng* 论衡, 17/55/8; *Guanzi,* 14.2/105/11.

**【原文】**

此天教也。日月之气，风雨不时，彗星之出，天为民之乱见之，故诏之妖祥，以戒不敬。今君若设文而受谏，谒圣贤人，虽不去彗，星将自亡。今君嗜酒而并于乐，政不饰而宽于小人，近逸好优，恶文而疏圣贤人，何暇在彗，茀又将见矣！"公忿然作色，不说。及晏子卒，公出（背）〔屏〕而泣曰："呜呼！昔者从夫子而游公阜，夫子一日而三责我，今谁责寡人哉？"

**【今译】**

天的告诫。时令节气的变化，有时会出现风不调雨不顺，彗星有时出现，都是上天因为百姓的动乱不安而显现的，用以诏示凶兆或者吉祥，警示不敬天命的人。现在您如果能因为天象的警示而虚心纳谏，拜谒圣明贤良的人，即使不去祈禳除去彗星，它也会自行消失。现在您酷爱喝酒，纵情享乐，不理国政而厚待小人，亲近奸佞的臣子，喜欢歌舞的优伶，厌恶天象而疏远圣明贤德的人，岂止彗星出现，茀星也会出现了！"景公生气的变了脸色，很不高兴。等到晏子去世的时候，景公走出屏风哭泣着说："唉！以前和晏子一起到公阜巡游，他一天之内三次责备我，现在谁能来责备我呢！"

of broom-comets are signs provided by Heaven on account of disorder among people. Therefore, Heaven decrees evil omens only in order to admonish those who lack respect. If you, my Lord draw support from this sign and accept remonstrations; if you pay courtesy visits to the sages and the worthy, then even if you do not try to exorcise the broom-comet, it will vanish by itself. But, you, my Lord, are fond of wine and overcome by pleasure. Your government is not in proper order [1] and you tolerate the petty. You associate with slanderers and you are fond of entertainers. You despise men of culture and you keep your distance from sages and worthy men. How can you have time to worry about the broom-comet when a blurred-comet[2] is about to appear?"

The Duke flushed with anger; he was displeased.

After Yanzi died, the Duke stepped out from behind his folding screen and said, crying:[3] "Oh, formerly when I followed the master and traveled around Gongfu, he found fault with me three times in a single day. Who will find fault with me now?"[4]

---

1   饰 → 饬 (*JS*, 71/28).

2   The *Guliangzhuan*, 榖梁传, 6.14.6/66/30, identifies between *bo* 孛 and *fu* 茀 — "bushy," "bristle," "fuzzy" or "blurred" comets – which are ominous signs for governments that are on the verge of ruin. A "broom comet" (彗星), may become "fuzzy" (茀; 孛) and change its appearance. See David W. Pankenier, ibid. See also *Hanshu* 汉书 , vol. 11, p. 3467; *JS,* 71/30.

3   立 → 泣 (*JS*, 71/33)

4   The gloomy end to this episode bears a striking resemblance to an anecdote found in BT *Baba Mezi'a* 84a, concerning the 3rd c. CE rabbinic antagonists Resh Lakish and R.Yohanan. In their last clash, R.Yohanan drove Resh Lakish into a state of mental anguish and, consequently, to his death. Only then did R.Yohanan realize that the world devoid of Resh Lakish's harsh criticism was empty and therefore not worth living in.

# 1.19 [19] 景公游寒涂不恤死胔晏子谏

齐景公巡游在寒冷的路上不抚恤没有掩埋的死尸，晏子进谏

【原文】

景公出游于寒涂，睹死胔，默然不问。晏子谏曰："昔吾先君桓公出游，睹饥者与之食，睹疾者与之财，使令不劳力，藉敛不费民。先君将游，百姓皆说曰：'君当幸游吾乡乎！'今君游于寒涂，据四十里之氓，殚财不足以奉敛，尽力不能周役，民氓饥寒冻馁，死胔相望，

【今译】

齐景公外出巡游，走在寒冷的路上，看见没有掩埋的尸体默不作声，不闻不问。晏子进谏说："以前我们的国君桓公出去巡游的时候，看见饥饿的人就给他们食物，看见生病的人就给他们财物，派遣差役不过度征用民力，征收赋税不虚费民财。因此桓公将要出游的时候，百姓们都说：'请国君到我们乡里巡游！'现在您巡游在寒冷的路上，住在周围四十里的百姓，倾尽家财也不够上缴赋税，竭尽人力也不能完成劳役，百姓们又冷又饿，死后没有掩埋的尸体一个挨着一个，但您却不闻不问，这已经丧失了为君之道。财富穷尽，人力枯竭，臣民不可能亲近国君；骄恣放纵，奢侈腐化，国君也不可能亲近臣民。国君和臣民离心离德，君臣之间不亲近，这是夏、商、周三代之所以衰

# 1.19 [19] DUKE JING WENT ON A PLEASURE EXCURSION TO HANTU[1] AND DID NOT TAKE PITY ON THE DECOMPOSING CORPSES. YANZI REMONSTRATED.[2]

When Duke Jing went on a pleasure excursion to Hantu and saw decomposing corpses, he kept silent and asked no questions.

Yanzi remonstrated, saying: "In the past, when our former ruler, Duke Huan, went on a pleasure excursion and saw hungry people, he gave them food, and when he saw sick people, he gave them money. His orders did not bring people to exhaustion and the taxes he collected did not burden the people too much. When our former ruler planned to go on a tour, all the people said joyfully: 'Could we be fortunate enough that our Lord will pass through our district?' But now you, my Lord, went on a pleasure excursion to Hantu, whose population consists of forty villages. They have given up their property and are unable to pay your taxes; they have exhausted their strength, and they cannot carry out your compulsory labor. The people are hungry and cold, frozen and famished; the decomposing corpses lie with eyes staring at each other — but you, my Lord, asked no questions and thereby failed in the way of a ruler. When means are reduced and strength is totally exhausted, then inferiors will have no way to feel close to their superiors. When superiors are arrogant and live extravagantly, they have no way to feel close to their inferiors. Mutual alienation between superiors and inferiors and lack of intimacy between a ruler and subjects were the reason for the decline of the Three Dynasties.[3] If you, my Lord, now continue to act like this, then I fear that the threat against your ruling lineage will give rise to the fortune of a different clan."

83

---

1   An unidentified place.

2   Item 1.19 [19] ↔ Item 7.8 [178].

3   The ancient Three Dynasties: Xia 夏 2205–1766 BCE, Shang 商 or Yin 殷 1766–1123 BCE, and Zhou 周 1122–249 BCE.

**【原文】**

而君不问，失君道矣。财屈力竭，下无以亲上；骄泰奢侈，上无以亲下。上下交离，君臣无亲，此三代之所以衰也。今君行之，婴惧公族之危，以为异姓之福也。"公曰："然，为上而忘下，厚藉敛而忘民，吾罪大矣。"于是敛死骴，发粟于民，据四十里之氓不服政其年，公三月不出游。

**【今译】**

亡的原因。现在您这样做，我担心公室的危亡，会变成异姓之族的福分啊。"景公说："好，身为国君只顾自己享乐而忘记了百姓的疾苦，加重赋税横征暴敛而不顾人民的死活，我的罪过太大了。"于是下令收敛死尸，发放粮食给百姓，并命令周围四十里之内的百姓一年之内不必服劳役，景公三个月没出去巡游。

The Duke said: "Yes. Because I, as a superior, thought little of inferiors, I imposed heavy taxes and forgot the people. My offence is great indeed."

Thereupon, he had the decomposing corpses collected and grain distributed among the people. The local population of the forty villages did not have to undergo compulsory labor for a whole year, and the Duke did not make any pleasure excursions for three months.

LIBRARY OF CHINESE CLASSICS

# 1.20 [20] 景公衣狐白裘不知天寒晏子谏

齐景公身穿名贵狐裘不知道天气寒冷，晏子进谏

## 【原文】

景公之时，雨雪三日而不霁。公被狐白之裘，坐〔于〕堂侧（陛）〔阶〕。晏子入见，立有间，公曰："怪哉！雨雪三日而天不寒。"晏子对曰："天不寒乎？"公笑。晏子曰："婴闻古之贤君饱而知人之饥，温而知人之寒，逸而知人之劳。今君不知也。"公曰："善。寡人闻命矣。"乃令出裘发粟〔以〕与饥寒〔者〕。（今）〔令〕所睹于涂者，无问其乡；所睹于里者，无问其家；循国计数，无言其名。士既事者兼月，疾者兼岁。孔子闻之曰："晏子能明其所欲，景公能行其所善也。"

## 【今译】

齐景公当政的时候，有一次大雪连续下了三天还不放晴。景公披着白色狐狸皮衣，坐在屋旁的台阶上。晏子进来拜见，站了一会儿，景公说："奇怪！大雪下了三天天气却不冷。"晏子说："天气真的不冷吗？"景公笑了笑。晏子说："我听说古时候的圣君贤主自己吃饱了而能想到别人的饥饿，自己穿暖了而能想到别人的寒冷，自己舒适了而能想到别人的辛劳。现在您想不到啊。"景公说："好！我听从您的教诲了。"于是命人发放皮衣和粮食给又冷又饿的百姓。又下令只要在路上看到饥寒交迫的百姓，不必问他是哪乡的人；在里中见到饥寒的百姓，不必问他是哪家的人；在国内调查统计饥寒的百姓，不必记录姓名。已有职业的发给两个月的粮食，因病不能劳作的发给两年的粮食。孔子听说这件事后说："晏子能够讲清楚他想做的事，景公能够实行他认为应该做的好事。"

## 1.20 [20] DUKE JING WORE A ROBE OF WHITE FOX FUR AND DID NOT KNOW THAT THE WEATHER WAS COLD. YANZI REMONSTRATED.

At the time of Duke Jing, there was a snowfall that lasted three days without stopping. The Duke, wrapped in a robe of white fox fur, sat on stairs at the side of the hall. Yanzi entered for an audience and stood still for a moment.

The Duke said: "How strange that it snows for three days and yet the weather is not cold."

Yanzi said: "Is the weather really not cold?"

The Duke laughed.

Yanzi said: "I have heard that the worthy rulers in ancient times ate to their fill, yet they knew that the people were hungry; they were warm, yet they knew that the people were cold; they were at ease, yet they knew that the people were toiling. But now you, my Lord, know nothing about that."

The Duke said: "Well said. I have now heard your instructions."

Thereupon, he ordered that fur robes be handed out and grain distributed among the hungry and the cold. He issued an order to refrain from questioning people seen on the road about their home districts and from questioning people seen in the villages about their families. He calculated the census throughout the state without asking for the names of people. Officers already in service received allotted sums for two months, and the sick among them received sums for two years.

When Confucius heard of this, he said: "Yanzi is capable of clarifying his wishes. Duke Jing is capable of carrying out what he considers good."

87

大中华文库

# 1.21 [21] 景公异荧惑守虚而不去晏子谏

齐景公惊异火星出现在虚宿而不离去，晏子进谏

## 【原文】

景公之时，荧惑守于虚，期年不去。公异之，召晏子而问曰："吾闻之，人行善者天赏之，行不善者天殃之。荧惑，天罚也，今留虚，其孰当之？"晏子曰："齐当之。"公不说，曰："天下大国十二，皆曰诸侯，齐独何以当〔之〕？"晏子曰："虚，齐野也。且天之下殃，固于富（疆）〔强〕。为善不用，出政不行；贤人使远，谗人反昌；百姓

## 【今译】

齐景公当政的时候，有一年火星出现在虚宿旁，过了一年也不离去。景公觉得古怪，就召见晏子问道："我听说，人做了善事上天就会给予奖赏，做了坏事上天就会降下灾祸。火星的出现，是上天降下惩罚的征兆，现在它留在虚宿，是谁要承受天降的灾祸呢？"晏子说："是齐国。"景公很不高兴，说："天下的大国足有十二个，都是一方诸侯，为什么偏偏是齐国承受天罚呢？"晏子说："虚宿所在的星位对应着齐国的分野。而且上天降下的灾祸，本来就是针对为政不善而又自恃富强的国家的。为善政的不被重用，制定的政策得不到贯彻实施；贤良的人被疏远，奸佞小人反而仕途通达；百姓怨声载道，自己还在祈祷吉祥；整天忙着文过饰非，走上绝路又有什么值得悲伤？所以众星宿次序混乱，变星发出光芒，火星回溯逆行，灾星就在一旁，有贤良的

# 1.21 [21] DUKE JING REGARDED IT ODD THAT MARS WAS STATIONED IN XU[1] AND DID NOT LEAVE THAT POSITION.[2] YANZI REMONSTRATED.

At the time of Duke Jing, Mars was stationed in Xu and for a whole year did not leave that position.

The Duke thought it odd, so he summoned Yanzi and asked: "I have heard that Heaven rewards people who do good and inflicts disaster upon those who do the opposite. Mars represents Heaven's punishment, and since Mars is now stationed in Xu, who should be held accountable for that?"

Yanzi said: "Qi should be held accountable for it."

The Duke was displeased and said: "There are twelve major states in the world, all of which are called the principalities. Why should Qi, in particular, be held accountable for it?"

Yanzi said: "Xu represents the celestial sphere of Qi.

Then,

Heaven sends down disasters,

---

1   *Xu* 虚 "Emptiness," the celestial sphere of Qi, is one of the twenty-eight lunar mansions or constellations in ancient Chinese astronomy.

2   The astronomical phenomenon described in Item 1.21 [21] is known as a "stationary point." It refers to a major planet that suddenly appears to be motionless in the night sky. This is caused by the relative motions between Earth and the planet. When a planet, such as Mars, is at near opposition, it is overtaken by Earth and then, because of its closeness to Earth, moves with higher relative velocity. Its normal direct motion seems to be temporarily retrograde, as if it were undergoing a loop or zigzag in the sky. The turning point between these motions, when the planet appears motionless against the star field, is known as a "stationary point." In ancient China, stationary points were called *ju* 居, *liu* 留, *su* 宿 or *shou* 守. See Needham, ibid, p. 399. The *Lüshi chunqiu*, 6.4/31/20, *the Xinxu*, 4.27/23/25, and the *Lunheng*, 17/54/13, records a similar episode in which Mars was stationed in the lunar mansion of Xin 心 – "Heart," the celestial sphere of Song, and thereby aroused the same negative reaction from the Duke of Song.

**【原文】**

疾怨，自为祈祥；录录（疆）〔强〕食，进死何伤？是以列舍无次，变星有芒，荧惑回逆，孽星在旁，有贤不用，安得不亡？"公曰："可去乎？"对曰："可致者可去，不可致者不可去。"公曰："寡人为之若何？"对曰："盍去冤聚之狱，使反田矣；散百官之财，施之民矣；振孤寡而敬老人矣。夫若是者，百恶可去，何独是孽乎？"公曰："善。"行之三月，而荧惑迁。

**【今译】**

人而不知重用，国家怎能不亡！"景公说："有什么办法能让它离去吗？"晏子说："凡是能招致的就能让它离去，不能招致的就不能让他离去。"景公说："那我应该怎么办呢？"晏子回答道："您为什么不平反冤假错案，让蒙冤的百姓回家种田；将百官聚敛的财物散发施舍给百姓；赈济孤寡而尊敬老人呢。如果能这样做，一切邪恶的事物都可以去除，何况这颗灾星呢？"景公说："好。"（于是按晏子说的）实行了三个月，火星就离去了。

they are certainly intended for the rich and powerful states.

Where people who do good are not employed,

and adopted administrative policies are not enforced.

The worthy are kept distant,

and slanderers, wrongly, prosper.

People hate, complain,

and pray for their own fortune.

The mediocre vigorously conceal[1] their faults,

they could go to their death and no one would care.

Therefore, the various constellations are not in sequence,

and variable stars emit flashes of light.[2]

Mars turns against its orbit,

and the inauspicious star[3] still lingers.

The worthy are not employed;

how could destruction be avoided?"

The Duke said: "Can Mars be made to leave?"

Yanzi responded: "Something that can be made to come can also be made to go; something that cannot be made to come cannot be made to go either."

The Duke said: "How should I deal with it?"

Yanzi answered: "You have to do away with the numerous unjust convictions and let the people return to their fields. Distribute the property of all officials and give it as charity to the people. Give money to the orphans and widows, and respect the old. Once you have accomplished this, all evils will be banished – let alone this inauspicious star, is this not so?"

The Duke said: "Well argued." He practiced this for three months and then Mars moved away.

---

1　食→ 饰 (JS, 67/12).

2　"Variable stars" (变星) are stars whose brightness as seen from Earth fluctuate.

3　Mars, the inauspicious planet.

# 1.22 [22] 景公将伐宋梦二丈夫立而怒晏子谏

齐景公将要讨伐宋国梦见两个人怒视自己，晏子进谏

## 【原文】

景公举兵将伐宋，师过泰山，公梦见二丈夫立而怒，其怒甚盛。公恐，觉，辟门召占瞢者，至。公曰："今夕吾梦二丈夫立而怒，不知其所言，其怒甚盛，吾犹识其状，识其声。"占瞢者曰："师过泰山而不用事，故泰山之神怒也。请趣召祝史祠乎泰山则可。"公曰："诺。"明日，晏子朝见，公告之如占瞢之言也。公曰："占梦者之言曰：'师过

## 【今译】

齐景公起兵要去讨伐宋国，大军经过泰山时，景公梦见两个人怒气冲冲地站在自己面前，气得很厉害。景公恐惧，从梦中惊醒，连忙关上门并悄悄召来解梦的人。景公说："今夜我梦见两个人怒气冲冲地站在我面前，不知道他们说了什么，只看见他们气得很厉害，我还能记得他们的模样，辨识出他们的声音。"解梦的人说："大军路过泰山而不举行祭祀，所以泰山的山神发怒了。请您赶快召见祝史祭祀泰山神就可以了。"景公说："好。"第二天，晏子来朝见景公，景公把解梦人的话告诉了晏子。景公说："解梦人讲：'大军路过泰山而不祭祀，所以泰山的山神发怒了。'现在我已经派人命令祝史去祭祀泰山山神了。"晏子低头想了一会儿，回答道："解梦的人不清楚，这两个人不是泰山的山神，

# 1.22 [22] DUKE JING WAS ABOUT TO ATTACK SONG. HE DREAMED OF TWO MEN STANDING BEFORE HIM WITH A FURIOUS DEMEANOR. YANZI REMONSTRATED.[1]

Duke Jing raised an army and was about to attack Song. When the army was passing Mount Tai,[2] he saw in his dream two men standing before him with a furious expression on their faces — their fury was extreme. The Duke woke up in fear, closed the door and summoned the diviner of dreams, who arrived.

The Duke said: "Tonight I dreamed that two men stood before me with a furious expression on their faces, and I did not understand their words. Their fury was extreme. I still retain their looks and voices in my mind."

The diviner of dreams said: "Your army passed Mount Tai without offering a sacrifice and therefore the spirits of the mountain are angry. Please immediately summon the Invocator and the Scribe to offer a sacrifice at Mount Tai and then everything will be in order."

The Duke said: "Very well."

The next day, Yanzi was received for an audience and the Duke told him what the diviner of dreams had said.

The Duke said: "These were the words of the diviner of dreams: 'Your army was passing along Mount Tai and you did not offer a sacrifice. Therefore, the spirits of Mount Tai are angry.' Now I am sending someone to summon the Invocator and the Scribe to offer a sacrifice to the spirits."

Yanzi bowed his head for a short while and replied: "This was beyond the understanding of the diviner of dreams. These were not the spirits of

---

1   Cf. *Lunheng*, 63/278/4.

2   One of the Five Sacred Peaks (五岳): Mount Tai 泰山 in Shandong (East); Mount Heng 衡山 in Hunan (South); Mount Hua 华山 in Shaanxi (West); Mount Heng 恒山 in Shanxi (North) and Mount Song 嵩山 in Henan (Center).

**【原文】**

泰山而不用事，故泰山之神怒也。'今使人召祝史祠之。"晏子俯有间，对曰："占梦者不识也，此非泰山之神，是宋之先，汤与伊尹也。"公疑，以为泰山神。晏子曰："公疑之，则婴请言汤、伊尹之状也。汤质皙而长，颜以髯，兑上〔而〕丰下，倨身而扬声。"公曰："然，是已。""伊尹黑而短，蓬而髯，丰上〔而〕兑下，偻身而下声。"公曰："然，

**【今译】**

而是宋国的先祖，商汤和伊尹。"景公不相信，认为他们就是泰山神。晏子说："您如果不信的话，那就让我描述一下商汤和伊尹的相貌吧。商汤皮肤白皙，身材高大，脸长有胡须，脸型上窄下丰，身体微曲但说话声音洪亮。"景公说："是的，就是这样。"晏子又说："伊尹皮肤黑个子矮，头发蓬松而有胡须，额头宽阔下巴略尖，身形佝偻，说话声音低沉。"景公说："是的，就是这样。那现在应该怎么办呢？"

Mount Tai, but rather Tang and Yi Yin, the ancestors of Song."[1]

The Duke remained skeptical and continued to think of them as the spirits of Mount Tai.

Yanzi said: "If you are skeptical, my Lord, then please let me describe the figures of Tang and Yi Yin. Tang had pale skin and was tall. He had whiskers on his chin.[2] The upper part of his face was narrow[3] and the lower part broad. He had upright posture and a high voice."

The Duke said: "Right, that's the one."

"Yi Yin had dark skin and was short. He had disheveled hair and whiskers. The upper part of his face was broad and the lower part narrow.[4] He had a humpback and a low voice."

The Duke said: "Right, that's the one. What should be done now?"

Yanzi said: "Tang, Taijia, Wuding and Zuyi[5] were mighty rulers of the world and it is improper that they have no successors. Yet, their successors have only Song, and you are going to attack it, my Lord. Therefore, Tang and Yi Yin are furious. Please disband your troops and make peace with Song."

Duke Jing did not heed the advice and ultimately attacked Song.

95

Yanzi said: "To attack a guiltless state and to infuriate the illustrious spirits thereby; to refuse to change a pattern of action and thereby to continue to accumulate distresses; to advance armies and in so doing suffer great misfortune[6]—all these are beyond my understanding. If in fact your army does advance, this will certainly have a disastrous effect

---

1   Tang is Emperor Cheng Tang. Yi Yin was his worthy minister.

2   颐 → 颜 (*YZCQ-ICS* , 9, n. 2).

3   锐 → 兑 ( *YZCQ-ICS*, 9, n.3).

4   锐 → 兑 ( *YZCQ-ICS*, 10, n.1).

5   Tang 汤 (1766–1754 BCE), Taijia 太甲 (1753–1721 BCE), Wuding 武丁 (1324– 1266 BCE) and Zuyi 祖乙 (1525 1507 BCE) were famous Emperors of the Shang (Yin) dynasty and the ancient forefathers of the State of Song.

6   过 → 祸, (*JS*, 83/16).

**【原文】**

是已。今若何？"晏子曰："夫汤、太甲、武丁、祖乙，天下之盛君也，不宜无后。今惟宋耳，而公伐之，故汤、伊尹怒，请散师以平宋。"景公不用，终伐宋。晏子（公）曰："伐无罪之国，以怒明神，不易行以续蓄，进师以近过，非婴所知也。师若果进，军必有殃。"军进再舍，鼓毁将殪。公乃辞乎晏子，散师，不果伐宋。

**【今译】**

晏子说："商汤、太甲、武丁、祖乙，这都是天下有名的圣君，不应该绝后。现在（他们的后裔）只有宋国，您却派兵去征讨，所以商汤和伊尹发怒，请您撤回军队和宋国和好吧。"景公不听晏子的谏言，终于伐宋。晏子说："讨伐无罪的国家来激怒神明，不改变伐宋的行为来和宋国重修旧好，进军就是靠近灾祸，这样的做法不是我所能理解的。军队如果坚持前进，那么士兵们一定会遭殃。"军队前进了六十里，果然鼓毁将亡。景公于是向晏子表示谢意，撤回军队，不再继续伐宋。

on the troops."

The troops advanced to a distance that required camping for two nights;[1] then, the drums were smashed and the general died.

Thereupon, the Duke apologized to Yanzi, disbanded the troops, and ultimately did not attack Song.

---

1  *She* 舍: a distance of about thirty *li* 里, or the area of a night encampment for the troops.

## 1.23 [23] 景公从畋十八日不返国晏子谏

齐景公田猎十八天不返回国都，晏子进谏

### 【原文】

景公畋于署梁，十有八日而不返。晏子自国往见公。比至，衣冠不正，不革衣冠，望游而驰。公望见晏子，下而急带曰："夫子何为遽〔乎〕？国家〔得〕无有故乎？"晏子对曰："不亦急也！虽然，婴愿有复也。国人皆以君为安野而不安国，好兽而恶民，毋乃不可乎？"

### 【今译】

齐景公到署梁去打猎，过了十八天还没有返回国都。晏子从国都出发去见景公。到了署梁，衣冠不整也不收拾，望见游猎的队伍就快马驰去。景公远远看见了晏子，赶忙下马束紧腰带，问道："您怎么这样急匆匆的？难道国内出了什么变故吗？"晏子回答说："也没什么急事！即便这样，我还是想向您汇报。国内的人都觉得您喜欢在野外打猎而不喜欢在都城内处理政务，喜欢野兽而厌恶百姓，这恐怕不可以吧？"景公说："为什么呢？是因为我审理夫妻间的诉讼案件不公正吗？那泰士子牛在呀；是因为社稷与宗庙没有得到祭祀吗？那泰祝子游在呀；是因为诸侯宾客的事宜没人处理吗？那行人子羽在呀；是因

# 1.23 [23] DUKE JING WENT ON A HUNTING EXPEDI-TION AND DID NOT RETURN TO THE CAPITAL FOR EIGHTEEN DAYS. YANZI REMONSTRATED.[1]

Duke Jing went hunting in Shuliang[2] and he did not return for eighteen days. Yanzi left the capital and went to see the Duke. When he arrived, his gown and headgear were awry, but he did not tie the belts of the gown and the headgear. When Yanzi saw the tassels of the Duke's flags, he galloped towards him.

When the Duke saw Yanzi, he stepped down from his chariot, hurriedly fastened his belt and said: "Master, why you are in such a rush, is there any alarming situation in the state?"

Yanzi answered: "Surely there is no emergency; and yet, I would like to report to you as follows: All the people in the state think that you, my Lord, are more at ease in the open fields than in the capital, and that you are fond of wild animals and dislike the people. Is that not unacceptable?"

The Duke said: "What can you possibly mean? Is it because of the unjust settlement of legal suits between man and wife? For that matter, Ziniu, the Judge, is there.[3] Is it because sacrifices are not offered at the altars of soils and grain, and in the ancestral temples? For that matter, Ziyou, the Senior Invocator, is there.[4] Is it because there is no one who receives the regional princes and official guests? For that matter, Ziyu, the Master of Protocol, is there. Is it because the fields are not cultivated and because the granaries are not full? For that matter, the Manager of Agriculture is

99

---

1   Item 1.23 [23] ↔ *Hanshi waizhuan*, 10.20/77/4.

2   An unidentified place.

3   泰 士 → 大 士 (*JS*, 856/15). The *Hanshi waizhuan*, ibid, reads 大理 Chamberlain for Law Enforcement.

4   泰祝 → 大祝 (*JS*, 86/16).

## 【原文】

公曰："何哉？（吾）为夫妇狱讼之不正乎？则泰士子牛存矣；为社稷宗庙之不享乎？则泰祝子游存矣；为诸侯宾客莫之应乎？则行人子羽存矣；为田野之不辟，仓库之不实〔乎〕？则申田存焉；为国家之有余不足聘乎？则吾子存矣。寡人之有五子，犹心之有四支，心有四支，故心得佚焉。今寡人有五子，故寡人得佚焉，岂不可哉！"晏子对曰："婴闻之，与君言异。若乃心之有四支，而心得佚焉，〔则〕可（得）；令四支无心，十有八日，不亦久乎！"公于是罢畋而归。

## 【今译】

为土地没有开辟，仓库中的粮食不够充足吗？那申田在呀；是因为国家的盈余不足无人管理吗？那有您在呀。我有你们五位辅佐，就像人的心有四肢一样，心有了四肢，所以心能得到安逸。现在我有你们五位大臣辅佐，所以我也能得到安逸，怎么不可以呢！"晏子回答道："我所听说的和您说的不一样。如果说心有四肢而能得到安逸，这是可以的；但让四肢失去心十八天，不是太久了吗！"景公于是停止田猎回到国都。

there.[1]  Is it because of surpluses or shortages in the state?[2]  For that matter, you, my Master, are there. My having these five masters is like the heart having four limbs. It is because the heart has four limbs that it can relax. It is because I now have five masters that I can relax. How could this not be proper?"

Yanzi said: "What I have heard is different from what you have said. As for the heart having four limbs and relaxing — this may well be. But if the four limbs are made to exist without the heart for eighteen days, is this not too long?"

Thereupon, the Duke stopped the hunt and came home.

---

1  申田 is not a name of a person. 申 is interchangeable with 司, and therefore 申田 is identical to 司田 ("Manager of Agriculture"), an official title in the state of Qi. See *Guanzi*, 8.2/66/7.

2  Erase 聘 (*JS*, 87/20).

# 1.24 [24] 景公欲诛骇鸟野人晏子谏

齐景公打算杀掉把鸟吓飞的乡下人，晏子进谏

## 【原文】

景公射鸟，野人骇之。公怒，令吏诛之。晏子曰："野人不知也。臣闻赏无功谓之乱，罪不知谓之虐。两者，先王之禁也，以飞鸟犯先王之禁，不可！今君不明先王之制，而无仁义之心，是以从欲而轻诛。夫鸟兽，固人之（養）〔养〕也，野人骇之，不亦宜乎？"公曰："善！自今已（后）〔来〕，弛鸟兽之禁，无以苛民也。"

## 【今译】

景公射鸟时，一个乡下人把鸟吓飞了。景公很生气，命令官吏把这个人杀掉。晏子说："这个乡下人不知道您在射鸟啊。我听说赏赐无功的人叫作乱，惩罚不知情的人叫作虐。这两件事都是先王禁止去做的，因为射鸟的缘故去触犯先王的禁令，这是不可以的！现在您既不明悉先王的制度，也没有慈爱百姓的仁义之心，所以放纵欲望轻易杀人。鸟兽本来就是人豢养的，乡下人把它吓飞了，不也是很正常的事吗？"景公说："好！从今以后解除捕杀鸟兽的禁令，不要因此而苛待百姓。"

## 1.24 [24] DUKE JING WANTED TO EXECUTE A PEASANT WHO FRIGHTENED AWAY BIRDS. YANZI REMONSTRATED.

Duke Jing was shooting birds when a peasant frightened them away. The Duke was furious and ordered an official to execute him.

Yanzi said: "The peasant is ignorant. I have heard that to reward those without merit is called 'fomenting disorder' and to punish the ignorant is called 'tyrannical oppression.' Both were prohibited by the former kings. It would not be right to transgress the prohibitions of the former kings simply because of birds. But now you, my Lord, fail to understand the regulations of the former kings and you lack the mind of humaneness and righteousness. For this reason, you indulge your desires and you execute capriciously. As for birds and animals, people certainly depend on them for support; so was it not fitting that the peasant frightened them away?"

The Duke said: "Well argued. From now on, the prohibition regarding birds and animals should be relaxed, eliminating the need to be harsh to the people."

103

# 1.25 [25] 景公所爱马死欲诛（圉人）〔养马者〕晏子谏

齐景公心爱的马死去打算杀掉养马的马夫，晏子进谏

## 【原文】

景公使（圉）人养所爱马，暴〔病〕死，公怒，令人操刀解（養）〔养〕马者。是时晏子侍前，左右执刀而进，晏子止〔之〕，而问于公曰："〔敢问古时〕尧舜支解人，从何躯始？"公（矍）〔惧〕然曰："从寡人始。"遂不支解。公曰："以属狱。"晏子曰："（此不知其罪而死），臣〔请〕为君数之，使知其罪，然后致之狱。"公曰："可。"晏子数之曰："尔罪有三：公使汝（養）〔养〕马而杀之，当死罪一也；

## 【今译】

齐景公让马夫饲养他心爱的一匹马，这匹马突然暴病死了，景公很生气，命人拿着刀去肢解养马的马夫。当时晏子正陪从在景公身边，左右的人拿着刀进来，晏子制止了他们，问景公说："冒昧地请问古时候尧舜肢解人，从谁开始的？"景公恐惧地说："从自己开始的。"于是就放弃了肢解马夫的打算。景公又说："把他投入监狱治罪。"晏子说："请让我为您历数他的罪行，让他知道自己犯了什么罪，然后再送进监狱。"景公说："可以。"晏子就历数马夫的罪过，说："你的罪有三

# 1.25 [25] THE FAVORITE HORSE OF DUKE JING DIED. DUKE JING WANTED TO EXECUTE ITS GROOM. YANZI REMONSTRATED.[1]

Duke Jing had commissioned someone to look after his favorite horse, but the horse died after a sudden illness. The Duke was furious and ordered his men to wield their knives and dismember the groom.

At the time, Yanzi was in attendance before the Duke, and when the Duke's entourage had taken hold of their knives and moved forward, Yanzi stopped them and asked the Duke: "May I ask, when Yao and Shun[2] dismembered people in ancient times, with which part of the body did they begin?"

The Duke, frightened, said: "It is I who initiated this punishment."

---

1  The present Item 1.25 [25], narrates a story about an unjust capital punishment. The Item probably contains later interpolations that give the whole narrated episode a more dramatic tone. These interpolations, however, conflict with the natural flow of the sequence of events of the episode as a whole. A more concise, alternative version of the episode appears in *Shuoyuan*, 9.16/72/14. It includes several lines that are marked in round brackets for deletion in the present *ICS* text of the *YZCQ*. These lines give the entire item a more consistent form and indeed seem to be integral to the original plot. They read: "Duke Jing had a horse. His groom let it die. The Duke was furious, took up his spear, and wanted to strike him himself. Yanzi said: 'If you do this, then he will die without knowing his crimes. May I list them, for you, my Lord, to make him realize his crimes, and then kill him?' Duke Jing said: 'Agreed.' Yanzi lifted the spear and, standing in front of the stableman, said: 'You groomed the horse for our Lord and you let it die — this crime deserves death. You make our Lord kill a stableman because of a horse — this crime again deserves death. You made our Lord kill a person because of a horse and let this become known to the four neighboring principalities — your crime again deserves death.' The Duke said: 'Master, please release him, please release him, do not let my humaneness be injured.'"

2  The legendary model emperors Yao and Shun of the Golden Age of Chinese antiquity, traditionally assumed to have reigned in the second half of the third millennium BCE.

【原文】

又杀公之所最善马，当死罪二也；使公以一马之故而杀人，百姓闻之，必怨吾君；诸侯闻之，必轻吾国。汝杀公马，使怨积于百姓，兵弱于邻国，当死罪三也。今以属狱。"公喟然（叹）曰："（夫子释之）！（夫子释之）！（勿伤吾仁也）。〔赦之〕。"

【今译】

条：国君让你养马而你把马养死了，这是第一条死罪；你养死的恰好是国君最喜爱的马，这是第二条死罪；让国君因为一匹马而杀人，百姓听说之后一定会怨恨国君，诸侯听说后一定会轻视我们齐国。你养死了国君的马，从而让国君被百姓怨恨，让齐国的军队弱于邻国，这是第三条死罪。现在就把你送进监狱。"景公听后长叹一声说："放了他。"

And so, they did not proceed to dismember the groom.

The Duke said: "Put him in jail."

Yanzi said: "Allow me to list his crimes for you, my Lord, so that he may know the crimes, and afterward send the man to jail."

The Duke said: "You may."

Yanzi listed them by saying: "Your crime is threefold. The Duke commissioned you to groom his horse, but you let it die — this is your first capital crime. Moreover, you allowed the best horse of the Duke to die — this is your second capital crime. And if you have caused the Duke to have a person killed because of a single horse — when the people hear of it, they will certainly bear resentment against our Lord; when the regional princes hear of it, they will certainly belittle our state. By allowing the Duke's horse to die you will cause the people's complaint against the Duke to grow and our military strength to be weakened with respect to the neighboring states — this is your third capital crime. But now, because of this, you will be put in jail."

The Duke sighed and said: "Pardon him."

# 第二卷 谏下

## 2.1 [26] 景公藉重而狱多欲托晏子晏子谏

齐景公赋税重而刑狱多打算把刑狱之事托付给晏子，晏子进谏

【原文】

景公藉重而狱多，拘者满圄，怨者满朝。晏子谏，公不听。公谓晏子曰："夫狱，国之重官也，愿托之夫子。"晏子对曰："君将使婴救其功乎？则婴有一妾能书，足以治之矣。君将使婴救其意乎？夫民无欲残其家室之生以奉暴上之僻者，则君使吏比而焚之而已矣。"景公不说，曰："救其功则使一妾，救其意则比焚，如是，夫子无所谓能治

【今译】

齐景公当政时，赋税重而冤案多，被拘捕的人填满了监狱，心怀怨愤的人遍布朝堂。晏子进谏，景公不听。景公对晏子说："监狱是国家的重要机构，我想把它托付给您去管理。"晏子回答说："您是想让我整顿刑狱吗？那么我有一个会写字的妾庸手下，完全能把这件事情办好。您是想让我整顿百姓的思想吗？既然百姓不愿意损害家庭的生计来供奉暴君的不良嗜好，那么您派人把他们犯罪的案卷一个个烧掉就可以了。"景公很不高兴，说："要清理刑狱就派一个小妾，要整顿百姓反抗的思想就把他们犯罪的案卷烧掉，如果这样的话，您又怎么谈得上能够治国呢？"晏子说："我的看法与您不同。如今胡貉戎狄养狗，多

# Chapter Two    Remonstrations — Part B

## 2.1 [26] UNDER DUKE JING, TAXES WERE SEVERE AND OPPRESSIVE AND LAWSUITS NUMEROUS. DUKE JING WANTED TO ENTRUST YANZI WITH THE LAWSUITS. YANZI REMONSTRATED.

Under Duke Jing, taxes were heavy and lawsuits numerous. The prison was full of detainees, and the court was filled with those who harbored resentments. Yanzi remonstrated, but the Duke did not pay heed.

The Duke said to Yanzi: "Handling lawsuits is an important official duty in the state. Master, I wish to entrust you with it."

Yanzi replied: "Do you, my Lord, wish to appoint me in order to manage these lawsuits? Then I have a concubine[1] who can write, and she will suffice to manage them. Or do you, my Lord, wish to appoint me in order to manage the minds of those who harbor resentments? Well now, since none of the people desire to destroy their family livelihood in order to comply with the perversities of cruel superiors, you should just order your officials to gather these lawsuits and burn them."

Duke Jing was displeased and said: "You say that in order to manage these lawsuits I could appoint a concubine, and in order to manage the minds of those who harbor resentments, I could gather these lawsuits and burn them; then, if that is all there is, have you none of what is called 'the ability to govern a state,' my Master?"

Yanzi replied: "This is different from what I have heard. Well now, the Hu, Mo,[2] Rong, and Di tribes[3] raise their dogs in packs ranging from

---

1  妄 → 妾 (*JS*, 98/5).

2  狢 → 貉 (*YZCQ-ICS*, 11, n. 4).

3  The Hu 胡, Mo 貉 and Di 狄 tribes were situated in the North; the Rong 戎 were situated in the West.

**【原文】**

国乎？"晏子曰："婴闻与君异。今夫胡狢戎狄之蓄狗也，多者十有余，寡者五六，然不相害。今束鸡豚妄投之，其折骨决皮，可立（得）〔待〕也。且夫上正其治，下审其论，则贵贱不相逾越。今君举千钟爵禄而妄投之于左右，左右争之，甚于胡狗，而公不知也。寸之管无当，

**【今译】**

的有十多只，少的有五六只，然而它们不会互相伤害。但如果将鸡肉或者猪肉随便扔给它们，那么它们（为了抢肉吃）马上就会互相撕咬得皮开肉绽、筋断骨折。而且国君端正自己的统治，百姓们懂得伦理，那么尊贵和卑贱才能各守本分而不互相逾越。现在您拿着高官厚禄随意赏赐给左右的亲信，他们抢夺起来比胡人的狗还要激烈，而您并不知道。一寸长的管子没有底，那么天下的粮食也装不满。现在齐国男子种田，女子织布，夜以继日的劳作，也不够供奉国君的开销，而您周围都是雕刻镂画装饰华美的景观。这就是没有底的管子，而您不知道。五尺高的小孩儿，拿着一寸来长的火把引火，天下的柴草加起来

groups larger than ten to groups as small as five or six. Yet these dogs do not harm and maim one another. But now, tie up a chicken or a suckling pig and recklessly fling it at them, and as you stand there, you would expect them to break each other's bones and tear each other's skins to pieces. Likewise, if superiors are correct in their governing and inferiors are clear as to their ranks,[1] the honored and lowly do not overstep their boundaries. But now you, my Lord, take ranks and emoluments amounting to a thousand *zhong* of grain and recklessly fling them at your entourage, and they fight for them more ferociously than the dogs of the Hu tribes; you, my Duke, fail to understand all this. All the grain in the state could not fill an inch-long[2] tube without a bottom. But now, in the state of Qi, the men plough and the women weave all through the night until dawn, and yet this is not enough to meet the demands of their superiors. Everywhere in your surroundings, my Lord, you have the most lovely carvings and engravings — this is the tube without a bottom; yet you, my Lord, certainly fail to understand all this. If a five-foot tall boy[3] were to hold an inch-long fire-spill,[4] then the entire realm could not supply enough firewood for the fires it would set. Yet your entire entourage, my Lord, is lighters of flames, but you persistently fail to understand all this. When bells and drums are arranged in order, and the dance of Shields and Axes[5] is presented, even Yu[6] could not prohibit people from watching. Likewise, even a sage would find it difficult to refine the desires of the people and still restrict their listening and restrain their hearts;

---

1   论 → 伦 (*JS*, 99/12).

2   *Cun* 寸, an "inch," approximately 2.3 centimeters, is equal to about one tenth of a *chi* 尺 ("a foot"), approximately 23 centimeters.

3   Approximately 115 cm. In other words, a fairly short and young child.

4   烟 → 燢 (*JS*, 99/16).

5   The Shields and Axes was a war dance in which the performers brandished shields and axes and mimicked a war scene. See *Liji* 礼记, 19.1/100/28; *Hanshi waizhuan*, 4.9/27/20.

6   Emperor Yu 禹 or the Great Yu, the legendary first ruler of the Xia dynasty.

**【原文】**

天下不能足之以粟。今齐国丈夫耕，女子织，夜以接日，不足以奉上，而君侧皆雕文刻镂之观。此无当之管也，而君终不知。五尺童子，操寸之烟，天下不能足以薪。今君之左右，皆操烟之徒，而君终不知。钟鼓成肆，干戚成舞，虽禹不能禁民之观。且夫饰民之欲，而严其听，禁其心，圣人所难也，而况夺其财而饥之，劳其力而疲〔之〕，常致其苦而严听其狱，痛诛其罪，非婴所知也。"

**【今译】**

也不够烧。现在您身边的亲信都是手持火把的人，而您不知道。当钟鼓排列奏起音乐，干戚挥动汇成舞蹈时，即便是大禹也不能禁止百姓观赏。而且压抑百姓的欲望，严格控制他们的见闻，禁锢他们的思想，这是圣人也难以办到的事，更何况掠夺他们的财物让他们挨饿，征用他们的劳力让他们疲乏，长期让他们受苦受难又严酷地判处他们入狱，狠心地治他们的罪，这些做法不是我所能理解的。"

all the more so when you, my Lord, rob the people of their property and starve them, exploit their strength and tire them, regularly bring suffering upon them, are harsh in dealing with their lawsuits, and punish their crimes severely. This is something beyond my understanding."

## 2.2 [27] 景公欲杀犯所爱之槐者晏子谏

齐景公打算杀掉碰到心爱槐树的人，晏子进谏

### 【原文】

景公有所爱槐，令吏谨守之，植木县之，下令曰："犯槐者刑，伤之者死。"有不闻令，醉而犯之者，公闻之曰："是先犯我令。"使吏拘之，且加罪焉。其子往辞晏子之家，托曰："负廓之民贱妾，请有道于相国，不胜其欲，愿得充数乎下陈。"晏子闻之，笑曰："婴其淫于色乎？何为老而见奔？虽然，是必有故。"令内之。女子入门，晏子望见之，曰："怪哉！有深忧。"进而问焉曰："所忧何也？"对曰："君树槐县令，犯之者刑，伤之者死。妾父不仁，不闻令，醉而犯之，吏将加罪焉。妾闻之，明君莅国立政，不损禄，不益刑，又不以私恚害公法，

### 【今译】

齐景公有棵心爱的槐树，命令官吏小心地守护着它，还在树旁立了个木桩，上面悬挂着令牌，令文写道："碰到这棵槐树的受刑，伤到这棵槐树的处死。"有个人不知道这道禁令，喝醉酒之后不小心碰到了这棵槐树，景公知道后说："这是第一个触犯我禁令的人。"于是命官吏把这人拘捕起来，准备严惩他。这人的女儿到晏子家去诉说情由，假装说道："我是城边百姓家的卑贱女子，有话向相国诉说，我不能克制自己的欲望，希望到相府中充当侍妾。"晏子听说此事后，笑道："难道我是个好色之徒？为什么我这么老了还有女子过来投靠？即便如此，这件事情也一定事出有因。"于是命人把女子叫进来。女子进门后，晏子看了看她，说："奇怪！她有深深的忧愁。"于是上前问道："什么事让你这么忧愁？"女子回答道："国君在槐树前悬挂了禁令，规定碰到槐树就要惩罚，伤到槐树就要处死。我父亲愚笨，不知道这项禁

## 2.2 [27] DUKE JING WANTED TO KILL SOMEONE WHO COLLIDED WITH HIS BELOVED PAGODA TREE. YANZI REMONSTRATED.[1]

Duke Jing had a Pagoda tree[2] that he loved. He ordered his officials to guard it carefully. He set up a wooden pole and posted the following order on it: "Whoever violates the tree will be punished; whoever damages it will die."

Some man did not hear of the order and, while drunk, violated the tree. When the Duke heard of this, he said: "This is the first violation against my order" and appointed officials to arrest the man and punish him.

The man's daughter went to Yanzi's house, saying:[3] "An unworthy woman of the people from beyond the city wall asks permission to speak to the Chief Minister. As I cannot contain my desires, I wish to occupy a place in the ranks of your lesser quarters."

When Yanzi heard this, he laughed and said: "Am I one who indulges in lewdness? How should I, in my old age, meet with some amorous woman? Nevertheless, she must have some reason for coming here." He ordered her to be let in. When she stepped through the gate, he looked at her from afar and said: "Strange, she is deeply troubled." He allowed her to enter the house and asked her: "What are you troubled about?"

The woman answered: "Our Lord planted a Pagoda Tree with an order posted on it that whoever violates the tree will be punished, and whoever damages it will die. My father is numb and did not pay heed to this command. He violated the Pagoda Tree while drunk, and the officials are

---

1  Item 2.2 [27] ↔ Item 7.9 [179]; *Gulienüzhuan* 古列女传, 6.4/53/20.

2  The Huai 槐 tree, *Styphnolobium japonicum*, or *Sophora japonica*, is known as the "Japanese Pagoda Tree," "Chinese Scholar Tree," or more simply as the "Pagoda Tree" or "Scholar Tree."

3  其子往辞晏子之家托曰 → 其子女往晏子家说曰 (*JS*, 103/8-9).

## 【原文】

不为禽兽伤人民，不为草木伤禽兽，不为野草伤禾苗。吾君欲以树木之故杀妾父，孤妾身，此令行于民而法于国矣。虽然，妾闻之，勇士不以众（疆）〔强〕凌孤独，明惠之君不拂是以行其所欲。此譬之犹自治鱼鳖者也，去其腥臊者而已。昧墨与人比居庾肆，而教人危坐。今君出令于民，苟可法于国而善益于后世，则父死亦当矣，妾为之〔收〕亦宜矣。甚乎！今之令不然，以树木之故，罪法妾父，妾恐其伤察吏之法，而害明君之义也。邻国闻之，皆谓吾君爱树而贱人，其可乎？愿相国察妾言，以裁犯禁者。"晏子曰："甚矣！吾将为子言之于君。"使

## 【今译】

令，醉酒之后碰到了槐树，官吏就要治他的罪了。我听说，贤明的君主治国理政，不损害百姓的利益，不增加刑罚，也不因为私人的怨恨损害国法，不为了禽兽伤害百姓，不为了草木伤害禽兽，不为了野草伤害禾苗。可我们的国君却因为一棵树的缘故要杀我的父亲，让我变成孤儿，这条法令在百姓中施行就变成国法了。即使如此，我听说英勇的人不会倚仗人多势强欺凌孤弱，圣明贤德的国君不违背原则去做自己想做的事。这譬如自己烹饪鱼鳖，去掉它腥臊的气味也就可以了。又比如有人在黑暗中比邻而居，在闹市上教人端坐。现在国君向百姓发出禁令，如果能够成为国法在全国施行而且有利于后世的话，那么我父亲理应被处死，我为他收尸也是应该的。可是现在的禁令并不是这样，因为一棵树的缘故要治我父亲的罪，我怕这样做会破坏严明官吏所遵守的法度，也会伤害圣明君主的仁义和威信。邻国如果知道这件事，都会说我们的国君喜爱树木，轻贱百姓，这怎么可以呢？希望相国您明察我的话，正确处理触犯禁令的人。"晏子说："太过分了！

going to punish him. I have heard that when an enlightened ruler oversees the state and establishes a government, he neither lowers salaries nor increases punishments. Moreover, he does not offend public laws because of personal spite. He does not hurt people for the sake of wild animals, or wild animals for the sake of plants, or crops for the sake of weeds. Our Lord wants to kill my father and orphan me because of a tree. This order is to be applied to the people and will become a state law. Nevertheless, I have heard: 'A courageous officer will not bully the lone individual with numerical superiority and strength; an enlightened and compassionate ruler will not cast aside what is right in order to carry out his desires.' This can be compared to one who prepares fish and tortoises by oneself and gets rid of their rancid and fetid odors, and nothing more; or to one who, in the dark of his shop in the market-quarter, instructs his neighbors to sit in a dignified manner.[1] Now our Lord has issued an order to the people. If the order is indeed turned into a state law whose positive effect would benefit future generations, then it would also be proper that my father die, and right that I place him in a coffin. Yet how different is the present order! My father is to be punished for the sake of a tree. I am afraid that this will hurt the lawfulness of the discerning officials and violate the righteousness of an enlightened ruler. If the neighboring states hear of this, they will all say that our Lord loves trees and disdains people. Is this right? It is my wish that you, the prime minister of the state, examine my words and thereby judge the offender of this prohibition."

Yanzi said: "This is indeed extreme. I will speak with our Lord about this on your behalf." He appointed someone to take her back. The next day, he went early in the morning for an audience with the Duke and reported to him: "I have heard that exhausting the property and the strength of

---

1   These two analogies do not appear in the parallel *Gulienüzhuan* version of this episode and, indeed, most commentators agree that these two analogies are not genuine but probably a later interpolation, see *JS*, 104-105/23-24.

**【原文】**

人送之归。明日，早朝，而复于公曰："婴闻之，穷民财力以供嗜欲谓之暴；崇玩好，威严拟乎君谓之逆；刑杀不（辜）〔称〕谓之贼。此三者，守国之大殃〔也〕。今君穷民财力，以羡（馁）〔饮〕食之具，繁钟鼓之乐，极宫室之观，行暴之大者〔也〕；崇玩好，县爱槐之令，载过者驰，步过者趋，威严似乎君，逆之明者也；犯槐者刑，伤槐者死，〔刑〕杀不称，贼民之深者〔也〕。君享国，德行未见于众，而三辟著于国，婴恐其不可以莅国子民也。"公曰："微大夫教寡人，几有大罪以累社稷，今子大夫教之，社稷之福，寡人受命矣。"晏子出，公令趣罢守槐之役，拔置县之木，废伤槐之法，出犯槐之囚。

**【今译】**

我将会替你向国君求情。"于是命人将女子送回家中。第二天早朝时，晏子对景公说："我听说，穷尽百姓的财富来满足自己的嗜好和欲望叫作'暴'；尊崇自己玩赏喜爱之物，使其具有国君般的威严叫作'逆'；责罚杀害无罪的人叫做'贼'。这三条，是守御国家的大灾难。现在您穷尽百姓的财力，制备多余的饮食器具，增加钟鼓乐器，修建极尽华美的宫室，施行的暴政很严重了；尊崇玩赏喜爱之物，悬挂出爱槐的禁令，使得乘车经过的人策马飞奔，走路路过的快步闪避，（这棵树）的威严已经像国君了，这是很明显的'逆'；碰到槐树要责罚，伤到槐树要处死，刑杀不当，残害百姓也很严重了。您尊享国君之位，没向百姓显示厚德善行，而这三种劣迹却举国皆知，我怕您不能再执掌国家，治理百姓了。"景公说："要不是您教我，我险些铸成大错危害社稷，现在我得到您到教导，真是国家的福气啊，我接受您的教诲了。"晏子离开之后，景公下令撤除看守槐树的差役，拔掉悬挂禁令的木桩，废除伤槐治罪的法令，释放伤到槐树的囚犯。

the people in order to satisfy cravings and desires is known as 'tyranny.' Adoring fine things and precious objects and giving them the same exalted position of authority as to the ruler himself is known as 'perversion.' Punishing or executing the innocent is known as 'predation.[1] These three characterizations are the principal disasters that can befall the safeguarding of the state. But now you, my Lord, exhaust the property and the strength of the people in order to create a surplus of your utensils for eating and drinking. You augment the music of bells and drums and you spend excessive amounts on the splendor of your palaces. This is an extremely tyrannical practice. You, my Lord, give priority to fine things and precious objects. You post an order that anyone who passes a beloved Pagoda Tree in a carriage has to gallop and anyone who passes it on foot has to run, so that the same honor is paid to it as to you; this is clearly a perversion. When you say that anyone who violates the Pagoda Tree will be punished and anyone who damages it will die, the punishment and the execution are inappropriate, amounting to treating the people with the most extreme kind of criminality. Ever since you have enjoyed the rule over this state, you have shown the multitude no sign of virtuous conduct, while these three forms of depravity have been clearly manifested in the state. I am afraid that these cannot be the means by which you oversee the state and rule the people as if they were your own children."

The Duke said: "Had you not instructed me, I might have committed a grave crime that would have had a disastrous effect on the altars of soil and grain. But now you, my High Officer, have instructed me on this matter; this is the good fortune of the altars of soil and grain. I accept your commands."

After Yanzi departed, the Duke ordered his officials to quickly dismiss the guards around the Pagoda Tree, to pull out the wooden pole that had been set up, to annul the law concerning the damaging of the Pagoda Tree, and to release the prisoner who violated the Pagoda Tree.

---

1   For a similar negative characterizations of government, cf. *Analects*, 20.2/57/30.

## 2.3 [28] 景公逐得斩竹者囚之晏子谏

齐景公追逐抓到砍伐自己竹子的人将其囚禁，晏子进谏

### 【原文】

景公树竹，令吏谨守之。公出，过之，有斩竹者焉，公以车逐，得而拘之，将加罪焉。晏子入见，曰："君亦闻吾先君丁公乎？"公曰："何如？"晏子曰："丁公伐曲（沃）〔城〕，胜之，止其财，出其民。公（曰）〔日〕自莅之，有舆死人以出者，公怪之，令吏视之，则其中〔有〕金与玉焉。吏请杀其人，〔收〕其人丁。公曰：'以兵降城，以众图财，不仁。且吾闻之，人君者宽惠慈众，不身传诛。'令舍之。"公曰："善！"晏子退，公令出斩竹之囚。

### 【今译】

齐景公种了一片竹林，命人小心看管。有一次景公外出，路过竹林，看见有人正在砍竹子，景公驱车追赶，抓住了砍竹子的人，准备治他的罪。晏子来见景公，说："您听闻过先代国君丁公的事迹吗？"景公说："丁公有什么事迹？"晏子说："丁公征伐曲城，取得了胜利，他下令禁止携带财物外出，只允许百姓出城。丁公每天亲自到城头巡视，有人用车子拉着死人的棺材出城，丁公感到很奇怪，就命令官吏去查看，发现棺材中装满了黄金和美玉。官吏请求杀掉这个人，没收他的财物。丁公说：'用武力占领城池，靠人多夺取财物，这样做不仁厚。况且我还听说，当国君的人应该对百姓宽厚仁慈，施以恩惠，不应该亲自传令杀人。'于是下令释放了那个人。"景公说："好！"晏子退走之后，景公下令释放砍竹子的囚犯。

## 2.3 [28] DUKE JING CHASED AND SEIZED SOMEONE WHO CUT DOWN A BAMBOO, AND IMPRISONED HIM. YANZI REMONSTRATED.[1]

Duke Jing had bamboo planted and ordered officials to guard it carefully. When the Duke went out and passed by the bamboo, he spotted someone cutting it down. The Duke in his carriage pursued the man, caught and arrested him, and was ready to punish him.

When Yanzi entered for an audience with the Duke, he said: "My Duke, have you heard of our former ruler, Duke Ding?"[2]

The Duke said, "What about him?"

Yanzi replied: "After Duke Ding attacked and defeated the town of Qu, he ordered that all property should remain in the city, while the population was made to leave. The Duke personally supervised this every day. Among the people departing was someone carting away a corpse. The Duke considered it strange. He ordered the officials to look into this matter, and they found gold and pieces of jade in the cart. The officials wanted to kill the man and confiscate his gold and pieces of jade.[3] The Duke said: 'Subduing a city with armed force, and conniving[4] in large numbers against property is inhumane. Furthermore, I have heard that a ruler should be generous, merciful, and kind to the multitude, and that he should not issue arbitrary[5] orders of execution.' Then he ordered the man to be released."

The Duke said: "Well argued."

Yanzi withdrew and the Duke ordered the release of the prisoner who cut down the bamboo.

*121*

---

1  Item 2.3 [28] ↔ Item, 7.9 [179].

2  Duke Ding succeeded Duke Tai (r. 1122–1078 BCE) and reigned in Qi between 1077–1051 BCE.

3  人丁 → 金玉 (*YZCQ-ICS*, 12, n. 9).

4  围 → 图 (*YZCQ-ICS*, 12, n. 10).

5  不身传诛 → 身不妄诛 (*YZCQ-ICS*, 12, n. 11).

## 2.4 [29] 景公以抟治之兵未成功将杀之晏子谏

齐景公因制砖的士兵没有成功打算杀掉他们，晏子进谏

### 【原文】

景公令兵抟治，当冰月之间而寒，民多（涷）〔冻〕馁，而功不成。公怒曰："为我杀兵二人。"晏子曰："诺。"少（为）间，晏子曰："昔者先君庄公之伐于晋也，其役杀兵四人，今令而杀兵二人，是杀师之半也。"公曰："诺！是寡人之过也。"令止之。

### 【今译】

齐景公命令士兵制砖，当时正是十一月和腊月之间，士兵们又冷又饿，没有完成任务。景公生气地说："给我杀两个士兵。"晏子说："是。"过了一会儿，晏子说："以前我们先代的国君庄公征讨晋国，那场战役一共杀了四名士兵，现在您下令杀两名士兵，这已经是那次出征所杀士兵的一半了。"景公说："是！这是我的过错。"于是下令停止杀士兵。

## 2.4 [29] DUKE JING WANTED TO KILL THE SOLDIERS ASSIGNED TO KNEADING CLAY FOR BRICKS WHO DID NOT COMPLETE THEIR TASK. YANZI REMONSTRATED.

Duke Jing ordered his soldiers to knead clay for bricks. This was during the twelfth month, in the dead of winter, and it was cold. Many people were freezing and hungry and therefore the work could not be finished.

The Duke became furious and said: "Kill two soldiers for me."

Yanzi said: "Very well!"

Shortly afterwards, Yanzi said: "In the past, when our former ruler Duke Zhuang launched an attack on Jin,[1] he had four of his soldiers killed. But now, if you order the killing of two soldiers, it would mean that you have killed merely half as many soldiers."

The Duke said: "Quite right, it was my mistake," and he ordered their execution terminated.

123

---

1  This attack on the state of Jin took place in 549 BCE. See *Zuozhuan*, B9. 23.4/276/26.

大中华文库

## 2.5 [30] 景公冬起大台之役晏子谏

齐景公冬天兴起修建大台的劳役，晏子进谏

### 【原文】

晏子使于鲁，比其返也，景公使国人起大台之役。岁寒不已，〔役之〕冻馁（之）者乡有焉，国人望晏子。晏子至，已复事，公（乃）〔延〕坐，饮酒乐，晏子曰："君若赐臣，臣请歌之。"歌曰："庶民之言曰：'冻水洗我，若之何？太上靡散我，若之何？'"歌终，喟然（叹而）流涕。公就止之曰："夫子曷为至此？殆为大台之役夫！寡人将速罢之。"晏子再拜，出而不言，遂如大台，执朴鞭其不务者，曰："吾

### 【今译】

晏子到鲁国出使，等他往回走的时候，齐景公下令让国都附近的百姓开始修建大台。到了寒冬季节还没有修好，参与修建大台的饥寒交迫的百姓每个乡都有，国都附近的百姓都盼望着晏子回来。晏子回到国都，向景公汇报了出使的情况，景公请晏子坐下，饮酒为乐，晏子说："您如果赐我饮酒，那我请求为您献歌一曲。"于是唱道："百姓的话说：'冰冷的水呀浇在我身上，怎么办？不仁的上天摧残我，怎么办？'"唱完之后，晏子长叹一声，泪流满面。景公靠近晏子劝慰他说："您为什么伤心到这种地步？大概是因为修建大台的事情吧！我这就下令停止修建它。"晏子拜了两拜，出去之后一言不发，直奔修建大台的工地，拿起木棍抽打那些不干活的人，说："我们这些微不足道的百姓都有房屋居住，以避免燥热和潮湿，国君修建

## 2.5 [30] DUKE JING LAUNCHED A CONSCRIPT LABOR PROJECT TO BUILD A LARGE TERRACE IN WINTER. YANZI REMONSTRATED.

Yanzi was sent on a mission to Lu. Before his return, Duke Jing had conscripted the people of his state for a labor project to build a large terrace. The wintry cold at the end of the year was unrelenting, and conscripted laborers from all the villages were freezing and hungry. The people looked to Yanzi for salvation.

When Yanzi arrived and finished reporting on the completion of his mission, the Duke invited him to sit down to have a drink and entertain himself.

Yanzi said, "If you, my Lord, grant me permission, I would like to sing a song," and he sang:

The words of the simple people say:

'Freezing water washes us,

what can we do about it?

The Supreme Ruler disperses us;

what can we do about it?'

At the end of the song, he sighed heavily and wept. The Duke moved toward Yanzi to stop him and said: "Master, how have you come to this? Perhaps it is because of the conscript labor at the large terrace? I will discontinue it immediately."

Yanzi bowed twice. Afterwards, he left without saying a word and went to the site of the large terrace. He seized a cane and flogged those who did not attend to their work and said: "We are slight people, and we all have our own small cottages, where we can shut ourselves up to escape the heat and the damp. Our Lord wants one terrace built and it is not finished promptly. What is the reason for this?"

**【原文】**

细人也，皆有盍庐，以避燥湿，君为一台而不速成，何为？"国人皆曰："晏子助天为虐。"晏子归，未至，而君出令趣罢役，车驰而人趋。仲尼闻之，喟然叹曰："古之善为人臣者，声名归之君，祸灾归之身。入则切磋其君之不善，出则高誉其君之德义。是以虽事惰君，能使垂衣裳，朝诸侯，不敢伐其功。当此道者，其晏子是耶！"

**【今译】**

一个大台而不尽快为他修好，这是为什么？"国都的百姓们都说："晏子帮着国君做坏事。"晏子回家，还没到，景公就已下令停止修建大台，于是车马人群都很快散开了。孔子听说这件事后，感慨地说："古时候善于做臣子的人，把好名声留给国君，把灾祸归咎于自身。进入朝堂就帮助国君改正缺点，离开朝堂就极力赞誉国君的美德和仁义。因此即使侍奉的是不贤的国君，但仍然能让他做到无为而治，让四方诸侯来朝，但他又不夸耀自己的功劳。能承担这种道义的人，也就是晏子了！"

All the people of the state said: "Yanzi is helping Heaven to inflict cruelties."

While Yanzi was on his way back, the Duke issued an order to immediately discontinue the conscript labor. Chariots hastened forward and people rushed away.

When Confucius heard about this, he heaved a deep sigh and said: "Those in ancient times who were good as ministers ascribed fame to their rulers' credit and ascribed disaster to their own discredit. When they entered for an audience, they reprimanded their rulers for doing what was not good, but upon exiting they praised them highly for their virtue and righteousness. For that reason, even when they served negligent rulers, they made it possible for the rulers to let their clothes hang down loosely,[1] and when they summoned the regional princes for an audience to their court, they did not presume to boast of their own achievements. Yanzi is indeed someone who undertook that very way — is he not?"

127

---

1 A metaphor for the effortless way in which the legendary emperors such as the Yellow Emperor and Yao and Shun achieved perfect rulership. See *Zhouyi* 周易, 66/82/5.

## 2.6 [31] 景公为长庲欲美之晏子谏

齐景公修建长庲打算把它装饰的精美一些，晏子进谏

### 【原文】

景公为长庲，将欲美之，有风雨作，公与晏子入坐饮酒，致堂上之乐。酒酣，晏子作歌曰："穗（乎）〔兮〕不得获，秋风至兮殚零落，风雨之弗杀也，太上之靡弊也。"歌终，顾而流涕，张躬而舞。公就晏子而止之曰："今日夫子为赐而诫于寡人，是寡人之罪。"遂废酒，罢役，不果成长庲。

### 【今译】

齐景公修建了一座名为"长庲"的台阁，正打算把它装饰的精美一些，有一次风雨大作，景公和晏子到长庲中饮酒，并让乐师到堂上奏乐。酒兴正浓时，晏子唱起歌来："庄稼有穗呀得不到收获，秋风吹来呀全都零落，风雨无情呀吹落了我的粮食，上天无情呀摧残了我的生活。"唱完歌，晏子环顾四周泪流满面，又伸出双臂起舞。景公走到晏子身边劝止他说："今天您因为赐酒宴乐而唱歌劝诫我，这是我的过失。"于是停止酒宴，罢去了（装饰长庲的）劳役，长庲的装饰最终没有完成。

## 2.6 [31] DUKE JING BUILT THE CHANGLAI[1] TERRACE AND WANTED TO DECORATE IT. YANZI REMONSTRATED. [2]

Duke Jing built the Changlai Terrace and wanted to have it decorated. Once, just as a storm was brewing, the Duke entered together with Yanzi and they sat down to drink wine; music was ordered to be played in the hall. After they had drunk enough and became tipsy, Yanzi sang a song:

The ears of grain cannot be harvested,

The autumn wind came; all have withered and fallen.

Wind and rain did not kill the crops,

It was the Supreme Ruler who ruined and destroyed them.

His song ended and he turned to look at the Duke with tears in his eyes; then he stretched to his full height and danced. The Duke moved toward Yanzi and stopped him, saying: "Today my Master has bestowed warnings upon me; this is my fault."

Consequently, the Duke gave up drinking, abolished the conscript labor, and did not bring the Changlai Terrace to completion.

---

1   While some dictionaries and commentators identify *lai* 庲 with *tai* 台 ("terrace"), others identify it with *she* 舍 ("dwelling house"); in the latter case, the sentence would read: "Duke Jing built a large dwelling house and wanted to decorate it."

2   Item 2.6 [31] ↔ Item 7.12 [182].

## 2.7 [32] 景公为邹之长涂晏子谏

齐景公修筑通往邹邑的道路，晏子进谏

### 【原文】

景公筑路寝之台，三年未息；又为长庲之役，二年未息；又为邹之长涂。晏子谏曰："百姓之力勤矣！公不息乎？"公曰："涂将成矣，请成而息之。"对曰："（明）君（不）屈民财者，不得其利；（不）穷民力者，不得其乐。昔者楚灵王作倾宫，三年未息也；又为章华之台，五年（又不）〔未〕息也；〔而又为〕乾溪之役，八年，百姓

### 【今译】

齐景公修建寝宫的高台，三年还没有完工；又修建长庲，两年还没有修好；又修筑通往邹地的道路。晏子劝谏说："百姓的劳役已经够多的了！您还不停止这些工程吗？"景公说："道路马上就要修好了，等完成之后再停止吧。"晏子说："国君如果耗尽民财，自己也得不到利益；耗尽民力，自己也得不到乐趣。从前楚灵王修建倾宫，三年没有完工；又修建章华之台，五年没有完工；又开始修建乾溪台的劳役，到了第八年，百姓实在疲惫不堪，于是这些工程被迫停止。楚灵王死在乾溪，但百姓不和他一起回国。现在您不遵行明君的道义，而走楚

## 2.7 [32] DUKE JING BUILT THE LONG ROAD TO ZOU. YANZI REMONSTRATED.

Duke Jing built a terrace over the Road Bedchamber,[1] and the work went on for three years without cessation. In addition, he conscripted laborers for the Changlai Terrace for two years without cessation, and he also built the Long Road to Zou.

Yanzi remonstrated and said: "The strength of the people is exhausted; shouldn't you cease?"

The Duke said: "The road is about to be completed; do let it be completed and then let the labor cease."

Yanzi replied: "A ruler who exhausts the wealth of the people cannot benefit from this act; a ruler who depletes the strength of the people cannot enjoy it. Formerly, King Ling of Chu[2] built the Towering-Leaning Palace, and the work went on for three years without cessation. He also built the Terrace of Zhanghua for five years without cessation, and he waged the War of Qianxi for eight years; the people's strength was overtaxed and so they ceased of their own accord. King Ling died in Qianxi, and the people did not take part in the return of his coffin. But now you, my Lord, are not guided by the righteousness of the enlightened rulers and you follow in the footsteps of King Ling. I am afraid, my Lord, that your conduct is oppressing the people and you will never see delights in Changlai. It would

---

1   路寝, either the "Road Bedchamber of the Right" (右路寝) or the "Road Bedchamber of the Left" (左路寝), one of the three royal bedchambers. For a detailed discussion of the nature, location and function of each of these three chambers, see *Shuoyuan*, 19.13/163/14; *Liji* 礼记, 22.3/115/1; *JS*, 116/1; James Legge, tr. *The Chinese Classics, Vol. V, The Ch'un Ts'ew with the Tso Chuen*. Reprint, Hong Kong University Press (1970): 121.

2   The notorious King Ling of Chu 楚灵王 lived in the same generation as Duke Jing. He reigned from 540–529 BCE.

**【原文】**

之力不足而〔自〕息也。灵王死于乾溪，而民不与君归。今君不遵明君之义，而循灵王之迹，婴惧君有暴民之行，而不睹长庲之乐也，不若息之。"公曰："善！非夫子者，寡人不知得罪于百姓深也。"于是令勿委坏，余财勿〔收〕，斩板而去之。

**【今译】**

灵王的老路，我怕您有残害百姓的行为，而看不到长庲中的乐事了，不如停止这些工程吧。"景公说："好！如果不是您，我还不知道已经把百姓得罪得这么严重了。"于是下令（百姓）不要损坏已经修好的路，已经发下去的财物也不收缴，拆掉筑路的模板后就可以自行离去。

be better to cease."

The Duke said: "Well argued. Were it not for someone like you, Master, I would never have known how gravely I had offended the people."

Thereupon, he ordered that the part of the road already built not be given over to ruin; that the remaining resources for the completion of the project should not be collected; and that the frame-boards be cut up and removed from the road.

LIBRARY OF CHINESE CLASSICS

133

## 2.8 [33] 景公春夏游猎兴役晏子谏

齐景公春夏之交巡游打猎兴起劳役，晏子进谏

### 【原文】

景公春夏游猎，又起大台之役。晏子谏曰："春夏起役，且游猎，夺民农时，国家空虚，不可。"景公曰："吾闻相贤者国治，臣忠者主逸。吾年无几矣，欲遂吾所乐，卒吾所好，子其息矣。"晏子曰："昔文王不敢盘游于田，故国昌而民安。楚灵王不废乾溪之役，起章华之台，而民叛之。今君不革，将危社稷，而为诸侯笑。臣闻忠不避死，谏不违罪。君不听臣，臣将（游）〔逝〕矣。"景公曰："唯唯，将弛罢之。"未几，朝韦囧解役而归。

### 【今译】

齐景公在春夏之交外出游猎，又开始修建大台。晏子进谏说："春夏之间发起劳役，而且外出游猎，会侵夺百姓耕作的时间，使国家空虚，这是不可以的。"景公说："我听说相国贤良国家就能太平，臣子忠诚君主就能安逸。我也活不了几年了，就想满足自己的乐趣，实现自己的喜好，您还是别管我了。"晏子说："以前周文王不敢迷恋于游玩和打猎，因此国家昌盛、百姓安乐。楚灵王不肯停止修建乾溪台的劳役，又修建章华台，所以百姓反叛。现在您如果不改变这些做法，就会危及社稷，被天下诸侯耻笑。我听说忠臣不怕死，进谏不怕获罪。您不听我的谏言，我就要离开您了。"景公说："是的是的，我马上就停止这些做法。"很快，景公就召见韦囧解除民工的劳役而使他们各自回家。

## 2.8 [33] DUKE JING CONDUCTED A HUNTING EXCURSION DURING THE SPRING AND SUMMER AND CONSCRIPTED A CORPS OF LABORERS. YANZI REMONSTRATED.

Duke Jing went on a hunting excursion during the spring and summer and, in addition, conscripted a corps of laborers to build a large terrace.

Yanzi remonstrated and said: "To raise a corps of conscript laborers and to conduct hunting excursions in the spring and summer is to rob the people of their busy seasons in the fields and deplete the resources of the state. This is not appropriate."

Duke Jing said: "I have heard that when the prime minister is worthy, the state is well ordered; when the ministers are loyal, the ruler is at ease. My years are numbered and I would like to achieve that which gives me pleasure and bring to completion what is to my liking. Master, you had better rest yourself."

Yanzi said: "In the past, King Wen[1] did not presume to spend his time in excursions and hunts;[2] therefore, the state was prosperous and the people were at peace. King Ling of Chu did not stop the Qianxi campaign and raised the Zhanghua Terrace, and the people rose up against him. Now if you, my Lord, do not change, you will endanger the altars of soil and grain and will become the laughingstock of the regional princes. I have heard that the loyal do not shun death and the remonstrator does not fear recrimination. If you, my Lord, do not listen to me, I will leave."

Duke Jing said: 'Yes, yes, I will stop it."

After a short while, Duke Jing summoned Wei Jiong[3] to court, released the conscript laborers, and returned.

135

---

1  The virtuous King Wen 文王 (1231–1135 BCE), whose son was King Wu 武王 (1169–1116 BCE), the first sovereign of the Zhou dynasty.

2  For an identical reference about King Wen's reserved attitude towards excursions and hunts, see *Shujing* 书经, 43/39/19.

3  An unidentified figure.

# 2.9 [34] 景公猎休坐地晏子席而谏

齐景公打猎休息时坐在地上，晏子拔草当席子坐而进谏

## 【原文】

景公猎休，坐地而食，晏子后至，左右灭葭而席。公不说，曰："寡人不席而坐地，二三子莫席，而子独搴草而坐之，何也？"晏子对曰："臣闻介胄坐阵不席，狱讼不席，尸（坐）〔在〕堂（上）不席，三者皆忧也。故不敢以忧侍坐。"公曰："（诺）〔善〕。"令人下席曰："大夫皆席，寡人亦席矣。"

## 【今译】

齐景公打猎休息时，坐在地上吃饭，晏子后到，就在旁边拔了些芦苇铺在地上当席子坐。景公很不高兴，说："我没坐席而是坐在地上，其他人也没有坐在席上，只有您拔草当席坐在上面，这是为什么？"晏子回答说："我听闻身披甲胄的将士在军阵前不坐席，打官司的人不坐席，祭祀之尸在堂上不坐席，这三种情况都是让人忧伤的。所以我不敢带着忧伤陪坐在您身边。"景公说："好。"于是让人铺下席子说："大夫们都坐到席上吧，我也要坐到席上。"

## 2.9 [34] DUKE JING SAT ON THE GROUND TO REST DURING A HUNT. YANZI SAT ON HIS MAT AND REMONSTRATED.[1]

During a pause in the course of a hunt, Duke Jing sat down on the ground to eat. Yanzi arrived later; the entourage tore off some reeds to make a mat for him to sit on.

The Duke was displeased and said: "I am not sitting on a mat, but on the bare ground; none of the gentlemen around me are sitting on a mat; only you, sir, have torn off some reeds to sit on. What is the meaning of this?"

Yanzi replied: "I have heard: when one puts on armor and takes one's place in a military formation, one does not sit on a mat. In a court of law, one does not sit on a mat, and also when a body is lying in one's house, one does not sit on a mat. All three cases are connected with troubling circumstances, thus I did not presume to serve you while sitting in a manner indicative of troubled feelings."

The Duke said: "Well argued." He ordered his people to spread mats on the ground and said: "All high officers are to sit on mats, and I will sit on a mat as well."

---

1   Item 2.9 [34] ↔ *Shuoyuan*, 17.55/150/9.

## 2.10 [35] 景公猎逢蛇虎以为不祥晏子谏

齐景公打猎遇到蛇和老虎认为是不祥之兆，晏子进谏

**【原文】**

　　景公出猎，上山见虎，下泽见蛇。归，召晏子而问之曰："今日寡人出猎，上山则见虎，下泽则见蛇，殆所谓不祥也？"晏子对曰："国有三不祥，是不与焉。夫有贤而不知，一不祥〔也〕；知而不用，二不祥〔也〕；用而不任，三不祥也。所谓不祥，乃若此者〔也〕。今上山见虎，虎之室也；下泽见蛇，蛇之穴也。如虎之室，如蛇之穴，而见之，曷为不祥也！"

**【今译】**

　　齐景公外出打猎，上山的时候看见了老虎，走到湖边又见到了蛇。回来后，景公召见晏子问道："今天我出去打猎，上山见到老虎，走到湖边又见到蛇，这大概就是所谓的不祥之兆吧？"晏子回答道："国家有三种不吉利的事，而这些是不包含在内的。有贤良的人而不知道，这是第一种不祥；知道贤良的人而不重用，这是第二种不祥；重用了又不信任，这是第三种不祥。所谓不祥之兆，说的就是像这类事情。现在您上山见到老虎，山是老虎的住处；走到湖边见到了蛇，湖边是蛇的洞穴。您去虎窝见到老虎，去蛇穴见到蛇，这哪是不祥之兆呢！"

## 2.10 [35] DUKE JING CAME UPON A SNAKE AND A TIGER DURING A HUNT.  HE CONSIDERED THEM INAUSPICIOUS. YANZI REMONSTRATED.[1]

Duke Jing went out on a hunt. He climbed a mountain and saw a tiger; he went down to a swamp and saw a snake. Upon his return, he summoned Yanzi and asked him: "Today I was out hunting. When I climbed a mountain I saw a tiger and when I went down to a swamp I saw a snake. May I assume this is what is called 'inauspicious'?"

Yanzi answered: "There are three inauspicious matters for a state and these are not among them. The first instance is if worthy people are not recognized as such; the second instance is if they are recognized as such but are not taken into service; and the third instance is if they are taken into service but they are not empowered to act. The so-called 'inauspicious matter' refers only to these three cases. But now, when you climbed a mountain and saw a tiger, you were at the tiger's lair. When you went down to the swamp and saw a snake, you were at the snake's hole. If one goes to the lair of the tiger and to the hole of the snake and sees them, why should these sightings be regarded as inauspicious?"

1   Item 2.10 [35] ↔ *Shuoyuan*, 1.23/6/19.

## 2.11 [36] 景公为台成又欲为钟晏子谏

齐景公修筑好高台又打算铸造大钟，晏子进谏

### 【原文】

景公为台，台成，又欲为钟。晏子谏曰："君国者不乐民之哀。君不胜欲，既筑台矣，今复〔欲〕为钟，是重敛于民，民必哀矣。夫敛民之哀，而以为乐，不祥，非所以君国者。"公乃止。

140

### 【今译】

齐景公修建了一座高台，建好之后，又想铸造大钟。晏子进谏道："当国君的人不应乐于见到百姓的哀痛。您不能克制自己的欲望，已经修筑了高台，现在又要铸造大钟，这样不断加重对百姓的征敛，百姓一定会痛苦不堪。加重百姓的赋税使他们哀痛，以此换来自己的快乐，这是不祥之兆，不是当国君的人应该做的事。"景公于是停止铸钟。

## 2.11 [36] DUKE JING FINISHED BUILDING A TERRACE AND ALSO WANTED TO CAST A BELL. YANZI REMONSTRATED.[1]

Duke Jing built a terrace and when it was completed, he wanted to cast a bell in addition.

Yanzi remonstrated and said: "He who rules a state should not delight in the people's suffering. You, my Lord, have given free rein to your desires and have built a terrace, and now you want to have a bell cast as well; this will only mean oppressive taxes for the people, and they will certainly suffer. To compound the people's suffering and to take delight in it is inauspicious and is not the way in which one rules a state."

Thereupon, the Duke desisted.

---

1   Item 2.11 [36] ↔ *Shuoyuan*, 9.15/72/11.

## 2.12 [37] 景公为泰吕成将以〔燕〕飨晏子谏

齐景公铸成大吕钟后打算举行宴饮，晏子进谏

### 【原文】

景公〔为〕泰吕成，谓晏子曰："吾欲与夫子燕。"对曰："未祀先君而以燕，非礼也。"公曰："何以礼为？"对曰："夫礼者，民之纪，纪乱则民失，乱纪失民，危道也。"公曰："善。"乃以祀焉。

### 【今译】

齐景公铸成大吕钟后，对晏子说："我想和您一起宴饮。"晏子回答说："没祭祀先代国君就举行宴饮，这不合礼法。"景公说："怎么做才算有礼呢？"晏子回答说："礼法是约束百姓的纲纪，纲纪混乱，百姓就失去了约束，纲纪混乱百姓离心，这是倾危之道。"景公说："好。"于是就举行祭祀。

## 2.12 [37] DUKE JING FINISHED CASTING THE TAILU[1] BELL AND WAS GOING TO HOLD A BANQUET TO CELEBRATE IT. YANZI REMONSTRATED.

When the making of the Tailü bell was completed, Duke Jing said to Yanzi: "I wish to hold a banquet with your participation, Master."

Yanzi answered: "It is a violation of the rites to hold a banquet without performing the proper sacrifice to the former rulers."

The Duke said: "Why does one have to follow the rites?"

Yanzi answered: "The rites are the basic guidelines of the people. When these guidelines fall into disorder, the people are lost. It is a dangerous course to allow the guidelines to fall into disorder and to lose the people."

The Duke said: "Well argued." Thereupon, he performed the appropriate sacrifice.

---

1  The Tailü 泰呂 and 大呂 are the names of an identical bell that was cast when Qi was in decline. See *Lüshi chunqiu*, 5.3/25/12.

大中华文库

## 2.13 [38] 景公为履〔而〕饰以金玉晏子谏

齐景公做了一双鞋用金玉来装饰，晏子进谏

### 【原文】

景公为履，黄金之綦，饰以银，连以珠，良玉之（胸）〔绚〕，其长尺，冰月服之以听朝。晏子朝，公迎之，履重，仅能举足，问曰："天寒乎？"晏子曰："君奚问天之寒也？古圣人制衣服也，冬轻而暖，夏轻而（清）〔清〕，今（君）〔金玉〕之履，冰月服之，是重寒也，履重不节，是过任也，失生之情矣。故鲁工不知寒温之节、轻重之量，以害

### 【今译】

齐景公做了一双鞋子，用金丝做鞋带，用白银来装饰鞋面，用珍珠来连接，又用美玉缀在鞋头，鞋子长一尺，（景公）腊月里穿着它临朝听政。晏子来朝见，景公起身相迎，但鞋子太重，只能抬起脚，他问晏子道："天气冷吗？"晏子说："您怎么问天气冷不冷？古时候的圣人制作衣服时，冬衣要轻而温暖，夏衣要轻而凉爽，现在您这双饰满金玉的鞋子，腊月天穿上它会更加寒冷，鞋子重量不合适，脚的负担也增加，这就脱离了生活的实际需求。所以（制作这双鞋的）鲁国鞋匠不知道冷暖的适度，也不知道轻重的适量，用这样的鞋子损害正常的生理，这是他的第一条罪名；做的鞋子不符合常制，让诸侯耻笑，

## 2.13 [38] DUKE JING COMMISSIONED SHOES DECORATED WITH GOLD AND JADE. YANZI REMONSTRATED.

Duke Jing commissioned shoes with golden laces and silver decorations. They had cords strung with pearls and their ornamental points were made of fine jade. They were one foot long.[1] He wore them for an audience in the winter. When Yanzi attended the audience, the Duke went to greet him but the shoes were so heavy that the Duke was barely able to lift his feet.

The Duke asked: "Is the weather cold?"

Yanzi replied: "Why do you ask if the weather is cold? In ancient times, clothes made for the sage were such that they were light and warm in winter, and light and cool in summer. Yet, wearing shoes that are made of gold and jade in the winter is heavy and leaves one cold. The weight of the shoes is inappropriate; it is beyond all bounds and constitutes losing touch with the reality of life. Apparently, the craftsman of Lu[2] did not know the correct proportions of cold and warm and did not know the correct measurement of light and heavy, and he thereby harmed orderly life. This is his first crime. That he produced an article that does not conform to proper norms and thereby made you the laughingstock among the regional princes. This is his second crime. That he utilized property without a useful result and thereby engendered resentment among the people. This is his third crime. Please have him arrested and judged by the court officers."

The Duke said: "The craftsman of Lu put hard work into making these shoes, please set him free."

145

---

1   The ancient Chinese foot, *chi* 尺, is said to be about 23 cm.

2   As the story of this item evolves, we learn that Yanzi blames a particular craftsman from Lu for the making of these shoes.

**【原文】**

正生，其罪一也；作服不常，以笑诸侯，其罪二也；用财无功，以怨百姓，其罪三也。请拘而使吏度之。"公〔曰〕："苦，请释之。"晏子曰："不可。婴闻之，苦身为善者，其赏厚；苦身为非者，其罪重。"公不对。晏子出，令吏拘鲁工，令人送之境，（吏）〔使〕不得入。公撤履，不复服也。

大中华文库

**【今译】**

这是他的第二条罪名；花掉很多财富却对国家不利，使得百姓怨恨，这是他的第三条罪名。请将他拘捕起来命官吏依法治罪。"景公说："鞋匠在制作鞋子时也付出了很多辛苦，请您放过他吧。"晏子说："不可以。我听说辛苦自己而去做善事的，应该重赏；辛苦自己而去做坏事的，应该重罚。"景公无言以对。晏子退出后，命令官吏拘捕鲁国鞋匠，派人把他送出齐国国境，不准他再到齐国来。景公也脱掉这双鞋，再也没有穿过。

Yanzi said: "It would not be appropriate. I have heard that if someone puts hard work into doing good, then he should be rewarded handsomely. But if someone puts hard work into wrongdoing, his punishment should be heavy."

The Duke did not answer. Yanzi went out and ordered the court officers to arrest the craftsman of Lu. He ordered someone to send the craftsman off to the border region and to make it impossible for him to return. The Duke removed the shoes and did not wear them again.

147

## 2.14 [39]（土）景公欲以圣王之居服而致诸侯晏子谏

齐景公打算用圣王的居室和服饰来招致诸侯，晏子进谏

### 【原文】

景公问晏子曰："吾欲服圣王之服，居圣王之室，如此，则诸侯其至乎？"晏子对曰："法其节俭则可，法其服（居其）室，无益也。三王不同服而王，非以服致诸侯也，诚于爱民，果于行善，天下怀其德而归其义，（若）〔善〕其衣服节俭而众悦也。夫冠足以修敬，不务其饰；衣足以掩形御寒，不务其美。衣不务于隅（肶）〔眦〕之削，冠无觚蠃之理，身服不杂彩，首服不镂刻。且古者尝有纮衣挛领而王天下

### 【今译】

齐景公问晏子说："我想穿古代圣王那样的服饰，住古代圣王那样的居室，这样的话，诸侯大概就都会归附了吧？"晏子说："您学习他们的节俭是可以的，学习他们的服饰和居室，并没有什么好处。夏禹、商汤、周文王没有穿一样的衣服却都建立王业，他们不是靠服饰使诸侯归附的，他们真诚地爱护百姓，成功地推行善政，天下人感念他们的德行，归附他们的仁义，所以虽然他们服饰节俭但百姓心悦诚服。帽子足够显示敬意就够了，不必追求修饰；衣服足够遮蔽身体抵御风寒就够了，不必追求华美。衣服不必追求斜角的剪裁，帽子不必追求狭窄有棱角的形状，穿在身上的衣服不要色彩斑斓，头上戴的帽子不要镂刻花纹。况且古时候曾经有人穿着缝制简朴衣领卷曲的衣服统一

## 2.14 [39] DUKE JING WANTED TO EMULATE THE DWELLINGS AND CLOTHES OF THE SAGE-KINGS AND TO HAVE THE REGIONAL PRINCES COME AND PAY COURT TO HIM ON THAT BASIS. YANZI REMONSTRATED.

Duke Jing queried Yanzi as follows: "I would like to be dressed like the sage-kings and live in houses similar in style to those they lived in. If I accomplish that, would I then bring other regional princes to pay court to me?"

Yanzi replied: "If you take as your model the frugality of the sage-kings, then it will be possible to achieve this, but if your model is their clothing and houses, the endeavor will be useless. The Three Kings[1] wore different clothes and still they ruled like true kings. It was not on account of their clothing that they drew the regional princes to them. They were sincere in loving the people and resolute in doing good. The whole realm cherished their virtue and all were drawn to their righteousness and approved of their modest clothing, which delighted the multitude. As for caps, one should suffice with cultivating a respectful demeanor, rather than striving for decoration. Clothing should merely cover the body and ward off the cold, rather than striving for beauty. One's dress should not strive for sharply cut angles and caps should not have a high and narrow shape.[2] The clothes on one's body should not be multicolored, and there should be no carved adornments on one's headgear. Moreover, in ancient times, some true kings of the realm used to have patched clothes and bent collars. Their righteousness lay in their love of life and their hatred of killing. They

149

---

1   The Three Kings of antiquity, Yu 禹, Tang 汤 and Wu 武, the founders of the Xia, Shang and Zhou royal dynasties.

2   贏 → 瀛 (*YZCQ-ICS*, 15, n. 4).

【原文】

者，其义好生而恶杀，节上而羡下，天下不朝其服，而共归其义。古者尝有处橧巢窟穴而不恶，予而不取，天下不朝其室，而共归其仁。及三代作服，为益敬也，首服足以修敬，而不重也，身服足以行洁，而不害于动作。服之轻重便于身，用财之费顺于民。其不为橧巢者，以避风也；其不为〔窟〕穴者，以避湿也。是故明堂之制，下之润湿，

【今译】

天下，他们爱惜生命、厌恶杀戮，节约君主的开销，追求百姓的富裕，天下人不朝拜他的服饰而是归附他的仁义。古时候曾经有人住在用柴堆的居室里和洞窟中而不嫌弃，给予他房屋他也不居住，天下人不朝拜他的房屋而是归附他的仁德。到三代制作衣服，是为了增加崇敬，头上戴的帽子足以表达敬意就够了，不必追求贵重，身上穿的衣服足以整洁、便于行动就够了，不要妨碍动作。服饰的轻重要穿戴方便，财物的花费要顺应民意。之所以不再用柴堆搭建居室，是为了躲避风雨；不再居于洞穴，是为了避免潮湿。所以建造明堂，让地下的潮湿之气上不来；让外边的寒暑之气进不来。土石建筑不作纹饰，竹木建筑不去雕镂，向百姓示范要懂得节俭。到了他们统治衰败的时候，服饰的奢侈大大超过了表达敬意的程度，宫室的华美超过了避免潮湿的

restricted superiors and aggrandize the inferiors; none of the residents made obeisance to them because of their clothing, but rather joined in being drawn to their righteousness. In ancient times, there were people[1] who did not detest to live in stick-made nests and caves; they gave and did not take; the whole realm made obeisance to them not on account of their housing, but rather of their humaneness. By the time of the Three Dynasties, official clothes were instituted to increase veneration; headgear was sufficient to inspire veneration, and was not heavy. The clothes on one's body were sufficient to practice modesty, but did not hinder movement. The weight of clothes was comfortable for the body, and was affordable to the people. The reason people of that period no longer framed stick-made nests was in order to avoid the wind, and the reason they no longer dug caves was to avoid dampness. Therefore, Ming Tang Hall's[2] regulations ensured that no dampness could rise from below and neither cold nor heat could enter from above. Earthworks were not embellished and woodwork had no carvings, in order to show the people that they knew frugality. When these dynasties approached their downfall, the luxury of their clothing exceeded what sufficed for veneration, and the beauty of palaces exceeded what sufficed for avoiding dampness. The use of manpower was enormous, and the

---

1  Yanzi's statement is in reference to the former kings as in *Liji*, 9.5/60/14: 昔者先王, 未有宫室, 冬则居营窟, 夏则居橧巢 ("In the past the former kings had no houses; in the winter they lived in caves that they had dug, and in the summer they lived in stick-made nests.").

2  The Ming Tang 明堂 — The Hall of Light — was a unique royal structure of the state of Qi, mentioned in many texts that deal with rituals and sacrifices. Mencius considered the Hall of Light to be the hall of a true king (*Mencius, 2.5/9/24*). For a detailed discussion of this hall, see James Legge; Ch'u Chai; Winberg Chai. *Li Chi: Book of Rites. An encyclopedia of ancient ceremonial usages, religious creeds, and social institutions*. New Hyde Park, N.Y., University Books (1967): vol. 1, 28-30. See also John S. Major, *et al.*, trs. *The Huainanzi: A Guide to the Theory and Practice of Government in Early Han China*. Translations from the Asian Classics. New York: Columbia University Press (2010): 882-883.

## 【原文】

不能及也；上之寒暑，不能入也。土事不文，木事不镂，示民（之）〔知〕节也。及其衰也，衣服之侈过足以敬，宫室之美过避润湿，用力甚多，用（则）〔财〕甚费，与民为雠。今君欲法圣王之服，不法其制，法其节俭也，则虽未成治，庶其有益也。今君穷台榭之高，极污池之深而不止，务于刻镂之巧，文章之观而不厌，则亦与民（而）〔为〕雠矣。若臣之虑，恐国之危，而公不平也。公乃愿致诸侯，不亦难乎！公之言过矣。"

## 【今译】

程度，动用了太多民力，花费了太多财富，以至于和百姓结为仇敌。现在您想学习圣王的服饰，不学习他们的制度，学习他们的节俭，那么即使不能成就治世，应该也还是有好处的。现在您一味追求高到不能再高的台廊，深得不能再深池塘，一味追求精巧的雕刻镂空、华美的花纹，不知满足，这也是与百姓为敌啊。如果真像我忧虑的那样，恐怕国家就危险了，国君您也无法安享太平。国君希望诸侯来朝，不是很困难吗！您的话说错了。"

resources applied were costly, and so the Kings made the people into their enemies. But now you, my Lord, wish to use as your criterion the clothes of the sage-kings, but not their regulations. If you take their frugality as a model, then even if you are unable to attain perfect order, it would probably be beneficial. But if you, my Lord, build the terraces as high as possible and ceaselessly dig ponds to a great depth; if you devote yourself insatiably to skillful carvings and to eye-catching emblems and ornaments, then you will transform the people into enemies as well. If my worries are realized, I am afraid that the state will be endangered and you yourself will not be safe. Would it not be a difficult matter, then, to wish the regional princes to come to pay court to you? Your words were wrong!"

## 2.15 [40] 景公自矜冠裳游处之贵晏子谏

齐景公自夸帽子衣服巡游居处的贵重，晏子进谏

### 【原文】

景公为西曲潢，其深灭轨，高三仞，横木龙蛇，立木鸟兽。公衣
黼黻之衣、素绣之裳，一（依）〔衣〕而五彩具焉；带球玉而冠且，被
发乱首，南面而立，傲然。晏子见，公曰："昔仲父之霸何如？"晏
子抑首而不对。公又曰："昔管文仲之霸何如？"晏子对曰："臣闻之，
维翟人与龙蛇比，今君横木龙蛇，立木鸟兽，亦室一就矣，何暇在霸
哉！且公伐宫室之美，（矜）〔矜〕衣服之丽，一衣而五彩具焉，带球

### 【今译】

齐景公命人挖了一个西曲池，池水的深度能没过车轴，又在池上
修筑了一座宫室，高达三仞，横梁上雕刻龙蛇，立柱上画满鸟兽。景
公穿着色彩斑斓的上衣，白色绣花的下裳，一身衣服上各种颜色都
齐备；衣带上佩戴着美玉，帽子上挂着冕缨，披散着头发，脸朝南站
着，神态傲慢。晏子来拜见景公，景公说："以前仲父的霸业怎么样？"
晏子低着头不回答。景公又问："以前管文仲的霸业怎么样？"晏子回
答道："我听说，只有翟人才与龙蛇为伍，现在您的横梁上雕刻着龙蛇，
立柱上画满了鸟兽，也可以说是和龙蛇鸟兽齐聚一室了，哪里还有时
间考虑霸业呢！而且您夸耀宫室的壮美，夸耀衣服的艳丽，一身衣服
兼具五彩，佩戴美玉但披头散发，也算是把各种仪容齐聚一室了，万
乘之国的国君，却一心向往歪门邪道，您已经丧失了魂魄，谁又能和

## 2.15 [40] DUKE JING TOOK PRIDE IN THE GREAT VALUE OF HIS CAP AND SKIRT AND THE LIVING QUARTERS OF HIS EXCURSIONS. YANZI REMONSTRATED.

When Duke Jing built the Curved Western Pool, it was so deep that it could submerge a carriage up to its axle. The crossbeams of his three-*ren*-high[1] house were decorated with dragons and snakes, and the vertical bars were decorated with birds and other animals. The Duke wore an upper garment made of colored and embroidered silk, and the material for his skirt was embroidered with white thread. His clothes featured all five colors; his belt was adorned with pearls and jade, and his cap with silk cords.[2]  His hair hung loose from his head to his shoulders. He stood facing south and looked thoroughly arrogant. Yanzi came for an audience.

The Duke said: "In the past, what was Zhongfu's Overlord like?[3]

Yanzi bowed his head and did not answer.

The Duke said again: "In the past, what was Guan Wenzhong's[4] Overlord like?"

Yanzi replied: "I have heard that only the Di people liken themselves

155

---

1  A *ren* 仞, an ancient measure of either five, seven or eight Chinese feet – *chi* 尺. The *Kongcongzi*, 3.4.10.1/4413, has four *chi* for one *ren*.

2  且→组 (*JS*, 137/8).

3  仲父 was one of the several appellations of Guan Yiwu 管夷吾 (720–645 BCE), cognomen Zhong 仲, the famous minister of the State of Qi. His reforms made the State of Qi the most powerful state in the realm and ultimately led Duke Huan 桓公 (d. 643 BCE) to be recognized as the first Overlord of all the princes. See Item 1.9 [9], note 53. For the *Guanzi*'s lengthy discussion of *ba* 霸 ("Overlord") see Allyn W. Rickett, tr. *Guanzi: Political, Economic, and Philosophical Essays from Early China*. Princeton Library of Asian Translations, Princeton (1985): vol. 1, pp. 348-365.

4  管 "文" 仲 → 管 "敬" 仲 (*JS*, 137/10). Obviously, Duke Jing mistakenly interprets Yanzi's silent response as a protest against the Duke's disrespectful reference to Guan Zhong's cognomen ("Zhong") 仲 rather to his posthumous name Jing "敬."

**【原文】**

玉而乱首被发，亦室一容矣，万乘之君，而一心于邪，君之魂魄亡矣，以谁与图霸哉？"公下堂就晏子曰："梁丘据、裔款以室之成告寡人，是以窃袭此服，与据为笑，又使夫子及，寡人请改室易服而敬听命，其可乎？"晏子曰："夫二子营君以邪，公安得知道哉！且伐木不自其根，则蘖又生也，公何不去二子者，毋使耳目淫焉。"

**【今译】**

您一起去建立霸业呢？"景公走下堂靠近晏子说："梁丘据、裔款告诉我这座宫室建好了，因此我私下穿上了这套衣服，和梁丘据等人取笑玩闹，又让您赶上了，请让我改个房间换身衣服再来恭恭敬敬地听您教诲，可以吗？"晏子说："那两个人总是用歪门邪道迷惑您，如此您怎么能懂得称霸诸侯的道理呢！而且砍伐树木如果不从根上着手，那么它还会生出新的枝条，您为何不除掉这二人，不要让您的耳目再被迷惑。"

to dragons and snakes. But now your house's crossbeams, my Lord, are decorated with dragons and snakes and its vertical bars with birds and other animals — all for the sake of completing a single house.[1] How could you have time to serve as an Overlord? Moreover, you brag of the beauty of your palaces and you boast of the elegance of your clothes, with all five colors in one outfit. Your belt is adorned with pearls and jade. Your hair hangs loosely from your head to your shoulders — all for the sake of posing in a single house.[2] You, my Lord, are a ruler of ten thousand chariots, yet you direct all your intentions towards vice, and your ethereal and earthly souls are lost. With whom would you plan to become an Overlord?"

The Duke descended to the hall, approached Yanzi and said: "Liangqiu Ju and Yi Kuan have informed me of the completion of the house and for this reason I have secretly dressed up in these clothes so as to have a laugh with Ju. Then I sent for you to come also. Allow me to remodel the house and change my clothes before I listen respectfully to your instructions. Would that do?"

Yanzi said: "These two gentlemen manipulated you with vice; how would you know the Way? Moreover, if one does not cut a tree from its root, the stump can yield sprouts again. Why don't you simply dismiss these two gentlemen so that your ears and eyes will not be subject to their blandishments?"

---

1 亦室一就矣 → 亦就一室矣 (JS, 137/12).

2 亦室一容矣 → 亦容一室矣 (JS, ibid).

## 2.16 [41] 景公〔为〕巨冠长衣以听朝晏子谏

齐景公做了巨大的帽子长长的衣服并穿戴着它们来上朝，晏子进谏

**【原文】**

景公为巨冠长衣以听朝，疾视矜立，日晏不罢。晏子进曰："圣人之服中，侻而不驵，可以导众，其动作，侻顺而不逆，可以奉生，是以下皆法其服，而民争学其容。今君之服，驵华不可以导众民，疾视矜立，不可以奉生，日晏矣，君不若脱服就燕。"公曰："寡人受命。"退朝，遂去衣冠，不复服。

**【今译】**

齐景公命人做了又高又大的帽子和长长的衣服并穿戴着它们来上朝，他瞪着眼睛做出傲然挺立的样子，天色很晚了还不退朝。晏子进谏说："圣人的衣服应该大小适中，简单而不华美，可以引导百姓，他的举动应该自然得体不违背常理，可以有益健康长寿，因此臣下都学习他的服饰，百姓争着学习他的仪容。现在您的服饰，华美长大不可以引导百姓，您瞪着眼睛站立也不利于健康长寿，天色很晚了，您不如脱掉这身衣服回去休息。"景公说："我接受您的建议。"于是退朝，脱去这套衣冠，再也没有穿过。

## 2.16 [41] DUKE JING COMMISSIONED A HUGE CAP AND A LONG ROBE AND HELD AN AUDIENCE WEARING THEM. YANZI REMONSTRATED.

Duke Jing commissioned a huge cap and a long robe and held an audience wearing them. Standing pompously, he looked around in an angry glare. The audience went on until the evening, without coming to an end.

Yanzi stepped forward and said: "The sages' clothing was modest: their clothes were simple and not showy and were suitable for guiding the multitude. Their actions were light, comfortable and unhindered, and suitable for nurturing life. For this reason, inferiors took these clothes as the style, and the people vied with one another in imitating their appearance. But now your clothes, my Lord, which are showy and colorful, are not suitable for guiding the multitude, and your angry glare and pompous posture are not suitable for nurturing life. It is quite late in the day, my Lord, so the best thing you can do is to take off these clothes and relax."

The Duke said: "I accept your instructions."

He withdrew from the audience and took off both his clothes and hat and never wore them again.

## 2.17 [42] 景公朝居严下不言晏子谏

齐景公在朝堂上太严厉臣下们不敢说话，晏子进谏

【原文】

晏子朝，复于景公曰："朝居严乎？"公曰："（严居朝）〔朝居严〕，则（害曷）〔曷害〕于治国家哉？"晏子对曰："朝居严则下无言，下无言则上无闻矣。下无言，则（无）〔吾〕谓之暗，上无闻，则吾谓之聋。聋暗，非害国家而如何也！且合升（豉）〔斗〕之微以满仓廪，合疏缕之纬以成帏幕，太山之高，非一石也，累卑然后高〔也〕。夫〔治天〕下者，非用一士之言也，固有受而不用，恶有拒而不受者哉？"

【今译】

晏子入朝，向齐景公禀报说："您在朝堂上是不是太严厉了？"景公说："在朝堂上严厉，对国家的治理有什么害处吗？"晏子回答说："在朝堂上太严厉，臣下们就不敢说话，臣下们不说话，国君就得不到汇报了。臣下们不说话，我们称之为哑，国君得不到汇报，我们称之为聋。又聋又哑，不是有害于治理国家又是什么呢！况且只有积累一升一斗的微小粮食才能装满粮仓，只有集合一丝一缕的绨线才能织成帏幕，泰山的高大，并不是只有一块石头，而是无数石头从低处累积然后才高大。治理天下，不是只听一个人的话就行的，当然有时候可以接受汇报而不采用，但哪有拒不接受汇报的呢？"

## 2.17 [42] DUKE JING ACTED STERNLY DURING AN AUDIENCE AND HIS INFERIORS DID NOT SPEAK OUT. YANZI REMONSTRATED.[1]

During a court audience, Yanzi addressed Duke Jing, saying:[2] "Should one act sternly during an audience?"

The Duke said: "If one is stern during an audience, what harm is done to the good governance of the state?"

Yanzi answered: "If an audience is conducted sternly, then inferiors will say nothing and superiors will heed nothing. When inferiors say nothing, I call this 'muteness'; when superiors heed nothing, I call this 'deafness.' If deafness and muteness do not constitute a danger to the state, what does? Furthermore, by accumulating grain in minute quantities of *sheng* and *dou*,[3] one can fill the public granaries; by collecting loose threads, one can form a curtain. The height of Mt. Tai was not made of a single rock; low layers were piled up until it became high. As for those who govern the realm, they do not rule by using the words of just one officer. Surely, there are cases of receiving without employing; but how could there be cases of rejecting without receiving?"

---

1   Item 2.17 [42] ↔ *Shuoyuan*, 9.26/76/13.

2   Omit 朝 following the *Shuoyuan* version.

3   A *sheng* 升 was 199.7 cubic centimeters. Ten *sheng* made one *dou* 斗.

## 2.18 [43] 景公登路寝台不终不悦晏子谏

齐景公攀登路寝台不能到达终点不高兴，晏子进谏

### 【原文】

景公登路寝之台，不能终，而息乎陛，忿然而作色，不说，曰："孰为高台？病人之甚也！"晏子曰："君欲节于身而勿高，使人高之而勿罪也。今高，从之以罪，卑亦从以罪，敢问使人如此可乎？古者之为宫室也，足以便生，不以为奢侈也，故节于身，（谓）〔调〕于民。及夏之衰也，其王桀背弃德行，〔作〕为璇室玉门。殷之衰也，其王纣作为倾宫灵台，卑狭者有罪，高大者有赏，是以身及焉。今君高亦有

### 【今译】

齐景公攀登路寝的高台，不能到达终点，中途在台阶上休息，他生气地变了脸色，不高兴地说："谁修建的高台？把人坑害的不浅啊！"晏子说："您要想节省体力就不要把它修这么高，既然让人把它修这么高就不要怪罪。现在修的高了有罪，修的低了也有罪，敢问有这样役使别人的吗？古时候修建宫室，是为了便于生活，不是为了奢侈享乐，因此自身节俭，百姓也受到教育。等到夏朝衰败的时候，它的王桀背弃了圣人的德行，建造了美玉装饰的宫室，白玉雕砌的大门。商朝衰败的时候，它的王纣建造了巍峨的宫殿和精美的台阁，修的低小的有罪，修的高大的有赏，因此灾祸殃及自身。现在您命人修台，

## 2.18 [43] DUKE JING ASCENDED THE TERRACE OVER THE ROAD BEDCHAMBER BUT COULD NOT REACH ITS TOP. HE WAS DISPLEASED AND YANZI REMONSTRATED.

Duke Jing ascended the terrace over the Road Bedchamber, and, unable to reach the top, he rested on the steps. The Duke was displeased and flushed with anger. He said: "Who built such a high terrace? It is extremely exhausting."

Yanzi said: "If you, my Lord, wanted this to be modest for your purposes, you would have not let it be built so high; but since you had people build it high, you should not blame them for it. But now, since it is high, you pursue them in blame; and if it were low, you would blame them also — I presume to ask, is it proper to employ people under such circumstances? In ancient times, the purpose of building palaces was to make life comfortable, rather than to demonstrate extravagance. Thus, we see that the ancients were thrifty themselves and taught[1] the people to act the same. But when the Xia declined and its King Jie turned his back on virtuous conduct, he built houses of precious stones and gates of jade. With the decline of the Yin, King Zhou built the Towering-Leaning Palace[2] and the Sacred Terrace. Those who built low and narrow structures were found guilty, and those who built high and large structures were rewarded. Therefore, disaster struck them. But now you, my Lord, blame both those who build high and those who build low; this is worse than the example of the kings of the Xia and Yin. The strength of the people is completely exhausted, and still they cannot evade blame. I am afraid that our state will

163

---

1   谓 → 诲 following *Mozi*, 1.6/6/24, which reads: 节于身诲于民.

2   The present "Towering-Leaning Palace" should not be confused with the "Towering-Leaning Palace" built by King Ling of Chu, mentioned in Item 2.7 [57].

**【原文】**

罪，卑亦有罪，甚于夏、殷之王；民力殚乏矣，而不免于罪，婴恐国之流失，而公不得亨也！"公曰："善！寡人自知诚费财劳民，以为无功，又从而怨之，是寡人之罪也！非夫子之教，岂得守社稷哉！"遂下，再拜，不果登台。

**【今译】**

修高了有罪，修低了也有罪，比桀、纣二王还要严苛；民力已经耗尽，还免不了受罚，我担心百姓离散，您就再也不能享乐了！"景公说："好！我自知这实在是劳民伤财又没有什么用处，又因此怪罪筑台的人，这是我的罪过！如果不是您的教诲，我又怎么能守住国家呢！"于是走下台来，向晏子拜了两拜，没有登上台顶。

be swept away and lost and you will not be able to enjoy the pleasures[1] of rule."

The Duke said: "Well argued. I myself know that I really wasted a great deal of resources and overworked the people. I considered the people to be of no merit and, furthermore, I resented them. This is my fault. How could I protect the altars of soil and grain without your instructions, Master?"

Thereupon he descended, bowed twice, and did not act upon his desire to ascend the terrace.

---

1   亨 → 享 (*YZCQ-ICS*, 17, n. 7).

## 2.19 [44] 景公登路寝台望国而（欢）〔叹〕晏子谏

齐景公攀登路寝台眺望国都而悲叹，晏子进谏

### 【原文】

　　景公与晏子登寝而望国，公愀然而（欢）〔叹〕曰："使后嗣世世有此，岂不可哉！"晏子曰："臣闻明君必务正其治，以事利民，然后子孙享之。《诗》云：'武王岂不事，贻厥孙谋，以燕翼子。'今君处佚怠，逆政害民有日矣，而犹出若言，不亦甚乎！"公曰："然则后世孰将把齐国？"对曰："服牛死，夫妇（笑）〔哭〕，非骨肉之亲也，为其利之大也。欲知把齐国者，则其利之者邪？"公曰："然，何以易〔之〕？"对曰："移之以善政。今公之牛马老于栏牢，不胜服也；车蠹于巨户，

### 【今译】

　　齐景公和晏子一起登上路寝台眺望国都，景公悲怆地叹息道："让后世子孙世代保有这个国家，难道不可以吗！"晏子说："我听闻贤明的国君一定致力于摆正他的治国理念，做有利于百姓的事，然后子孙后代才能安享国家。《诗经》中说：'武王怎么能不做（有利于百姓的）事呢，他为子孙的将来做好了安排，并庇佑保护他们。'现在您安逸怠惰，倒行逆施，侵害百姓已经很长时间了，还能说出这样的话来，这不是太过分了吗！"景公说："既然这样，那么后世谁将执掌齐国呢？"晏子说："拉车的牛死了，主人夫妇伤心地哭泣，这并不是因为他们跟牛之间有骨肉之亲，而是因为牛给他们带来的利益太大了。

## 2.19 [44] DUKE JING ASCENDED THE TERRACE OVER THE ROAD BEDCHAMBER. HE LOOKED OVER THE CAPITAL AND SIGHED. YANZI REMONSTRATED.

Duke Jing climbed the terrace over the Road Bedchamber[1] together with Yanzi and surveyed his capital. The Duke sighed sadly and said: "Oh, if only every generation of my descendants could possess this how could this not be proper?"

Yanzi said: "I have heard that the enlightened ruler must strive to rectify his governance so that his acts will benefit the people. Only then may his sons and grandsons enjoy it. As it says in the *Odes*:

Did King Wu not work?

He handed down his plans to his grandsons,

To bring peace and security to his sons.[2]

But now you, my Lord, indulge in idle pleasures, and your perverse policies have harmed the people for quite some time; yet you still express yourself in such words — is this not excessive?"

The Duke said: "If so, then who will hold power in the state of Qi in later generations?"

Yanzi answered: "When a yoked ox dies, then the owner and his wife weep, not because it was their own flesh-and-bone relative, but because it brought them great benefits. If you now want to know who will hold power in the state of Qi, will it not be the one who brings it benefit?"

The Duke said: "Agreed. How can I change all this?"

Yanzi answered: "You can avert all this by means of good governance. Now, my Lord, your cattle and horses have become old in the animal

---

1   Add 路 before 寝 (*JS*, 146/2).

2   The *Shijing*, 244/123/29, reads 仕 instead of 事 and 诒 instead of 贻.

大中华文库

## 【原文】

不胜乘也；衣裘襦袴，朽弊于藏，不胜衣也；醓醢腐，不胜沽也；酒醴酸，不胜饮也；府粟郁，而不胜食。又厚藉敛于百姓，而不以分馁民。夫藏财而不用，凶也，财苟失守，下其报环至。其次昧财之失守，委而不以分人者，百姓必进自分也。故君人者与其请于人，不如（于请）〔请于〕己也。"

## 【今译】

您想知道将来执掌齐国的人，那么应该就是给齐国人带来利益最大的人吧！"景公说："既然这样，有什么办法能改变这种局面呢？"晏子说："用好的政策来改变。现在您的牛马在圈里关老了，不能拉车；您的车子在车库中生了蠹虫，不能乘坐；您的皮衣皮袄在藏衣柜中朽坏了，不能再穿；肉酱腐烂了，不能再卖；美酒放酸了，不能再喝；仓库中的粮食堆的发了霉，不能再吃。可您还加重赋税，对百姓横征暴敛，而不肯把聚敛的财物分发给贫穷饥饿的人。储藏财物而不使用，是不吉利的，这些财物一旦失去，随后而来的报复行动就会连续不断。再说暗藏的财物守不住，丢弃了而不分给别人，那么百姓一定会自己前来把它分掉。因此做国君的人与其求助于别人，不如求助于自己。"

enclosures and cannot be yoked; the carriages behind the huge doors are eaten by worms and cannot be used for driving; items of clothing, furs, jackets and trousers decay in the storehouses and cannot be worn; vinegar and meat sauce spoil and cannot be sold; wine and fine liquor turn into vinegar and cannot be drunk; the grain in your store house becomes moldy and cannot be eaten. Furthermore, you heavily tax the people and do not share any of the gains with the starving. Accumulating goods and making no use out of them is disastrous. If indeed one fails to safeguard these accumulated goods, then one will be targeted by the inferiors' revenge. Worse, if one is unaware that one has failed to safeguard the goods, and the goods lie about without being distributed among the people, then people will certainly take the initiative and distribute these goods by themselves. Therefore, nothing is better for the ruler of the people than to make demands on himself rather than on the people."

169

## 2.20 [45] 景公路寝台成逢于何愿合葬晏子谏而许

齐景公修成路寝台，逢于何希望父母合葬，晏子进谏而被准许

### 【原文】

景公成路寝之台，逢于何遭丧，遇晏子于途，再拜乎马前。晏子下车挹之，曰："子何以命婴也？"对曰："于何之母死，兆在路寝之台牖下，愿请命合骨。"晏子曰："嘻！难哉！虽然，婴将为子复之，适为不得，子将若何？"对曰："夫君子则有以，如我者侪小人，吾将左手拥格，右手栖心，立饿枯槁而死，以告四方之士曰：'于何不能葬其母者也。'"晏子曰："诺。"遂入见公，曰："有逢于何者，母死，兆在

### 【今译】

齐景公命人修好了路寝台，有个叫逢于何的人遇上了丧事，他在路上遇到晏子，在马前拜了两拜。晏子下车作揖还礼，问道："您有什么事情让我去做吗？"逢于何回答说："我的母亲去世了，墓穴在路寝台的墙下面，我请求将父亲母亲合葬。"晏子说："唉！难啊！即便如此，我仍然要替您向国君禀报，如果偏巧得不到同意，您将怎么办呢？"逢于何回答说："君子总会有办法的，像我这样的普通百姓，只能左手扶着灵车，右手捶着胸口，站在那里饥饿枯槁而死，用这种方式告诉天下人说：'逢于何是不能埋葬母亲的人。'"晏子说："知道了。"于是进宫去见景公，说："有一个叫逢于何的人，他的母亲去世了，墓穴在路寝台的墙下面，他请求将父亲和母亲合葬。这件事应该怎么处理？"景公听后变了脸色，不高兴地说："从古至今，您听

## 2.20 [45] DUKE JING COMPLETED THE TERRACE OVER THE ROAD BEDCHAMBER. PENG YUHE WISHED TO BURY HIS PARENTS TOGETHER. YANZI REMONSTRATED AND PERMISSION WAS GRANTED. [1]

Duke Jing completed the terrace over the Road Bedchamber. Peng Yuhe, [2] who was experiencing the loss of a loved one, met Yanzi on the road and bowed twice in front of his horses. Yanzi stepped down from his carriage, folded his hands in salute, and said: "What is it that you command me to do, Sir?"

Peng Yuhe replied: "My mother died and the gravesite is below the wall [3] of the terrace over the Road Bedchamber. I would like to ask the Duke to issue an order allowing me to mingle her bones with those of my father."

Yanzi said: "Oh! That is very difficult! Even so, I will report the matter to him for you. And if, by chance, you are not granted permission, what would you do?"

Peng Yuhe answered: "A man of noble character would have the means to act; a man like myself is merely a person of no account. I would hold the cross-pole of the hearse with my left hand and beat upon my heart with my right hand, stand and starve until I withered and died, in order to make it clear to the officers of all four quarters: 'Yuhe is a person who was unable to bury his mother.'"

Yanzi said: "Very well." Thereupon, he went to his audience with the Duke and said: "There is a man named Peng Yuhe; his mother died and her gravesite is situated below the wall of the Road Bedchamber. I would like to ask for your permission to let him mingle the bones."

171

---

1   Item 2.20 [45] ↔ Item 7.11 [181].

2   An unidentified figure.

3   牖 → 墉 (*JS*, 150/5).

**【原文】**

路寝，当（如之何）〔牖下〕？愿请合骨。"公作色不说，曰："〔自〕古（之）及今，子亦尝闻请葬人主之宫者乎？"晏子对曰："古之人君，其（室宫）〔宫室〕节，不侵生（民）〔人〕之居，〔其〕台榭俭，不残死人之墓，故未尝闻诸请葬人主之宫者也。今君侈为宫室，夺人之居，广为台榭，残人之墓，是生者悉忧，不得安处，死者离易，不得合骨。

**【今译】**

说过请求把死人埋葬在君主宫殿中的事吗？"晏子回答说："古时候的君王，他们的宫室很狭小，不侵占百姓的居所，他们的台榭很朴素，不破坏死人的坟墓，所以没有听说过请求把死人埋葬在君主宫殿中的事。现在您修建奢华的宫殿，侵夺了百姓的居所，大量修筑亭台廊榭，破坏了死人的坟墓，这就使得活着的人忧愁，没有地方安居，死了的人分离，得不到合葬。纵情享乐游玩，对活人和死人都傲慢轻视，这不是君王的行为。只顾满足自己的欲望和要求，不顾百姓，这不是保存国家的方法。而且我听说，让活人得不到安居，叫作积蓄忧愁；让死人得不到安葬，叫作积蓄哀痛。积蓄忧愁导致怨恨，积蓄哀痛导致危亡，您不如答应他的要求。"景公说："好吧。"晏子出去后，梁丘

The Duke's facial expression revealed his displeasure and he said: "From antiquity until today, have you ever heard of anyone asking to conduct a burial on the grounds of the sovereign's palace?"

Yanzi answered: "The palaces and the halls of the rulers of ancient times were modest and did not encroach upon the dwellings of the people living in them.[1] Their terraces and terrace-halls were modest and did not harm the tombs of the dead. That is why no one has ever heard of someone asking to be allowed to conduct a burial in the grounds of the palace of the sovereign. But now you, my Lord, are building palaces and halls extravagantly, and you rob the people of their dwellings. You build terraces and terrace-halls on a grand scale and destroy the tombs of the people. The living are aggrieved and worried and cannot live in peace, while the dead are separated from each other and their bones cannot be mingled. An excess of pleasure and extravagant excursions and showing haughty disregard for the living and the dead alike are not a ruler's proper conduct. Following one's desires and satisfying one's own demands without caring for the common people is not the way to survive. Furthermore, I have heard that if the living cannot obtain peace of mind, this is called 'accumulating sorrow.' If the dead cannot be buried, this is called 'accumulating grief.' He who accumulates sorrow will inspire resentment; he who accumulates grief will be in peril. My Lord, it would be better to permit his request."

The Duke said: "Very well." After Yanzi went out, Liangqiu Ju said: "From antiquity until the present day, I have never heard of anyone asking to conduct a burial in the grounds of the palace of his Duke. Why did you permit it?"

The Duke said: "Cutting off the dwellings of the people and destroying their tombs, humiliating people in mourning and preventing burials means not granting favors to the living and not performing the rites for the dead.

---

1   For an identical view of the way the ancients built their dwelling houses, see *Mozi*, 1.6/20-27.

**【原文】**

丰乐侈游，兼傲生死，非人君之行也。遂欲满求，不顾细民，非存之道〔也〕。且婴闻之，生者不得安，命之曰蓄忧；死者不得葬，命之曰蓄哀。蓄忧者怨，蓄哀者危，君不如（详）〔许〕之。"公曰："诺。"晏子出，梁丘据曰："自古及今，未尝闻求葬公宫者也，若何许之？"公曰："削人之居，残人之墓，凌人之丧，而禁其葬，是于生者〔无〕施，于死者无礼。《诗》云：'谷则异室，死则同穴。'吾敢不许乎？"逢于何遂葬其母路寝之牖下，解衰去绖，布衣縢履，玄冠芒武，踊而不哭，躃而不拜，已乃涕洟而去。

**【今译】**

据说："从古至今，没听说过请求把死人埋在国君宫里的，您为什么要答应呢？"景公说："削夺百姓的居所，破坏百姓的坟墓，侵犯百姓的丧事，而又禁止他合葬父母，这样做对生者是没有施恩，对死者是无礼。《诗经》里说：'活着的时候不能住在一起，死去之后也要葬在一起。'我怎么能不答应呢？"逢于何于是就把他的母亲葬在路寝台的墙下，他解下丧服，穿上布衣藤鞋，戴上黑色的帽子，紫草结带，极为哀伤但没有痛哭，扑倒在地而没有下拜，葬礼结束之后才流着眼泪离开。

As it says in the *Odes*:

> 'During their lifetime they lived in separated chambers,
>
> But in death they were buried in the same grave.' [1]

How would I presume not to permit this?" Thereupon, Peng Yuhe buried his mother under the wall of the Road Bedchamber. He took off his mourning garment and removed the mourning band.  He clad himself in plain clothes and wore straw sandals and a dark hat with white ribbons. Then, without weeping, he stamped on the ground and beat his breast without bowing. When he had finished with this, he burst into tears and left.

---

1   *Shijing*, 73/33/28.

## 2.21 [46] 景公嬖妾死守之三日不敛晏子谏

齐景公的嬖妾去世，景公守了三天不收敛，晏子进谏

### 【原文】

景公之嬖妾婴子死，公守之，三日不食，肤著于席不去。左右以复，而君无听焉。晏子入，复曰："有术客与医俱言曰：'闻婴子病死，愿请治之。'"公喜，遽起曰："病犹可为乎？"晏子曰："客之道也，以为良医也，请尝试之。君请屏洁，沐浴饮食，间病者之宫，彼亦将有鬼神之事焉。"公曰："诺。"屏而沐浴。晏子令棺人入敛，已敛，而复曰："医不能治病，已敛矣，不敢不以闻。"公作色不说，曰："夫子

### 【今译】

齐景公的爱妾婴子去世了，景公守着尸体，三天没有进食，皮肤沾到席子也不离开。左右的人劝说，但景公不听。晏子来见景公，禀报说："有懂巫术的外来人和医生都说：'听闻婴子病死了，请让我们来救治她。'"景公很高兴，赶忙站起来说："病死的人还能救治吗？"晏子说："外来人懂得巫术，自认为是不错的医生，请求试一试。请您回避一下，沐浴更衣，吃些食物，远离婴子的房间，他们可能会进行祭祀鬼神的活动。"景公说："好。"于是离开这里去沐浴更衣。晏子命令负责丧葬的人把婴子的尸体入殓，装殓好之后，向景公回禀说："医生不能治疗婴子的病，已经入殓了，不敢不把这件事告诉您。"景公变了脸色，不高兴地说："您用医治她为借口让我离开，不让我看，将要

## 2.21 [46] DUKE JING'S FAVORITE CONCUBINE DIED. HE HELD A VIGIL OVER HER BODY FOR THREE DAYS WITHOUT PUTTING HER IN A COFFIN. YANZI REMONSTRATED.

Yingzi, a favorite concubine of Duke Jing, died. The Duke held vigil over her body and did not eat for three days. Her skin stuck to the mat but he did not leave. The Duke's entourage tried to bring the situation to his awareness, but he would not listen to them. Yanzi entered the court and reported: "There is a master of supernatural skills[1] and a physician and they both say: 'We have heard that Yingzi died from an illness and we would like to ask permission to remedy her.'"

The Duke rejoiced; he got up immediately and said: "Can anything still be done about this illness?"

Yanzi said: "I consider the method of these two to be good medicine; please try it. I ask you, my Lord, to separate yourself from her body and to purify yourself by bathing. Drink and eat and keep a distance from the palace where the infirmity is present because there will surely be some interaction of spirits and demons there."

The Duke said, "Very well." He separated himself from her body and bathed. Yanzi ordered the coffin attendants to put her into a coffin. After she had been put into the coffin, Yanzi reported to the Duke: "The physician was not able to treat her illness and she has already been put into a coffin. I dare not conceal this from you."

The Duke's facial expression revealed his displeasure and he said: "You, Master, gave me instructions based on medical arguments and did not let me observe the administrations. When you were about to put her into a coffin you did not let me know about it. I am a ruler in name only."

177

---

1  术客 → 客有术者 (*JS*, 156/4).

【原文】

以医命寡人，而不使视，将敛而不以闻，吾之为君，名而已矣。"晏子曰："君独不知死者之不可以生邪？婴闻之，君正臣从谓之顺，君僻臣从谓之逆。今君不道顺而行僻，从逆者迩，（导害）〔道善〕者远，谗谀萌通，而贤良废灭，是以（谄）〔诌〕谀繁于（间）〔闾〕，邪行交于国也。昔吾先君桓公用管仲而霸，嬖乎竖刁而灭，今君薄于贤人之礼，

【今译】

入殓的时候也不告诉我，我当国君，只不过虚有其名而已。"晏子说："您难道不懂得死去的人不可以再复活的道理吗？我听说，国君行为端正臣子服从叫作顺，国君行为邪僻臣子服从叫作逆。现在您不行正道而行邪僻，跟着您行邪僻的您就亲近，劝导您向善的您就疏远，谗佞阿谀泛滥流行，贤良正直废弃消失，因此谗佞阿谀之人充斥闾巷，行为奸邪的人遍布京城。以前我们先代的国君桓公任用管仲而称霸诸侯，宠信竖刁就身死国衰，现在您对待贤臣礼敬不够，对待侍妾之死却过于哀伤。况且古时候的圣王蓄养私宠而不损伤德行，人死即敛而不有损宠爱，送别死者而不过度哀伤。德行损伤就会沉溺于私欲，宠爱失度就会损伤身体，哀伤过度就会损伤性情。因此圣王对这些都很节制。人死了就埋葬，不应停留太久给活着的人增加事端，棺材衣物应该适

Yanzi said: "My Lord, do you of all people not know that the dead cannot be revived? I have heard that if the ruler is upright and his ministers follow his example, it is called 'obedient.' If the ruler is aberrant and the ministers follow his example, it is called 'defiant.' But now you, my Lord, do not lead your ministers to be obedient and your conduct is aberrant. Those who walk in the ways of evil are close to you and those who are guided by the good keep their distance. Slanderers and flatterers sprout up; the worthy and the good are dismissed and perish. For that reason, the slanderers and flatterers flourish within your gates, and evil men go to and fro within the capital. In the past, our former ruler Duke Huan employed Guan Zhong and became overlord. But when he favored Shu Diao, he perished. But now you, my Lord, pay meager attention to the rites of the worthy and lavish attention to mourning for a favored concubine. Furthermore, the ancient sage-kings had wives and concubines, but this did not harm their behavior;[1] they put the dead in coffins without diminishing their love, and they escorted their dead without diminishing their grief. When conduct is harmed, one sinks into self-indulgence; when love diminishes, life is harmed; and when grief diminishes, the inborn nature is impaired. Therefore, the sage-kings moderated their mourning. If someone died, they would put him immediately into a coffin, so that the life of the people was not disturbed. The costs of inner coffin, outer coffin, shrouds, and winding sheets did not interfere with the support of life.[2] Weeping and

---

1  The *Mozi*, 1.6/8/8, expresses an identical view of the way the ancient kings understood the interplay between their intimate life and public conduct.

2  The rabbinical masters make a similar statement in BT *Ketubot* 8b, noting that the funeral of the dead person was harder for relatives to bear than his death itself, because of the great expense of the costly garments for the dead. The relatives therefore used to run away from the funeral, leaving the dead person lying on the ground, until the rule of Rabban Gamaliel II of Yavne (2nd century CE) was adopted at his own funeral and he was carried out for burial in garments of linen alone. Then all the people followed his example and carried out the dead in such garments.

## 【原文】

而厚嬖妾之哀。且古圣王畜私不伤行，敛死不失爱，送死不失哀。行（荡）〔伤〕则溺己，爱失则伤生，〔哀〕失则害性。是故圣王节之也。〔死〕即毕葬，不留生事，棺椁衣衾，不以害生（养）〔养〕，哭泣处哀，不以害生道。今朽尸以留生，广爱以伤行，（修）〔循〕哀以害性，君之失矣。故诸侯之宾客惭入吾国，本朝之臣惭守其职，崇君之行，不可以导民；从君之欲，不可以持国。且婴闻之，朽而不敛，谓之僇尸，臭而不〔收〕，谓之陈胔。反明王之性，行百姓之诽，而内嬖妾于僇胔，此之为不可。"公曰："寡人不识，请因夫子而为之。"晏子复〔曰〕："国之士大夫，诸侯四邻宾客皆在外，君其哭而节之。"仲尼闻之曰："星之昭昭，不若月之曀曀，小事之成，不若大事之废，君子之非，贤于小人之是也。其晏子之谓欤！"

## 【今译】

度，不要因此损耗活人的供养之资，哭泣表达哀伤，不要过分悲痛妨害生存之理。现在腐朽的尸体还留给活着的人服侍，太多的私情损伤自己的德行，无休止的哀伤损害自己的性情，这是您的过失！因此诸侯国的使节羞于来到我国，本国的臣子也耻于安守本职，推崇您的行为，不可以教导百姓；顺从您的欲望，也不可以执掌国家。而且我听说，尸体腐朽而不收敛，叫作僇尸（侮辱尸体），尸体发臭而不收敛，叫作陈胔（陈列腐肉）。您违反圣王的原则，做百姓非议的事情，把爱妾纳入腐尸烂肉的行列，这样做是不行的。"景公说："我没什么见识，就按您说的去办吧。"晏子又说："本国的士大夫和相邻诸侯国的使节都在外边等着举行丧礼，您哭的时候要节哀啊。"孔子听说后说："闪烁的星辰亮不过被云遮住的月亮，小事的成功比不上大事的失误，君子的过错，好过小人的正确。这大概说的就是晏子吧！"

engaging in mourning were not used to harm the way of the living. But now you let the corpse decay and you disturb the life of the living. Your exaggerated love has impaired your behavior and your prolonged grief has harmed your inborn nature. My Lord, this is your failure. Therefore, foreign visitors sent by the regional princes are ashamed to enter our state, and the ministers of your own court are ashamed to retain their positions. One cannot guide the people based on respect for conduct such as yours, my Lord, and one cannot control the state, my Lord, by granting free reign to one's desires. Further, I have heard that not putting a decayed corpse into a coffin is called 'humiliating a corpse.' If the corpse already stinks and has not been encoffined, it is called 'exhibiting a decomposing corpse.' Acting contrary to the inborn nature of the enlightened kings and practicing what people scorn — letting a favorite concubine's decomposing corpse lie in court in a humiliating fashion — is unacceptable."

The Duke said: "I did not realize this. I request to be allowed to act in accordance with your instructions."

Yanzi responded: "The officers and the high officers of the state as well as delegates of all the neighboring states' sovereigns are all waiting outside. My Lord, you may weep, but with moderation."

When Confucius heard of this, he said: "The brightness of the stars is not yet as intense as the shadowy light of the moon. Accomplishment of insignificant undertakings cannot be compared to failure in great matters. The wrong acts[1] of a man of noble character are worthier than the correct acts of a petty man. Does this not refer to Yanzi?"

---

1   These "wrong acts" refer to Yanzi's success in placing Yingzi's body in coffin by tricking his Duke into believing that she could be resurrected.

## 2.22 [47] 景公欲厚葬梁丘据晏子谏

齐景公打算厚葬梁丘据，晏子进谏

### 【原文】

梁丘据死，景公召晏子而告之，曰："据忠且爱我，我欲丰厚其葬，高大其垄。"晏子曰："敢问据之忠与爱于君者，可得闻乎？"公曰："吾有喜于玩好，有司未能我共也，则据以其所有共我，〔吾〕是以知其忠也；每有风雨，暮夜求〔之〕必存，吾是以知其爱也。"晏子曰："婴对则为罪，不对则无以事君，敢不对乎！婴闻之，臣专其君，谓之不忠；子专其父，谓之不孝；妻专其夫，谓之（不）嫉。事（父）〔君〕之道，导亲于父兄，有礼于群臣，有惠于百姓，有信于诸侯，谓之忠；为子之道，以钟爱其兄弟，施行于诸父，慈惠于众子，诚信于朋友，

### 【今译】

梁丘据去世了，齐景公召见晏子，告诉他说："梁丘据忠诚而且爱戴我，我打算隆重地安葬他，把他的坟墓修的高大气派。"晏子说："请问梁丘据对您忠诚和爱戴的表现，可以让我听听吗？"景公说："我喜欢玩赏的东西，主管的官员不能给我提供的，梁丘据就把他自己的拿来供奉给我，所以我知道他对我的忠诚；或者刮风下雨的夜晚我召见他，他一定会来，所以我知道他爱戴我。"晏子说："我回答就会得罪您，不回答又是没有侍奉好国君，怎么敢不回答呢！我听说，臣子集中全部精力侍奉君王，叫作不忠；儿子集中全部精力侍奉父亲，叫作不孝；妻子集中全部精力侍奉丈夫，叫作嫉妒。侍奉君王的原则，是要引导君王和父兄亲近，对群臣有礼，对百姓施以恩惠，对诸侯有信

## 2.22 [47] DUKE JING WANTED TO BURY LIANGQIU JU LAVISHLY. YANZI REMONSTRATED.

Liangqiu Ju died. Duke Jing summoned Yanzi and informed him about it, saying: "Ju was bound to me by ties of loyalty and affection. Therefore, I want to give him a rich burial and make his grave mound enormous."

Yanzi said: "Dare I, my Lord, ask about Ju's loyalty and love for his ruler? May I hear about it?"

The Duke said: "When there were fine things and precious objects that I fancied and the office in charge of these objects was not able to provide me with them, then Ju provided me with them out of his own resources. In this I recognized his loyalty. Every time I sought him, whether it was stormy or late at night, he surely stayed by my side. In this I recognized his love."

Yanzi said: "If I reply to this, I will commit an offence. If I do not reply, I will have nothing with which to serve my ruler. How dare I not reply? I have heard that if a minister monopolizes his ruler, he is called 'disloyal.' If a son monopolizes his father, he is called 'unfilial.' If a wife monopolizes her husband, she is called 'jealous.' The way to serve a ruler is to direct him to uphold close relations with his father and elder brothers, to deal with his various ministers according to the rites, and to show generosity toward the people and good faith toward the regional princes. This is called 'loyalty.' The way to be a son is to love one's brothers unstintingly, to manifest good conduct among all one's uncles, and to have a merciful and generous attitude toward all of one's sons and a sincere and faithful attitude toward one's friends. This is called 'filial piety.' The way to be a wife is to let all the concubines take pleasure in one's husband. This is called 'a lack of jealousy.' Now, all people within the four borders are your subjects, yet only Ju loved you with all his might. Why, then, do so few people love you? All the goods within the four borders belong to you, my Lord, and

**【原文】**

谓之孝；为妻之道，使其众妾皆得欢忻于其夫，谓之不嫉。今四封之民，皆君之臣也，而维据尽力以爱君，〔何爱者之少邪〕？〔四封之货〕，〔皆君之有也〕，〔而维据也以其私财忠于君〕，〔何忠者之寡邪〕？〔据之防塞群臣〕，〔雍蔽君〕，〔无乃甚乎〕？"〔公曰〕："〔善哉〕！〔微子〕，〔寡人不知据之至于是也〕。"〔遂罢为垒之役〕，〔废厚葬之令〕，〔令有司据法而责〕，〔群臣陈过而谏〕。〔故官无废法〕，〔臣无隐忠〕，〔而百姓大说〕。

**【今译】**

誉，这才叫忠诚。做儿子的原则，是要劝导父亲钟爱兄弟，对伯父、叔父施以善行，对所有儿子施以仁爱，对朋友忠诚守信，这才叫孝顺；做妻子的原则，是要让众侍妾都能得到丈夫的欢心，这才叫不嫉妒。现在四方疆域内的百姓，都是您的臣民，而只有梁丘据竭尽全力来爱戴您，为什么爱戴您的人这么少呢？四方疆域内的财货，都归您所有，而只有梁丘据用他的私财来表达对您的忠诚，为什么忠诚的人这么少呢？梁丘据防范群臣、堵塞言路，蒙蔽国君，是不是太严重了呢？"景公说："对啊！如果不是您这番话，我还不知道梁丘据已经坏到这种地步了。"于是罢去了修造坟墓的劳役，废除了厚葬的命令，下令有关部门根据法律来明确职责，群臣陈述君王的过失而进谏。因此朝廷没有无用的法律，群臣没有隐没的忠诚，百姓们极为高兴。

only Ju expressed his loyalty to you with all his personal means; why are so few people loyal to you? In blocking the access of all ministers to you and screening you off, was Ju not going too far?"

The Duke said: "Well argued! Without you, sir, I would have never known how far things had gone with Ju." Thereupon, he rescinded the call for conscript labor to make the grave's mound, and withdrew his order for a lavish burial. He ordered the relevant officers to censure misbehavior in accordance with the law. He ordered the ministers to point out faults and remonstrate with him. As a result, no laws were disregarded in the administration, ministers had no hidden loyalties, and the people were extremely content.

## 2.23 [48] 景公欲以人礼葬走狗晏子谏

齐景公打算用人的礼节安葬猎狗，晏子进谏

**【原文】**

　　景公走狗死，公令外共之棺，内给之祭。晏子闻之，谏。公曰："亦细物也，特以与左右为笑耳。"晏子曰："君过矣！夫厚藉敛不以反民，弃货财而笑左右，傲细民之忧，而崇左右之笑，则国亦无望已。且夫孤老冻馁，而死狗有祭，鳏寡不恤，而死狗有棺，行辟若此，百姓闻之，必怨吾君，诸侯闻之，必轻吾国。怨聚于百姓，而权轻于诸侯，而乃以为细物，君其图之。"公曰："善。"趣庖治狗，以会朝属。

**【今译】**

　　齐景公的猎狗死了，景公下令在宫外给它准备棺材，在宫内给它准备祭品。晏子听说后，前来进谏。景公说："这只不过是一件小事，特意拿来和身边的人取乐的。"晏子说："您错了！加重赋税聚敛财富而不回馈百姓，舍弃财物而与身边的人取笑为乐，轻视百姓的忧愁，重视近臣的玩乐，那么国家就没什么希望了。况且孤儿老人受冷受饿，而死狗却享有祭祀，鳏夫寡妇不知抚恤，而死狗却拥有棺材，行为邪僻到这个样子，百姓听说的话，一定会怨恨您，诸侯听说的话，一定会轻视我们的国家。百姓聚积怨恨，诸侯轻视国家，却认为是小事，请您好好考虑吧。"景公说："好。"于是命令厨师杀狗烹肉，用来会宴群臣。

## 2.23 [48] DUKE JING WANTED TO BURY HIS HOUND IN ACCORDANCE WITH HUMAN RITES. YANZI REMONSTRATED.

One of Duke Jing's hunting hounds died. The Duke ordered that a coffin to be supplied for it from outside the court and a sacrifice be made for it within the court. Yanzi heard of this and remonstrated.

The Duke said: "This is only an insignificant matter. I merely wanted to use this occasion to amuse my entourage."

Yanzi said: "You, my Lord, are wrong. If one taxes lavishly and returns none of the revenue to the people, if one wastes property and goods in order to amuse one's entourage, if one arrogantly disregards the worries of the common people and values highly the laughter of one's entourage, then there will surely be no hope for one's state. Furthermore, when orphans and the elderly freeze and starve, yet sacrifice is made to a dead dog; and widowers and widows are not treated with compassion, but dead dogs receive a coffin — if such perverse conduct becomes known to the people, they will certainly feel resentment towards you, my Lord; and if the regional princes hear of it, they certainly will think little of our state. When the resentments accumulate among the people and the regional princes take lightly your authority, yet you still regard this as an insignificant matter — you should give it your careful consideration, my Lord."

The Duke said: "Well argued." Then he urged the cook to prepare the dog and with this dish he met his ministers in a court audience.[1]

---

1  For a completely different, sentimental attitude towards the death of a one's dog, see *Liji*, 4.65/29/23, where Confucius instructs Zigong regarding the proper way to bury Confucius' own pet dog.

## 2.24 [49] 景公养勇士三人无君臣之义晏子谏

齐景公豢养的三个勇士没有君臣之义，晏子进谏

**【原文】**

　　公孙接、田开疆、古冶子事景公，以勇力搏虎闻。晏子过而趋，三子者不起，晏子入见公曰："臣闻明君之蓄勇力之士也，上有君臣之义，下有长率之伦，内可以禁暴，外可以威敌，上利其功，下服其勇，故尊其位，重其禄。今君之蓄勇（士）〔力〕之（力）〔士〕也，上无君臣之义，下无长率之伦，内不〔可〕以禁暴，外不可〔以〕威敌，此危国之器也，不若去之。"公曰："三子者，搏之恐不得，刺之恐不中也。"晏子曰："此皆力攻勍敌之人也，无长幼之礼。"因请公使人少馈

**【今译】**

　　公孙接、田开疆和古冶子一块儿侍奉齐景公，因为勇猛有力能和猛虎搏斗而闻名。有一次晏子从他们面前快步走过，三人没有起来行礼，晏子进见景公说："我听闻贤明的君主蓄养的勇士，上能遵守君臣之间的道义，下能遵守长幼之间的伦理，对内可以制止凶暴，对外可以威慑敌人，君主因为他们的功劳而获利，臣民因为他们的勇武而服膺，因此尊崇他们的地位，增加他们的俸禄。现在您蓄养的勇士，上不能遵守君臣之间的道义，下不能遵守长幼之间的伦理，对内不能制止凶暴，对外不能威慑敌人，这是危害国家的人，不如除掉他们。"景公说："这三个人，靠搏斗来击败他们恐怕做不到，派人刺杀他们又怕刺不中。"晏子说："他们都是些靠蛮力攻打强敌之人，不懂得长幼尊卑之礼。"于是请景公派人送去两个桃子给他们，说："三位勇士为什

## 2.24 [49] DUKE JING SUPPORTED THREE COURAGEOUS OFFICERS WHO DID NOT OBSERVE NORMS OF RIGHTEOUS BEHAVIOR BETWEEN RULER AND MINISTERS. YANZI REMONSTRATED.

Gongsun Jie, Tian Kaijiang and Gu Yezi served Duke Jing and were famous for having the courage and strength to capture tigers. When Yanzi respectfully hastened by them, they did not rise. Yanzi entered the Duke's audience and said: "I have heard that when the enlightened ruler cultivates courageous, strong officers and superiors observe norms of righteousness between ruler and ministers, and inferiors maintain the norm of following the lead of their elders. Thereby, violence is prevented inside the state while external enemies are intimidated. Superiors benefit from their achievements, and inferiors submit to their courageous deeds. Hence, the ruler elevates them to an honored position and gives them a large emolument. But now, the way you, my Lord, cultivate courageous, strong officers is the following: superiors do not observe norms of righteousness between a ruler and ministers, and inferiors do not maintain the norm of following the lead of their elders. Violence is not prevented inside the state, and external enemies are not intimidated. These three officers are instruments for the endangerment of the state. There is no better course than to get rid of them."

The Duke said: "I am afraid that if I try to capture these three I will fail, while if I try to kill them, the strike might miss."

Yanzi said: "They are all men who attack and overpower their enemies with strength; they lack the proper rites between senior and junior."

And so he asked the Duke to send someone to offer them a small present of two peaches, with the following words: "Why don't the three of you eat from these peaches, each an amount relating to his respective achievements?" Gongsun Jie looked up, sighed and said: "Yanzi is a

**【原文】**

之二桃，曰："三子何不计功而食桃？"公孙接仰天而叹曰："晏子，智人也！夫使公之计吾功者，不受桃，是无勇也，士众而桃寡，何不计功而食桃矣。接一搏猏而再搏乳虎，若接之功，可以食桃而无与人同矣。"援桃而起。田开疆曰："吾（伏）〔仗〕兵而却三军者再，若开疆之功，亦可以食桃，而无与人同矣。"援桃而起。古冶子曰："吾尝

**【今译】**

么不按功劳大小来吃桃子呢？"公孙接仰天叹息道："晏子真是个聪明人啊！他让景公用这种办法来计算我们的功劳，不能得到桃子，就是没有勇力，人多而桃少，怎能不按功劳大小来吃桃呢？我公孙接曾经搏杀了一只体大力强的野猪，又搏杀了一只正在哺乳的老虎，像我公孙接这样的功劳，可以吃桃子而且不用和别人同享了。"于是拿了个桃子站起来。田开疆说："我手持兵器击退敌军两次，像我田开疆这样的功劳，也可以吃桃，不必和他人同享（桃子）。"于是拿了另一个桃子站起来。古冶子说："我曾经跟随国君渡黄河，有一只大鼋咬住左边拉车的马潜入砥柱激流之中。那时候，我年纪还小不会游泳，可我潜入水中逆流行进百步，又顺流行进九里，找到大鼋杀了它，我左手拿着马尾，右手拿着鼋头，像仙鹤一样从水中跃出。渡口的人都说：'河神！'在我看来，他们说的河神就是大鼋的头。像我古冶子这样的功劳，也可以吃桃子而不用和他人共享。二位为何不把桃子还回来！"说完拔

clever man. It was he who made the Duke have us assess our relative achievements. Refusing to accept a peach would indicate a lack of courage: too many officers; too few peaches. Why don't we measure our respective achievements and then each eat from the peaches in accordance with that amount? Once I captured a fully grown wild boar, and another time a nursing tigress. For such an achievement I can eat a peach without sharing it with anyone else." He grabbed a peach and stood up.

Tian Kaijiang said: "Twice I held a weapon and made the Three Armies[1] withdraw. For such achievements, I should also eat a peach without sharing it with someone else." He grabbed a peach and stood up.

Gu Yezi said: "Once, when I followed my ruler across the Yellow River, a giant turtle seized the left outer horse of the carriage in his jaws and plunged with it into a strong current as strong as that of the Polished Pillar stream.[2] At that time I was still young and could not swim, so I waded in the water against the current a hundred paces, and then floated with the current nine *li* downstream. There, I overtook the turtle and killed it. I held the tail of the horse tightly with my left hand and seized the head of the turtle in my right hand. I jumped out of the water high-stepping like a crane and all the ferrymen said: 'This is Hebo,'[3] but as I saw it, it was the head of the giant turtle. For such an achievement, I can also eat a peach without sharing it with others. Why don't you two gentlemen return the peaches?" He drew his sword and stood up. Gongsun Jie and Tian Kaijiang said: "Our courage is not as good as yours, nor do our achievements equal to yours. To take the peaches and not to yield precedence would be greedy. However, choosing not to die under such circumstances would be a lack of courage.

---

1  I.e., the joint military forces of a large state.

2  The Polished Pillar 砥柱 is a name of a boulder in the middle of the Yellow River. It was not located in Qi but in the minor state of Guo 虢, in the present-day province of Henan.

3  Hebo 河伯, the River God.

**【原文】**

从君济于河，鼋（御）〔衔〕左骖以入砥柱之流。当是时也，冶少不能游，潜行逆流百步，顺流九里，得鼋而杀之，左操骖尾，右挈鼋头，鹤跃而出。津人皆曰：'河伯也！' 若冶视之，则大鼋之首。若冶之功，亦可以食桃而无与人同矣。二子何不反桃！" 抽剑而起。公孙接、田开疆曰："吾勇不子若，功不子逮，（耻）〔取〕桃不让，是贪也；然而不死，无勇也。" 皆反其桃，挈领而死。古冶子曰："二子死之，冶独生之，不仁；耻人以言，而夸其声，不义；恨乎所行，不死，无勇。虽然，二子同桃而节，冶专〔其〕桃而宜。" 亦反其桃，挈领而死。使者复曰："已死矣。" 公殓之以服，葬之以士礼焉。

**192**

**【今译】**

剑而起。公孙接和田开疆说："我们不如您勇武，不如您功高，没有谦让就先拿了桃，这是贪婪；这样还不去死，就是不勇敢。" 于是二人都将桃子还回去，自刎而死。古冶子说："二人因桃而死，只有我还活着，这是不仁；用言语羞辱人，而夸耀自己的名声，这是不义；怨恨自己的行为，而不赴死，这是不勇敢。即便如此，但还是他们二人同吃一个桃子，我独自吃一个桃子最合适。" 于是也还回桃子，自刎而死。送桃的使者回报景公："三人都已经死了。" 于是景公命人给他们穿官服入殓，用安葬士的礼节埋葬了他们。

So both men returned their peaches, cut their own throats and died.

Gu Yezi said: "For this, these two died, and, for this, only I am still alive. This is not humaneness. To shame others with one's words and to show off with one's own fame is not righteous. To regret what you did and not to die is to lack courage. Nevertheless, if these two would have been modest and shared one peach, or if I alone had taken one peach, it would have been appropriate." Then he too returned the peach, cut his own throat, and died. The messenger, who reported this, said: "They are dead." The Duke had them clad in shrouds and buried them with the rites ordained for officers.

## 2.25 [50] 景公登射思得勇力〔士〕与之图国晏子谏

齐景公举行大射礼想要得到勇武有力的猛士和他们谋划国家大事，晏子进谏

【原文】

景公登射，晏子修礼而侍。公曰："选射之礼，寡人厌之矣！吾欲得天（勇下）〔下勇〕士，与之图国。"晏子对曰："君子无礼，是庶人也；庶人无礼，是禽兽也。夫〔臣〕勇多则弑其君，〔子〕力多则杀其长，然而不敢者，维礼之谓也。礼者，所以御民也；辔者，所以御马也。无礼而能治国家者，婴未之闻也。"景公曰："善。"乃饰射更席，以为上客，终日问礼。

【今译】

齐景公举行大射礼，晏子按照大射礼的规定做好了准备等待景公。景公说："选射的礼节，我早已厌倦了！我想得到天下的勇士，和他们共同谋划国家大事。"晏子回答道："君子不遵守礼仪，就成了平民百姓；百姓不遵守礼仪，就成了禽兽。臣下勇武太盛就会弑杀君主，年轻人力量太大就会杀戮尊长，然而他们之所以不敢这样做，就是因为有礼仪啊。礼仪是用来控御百姓的，辔头是用来控御马匹的。不讲礼仪而能治理好国家的，我没有听说过。"景公说："好。"于是郑重参加大射礼，改变了晏子的座席，将其奉为上宾，整天询问礼仪的事。

# 2.25 [50] DUKE JING PRACTICED ARCHERY,[1] INTENDING TO RECRUIT COURAGEOUS, STRONG OFFICERS AND PLAN WITH THEM THE AFFAIRS OF THE STATE. YANZI REMONSTRATED.[2]

Duke Jing practiced archery. Yanzi stood in attendance in full compliance of the rites.[3]

The Duke said: "I find the process of selecting officers through archery rites tedious. What I want is to recruit courageous officers of the realm and to plan with them the affairs of state."

Yanzi replied: "A gentleman devoid of the rites is nothing more than a commoner. In the absence of the rites, a commoner is nothing more than a wild beast.[4] If ministers are excessively courageous, they commit regicide; if children are excessively strong, they kill their elders. Only what we know as the rites prevents them from daring to do so. The rites are the means by which the people are held in check. Reins are the means by which horses are held in check.[5] I have never heard of someone devoid of the rites who was able to put his state into good order."

Duke Jing said: "Well argued." Thereupon, he applied himself to the rectification of Archery Rites.[6] He rearranged the order of mats so as to give Yanzi the most honorable seat, and throughout the whole day he posed questions about the Archery Rites.

195

---

1   登 → 得 (*JS*, 171/2).

2   Item 2.25 [50] ↔ *Shuoyuan*, 19.6/161/23.

3   For a list of the archery Rites, see *Liji*, 47.1-12/170-172; *Yili*, 仪礼, 7/36/20.

4   An almost identical statement appears in Item 1.2 [2].

5   Cf. *Kongcongzi* 孔丛子, 2.1/8/22.

6   饰 → 饬 (*YZCQ-ICS*, 21, n. 4).

# 第三卷 问上

## 3.1 [51] 庄公问威当世服天下时耶晏子对以行也

齐庄公问威震当世使天下归服是不是因为天时，晏子回答是因为德行

【原文】

庄公问晏子曰："威当世而服天下，时耶？"晏子对曰："行也。"公曰："何行？"对曰："能爱邦内之民者，能服境外之不善；重士民之死力者，能禁暴国之邪逆；〔中〕听（赁）〔任〕贤者，能威诸侯；安仁义而乐利世者，能服天下。不能爱邦内之民者，不能服境外之不善；

【今译】

齐庄公问晏子说："威震当代而使天下归服，是因为天时吗？"晏子回答说："是因为德行。"庄公问："什么德行？"晏子回答说："能爱护国内的百姓，就能使境外不好的人归服；能重视臣民百姓的生死劳苦，就能禁除残害国家的邪逆；能听取中正之言而任用贤能，就能威震诸侯；能安于施行仁义而乐于为世间谋福利，就能使天下归服。不能爱护国内的百姓，就不能使境外不好的人归服；轻视臣民百姓的生死劳苦，就不能禁除残害国家的邪逆；刚愎自用轻视贤良之臣的谏

# Chapter Three    Queries — Part A

## 3.1 [51] DUKE ZHUANG ASKED WHETHER INSTILLING AWE IN ONE'S CONTEMPORARIES AND SUBJUGATING THE REALM DEPENDS ON AN OPPORTUNE MOMENT. YANZI REPLIED THAT IT IS A MATTER OF CONDUCT.

Duke Zhuang queried Yanzi as follows: "Does instilling awe in one's contemporaries and subjugating the realm depend on an opportune moment?"

Yanzi replied: "It is a matter of conduct."

The Duke said: "What kind of conduct?"

Yanzi replied: "Whoever is able to love the people within the state will be able to subjugate those who do evil beyond its border.[1] Whoever regards the death and toil of his officers and his people with due gravity will be able to suppress the wicked and subversive activities of aggressor states. Whoever pays heed to the upright[2] and employs the worthy will be able to instill awe upon the regional princes. Whoever rests content with humaneness and righteousness and delights in benefiting his contemporary generation will be able to subjugate the realm.[3] Whoever is incapable of

197

---

1 *Guanzi*, 8.1/58/6, parallel statement.

2 中听 → 听中正之言也 (*JS*, 174/2).

3 This statement is most probably a critical reaction to the lesser status of 利 — profit and 知 — knowledge, which Confucius and Mencius commonly held inferior to 仁 — humaneness. The *Analects*' distinctive statement (*Analects* 4.2/7/7) that the humane person rests content in humaneness while the knowledgeable person profits from humanness (仁者安仁, 知者利仁), is paraphrased here as a complementary rather than an antithetical statement. In other words, while Confucius of the *Analects* states that the knowledgeable person (知者) manipulate humanness for personal profit, Yanzi assigns an identical status to both 仁 — humaneness and 利 — profit by arguing that the "awe inspiring ruler" not only rests content in humaneness and righteousness, but also delights in unselfishly benefiting the entire realm.

大中华文库

**【原文】**

轻士民之死力者，不能禁暴国之邪逆；愎谏傲贤者（之言），不能威诸侯；倍仁义而贪名实者，不能威当世。而服天下者，此其道也已。"而公不用，晏子退而穷处。公任勇力之士，而轻臣仆之死，用兵无休，国罢民害，期年，百姓大乱，而身及崔氏祸。君子曰："尽忠不豫交，不用不怀禄，（其）晏子可谓廉矣！"

**【今译】**

言，就不能威震诸侯；违背仁义之政而贪图名利，就不能威震当世。这就是使天下归服的方法。"但是庄公不采纳，于是晏子退出朝廷过着穷困的生活。庄公任用勇武有力的猛士，轻视臣民的死亡，不停地出兵征讨，导致国家疲敝百姓遭殃，一年后，百姓大乱，庄公自己也被崔杼杀害。君子说："竭尽忠诚而不提前结交国君，不被任用也不贪恋禄位，晏子可以说是廉正了！"

love for the people within the state will not be able to subjugate those who do evil from beyond it. Whoever regards the death and toil of his officers and his people lightly will not be able to suppress the wicked and subversive activities of aggressor states. Whoever is deaf to all remonstrations and is arrogant towards the worthy will not be able to instill awe upon the regional princes. Whoever turns his back on humaneness and righteousness and is greedy for fame and property will not be able to instill awe upon his contemporaries and subjugate the realm. This is the only way."

But the Duke declined to put Yanzi's advice into effect and Yanzi withdrew and lived in dire straits. The Duke employed officers for their courage and strength and took lightly the death of his ministers and servants. He was perpetually engaged in warfare, the state was exhausted, and the people suffered as a consequence. After one year, the people were in great disorder and a disaster came upon the Duke in the person of Cui Zhu.[1]

The man of noble character said:[2] "Loyal to the utmost, he did not strive to maintain his relationship with the ruler. When his advice was not implemented, he was not preoccupied with his emolument. Yanzi can be called a man of integrity."

---

1   For Duke Zhuang of Qi 齐庄公, see above, n.3.

2   For a detailed and refined analysis of the six occurrences of the statement "The man of noble character said" (君子曰) in the *YZCQ*, see David Schaberg, "Platitude and Persona: *Junzi* Comments in *Zuozhuan* and Beyond." In Helwig Schmidt-Glintzer, *et al.*, eds. *Historical Truth, Historical Criticism, and Ideology: Chinese Historiography and Historical Culture from a New Comparative Perspective*. Leiden Studies in Comparative Historiography 1. Leiden and Boston: Brill, (2005): 177-96.

## 3.2 [52] 庄公问伐晋晏子对以不可若不济国之福

齐庄公问讨伐晋国的事，晏子回答说不可以，如果不成功是齐国的福气

### 【原文】

庄公将伐晋，问于晏子，晏子对曰："不可。君得合而欲多，（養）〔养〕欲而意骄。得合而欲多者危，（養）〔养〕欲而意骄者困。今君任勇力之士，以伐明主，若不济，国之福也，不德而有功，忧必及君。"

### 【今译】

齐庄公将要讨伐晋国，向晏子征求意见，晏子回答说："不行。您应该得到的已经得到了却还想要更多，欲望增长就会意气骄横。应得的已经得到却想要更多就会危险，欲望增长而意气骄横就会陷入困境。现在您任用勇武有力的猛士去攻打贤明的君主，如果不胜，则是国家的福气，没有仁德而有战功，忧患一定会殃及到您身上。"庄公变了脸色，很不高兴。晏子辞去官职不再做大臣，退出宫廷过着穷困的生活，

## 3.2 [52] DUKE ZHUANG CONSULTED ABOUT LAUN-CHING AN ATTACK ON JIN. YANZI REPLIED THAT IT WOULD NOT BE APPROPRIATE AND THAT IT WOULD BE FORTUNATE FOR THE STATE IF THE DUKE DID NOT SUCCEED.[1]

Duke Zhuang was about to launch an attack on Jin and consulted Yanzi about it.

Yanzi replied: "It would not be appropriate. My Lord, what you possess is sufficient, and yet you wish to possess more. You indulge your desires, and your intentions are arrogant. He who possesses what is sufficient and wishes for more imperils himself. He who indulges his desires and whose intentions are arrogant meets difficulties. But now you, my Lord, are employing officers for their courage and strength in order to launch an attack on the covenant chief.[2] If you do not succeed, it will be fortunate for the state. For if you achieve success without virtue, distress will surely fall upon you, my Lord."

The Duke's face flushed in anger; he was displeased. Yanzi resigned and stopped serving as minister. He withdrew and lived in dire straits. Pigweed and goosefoot grew beneath his home and thorny scrubs grew outside his gate. Duke Zhuang did appoint officers for their courage and strength after all, and marched westward to launch an attack on Jin. He

201

---

1  Item 3.2 [52] ↔ *Zuozhuan*, B9.23.4/276/28.

2  明 → 盟 according to the *Zuozhuan*, ibid. The alliance was led by the state of Jin. For a discussion of the interchangeability between 盟 and 霸, see Taeko A. Brooks, "Evolution of the Ba 霸 'Hegemon' Theory;" *Warring States Papers*, 1 (2010): 220-2. For a detailed discussion of the system of alliances in the period under consideration, see Yuri Pines, *Foundations of Confucian Thought: Intellectual Life in the Chunqiu Period, 722–453* BCE Honolulu: University of Hawaii Press (2002): 119-125.

**【原文】**

公作色不说。晏子辞不为臣，退而穷处，堂下生（蓼藿）〔藜藋〕，门外生荆棘。庄公终任勇力之士，西伐晋，（耻）〔取〕朝歌，及太行、孟门，兹于兑，期而民散，身灭于崔氏。崔氏之期，逐群公〔子〕，及庆氏亡。

**【今译】**

院子里长满了野草，门外长满了荆棘。庄公最终还是任用勇武有力的猛士向西攻打晋国，夺取了朝歌，到达了太行、孟门，进入兹于隧道，一年之后百姓离散，庄公被崔杼所杀。崔杼执政时，驱逐了齐国王室诸公子，直到庆封逃亡。

conquered Chaoge and got as far as Taihang, Mengmen, and the Chieyu tunnel gate.[1] A year later, his population was scattered and the Duke himself lost his life to Cui Zhu. During the period of unrest initiated by Cui Zhu, all the sons of the Duke were expelled and also Qing Feng[2] was driven into exile.[3]

---

1  兌 → 隧 (*YZCQ-ICS*, 21, n. 5).

2  Qing Feng, 庆封, was a minister of great wealth and influence at the Qi court. He was Cui Zhu's ally in the revolt against and the assassination of Duke Zhuang in 548 BCE. He later exterminated the Cui Zhu's lineage and eventually was forced to flee into exile in 545 BCE and was executed in 538 BCE by King Ling of Chu 楚灵王 (r. 540-529 BCE). For Qing Feng's forced exile and execution see, *Lüshi chunqiu*, 22.1/144/18.

3  At this point, the text of Item 3.2 [52] abruptly comes to its end. However, the *Zuozhuan*'s version of Cui Zhu's revolt, B9. 28.11/299/10, adds the following three characters 皆召之 after 及庆氏亡, which make the ending of this item more intelligible: "By the time that Qing Feng was driven into exile, the Duke's sons were all summoned back to the capital."

## 3.3 [53] 景公问伐鲁晏子对以不若修政待其乱

齐景公问讨伐鲁国的事，晏子回答说不可以，不如修明政教等待鲁国内乱

### 【原文】

景公举兵欲伐鲁，问（以）〔于〕晏子，晏子对曰："不可。鲁公好义而民戴之，好义者安，见戴者和，伯禽之治存焉，故不可攻。攻义者不祥，危安者必困。且婴闻之，伐人者德足以安其国，政足以和其民，国安民和，然后可以举兵而征暴。今君好酒而辟，德无以安国，厚藉敛，意使令，无以和民。德无以安之则危，政无以和之则乱。未

### 【今译】

齐景公起兵想要征伐鲁国，向晏子询问，晏子回答说："不行。鲁国国君喜好礼义而且百姓拥戴他，喜好礼义的人能使国家安定，被拥戴的人能使百姓和乐，伯禽治国的传统还在，因此不能攻打。攻打讲礼义的国家不吉祥，危害安定的国家一定会陷入困境。而且我听说，攻打别的国家的人德行足够安定自己的国家，政教足够和睦本国的百姓，国家安定百姓和乐，然后才能够出兵征讨凶暴。现在您喜好饮酒而且行为邪僻，德行不能使国家安定，加重赋税聚敛财富，任意驱使命令百姓，不能让百姓和乐。德行不能使国家安定那就会出危险，政教不能使百姓和乐那就会出祸乱。不能在危机和祸乱的规律下幸免，而想要征伐安定和乐的国家，这是不可以的，不如修明政教来等待鲁

## 3.3 [53] DUKE JING CONSULTED ABOUT ATTACKING LU. YANZI REPLIED THAT IT WOULD BE PREFERABLE TO CULTIVATE GOOD GOVERNMENT AND WAIT FOR INTERNAL DISORDER IN LU TO ARISE.

Duke Jing conscripted an army, intending to attack Lu, and consulted Yanzi about it.

Yanzi replied: "It would not be appropriate. The Duke of Lu admires righteousness, and the people support him. Whoever loves righteousness is at peace. Whoever is supported by the people achieves harmony. Boqin's[1] governance method is observed there. Therefore, it would not be appropriate to attack it. One who attacks the righteous will be unlucky. One who endangers the peaceful will certainly face difficulties. Furthermore, I have heard that those who attack others have virtue sufficient to keep their state peaceful and a government capable of making their people harmonious. Once one's state is peaceful and its people harmonious, one can cultivate an army and attack an aggressor. But now you, My Lord, love wine, and you stray from the proper path. You have no virtue with which to keep your state peaceful. You collect heavy taxes, give arbitrary orders, and lack what it takes to make people harmonious. If your virtue is insufficient to make your state peaceful, then the state will be imperiled. When the government is insufficient to make the people harmonious, havoc ensues. It is inadvisable for one whose guiding principles are liable to peril and havoc to seek to attack a state that is peaceful and harmonious. It would be better for you to cultivate your own government and wait for internal disorder to arise against the ruler of Lu. When the people distance themselves from their ruler, when superiors resent their inferiors, only then should you attack him.

205

---

1 Boqin 伯禽 was the son of the exemplary Duke of Zhou 周公, who was the regent of the young King Cheng 成王, the son of King Wu 武王, founder of the Zhou dynasty.

**【原文】**

免乎危乱之理，而欲伐安和之国，不可，不若修政而待其君之乱也。〔民离〕其君（离），上怨其下，然后伐之，则义厚而利多，义厚则敌寡，利多则民欢。"公曰："善。"遂不果伐鲁。

**【今译】**

国国君的乱政。到时候百姓离开他们的君主，国君怨恨他的臣下，然后再兴兵讨伐，那（我军）德义厚重而且获利更多，德义厚敌人就少，获利多百姓就高兴。"景公说："好。"于是就没有攻打鲁国。

Then your righteousness will be great and your benefit abundant. When righteousness is great, then enemies are few; when benefit is abundant, then the people are happy."

The Duke said: "Well argued." Consequently, he did not carry out the attack on Lu.

# 3.4 [54] 景公伐斄胜之问所当赏晏子对以谋胜禄臣

齐景公讨伐莱国取胜问应当如何赏赐功臣，晏子回答说用智谋战胜敌国应该增加臣子的俸禄

## 【原文】

景公伐斄，胜之。问晏子曰："吾欲赏于斄何如？"对曰："臣闻之，以谋胜国者，益臣之禄；以民力胜国者，益民之利。故上有羡获，下有加利，君上享其（民）〔名〕，臣下利其实。故用智者不偷业，用力者不伤苦，此古之善伐者也。"公曰："善。"于是破斄之臣，东邑之卒，皆有加利。是上独擅名，利下流也。

## 【今译】

齐景公攻打莱国，获得了胜利，问晏子说："我想赏赐伐莱有功的臣子，应该怎么做？"晏子回答道："我听说，靠智谋战胜敌国，应该增加臣子的俸禄；靠百姓的力量战胜敌国，应该增加百姓的利益。因此国君有更多的收获，臣民也有更多的利益，国君享有美名，臣民获得实利。所以付出智谋的人尽心尽责，付出劳力的人不怕辛苦，这就是古时候善于征伐的人的做法。"景公说："好。"于是参与讨伐莱国的臣子，东部城邑的士卒，全都增加了赏赐。就这样国君独占了战胜者的威名，臣民们则获得了实利。

## 3.4 [54] DUKE JING ATTACKED LI AND DEFEATED IT. HE ASKED WHO SHOULD BE REWARDED. YANZI REPLIED THAT EMOLUMENTS SHOULD BE GIVEN THOSE MINISTERS WHOSE PLANS LED TO THE VICTORY.

Duke Jing attacked Li and defeated it.[1] He asked Yanzi: "I would like to grant a reward to those who were involved in Li — what do you think?"

Yanzi replied: "Here is what I have heard: those who defeat a state by means of planning increase the emoluments of their ministers; those who defeat a state through the people's strength increase the benefits to the people. Therefore, superiors receive excess gains and inferiors receive additional benefits. The high-ranking ruler enjoys fame and his subjects benefit from its fruits. Therefore, those who use their intelligence do not shirk their obligations, and those who use their strength are not hurt by hardship. Such was the situation in ancient times for those who were skillful at attacking."

The Duke said: "Well argued." Thereupon, he provided additional benefits to the ministers who crushed Li and the soldiers who fought in this Eastern city-state. In this way, the superior was the only one who enjoyed fame, while the benefits trickled down.

---

1  Li 棃 is identical with Lai 莱, a city-state located east of Qi.

## 3.5 [55] 景公问圣王其行若何晏子对以衰世而讽

齐景公问圣王的德行是什么样的，晏子用世道衰败来回答，进而讽谏

**【原文】**

景公外傲诸侯，内轻百姓，好勇力，崇乐以从嗜欲，诸侯不说，百姓不亲。公患之，问于晏子曰："古之圣王，其行若何？"晏子对曰："其行公正而无邪，故谗人不得入；不阿党，不私色，故群徒之卒不得容；薄身厚民，故聚敛之人不得行；不侵大国之地，不耗小国之民，故诸侯皆欲其尊；不劫人以兵甲，不威人以众强，故天下皆欲其强；德行教诲加于诸侯，慈爱利泽加于百姓，故海内归之若流水。今

**【今译】**

齐景公对外傲视诸侯，对内轻视百姓，喜好勇武有力的猛士，追求享乐放纵嗜欲，诸侯不高兴，百姓不亲附。景公很忧虑，向晏子询问道："古时候的圣王，他们的行为是什么样的？"晏子回答说："他们的行为公平正直而且没有邪念，因此谗谄的人无机可乘；不结党营私，不偏爱美色，因此拉帮结派的人不被容忍；自身节俭而对百姓宽厚，因此聚敛财物的人不能胡作非为；不侵夺大国的土地，不损耗小国的百姓，因此诸侯们都希望他地位尊贵；不靠武力强大劫掠别人，不靠人多势众威胁别人，因此天下人都希望他强大；德行教训施加给诸侯，慈爱恩泽施加给百姓，因此四海之内的人都像流水入海一样归附他。现在在衰败世道做国君的人，乖谬不正，结党营私，因此谗谄奸佞，拉帮结派的人多；重视自身的享受，轻视百姓的生计，因此聚敛财物的人大行其道；侵占大国的土地，消耗小国的百姓，因此

## 3.5 [55] DUKE JING ASKED WHAT CHARACTERIZED THE CONDUCT OF THE SAGE-KINGS. YANZI REPLIED WITH AN ANALOGICAL REMONSTRATION REFERRING TO THE PRESENT AGE OF DECLINE.

Duke Jing behaved arrogantly toward the external regional princes and thought little of the state's residents. He favored the courageous and the strong, placed supreme value on pleasures and, accordingly, indulged his desires. The regional princes were displeased, and the people felt no kinship with him. The Duke was troubled by this, and he asked Yanzi: "What characterized the conduct of the sage-kings of ancient times?"

Yanzi replied: "Their conduct was upright and not corrupt, and therefore slanderers could not have insinuated themselves. They did not cater to factions and did not indulge in illicit sex, and therefore followers of partisan groups were not tolerated. They restrained themselves, but enriched the people, and therefore the venal tax-collectors were unable to act. They did not invade the territories of large states, and they did not exhaust the people of small states, and therefore all the regional princes wanted them to be honored. They did not devastate people through armed force and did not overawe them through numerical superiority and strength, and therefore everyone in the realm wished them to be strong. They bestowed their virtuous conduct and moral instructions upon the regional princes; their compassion and beneficence were bestowed upon the common people, and therefore people everywhere rushed to them like a torrent. But now, the rulers of the present era of decline are evil and cater to factions. Therefore, the followers of partisan groups of slanderers and flatterers are numerous. They enrich themselves amply, but restrain the people, and therefore the venal tax-collectors are able to act. They invade the territories of large states and they exhaust the people of small states; therefore, the regional princes do not wish them to be honored. They devastate people through armed force

**【原文】**

衰世君人者，辟邪阿党，故谗（谣）〔诏〕群徒之卒繁；厚身（养）〔养〕，薄视民，故聚敛之人行；侵大国之地，耗小国之民，故诸侯不欲其尊；劫人以兵甲，威人以众强，故天下不欲其强；灾害加于诸侯，劳苦施于百姓，故雠敌进伐，天下不救，贵戚离散，百姓不（兴）〔与〕。"公曰："然则何若？"敡曰："请卑辞重币，以说于诸侯，轻罪省功，以谢于百姓，其可乎？"公曰："诺。"于是卑辞重币，而诸侯附，轻罪省功，而百姓亲，故小国入朝，燕鲁共贡。墨子闻之曰："晏子知道，道在为人，而失为己。为人者重，自为者轻。景公自为，而小国不（为）与，（在）为人，而诸侯为役，则道在为人，而行在反己矣，故晏子知道矣。"

**【今译】**

诸侯们不希望他地位尊贵；靠武力强大劫掠别人，靠人多势众威胁别人，因此天下人都不希望他强大；把灾祸损害带给诸侯，把劳累苦难带给百姓，因此仇敌来攻伐时，天下无人援救，王公贵族离散，百姓也不支持。"景公说："这样的话那要怎么办？"晏子回答说："请您用谦逊的语言和厚重的礼物来游说诸侯，减轻刑徒免去劳役来向百姓谢罪，这样可以吗？"景公说："好。"于是用谦逊的语言和厚重的礼物游说而诸侯归附，减轻刑徒免去劳役而百姓亲附，因此小国来朝见，燕国和鲁国也一起来进贡。墨子听说这件事之后说："晏子懂得治国的道理，得道在于为别人，而失道在于为自己。为别人着想的人被尊重，为自己着想的人被轻视。景公为自己着想，而小国不亲附，为别人着想，而诸侯们都被他役使，这就是在道义上为了别人，而行为上不为自己，所以说晏子懂得治国的道理啊。"

大中华文库

and overawe other people with numbers and strength; therefore, the realm does not wish them to be strong. Their calamities affect the regional princes, and they impose hardships on the people. Therefore, when enemies mount an attack them, the realm will not come to their rescue, ministers of ducal blood will disperse, and the people will not support them."

The Duke said: "If so, what can be done about this?"

Yanzi replied: "My request is that you seek favor with the regional princes by using humble words and lavish gifts. Alleviate punishments, reduce compulsory labor, and thereby mollify the people. Is this acceptable?"

The Duke said: "Very well."

Thereupon, the Duke used humble words and lavish gifts, and the regional princes allied themselves with him. He alleviated punishments and reduced compulsory labor, and the people cleaved to him. Hence, small states came to his court and both the states of Yan and Lu offered him tribute.

When Mozi heard about this, he said: "Yanzi knew the Way. The Way lies in deeds on behalf of others, but is lost in deeds on one's own behalf. Those who act on behalf of others carry considerable weight, and those who act on behalf of themselves carry little weight. When Duke Jing acted on his own behalf, small states did not support him, but when he acted on behalf of others, the regional princes served him. Thus, the Way is found through acting on behalf of others, and its practice is in examining one's self critically. Yanzi knew the Way."

## 3.6 [56] 景公问欲善齐国之政以干霸王晏子对以官未具

齐景公打算搞好齐国的政治行霸王之道，询问晏子的意见，晏子回答说官吏尚未具备

**【原文】**

景公问晏子曰："吾欲善治齐国之政，以干霸王之诸侯。"晏子（作色）对曰："官未具也。臣数以闻，而君不肯听也。故臣闻仲尼居处惰倦，廉隅不正，则季次、原宪侍；气郁而疾，志意不通，则仲由、卜商侍；德不盛，行不厚，则颜回、骞、雍侍。今君之朝臣万人，兵车千乘，不善政之所失于下，贾坠于民者众矣，未有能士敢以闻者。臣

**【今译】**

齐景公问晏子说："我想把齐国的国政治理好，称霸于诸侯。"晏子回答说："辅佐的官员没有具备。我多次进谏，而您不肯听从。我听说孔子生活倦怠，品行不端庄不公正时，就有季次和原宪在旁陪侍；气血郁结成疾，思想不通畅时，就有仲由和卜商在旁陪侍；品德不够高尚，行为不够宽厚时，就有颜回、闵子骞和冉雍在旁陪侍。现在您有臣子不下万人，兵车千乘，不好的政策给下面带来损失，落到百姓身上的太多了，却没有敢于向您报告的人。因此我说：官吏没有具备。"景公说："我现在想听从您的意见来整顿好齐国的国政，可以吗？"晏子回答道："我听说，国家拥有齐备的官员，然后就能把政治

# 3.6 [56] DUKE JING INQUIRED ABOUT HIS WISH TO IMPROVE THE GOVERNANCE EFFICIENCY OF THE STATE OF QI IN ORDER TO SEEK THE POSITION OF OVERLORD. YANZI REPLIED THAT THE DUKE'S STAFF WAS NOT YET COMPLETE.[1]

Duke Jing queried Yanzi as follows: "I want to improve the governance efficiency of the state of Qi in order to seek the position of overlord among the regional princes — how should I accomplish this?"[2]

Yanzi replied: "Your staff is not yet complete. I have repeatedly reminded you about this, but you have been unwilling to pay heed. I have heard[3] that when Confucius was idle and left lethargic at home, and cultivation was not being pursued in every nook and cranny, he had Jici and Yuanxian attend him.[4] When he was gloomy and ill, and when his thinking and aspirations were inhibited, he had Zhongyou and Bushang[5] attend him. When his virtue was not flourishing and his conduct not generous, he had Yan Hui, Qian, and Yong[6] attend him. Now you have in attendance at court ten thousand ministers, and your standing army[7] of one thousand chariots; the people suffer from numerous harmful policies. Until now, no capable officer has ever dared to tell you all this. Therefore, I say that your staff is

215

---

1 Item 3.6 [56] ↔ *Shuoyuan*, 1.18/5/1; *Kongcongzi*, 6.1/62/22.

2 以干霸王之诸侯 → 吾欲霸诸侯若何 (*JS*, 184/2).

3 Omit 故 (*JS*, 184/5).

4 Two of Confucius' disciples. For all the disciples and other figures who surrounded Confucius throughout his lifetime, see Bruce E. Brooks and Taeko A. Brooks, *The Original Analects: Sayings of Confucius and His Successors*. Translations from the Asian Classics. New York: Columbia University Press (1998): 272-284.

5 I.e., Zilu 子路 and Zixia 子夏, prominent disciples of Confucius.

6 I.e., Yan Hui 颜回, Min Ziqian 闵子骞 and Zhonggong 仲弓, prominent disciples of Confucius.

7 兵 → 立 (*JS*, 185/14).

**【原文】**

故曰：官未具也。"公曰："寡人（今）欲从夫子而善齐国之政，可乎？"对曰："婴闻〔之〕，国有具官，然后其政可（喜）〔善〕。"公作色不说，曰："齐国虽小，则可谓官不具？"对曰："此非臣之所复也。昔吾先君桓公身体惰懈，辞令不给，则隰朋昵侍；（右左）〔左右〕多

**【今译】**

治理好。"景公变了脸色，不高兴地说："齐国虽然小，怎么能说官吏不具备？"晏子回答道："这不是我所能回答的。以前我们的国君桓公身体懒惰懈怠，应酬时词不达意时，就有隰朋在一旁亲切服侍；左右近臣多有过失，刑罚不公正时，就有弦宁在一旁亲切服侍；土地不修整，百姓不安乐时，就有宁戚在一旁亲切服侍；军吏懈怠，士兵偷懒时，就有王子成甫在一旁亲切服侍；生活安逸怠惰，左右近臣畏惧，乐舞不断，理正不勤，就有东郭牙在一旁亲切服侍；道德礼义不恰当，信

not yet complete."

The Duke said:[1] "I would like to follow your advice and improve the governance of the state of Qi. Is this possible?"

Yanzi replied: "I have heard that only after a state has a complete staff of officers can its government improve."

The Duke's face flushed in anger. He was displeased and said: "However small the state of Qi may be, could one ever say that its staff is not complete?"[2]

Yanzi replied: "This was not what I meant. In the past, when our former ruler, Duke Huan, became decrepit and feeble in body and his orders were not forthcoming, he made Xi Peng[3] his close attendant. When his entourage made many mistakes and their legal judgments were not pertinent, he made Xian Ning[4] his close attendant. When fields and open land were not cultivated and the common people were not at peace, he had Ning Qi[5] as his close attendant. When the army officers were lazy and the soldiers rapacious, he had Prince Cheng Fu[6] as his close attendant. When Duke Huan was indolent at home and his entourage was menacing, and he indulged profusely in pleasure and took very little part in governing, he

217

---

1  *JS*, 183/1 suggests that this line is the beginning of a completely new, separate item.

2  则可 → 则何 (*YZCQ-ICS*; 23, n. 3/B).

3  According to *Hanfeizi*, 12/92/8, Duke Huan appointed Xi Peng as an administrator of home affairs and Guan Zhong as an administrator of foreign affairs, so that the two would watch each other. According to *Guanzi*, 8.2/63/17, however, Xi Peng served Duke Huan as an administrator of foreign affairs.

4  The *Shuoyuan*, ibid, describes Xian Zhang 弦章, who appears several times in the *YZCQ,* as a man of eloquence and integrity. The *Hanefizi*, ibid, has Xian Shang 弦商, who was a 大理 "Chamberlain of Law Enforcement," at Duke Huan's court.

5  Ning Qi or Ning Wu 武 in *Hanfeizi*, ibid, served Duke Huan as a 大田, "Grand Minister of Agriculture."

6  In *Hanfeizi*, ibid, Prince Cheng Fu is referred to as 公子成父 "Noble Scion Cheng Fu," Duke Huan's 大司马 "Grand Marshal."

**【原文】**

过，狱谳不中，则弦宁昵侍；田野不修，民氓不安，则宁戚昵侍；军吏怠，戎士偷，则王子成甫昵侍；居处佚怠，左右慑畏，繁乎乐，省乎治，则东郭牙昵侍；德义不中，信行衰微，则管子昵侍。先君能以人之长续其短，以人之厚补其薄，是以辞令穷远而不逆，兵加于有罪而不顿，是故诸侯朝其德，而天子致其胙。今君之过失多矣，未有一士以闻〔者〕也。故曰：官不具。"公曰："善。"

**【今译】**

誉德行衰微时，就有管仲在一旁亲切服侍。桓公能够用他人的长处弥补自己的短处，能用他人的优点弥补自己的缺点，因此他的命令传到很远的地方也没人反对，出兵攻打有罪的人也不会遇到挫折，因此诸侯们朝贺他的德行，天子赐给他祭肉。现在您的过失太多了，没有一个人告诉您。因此说：辅佐的官员不具备。"景公说："好。"

made Dongguo Ya[1] his close attendant. When his virtue and righteousness were improper and his trustworthy conduct in decline, he nominated Guanzi as his close attendant. Our former ruler would complement his shortcomings with the strengths of others and compensate his limitations with the abundant talents of others. Therefore, his orders were far-reaching and no disobedience emerged. His military power extended to the guilty without obstruction. Hence, the regional princes paid homage to his virtue and the Son of Heaven sent him portions of the sacrificial meat.[2] But now your mistakes, my Lord, are many, yet there is not a single officer who informs you of this. Therefore, I said that your staff is not yet complete.

The Duke said: "Well said."

---

1  Dongguo Ya was Duke Huan's 谏臣, "Minister of Remonstration." See *Hanfeizi*, ibid.

2  *Zuozhuan*, B5.9.2/81/27, records the sending of the sacrificial meat from the Zhou king to Duke Huan.

## 3.7 [57] 景公问欲如桓公用管仲以成霸业晏子对以不能

齐景公打算像桓公重用管仲那样重用晏子以成就王霸之业，晏子回答说不可以

【原文】

景公问晏子曰："昔吾先君桓公，有管仲夷吾保（义）〔乂〕齐国，能遂武功而立文德，（纠）〔纠〕合兄弟，抚存（翌）〔冀〕州，吴越受令，荆楚惛忧，莫不宾服，勤于周室，天子加德。先君昭功，管子之力也。今寡人亦欲存齐国之政于夫子，夫子以佐佑寡人，彰先君之功烈，而继管子之业。"晏子对曰："昔吾先君桓公，能任用贤，固有

【今译】

齐景公问晏子道："以前我们先代的国君桓公，有管仲辅佐治理齐国，能够通过武力建功立业也能通过文治建立德政，联合诸侯，安抚保有冀州，吴国越国都接受他的号令，楚国感到恐惧，诸侯们无不服从归顺，尽力效忠周王室，因此周天子嘉奖他的德行。先君桓公建立显赫的功业，全靠管仲的力量啊。现在我想把齐国的国政交给您，请您辅佐我，以发扬先君的功德，继承管仲的事业。"晏子回答说："以前我们的先君桓公，能够选贤任能，国家有什五的管理体制，治理遍及百姓，身份尊贵的人不欺凌身份卑贱的人，富有的人不轻视贫穷的

# 3.7 [57] DUKE JING CONSULTED REGARDING HIS ASPIRATION TO BE LIKE DUKE HUAN, WHO MADE USE OF GUAN ZHONG IN ORDER TO ATTAIN THE STATUS OF OVERLORD. YANZI REPLIED THAT THE DUKE WAS UNABLE TO FULFILL THIS ROLE.

Duke Jing queried Yanzi as follows: "In the past, our former ruler Duke Huan had Guan Zhong, also known as Yi-wu,[1] to protect and regulate the state of Qi, and so eventually he was able to achieve military success and establish civil virtues. He allied with the fraternal regional princes,[2] pacifying and protecting Ji Zhou.[3] Wu and Yue obeyed his orders, and Jing-Chu[4] dreaded him. All obeyed him. He was sedulous in the service to the house of Zhou and the Son of Heaven granted him favor. The brilliant achievements of our former ruler resulted from the strength of Guanzi. Now I too want to entrust the government of Qi to you, Master, so that you, my Master, may help me to display our former ruler's achievements and continue the enterprise of Guanzi."

Yanzi replied: "In the past, our former ruler Duke Huan was able to employ the worthy and entrust responsibility to them, and so the state[5] had the ten and five household divisions.[6] The administration was all-

221

---

1   I.e., Guan Zhong. Yiwu was the courtesy name (字) of Guan Zhong.

2   I.e., the "princes" (诸侯). The *Zuozhuan*, B5. 26.3/10723, reads: 桓公是以纠合诸侯 ("For this reason Duke Huan called in the princes").

3   Ji Zhou — the Ji Province — located between the two parts of the Yellow River (*Lüshi chunqiu*, 13.1/63/5), which refers to the region that covers the central plains of ancient China.

4   Jing — 荆 was the older name of the state of Chu — 楚.

5   固 → 国 (*YZCQ-ICS*, 23, n. 5).

6   For a description of this organizational structure of villages into groups of ten and five households, see *Guanzi*, 1.4/8/7; Allyn W. Rickett, tr. *Guanzi: Political, Economic, and Philosophical Essays from Early China*. vol. 1, Princeton Library of Asian Translations, Princeton (1985): 103.

【原文】

什伍，治遍细民，贵不凌贱，富不傲贫，功不遗罢，佞不吐愚，举事不私，听狱不阿，内妾无羡食，外臣无羡禄，鳏寡无饥色；不以饮食之辟害民之财，不以宫室之侈劳人之力；节（耴）〔取〕于民，而普施之，府无藏，仓无粟，上无骄行，下无（谄）〔谄〕德。是以管子能以

【今译】

人，有功的人不谴责无功的人，有才的人不唾弃愚笨的人，办事不徇私情，断案公平公正，宫内的姬妾没有多余的食物，外朝的臣子没有多余的俸禄，鳏夫寡妇也没有饥饿的面色；先君不因饮食上的偏好损害百姓的财物，不因宫室的奢侈加重百姓的劳役；向百姓索取的少，而普遍施恩于百姓，府库中没有储藏，仓库中也没有粮食，君上没有骄傲的言行，臣下也没有谄佞的品质。因此管仲能让齐国避免灾祸，让先君桓公参决于天子。现在您想发扬先君的功德，继承管仲的事业，那就不要用太多的偏好去损伤百姓，不要放纵欲望纵情享乐和诸侯结怨，大臣们谁敢不秉持为善的理念尽力把事情做好，来顺从君王的心意呢？现在您疏远贤人，而任用谄谀之人；役使百姓唯恐不多，聚敛财

inclusive, reaching the common people. The nobles did not humiliate the lowly, and the rich were not haughty towards the poor. Those with accomplishments did not reprimand[1] the weary, and the eloquent did not scold the foolish. Official undertakings were free of personal preferences, and lawsuits were heard without favoritism. Concubines within the palace did not enjoy expensively abundant food, and ministers outside the palace did not enjoy over-generous, abundant emoluments. Widows and widowers did not did not have famished faces. The people's property was not harmed by the misappropriation of food and drink, and the people's strength was not exhausted with extravagant palaces. He was moderate in taking from the people and bestowed favors extensively. Nothing was hoarded in the warehouses, and grain was not stored in the granaries. Superiors did not exhibit arrogant conduct, and inferiors avoided sycophancy. This is why Guanzi was able to keep the state of Qi free of disasters and allowed our former ruler to take part in the Son of Heaven's rule. Now if you, My Lord, want to manifest the achievements of our former ruler and carry on the enterprises of Guanzi, then you should not harm the people with your great profligacy, and you should not provoke resentment among the regional princes with your desire for fine things and precious objects; and who then, among your ministers, would dare not accept your goodness and not exhaust his strength in order to follow your will? But now you, my Lord, distance yourself from the worthy, and you employ slanderers and flatterers. You over use the people so much that they cannot bear it, and you collect such high taxes that they cannot afford them. You take a great deal from the people, but bestow very little upon them. You demand much from the regional princes, but you think little of the rites due to them. The stores in your warehouse are spoiled by insects, and your attitude to the regional princes is contrary to the rites. Beans and millet are stored and hidden away,

---

1   遗 → 遣 (*YZCQ-ICS*, 23, n. 7).

**【原文】**

齐国免于难，而以吾先君参乎天子。今君欲彰先君之功烈，而继管子之业，则无以多辟伤百姓，无以嗜欲玩好怨诸侯，臣孰敢不承善尽力，以顺君意？今君疏远贤人，而任谗谀；使民若不胜，藉敛若不得；厚（耴）〔取〕于民，而薄其施，多求于诸侯，而轻其礼；府藏朽蠹，而礼悖于诸侯，菽粟藏深，而怨积于百姓；君臣交恶，而政刑无常。臣恐国之危失，而公不得享也。又恶能彰先君之功烈而继管子之业乎！"

**【今译】**

物唯恐不得；向百姓索取的太多，而施恩太少，向诸侯们索取的太多，而轻视对他们的礼敬；府库里储藏的东西朽坏生了蛀虫，和诸侯们交往违背了礼仪，粮食储藏了很多，而在百姓中积蓄了怨恨；君臣之间互相怀恨，而政令刑律变化无常。我怕国家有覆亡的危险，而您也不能享有国君之位。又怎么能发扬先君的功德而继承管仲的事业呢！"

while resentment mounts up among the people. The ruler and his ministers hate each other, and administration and punishments are inconsistent. I fear that the state will be endangered and fall to ruin and that you will not be able to take pleasure in it. How, then, are you able to manifest our former ruler's achievements and continue the enterprise of Guanzi?"

## 3.8 [58] 景公问莒鲁孰先亡晏子对以鲁后莒先

齐景公问莒国和鲁国谁先灭亡，晏子回答说鲁国后亡莒国先亡

### 【原文】

景公问晏子："莒与鲁孰先亡？"对曰："以臣观之也，莒之细人，变而不化，贪而好假，高勇而贱仁，士武以疾，忿急以速竭，是以上不能（養）〔养〕其下，下不能事其上，上下不能相〔收〕，则政之大体失矣。故以臣（之观）〔观之〕也，莒其先亡。"公曰："鲁何如？"对曰："鲁之君臣，犹好为义，下之妥妥也，奄然寡闻，是以上能（其养）〔养其〕下，下能事其上，上下相〔收〕，政之大体存矣。故鲁犹

### 【今译】

齐景公问晏子："莒国和鲁国哪个先灭亡？"晏子回答道："在我看来，莒国的百姓，改变常理而不遵从教化，生性贪婪而喜好作假，推崇勇武而轻视仁德，士人们（处理事情）急于动用武力，忿恨急躁而很快衰竭，因此国君不能豢养他的臣下，臣下也不能侍奉他的国君，上下不能互相配合，那么国家的根本就丧失了。所以在我看来，莒国应该会先灭亡。"景公说："鲁国怎么样呢？"晏子回答说："鲁国的君臣，仍然喜好推行仁义，臣民很安定，见闻也少，因此国君能豢养他的臣下，臣下也能侍奉国君，上下之间可以互相配合，国家的根本还存在。因此鲁国还可以长期守住国家，但他也有一个失误。邹国和滕国都是小国，野鸡奔跑就能穿过它们的国境，还能称为公侯，小国侍奉大国，弱国侍奉强国，由来已久，宋国是周朝分封建立的国家，鲁

# 3.8 [58] DUKE JING ASKED: WHICH WILL PERISH FIRST, JU OR LU?  YANZI REPLIED THAT LU WOULD PERISH LATER AND JU FIRST.

Duke Jing queried Yanzi as follows: "Which will be the first to perish, Lu or Ju?"[1]

Yanzi replied: "As I see it, the common people of Ju change, but they are not transformed for the better. They are greedy and fond of falsehood. They value courage highly and hold humaneness in contempt. Their officers are fast, quick-tempered, and quickly exhausted. Therefore, the superiors cannot nurture their inferiors, while the inferiors cannot serve their superiors. When superiors and inferiors cannot get on close terms with each other, then the fundamental structure of the government is lost. Therefore, as I see it, Ju will probably be the first to perish."

The Duke said: "What about Lu?"

Yanzi said: "The ruler and ministers of Lu seem to be fond of acting righteously; their inferiors are docile, weak, and seldom heard from. Therefore, the superiors can nurture their inferiors, while the inferiors can serve their superiors. When superiors and inferiors get on close terms with each other, the fundamental structure of the government survives. Hence, it looks as if Lu may be preserved for a long time — though there is one reason why they might fail[2] after all. The territories of Zou and Teng[3] are so small that pheasants who merely flutter about are already beyond the borders, and still their rulers are called 'dukes' and 'lords.' It has been the rule for long that the small serves the big and the weak serves the strong;

227

---

1   Ju 莒 was a small state located in the present day Ju County, which was destroyed by the state of Chu 楚 in 431.

2   亦 → 失 (*JS*, 194/8 ).

3   Zou 邹 — identical with Zhu 邾 — and Teng 滕 were two tiny princedoms located in Lu and Song, respectively.

**【原文】**

可长守，然其亦有一焉。彼邹滕雏奔而出其地，犹称公侯，（大）〔小〕之事（小）〔大〕，弱之事强，久矣，彼周者，殷之树国也，鲁近齐而亲殷，以变小国，而不服于邻，以远望鲁，灭国之道也。齐其有鲁与莒乎？"公曰："鲁与莒之事，寡人既得〔而〕闻之矣，寡人之德亦薄，然后世孰践有齐国者？"对曰："田无宇之后为几。"公曰："何故也？"对曰："公量小，私量大，以施于民，其与士交也，用财无筐箧之藏，国人负携其子而归之，若水之流下也。夫先与人利，而后辞其难，不亦寡乎？若苟勿辞也，从而抚之，不亦几乎？"

大中华文库

**【今译】**

国靠近齐国而去亲附宋国，以狭小的国土而不归附强大的邻国而寄希望于远方的晋国，这是使国家灭亡的政策。齐国大概会占有鲁国和莒国吧！"景公说："鲁国和莒国的情况，我大概了解了，我的德行浅薄，然而后世谁能登上齐国的国君之位呢？"晏子回答说："田无宇的后人差不多。"景公说："为什么呢？"晏子说："田氏收粮时用小斗，贷粮时用大斗，用这种办法施恩于百姓，他和士人交往，用钱时能倾尽所有，国内的百姓带着儿子去归附他，就像水往低处流一样。先给百姓利益，然后推辞为百姓作君主，这种事不是太少了吗？假如不想推辞作君主，又去顺从民意安抚百姓，这不是已经接近享有齐国了吗？"

even the Zhou Kingdom was previously a state enfeoffed by Yin.[1] Lu is located near Qi but feels kinship to Yin,[2] and thereby contravenes the rule of conduct for small states, and is no longer subjected to its strong neighbor. From a distant vantage-point, this is how Lu will be destroyed. Qi will take possession of both Lu and Ju."

The Duke said: "I have already heard of the situation in Lu and Ju. My virtue, too, is slight, so who in later generations will ascend the throne and take possession of the State of Qi?"

Yanzi replied: "Probably the descendants of Tian Wuyu."[3]

The Duke said: "Why?"

Yanzi replied: "The standard, public measures are small, but their own private measures are large, and they distribute to the people accordingly.[4] In dealing with officers, they make use of property without depositing it in boxes and trunks. The people of the state turn to them, as water flows downhill, carrying their children on their backs and arms. Isn't it unlikely for people to first benefit from others and then turn away from them in time of difficulty? And if, indeed, they do not ignore their beneficiaries' difficulties, and their beneficiaries continue to pacify them, are they not coming close to gaining possession of Qi?"

229

---

1  The Yin (Shang) dynasty enfeoffed the Zhou as a city-state, which developed as a kingdom situated to the west of the Yin and subservient to them. Later, the Zhou overthrew the Yin and enfeoffed their descendants in the state of Song 宋.

2  I.e., they feel kinship to the small and weak state of Song 宋. The *JS*, 194/11, suggests to replace Yin 殷 with Jin 晋 since during the period under consideration, the ruler of Lu paid many tribute visits to the state of Jin.

3  Tian Wuyu or Chen Huanzi 陈桓子, the fifth head of the Chen lineage in Qi. For a similar discussion between Duke Jing and Yanzi concerning the future of Qi and the Tian (Chen) family, see, *Hanfeizi*, 34/98/22.

4  Item 4.17 [97], and the *Zuozhuan*, B10. 3/323/23-26, say that the private measures of the Chen (Tian) clan such as *dou* 豆, *qu* 区, *fu* 釜 and *zhong* 钟 are a quarter bigger than the standard public measures. Both texts continue to explain that the members of the clan lend to the people according to their own private measures and take back according to the standard, public measures; hence their popularity.

## 3.9 [59] 景公问治国何患晏子对以社鼠猛狗

齐景公问治理国家忧患的是什么，晏子回答说土地庙里的老鼠和凶猛的狗

### 【原文】

景公问于晏子曰："治国〔何〕患？"晏子对曰："患夫社鼠。"公曰："何谓也？"对曰："夫社，束木而涂之，鼠因往托焉，熏之则恐烧其木，灌之则恐败其途，此鼠所以不可得杀者，以社故也。夫国亦有焉，人主左右是也。内则蔽善恶于君上，外则卖权重于百姓，不诛之则为乱，诛之则为人主所案据，腹而有之，此亦国之社鼠也。人有酤

### 【今译】

齐景公问晏子说："治理国家的人忧患什么？"晏子回答说："忧患是藏身于土地庙中的老鼠。"景公说："为什么这样说呢？"晏子回答说："土地庙是用捆绑好的木材涂抹上泥土修成的，老鼠藏身在其中，用火熏烤怕烧毁木材，用水浇灌又怕冲毁泥土，这些老鼠之所以不能被杀死，就是因为土地庙的缘故。国家也有这种老鼠，就是国君左右的近臣。他们对内混淆善恶，蒙蔽国君，对外玩弄威权，欺压百姓，不诛杀他们国家就会混乱，诛杀他们国君又坚持不从，或平反其狱以宥其辜，这些人就是国家的社鼠。有个卖酒的人，他用来装酒的器皿非常整洁，店铺外挂着高高的酒幌，但他的酒放酸了也卖不出去，他问乡里的人这是什么原因，乡里人说：'你养的狗太凶猛，别人拿着酒器进了你的店，要买你的酒，你的狗迎面冲上来就咬人，这就是酒放酸了也卖不出去

# 3.9 [59] DUKE JING ASKED YANZI WHAT SHOULD CONCERN A LEADER IN GOVERNING THE STATE. YANZI REPLIED: ALTAR RATS AND FEROCIOUS DOGS.[1]

Duke Jing queried Yanzi as follows: "What should one be concerned about in governing the state?"

Yanzi replied: "One should be concerned about the rats in the Altar of the Soil."

The Duke said: "What do you mean?"

Yanzi replied: "The Altar of the Soil consists of pieces of wood that are tied together and plastered. Hence, rats can go inside and find shelter in it. If you wanted to smoke them out, there would be the fear of setting the Altar's wood on fire. If you flooded them out, there would be the fear of damaging its plaster.[2] That is why these rats cannot be killed for the sake of the Altar of the Soil. States also have rats, which are the entourage surrounding the ruler. Internally, they conceal good and evil from their rulers; externally, they sell their excess power to the people.[3] If you do not punish them, they will wreak havoc; if you punish them, then they are given shelter by the ruler, who fosters and preserves them. These are the altar rats of the state.

There was a wine merchant who cleaned his wine container thoroughly and set up a very long banner, but the wine did not sell and it soured. He asked the people of his village why this was, and they said: 'Your dog, sir, is ferocious; when people enter your shop with containers to buy your wine,

231

---

1   Item 3.9 [59] ↔ *Hanshi waizhuan* 7.9/51/21. In the parallel texts of the *Shuoyuan*, 7.35/54/22 and *Hanfeizi*, 34/103/3-13, this dialogue takes place between Duke Huan and Guan Zhong.

2   途 → 塗 (*YZCQ-ICS*, 24, n. 5).

3   The *Hanshi waizhuan*, 7.9/51/23, has: 卖君以要利 "They sell you, my Lord, for profit."

**【原文】**

酒者，为器甚洁清，置表甚长，而酒酸不售，问之里人其故，里人云：'公（狗之）〔之狗〕猛，人挈器而入，且酤公酒，狗迎而噬之，此酒所以酸而不售也。'夫国亦有猛狗，用事者是也。有道术之士，欲干万乘之主，而用事者迎而龁之，此亦国之猛狗也。左右为社鼠，用事者为猛狗，（主安得无壅），（国安得无患乎）？〔则道术之士不得用矣〕，〔此治国之所患也〕。"

**【今译】**

的原因。'国家也有凶猛的狗，就是那些当权的人。懂得治国方略的人，想要见万乘之国的国君，但这些人迎上来就咬人，他们就是国家的猛狗。国君左右的近臣是社鼠，当权的人是猛狗，懂得治国方略的人得不到任用，这就是治理国家的忧患。"

your dog comes out and bites them. This is why your wine soured and did not sell.' States, too, have ferocious dogs — these are the functionaries. Officers who practice the arts of the Way seek out a ruler of ten-thousand chariots, but the functionaries come out and bite them. These, too, are the ferocious dogs of the state. When the entourage is composed of rats of the Altar of the Soil and the functionaries are 'ferocious dogs,' then officers practicing the arts of the way of ruling are not put to good use. These are a source of concern with regard to putting the state in order."

LIBRARY OF CHINESE CLASSICS

233

## 3.10 [60] 景公问欲令祝史求福晏子病以常辞罪而无求

齐景公打算让祝史祈求福运询问晏子的意见，晏子诟病这种做法，劝景公平常多向神灵谢罪不要祈求福运

### 【原文】

景公问晏子曰："寡人意气衰，身病甚。今吾欲具珪（璋）〔璧〕牺牲，令祝宗荐之乎上帝宗（朝）〔庙〕，意者礼可以干福乎？"晏子对曰："婴闻之，古者先君之干福也，政必合乎民，行必顺乎神；节宫室，不敢大斩伐，〔以〕无逼山林；节饮食，无多畋渔，以无逼川泽；祝宗用事，辞罪而不敢有所求也。是以神民俱顺，而山川纳禄。今君政

### 【今译】

齐景公问晏子道："我的精气神衰弱，身体病得很厉害。现在我想准备珪璧、牺牲等祭品，让祝宗用它祭祀上帝、宗庙，心中以为用礼可以求福吧？"晏子回答说："我听闻，古时候的君王求福，政事一定合乎百姓的心愿，行为一定顺从神灵的意志；建造宫室要节俭，不敢大量砍伐树木，以免危害山林；饮食节制，不能过度渔猎，以免危害河流湖泊；祝宗祭祀的时候，只能向神灵谢罪而不敢有所祈求。因此神灵和百姓都很和顺，山林川泽送来福禄。现在您的政事违背百姓的心愿，行为违背神灵的意志；扩建宫室，大量砍伐树木，危害山林；饮食过于丰盛，大量渔猎，危害了河流和湖泊。因此百姓和神灵都心怀

# 3.10 [60] DUKE JING INQUIRED REGARDING HIS INTENTION TO ASSIGN THE INVOCATOR AND THE ANCESTRAL ATTENDANT TO SEEK GOOD FORTUNE. YANZI REPLIED[1] THAT THE DUKE SHOULD[2] ASK FORGIVENESS FOR HIS GUILT RATHER THAN SEEK GOOD FORTUNE.

Duke Jing queried Yanzi as follows: "My will power and vitality are in decline, and I am physically very ill. Now I intend to prepare sacrificial animals, the *gui* jade baton and the *bi* jade disk, and assign the Invocator and the ancestral attendant to offer them to God on High and to the spirits in the ancestors' temple. I hope that through this Rite, I may perhaps seek good fortune."

Yanzi replied: "I have heard that in ancient times when our former rulers sought to gain good fortune, it was necessary for their government to be in accord with the people and to submit to the spirits in their conduct. They were frugal with their palaces and did not dare to cut trees excessively and thus avoided encroaching upon the mountain forests. They were sparing in their drinking and eating, and so excessive hunting and fishing did not take place; thus, they avoided encroaching on rivers and lakes. When the Invocator and the ancestral attendant performed their service, they would ask forgiveness for guilt and did not presume to ask for anything more. That is why both the spirits and the people acceded to them, and the mountains and rivers brought blessings. But now your government, my Lord, is directed against the people, and your conduct offends the spirits. Your palaces are vast, and you cut trees excessively and thereby encroach upon the mountain forests. You drink and eat gluttonously, and you hunt and

235

---

1  病 → 对 (*JS*, 202/1).

2  常 → 当 (*JS*, 202/1).

**【原文】**

反乎民，而行悖乎神；大宫室，多斩伐，以逼山林；羡饮食，多畋渔，以逼川泽。是以民神俱怨，而山川〔收〕禄，司过荐罪，而祝宗祈福，意者逆乎！"公曰："寡人非夫子无所闻此，请革心易行。"于是废公阜之游，止海食之献，斩伐者以时，畋渔者有数，居处饮食，节之勿羡，祝宗用事，辞罪而不敢有所求也。故邻国忌之，百姓亲之，晏子没而后衰。

**【今译】**

怨恨，山林川泽收回福禄，司过之官向神灵告罪，而祝宗又来祈福，恐怕相互矛盾吧！"景公说："没有您我就不会听到这些，请允许我洗心革面，改变行为。"于是废掉了去公阜游玩的计划，停止了海中食物的进献，按时砍伐树木，适度渔猎，宫室饮食都注重节约而不过多地要求，祝宗祭祀的时候，只是谢罪而不敢有所祈求。因此邻国忌惮，百姓亲附，晏子死后齐国才逐渐衰败。

fish excessively, thereby encroaching upon rivers and marshes. Therefore, both the people and the spirits resent you, and the mountains and rivers retract their blessings. The officer in charge of fault-finding proclaims your guilt, yet the Invocator and the ancestral attendant pray for good fortune—I suppose that this is contradictory, is it not?"

The Duke said: "Were it not for you, I would never have heard this. I would like to reform my heart and change my conduct."

Thereupon, he canceled his excursion to Gong-fu[1] and suspended the contributions of sea food.[2] The forests were hewn in accord with the seasons, and hunting and fishing was limited to set quotas. Dwellings and eating and drinking were modest, without excess. When the invocator and the ancestral attendant performed their service, they asked forgiveness for guilt without presuming to ask for anything more. As a result, the neighboring states stood in awe of the Duke, and his people felt kinship to him. After Yanzi's death, however, the state declined.

237

---

1   A recreation area of Duke Jing. See above 1.18.

2   According to the *Shuoyuan*, 1.40/10/4, Duke Jing received a fishing contribution and then loaded it on fifty carriages and gave it as a gift to Xian Zhang.

## 3.11 [61] 景公问古之盛君其行如何晏子对以问道者更正

齐景公问古时候的圣明君主的德行是什么样的，晏子回答说询问道义的人都改行正道

**【原文】**

景公问晏子曰："古之盛君，其行如何？"晏子对曰："薄于身而厚于民，约于身而广于世；其处上也，足以明政行教，不以威天下；其取财也，权有无，均贫富，不以养嗜欲；诛不避贵，赏不遗贱；不淫于乐，不遁于哀；尽智导民而不伐焉，劳力（岁事）〔事民〕而不责焉；（为）政尚相利，故下不以相害〔为〕行；教尚相爱，故民不以相恶为

**【今译】**

齐景公问晏子说："古时候的圣君，他们的行为是什么样的？"晏子回答说："他们薄待自己但厚待百姓，约束自身但宽待天下；他们居于国君之位，足以澄明政治推行教化，不用靠武力威慑天下；他们征收财物，权衡有无，均匀贫富，不以此满足自己的嗜好和欲望；诛罚不避权贵，恩赏不忘贫贱；不过度沉迷于享乐，不过分沉浸于哀痛；竭尽智慧教导百姓而不自我夸耀，劳心费力治理百姓而不胡乱责罚；治国理政崇尚互利，因此百姓之间以不相互损害为行为准则；推行教化崇尚相爱，因此百姓之间不以恶名相加。刑罚适度而且符合法律，废刑和问罪都要顺应民意。因此贤能的人居于上层而不哗众取宠，没有才能的人居于下层而没有怨言，四海之内，全国之中，平民百姓同心同德。像这样仿佛处理家事的政事，活着的时候对百姓有厚利，死

# 3.11 [61] DUKE JING INQUIRED REGARDING THE CONDUCT OF THE GREAT RULERS OF ANCIENT TIMES. YANZI REPLIED THAT THOSE WHO ASK ABOUT THE WAY CHANGE THEIR HEARTS.[1]

Duke Jing queried Yanzi as follows: "What characterized the conduct of the great rulers of ancient times?"

Yanzi replied: "They restricted themselves, but were generous to the people. As for themselves, they were restrained, but towards the world, they were generous. In their position as superiors, they were fit to practice enlightened rule and moral instructions. They did not use their position to intimidate the world. In collecting money and goods, they balanced the weight of the haves and the have-nots; they treated the poor and the rich with equity; and they did not use their positions to indulge their own desires. When they applied punishments, they did not shy away from the nobles, and when they gave rewards, they did not neglect the lowly. They were not extravagant in their pleasures, and they did not get mired in grief. They used their wisdom to the fullest in guiding the people, but they were not boastful in doing so. They worked extremely hard to serve the people and did not find fault with them. Their government promoted mutual benefit; therefore, their subjects did not consider mutual harm to be acceptable conduct. Their moral teaching promoted mutual love; therefore, the people did not regard mutual hatred as a way to gain fame. Punishments followed the law precisely, and dismissals and indictments were made in accordance with the circumstances of the people. Therefore, the worthy occupied superior positions without ostentation, and the unworthy occupied inferior positions without resentment. Within the Four Seas and the domain of the altars of soil and grain, the people who lived on grain[2] shared a common purpose

239

---

1   正 → 心 (*JS*, 206/13).

2   I.e., the Chinese, as opposed to tribes surrounding China.

【原文】

名。刑罚中于法，废罪顺于民。是以贤者处上而不华，不肖者处下而不怨，四海之内，社稷之中，粒食之民，一意同欲。若夫私家之政，生有〔厚利〕，〔死有〕遗教，此盛君之行也。"（公不图），晏子曰："臣闻问道者更正，闻道者更容。今君税敛重，故民心离；市买悖，故（商）〔商〕旅绝；玩好充，故家货殚。积邪在于上，蓄怨藏于民，嗜欲备于侧，毁非满于国，而公不图。"公曰："善。"于是令玩好不御，公市不豫，宫室不饰，业土不成，止役轻税，上下行之，而百姓相亲。

【今译】

后还遗留下教化，这就是圣君的德行。"（景公不想这样做）晏子说："我听闻询问道义的人是要更改正道，听到道义的人要更改仪容。现在您赋税聚敛过重，因此民心离散；买卖贸易混乱，因此商旅断绝；国君的玩好之物充盈，因此百姓家中财货竭尽。邪僻累积隐藏于朝堂，怨恨滋生隐藏于民间，嗜欲之物放在身边，诽谤非议遍布全国，而您却不去考虑。"景公说："好。"于是下令玩好之物不再使用，市场贸易不许欺诈，宫室不再装饰，未完成的工程不再修建，停止劳役减轻税赋，上下一起行动，而百姓相亲相爱。

and identical desires. This was like the managing of a private family: during their lifetime, they had large benefits; when they died, they left their moral teaching. Such was the conduct of the mighty rulers. I have heard that those who ask about the Way change their hearts,[1] and those who hear about the Way change their countenance. But now, your tax collections, my Lord, are heavy; therefore, the hearts of the people turn away from you. Market conditions are adverse, and therefore tradesmen and traveling merchants abandon you. Fine things and precious objects abound, and therefore the wealth of households is exhausted. Those in superior positions amass wickedness, and the people horde up resentments. You have all that you desire within your palace, while slander and defamation spread throughout your capital, yet you still do not try to resolve all this."

The Duke said: "Well argued."

Thereupon, he prohibited the carrying of fine things and precious objects, inflated prices in the market, decoration of palaces, and completion of the earthworks for construction. He stopped compulsory labor and lowered taxes. Superiors and inferiors followed these decrees, and the people felt kinship with one another.

---

1   正 → 心 (*JS*, 206/13).

大中华文库

## 3.12 [62] 景公问谋必得事必成何术晏子对以度义因民

齐景公问谋划一定有收获做事情一定成功有什么办法，晏子回答说要符合道义顺从百姓

### 【原文】

景公问晏子曰："谋必得，事必成，有术乎？"晏子对曰："有。"公曰："其术如何？"晏子曰："谋度于义者必得，事因于民者必成。"公曰："奚谓也？"对曰："其谋也，左右无所系，上下无所靡，其声不悖，其实不逆，谋于上，不违天，谋于〔下〕，不违民，以此谋者必得矣；事大则利厚，事小则利薄，称事之大小，权利之轻重，国有义劳，民

### 【今译】

齐景公问晏子说："谋划一定实现，办事一定成功，有这样的办法吗？"晏子回答说："有。"景公说："那方法是怎样的？"晏子说："谋划符合道义就一定会实现，办事顺从百姓就一定能成功。"景公道："为什么这样说呢？"晏子回答说："谋划事情不受左右的干扰，不受上下的牵连，言论不违背礼仪，行为不逆反道义，谋划的事情上不违背天意，下不违背民心，用这样的方法谋划的事情一定能实现；事情大则利益丰厚，事情小则利益微薄，估量事情的大小，权衡利益的轻重，国家有道义，百姓有利益，用这样的方法做事情就一定能成功。不讲道义去谋划，即使成功也不会安宁；轻视百姓去做事，即使成功也不光荣。因此我听闻道义是谋划的法则，百姓是做事的根本，因此违背道义去谋划，违背百姓去做事，没有听说过有留存的。以前夏商周三代兴盛的时候，谋划一定考虑道义，做事一定顺从百姓。等到三

# 3.12 [62] DUKE JING INQUIRED REGARDING THE METHOD BY WHICH PLANS ARE CERTAIN TO ACHIEVE THEIR PURPOSE AND UNDERTAKINGS TO BE ACCOMPLISHED. YANZI REPLIED THAT THESE PLANS AND UNDERTAKINGS SHOULD BE MEASURED BY RIGHTEOUSNESS AND CONFORMANCE TO THE NEEDS OF THE PEOPLE.

Duke Jing queried Yanzi as follows: "Is there a method by which plans are certain bound to achieve their purpose and undertakings bound to be accomplished?"

Yanzi replied: "There is."

The Duke said: "What is this method?"

Yanzi said: "Those plans that are based on righteousness are certain to succeed, and undertakings that conform to the needs of the people are certain to be accomplished."

They Duke said: "What do you mean?"

Yanzi replied: "One who makes plans, with no one among his entourage to tie him down and no one among the superiors and inferiors to harness[1] him; whose words are not contradictory and whose deeds are not perverse; and who in consultation with superiors, does not defy Heaven, and with inferiors does not defy the people — one who plans thus is sure to achieve his purpose. When one's undertakings are great, then benefits are abundant; when they are small, benefits are meager. Measure the size of the undertaking, reckon the weight of benefits, and the state will have fair labor and the people will have additional benefits. Those who initiate undertakings in this way will certainly accomplish them. If one avoids righteousness in making plans, even if these plans are accomplished, one will not be at

243

---

1 靡 → 縻 (*YZCQ-ICS*, 26, n. 1).

## 【原文】

有（如）〔加〕利，以此举事者必成矣。夫逃（人）〔义〕而谟，虽成不安；傲民举事，虽成不荣。故臣闻义、谋之法（者）〔也〕，民、事之本也，故（及）〔反〕义而谋，（信）〔倍〕民而动，未闻存者也。昔三代之兴也，谋必度（其）〔于〕义，事必因于民。及其衰也，建谋者（及）〔反〕义，兴事〔者〕伤民。故度义因民，谋事之术也。"公曰："寡人不敏，闻善不行，其（已）〔危〕如何？"对曰："上君全善，其次出入焉，其次结邪而羞问。全善之君能制；出入之君、时问之君，虽日危，尚可以没身；羞问之君，不能保其身。今君虽危，尚可没其身也。"

## 【今译】

代衰亡的时候，谋划的人不考虑道义，做事的人损害百姓。因此考虑道义和顺从百姓，是谋划做事的方法。"景公说："我不聪明，听到善言也没施行，已经出现危险该怎么办呢？"晏子回答说："上等的君王全部事情都择善而行，稍差一些的君王和全善有一些差异，再差一些的君王行为邪僻而羞于询问。全部择善而行的君王能够掌控局面；和全善有差异的君王、能够经常问询的君王，虽然日渐危险，但尚且可以善终；羞于问询的君王，不能保全自身。现在您虽然日渐危险，但还能得以善终。"

peace. If one initiates undertakings with an attitude of arrogance towards the people, even if these undertakings are accomplished, one will not be glorified. Hence, I have heard that righteousness is the correct model for planning and the people are the foundation of all undertakings. Therefore, to my knowledge, no one who makes plans contrary to righteousness and takes action that is hostile to the people has ever survived. Formerly, in the heyday of the Three Dynasties, plans were always measured by standards of righteousness and undertakings were always grounded in the people. When these dynasties declined, those who promoted plans acted against righteous principles, and those who initiated undertakings harmed the people. Therefore, righteous measurement and conformance to the needs of the people constitute the art of planning and undertaking affairs."

The Duke said: "I am not that bright. I am taught to do good, but do not act on it—is this a cause for danger?"

Yanzi replied: "The best ruler is perfect; the next best is mediocre; and the one that comes next is he who allies himself with evil and is embarrassed to raise questions. The perfect ruler is able to control; the mediocre ruler raises questions occasionally;[1] although he may face danger, his life may still end from natural causes. The ruler who is embarrassed to raise questions cannot die naturally. Now you, my Lord, although you are in danger, you can still die naturally."

---

1   出入之君时问 (*YZCQ-ICS*, 26, n. 5).

## 3.13 [63] 景公问〔善〕为国家者何如晏子对以举贤官能

齐景公问善于治理国家的方法是什么，晏子回答说要举用贤人授官给有才能的人

### 【原文】

景公问晏子曰："莅国治民，善为国家者何如？"晏子对曰："举贤以临国，官能以救民，则其道也。举贤官能，则民与若矣。"公曰："虽有贤能，吾庸知乎？"晏子对曰："贤而隐，庸为贤乎，吾君亦不务乎是，故不知也。"公曰："请问求贤。"对曰："观之以其游，说之以其行，君无以靡曼辩辞定其行，无以毁誉非议定其身，如此，则不为

### 【今译】

齐景公问晏子说："当国君治理百姓，善于治国的方法是什么？"晏子回答说："选任贤明的人来治理国家，授官给有才能的人来治理百姓，这就是治国的方法。选任贤人，授官给有才能的人，那百姓就会办善事了。"景公说："即使有贤能的人，我怎么才能知道呢？"晏子回答说："贤明而隐居，怎么还能称得上贤人呢，国君也没有注意这些，所以不知道。"景公说："请问寻求贤人的方法。"晏子回答说："观察与他交游的人，注意他的言行举止，您不要依靠华丽的言辞来判定他的品行，也不要因为别人的诋毁或赞美来评定他本人，这样，他就

# 3.13 [63] DUKE JING INQUIRED REGARDING THOSE WHO ARE GOOD AT RULING THE STATE. YANZI REPLIED THAT THEY PROMOTE THE WORTHY AND APPOINT THE CAPABLE.

Duke Jing queried Yanzi as follows: "In administrating a state and governing the people, what must those who are good at ruling the state be like?"

Yanzi replied: "If you manage the state by promoting the worthy and administer the people by appointing the capable, then you follow the Way. If you promote the worthy and appoint the capable, then goodness will be fostered among the people."[1]

The Duke said: "Even if there are worthy and capable people, how can I find out about them?"

Yanzi replied: "If they are worthy but remain hidden, how can they be worthy? It seems that you, my Lord, do not apply your efforts to this; therefore, you cannot find out about them."

The Duke said: "May I ask about seeking the worthy?"

Yanzi replied: "Observe them according to their associations, and comment about them on the basis of their conduct. You, my Lord, should not form a judgment regarding their conduct on the basis of their charm and eloquence and should not determine their character on the basis of praise, blame, and criticism. In this way, their conduct will not be falsified into a misleading reputation and they will not conceal their desires in order to manipulate their ruler.[2] Therefore, with regard to those who are successful: observe whom they recommend, what those who are hard-pressed refuse to do, what those who are rich distribute, and what those who are poor refuse

247

---

1   与若 → 兴善 (*YZCQ-ICS*, 26, n. 6).

2   荣 → 营 (*YZCQ-ICS*, 26, n. 7).

**【原文】**

行以扬声，不掩欲以荣君。故通则视其所举，穷则视其所不为；富则视其所〔分〕，〔贫则视其所〕不（耴）〔取〕。夫上士，难进而易退也；其次易进易退也；其下易进难退也。以此数物者（耴）〔取〕人，其可乎！"

**【今译】**

不能故作高行来张扬名声，不能掩盖私欲来迷惑君主。因此在他得意时要观察他的所作所为，在他失意时要观察他不愿做的事；富有时要观察他分财物给什么人，贫穷时要观察他不愿取的财物。最上等的士难以引进而容易退去；次一等的容易引进也容易退去；最下等的容易引进难以退去。用这几条标准来选取人才，大概就可以了吧！"

to take.[1] The best officer would be the one who advances with difficulty and withdraws with ease; next comes the one who advances with ease and withdraws with ease; and the lowest is the one who advances with ease and retires with difficulty. Selecting people with these various traits is most likely the proper way — is this acceptable?"

---

1   Item 3.13 [63] ↔ *Hanshi waizhuan* 3.6/17/3; *Shuoyuan*, 2.5/7/7; *Lüshi chunqiu*, 3.4./15/14.

# 3.14 [64] 景公问君臣身尊而荣难乎晏子对以易

齐景公问做国君受到尊重做臣子获得荣耀是否困难，晏子回答说容易

【原文】

景公问晏子曰："为君，身尊民安，为臣，事治身荣，难乎，易乎？"晏子对曰："易。"公曰："何若？"对曰："为君节（養）〔养〕其余以顾民，则（君）〔身〕尊而民安；为臣忠信而无逾职业，则事治而身荣。"公又问："为君何行则危？为臣何行则废？"晏子对曰："为君，

【今译】

齐景公问晏子说："做国君，让自身受到尊重百姓得到安乐，做臣子，办好国家大事让自身获得荣耀，这是困难呢还是容易呢？"晏子回答说："容易。"景公问："为什么？"晏子回答说："当国君就生活节俭用多余的财物照顾百姓，那么国君就会受到尊重而百姓得到安乐；做臣子忠诚守信而不逾越职权，那么就能办好国家大事而自身获得荣耀。"景公又问："做国君什么行为会有危险？做臣子什么行为会被罢免？"晏子回答说："做国君，加重赋税聚敛财物还借口说是为了百姓，任用谗谀之人还借口说是任用贤臣，疏远公平正直的人还借口说他们不顺从，国君办了这三件事就危险；做臣子，结党营私以求进身，逾越职权，提防百姓隐瞒利益而求自己多得，跟从在国君身边不陈述国

# 3.14 [64] DUKE JING ASKED IF IT IS DIFFICULT FOR RULERS AND MINISTERS TO BE HONORED AND GLORIFIED. YANZI REPLIED THAT IT IS EASY.

Duke Jing queried Yanzi as follows: "Is it difficult or easy to be a ruler who is honored, and whose people are at peace; to be a minister who is glorified, and whose undertakings are ordered?"

Yanzi replied: "It is easy."

The Duke said: "In what sense?

Yanzi replied: "If a ruler is frugal in building up a surplus to care for the people, then he will be honored and the people will be at peace. If a minister is loyal and trustworthy and does not overstep the duties of office, then his undertakings will be orderly and he will be glorified."

The Duke again asked: "What conduct endangers a ruler, and what conduct results in dismissal of a minister?"

Yanzi replied: "A ruler who collects heavy taxes, pretending that this is in the people's interest; who promotes slanderers and sycophants, pretending that he is employing the worthy; who distances himself from those who are impartial, pretending that they are not obedient—such a ruler who practices these three acts is placing himself in danger. A minister who forms alliances in cliques in order to seek promotion and oversteps his duty as an official; who prevents his subordinates from gaining benefits and seeks to increase his own wealth; and who, in following his ruler, does not criticize faults and thereby seeks favor with the ruler—such a minister who practices these three acts is dismissed. For this reason, the enlightened ruler does not demonstrate[1] depravities to the people; he protects the people's property and does not suffer losses. He establishes laws and regulations and does not violate them. If indeed he seeks something from the people,

251

---

1   观 → 示 (*JS*, 215/7).

**【原文】**

厚藉敛而托之为民，进谗谀而托之用贤，远公正而托之不顺，君行此三者则危；为臣，比周以求（寸）〔进〕，逾职业，防下隐利而求多，从君不陈过而求亲，人臣行此三者则废。故明君不以邪观民，守则而不亏，立法仪而不犯，苟有所求于民，（而）不以身害之，是故刑政安于下，民心固于上。故察士不比周而进，不为苟而求，言无阴阳，行无内外，顺则进，否则退，不与上行邪，是以进不失廉，退不失行也。"

**【今译】**

君的过失而只求亲近，臣子做了这三件事就该被罢免。因此贤明的君主不做邪僻之事让臣民观看，守护百姓的财物而不损害其利益，树立了法律礼仪而自己不触犯，如果向百姓有所求取，也不因自身需求而损害百姓，因此刑律政教使百姓安定，民心团结在国君周围。所以明察之士不结党营私来求进身，不做苟且之事来求取名物，言语无阴阳之分，行为无内外之别，顺利时就进身，不顺时就引退，不和国君一起做邪僻之事，因此进身不失廉洁，引退不失德行。"

he does not harm them for the sake of his interests. For this reason, punishments and governmental measures have a calming effect on inferiors, and the people's hearts are firmly united with him. Therefore, circumspect officers do not form alliances in cliques in order to be promoted and do not act unscrupulously in order to seek advantage for themselves. What they say face to face is not different than what they say in an anonymous forum, and their norms of conduct do not apply differently inside and outside of their household domain.  If their words are followed, they advance; if not, they withdraw. They do not practice evil in collusion with their superior and so, when they advance, they do not lose their integrity, and when they withdraw, they do not act incorrectly."

253

## 3.15 [65] 景公问天下之所以存亡晏子对以六说

齐景公问天下兴盛衰亡的原因，晏子用六种说法回答

### 【原文】

景公问晏子曰："寡人持不仁，其无义耳也。不然，北面与夫子而义。"晏子对曰："婴，人臣也，公曷为出若言？"公曰："请终问天下之所以存亡。"晏子曰："缦密不能，麓苴〔不〕学者诎，身无以用人，

### 【今译】

齐景公问晏子说："我不仁德，不足以议政。不如面向北和您议论。"晏子回答说："我是臣子，您为什么说出这样的话？"景公说："我请求最终向您询问天下之所以兴盛衰亡的原因。"晏子说："不能细心做事，粗心不愿学习的人屈居人下，自己不会用人，而又不能为人所用的人身份卑贱。不能亲近好人而又不能疏远坏人的人是危险的。和朋友交游，没有被人喜爱的长处而又不能欣赏他人长处的人注定穷困。

# 3.15 [65] DUKE JING INQUIRED ABOUT THE CAUSES LEADING TO THE SURVIVAL AND DESTRUCTION OF THE REALM. YANZI REPLIED WITH SIX ARGUMENTS.

Duke Jing queried Yanzi as follows: "I lack humaneness by my nature, so perhaps we should not discuss[1] this anymore? Otherwise, I should rather face north and express my views to you, my Master."[2]

Yanzi replied: "I am a minister; why do you utter such words, my Lord?"

The Duke said: "Then let me, once and for all, ask you about the causes leading to the survival and destruction of the realm."

Yanzi replied: "Those who are neither able to deal with what is refined and delicate nor able to learn what is coarse should be dismissed. Those who have the capacity neither to employ others nor to be employed by others should be demoted. Those who are neither able to be intimate with good people nor able to distance themselves from evil people will find themselves in danger. In social exchanges with friends,[3] those who are not pleased by anything that people can do nor have the ability themselves to please people will find themselves in dire straits. Those who serve the ruler for the sake of

---

1 义 → 议 (*YZCQ-ICS*, 27, n. 2).

2 All sovereigns of traditional China sat facing south when holding audience, and ministers and subjects faced north. In this Item, we find Duke Jing worn out by the countless audiences he held with Yanzi during which he heard time and again about his failings as a humane ruler. The Duke therefore states that he would rather continue his discussions with Yanzi facing north, namely, that he relinquishes all his privileges as ruler and becomes an ordinary person. Yanzi obviously refuses to take part in Duke Jing's farce and forces him to continue to play his role as ruler. Duke Jing then seizes the opportunity and addresses Yanzi with a question regarding the reasons leading to the destruction of the realm — a question he has held in his mind throughout.

3 Omit 从 (*YZCQ-ICS*, 27, n. 3).

**【原文】**

而又不为人用者卑。善人不能戚，恶人不能疏者危。交游朋友，从无以说于人，又不能说人者穷。事君要利，大者不得，小者不为者馁。修道立义，大不能专，小不能附者灭。此足以观存亡矣。"

**【今译】**

侍奉国君只求利益，大事做不了，小事又不愿做的人要挨饿。修身行道，树立礼义，大的事情不能单独负责，小的事情不能依附合作的人一定灭亡。这些足以观察兴盛衰亡了。"

profit and are neither able to attain what is great nor are engaged in lesser matters will starve. Those who perfect the Way and establish righteousness but are unable to devote themselves wholeheartedly to great undertakings and to ally themselves with others to do lesser undertakings will be wiped out. These points should be sufficient to show the reasons for survival and destruction."

## 3.16 [66] 景公问君子常行曷若晏子对以三者

齐景公问君子的日常行为是什么样的，晏子用三件事来回答

**【原文】**

景公问晏子曰："君子常行曷若？"晏子对曰："衣冠不中，不敢以入朝；所言不义，不敢以要君；（行己）〔身行〕不顺，（不敢）治事不公，不敢以莅众。衣冠无不中，故朝无奇辟之服；所言无不义，故下无伪上之报；身行顺，治事公，故国无阿党之义。三者，君子之常行（者）也。"

**【今译】**

齐景公问晏子说："君子日常的行为是什么样的？"晏子回答说："衣冠不端正，不敢进入朝堂；言论不合道义，不敢要求国君听从；自身的行为不符合规矩，做事不公正，不敢管理百姓。衣冠没有不端正的，所以朝堂上没有奇装异服；言论没有不符合道义的，所以臣下不会向国君做假报告；自身行为符合规矩，办事公正，所以国家没有结党营私的活动。这三条，就是君子的日常行为。"

# 3.16 [66] DUKE JING ASKED WHAT CHARACTERIZES THE STANDARD CONDUCT OF A MAN OF NOBLE CHARACTER. YANZI REPLIED THAT IT CONSISTS OF THREE CHARACTERISTICS.

Duke Jing queried Yanzi as follows: "What characterizes the standard conduct of a man of noble character?"

Yanzi replied: "If his clothing and hat do not fit, he dares not enter the court for an audience. If his words are not righteous, he does not dare to coerce his ruler. If his conduct is contrary to what is required, and he is biased in taking care of things, he dares not face the masses. Since his clothing and hat always fit, no one else appears in outlandish outfits during a court audience. Since his words always accord with righteousness, inferiors present no false reports to superiors. Since his conduct follows what is required, and he is unbiased when he puts affairs in order, there are no disputes in the state among various factions. These three acts characterize the standard conduct of a man of noble character."

259

## 3.17 [67] 景公问贤君治国若何晏子对以任贤爱民

齐景公问贤明君主怎样治理国家，晏子用任用贤臣仁爱百姓来回答

大中华文库

### 【原文】

景公问晏子曰："贤君之治国若何？"晏子对曰："其政任贤，其行爱民，其（耻）〔取〕下节，其自养俭；在上不犯下，在治不傲穷；从邪害民者有罪，进善举过者有赏。其政，刻上而饶下，赦过而救穷；不因喜以加赏，不因怒以加罚；不从欲以劳民，不修怒而危国；上无骄行，下无谄德；上无私义，下无窃权；上无朽蠹之藏，下无冻馁之民；不事骄行而尚司，其民安乐而相亲。贤君之治国若此。"

### 【今译】

260

齐景公问晏子说："贤德的君主是怎样治理国家的？"晏子回答说："他们在政治上选贤任能，在行为上爱护百姓，在向百姓索取时懂得节制，在供养自己时比较节俭；居于上位而不侵犯下面的利益，居于管理位而不轻视穷困百姓；放纵奸邪之行侵害百姓的有罪，进献善言检举过失的有赏。他们在政治方面，对上严格而对下宽厚，赦免有过失的而救助穷困的；不因为喜好而增加赏赐，不因为愤怒而加重处罚；不放纵私欲来劳损百姓，不和诸侯结怨以危害国家；国君没有骄纵的行为，臣下没有谄媚的品行；国君没有私人关系的道义，臣下没有私下利用职权的行为；国家上没有腐朽生蠹的库藏，下没有饥寒交迫的百姓；不侍奉骄纵的行为而崇尚大同，百姓安居乐业而互相亲爱。贤明的君主就是这样治理国家的。"

# 3.17 [67] DUKE JING ASKED HOW A WORTHY RULER GOVERNS HIS STATE. YANZI REPLIED THAT WORTHY GOVERNANCE CONSISTS OF APPOINTING WORTHY AND LOVING THE PEOPLE.

Duke Jing queried Yanzi as follows: "How does a worthy ruler govern his state?"

Yanzi replied: "His governing consists of appointing the worthy and his conduct consists of loving the people. He is restrained in taking from inferiors and frugal in creating himself wealth. His superiors do not offend inferiors and those in administrative control are not arrogant to the destitute. Those who walk in the way of evil and harm the people are held guilty, and those who present good advice and point out mistakes are rewarded. His government is severe with those in a high position and lenient to those of low status, pardoning offences and assisting the destitute. He does not grant rewards based on personal pleasure and he does not inflict punishments based on anger. He refrains from giving in to desires, thereby overworking the people labor, and he does not incur enmity[1] thereby endangering the state. Under his government, those in positions of high status are free of arrogant conduct, and those in low status positions are free of sycophancy.[2] Those in high status positions have no egoistic morality and those in low status positions do not usurp power. Superiors do not store goods to be spoiled by insects in the warehouses, and none of the inferior people suffer cold and hunger. He does not act arrogantly, and he exalts unity.[3] The people are at peace and happy and they esteem kinship. This is how the worthy ruler governs his state."

261

---

1　怒 → 怨 (*JS*, 221/4).

2　谄 → 讇 (*YZCQ-ICS*, 3.7/24/2).

3　司 → 同 (*JS*, 221/7). "Exalting Unity" (尚同) is the title of three consecutive chapters (11-13) in the *Mozi*. For a brief discussion of the meaning of this title, see Ian Johnston, tr. *Mozi: A Complete Translation*. Hong Kong: Chinese University Press (2010): 90.

# 3.18 [68] 景公问明王之教民何若晏子对以先行义

齐景公问贤明君主怎样教化百姓，晏子回答说要先施行德义

## 【原文】

景公问晏子曰："明王之教民何若？"晏子对曰："明其教令，而先之以行义；（養）〔养〕民不苛，而防之以刑辟；（求所）〔所求〕于下者，（不）〔必〕务于上；所禁于民者，不行于身。守于民财，无亏之以利，立于仪法，不犯之以邪，苟所求于民，不以身害之，故下（之）劝从其教也。称事以任民，中听以禁邪，不穷之以劳，不害之以（实）〔罚〕，苟所禁于民，不以事逆之，故下不敢犯其上也。古者百里而异习，千里而殊俗，故明王修道，一民同俗，上〔以〕爱民为法，下〔以〕相亲为义，是以天下不相遗，此明王〔之〕教民（之理）也。"

## 【今译】

齐景公问晏子说："贤明的君王是怎样教化百姓的？"晏子回答说："阐明政教和法令的要求，自己率先执行；养育百姓不苛刻，而用刑罚防止他们犯罪；对下面提的要求，上面从先做到；禁止百姓做的事情，自己也不能去做。守护百姓的财产，不要损害他们的利益，树立礼仪法度，不做奸邪的事情去触犯，如果对百姓有所求取，不因自身的需求损害他们的利益，因此百姓听从他的教化。估量事情的大小来使用民力，公正听讼断案来禁除奸邪，不用劳役穷竭民力，不用刑罚侵害百姓，如果有对百姓的禁令，不能因为任何事由违反，因此下边的臣民不敢冒犯君上。古时候百里之内习惯不同，千里之内风俗不同，因此贤明君王修定道义，要和百姓的风俗相一致，君上以爱护百姓为法度，臣民以相亲相爱为义理，因此天下之人不互相遗弃，这就是贤明君王教化百姓的方法。"

# 3.18 [68] DUKE JING ASKED WHAT MORAL INSTRUCTIONS SHOULD BE GIVEN TO THE PEOPLE BY AN ENLIGHTENED KING. YANZI REPLIED THAT THE ENLIGHTENED KING FIRST PUTS RIGHTEOUSNESS INTO EFFECT.

Duke Jing queried Yanzi as follows: "What should the moral instructions given to the people by an enlightened king be?"

Yanzi replied: "The enlightened king elucidates his moral instructions and regulations, but first he puts righteousness into effect. He nurtures the people; he is not harsh, and he protects them through his penal system. What he demands from inferiors he strives to attain from superiors; that which is forbidden of the people, he himself does not practice. He protects the people's property and does not incur losses for the sake of his own benefit. He bases himself on rules of etiquette and a system of laws and does not contravene them for evil purposes. If indeed he seeks something from the people, then he does not harm them for the sake of his interests. Therefore, the inferiors are motivated to follow his moral instructions. He weighs objective facts in the process of hiring people; he is just in adjudicating cases to prevent evil; he does not bring destitution on the people by compulsory labor; and he does not harm the people with punishments. If he indeed prohibits the people from doing something, he does not violate the prohibition in his own affairs. Therefore, inferiors do not dare to offend their superiors. In ancient times, people in every one hundred *li* had different practices and in every one thousand *li* had different customs. Therefore, the enlightened kings perfected the way to unify the people and made customs uniform. Superiors regarded love of the people as a model, and inferiors regarded mutual consideration as righteousness. Therefore, no disobedience[1] existed in the world at that time. These are the moral instructions given to the people by an enlightened king."

---

1 遗 → 违 (*YZCQ-ICS*, 28, n. 1).

# 3.19 [69] 景公问忠臣之事君何若晏子对以不与君陷于难

齐景公问忠臣怎样侍奉国君，晏子回答说不和国君一起陷于危难

## 【原文】

景公问于晏子曰："忠臣之事君也何若？"晏子对曰："有难不死，出亡不送。"公不说，曰："君裂地而封之，疏爵而贵之，君有难不死，出亡不送，（可谓忠乎），〔其说何也〕？"对曰："言而见用，终身无难，臣奚死焉；谋而见从，终身不出，臣奚送焉。若言不〔见〕用，有难而死之，是妄死也；谋而不〔见〕从，出亡而送之，是诈伪也。故忠臣也者，能纳善于君，〔而〕不能与君陷于难。"

## 【今译】

齐景公问晏子说："忠臣是怎样侍奉国君的？"晏子回答说："国君有灾难不为国君去死，国君出国逃亡也不护送。"景公很不高兴，说："国君分割土地来封赏他，分出爵位来使他显贵，国君有了灾难不为国君去死，国君出逃也不护送，为什么这样说呢？"晏子回答说："忠臣的谏言被采纳，国君一生不会有灾难，臣子怎么会去死；忠臣的计谋被听从，国君一生不会出国逃亡，臣子怎么会去护送。如果忠臣的谏言不被采纳，国君有了灾难而为国君去死，这是没有意义的死；如果忠臣的计谋不被听从，国君出国逃亡而去护送，这是狡诈虚伪的行为。因此忠臣能够向国君进献善言，而不能和国君陷入灾难。"

## 3.19 [69] DUKE JING ASKED WHAT A LOYAL MINISTER'S SERVICE TO A RULER SHOULD BE LIKE. [1] YANZI REPLIED THAT A LOYAL MINISTER DOES NOT FALL INTO DISASTER ALONG WITH HIS RULER.

Duke Jing queried Yanzi as follows: "What should a loyal minister's service to a ruler be like?"

Yanzi replied: "If the ruler faces disaster, the minister does not die with him; if he flees into exile, he does not accompany him."

The Duke was displeased and said: "A ruler divides the land and parcels it out to his ministers as fiefs, bestowing upon them titles and honors; yet when he faces disaster they will not die with him and when he flees into exile they will not accompany him? What is the line of reasoning here?"

Yanzi replied: "If a minister's words are put into practice, the ruler will face no disaster throughout his life, so why should a minister die? [2] If the ministers' plans are followed, then the ruler will not be forced into exile throughout his life, so why should the minister accompany his ruler into exile? If the minister's words are not practiced and the minister dies during the disaster—this is a senseless death; if his plans are not followed and he accompanies his ruler into exile—this is deception and falsity. Therefore, those who are loyal ministers, able to provide their ruler with good counsel, cannot fall into disaster along with their ruler."

---

1  As in the text, 何若 → 若何 (*YZCQ-ICS*, 28, n. 2).

2  For the same idea regarding the degree of self-sacrifice ministers should or should not make for their ruler, see *Kongcongzi,* 3.3/22/8; Yoav Ariel, tr. *K'ung-ts'ung-tzu: The K'ung Family Master's Anthology*. Princeton Library of Asian Translations. Princeton (1989): 128.

# 3.20 [70] 景公问忠臣之行何如晏子对以不与君行邪

齐景公问忠臣的行为是什么样的，晏子回答说不和国君一起行奸邪之事

## 【原文】

景公问晏子曰："忠臣之行何如？"对曰："不掩君过，谏乎前，不华乎外；选贤进能，不私乎内；称身就位，计能（定）〔受〕禄；睹贤不居其上，受禄不过其量；不权（居）〔君〕以为行，不称位以为忠；不掩贤以隐长，不刻下以谀上；君在不事太子，国危不交诸侯；顺则进，否则退，不与君行邪也。"

## 【今译】

齐景公问晏子道："忠臣的德行是什么样的？"晏子回答说："不掩饰君主的过失，在君主面前进谏，不对外宣扬君主的过失；选贤任能，不偏爱内亲；估量自身的德行就任官职，权衡自己的才能接受俸禄；看到贤能的人而不居于其上，接受俸禄不超过应得的数量；不权衡君王的意志来决定自己的行为，不估量职位的高低来决定自己的忠诚；不掩盖贤才而隐瞒他的长处，不刻薄下属而谄谀上级；国君在位时不侍奉太子，国家危难时不结交诸侯；顺利时就进身，不顺时就引退，不和国君一起做奸邪的事。"

## 3.20 [70] DUKE JING ASKED WHAT THE CONDUCT OF A LOYAL MINISTER SHOULD BE LIKE. YANZI REPLIED THAT A LOYAL MINISTER DOES NOT PRACTICE EVIL IN COLLUSION WITH THE RULER.

Duke Jing queried Yanzi as follows: "What should the conduct of a loyal minister be like?"

Yanzi replied: "A loyal minister does not conceal the ruler's mistakes; within the court, he remonstrates openly in front of him, but he keeps his criticism discrete outside the court. He selects the worthy and promotes the capable; he does not favor those who belong to his inner circle; he takes a position based upon correct self-assessment; and he evaluates whether his ability merits his emolument. If he sees the worthy, he does not exalt himself above them. He refuses to accept a greater emolument than what is his due. He does not take into account his ruler's views when shaping his own conduct, and he does not weigh the responsibilities of his office in order to appear loyal. He does not conceal other worthies from his superiors by obscuring their merit. He is not malicious towards inferiors in order to flatter his superiors. When the ruler is alive, he does not serve the crown prince. When the state is in peril, he does not make contact with the regional princes. If his advice is followed, he advances; if not, he withdraws. He does not practice evil in collusion with the ruler."

267

## 3.21 [71] 景公问佞人之事君何如晏子对〔以〕愚君所信也

齐景公问奸佞之人怎样侍奉国君，晏子回答说他们是愚昧国君所信任的

【原文】

景公问："佞人之事君如何？"晏子对曰："意难，难不至也。明言行之以饰身，伪言无欲以说人，严其交以见其爱；观上之所欲，而微为之偶，求君逼尔，而阴为之与；内重爵禄，而外轻之以诬行，下事左右，而面示正公以伪廉；求上采听，而幸以求进；傲禄以求多，辞

【今译】

齐景公问晏子："奸佞之人是怎样侍奉国君的？"晏子回答说："很难说，难在说不到位。他们公开的言行是为了修饰自身，假说没有欲望以取悦于人，对交往的人严格以体现他的关爱；观察国君的欲求，而暗中与他偶合，求见国君亲近的人，而暗地里和他们结交；内心里重视爵位和俸禄，而表面上轻视以欺骗他人，小心地侍奉国君左右的近臣，而表面上展示公平公正以假装廉洁；祈求国君采纳听取他们的意见，有幸被宠信以求进身；轻视俸禄以求更多，辞去任职以求重用；巧于索取，鄙弃给予；喜欢新的，怠慢旧的；吝惜财物，施舍很少；看见贫穷的亲友好像不认识，追逐利益唯恐来不及；对外结交来宣扬自己，背弃至亲厚待自身；积攒了礼仪的修养，而声称有怜悯贫苦的

# 3.21 [71] DUKE JING ASKED WHAT CHARACTERIZES THE SYCOPHANTS WHO SERVE THEIR RULER. YANZI REPLIED THAT SYCOPHANTS ARE THOSE WHOM A FOOLISH RULER TRUSTS.

Duke Jing asked Yanzi: "What characterizes the sycophants who serve their ruler?"

Yanzi replied: "Ah, a difficult question, yet not exceptionally difficult.[1] The sycophants openly speak about their activities so that their own position may be enhanced; they falsely state that they have no desires, in order to please people; they maintain strict formalities in relationships with the ruler in order to gain his favor; they observe the desires of the ruler and in their petty dealings become his collaborators; they seek out the ruler's intimate courtiers and secretly form alliances with them; inwardly, they highly value titles and emoluments, yet outwardly they belittle both in order to create the opposite impression; they humbly serve the entourage of the ruler and appear to give expression to justice and fairness, as a pretense for integrity; they aspire to have their superiors heed their advice, so that they may be promoted by luck; they speak contemptuously of their emoluments, in order to pursue more; they resign from a position, in order to aim for a more important one; they are skillful in taking and sparing in giving; they are happy with what is new, and neglect what is old; they are frugal with property and give scant charity; they look upon the destitute as if they do not recognize them, yet they scurry after profit as if chasing something beyond their reach. They seek relations with outsiders in order to spread their own fame, yet turn their backs on their relatives for their own benefit; they

269

---

1  意 → 噫. (*JS*, 228/2). The same rhetorical style is replicated also in Item 2.20 [45] (*YZCQ-ICS*, 18/9) which reads: 晏子曰: 嘻! 难哉! 难然，婴将为子复之. (Yanzi said: "Oh! That is very difficult! Even so, I will report the matter to him for you.").

**【原文】**

任以求重；工乎取，鄙乎予；欢乎新，慢乎故；惏乎财，薄乎施；睹贫穷若不识，趋利若不及；外交以自扬，背亲以自厚；积丰义之（養）〔养〕，而声矜恤之义；非誉乎情，而言不行身，涉时所议，而好论贤不肖；有之己，不难非之人，无之己，不难求之人；其言强梁而信，其进敏逊而顺：此佞人之行也。明君之所诛，愚君之所信也。"

**【今译】**

美德；诋毁和赞美虽然合乎情理，但言论从不见于行动，涉及时政所发的议论，喜欢评论他人贤德或不肖；自己有，就轻易责备别人，自己没有，就轻易要求别人；他们的言语强横而自信，他们的进身迅速而顺利：这些就是奸佞之人的行为。这是贤明君主要诛除的，却是愚昧君主所信任的。"

hoard[1] an abundance of provisions but loudly proclaim the righteousness of compassion; they criticize and praise according to their emotions yet in their personal conduct do not conform to what they say. They become involved in current debates, and they love judging who is worthy and who is unworthy; if they have undesirable traits, they have no trouble criticizing others who have such traits, yet if they do not possess desirable traits, they do not find it difficult to demand these traits from others.[2] Their words are forceful and convincing, and they are swift, yielding, and obedient in their career advancement. Such is the conduct of sycophants. They are the ones the enlightened ruler punishes and the foolish ruler trusts."

---

1   義 → 羨 (*JS*, 229/13).

2   This is in direct opposition to the *Daxue* 大学 (*Liji*, 43.2/165/27), which refers to the man of noble character (君子) as someone who "must first possess a quality within himself before he can demand it of other men, and he must himself be free of a certain undesirable trait before he can censure it in others." Andrew Plaks, tr. *Ta Hsüeh and Chung Yung (The Highest Order of Cultivation and On the Practice of the Mean)*. Harmondsworth: Penguin, (2003): 14.

## 3.22 [72] 景公问圣人之不得意何如晏子对以不与世陷乎邪

齐景公问圣贤之人不得意的时候怎么做，晏子回答说不和世俗一起陷入奸邪

**【原文】**

景公问晏子曰："圣人之不得意〔也〕何如？"晏子对曰："上作事反天时，从政逆鬼神，藉敛殚百姓；四时易序，神祇并怨；道忠者不听，荐善者不行，谀过者有赏，救失者有罪。故圣人伏匿隐处，不干长上，洁身守道，不与世陷乎邪，是以卑而不失义，瘁而不失廉。此圣人之不得意也。"〔公曰〕："圣人之得意何如？"对曰："世治政平，举事调

**【今译】**

齐景公问晏子说："圣人不得意的时候是什么样的？"晏子回答说："君上作事违反天时，处理政事悖逆鬼神，赋税聚敛穷竭百姓；四时改变顺序，天神地祇一起怨怒；说出的忠言不被听从，提出的善政不被推行，阿谀过失的有赏，补救过失的有罪。因此圣人藏匿隐居，不干预国君的事务，洁身自好，坚守道义，不和世俗一起陷入邪恶，因此地位卑下但不失正义，身心疲惫但不失廉洁。这就是圣人不得意时的样子。"景公说："圣人得意的时候又是什么样的？"晏子回答说："国家治理政治清平，国君办事与上天协调，赋税聚敛合乎民意，百姓喜欢这种整治措施，远方的人也怀念这种德行；四时不失顺序，风雨不

# 3.22 [72] DUKE JING ASKED WHAT CHARACTERIZES THE SAGE WHO DOES NOT FULFILL HIS ASPIRATIONS. YANZI REPLIED THAT THE SAGE DOES NOT FALL INTO EVIL ALONG WITH HIS FELLOW MEN.

Duke Jing queried Yanzi as follows: "What characterizes the sage who does not fulfill his aspirations?"

Yanzi replied: "Superiors act in opposition to the temporal order of the world; they defy the spirits when carrying out the affairs of state; tax collection drains the people; the four seasons change their proper order, the spirits of both Heaven and Earth are resentful; those who follow the way of loyalty are not heeded; those who give good advice have no impact; those who praise mistakes are rewarded; and those who try to correct mistakes are held guilty. Therefore, the sage goes into hiding in secret places and does not involve himself with those who are in charge and with his superiors. He keeps himself pure and guards the Way in order not to fall into evil with his fellow men. For this reason his status is low, yet he does not abandon righteousness; he is exhausted and sick, yet he does not lose his integrity. This is what characterizes the sage who does not fulfill his aspirations."

The Duke said: "What would it be like if the sage were to fulfill his aspirations?"

Yanzi replied: "The world would be well ordered and the government stable; whatever they would do is in harmony with Heaven; taxes would be collected in conformance with the people's need; the people would be happy with their government; even distant people would cherish the ruler's virtues; the four seasons would not miss their proper order; wind and rain would not be devastating, Heaven would manifest astronomical phenomena in the ruler's praise, the earth would grow, and crops and all goods would be available; the spirits would confer endless bounty; the people would submit to moral instructions and not merely pretend to do so; no government

273

**【原文】**

乎天，藉敛和乎〔民〕，百姓乐（及）其政，远者怀其德；四时不失序，风雨不降（雪）〔虐〕；天明象而〔致〕赞，地长育而具物；神降福而不靡，民服教而不伪；治无怨业，居无废民：此圣人之得意也。”

**【今译】**

成灾害；天象吉祥以示赞美，土地长育万物具备；神灵不断降下福气，百姓服从教化而不虚伪；治理国家没有被埋怨的事业，居所之中没有游手好闲的百姓，这就是圣人得意时的样子。”

enterprise would cause resentment; and there would be no homes with unemployed people. This is what characterizes the world of a sage who fulfills his aspirations."

# 3.23 [73] 景公问古者君民用国不危弱晏子对以文王

齐景公问古时候的君主治理百姓不招致危险和削弱国力，晏子用文王的事迹来回答

【原文】

景公问晏子曰："古者君民而（不）危，用国而（不）弱，恶乎失之？"晏子对曰："婴闻之，以邪莅国、以暴和民者危，修道以要利，得求而返邪者弱。古者文王修德，不以要利，灭暴不以顺纣，干崇侯之暴，而礼梅伯之醢，是以诸侯明乎其行，百姓通乎其德，故君民而不危，用国而不弱也。"

【今译】

齐景公问晏子说："古时候的君王治理百姓而招致危险，使用国力而削弱，在哪里失败的？"晏子回答说："我听闻，用邪恶的人管理国家、用暴力的手段统治百姓就会招致危险，推行道义是为了索取利益、得到所求之后又返回邪恶就会削弱国力。古时候的周文王推行德政，不是为了索取利益，消灭凶暴不让他去顺从商纣，干预崇侯的暴政，而礼敬梅伯被粉碎的遗骸，因此诸侯们明察他的德行，百姓们了解他的品德，所以治理百姓而不招致危险，使用国力而不削弱。"

# 3.23 [73] DUKE JING INQUIRED ABOUT RULERS IN ANCIENT TIMES WHO RULED THE PEOPLE WITHOUT ENDANGERING THEMSELVES AND MANAGED THE STATES WITHOUT ENFEEBLING THEMSELVES. YANZI REPLIED WITH THE EXAMPLE OF KING WEN.[1]

Duke Jing queried Yanzi as follows: "How was it that rulers in ancient times who endangered themselves in ruling the people and enfeebled themselves in managing their states still managed to lose their states?"

Yanzi replied: "I have heard that those who rule a state by wickedness and pacify the people through brutality endanger themselves. Those who cultivate the Way in order to seek profit[2] and revert to evil when they achieve it become enfeebled. In ancient times, King Wen cultivated virtue but did not seek personal gain; he eliminated brutality and did not obey Zhou.[3] He blocked the brutality of the Marquis of Chong[4] and honored, according to the rites, mincemeat made from the remains of the Earl of Bo.[5] For this reason, the regional princes were enlightened by his conduct and the people understood his virtue thoroughly. Therefore, he was not endangered in ruling the people and was not weakened in managing the state."

277

---

1   The title of the present item (用国不危弱), refers to the statement that ends this Item (用国而不弱也) and not to the contrary statement (用国而弱) embodied in the question put forward to Yanzi by Duke Jing at the beginning of the Item.

2   Cf. Item 3.1 [51], note 3.

3   Zhou is Zhou Xin 纣辛, the last tyrant of the Shang (Yin) dynasty. The virtuous King Wen 文王 (1231–1135 BCE) and his son, King Wu 武王 (1169–1116 BCE), rebelled against Zhou Xin and overthrew his dynasty.

4   Hu 虎, the Marquis of Chong 崇侯, was one of Zhou Xin's 纣辛 princes.

5   Zhou Xin presented mincemeat made from the remains of the Earl of Bo, whom he murdered, as a ritual gift to the princes. King Wen, who was then one of the princes, wept and wailed over this, but ceremoniously accepted the "gift" in order to report it to his fellow princes.

# 3.24 [74] 景公问古之莅国者任人如何晏子对以人不同能

齐景公问古时候治理国家的人怎样用人，晏子回答说每个人都有不同的才能

## 【原文】

景公问晏子曰："古之莅国治民者，其任人何如？"晏子对曰："地不同（生）〔宜〕，而任之以一种，责其俱生不可得；人不同能，而任之以一事，不可责遍成。责焉无已，智者有不能给，求焉无餍，天地有不能赡也。故明王之任人，（谄）〔诎〕谀不迩乎左右，阿党不治乎本朝；任人之长，不强其短，任人之工，不强其拙。此任人之大略也。"

## 【今译】

齐景公问晏子说："古时候管理国家治理百姓的人，他们是怎样用人的？"晏子回答说："土地有不同的品质，因而只能让它栽种一种作物，要求它什么作物都能生长是不可能的；人有不同的才能，因而只能让他去做一件事，不能要求他什么事都能办成。要求没完没了，聪明人也有不能办到的，求取不知满足，天地也有不能满足的。因此贤明的君王在用人的时候，谄谀之人不能靠近他左右，结党营私的人不能管理本朝的事务；任用别人的长处，不强求他的短处，任用别人的灵巧之处，不强求他的笨拙之处。这就是用人的大致原则。"

## 3.24 [74] DUKE JING INQUIRED HOW STATE RULERS OF ANCIENT TIMES APPOINTED FUNCTIONARIES. YANZI REPLIED THAT THEY DID SO IN ACCORDANCE WITH THE DIFFERENT ABILITIES OF THE PEOPLE.

Duke Jing queried Yanzi as follows: "In ancient times, how did those rulers who kept the people in good order appoint functionaries?"

Yanzi replied: "Regions do not all share the same suitability, and if you plant an identical seed in each of them, the expectation that they will sprout at the same time is not fulfilled. People do not have identical abilities. Hence, if you charge them with the same tasks, the expectation that they will all succeed cannot be fulfilled. If expectations are unlimited, even the clever will be unable to satisfy on all accounts. If demands are insatiable, even Heaven and Earth will be unable to satisfy them. Therefore, when the enlightened kings appointed officials, they did not allow flatterers and toadies to approach their entourages, and those who formed factions did not exercise any power in their courts. They leveraged people's strengths and did not take advantage of their weaknesses. They put people's skills to good use and did not dwell on their ineptness. Such are the broad guidelines of the way of appointing functionaries."

279

## 3.25 [75] 景公问古者离散其民如何晏子对以今闻公令如寇雠

齐景公问古时候使百姓离散的人是什么样的，晏子回答说现在百姓听到您的命令就像遇到了仇敌

大中华文库

【原文】

景公问晏子曰："古者离散其民，而隕失其国者，其常行何如？"晏子对曰："国贫而好大，智薄而好专；贵（无贱）〔贱无〕亲焉，大臣无礼焉；尚谗谀而贱贤人，乐简慢而玩百姓；国无常法，民无经纪；好辩以为智，刻民以为忠，流湎而忘国，好兵而忘民；肃于罪诛，而慢于庆赏；乐人之哀，利人之（德）〔难〕；（难）〔德〕不足以怀人，政不足以惠民；赏不足以劝善，刑不足以防非，亡国之行也。今民闻公令如寇雠，此古〔之〕离散其民，隕失其国〔者〕（所）〔之〕常行者也。"

【今译】

齐景公问晏子说："古时候使百姓离散，而失去国家的人，他们日常的行为是什么样的？"晏子回答说："国家贫穷而好大喜功，智谋浅薄而喜欢独断；贵戚和平民都不亲附，大臣们也不讲礼义；崇尚谗谀之人而轻视贤能之人，乐于怠慢而轻视百姓；国家没有固定的法令，百姓没有可以遵行的秩序；认为喜欢与人辩论的人有才智，苛待百姓的人是忠臣，沉湎酒色而忘记了国家，喜好打仗而忘记了百姓；严正于治罪杀人，而轻慢于庆功赏赐；把别人的哀痛视为快乐，把别人的苦难视为有利可图；德行不足以让人怀念，政教不足以让百姓受惠；赏赐不足以劝人行善，刑罚不足以防止坏事，这就是亡国的行为。现在百姓听到您的命令就像遇到了仇敌，这就是古时候使百姓离散，失去国家的人的日常行为。"

## 3.25 [75] DUKE JING ASKED HOW THE ANCIENTS DISPERSED THE PEOPLE. YANZI REPLIED THAT NOW PEOPLE HEAR THE DUKE'S COMMANDS AS IF FROM AN ENEMY.

Duke Jing queried Yanzi as follows: "In ancient times, what were the habitual practices that led some rulers to scatter their people and destroy their states?"

Yanzi replied: "Their states were poor, yet they loved ostentation; their wisdom was meager, yet they loved arbitrary dictates; neither the nobility nor the lower class were close to them, and they did not treat their high ministers according to the rites; they highly valued slanderers and flatterers, and despised the worthy; they enjoyed negligence and laziness and they trifled with the people; their states lacked stable laws, and the people had no standards and regulations; they considered wise those who were fond of sophistry, and loyal those who treated the people harshly; they unceasingly wallowed in indulgence and forgot their states; they loved militarism and forgot the people; they were stern in incriminating and punishing and languid in congratulating and rewarding; they found delight in the sorrow of others and profited from people's difficulties; their virtue was insufficient to bring people into their fold, and their government was insufficient to confer benevolence on them; their rewards were insufficient to encourage good behavior, and their punishments were insufficient to prevent wrongdoing. This conduct destroyed their states. And now, my Lord, the people hear your commands as if from an enemy — these were the habitual practices that led some rulers to scatter their people and destroyed their states in ancient times."

## 3.26 [76] 景公问欲和臣亲下晏子对以信顺俭节

齐景公打算与大臣和睦与百姓亲近，询问晏子的意见，晏子回答说要诚信和顺俭朴节用

【原文】

景公问晏子曰："吾欲和（民）〔臣〕亲下奈何？"晏子对曰："君得臣而任使之，与言信，必顺其令，赦其过，任大臣无多责焉，使迩臣无求壁焉，无以嗜欲贫其家，无信谗人伤其心，家不外求而足，事君不因人而进，则臣和矣。俭于藉敛，节于货财，作工不历时，使民不尽力，百官节适，关市省征，山林陂泽，不专其利，领民治民，勿

【今译】

齐景公问晏子说："我想与大臣和睦与百姓亲善要怎么做？"晏子回答说："国君得到大臣而任用他们，与他们谈话要言而有信，一定要听从他们的善言，赦免他们的过失，任用大臣不要过多要求，使用近臣不要求于壁幸，不要因为自己的嗜欲使大臣家贫穷，不要听信奸人的谗言伤害大臣的心，家庭开销不用向外求助而得到满足，侍奉国君不靠人情而得以进升，那么君臣之间就和睦了。减轻赋敛，节约财物，兴办工程不要历时过久，役使百姓不要穷竭其力，官员们要适度节约，关卡市场要减少征税，山林湖泽产出的物品，不要独占它的利益，领导和治理百姓，不要让他们感到烦乱，要了解他们的贫富情况，不要

# 3.26 [76] DUKE JING CONSULTED REGARDING HIS WISH TO BE IN HARMONY WITH HIS MINISTERS AND TO MAINTAIN CLOSE RELATIONSHIPS WITH HIS INFERIORS. YANZI REPLIED THAT THIS COULD BE ATTAINED THROUGH TRUTHFULNESS, OBEDIENCE, FRUGALITY AND MODERATION.

Duke Jing queried Yanzi as follows: "I wish to be in harmony with my ministers and to maintain close relationships with my inferiors; how should I go about this?"

Yanzi replied: "If you, My Lord, recruit ministers and appoint them for service and have truthful conversations with them, their edicts should be obeyed and their errors pardoned. When you employ important ministers,[1] do not expect too much of them; if you take into service ministers to be your close aides, do not seek out favorite intimates among them. Do not allow your inclinations and desires to impoverish their families; do not trust slanderers and thus hurt the ministers' feelings; their families should not look afar in order to have what is sufficient; in their service of the ruler, they should not be promoted through the mediation of third persons. In this way, the ministers will be in harmony with you. Be frugal in levying taxes and moderate with your properties; a labor project that you start should not last too long; your use of people should not exhaust their strength; the number of offices you maintain should be limited and appropriate; taxes should be reduced at the barrier gates and marketplaces; and you should not monopolize the profits from mountains, forests and ponds. Lead the people and create good order among them; do not cause them be troubled and chaotic; be informed about their poverty and prosperity and do not allow them to go cold and hungry; then the people will become close to you."

283

---

1　Add 臣 (*YZCQ-ICS*, 3.26/30/13, n. 1).

【原文】

使烦乱，知其贫富，勿使冻馁，则民亲矣。"公曰："善！寡人闻命矣。"故令诸子无外亲谒，辟梁丘据无使受报，百官节适，关市省征，陂泽不禁，冤报者过，留狱者（诸）〔请〕焉。

【今译】

让他们受冻挨饿，那么君民之间就亲善了。"景公说："好！我接受您的教诲了。"因此下令诸子不要接受外人的亲近拜谒，驳斥梁丘据不让他接受举报，官员们适度节约，关卡市场减少征税，山林湖泽不禁止百姓进入，惩罚那些判罪不当使人蒙受冤屈的人，留在监狱中的可以请求申诉。

The Duke said: "Well argued. I have heard your commands." Therefore, he gave orders to the various ministers not to become intimate with the receptionists stationed outside the court, and he kept at a distance Liangqiu Ju and did not let him receive the reports of legal cases. The number of offices was limited and appropriate; taxes at barrier gates and marketplaces were reduced; fishing was allowed in ponds and marshes; those whose reports led to unjust rule were blamed; and those who had languished in prison were pardoned.

# 3.27 [77] 景公问得贤之道晏子对以举之以语考之以事

齐景公问得到贤能的办法，晏子回答说要用言辞选拔用办事能力考核

## 【原文】

景公问晏子曰："（耶）〔取〕人得贤之道何如？"晏子对曰："举之以语，考之以事，能谕，则尚而亲之，近而勿辱以（耶）〔取〕人，则得贤之道也。是以明君居上，寡其官而多其行，拙于文而工于事，言不中不言，行不法不为也。"

大中华文库

## 【今译】

齐景公问晏子说："选取人才得到贤臣的方法是什么？"晏子回答说："根据他说的话来选拔，根据他做的事来考察他的能力，能晓谕事理的，就尊重而亲近他，亲近而不使人感到屈辱地选用，这就是得到贤臣的方法。因此贤明的国君主政时，用的官员少但做出的成绩多，他们不善言辞但很会办事，说话不公正就不说，做事不合法度就不做。"

## 3.27 [77] DUKE JING ASKED HOW TO OBTAIN THE SERVICES OF WORTHY FUNCTIONARIES. YANZI REPLIED THAT THE DUKE SHOULD PROMOTE PEOPLE ACCORDING TO THEIR WORDS AND EXAMINE THEM ACCORDING TO THEIR DEEDS.

Duke Jing queried Yanzi as follows: "What is the way of selecting functionaries and obtaining worthy ones?"

Yanzi replied: "Promote them according to their words and examine them according to their deeds. If their abilities are clearly manifested, then value them highly and draw them near to you. If you become close to them, without being abusive, you could select among them and, ultimately, perfect the way of obtaining the worthy. Therefore, when the enlightened ruler resides at the top, he reduces his number of his officials and increases the weight of his own actions. He is unhurried in the writing of documents but industrious in deeds. He does not utter words that fail to hit the mark and does not conduct himself unlawfully."

## 3.28 [78] 景公问臣之报君何以晏子对以报以德

齐景公问大臣怎样报效君主，晏子回答说报效君主要用德行

大中华文库

### 【原文】

景公问晏子曰："臣之报其君何以？"晏子对曰："臣虽不知，必务报君以德。士逢有道之君，则顺其令；逢无道之君，则争其不义。故君者择臣而使之，臣虽贱，亦得择君而事之。"

### 【今译】

齐景公问晏子说："臣子用什么来报效国君？"晏子回答说："我虽然不聪明，但知道务必用德行来报效国君。士人如果遇上了有道之君，就顺从他的政令；如果遇上了无道之君，就诤谏他的不义之举。因此国君要选择臣子来使用，臣子即使地位卑贱，也可以选择国君而侍奉他。"

## 3.28 [78] DUKE JING ASKED HOW A MINISTER SHOULD EXPRESS GRATITUDE TO HIS RULER. YANZI REPLIED THAT HE REPAYS HIS RULER BY BEING VIRTUOUS.

Duke Jing queried Yanzi as follows: "How does a minister express gratitude to his ruler?"

Yanzi replied: "Even if a minister is not wise, he must express gratitude to his ruler by being virtuous. If an officer encounters a ruler who possesses the Way, then he should follow his orders; but if he encounters a ruler who does not possess the Way, then he should remonstrate with him for being unrighteous. Therefore, a ruler chooses ministers and takes them into service; ministers, even if low in rank, can also choose a ruler and serve him."

# 3.29 [79] 景公问临国莅民所患何也晏子对以患者三

齐景公问亲临国政治理百姓所忧虑的是什么，晏子用三个忧虑来回答

【原文】

景公问晏子曰："临国莅民，所患何也？"晏子对曰："所患者三：忠臣不信，一患也；信臣不忠，二患也；君臣异心，三患也。是以明君居上，无忠而不信，无信而不忠者。是故君臣同欲，而百姓无怨也。"

【今译】

齐景公问晏子说："亲临国政治理百姓，所忧虑的是什么？"晏子回答说："所忧虑的有三件事：忠诚的大臣不被信任，这是第一个忧虑；信任的大臣不忠诚，这是第二个忧虑；国君和大臣心思不同，这是第三个忧虑。因此贤明的国君主政时，没有忠诚而不被信任的大臣，也没有信任而不忠诚的大臣。因此君臣之间同心同德，而百姓也就没有怨恨了。"

## 3.29 [79] DUKE INQUIRED REGARDING THE WORRIES INVOLVED IN RULING THE STATE AND GOVERNING THE PEOPLE. YANZI REPLIED THAT THERE ARE THREE KINDS OF WORRIES.

Duke Jing asked Yanzi: "What should one be worried about in ruling the state and governing the people?"

Yanzi replied: "These worries are threefold. The first worry is when loyal ministers do not enjoy trust. The second worry is when ministers who enjoy trust are not loyal. The third worry is when the ruler and his ministers are of different minds. Therefore, when an enlightened ruler resides at the top, there are no loyal ministers who do not enjoy trust, and there are no trustworthy ministers who are not loyal. Therefore, the ruler and his ministers share identical desires and the people bear no resentment."

## 3.30 [80] 景公问为政何患晏子对以善恶不分

齐景公问治国理政的忧患是什么，晏子用善恶不分来回答

### 【原文】

景公问于晏子曰："为政何患？"晏子对曰："患善恶之不分。"公曰："何以察之？"对曰："审择左右。左右善，则百僚各得其所宜，而善恶分。"孔子闻之曰："此言也信矣！善进，则不善无由入矣；不善进，则善无由入矣。"

### 【今译】

齐景公问晏子说："治国理政怕的是什么呢？"晏子回答说："怕的是善恶不分。"景公说："怎么才能看出来呢？"晏子回答说："要谨慎挑选左右的近臣。近臣良善，那么百官就会得到各自适宜的位置，而善与恶就分清了。"孔子听闻这件事后说："这话说得对呀！良善的人进到国君身边，那么不善的人就没有机会进入了；不善的人进到国君身边，那么良善的人就没有机会进入了。"

## 3.30 [80] DUKE JING INQUIRED REGARDING THE WORRIES INVOLVED IN GOVERNING. YANZI REPLIED THAT ONE SHOULD WORRY WHEN GOOD AND EVIL ARE NOT CLEARLY DISTINGUISHED.[1]

Duke Jing asked Yanzi: "What are the main concerns in governing?"

Yanzi replied: "One should be concerned when good and evil are not clearly distinguished."

The Duke said: "How can this be observed?"

Yanzi replied: "By carefully choosing one's entourage. If one's entourage is good, then each of the surrounding officials will receive his proper share and so good and evil will not be clearly distinguished."

When Confucius heard this he said: "These words are true. When the good advance, the bad have no way to gain access; when the bad advance, the good have no way to gain access."

293

---

1   Item 3.30 [80] ↔ *Shuoyuan*, 7.36/55/1.

国家出版基金项目
NATIONAL PUBLICATION FOUNDATION

大中华文库
LIBRARY
OF CHINESE CLASSICS

大中华文库

汉英对照

**Library of Chinese Classics**
**Chinese-English**

# 晏子春秋

# THE SPRING AND AUTUMN
# ANNALS OF MASTER YAN
# （Ⅱ）

[以色列] 欧永福　导言、注释、翻译

张　飘　刘　喆　今译

INTRODUCED, COMMENTED AND TRANSLATED BY Yoav Ariel
MODERN CHINESE TEXT BY Zhang Piao and Liu Zhe

中国人民大学出版社

China Renmin University Press

## The Inner Chapters

## The Outer Chapters

# 第四卷 问下

## 4.1 [81] 景公问何修则夫先王之游晏子对以省耕实

齐景公问怎样做才能仿效先王的巡游，晏子回答说要观察耕种和收获

### 【原文】

景公出游，问于晏子曰："吾欲观于转附、朝舞，（遵）〔循〕海而南，至于琅邪，寡人何修则夫先王之游？"晏子再拜曰："善哉，君之问也！〔婴〕闻〔之〕，天子之诸侯为巡狩，诸侯之天子为述职。故春省耕而补不足者谓之游，秋省实而助不给者谓之豫。夏（谚）〔语〕曰：

### 【今译】

齐景公出游，向晏子问道："我想观赏转附、朝舞，然后沿海南下，到达琅邪，我应该怎样做才能仿效先代君王的巡游呢？"晏子拜了两拜说："您问得好啊！我听闻，天子到诸侯的领地叫巡狩，诸侯来朝拜天子叫述职。因此春天察看耕地补助那些种不上庄稼的叫作游，秋天察看收成而帮助那些不能自给的叫作豫。夏朝的谚语说：'我们的君王不春游，我怎么能得到休息？我们的君王不秋游，我怎么能得到帮助？春天巡游秋天巡游，成为诸侯们的法度。'现在您的巡游不是这样，兴师动众耗去大量粮食，贫穷的人得不到补助，辛劳的人得不到

# Chapter Four   Queries — Part B

## 4.1 [81] DUKE JING ASKED HOW ONE SHOULD GO ABOUT EMULATING THE TOURS OF THE FORMER KINGS. YANZI REPLIED BY REFERENCE TO INSPECTION OF PLOUGHING AND HARVESTING.[1]

Duke Jing went on a pleasure excursion, and queried Yanzi as follows: "I would like to follow the sea southward and as far as Langye.[2] How should I go about emulating the way in which the former kings conducted their excursions?"

Yanzi bowed twice and said: "Your question, My Lord, is excellent. I have heard that when the Son of Heaven went to the regional princes, this was known as an Inspection Tour. When the regional princes went to pay homage to the Son of Heaven, this was known as a Duty Report. Therefore, in spring, the aim was to inspect the ploughing, so that the deficiencies could be made up for, this was called the 'Spring Tour.' And in the autumn, the aim was to inspect the harvest, so that farmers who did not bring in enough could be given aid, this was called the 'Autumn Excursion.' As the saying of the Xia Dynasty puts it:

If our Lord does not go on tour,

How are we to get rest?

If our Lord does not make excursions,

How are we to get help?

---

1   Item 4.1 [81] ↔ *Mencius*, 2.4/9/9; *Guanzi*, 10.1/73/25. For a short comparison of these two parallel texts and the present item, and for a discussion of the locations of Zhuanfu 转附 and Langye 琅邪, see Allyn W. Rickett, tr. *Guanzi: Political, Economic, and Philosophical Essays from Early China*. Princeton Library of Asian Translations, Princeton (1985): vol. 1, pp. 377, n. 4-6.

2   琅琊 → 琅邪 (*JS*, 242/4).

大中华文库

**【原文】**

'吾君不游，我曷以休？吾君不豫，我曷以助？一游一豫，为诸侯度。'今君之游不然，师行而粮食，贫苦不补，劳者不息。夫从（南）〔高〕历时而不反谓之流，从下〔历时〕而不反谓之连，从兽而不归谓之荒，从乐而不归谓之亡。古者圣王无流连之游、荒亡之行。"公曰："善。"命吏计公（掌）〔禀〕之粟，藉长幼贫氓之数。吏所委发廪出粟，以与贫民者三千钟，公所身见癃老者七十人，振赡之，然后归也。

**【今译】**

休息。从高处向下游玩长时间不知返回叫作流，从下向上游玩长时间不知返回叫作连，沉迷打猎而不归朝叫作荒，纵情享乐而不归朝叫作亡。古时候的圣王没有流连的巡游、荒亡的出行。"景公说："好。"于是命令官吏统计仓库中的粮食，登记年老、年幼和贫困百姓的人数。官吏受命开仓放粮，给予贫民的有三千钟，景公亲自接见了七十个年老体弱的人，都予以赈济，然后就回了都城。

With each tour, with each excursion,

He sets a model for the regional princes.

But now your tours, My Lord, are different:

When the army marches, it is allotted rations,

But the poor are not helped;

And the weary have no rest. [1]

'Drifting' means following an upward course for lengthy periods without returning; 'lingering' is following a downward course for lengthy periods without returning; 'recklessness' is going to hunt without returning; 'wantonness' is pursuing pleasure without returning. In ancient times, the sage kings did not have tours of 'drifting' and 'lingering,' nor did they practice 'recklessness' and 'wantonness.'"

The Duke said "Well argued" and ordered the officials to issue an inventory of the millet in the public granary and register the number of the poor among the old and young. The millet for which the officials were commissioned to open the granary and take out to give to the poor amounted to three thousand *zhong*. The Duke in person met seventy infirm old people. He offered support to relieve them and only then did he return to court.

---

1  Both *Mencius* (2.4/9/13-14) and *YZCQ* (4.1/31/20-21) feature the same twenty-four characters for the Xia Dynasty's saying. However, Yanzi's explication of this saying, with which he portrays the nature of Duke Jing's excursions, consists of only thirteen rhymed characters in the *YZCQ*, while in the *Mencius* they are followed by twenty-four more rhymed characters. Since in both *Mencius* (2.4/9/15-17) and *YZCQ* (4.1/31/21-23) Yanzi makes a semantic analysis of the words 流 ("meandering"), 连 ("lingering"), 荒 ("reckless"), and 亡 ("ruined") — that is, a semantic analysis of words that do not appear in the thirteen rhymed characters of the *YZCQ* at all, but rather in the additional twenty-four rhymed characters of the *Mencius* (2.4/9/15-16) — we might assume that the compiler of the present item was very well-acquainted with the Mencius' full version of the episode and probably considered Mencius' twenty-four additional rhymed characters redundant.

# 4.2 [82] 景公问桓公何以致霸晏子对以下贤以身

齐景公问桓公怎样成为霸主，晏子回答说要亲身礼敬贤士

**【原文】**

景公问于晏子曰："昔吾先君桓公，善饮酒穷乐，食味方丈，好色无别。辟若此，何以能率诸侯以朝天子乎？"晏子对曰："昔吾先君桓公，变俗以政，下贤以身。管仲，君之贼者也，知其能足以安国济功，故迎之于鲁郊，自御，礼之于庙。异日，君过于康庄，闻宁戚歌，

**【今译】**

齐景公向晏子问道："以前我们的先代国君桓公，善于饮酒纵情享乐，吃的美味佳肴足有一丈见方，喜好女色没有差别。像这样邪僻，怎么能够率领诸侯去朝拜天子呢？"晏子回答说："以前我们的先代国君桓公，用政教移风易俗，亲身礼敬贤士。管仲，是害过桓公的人，桓公知道他的才能足以安定国家成就功业，因此到鲁国的郊外去迎接他，还亲自驾车，在庙堂中对他礼遇有加。过了一段时间，桓公在大路上经过，听到宁戚唱歌，就停下车驾仔细听他唱，宁戚的歌有贤人

## 4.2 [82] DUKE JING ASKED HOW DUKE HUAN ATTAINED THE STATUS OF OVERLORD. YANZI REPLIED THAT HE WAS PERSONALLY COURTEOUS TO THE WORTHY.

Duke Jing queried Yanzi as follows: "In the past, our former ruler Duke Huan was fond of drinking wine and pursuing pleasures to the limit. His food was spread out over ten square feet[1] and his fondness for women was indiscriminate.[2] I wonder how a man of such a perverse nature was capable of leading the regional princes to pay homage to the Son of Heaven."

Yanzi replied: "In the past, our former ruler Duke Huan transformed customs for the better through proper government, and he was personally courteous to the worthy. Guan Zhong was an enemy of our former ruler, but Duke Huan knew that Guan Zhong's ability was great enough to make the state peaceful and successful in his undertaking. Therefore, he welcomed him on the outskirts of Lu. Our ruler himself drove there, and he treated Guan Zhong with the proper rites in the ancestral temple.[3] On another day, our ruler, riding on a highway, heard Ning Qi singing. He stopped his carriage and listened, realized the singing voice was the voice of a worthy person, and then raised Ning Qi to the position of Grand Minister of Agriculture.[4] Whenever our former ruler met the worthy person, he did not leave him behind; he tirelessly appointed the capable. Therefore, within the state, the people submitted to him, and wherever he launched invasions, the

---

1   Cf. *Mencius*, 14.34/77/10.

2   Most commentaries suggest that Duke Huan's indiscriminate desire for women implies that he was involved in incest.

3   For a full description of the welcoming ceremony that Duke Huan gave Guan Zhong at the outskirts of Lu see *Lüshi chunqiu*, 24.2/155/27.

4   According to the *Huainanzi*, 10/91/8; 12.14/109/3, Ning Qi struck a profound emotional response in Duke Huan by tapping on a cow's horn and singing along.

## 【原文】

止车而听之，则贤人之风也，举以为大田。先君见贤不留，使能不怠，是以内政则民怀之，征伐则诸侯畏之。今君闻先君之过，而不能明其大节，桓公之霸也，君奚疑焉？"

## 【今译】

的风范，桓公因此任命他为大田。桓公见到贤良的人就不让他留在民间，任用有才能的人毫不怠慢，因此对内施政则百姓怀念，对外征伐则诸侯畏惧。现在您只知晓桓公的过失，而不能明白他治国理政的大方略，桓公的霸业，您怎么能怀疑呢？"

regional princes were afraid of him. Now you, My Lord, have heard about the faults of our former ruler, yet you are not able to discern his decisive principles. Why are you, My Lord, suspicious about the overlordship of Duke Huan?"

## 4.3 [83] 景公问欲逮桓公之后晏子对以任非其人

齐景公想成为桓公的后继者，问晏子的意见，晏子回答说任用的人不对

【原文】

景公问晏子曰："昔者先君桓公，从车三百乘，九合诸侯，一匡天下。今吾从车千乘，可以逮先君桓公之后乎？"晏子对曰："桓公从车三百乘，九合诸侯，一匡天下，左有鲍叔，右有仲父。今君左为倡，右为优，谗人在前，谀人在后，又焉可逮桓公之后者乎？"

【今译】

齐景公问晏子说："以前我们的先代国君桓公，只有三百辆战车随从，便多次会盟诸侯，匡正天下。现在我有千辆战车随从，可以在先代国君桓公之后称霸诸侯吗？"晏子回答说："桓公只有三百辆战车跟从，便多次会盟诸侯，安定天下，是因为他左有鲍叔，右有管仲辅佐。现在您左边是倡伎，右边是优伶，进谗之人在前，阿谀之人在后，又怎么能在桓公之后称霸诸侯呢？"

## 4.3 [83] DUKE JING CONSULTED REGARDING HIS WISH TO QUALIFY AS DUKE HUAN'S SUCCESSOR. YANZI REPLIED THAT HE DID NOT APPOINT THE RIGHT PEOPLE.

Duke Jing queried Yanzi as follows: "In the past, our former ruler, Duke Huan, had in his train three hundred chariots. He gathered the regional princes nine times and had brought unity and order to the entire realm.[1] Now, my train is a thousand chariots; might I qualify as Duke Huan's successor?"

Yanzi replied: "What enabled Duke Huan, with three hundred chariots in his train, to gather together the regional princes nine times and to bring unity and order to the entire realm, was that Bao Shu[2] was on his left side and Zhong Fu[3] was on his right. But now you, My Lord, have on your left there women singers and on your right women actors; slanderers are in front of you and flatterers are behind you. So how can you qualify as Duke Huan's successor?"

---

1 Cf. *Analects*, 14.17/38/24.

2 Bao Shuya 鮑叔牙 was a close colleague of Guan Zhong and an early adherent of Duke Huan.

3 Zhongfu 仲父 — "Uncle" — is the honorary title Duke Huan gave to Guan Zhong.

大中华文库

## 4.4 [84] 景公问廉政而长久晏子对以其行水也

齐景公问廉洁正直而且能够长久的人的行为，晏子回答说他们的行为像水一样

**【原文】**

景公问晏子〔曰〕："廉政而长久，其行何也？"晏子对曰："其行水也。美哉水乎清清，其浊（不无）〔无不〕雩途，其清无不洒除，是以长久也。"公曰："廉政而邀亡，其行何也？"对曰："其行石也。坚哉石乎落落，视之则坚，循之则坚，内外皆坚，无以为久，是以邀亡也。"

**【今译】**

齐景公问晏子说："廉洁正直而且能够长久的人，他们的行为是什么样的？"晏子回答说："他们的行为就像水一样。流水清清澈澈的多么美好，它混浊的时候无不可以用来涂抹墙屋，它清澈的时候无不可以用来洒扫除垢，因此可以长久。"景公说："廉洁正直但迅速灭亡的人，他们的行为是什么样的？"晏子回答说："他们的行为就像石头。石头起起落落的多么坚硬，它看起来坚硬，摸起来坚硬，里里外外都很坚硬，没办法让自己久存，因此迅速灭亡。"

## 4.4 [84] DUKE JING INQUIRED REGARDING SCRU-
## PULOUS GOVERNANCE THAT WOULD BE LONG-LAS-
## TING. YANZI REPLIED THAT ITS CONDUCT SHOULD
## BE LIKE WATER.

Duke Jing queried Yanzi as follows: "What conduct should a scrupulous government pursue so that it endures?"

Yanzi replied: "Its conduct should be like water. Beautiful indeed is water when it is limpid. There is nothing that the muddiness of water will not obscure; there is nothing that its limpidness will not clarify. That is why it is enduring."

The Duke said: "What actions does a scrupulous government pursue that lead it to perish rapidly?"

Yanzi replied: "Its actions are like stones. Hard indeed is the appearance of stones. When viewed, they are hard; when touched, they are hard; inside and out, they are all hard. They possess nothing of an enduring nature, therefore they perish rapidly."[1]

305

---

1   The philosophical force behind Item 4.4 [84] is similar to the one that runs through Chapter 39 of the *Dao De Jing* 道德经 (39.20B/97/4), where it is stated that rulers should realize that their high, noble position is rooted in its opposite — lowliness. In the present paragraph, the nature of water is portrayed in accord with its polar characteristics: it can be both limpid and muddy. It is multi-functional and therefore lasting. The stone, however, is always hard and, having only this one function, is quick to perish. The strikingly similar reference to a stone in both texts (*YZCQ*: 石乎落落; *Dao De Jing*: 落落乎石) also suggests a relationship between the two texts. See also *Kongcongzi*, 3.3/22/1; Yoav Ariel, tr. *K'ung-ts'ung-tzu: The K'ung Family Master's Anthology*. Princeton Library of Asian Translations. Princeton (1989): 129.

## 4.5 [85] 景公问为臣之道晏子对以九节

齐景公问做臣子的原则，晏子用九条节义回答

### 【原文】

景公问晏子曰："请问为臣之道。"晏子对曰："见善必通，不私其利，（庆）〔荐〕善而不有其名；称身居位，不为苟进；称事授禄，不为苟得；体贵侧贱，不逆其伦，居贤不肖，不乱其序；肥利之地，不为私邑，贤质之士，不为私臣；君用其所言，民得其所利，而不伐其功。此臣之道也。"

大中华文库

### 【今译】

齐景公问晏子说："请问做臣子的原则。"晏子回答说："见到好的事情一定要推广，不要把利益据为己有，举荐贤能之人而不贪图名声；估量自己的才能而担任相应的职位，不做苟且求进身的事；估量自己所做的事情来接受俸禄，不要贪图多得财物；列位分清尊贵和卑贱，不违逆伦常，使贤良之士和不肖之人各得其所，不打乱次序；肥沃有利的土地，不占为自己的食邑，贤德质直的人，不充作自己的家臣；国君采纳了自己的意见，百姓得到了自己的好处，而不夸耀自己的功劳。这就是做臣子的原则。"

## 4.5 [85] DUKE JING ASKED ABOUT THE WAY TO BE A MINISTER. YANZI REPLIED WITH NINE MORAL POINTS.

Duke Jing queried Yanzi as follows: "I would like to ask about the way to be a minister."

Yanzi replied: "If a minister sees good, he must share it and not keep its profit to himself. He recommends the good and does not claim fame on account of it; he weighs his qualifications before he takes a post and does not promote himself wantonly; he weighs his deeds when receiving an emolument and does not accept it wantonly; he emphasizes with the noble and sets aside the lowly; he does not contravene their proper positions; he arranges the worthy and the unworthy without confusing their order; he does not take fertile, profitable land for his own town, and he does not make worthy, qualified officers his own trusted followers. The ruler applies what the minister says, and the people gain benefits from him, but he does not boast of his own achievements. Such is the way of a minister."

307

## 4.6 [86] 景公问贤不肖可学乎晏子对以勉强为上

齐景公问贤能或不贤是否可以学习，晏子回答说要坚持向贤者学习

### 【原文】

景公问晏子曰："人性有贤不肖，可学乎？"晏子对曰："《诗》云：'高山仰（止）〔之〕，景行行（止）之。'〔乡〕者，其人也。故诸侯并立，善而不怠者为长；列士并学，终善者为师。"

### 【今译】

齐景公问晏子说："人性有贤德的有不好的，可以学习吗？"晏子回答说："《诗经》说：'德如高山人人景仰，行如大路人人遵循。'心中向往的应是那样的人。因此诸侯并立时，推行善政而不怠惰的人成为首领；士人们一起学习时，把善行坚持到底的成为师长。"

## 4.6 [86] DUKE JING INQUIRED REGARDING THE RELEVANCE OF LEARNING TO WORTHINESS AND UNWORTHINESS. YANZI REPLIED THAT EXERTING ONESELF IS BEST.

Duke Jing asked Yanzi: "By nature, some are worthy, but some are unworthy. Can one acquire worthiness by learning?"

Yanzi replied: "As it says in the *Odes*:

I look up at the high mountain,

I travel the great road.[1]

This ode refers to a person who has made these his vocation. Therefore, when the regional princes convene, the one who does well and is not idle becomes the chief; when officers study together, the one who does well all his days becomes the teacher."[2]

309

---

1  *Shijing*, 218/107/14.

2  The *Hanshi waizhuan*, 7.23/55/13, presents a similar argument by using the same quotations from the *Shijing*.

## 4.7 [87] 景公问富民安众晏子对以节欲中听

齐景公问如何使百姓富足民众安定，晏子回答说要节制欲望公正听讼

### 【原文】

景公问晏子曰："富民安众难乎？"晏子对曰："易。节欲则民富，中听则民安，行此二者而已矣。"

### 【今译】

齐景公问晏子说："让百姓富足民众安定困难吗？"晏子说："容易。国君节制欲望百姓就会富足，公正听讼断案民众就会安定，做好这两件事就行了。"

## 4.7 [87] DUKE JING ASKED ABOUT ENRICHING THE PEOPLE AND MAKING THE MASSES PEACEFUL. YANZI REPLIED THAT LIMITING DESIRES AND MAKING JUST ADJUDICATIONS SUFFICES.

Duke Jing queried Yanzi as follows: "Is it difficult to enrich the people and make the masses peaceful?"

Yanzi replied: "It is easy. If desires are limited, then people will be rich; and when adjudications are just, then people will be peaceful. It is sufficient to put these two conditions into practice."

## 4.8 [88] 景公问国如何则谓安晏子对以内安政外归义

齐景公问国家怎样才算安定，晏子回答说百姓安定诸侯归附

大中华文库

### 【原文】

景公问晏子曰："国如何则可谓安矣？"晏子对曰："下无讳言，官无怨治；通人不华，穷民不怨；喜乐无羡赏，忿怒无羡刑；上有礼于士，下有惠于民；地博不兼小，兵强不劫弱；百姓内安其政，诸侯外归其义：可谓安矣。"

### 【今译】

齐景公问晏子说："国家怎样才可以算得上安定呢？"晏子回答说："臣民说话没有忌讳，官员治理使百姓没有怨言；显贵的人不奢华，贫困的百姓没有怨恨；高兴时不增加赏赐，愤怒时不加重刑罚；在上能礼敬贤人，在下能施恩于百姓；土地辽阔不去兼并小国，兵力强盛不去劫掠弱国；国境内的百姓安于他的政策，国境外的诸侯归附他的德义。这样就可以说是安定了。"

## 4.8 [88] DUKE JING ASKED WHAT A STATE MUST BE LIKE IN ORDER TO BE CALLED PEACEFUL. YANZI REPLIED THAT DOMESTIC PEACE IS CREATED BY THE GOVERNMENT, AND PEOPLE ARE DRAWN FROM BEYOND THE STATE BY ITS RIGHTEOUSNESS.

Duke Jing queried Yanzi as follows: "What must a state be like in order to be called peaceful?"

Yanzi replied: "Inferiors have nothing to conceal, and the officials do not generate resentment in their administration; successful functionaries are not gaudy, and the destitute do not bear resentment; when the ruler is pleased, he does not generate unrestrained rewards; when he is angry, he does not apply unrestrained punishment; rites are observed towards officials in the upper classes, and kindness is shown to people in the inferior classes; though the territory is large, a small one is not annexed; the army is strong, and the weak are not robbed; the government makes the people residing within state peaceful, and the state's righteousness attract those beyond the state. This is what is meant by 'stability.'"

## 4.9 [89] 景公问诸侯孰危晏子对以莒其先亡

齐景公问诸侯国哪个危险，晏子回答说莒国大概先灭亡

【原文】

　　景公问晏子曰："当今之时，诸侯孰危？"晏子对曰："莒其先亡乎！"公曰："何故？"对曰："地侵于齐，货（谒）〔竭〕于晋，是以亡也。"

【今译】

314
　　齐景公问晏子说："当今的形势，诸侯之中哪个国家更危险？"晏子回答说："莒国大概会先灭亡吧！"景公问："为什么呢？"晏子回答说："莒国的土地临近齐国，却穷竭财物送给晋国，因此会灭亡。"

## 4.9 [89] DUKE JING ASKED WHO WAS IN DANGER AMONG THE REGIONAL PRINCES. YANZI REPLIED THAT JU WOULD PERHAPS BE FIRST TO PERISH.

Duke Jing queried Yanzi as follows: "At the present time, who among the regional princes is in danger?"

Yanzi replied: "Ju will perhaps be first to perish."[1]

The Duke said: "Why is this so?"

Yanzi replied: "Qi is invading its territories and Jin is decimating its properties. This is why it is perishing."

*315*

---

1  Cf. item 3.8 [58], above.

大中华文库

# 4.10 [90] 晏子使吴吴王问可处可去晏子对以视国治乱

晏子出使吴国，吴王问国家什么时候可以居处什么时候应该离去，晏子回答说要看国家的治平或丧乱

## 【原文】

晏子聘于吴，吴王曰："子大夫以君命辱在敝邑之地，施贶寡人，寡人受贶矣，愿有私问焉。"晏子巡遁而对曰："婴，北方之贱臣也，得奉君命，以趋于末朝，恐辞令不审，讥于下吏，惧不知所以对者。"吴王曰："寡人闻夫子久矣，今乃得见，愿终其问。"晏子避席对曰："敬

## 【今译】

晏子出使吴国，吴王说："大夫您因为齐君的命令屈尊来到我们这个国家，赠予我礼物，我接受馈赠，还有一些私下的问题希望向您请教。"晏子有些迟疑地说："我只不过是北方齐国的一个卑贱臣子，奉国君的命令，从末朝来到贵国，恐怕我的言辞不够审慎，被贵国官员耻笑，心中恐惧不知道该怎么回答。"吴王说："我听闻您的大名已经很久了，今天才得以相见，希望能坚持向您请教。"晏子离开座席站起来回答说："那我就恭敬地接受您的命令了。"吴王说："国家在什么情况下可以居处，在什么情况下可以离开？"晏子回答道："我听说，亲近和疏远的人都能够处于他们应得的位置，大臣们能够竭尽忠诚，百

# 4.10 [90] YANZI WAS SENT ON A DIPLOMATIC MISSION TO WU. THE KING OF WU INQUIRED REGARDING THE CRITERION FOR LIVING IN A STATE OR FLEEING FROM IT. YANZI REPLIED THAT ONE SHOULD OBSERVE THE ORDER OR DISORDER IN A GIVEN STATE.

Yanzi was on an official visit to Wu. The King of Wu[1] said: "On the command of your ruler, you, my distinguished Master, grace me by your visit to my insignificant city. In accepting this bounty, I would like to ask you a confidential question."

Yanzi was taken aback and replied: "I am the lowest kind of minister from the North, ordered by his ruler to come to this[2] court; I'm afraid that I will become a laughingstock to the low functionaries if I do not choose my words carefully. I fear that I will not know how to respond."

The King of Wu said: "I have heard of you, Master, for a long time, and now that you appear before me, I would like to complete my question."

Yanzi rose up from his mat and replied: "I respectfully receive your command."

The King of Wu said: "What kind of state would one want to live in, what kind of state would one want to flee from?"

Yanzi replied: "I have heard that one should live in a state where those who are close to the ruler — as well as those who are not — receive their proper stature; grand ministers can maintain their loyalty to the fullest; the people do not bear resentment towards the government; and no cruel punishment is inflicted. This is why a man of noble character cherishes a ruler who is not deviant, and on this basis occupies his proper position in the

---

1   The King of Wu mentioned here is Helü, 阖闾, an assassin and a warmonger who reigned in Wu between 514–496 BCE.

2   末 → 本 (*YZCQ-ICS*, 33, n. 4).

**【原文】**

受命矣。"吴王曰："国如何则可处，如何则可去也？"晏子对曰："婴闻之，亲疏得处其伦，大臣得尽其忠，民无怨治，国无虐刑，则可处矣。是以君子怀不逆之君，居治国之位。亲疏不得居其伦，大臣不得尽其忠，民多怨治，国有虐刑，则可去矣。是以君子不怀暴君之禄，不处乱国之位。"

**【今译】**

姓们不怨恨国家的统治，国家没有暴虐的刑罚，（这样的国家）就可以居处了。因此君子归附不行悖逆的国君，出任治平国家的职位。亲近与疏远的人不能居于其应得的位置，大臣们不能竭尽忠诚，百姓们大多怨恨国家的统治，国家有暴虐的刑罚，（这样的国家）就可以离开了。因此君子不怀念凶暴君主的俸禄，不出任混乱国家的职位。"

government of the state. One should flee a state where those who are close to the ruler — as well as those who are not — fail to receive their proper stature; grand ministers cannot maintain their loyalty to the fullest; people bear intense resentment towards the government; or cruel punishment is inflicted. Therefore, a man of noble character does not cherish emoluments given by a cruel ruler and does not occupy a position in a disordered state."

## 4.11 [91] 吴王问保威强不失之道晏子对以先民后身

吴王问保持国威强盛不衰的办法，晏子回答说要先考虑百姓后考虑自身

【原文】

晏子聘于吴，吴王曰："敢问长保威强勿失之道若何？"晏子对曰："先民而后身，先施而后诛；强不暴弱，贵不凌贱，富不傲贫；百姓并进，有司不侵，民和政平；不以威强退人之君，不以众强兼人之地；其用法，为时禁暴，故世不逆其志；其用兵，为众屏患，故民不疾其劳：此长保威强勿失之道也。失此者危矣！"吴王忿然作色，不说。晏子曰："寡君之事毕矣，婴无斧锧之罪，请辞而行。"遂不复见。

【今译】

晏子出使吴国，吴王问："请问长久保持国威强盛不衰的办法是什么？"晏子回答说："国君要先考虑百姓后考虑自身，先施行教化而后再行诛罚；强大的不欺负弱小的，高贵的不凌辱卑贱的，富有的不轻视贫穷的；百姓都有进身做官的机会，官吏之间不互相侵犯，人民和乐政治清平；不靠威势强盛逼退他国的君主，不靠人多势强兼并他国的土地；制定法令，是为当世禁除凶暴，所以世人不违逆他的意志；发动战争，是为大众屏除祸患，所以百姓不厌恶他的劳役：这就是长久保持国威强盛不衰的办法。失去这些就危险了！"吴王愤怒地变了脸色，很不高兴。晏子说："我们国君交代的事情已经办完了，我没有犯杀头的罪过，请允许我告辞回国。"于是再也没见吴王。

## 4.11 [91] THE KING OF WU ASKED HOW ONE PRESERVES ONE'S POWER AND STRENGTH WITHOUT LOSING ONE'S TRUE FOUNDATION. YANZI REPLIED, PUT THE PEOPLE FIRST AND ONESELF LAST.

Yanzi was on an official visit to Wu. The King of Wu said: "May I ask how one preserves one's power and strength for a long time without losing one's true foundation?"

Yanzi replied: "By putting the people first and oneself last; giving top priority to bestowing and lowest to punishing. When the strong do not oppress the weak, the noble do not humiliate the lowly, and the rich are not arrogant to the poor. When people make progress together; functionaries are not aggressive, the people are harmonious, and the government is peaceful. When the ruler does not drive away other people's rulers by means of power and strength, nor does he annex other people's lands with his large and strong army. He implements timely laws to restrain the violent, and therefore his contemporaries do not object to his ambition. He deploys troops to ward off worries from the masses, and therefore people are not crushed by their toil. This is how one preserves one's power and strength for a long time without losing one's true foundation. Those who lose their true foundation will be in danger."

The King of Wu flushed with anger and was displeased.

Yanzi said: "I have fulfilled my duty to my ruler's affairs. I committed no crime that deserves the axe on the execution block. May I be granted to leave?"

Consequently, he did not see the King again.

## 4.12 [92] 晏子使鲁鲁君问何事回曲之君晏子对以庇（秩）〔族〕

晏子出使鲁国，鲁国国君问他为什么侍奉邪僻的君主，晏子回答说要庇护族人

**【原文】**

晏子使鲁，见昭公，昭公说曰："天下以子大夫语寡人者众矣，今得见而羡乎所闻，请私而无为罪。寡人闻大国之君，盖回曲之君也，曷为以子大夫之行，事回曲之君乎？"晏子逡循对曰："婴不肖，婴之族又不若婴，待婴而祀先者五百家，故婴不敢择君。"晏子出，昭公语

**【今译】**

晏子出使鲁国，见到鲁昭公，昭公高兴地说："天下人已经多次把大夫您的情况告诉我，今日相见才知道您的才能远远超过传闻，请允许我私下询问而不要怪罪。我听闻大国的国君，大多是邪僻不公正的君主，为什么凭借大夫您的德行，却侍奉邪僻不公正的君主呢？"晏子恭敬地回答说："我不贤德，我的族人还不如我，等待我的帮助来祭祀祖先的有五百家，因此我不敢选择国君。"晏子出去后，昭公对人说："晏子是位仁德的人啊，他使逃亡的国君返回国内，使倾危的国家安定，

## 4.12 [92] YANZI WAS SENT ON A DIPLOMATIC MISSION TO LU. THE RULER OF LU ASKED HIM WHY HE SERVES A WICKED RULER. YANZI REPLIED THAT HE HAD TO PROTECT HIS OWN CLAN.

Yanzi was sent on a diplomatic mission to Lu and had an audience with Duke Zhao.[1] Duke Zhao was delighted and said: "Many people in the world told me about you, my distinguished Master. Now I can see that you surpass what I have heard so please do not be offended if I offer here a personal word. I have heard that the ruler of a great state is oftentimes a wicked ruler.[2] How is it that such a distinguished Master as yourself actively serves a wicked ruler?"

Yanzi was taken aback and replied: "I am unworthy, and still, there is none in my clan who can measure up to me. No less than five hundred families depend on me for their sacrifices to the ancestors and therefore I dare not be selective about a ruler."

When Yanzi left, Duke Zhao said to his people: "Yanzi is a humane person; he wept over his deceased ruler[3] and brought peace to an endangered state without gaining any personal profit from any of it. He desecrated Cui Zhu's corpse by exposing it,[4] and exterminated Cui Zhu's

323

---

1   Duke Zhao 昭公 reigned in Lu between 541–510 BCE.

2   Duke Zhao's personal question obviously refers to Yanzi's ruler, Duke Jing, the ruler of Qi.

3   The text reads 反亡君, "He made his ruler return from exile;" however, no source mentions such an event. For this reason *JS*, 258/5, suggests replacing 反 ("return") with 哭 ("wept") in accordance with the spirit of the event that is portrayed in the following Item 5.2, where Yanzi sits over the remains of his ruler, Duke Zhuang, and weeps.

4   The *Zuozhuan*, B9.28.11/299/19, provides a full account of the desecration of Cui Zhu's corpse, without making any mention of Yanzi as one of the participants in this event.

## 【原文】

人曰："晏子，仁人也，反亡君，安危国，而不私利焉；僇崔杼之尸，灭贼乱之徒，不获名焉；使齐外无诸侯之忧，内无国家之患，不伐功焉；鍥然不满，退托于族，晏子可谓仁人矣。"

## 【今译】

却不图私利；斩戮崔杼的尸体，剿灭乱臣贼子，却不获取美名；使齐国外无诸侯侵犯的忧虑，内无国家倾危的祸患，而不自夸功绩；没有自满的样子，却托词为了家族，晏子可以说是仁德的人啊。"

rebellious followers, and did not gain fame for himself by any of this. He made Qi a state that was not aggrieved by the external regional princes, and faced no worries for the state and ruling families from within. He did not boast about his own merits; he was humble and in no way self-satisfied. He retired using his clan as a pretext. Yanzi may be called a humane person."

## 4.13 [93] 鲁昭公问鲁一国迷何也晏子对以化为一心

鲁昭公问鲁国上下为什么迷惑，晏子回答说因为国家上下化为了一种心思

### 【原文】

晏子聘于鲁，鲁昭公问焉〔曰〕："吾闻之，莫三人而迷，今吾以（鲁）一国（迷）虑之，〔鲁〕不免于乱，何也？"晏子对曰："君之所尊举而富贵，入所以与图身，出所以与图国，及左右偪迩，皆同于君之心者也。犒鲁国化而为一心，曾无与二，其何暇有三？夫偪迩于君之侧者，距本朝之势，国之所以〔不〕治也；左右谗谀，相与塞善，

### 【今译】

晏子出使鲁国，鲁昭公问他说："我听闻，做事情不和三个人商量就会迷惑，现在我和鲁国全国人商量国事，但还是不能避免混乱，这是为什么？"晏子回答说："您尊崇举任而得到富贵的人，召入宫中和他谋划自身私事的人，到了外朝和他谋划国家大事的人，以及您左右亲近的臣子，都是和您同一条心的人。把鲁国人的心矫正同化为一个，您就听不到第二种心声，哪里还有空暇了解第三种？君王身侧的近臣，能够抗拒朝中的群臣，国家因此不能治理；君王左右的谗谀之臣，相互勾结堵塞善言，德行因此衰败；做官的人只求禄位，游荡的人豢养

# 4.13 [93] DUKE ZHAO OF LU ASKED WHY THE WHOLE STATE OF LU HAD LOST ITS WAY. YANZI REPLIED THAT THE DUKE HAS TRANSFORMED LU INTO A SINGLE-MINDED STATE.

During Yanzi's official visit to Lu, Duke Zhao asked him: "I have heard that without three people to consult with, a person will lose his way. Now I have an entire populace I may confer with, and yet Lu has not avoided disorder. Why is that?"[1]

Yanzi replied: "When those whom you, My Lord, honor, promote, enrich and ennoble — enter your court, they make plans for themselves; when they leave your court, they make plans for their fiefdoms. As for your entourage and intimate courtiers, they all conform to your mind's wishes, so that you reform[2] the whole state of Lu, transforming it into a single-minded state. You have never consulted with two of them; how could you find time to consult with three? As for your intimate courtiers standing by your side, My Lord, they distance themselves from the power of your own court, and for this reason the state is not well governed. Your entourage slanders and flatters; they join forces and block the good; for this reason, standards of conduct are declining. Your officers retain their emoluments, and those who serve you abroad form clandestine alliances. For this reason, you are in personal danger. As it says in the *Odes*:

Luxuriant are the oak clumps;

We make firewood of them, we pile them up.

Stately is our Lord King;

---

1   Cf. *Hanfeizi*, 30/63/1.

2   犒 → 矫 (*YZCQ-ICS*, 34, n. 3). *Hanfeizi*, 30/62/30, reads: 举鲁国尽化为一 ("The whole state of Lu has been transformed into a unit").

**【原文】**

行之所以衰也；士者持禄，游者（養）〔养〕交，身之所以危也。《诗》曰：'芃芃棫朴，薪之槱之，济济辟王，左右趋之。'此言古者圣王明君之使以善也。故外知事之情，而内得心之诚，是以不迷也。"

**【今译】**

私党相互结交，国君因此身处险境。《诗经》中说：'茂盛的棫树，砍下来做柴木，庄严肃静的君王，群臣赶来亲附。'这是说古时候的圣王明君根据善行用人。因此外能知晓事物的情形，内能得到心灵的真诚，因此就不迷惑了。"

On left and right[1] they rush to him.[2]

These words show that in ancient times, the sage-kings and enlightened rulers caused everything to turn to good. Therefore, outside the court, they could know the true state of affairs, and from within the court, they could realize the sincerity of the people's minds. That is why they did not lose their way."

329

---

1   左右 "To left and right," that is, the king's entourage.

2   *Shijing*, 238/119/16.

## 4.14 [94] 鲁昭公问安国众民晏子对以事大养小谨听节俭

鲁昭公问怎样使国家安定百姓增多，晏子回答说要侍奉大国豢养小国谨慎听讼节约俭朴

### 【原文】

晏子聘于鲁，鲁昭公问曰："〔大〕夫俨然辱临敝邑，窃甚嘉之，寡人受贶，请问安国众民如何？"晏子对曰："婴闻傲大贱小则国危，慢听厚敛则民散。事大（养）〔养〕小，安国之器也；谨听节俭，众民之术也。"

### 【今译】

晏子出使鲁国，鲁昭公问道："大夫您庄重地屈尊来到我们鲁国，我内心非常高兴，我接受您的馈赠，请问怎样才能使国家安定百姓增多呢？"晏子回答说："我听闻傲视大国轻视小国国家就会危险，轻慢听讼厚敛财富百姓就会离散。因此侍奉大国豢养小国，是使国家安定的利器；认真听讼躬行节俭，是使百姓增加的方法。"

# 4.14 [94] DUKE ZHAO OF LU INQUIRED ABOUT BRINGING PEACE TO THE STATE AND INCREASING THE POPULATION. YANZI REPLIED THAT THIS IS ACHIEVED BY SERVING GREAT STATES, CARING FOR SMALL STATES, CAREFULLY HEARING COURT CASES, AND COLLECTING TAXES SPARINGLY.

When Yanzi was on an official mission to Lu, Duke Zhao asked him: "A high officer like yourself conferred an honor on me by your solemn visit to my insignificant city. I humbly express my deep appreciation of this visit, which I accept as a gift. I would like to ask, what is the way to bring peace to the masses and increase the population?"

Yanzi replied: "I have heard that if one is arrogant to great states and despises small states, this brings danger upon one's own state. If one is negligent in hearing court cases and one collects heavy taxes, then one's people will be dispersed. Serving great states and caring for small states is the tool for bringing peace to one's state; the careful hearing of court cases and sparing tax is the art of increasing the population."

## 4.15 [95] 晏子使晋晋平公问先君得众若何晏子对以如美渊泽

晏子出使晋国，晋平公问晋国先代国君获得民众拥护的样子，晏子回答说像雨水汇入江河湖泊

### 【原文】

晏子使晋，晋平公飨之文室，既静矣，晏以，平公问焉，曰："昔吾先君得众若何？"晏子对曰："君飨寡君，施及使臣，御在君侧，恐惧不知所以对。"平公曰："闻子大夫数矣，今乃得见，愿终闻之。"晏子对曰："臣闻君子如美，渊泽容之，众人归之，如鱼有依，极其游泳之乐；若渊泽决竭，其鱼动流，夫往者维雨乎，不可复已。"公又问曰：

### 【今译】

晏子出使晋国，晋平公在文室举行飨礼，飨礼结束，又举行宴礼，晋平公问晏子说："以前我晋国的先代国君得到众人拥护的情况是什么样的？"晏子回答说："您用飨礼对待我国国君，施恩惠及使臣，我侍候在您的身边，诚惶诚恐不知道怎么回答。"晋平公说："我听闻大夫您的名声已经很多次了，今天才得以相见，希望最终能够听到您的教诲。"晏子回答说："我听闻君子就像雨水，江河湖泊容纳他，众人归附他，就像鱼有了水为依靠，才能极尽游泳的快乐；如果江河湖泊决口枯竭，其中的鱼也随着水流走，以往维系的雨水啊，就再也不能恢复了。"晋平公又问道："请问齐庄公和现在的国君景公相比谁更贤明？"晏子说：

# 4.15 [95] YANZI WAS SENT ON A DIPLOMATIC MISSION TO JIN. DUKE PING OF JIN ASKED HOW HIS FORMER RULER WON OVER THE PEOPLE. YANZI REPLIED THAT HE WAS LIKE RAIN1 POOLED IN DEEP MARSHES.

Yanzi was sent on a diplomatic mission to Jin. Duke Ping of Jin[2] received him with a banquet in a decorated room. When the banquet grew quiet, Duke Ping asked him:[3] "How did my former ruler win over the multitudes?"

Yanzi replied: "The banquet you arranged for my ruler was extended to me, his envoy. Since I am now standing in attendance at your side, I fear that I may not know how to respond properly."

Duke Ping said: "I have repeatedly heard of you, Master. Now that I have finally succeeded in seeing you, I would like to hear you in full."

Yanzi replied: "A man of noble character is like the rain,[4] which pools in deep marshes. The multitude turns to him as fish rely on marshes, enjoying themselves to the utmost by swimming. But if the marshes dry up, then the fish in them flap helplessly. They need rain to get anywhere. They will never return."

The Duke asked further: "May I ask you who was worthier, Duke Zhuang or your present ruler?"

Yanzi replied: "Those two rulers conducted themselves differently. This is not something I would presume to understand."

333

---

1   美 → 雨 (*JS*, 265/4).

2   The lustful, incompetent Duke Ping of Jin 晋平公 reigned in Jin between 557–532 BCE.

3   Omit 晏以 (*YZCQ-ICS*, 35, n.1).

4   美 → 雨 (*JS*, 265/4).

大中华文库

## 【原文】

"请问庄公与今〔君〕孰贤？"晏子曰："两君之行不同，臣不敢（不）知也。"公曰："王室之正也，诸侯之专制也，是以欲闻子大夫之言也。"对曰："先君庄公不安静处，乐节饮食，不好钟鼓，好兵作武，士与同饥渴寒暑，君之强，过人之量，有一过不能已焉，是以不免于难。今君大宫室，美台榭，以辟饥渴寒暑，畏祸敬鬼神，君之善，足以没身，不足以及子孙矣。"

## 【今译】

"两位国君的德行不同，我不敢自作聪明去评论。"晋平公说："王室里有不正之风，诸侯们专横跋扈，因此想听听您的高论。"晏子回答说："先代国君庄公不安于平静的生活，喜欢节制饮食，不喜欢钟鼓乐舞，喜好兴兵动武，能和将士们一起共度饥渴寒暑，庄公身强体壮，有超过一般人的力量，有过人之处而不能控制自己，因此不能避免灾难。现在的景公大建宫室，把台榭装饰的精美，用来避免饥渴寒暑，畏惧灾祸敬奉鬼神，景公的善行，足够得以善终，但不足以惠及子孙。"

The Duke said: "At present, the royal house of Zhou is not rectified,[1] and the regional princes misuse their power; for this reason, I would like to hear your words as a high officer."

Yanzi replied: "My former ruler, Duke Zhuang, was not at ease when living quietly. He gladly curtailed drink and food, and did not like bells and drums. He liked weapons and the conduct of military affairs; with his warriors, he shared hunger and thirst, cold and heat. His physical powers exceeded the capacity of normal persons. His one mistake was that he could not stop; therefore, he was not saved from catastrophe. The present ruler expands palaces and chambers and decorates terraces beautifully in order to take refuge from hunger, thirst, cold, and heat. He fears calamity and worships spirits and demons. His good traits are sufficient for him to find a peaceful end, but not to benefit his descendants."

335

---

1   Add 不 before 正 (*JS*, 266/10).

## 4.16 [96] 晋平公问齐君德行高下晏子对以小善

晋平公问齐国国君德行的高低，晏子回答说有小的善行

### 【原文】

晏子使于晋，晋平公问曰："吾子之君，德行高下如何？"晏子对以"小善"。公曰："否，吾非问小善，问子之君德行高下也。"晏子蹴然曰："诸侯之交，绍而相见，辞之有所隐也。君之命质，臣无所隐，婴之君无称焉。"平公蹴然而辞送，再拜而反曰："殆哉吾过！谁曰齐君不肖！直称之士，正在本朝也。"

### 【今译】

晏子出使晋国，晋平公问道："先生您的国君，德行的高低怎么样？"晏子用"小善"来回答。晋平公说："不，我不是问有没有小的善行，我是在问您的国君德行的高低。"晏子不安地说："诸侯之间交往，第一次相见，言辞之中有所隐瞒。您的询问很质直，我不敢有所隐瞒，我的国君在德行方面没什么值得称道的。"晋平公不安地送别晏子，拜了两拜后返回说："我的过失太危险了！谁说齐国的国君不贤明！敢于直言的士人，正在我们朝中啊。"

# 4.16 [96] DUKE PING OF JIN INQUIRED REGARDING THE RULER OF QI'S VIRTUOUS DEEDS, WHETHER THEY SHOULD BE CONSIDERED LOFTY OR LOWLY. YANZI REPLIED WITH RESPECT TO THE DUKE'S MINOR ACTS OF GOODNESS.

Yanzi was sent on a diplomatic mission to Jin. Duke Ping of Jin asked: "How would you rank the virtuous acts of your ruler — lofty or lowly?"

Yanzi referred in his answer to the Duke's minor acts of goodness.

Duke Ping said: "No, I am not asking about his minor acts of goodness, I am asking whether your ruler's virtuous acts are highly commendable or not."

Yanzi winced and said: "The relationships between the regional princes are such that they meet each other through mediators. There is something hidden in their words. Your order is blunt and I have nothing to hold back: there is nothing praiseworthy about my ruler."

Duke Ping winced and dismissed Yanzi with polite words. He escorted him on his way out, bowed twice, returned, and said: "Oh how dangerous are my mistakes. Who may say that the ruler of Qi is unworthy if such a straightforward officer is present at his court?"

337

# 4.17 [97] 晋叔向问齐国若何晏子对以齐德衰民归田氏

晋国的叔向问齐国的情况，晏子回答说齐国德运衰败百姓归附田氏

## 【原文】

晏子聘于晋，叔向从之宴，相与语。叔向曰："齐其何如？"晏子对曰："此季世也，吾弗知，齐其为田氏乎！"叔向曰："何谓也？"晏子曰："公弃其民，而归于田氏。齐旧四量：豆、区、釜、钟。四升为豆，各自其四，以登于釜，釜十则钟。田氏三量，皆登一焉，钟乃巨矣。以家量贷，以公量收之。山木如市，弗加于山，鱼盐（唇）

## 【今译】

晏子出使晋国，叔向陪他宴饮，二人相互聊天。叔向问："齐国情况怎么样？"晏子回答说："这就到了末世了，我不智慧，齐国大概要被田氏夺取了！"叔向问："为什么这样说呢？"晏子说："国君抛弃了百姓，而使他们归附田氏。齐国原有四种量器：豆、区、釜、钟。四升为一豆，四豆为一区，四区为一釜，十釜为一钟。田氏的前三种量器，都在原有量器的基础上加一进位，因此钟的数量就很巨大了。田氏用私家的量器借贷，用公家的量器回收。山上的木材运到市场上卖，价格不会比在山上的时候增加，鱼、盐、蛤蜊运到市场上卖，价格不会比在海边的时候增加。百姓把劳动成果分成三份，两份都给了公家，

# 4.17 [97] SHUXIANG[1] OF JIN ASKED ABOUT THE STATE OF QI. YANZI REPLIED THAT THE VIRTUE OF QI IS IN DECLINE, WITH THE PEOPLE TURNING TO THE TIAN LINEAGE.[2]

When Yanzi was on an official visit to Jin, Shuxiang accompanied him to a banquet and they engaged in conversation with each other.

Shuxiang said, "What do you make of the present situation in Qi?"

Yanzi said: "These are the final days of its existence. I don't know, but that Qi is bound to become the possession of the Tian lineage."[3]

Shuxiang asked: "What do you mean?"

Yanzi said, "The Duke has deserted his people, leaving them to submit to the Tian linage. Qi has long had four measurement units — *dou*, *qu*, *fu* and *zhong*. Four *sheng*[4] make one *dou*, and each successive unit is four times larger than the preceding one, up to the *fu* unit. Ten units of *fu* make one unit of *zhong*. The Tian lineage increased the first three measurement units by one unit each, and thus their unit of *zhong* became huge.[5] They gave loans according to their clan's units but collected debts according to public measurement units. Their timber arrived from the mountains to the markets with no extra charge for transportation; their fish, salt, clams, and oysters arrived from the sea to the markets with no extra charge for

339

---

1   Shuxiang 叔向 (d. 528) is the cognomen of Yangshe Xi 羊舌肸, a prominent statesman and one of the most influential officials in Jin at the time.

2   Item 7.10 [180] ↔ *Zuozhuan*, B10.3.3/323/23. An account and a moral evaluation of this discussion is also recorded in the *Kongcongzi*, 5.3/59/4.

3   The *Zuozhuan* has Chen linage 陈氏, which is identical with the *YZCQ*'s Tian linage 田氏. For a discussion of the interchangeability of these two linages names, see Legge, V, 840.

4   One s*heng* 升 equals one liter.

5   One traditional Qi's unit of *zhong* would therefore contain 640 liters while the *zhong* unit of the Tian lineage would contain no less than 1,250 liters.

**【原文】**

〔蜃〕蛤，弗加于海。民参其力，二人于公，而衣食其一；公积朽蠹，而老少（涷）〔冻〕馁；国（都之）〔之都〕市，屦贱而踊贵；民人痛疾，或燠休之。昔者殷人诛杀不当，僇民无时，文王慈惠殷众，收恤无主，是故天下归之，民无私与，维德之授。今公室骄暴，而田氏慈惠，其爱之如父母，而归之如流水，欲无获民，将焉避？箕伯、直柄、虞遂、伯戏，其相胡公、太姬，已在齐矣。"叔向曰："虽吾公室，

340

**【今译】**

只留下一份作衣食之用；公家积聚的财物腐朽生蠹，而老人小孩却饥寒交迫；国都的市场上，鞋子便宜而假腿昂贵；百姓痛苦怨恨，偶尔会从田氏那里得到慰藉。以前商朝诛杀不适当，杀戮百姓不分时节，周文王仁爱商朝的民众，收养抚恤无家可归的人，因此天下人都归附他，百姓并不偏向谁，谁推行德政就拥护谁。现在齐国公室骄横残暴，而田氏却仁爱百姓，如同父母爱护子女，百姓归附田氏就像流水涌来，即使田氏不想获得百姓的拥护，又怎么避得开呢？田氏的祖先箕伯、

transportation. The people's labor in Qi is apportioned three ways — two parts go to the Duke and one provides for the people's clothing and food. The Duke's hoarded grain is contaminated by insects, while elders and children suffer from cold and hunger. In the market of the state capital, shoes for people with amputated toes are expensive, while regular shoes are cheap.[1] People suffer gravely, some moan and then groan for respite. In the past, the Yin rulers' punishments were inappropriate, and they massacred people unceasingly. King Wen[2] was compassionate toward Yin's large population. He received and comforted those who no longer had a real ruler, and therefore the realm turned to him. The people do not confer power for the sake of affiliations — only the virtuous receive their authority. But now the ducal house is arrogant and violent, while the Tian lineage is compassionate. They love the people as if they were their parents, and the people rush to them like a torrent. Even if they do not aspire to win the people's allegiance, how would this be avoided? Jibo, Zhibing, Yusui, and Boxi have followed Duke Hu and his consort Tai Ji.[3] Their presence is already ingrained in Qi."

Shuxiang said: "The house of my Duke, as well, is in its final days of existence. Armored horses are not yoked to chariots; the chief ministers do not deploy the army. The Duke's chariots have no drivers, and the ranks have no officers. Most of the people are tired and worn out, while

---

1  The high demand for pricey shoes for people with amputated toes is explained in Item 6. [161] as follows: "At that time, the Duke imposed numerous corporal punishments, and so there were traders who sold shoes catering to those whose toes were chopped off as a punishment."

2  The virtuous King Wen 文王 (1231–1135 BCE), whose son, King Wu 武王 (1169–1116 BCE), was the first sovereign of the Zhou dynasty.

3  According to the *Shiji*,1575, Duke Hu (personal name Man 满) was a descended of the Sage Emperor Shun. He was enfeoffed in Chen 陈 by King Wu. According to Du Yu's 杜预 commentary on the parallel text in the Zuozhuan (B10.3.3/323/23), Jibo, Zhibing, Yusui, and Boxi were descendants of Emperor Shun and ancestors of the Chen 陈 (田) lineage.

**【原文】**

亦季世也。戎马不驾，卿无军行，公乘无人，卒列无长；庶民罢弊，宫室滋侈，道殣相望，而女富溢尤；民闻公命，如逃寇雠；栾、郤、（晋）〔胥〕、原、孤、续、庆、伯，降在皂隶；政在家门，民无所依，而君日不悛，以乐慆忧；公室之卑，其何日之有！谗鼎之铭曰：'昧旦

**【今译】**

直柄、虞遂、伯戏的神位辅佐着陈胡公和大姬的灵位，已经安居在齐国了。"叔向说："即使是我们晋国的公室，也到了末世了。战马不驾战车，上卿不能指挥军队，战车上没有打仗的士兵，士兵队列中没有长官；百姓疲惫困苦，宫室却日渐奢侈，道路上饿死的人比比皆是，而公室却更加富足；百姓听到国君的命令，如同逃避强盗和仇敌；栾、郤、胥、原、孤、续、庆、伯这些晋国的世家，地位已经下降为吏役；政事落入权臣手中，百姓没有依靠，然而国君每日不知悔改，用享乐来忘记忧虑；

the palaces and chambers increase extravagantly. People who have starved to death lie on the roads with eyes staring at each other, while the wealth of the families of favorite female companions becomes excessive great.[1] When people hear the Duke's orders, they run from them as from enemies. The clans of Luan, Xi, Xu, Yuan, Hu, Xu, Qing and Bo[2] have been demoted to the status of menial servants. The great families control the government, and the people have no one to rely on. Instead of repenting, the ruler goes on day after day amusing himself to hide his malaise. How many days are then still required for the downfall of the ducal house? The inscription on the Chan tripod[3] says,

> You may arise at early dawn and do glorious deeds,
>
> yet your descendants will still become idlers.

All the worse when the Duke never shows remorse; how could he possibly survive for long?"

Yanzi said, "What then will you do, my Master?"

Shuxiang said: "All human efforts have been exhausted; there is nothing else I can now do except wait for Heaven. The clan of the Duke of Jin has come to its end. I have heard that when a ducal house is about to fall, its clan lineage will first fall like leaves from a tree and then the Duke will

343

---

1   I follow Du Yu's 杜预 commentary on the parallel text in the Zuozhuan (B10.3.3/323/23), which has 嬖宠之家 for 女. The *JS*, 272/29, however, replaces 女 with 如; in that case, the sentence would translate: "While the wealth of the ducal house seems to become staggeringly high."

2   This segment, which consists of eight characters, is punctuated in the *YZCQ-ICS*, 4.17/36/2-3 in pairs (栾郤, 胥原, 孤续, 庆伯). However, in the parallel *Zuozhuan*'s segment (B10.3.3/324/1), it is punctuated by the same *ICS* concordance editorial team in eight separate characters. I follow both the later punctuation and the explanation given by the *JS*, 272/31 that these characters denote eight clan names in ancient Jin of prominent ministerial lineages.

3   The Chan tripod is one of the nine tripods which, according to legend, were cast by Emperor Yu and handed down from dynasty to dynasty as symbols of imperial authority.

**【原文】**

丕显，后世犹怠'，况（曰）〔日〕不悛，其（竜）〔能〕久乎？"晏子曰："然则子将若何？"叔向曰："人事毕矣，待天而已矣！晋之公族尽矣。肸闻之，公室将卑，其宗族枝叶先落，则公从之。肸之宗十一族，维羊舌氏在而已，肸又无子，公室无度，幸而得死，岂其获祀焉！"

**【今译】**

公室的衰败，还有几天呢！谗鼎上的铭文说：'天不亮就起来办事，后世子孙还是会懈怠'，更何况不知悔改，又怎么能长久！"晏子说："那您打算怎么办？"叔向说："人能做的事已经做完了，只能等待上天的安排了！晋国的公族气数已尽。我听说，公室将要衰败的时候，他的宗族就像大树的枝叶先凋落，然后公室跟着衰亡。我的宗族有十一支，只有羊舌氏留存到现在，我又没有儿子，公室荒淫无度，我能够善终就是侥幸，哪里还奢望得到后人的祭祀！"

follow them. My ancestry consisted of eleven lineages, of which Yang-she, my house, is the only one that remains. Furthermore, I have no son, and the ducal house acts without proper standards. I shall be lucky to die a natural death; surely I cannot hope to be offered sacrifices by my descendants."

# 4.18 [98] 叔向问齐德衰子若何晏子对以进不失忠退不失行

叔向问齐国德运衰败您打算怎么办，晏子回答说进身不丧失忠义引退不丧失德行

## 【原文】

叔向问晏子曰："齐国之德衰矣，今子何若？"晏子对曰："婴闻事明君者，竭心力以没其身，行不逮则退，不以诬持禄；事惰君者，优游其身以没其世，力不能则去，不以谀持危。且婴闻君子之事君也，进不失忠，退不失行。不苟合以隐忠，可谓不失忠；不持利以伤廉，可谓不失行。"叔向曰："善哉！《诗》有之曰：'进退维谷。'其此之谓欤！"

## 【今译】

叔向问晏子说："齐国的德义已经衰败了，现在您有什么打算？"晏子回答说："我听闻侍奉贤明的君主，应该竭尽心力直至身死，德行不够就主动引退，不用欺骗的行为取得俸禄；侍奉怠惰的君主，应该独善其身直至死亡，能力不能胜任就主动离去，不靠阿谀奉承招致危险。而且我听闻君子侍奉国君，进身不丧失忠诚，引退不丧失德行。不同流合污而隐没忠诚，可以说是不丧失忠诚；不获取私利而损伤廉洁，可以说是不丧失德行。"叔向说："好啊！《诗经》中说：'进退维谷。'说的就是这个意思吧！"

# 4.18 [98] SHUXIANG ASKED YANZI WHAT CAN BE DONE REGARDING THE DECLINE OF VIRTUE IN QI. YANZI REPLIED, NOT LOSING SIGHT OF ONE'S LOYALTY WHILE ADVANCING AND NOT LOSING SIGHT OF PROPER GOOD CONDUCT WHILE WITHDRAWING.

Shuxiang queried Yanzi as follows: "The virtue of the state of Qi has declined. What are you, master, going to do now?"

Yanzi replied: "I have heard that he who serves an enlightened ruler should expend his mental and physical power through his moment of death. If such a person's conduct is unequal to his task, then he should withdraw and not hold on to his emolument and position by deceptive means. If he serves an indolent ruler, he could live carefree until the end of his life; however, if he is unable to continue this, then he should leave him and not cling to this endangered condition by means of flattery. Furthermore, I have heard that when a man of noble character in service to a ruler advances, he should not lose sight of his loyalty; when he withdraws, he should not lose sight of proper good conduct. If one superficially conform while hiding his true loyalties, then one can be referred to as not having lost sight of one's loyalty. If one does not abuse integrity by clinging to personal gain, then one can be referred to as not having lost sight of proper good conduct."

Shuxiang said: "Excellent! As it says in the *Odes*:

Both ahead and behind there are nothing but ravines. [1]

Is this not what is meant here?"

347

---

1   *Shijing*, 257/134/22.

## 4.19 [99] 叔向问正士（人邪）〔邪人〕之行如何晏子对以使下顺逆

叔向问正人君子和奸邪小人的行为各是什么样的，晏子用被任官或居民间的顺逆情况来回答

### 【原文】

叔向问晏子曰："正士之义，邪人之行，何如？"晏子对曰："正士处势临众不阿私，行于国足（養）〔养〕而不忘故；通则事上，使恤其下，穷则教下，使顺其上；事君尽礼行忠，不（正）〔句〕爵禄，不用则去而不议。其交友也，论身义行，不为苟戚，不同则踈而不悱；不

### 【今译】

叔向问晏子说："正人君子的义行，奸邪小人的行为，都是什么样的？"晏子回答说："正人君子居于有权势的高位治理百姓而不偏袒亲私，行走于国中衣食无忧而不忘记故旧；通达时就侍奉国君，让国君抚恤百姓，困厄时就教化百姓，让百姓顺从国君；侍奉国君礼仪周到行为忠诚，不贪图爵位和俸禄，不被任用就离开而不非议。他们和朋友交游的时候，劝说朋友躬身行义，不苟求亲近，道不同就疏远而不诽谤朋友；不向国君诋毁他人来进身，不在国内靠刻薄百姓获取尊位。因此正人君子被国君重用时百姓安居乐业，行走于民间时国君受到尊重；因此他们得到百姓拥护时国君不怀疑，被国君任用时不会做违背

# 4.19 [99] SHUXIANG ASKED WHAT CHARACTERIZES THE CONDUCT OF THE UPRIGHT OFFICER AND THE WICKED PERSON. YANZI REPLIED THAT IT IS A MATTER OF MAKING ONE'S INFERIORS FOLLOW INSTRUCTIONS OR DEFY THEIR SUPERIORS.

Shuxiang queried Yanzi as follows: "What characterizes the righteousness of the upright officer and the conduct of the wicked?"

Yanzi replied: "When an upright officer occupies an advantageous position and stands over the multitude, he is not partial. When his policies are carried out in the state and he has enough supplies for himself, he does not forget his veteran associates. If he is successful, then he will serve his superior and influence him to take affectionate care of his inferiors. If he is in difficult circumstances, then he will instruct his inferiors and influence them to follow their superiors. When he serves a ruler, he performs the rites thoroughly and acts out of loyalty, rather than for the sake[1] of titles and emoluments. When he is not employed, he withdraws and does not express critical views. In his association with friends, he manifests trustworthiness and practices righteousness;[2] he does not establish close ties wantonly. If he and his friends disagree, then he keeps his distance from them and is reluctant to slander them. He does not receive promotion from a ruler by slanderous conduct, and he does not gain honor in the state by being malevolent towards people. Therefore, when superiors employ him, the people are in peace, and when he acts among the inferiors, the ruler is respected. Therefore, he wins over the multitudes, yet the ruler has no misgivings over his personal allegiance; he is the ruler's employee, yet his conduct is not perverse. For this reason, he does not lose his own scruples

---

1   正 → 句 (*YZCQ-ICS*, 36, n. 3).

2   论身义行 → 论信行义 (*JS*, 176/3).

**【原文】**

毁进于君，不以刻民尊于国。故用于上则民安，行于下则君尊；故得众上不疑其身，用于君不悖于行。是以进不丧（亡）〔己〕，退不危身，此正士之行也。邪人则不然，用于上则虐民，行于下则逆上；事君苟进不道忠，交友苟合不道行；持谀巧以正禄，比奸邪以厚养；矜爵禄以临人，夸礼貌以华世；不任于上则轻议，不笃于友则好诽。故用于上则民忧，行于下则君危，是以其事君近于罪，其交友近于患，其得上辟于辱，其为生债于刑，故用于上则诛，行于下则弑。是故交通则辱，生患则危，此邪人之行也。"

**【今译】**

德行的事。因此他们进身时不会丧失自我，引退时不会危及自身，这就是正人君子的义行。奸邪的人就不是这样，他们被国君任用时就会虐待百姓，行走于民间时就会违逆君上；侍奉国君苟且求进不讲忠诚，结交朋友苟求相合不讲德行；靠阿谀取巧来获得俸禄，靠勾结奸邪获取丰厚供养；在人前炫耀爵位俸禄，过分修饰庄肃和顺的仪容来哗众取宠；不被国君任用时就轻率议论，不被朋友笃信时就喜好诽谤。所以他们被国君任用时百姓忧虑，行走于民间时国君危险，因此他侍奉国君时接近罪恶，结交朋友时接近忧患，他们身处高位就会邪僻背理，做底层官吏就会滥用刑罚，因此被国君任命就会诛杀百姓，行走于民间就会犯上弑君。因此和他们来往就会受辱，发生祸患就会危害自身，这就是奸邪之人的行为。"

as he advances, nor does he endanger himself in withdrawal. Such is the conduct of an upright officer. The wicked are not so. When a wicked man is employed by a superior, he is cruel to the people; when he acts among inferiors, he is defiant to his superior. When serving his ruler, he seeks undeserved advancement and he does not pursue loyalty. In his association with friends, he wantonly associates with them and does not follow the way of proper conduct. He seeks[1] after emoluments by flattery and deceit and increases his livelihood by allying with the villainous and the treacherous. He stands over others while taking pride in his titles and emoluments; he boasts of his rites and appearance in order to flaunt himself to the world. When he is not appointed by superiors, he is quick to express critical views. When he is undependable to his friends, he is prone to slander. Therefore, when he is employed by a superior, the people are anxious. When he is active amongst inferiors, the ruler is endangered. For this reason, his service of the ruler borders on criminal conduct and his association with friends borders on disaster. When he reaches a higher position, he sinks into disgrace; when he earns his livelihood, he stumbles into punishable acts. Therefore, when he is employed by a superior, it will result in execution, and when he is active among inferiors, he will commit regicide. Therefore, his social interactions result in humiliation and his stirring up of trouble results in peril. This is the conduct of the wicked."

---

1　正 → 勾 (*JS*, 276/2).

## 4.20 [100] 叔向问事君徒处之义奚如晏子对以大贤无择

叔向问侍奉国君或居处无为时应该怎么做，晏子回答说大贤者没有选择

【原文】

叔向问晏子曰："事君之伦，徒处之义奚如？"晏子对曰："事君之伦，知虑足以安国，誉厚足以导民，和柔足以怀众，不廉上以为名，不倍民以为行，上也；洁于治己，不饰过以求先，不谗谀以求进，不阿（久）〔所〕私，不诬所能，次也；尽力守职不怠，奉官从上不敢隋，畏上故不苟，忌罪故不辟，下也。三者，事君之伦也。及夫大贤，

【今译】

叔向问晏子说："侍奉国君时的伦序，居处无为时的德义是什么？"晏子回答说："侍奉国君时的伦序，智慧谋虑足以安定国家，德高望重足以引导百姓，和蔼温柔足以安抚民众，不向国君自诩清廉以获取名声，不违背民意来推行政令，这是上等；洁身自好严于律己，不掩饰过失来求胜争先，不谗佞阿谀来请求进身，不偏爱亲私，不诬陷贤能，这是次等；竭尽全力做好本职工作不懈怠，服从上级顺从国君不敢偷懒，畏惧国君因此不行苟且之事，忌惮罪责因此不行邪僻之事，这是下等。这三个等次，就是侍奉国君的伦序。至于那些有大贤德的人，居处无为与侍奉国君没有选择，只能根据时势采取适宜的做法。有一些被称为君子的人，才能不足以辅佐国君，引退居处不顺从国君，耕治田园，

## 4.20 [100] SHUXIANG ASKED WHAT CHARACTERIZES THE NORMS OF SERVING A RULER OR LIVING IN WITHDRAWAL. YANZI REPLIED THAT FOR THE GREAT WORTHIES, IT MAKES NO DIFFERENCE WHETHER THEY LIVE IN WITHDRAWAL OR ENTER SERVICE.

Shuxiang queried Yanzi as follows: "What characterizes the norms of serving a ruler and the righteousness of living in withdrawal?"

Yanzi replied: "The best norms of serving a ruler are: understanding and concern sufficient to keep the state at peace; great fame sufficient to guide the people; mildness and compliance sufficient to cherish the multitudes; avoidance of mock honesty to one's superior in order to make a name for oneself; avoidance of action against the people in order to go one's own way. Of a lesser order there are: to be pure in self-control and not conceal mistakes to seek supremacy; avoidance of slander and flattery in seeking advancement; avoidance of favoritism to one's intimates and defamation of those who are competent. The least important norms are: to exhaust one's strength and remain dutiful without indolence; to obey superiors in official posts and not dare to be negligent; not to act wantonly out of awe of superiors; not to be led astray out of fear of being prosecuted. These three categories are the norms for serving a ruler. As for the great worthies, it makes no difference whether they live in withdrawal or enter into service—they react as fitting to the circumstances of their time. There are those who are called 'people of noble character' whose ability is not sufficient to assist their superiors, and when they withdraw from office and live in retreat, they do not follow the guidelines of their superiors. They then dedicate themselves to tending their vegetable gardens and wearing straw sandals; they respectfully[1] and cautiously attend to the commands of their

353

---

1   共 → 恭 (*JS*, 279/7).

## 【原文】

则徒处与有事无择也，随时宜者也。有所谓君子者，能不足以补上，退处不顺上，治唐园，考菲履，共恤上令，第长乡里，不夸言，不愧行，君子也。不以上为本，不以民为忧，内不恤其家，外不顾其（身）游，夸言愧行，自勒于饥寒，不及丑俦，命之曰狂僻之民，明上之所禁也。进也不能及上，退也不能徒处，作穷于富利之门，毕志于畎亩之业，穷通行无常处之虑，佚于心，利通不能，穷业不成，命之曰处

## 【今译】

编织草鞋，敬守国君的法令，友爱乡里百姓，言辞不夸张，行为不怪异，这是君子。不把国君视为根本，不把百姓之事视为忧患，对内不体恤家人，在外不顾惜朋友，言辞夸张行为怪异，只关心自己的饥寒，不顾及众人的疾苦，这种人叫作狂妄邪僻之民，这是圣明君主所禁用的。进身不能顾及国君，引退不能居处无为，在富贵门前故作贫穷姿态，无心于农耕之业，做事情没有稳定长远的考虑，内心安逸，通达时不能获取利益，困厄时不能成就功业，这种人叫作僻处封闭之民，这是

superiors and show a young brother's respect to the elders of their villages. They do not boast and are not involved in shameful acts. These are people of noble character.

There are those who do not take their superiors as their foundation and the people as their source of worry; in private life they do not extend special consideration to their families, and in public they do not pay heed to their conduct; they speak boastfully and are involved in shameful acts. They are assiduous[1] in tending to their own hunger and cold, but their effort does not extend to their peers. They should be called 'insane, perverse people'; the enlightened ruler bans them. There are those who while advancing in office cannot reach high status, and when they withdraw, they are unable to cope with their life in withdrawal. They exhaust their power in the realm of riches and profit, and their ambition is devoured by work in the field. They act without consideration for constant position;[2] they are given to ease in their hearts; when they profit and become wealthy they are of no benefit for others, and when they are in difficult circumstances they cannot accomplish their own tasks. They should be called 'people who live for wealth alone.' The enlightened ruler punishes them. There are those who are wise, but not sufficiently so to benefit the ruler; they are capable, but not sufficiently so to prompt the people to labor; they please[3] themselves and live in withdrawal; they are called arrogant to their superiors. There are people who advance in a wanton manner with no regard for the method they use; have undeserved gain with no understanding of what is loathsome. They are called 'rebellious and treacherous.' There are people who have nothing to do with the ruler – they cannot induce the people to labor, they embellish the righteousness of living in withdrawal and noisily belittle the fame of their ruler. They are called 'people who bring chaos to their states.' When the enlightened ruler

355

---

1  勒 → 勤 (*YZCQ-ICS*, 37, n. 4).

2  Delete 穷通 (*JS*, 280/16).

3  俞 → 愉 (*JS*, 281/19).

## 【原文】

封之民，明上之所诛也。有智不足〔以〕补君，有能不足以劳民，俞身徒处，谓之傲上，苟进不择所道，苟得不知所恶，谓之乱贼。身无以与君，能无以劳民，饰徒处之义，扬轻上之名，谓之乱国。明君在上，三者不免罪。"叔向曰："贤不肖，性夫！吾每有问，而未尝自得也。"

## 【今译】

贤明国君所诛罚的。有智谋不足以辅佐国君，有才能不足以服务百姓，偷懒散漫无所事事，这叫作傲上，为了进身不择手段，为了获利不顾廉耻，这叫作乱贼。自身不能为国君分忧，才能不足以为百姓效劳，却美化居处无为的德义，宣扬轻视国君的名声，这叫作乱国。贤明国君执政，这三种人都不能免于治罪。"叔向说："贤德或者不贤德，是天性吧！我经常提出问题，却从来没有自己得出答案。"

occupies a supreme position, the crimes of these three kinds of people will not avoid punishment."

Shuxiang said: "The distinction between worthiness and unworthiness is a matter of inborn disposition. I often ask this question, but have never been able to attain this in my own life."

大中华文库

## 4.21 [101] 叔向问处乱世其行正曲晏子对以民为本

叔向问身处乱世应该公正还是曲从，晏子说应该以百姓为根本

### 【原文】

叔向问晏子曰："世乱不遵道，上辟不用义；正行则民遗，曲行则道废。正行而遗民乎？与持民而遗道乎？此二者之于行何如？"晏子对曰："婴闻之，卑而不失尊，曲而不失正者，以民为本也。苟持民矣，安有遗道？苟遗民矣，安有正行焉？"

### 【今译】

叔向问晏子说："世风混乱不遵行道义，国君邪僻不行用礼义；行为正直就会脱离民众，行为不正就会废弃道义。是行为正直脱离民众呢？还是拥有民众脱离道义呢？这两种行为应该怎样选择？"晏子回答说："我听闻，谦卑而不失尊严，曲从而不失正道的人，都把百姓视为根本。如果能够拥有民众，又怎么会脱离道义呢？如果脱离了民众，又怎么会有正直的行为呢？"

# 4.21 [101] SHUXIANG INQUIRED REGARDING THE CHOICE OF CONDUCT BETWEEN HONESTY AND CROOKEDNESS WHILE LIVING IN A WORLD IN CHAOS. YANZI REPLIED THAT ONE SHOULD TAKE THE PEOPLE AS ONE'S ROOT.

Shuxiang queried Yanzi as follows: "When the world is in chaos and does not adhere to the Way, superiors are perverse and do not employ the righteous; if one conducts oneself uprightly, one will lose the people's favor; if one acts crookedly, the Way will be abandoned. Should one adhere to upright conduct and lose the people, or rather maintain the people's favor and lose the Way? How is this dilemma reflected in proper conduct?"

Yanzi replied: "I have heard it said that those who manage not to lose their dignity when they hit rock-bottom and not to lose their uprightness when subjected to crookedness take root in the people. If you indeed cling to the people, how would the Way be lost? If you indeed lose the people, how would upright conduct exist?"

## 4.22 [102] 叔向问意孰为高行孰为厚晏子对以爱民乐民

　　叔向问什么样的品德高尚，什么样的行为宽厚，晏子回答说仁爱百姓是高尚，让百姓快乐是宽厚

### 【原文】

　　叔向问晏子曰："意孰为高？行孰为厚？"对曰："意莫高于爱民，行莫厚于乐民。"又问曰："意孰为下？行孰为贱？"对曰："意莫下于刻民，行莫贱于害身也。"

### 【今译】

　　叔向问晏子说："什么样的品德最高尚？什么样的行为最宽厚？"晏子回答说："没有比仁爱百姓更高尚的品德，没有比让百姓快乐更宽厚的行为。"叔向又问道："什么样的品德最低下？什么样的行为最卑贱？"晏子回答说："没有比刻薄百姓更低下的品德，没有比残害百姓更卑贱的行为。"

## 4.22 [102] SHUXIANG ASKED WHICH IDEA IS THE LOFTIEST AND WHICH CONDUCT IS THE MOST GENEROUS. YANZI REPLIED, LOVING AND MAKING THE PEOPLE HAPPY.

Shuxiang queried Yanzi as follows: "Which idea is the loftiest? Which conduct is the most generous?"

Yanzi replied: "No idea is loftier than loving the people; no conduct is greater than making the people happy."

Shuxian asked again: "Which idea is the lowliest? Which conduct is the most degenerate?"

Yanzi replied: "No idea is lowlier than being mean to the people; no conduct is more degenerate than hurting the people."[1]

361

---

1  身 → 民 (*JS*, 283/3).

## 4.23 [103] 叔向问啬吝爱之于行何如晏子对以啬者君子之道

叔向问啬、吝、爱表现在行为上是什么样，晏子回答说啬是君子的做法

【原文】

叔向问晏子曰："啬、吝、爱之于行何如？"晏子对曰："啬者，君子之道，吝、爱者，小人之行也。"叔向曰："何谓也？"晏子曰："称财多寡而节用之，富无金藏，贫不假贷，谓之啬；积多不能分人，而厚自养，谓之吝；不能分人，又不能自养，谓之爱。故夫啬者，君子之道；吝、爱者，小人之行也。"

【今译】

叔向问晏子说："啬、吝、爱表现在行为上是什么样的？"晏子回答说："啬是君子的行为，吝、爱是小人的行为。"叔向问："为什么这样说呢？"晏子说："估量财富的多少而节约使用，富有时没有金钱储藏，贫穷时不向人借贷，这称作啬；积聚很多不能分给别人，而优厚地供养自己，这称作吝；不能分给别人，也不供养自己，这称作爱。因此啬是君子的行为；吝、爱是小人的行为。"

# 4.23 [103] SHUXIANG ASKED HOW THRIFT, MISER-LINESS AND COVETOUSNESS ARE REFLECTED IN CONDUCT. YANZI REPLIED THAT THRIFT IS THE WAY OF A MAN OF NOBLE CHARACTER.

Shuxiang queried Yanzi as follows: "How are thrift, miserliness and covetousness reflected in conduct?"

Yanzi replied: "To be thrifty is the way of the man of noble character; to be miserly or covetous is the conduct of the petty man."

Shuxiang asked: "What does that mean?"

Yanzi replied: "Calculating the amount of property and using it with restraint, not hoarding gold in prosperity and not taking loans in poverty is called thrift. Accumulating wealth and failing to share with others and caring only for the nourishment of oneself is called miserliness. Failing to share with others and failing to care for one's own upkeep is called covetousness. Therefore, thrift is the way of the man of noble character; miserliness and covetousness are the conduct of the petty man."

363

## 4.24 [104] 叔向问君子之大义何若晏子对以尊贤退不肖

叔向问君子的正道是什么，晏子回答说要尊敬贤能斥退不贤的人

**【原文】**

叔向问晏子曰："君子之大义何若？"晏子对曰："君子之大义，和调而不缘，溪盎而不苛，庄敬而不狡，和柔而不铨，刻廉而不刿，行精而不以明污，齐尚而不以遗罢，富贵不傲物，贫穷不易行，尊贤而不退不肖。此君子之大义也。"

**【今译】**

叔向问晏子说："君子的正道是什么？"晏子回答说："君子的正道是：和睦协调而不随波逐流，明察而不苛求，庄严敬肃而不狡诈，和蔼温柔而不卑躬屈膝，严正廉洁而不伤害别人，行为清白而不彰明别人的污浊，崇尚同一而不遗弃疲弱，富贵时不轻视财物，贫穷时不改变德行，尊重贤能而斥退不贤的人。这就是君子的正道。"

大中华文库

## 4.24 [104] SHUXIANG ASKED WHAT CHARACTERIZES THE GREATEST RIGHTEOUSNESS OF THE MAN OF NOBLE CHARACTER. YANZI REPLIED THAT HE HONORS THE WORTHY BUT DOES NOT REJECT THE UNWORTHY.

Shuxiang queried Yanzi as follows: "What characterizes the greatest righteousness of the man of noble character?"

Yanzi replied: "The greatest righteousness of the man of noble character lies in the fact that that he is harmonious but does not shrink from danger.[1] He does not act wantonly;[2] he is solemn and respectful but not excessively demanding;[3] he is kind and yielding but not lowly;[4] he is strict and honest but does not inflict suffering; his conduct is spotless but he does not use this fact to shed light on other's corruption; he has high regard for unity[5] without overlooking the incompetent. When rich and honored, he is not arrogant to others; when poor and hard-pressed, he does not change his attitudes; he honors the worthy but does not reject the unworthy. This is the greatest righteousness of the man of noble character."

---

1  溪益 → 徯醢 (*JS*, 285/1). According to the *Fangyan* 方言, *SBCK*, VI, 5/a7, the compound 徯醢 means 危 "danger" in southern Qi.

2  苛 → 苟 (*JS*, ibid.).

3  狡 → 急 (*YZCQ-ICS*, 38, n. 3).

4  銓 → 卑 (*YZCQ-ICS*, 38, n. 4).

5  齐尚 → 同尚 → 尚同 (*JS*, 285/2).

## 4.25 [105] 叔向问傲世乐业能行道乎晏子对以狂惑也

叔向问傲视世人独自安居乐业能否坚持道义，晏子回答说这种行为是狂妄迷惑

### 【原文】

叔向问晏子曰："进不能事上，退不能为家，傲世乐业，枯槁为名，不疑其所守者，可谓能行其道乎？"晏子对曰："婴闻古之能行道者，世可（正以）〔以正〕则〔正〕，不可以正则曲。其正也，不失上下之伦；其曲也，不失仁义之理。道用，与世乐业；不用，有所依归。不以傲上华世，不以枯槁为名。故道者，世之所以治，而身之所以安也。今

### 【今译】

叔向问晏子说："进身不能侍奉国君，引退不能管好家族，傲视世人独自安居乐业，弃世隐居以获取美名，不怀疑自己坚守的做法，这样的人可以说是坚持了他的道义吗？"晏子回答说："我听闻古时候能够奉行正道的人，世风可以矫正就去矫正，不可以矫正就委曲求全。他矫正，不丧失上下尊卑的伦常；他曲从，不丧失仁德礼义的原则。他坚守的道义被采用时，就和世人一同安居乐业；不被采用时，也有所依托和归附。不靠傲视君上来哗众取宠，不用弃世隐居来获取美名。因此道义，是世间能被治理，自己能够安身立命的原因。现在把不侍奉国君视为道义，把不顾家族视为德行，用弃世隐居来获取美名，世

## 4.25 [105] SHUXIANG ASKED IF THOSE WHO TAKE JOY IN THEIR TASKS WITH AN ATTITUDE OF CONTEMPT FOR THEIR PEERS ARE CAPABLE OF PRACTICING THE WAY. YANZI REPLIED THAT THEY ARE INSANE AND BAFFLED.

Shuxiang queried Yanzi as follows: "Concerning those who when advancing in office are not able to serve their superiors, or who when withdrawing are not able to take care of their families; who take joy in their tasks with an attitude of contempt for their peers; who make a name for themselves with their emaciated appearance and have no doubt about what they are preserving — can we say that they are capable of putting their Way into practice?"

Yanzi replied: "I have heard concerning those who were able to put the Way into practice in ancient times: if the world could have been rectified, they would have rectified it; if it could not, then they dealt with it in a roundabout way. When they managed to rectify it, they did not lose sight of the hierarchy of superiors and inferiors, and when their way was roundabout, they did not lose sight of the principles of humaneness and righteousness. If the Way was applied, they shared with the world their joy in their tasks; if the Way was not applied, they had a place to seek refuge. They did not flaunt themselves around their peers by being supercilious to their superiors, and they did not make names for themselves with an emaciated appearance. Therefore, the Way is that by which the world becomes well-ordered and the life of the individual becomes peaceful. But now, to consider not serving a superior, not taking care of the family, and making a name for oneself through an emaciated appearance as the Way — if the world practices all this, the Way will fall into chaos; if individuals practice this, they will be in peril. Furthermore, as with Heaven and Earth, an order exists between superiors and inferiors; when the enlightened

**【原文】**

以不事上为道，以不顾家为行，以枯槁为名，世行之则乱，身行之则危。且天之与地，而上下有衰矣；明王始立，而居国为制矣；政教错，而民行有伦矣。今以不事上为道，（及）〔反〕天地之衰矣；以不顾家为行，倍先圣之道矣；以枯槁为名，则世塞政教之途矣。有明上，〔不〕可以为下；遭乱世，不可以治乱。说若道，谓之惑，行若道，谓之狂。惑者狂者，木石之朴也，而道义未戴焉。"

**【今译】**

间推行这种道义就会混乱，自身奉行这种道义就会危险。况且天和地，上下之间本来就有等衰；圣明君王开始建立国家，便制定了一整套典章制度；政教措施施行得当，百姓的行为就有准则了。现在把不侍奉国君视为道义，违反了天地之间的等衰；把不顾家族视为德行，违背了先代圣王的规则；用弃世隐居获取美名，那么就堵塞了世间政教的途径了。贤明君主执政，不可以用它治理百姓；遭逢乱世，不可以用它治理祸乱。欣赏这种道义，就是迷惑，奉行这种道义，就是狂妄。迷惑的人和狂妄的人，就像没有经过雕琢的木头和石头，是不能承载道义的。"

kings first ascended the throne and their rule over their states had already been regulated, they implemented their governance and moral teachings and the people's conduct was ordered according to their norms. But now, those who take as the Way not serving superiors are acting contrary to the order between Heaven and Earth. Those who regard not taking care of their families to be proper conduct turn their back on the way of the former sages. If they try to make a name for themselves by an emaciated appearance, then the paths of government and moral teaching will be blocked in the world. Even if an enlightened ruler exists, they cannot be his subjects; when they confront a chaotic world, they cannot set it in order. When they claim that such is the Way, they can be called baffled; when they put such a Way into effect, they can be called insane. Bafflement and insanity correspond to wood and stone in their coarse states; neither bears the true meaning of the Way."

369

# 4.26 [106] 叔向问人何若则荣晏子对以事君亲忠孝

叔向问什么人光荣，晏子回答说忠诚国君孝顺父母的人

## 【原文】

叔向问晏子曰："何若则可谓荣矣？"晏子对曰："事亲孝，无悔往行，事君忠，无悔往辞；和于兄弟，信于朋友，不谄过，不责得；言不相坐，行不相反；在上治民，足以尊君，在下莅修，足以变人，身无所咎，行无所创，可谓荣矣。"

## 【今译】

叔向问晏子说："什么样的人可以称为光荣？"晏子回答说："侍奉父母孝顺，没有可后悔的行为，侍奉国君忠诚，没有可后悔的言辞；对兄弟和睦，对朋友诚信，不隐瞒过失，不索取私利；言谈不互相争论，行为不和语言相违背；在朝廷做官治理百姓，足以让百姓尊重国君，在民间进行自我修养，足以改变百姓的习俗，自身没有过错，德行不受损伤，这就可以说是光荣了。"

## 4.26 [106] SHUXIANG ASKED WHAT CHARACTERIZES A PERSON WHO IS DEEMED GLORIOUS. YANZI REPLIED THAT SUCH A MAN SERVES HIS RULER LOYALLY AND HIS PARENTS FILIALLY.

Shuxiang queried Yanzi as follows: "A person who is deemed glorious — what characterizes such a person?"

Yanzi replied: "He serves his parents filially; he has no cause for regret in his past conduct. He serves the ruler loyally; he has no regrets over his past statements. He is harmonious with his brothers; he is trustworthy to friends. He does not conceal mistakes; he does not seek gain. His words are not in conflict, and his conduct is not contradictory. When in a lofty position, he regulates the people into sufficient good order so as to honor the ruler; when lowly, he cultivates himself sufficiently so as to change others for the better; he is faultless as a person, and his conduct does not inflict any wounds: such a one is deemed glorious."

## 4.27 [107] 叔向问人何以则可保身晏子对以不要幸

叔向问人怎样做事才可以保全自身，晏子回答说不要强求宠幸

### 【原文】

叔向问晏子曰："人何以则可谓保其身？"晏子对曰："《诗》曰：'既明且哲，以保其身，夙夜匪懈，以事一人。'不庶几，不要幸，先其难乎而后幸，得之时其所也，失之非其罪也，可谓保其身矣。"

### 【今译】

叔向问晏子说："一个人怎样做事才可以称之为保全自身？"晏子回答说：《诗经》中说：'既聪明又睿智，可以保全自身，从早到晚不懈怠，用来侍奉周天子。'不抱希望，不怀侥幸，先历经艰难而后得到宠幸，得到了是他应该得到，失去了也不是他的罪过，这样做就可以称之为保全自身了。"

## 4.27 [107] SHUXIANG ASKED, WHAT CHARACTERIZES A MAN WHO PROTECTS HIS OWN SELF? YANZI REPLIED THAT SUCH A MAN SHOULD NOT SEEK FAVORS.

Shuxiang queried Yanzi as follows: "What kind of a man is considered to be 'protecting his own self'?"

Yanzi replied: "As it says in the *Odes*:

He was enlightened and wise,

He protected his own self;

Morning and night he never slackened,

Serving the One Man.[1]

A man who does not chase vain hopes and does not seek favors from the ruler; who first thinks of difficulties, and only afterwards of favorable outcomes; who deserves what he gains[2] and is not blamed when he loses — such a person can be called 'protecting his own self.'"

373

---

1   *Shijing*, 260/137/25.

2   时 → 是 (*JS*, 289/6).

## 4.28 [108] 曾子问不谏上不顾民以成行义者晏子对以何以成也

曾子问不进谏国君不顾及百姓来保持德行礼义的人，晏子回答说用什么办法保持啊

**【原文】**

曾子问晏子曰："古者尝有上不谏上，下不顾民，退处山谷，以成行义者也？"晏子对曰："察其身无能也，而托乎不欲谏上，谓之诞意也。上惛乱，德义不行，而邪辟朋党，贤人不用，士亦不易其行，而从邪以求进，故有隐有不隐。其行法，士也，乃夫议上，则不取也。夫上不谏上，下不顾民，退处山谷，婴不识其何以为成行义者也。"

**【今译】**

曾子问晏子说："古时候曾经有上不进谏国君，下不顾及百姓，退隐居住在山谷，以此保持德行礼义的人吗？"晏子回答说："明知自己没有能力辅佐国君，却推托说不愿向国君进谏，这叫作荒诞虚妄。国君昏庸淫乱，德行礼义得不到施行，而邪僻之人结为朋党，贤能的人得不到任用，士人也不改变他们的品行，而跟从奸邪之人以求进身，因此有隐居的也有不隐居的。他们的行为符合礼法，就是士人，至于非议国君的，就不可取了。对于那些上不进谏国君，下不顾及百姓，退隐居住在山谷的，我不知道他用什么办法成为保持德行礼义的人。"

## 4.28 [108] ZENGZI[1] ASKED WHETHER PEOPLE WHO DID NOT REMONSTRATE WITH THEIR SUPERIORS AND DID NOT TAKE CARE OF THE PEOPLE COULD FULFILL THEIR PRACTICE OF RIGHTEOUSNESS. YANZI REPLIED THAT HE DOES NOT KNOW HOW THEY COULD POSSIBLY HAVE FULFILLED IT.

Zengzi queried Yanzi as follows: "Were there people in ancient times who did not remonstrate with their superiors and did not take care of their inferior people; who withdrew and dwelt the valleys in order to fulfill their practice of righteousness?"

Yanzi replied: "When one realizes after self-examination that one has no capabilities and, as a pretext, says that one does not want to remonstrate against his superior — this, we may say, is an absurd notion. If a ruler is dazed and confused, and virtue and righteousness are not practiced, the perverse unite in cliques and the worthy are not employed. Even officers do not change their conduct but rather follow the wicked in seeking advancement; and under such circumstances, there are those who hide and those who do not hide.[2] If people neither remonstrate with their ruler above nor care for the people below, but rather live in withdrawal in the valleys — I do not know how such people can fulfill the practice of righteousness."

375

---

1  Zengzi 曾子, personal name Shen 参, courtesy name Ziyu 子舆, was one of Confucius' most prominent disciples. The authorship of a large part of the *Great Learning* 大学 is traditionally ascribed to him.

2  Omit 其行法, 士也, 乃夫议上, 则不取也. (*JS*, 289).

## 4.29 [109] 梁丘据问子事三君不同心晏子对以一心可以事百君

梁丘据问您如何侍奉三个不同心思的国君，晏子回答说一个心思可以侍奉一百个国君

### 【原文】

梁丘据问晏子曰："子事三君，君不同心，而子俱顺焉，仁人固多心乎？"晏子对曰："婴闻之，顺爱不懈，可以使百姓，强暴不忠，不可以使一人。一心可以事百君，三心不可以事一君。"仲尼闻之曰："小子识之！晏子以一心事百君者也。"

### 【今译】

梁丘据问晏子说："您先后侍奉了三个国君，国君有不同的心思，而您侍奉他们却都很顺利，仁德的人本来就有很多心思吧？"晏子回答说："我听闻，顺从国君爱护百姓不松懈，就可以驱使百姓，暴虐百姓不忠诚国君，就不能驱使一个人。一个心思能够侍奉一百个国君，很多个心思不能侍奉一个国君。"孔子听说这件事之后说："年轻人要记住！晏子是用一个心思能够侍奉一百个国君的人。"

## 4.29 [109] LIANGQIU JU QUESTIONED YANZI REGARDING HIS SERVICE TO THREE DIFFERENT RULERS WHO DID NOT SHARE THE SAME MIND. YANZI REPLIED THAT IF ONE IS OF A SINGLE MIND HE CAN SERVE A HUNDRED RULERS.[1]

Liangqiu Ju queried Yanzi as follows: "You have served three different rulers who were not of the same mind and yet you attached yourself to all of them — can a humane person really be said to be of several minds?"

Yanzi replied: "I have heard that one who is unflaggingly compliant and caring can take the people into his service. One who is fierce, brutal, and disloyal cannot employ even a single person. If one is of a single mind he can serve a hundred rulers; if one is of three minds he cannot serve one ruler."

When Confucius heard this, he said: "My young friends, you must know this: Yanzi is a person of a single mind with which he can serve a hundred rulers."

---

1   Item 4.29 [109] ↔ Item 7.19 [189]; Item 8.3 [200]; Item 8.4 [201]; *Kongcongzi*, 6.1/62/3.

## 4.30 [110] 柏常骞问道无灭身无废晏子对以养世君子

伯常骞问道义不灭绝自身也不毁废的办法，晏子用教养世人的君子来回答

【原文】

柏常骞去周之齐，见晏子曰："骞，周室之贱史也，不量其不肖，愿事君子。敢问正道直行则不容于世，隐道危行则不忍，道亦无灭，身亦无废者何若？"晏子曰："善哉！问事君乎。婴闻之，执二法裾，则不取也；轻进苟合，则不信也；直易无讳，则速伤也；新始好利，

【今译】

伯常骞离开周朝到了齐国，见到晏子说："我是周王室一个地位卑贱的史官，不估量自己的不贤德，愿意侍奉您。请问坚持正道行为正直就不能容于世人，违背道义诡诈行事又于心不忍，道义也不灭绝，自身也不毁废的办法是什么？"晏子说："好啊！您问的是怎样侍奉君主吧？我听闻，心高气傲刚愎自用，就不能听取意见；轻率进言随意附和，就不能忠诚有信；正直平易没有忌讳，就会很快受到伤害；标

## 4.30 [110] BOCHANG QIAN[1] ASKED HOW TO AVOID BOTH THE EXTINCTION OF THE WAY AND THE ABANDONMENT OF SELF. YANZI REPLIED: BY BEING A MAN OF NOBLE CHARACTER WHO FOSTERS THE GOOD OF THE WORLD.[2]

When Bochang Qian left Zhou and went to Qi, he was received by Yanzi and said to him: "I am a lowly scribe of the House of Zhou. Regardless of my pettiness, I wish to serve a man of noble character. Dare I ask: on the one hand, if I follow the correct Way and conduct myself in a straightforward manner, I may not be accepted by the world; if, on the other hand, I hide my Way and conduct myself deceitfully,[3] I will not bear it. How can I avoid both the extinction of the Way and the abandonment of myself?"

Yanzi replied: "This is an excellent question concerning how one should serve a ruler. I have heard that those who cling to one[4] extreme and take arrogance[5] as their model will not be chosen for office; those who advance with ease and unite wantonly will not be trusted; those who are straightforward, who speak with no inhibitions[6] and have nothing to hide, will be speedily harmed; those who aspire to innovation and are fond of profit will in no case[7] escape ruin. Furthermore, I have heard that the man of noble character who fosters the world does not take the easy way in order to advance, and does not withdraw in the face of difficulties;[8] he critically

---

1   Regarding Bochang Qian, see, the preceding item 1.18.

2   Item 4.30 [110] ↔ *Kongzi jiayu* 孔子家语, 9.3/14/28.

3   危 → 诡 (*YZCQ-ICS*, 39, n. 2).

4   执二 → 执一 (*YZCQ-ICS*, 39, n. 4).

5   裾 → 倨 (*JS*, 292/8).

6   *Mencius*, 7.22/39/17, expresses the same idea.

7   Add 不 after 无 (*JS*, 293/10).

8   重 → 难 (*YZCQ-ICS*, 39, n. 6).

**【原文】**

则无敝也。且婴闻养世之君子，从（重）〔轻〕不为进，从（轻）〔重〕不为退，省行而不伐，让利而不夸，陈物而勿专，见象而勿强，道不灭，身不废矣。"

**【今译】**

新立异贪图获利，就无不破败。而且我听闻教养世人的君子，不会见易而进，不会知难而退，反省自己的行为而不夸耀功劳，出让利益而不自夸，陈述事理而不专断，见到天象而不违抗，道义就不会灭绝，自身也就不会毁废了。"

examines his conduct without praising himself; he forgoes profit and does not boast; he explains everything in detail, without being arbitrary; he shows by way of personal example but does compel others. Hence, his Way will not be extinguished nor will his person be abandoned."

# 第五卷　杂上

## 5.1 [111] 庄公不说晏子晏子坐地讼公而归

庄公不喜欢晏子，晏子坐在地上和庄公争论然后离开

### 【原文】

晏子臣于庄公，公不说，饮酒，令召晏子。晏子至，入门，公令乐人奏歌曰："已哉，已哉！寡人不能说也，尔何来为？"晏子入坐，乐人三奏，然后知其谓己也。遂起，北面坐地。公曰："夫子从席，曷为坐地？"晏子对曰："婴闻讼夫坐地，今婴将与君讼，敢毋坐地乎？婴闻之，众而无义，强而无礼，好勇而恶贤者，祸必及其身，若公者之谓矣。且婴言不用，愿请身去。"遂趋而归，管籥其家者纳之公，财在

晏子春秋　第五卷　杂上

### 【今译】

晏子是齐庄公的臣子，齐庄公不高兴，饮酒时，下令召见晏子。晏子到来，进入殿门，齐庄公让乐队演奏歌曲，唱道："罢了，罢了，我不开心，你来干什么？"晏子入座后，乐队又演奏了三遍，然后晏子才明白是唱给自己听的。于是站起来，面向北方坐到地上。齐庄公问他："您不坐在席上，为什么要坐在地上呢？"晏子回答说："我听说讼争的人坐在地上，今天我要和您争论是非，怎么敢不坐在地上呢？我听说，人多了便不讲道义，势力强大了就不讲礼仪，崇尚勇力而厌恶贤能的人，祸患一定会落到他身上，像您就是这样的人。而且我的

# Chapter Five   Miscellany — Part A

## 5.1 [111] DUKE ZHUANG WAS DISPLEASED WITH YANZI. YANZI SAT ON THE BARE GROUND, ACCUSED BY THE DUKE, AND THEN RETURNED HOME.

Once, when Yanzi was serving Duke Zhuang as a minister, the Duke became displeased. During a banquet, he ordered that Yanzi be summoned to court. When Yanzi arrived and entered the gate, the Duke ordered the musicians to play and sing the following tune: "Enough! Enough! I am unable to find pleasure; what have you come here to do?"

Yanzi entered and took his seat, but only after the musicians performed the song three times did he realize that it was directed towards him. Then he rose and sat down again, on the bare ground, facing north.

The Duke said: "Master, take your place on the mat; why do you sit on the bare ground?"

Yanzi said: "I have heard that the accused sits on the bare ground. As I am about to be accused by you, My Lord, how could I dare not sit on the bare ground? I have heard: He who is supported by many but devoid of righteousness, who is strong but devoid of the rites, who is fond of men of courage but hates the worthy, will certainly encounter personal disaster. This refers to people like you, My Duke. Furthermore, as my words have not been put into effect, I wish to request to be allowed to leave."

With that, he returned home hurriedly. He locked his house along with its contents and turned over the keys to the Duke; he put on the market all the property he had outside his house, saying: "If a man of noble character directs his efforts toward the people, then titles and emoluments are due him — he need not decline a noble position and wealth. Yet, if he does not direct his efforts toward the people, he should eat the same kind of food as the

**【原文】**

外者斥之市，曰："君子有力于民，则进爵禄，不辞富贵；无力于民而旅食，不恶贫贱。"（逐）〔遂〕徒行而东，耕于海滨。居数年，果有崔杼之难。

**【今译】**

建议您都不接受，所以请求离开。"然后快步走回家，将家中锁钥交还公家，把外在财物放到市场上出售，并说："君子能够为民众出力，那么就接受爵位和俸禄，不拒绝富贵；不能为民众出力就不接受俸禄，不厌恶贫贱。"于是就徒步向东走，在海边以耕田为生。过了几年，果然就发生了崔杼杀死齐庄公的事情。

common people and may not disdain poverty and lowliness."

Thereupon, he headed East by foot and farmed on the sea-coast. He lived there for several years, and then, indeed, the disaster with Cui Zhu occurred.

# 5.2 [112] 庄公不用晏子〔晏子〕致邑而退后有崔杼之祸

庄公不任用晏子，晏子归还封邑而离开，后来发生了崔杼的祸患

## 【原文】

晏子为庄公臣，言大用，每朝，赐爵益邑；俄而不用，每朝，致邑与爵。爵邑尽，退朝而乘，喟然而叹，终而笑。其仆曰："何叹笑相从数也？"晏子曰："吾叹也，哀吾君不免于难；吾笑也，喜吾自得也，吾亦无死矣。"崔杼果弑庄公，晏子立崔杼之门，从者曰："死乎？"晏子曰："独吾君也乎哉？吾死也！"曰："行乎？"曰："独吾罪也乎

## 【今译】

晏子做齐庄公的臣子时，所提出的意见被大加采用，每次朝见，都被赐予爵位，增加封地；后来不再采纳他的意见，每次朝见，就逐渐归还所赏赐的封地和爵位。爵位和封地都返还后，晏子退朝后乘上马车，长叹一声，最终还是笑了。他的仆人问道："您为什么屡次一会儿叹息，一会儿发笑呢？"晏子说："我叹息，是哀叹我的国君没能免于死难；我笑，是欣喜我得到自由，也免去死亡了。"崔杼果然杀死了庄公，晏子站在崔杼的门外，随从说："死吗？"晏子说："是我一个人的国君吗？我死？"随从说："逃吗？"晏子说："是我一个人的罪过吗？我逃？"随从说："回吗？"晏子说："我的国君死了，怎么能回去呢？作为百姓的君主，怎么能以地位欺压百姓，应当主持国政；作为君主的臣子，怎么能只求自己的俸禄，应该建设自己的国家。所以国君是为社稷而死的话，那么就为他而死，为了社稷而逃亡的话，那么就跟

## 5.2 [112] DUKE ZHUANG PAID NO HEED TO YANZI'S ADVICE. YANZI RETURNED HIS FIEF-CITIES AND WITHDREW FROM SERVICE. THEN THE CALAMITY OF CUI ZHU OCCURRED.[1]

When Yanzi served as a minister of Duke Zhuang, his words were highly regarded. Each time he attended a court audience, the Duke conferred on him titles and granted him additional fief-cities. Then suddenly, his words were not heeded anymore and every time he attended a court audience he ceded back some fief-cities and titles, until there were none left. He then withdrew from court and mounted his carriage, sighing heavily and then finishing with a laugh.

His driver said: "How can you both sigh and laugh one after another?"

Yanzi replied: "My sigh was for lamenting my ruler, who, sadly, will not avoid calamity, and my laugh was because I was pleased with my own self-assurance, for I will, surely, not have to face death."[2]

Ultimately, Cui Zhu really did assassinate Duke Zhuang. Yanzi stood at Cui Zhu's gate. His followers said: "Do you intend to die?"

Yanzi replied: "Was he my ruler exclusively? Why should I die for him?"

His followers said: "Do you intend to leave the country?"

Yanzi replied: "Was his crime mine alone? Why should I flee into exile?"

His attendant said: "Then would you return to your home?"

Yanzi replied: "My ruler is lying dead, how can I return home? A true ruler of the people is surely not someone who rules in order to abuse the people, but rather to make the altars of soil and grain his chief concern;

---

1   Item 5.2 [112] ↔ *Zuozhuan*, B9.25/283/12; *Shiji*, 1502.

2   For a less dramatic prescription of the role a self-assured minister should play during a chaotic period, see Item 7.16 [186].

**【原文】**

哉！吾亡也！"曰："归乎？"曰："吾君死，安归！君民者，岂以陵民，社稷是主；臣君者，岂为其口实，社稷是养。故君为社稷死，则死之，为社稷亡，则亡之；若君为己死而为己亡，非其私暱，孰能任之。且人有君而弑之，吾焉得死之？而焉得亡之？将庸何归！"门启而入，崔子曰："子何不死？子何不死？"晏子曰："祸始，吾不在也；祸终，吾不知也，吾何为死？且吾闻之，以亡为行者，不足以存君；以死为义者，不足以立功。婴岂其婢子也哉！其缢而从之也！"遂袒免，坐，枕君尸而哭，兴，三踊而出。人谓崔子必杀之，崔子曰："民之望也，舍之得民。"

**【今译】**

随他逃亡；如果国君是为了自己而死，为了自己而逃亡，不是他宠幸的人，谁能陪伴他呢？况且有的人连国君都杀了，我怎能为他而死，怎能为他而逃亡呢？又能回到哪里去呢？"开门后，晏子走进去，崔杼说："你为何不死？你为何不死？"晏子说："祸乱开始的时候，我并不在；祸乱结束的时候，我也不知道，我为什么要死呢？况且我听说，以逃亡为行径的人，不能保存国君；以死为义行的人，不能建立功勋。晏婴难道是他的奴婢吗？怎么能自缢去跟随国君呢？"于是袒露左臂，坐到地上，枕着国君的尸体而哭，起来后，向国君跳脚号哭后离开。有人劝说崔杼一定要杀了他，崔杼说："晏子为民众所景仰，放他走可得到民众拥护。"

a true minister is surely not someone who serves his ruler for the sake of material gain, but rather to nurture the altars of soil and grain. Therefore, if the ruler dies for the sake of the altars of soil and grain, one should die with him; if the ruler flees into exile for the sake of the altars of soil and grain, one should flee with him. But if the ruler dies or flees into exile for personal reasons — except for his close intimates, who should share the responsibility with him? Besides, a man had a ruler but nonetheless he killed him — why should I die or flee into exile because of him? And yet, how could I return home now?"

When the gate of Cui Zhu's house was open and Yanzi entered, Cui Zhu said: "Master, why don't you die, why don't you die?"

Yanzi replied: "I was not present at the time the calamity started, nor did I know about it when it ended. Why, then, should I die? Furthermore, I have heard that fleeing into exile with one's ruler will not help to save him, just as dying for a righteous cause will not help to establish one's merit. Am I a maid-servant that I should hang myself and follow him into death?"

With that, he sat down, baring his left arm and taking off his cap. He cradled the Duke's corpse and wept. Then he rose, performed the three stamps of the foot prescribed for mourning and left. Someone told Cui Zhu that he must kill Yanzi, but Cui Zhu replied: "The people look up to him. If I release him, I will win over the people."

## 5.3 [113] 崔庆劫齐将军大夫盟晏子不与

崔庆劫持齐国的将军和大夫一起盟誓，晏子不参与

### 【原文】

崔杼既弑庄公而立景公，杼与庆封相之，劫诸将军大夫及显士庶人于太宫之坎上，令无得不盟者。为坛三仞，陷其下，以甲千列环其内外，盟者皆脱剑而入。维晏子不肯，崔杼许之。有敢不盟者，戟拘其颈，剑承其心，令自盟曰："不与崔庆而与公室者，受其不祥。言不疾，指不至血者死。"所杀七人。次及晏子，晏子奉杯血，仰天叹曰："呜呼！崔子为无道，而弑其君，不与公室而与崔庆者，受此不详。"俛而饮血。崔杼谓晏子曰："子变子言，则齐国吾与子共之；子不变子言，

### 【今译】

崔杼杀死了庄公而立景公为国君后，与庆封任齐相。他们劫持齐国诸位将军大夫以及有名望的士人百姓到太庙的门前，下令全部参与盟誓。建造了五米多高的高台，下面挖出大坑，用千名士兵环绕内外，参与盟誓的人都要摘下佩剑进入。只有晏子不肯摘下佩剑，崔杼同意了。有敢不参与盟誓的，就用戟钩住他的脖子，用剑指着他的心口。崔杼命令他们自己盟誓说："不交好崔庆而交好齐国公室的人，就会遇到灾祸。发誓不果断的，手指没有刺出血的都要被处死。"一共杀了七个人。轮到晏子了，晏子捧起盛血的杯子，抬头对着天空长叹说："唉！崔杼做了不符合道义的事，杀了他的国君，不交好齐国公室而交好崔庆的人，就会遇到灾祸。"然后俯身喝下杯中的血。崔杼对晏子说："改变你的誓言，那么齐国就是你与我所共有的；如果不改变你的誓言，戟

# 5.3 [113] CUI ZHU AND QING FENG[1] FORCED THE GENERALS AND HIGH OFFICERS OF QI TO SWEAR TO A COVENANT. YANZI DID NOT TAKE PART.[2]

After Cui Zhu assassinated Duke Zhuang and installed Duke Jing in his place, he and Qing Feng appointed themselves as his Premiers. They forced all the various generals and high officers along with other distinguished officers and commoners to stand over the open grave in the ancestral temple and ordered that they had no choice but to keep the covenant. An altar three *ren*[3] in height was constructed, under which a trench was dug, surrounded by ranks of a thousand armored soldiers, inside and outside. All those who swore to keep the covenant removed their swords and entered. Only Yanzi was unwilling to do so, and Cui Zhu permitted him to refuse. Anyone who dared to refuse to swear to keep the covenant had a halberd hook placed[4] over his throat and a sword directed at his heart, and he was ordered to repeat individually the following covenant: "If I am not allied with Cui Zhu and Qing Feng, but rather with the former ducal house, may I suffer the same calamity." Those who did not utter these words quickly enough and did not dip their finger in blood[5] were put to death. Seven men had been killed when Yanzi's turn came. Yanzi raised up the cup of blood, faced Heaven, and sighed: "Woe! Cui Zhu has been so unprincipled as to assassinate his ruler. If I do not ally myself with the former ducal house, but rather with Cui Zhu and Qing Feng, may I suffer the same calamity." He then lowered his head and drank the blood. Cui Zhu said to Yanzi: "If

391

---

1   For Qing Feng see Item 3.2 [52].

2   Item 5.3 [113] ↔ *Lüshi chunqiu*, 20.3/131/13; *Xinxu* 新序, 8.4/44/19; *Hanshi waichuan*, 2.13/10/9.

3   A *ren* 仞 is an ancient measure of five, seven or eight Chinese feet — *chi* 尺.

4   拘 → 鉤 (*JS*, 299/5).

5   The ancient method of confirming an oath consisted of smearing the blood of a sacrifice with a finger on one's mouth.

## 【原文】

戟既在脰，剑既在心，维子图之也。"晏子曰："劫吾以刃，而失其志，非勇也；回吾以利，而倍其君，非义也。崔子！子独不为（天讨）〔夫《诗》〕乎！《诗》云：'莫莫葛藟，施于条枚，恺恺君子，求福不回。'今婴且可以回而求福乎？曲刃钩之，直兵推之，婴不革矣。"崔杼将杀之，或曰："不可！子以子之君无道而杀之，今其臣有道之士也，又从而杀之，不可以为教矣。"崔子遂舍之。晏子曰："若大夫为大不仁，

## 【今译】

已经在你的脖子上了，剑也指着你的心口，你自己考虑吧！"晏子说："用兵刃来威胁我，让我放弃自己的志向，这不是勇者所做的事；用利益来回报我，让我背叛国君，这是不符合道义的。崔杼！难道你不读《诗经》吗？《诗经》上说：'生长茂盛的葛藤，依托在树枝之上，温文尔雅的君子，不会通过不正当的方式追求福祉。'难道今天我晏婴能够以这种不正当的方式求福吗？请用戟钩断我的脖颈，用剑刺穿我的心口，我是不会改变的。"崔杼想要杀了他，有人反对说："不能杀他，您因君主行无道之事而杀了他，现在他的臣子是有道之人，如果再杀了他，那么就无法教化百姓了。"于是崔杼放他走了。晏子接着说："像崔杼这样做了大坏事，又做件小好事，怎么能抵消呢？"快步离开太

you change your words, I will share the state of Qi with you, but if not, the halberd is already placed on your throat and the sword on your heart — it is up to you to choose your course of action!"

Yanzi replied: "If I am forced by the blade to relinquish my personal ideals, it will be a lack of courage; if I am deflected by personal gain and turn my back on my former ruler, it will be a lack of righteousness. Have you, Cui Zhu, of all people, not studied the *Odes*? As it says in the *Odes*:

> Dense grow the tendrils and the wild vine,
>
> Spread out over branches and stems;
>
> Our lord is cheerful and contented, [1]
>
> In quest of fortune he does not change course. [2]

Now, should I change course because I seek my fortune? Even if hooked by a curved blade or pierced by a pointed weapon, I will not change."

Cui Zhu wanted to have him killed, but someone said: "This would be improper. It was you who killed your ruler on the grounds that he was unprincipled. But now, that ruler's minister is an officer who possesses the Way. If you also proceed to kill him, this will not be accepted as moral teaching." Consequently, Cui Zhu released him.

Yanzi said: "A high officer such as yourself has been very ruthless, and has performed a small act of kindness — how can you be deemed loyal?" He then ran out in small steps and grabbed the strap so as to pull himself up into the chariot. His driver wanted to gallop ahead but Yanzi held his hand and said: "Slow down, we should not break the pace; swiftness does not guarantee life and slowness does not necessarily lead to death. The fate of a deer born in the wild is to be hung in the kitchen. My fate too hangs by a thread."

---

1   Retain 恺悌 (*SBCK*, V/6b2).

2   *Shijing*, 239/120/15.

**【原文】**

而为小仁，焉有中乎！"趋出，授绥而乘。其仆将驰，晏子抚其手曰："徐之！〔毋失节〕，疾不必生，徐不必死，鹿生于野，命悬于厨，婴命有〔所〕系矣。"按之成节而后去。《诗》云："彼己之子，舍命不渝。"晏子之谓也。

**【今译】**

庙，接过登车的绳索乘上马车，他的仆从想要驾车快跑，晏子按住他的手说："慢慢走，走得快了未必能活，走得慢了也未必会死，鹿虽然生活在田野之中，但它的命却是掌握在厨师手中，我的命自己已经掌握不了了。"然后按照应有的速度驾车离开。《诗经》说："有些人，就算死也不会改变他的志向。"说的就是晏子这种人。

The driver then restrained the horses and they drove away at a measured pace.

As it says in the *Odes*:

That gentleman over there,

Would give up his life and not change.[1]

This describes Yanzi perfectly.

---

1    *Shijing*, 80/36/2.

# 5.4 [114] 晏子再治阿而（见信）〔见信〕景公任以国政

晏子再次治理东阿，而被景公所信任，景公让他来治理国家

## 【原文】

景公使晏子为（东）阿宰，三年〔而〕毁闻于国。景公不说，召而免之。晏子谢曰："婴知婴之过矣，请复治阿，三年而誉必闻于国。"景公不忍，复使治阿，三年而誉闻于国。景公说，召而赏之。景公问其故，对曰："昔者婴之治阿也，筑蹊径，急门闾之政，而淫民恶之；举俭力孝弟，罚偷窥，而惰民恶之；决狱不避〔贵强〕，贵强恶之；左右所求，法则予，非法则否，而左右恶之；事贵人体而不过礼，而贵

## 【今译】

景公让晏子担任东阿的地方长官，三年后，批评他的言论传到国都。景公很生气，就召回晏子并要免除他的职务。晏子道歉说："我知道我做错了什么，请求让我再次治理东阿，三年后您一定能听到夸赞我的言论。"景公不忍心免去他的职务，就让他再次治理东阿，三年后夸赞他的话果然传到了国都。景公很高兴，召回晏子并赏赐他。景公问他发生变化的原因，晏子回答说："以前我治理东阿的时候，修筑道路，加强对乡里大门的管理，喜欢游乐的人就会憎恨我；表彰节俭勤劳孝顺父母兄长的人，处罚偷懒的人，懒惰的人就会憎恨我；在判决诉讼的时候保持公正，有权势的人就会憎恨我；身边的人有所请求，合乎法律的就给他，不符合的就不给，身边的人也会憎恨我；接待显贵的人而不用超越规格的礼节，显贵之人也会憎恨我。因此有三类不合正道的人在外批评我，有两类小人在内说我的坏话，三年后国君就会听

## 5.4 [114] WHEN YANZI GOVERNED DONG-E FOR THE SECOND TIME, HE GAINED TRUST. DUKE JING APPOINTED HIM TO GOVERN THE WHOLE STATE. [1]

Duke Jing commissioned Yanzi to serve as a governor in Dong-e County. [2] Three years later, Yanzi was defamed throughout the state. Duke Jing was displeased. He summoned Yanzi and dismissed him, but Yanzi apologized: "I am well aware of my faults, yet I request to be commissioned to govern Dong-e, and in three years, my good name will certainly be spread throughout the state." Duke Jing could not bear to refuse him and once again commissioned Yanzi to govern Dong-e again. Three years later, Yanzi's fame had spread throughout the state. Duke Jing was pleased; he summoned Yanzi in order to reward him, but Yanzi declined to accept the reward. [3] When Duke Jing asked Yanzi his reasons, Yanzi replied: "In the past, when I governed Dong-e, I built alleyways and byways and expedited the application of governmental rules at all gateways; but the licentious people hated this. I praised the frugal and the industrious, the filial son and the good brother; I punished the lazy and the decadent, but the indolent hated this. When I passed judgment, I did not flinch from the noble and the powerful, and so the noble and the powerful hated this. I granted whatever my entourage sought, provided it was lawful; if it wasn't, I denied their request, and so my entourage hated this. When I served honored people, I personally did not exceed the rites, and so the honored people hated this. For these reasons, three evil cliques slandered me from outside, and two malicious cliques slandered me from within. Three years later, all these slanderers were brought to your attention, my Lord. But

---

1   Item 5.4 [114] ↔ Item 7.20 [190]; *Shuoyuan*, 7/.29/53/11.

2   Retain 东 in accordance with Item 7.20 [190] and with the *Shuoyuan* parallel item, ibid.

3   Add 辞而不受 (*YZCQ-ICS*, 41, n. 2).

**【原文】**

人恶之。是以三邪毁乎外，二谗毁于内，三年而毁闻乎君也。今臣谨更之，不筑蹊径，而缓门闾之政，而淫民说；不举俭力孝弟，不罚偷窳，而惰民说；决狱阿贵强，而贵强说；左右所求言诺，而左右说；事贵人体过礼，而贵人说。是〔以〕三邪誉乎外，二谗誉乎内，三年而誉闻于君也。昔者婴之所以当诛者宜赏，今所以当赏者宜诛，是故不敢受。"景公知晏子贤。乃任以国政，三年而齐大兴。

**【今译】**

到批评我的言论。现在我慎重地改变了这种做法，不再修筑道路，放松对乡里大门的管理，喜欢游乐的人就满意了；不再表彰节俭勤劳孝顺父母兄长的人，不处罚偷懒的人，懒惰的人也满意了；判决诉讼的时候偏袒有权势的人，有权势的人就满意了；对身边人的要求都满足，身边的人也满意了；接待显贵的人用超规格的礼节，显贵之人也满意了。所以有三类不和正道的人在外夸赞我，两类小人在内夸赞我，三年后国君就能听到夸赞我的话了。以前我要被责罚的时候应该赏赐，现在要被赏赐的时候应该责罚，因此不敢接受您的赏赐。"景公知道晏子是一位贤臣，于是就让他处理国家政务，三年后齐国逐渐强盛起来。

now I have carefully changed my approach; I did not build alleyways and byways and delayed implementing governmental rules at the gateways, and the licentious people were pleased. I did not praise the frugal and the industrious, the filial son and the good brother; I did not punish the lazy and the degenerate, and the indolent were pleased. I refrained from passing judgment on the noble and the powerful people of Dong-e, and they were pleased. Whatever my entourage sought, I approved, and they were pleased. When serving honored people I went beyond the rites, and they were pleased. For this reason, three evil cliques praised me from outside and two malicious cliques praised me from within. Three years later, all these praises were brought to your attention, my Lord. My former actions that resulted in punishment were in fact worthy of reward, and my actions now that resulted in reward were in fact punishable. Therefore, I do not presume to accept."

Duke Jing realized that Yanzi was worthy; he then appointed him to govern the whole state, and within three years' time, Qi prospered.

## 5.5 [115] 景公恶故人晏子退国乱复召晏子

景公厌恶原有的人，晏子辞去职位，齐国混乱景公又召回晏子

【原文】

景公与晏子立于曲潢之上，晏子称曰："衣莫若新，人莫若故。"公曰："衣之新也，信善矣，人之故，相知情。"晏子归，负载使人辞于公曰："婴故老耄无能也，请毋服壮者之事。"公自治国，身弱于高国，百姓大乱。公恐，复召晏子。诸侯忌其威，而高国服其政，田畴垦辟，蠹桑豢〔牧〕之处不足，丝蠹于燕，牧马于鲁，共贡入朝。墨子闻之曰："晏子知道，景公知穷矣。"

【今译】

景公和晏子一起站在潢河弯曲的地方，晏子说："衣服最好的莫过于新衣服，人最好的还是故人。"景公说："新的衣服，的确是更好的，但故友之间，互相了解的就太多了。"晏子回去后，收拾自己的行李并派人向景公告辞说："晏婴已经年迈无能了，请不要让他再做壮年人的事了。"景公治理国家，自己的势力比高、国两家大夫还要弱，国内百姓大乱。景公十分恐慌，又再次召回晏子。各国诸侯忌惮他的威望，高、国两家大夫也服从他的治理，百姓开垦荒地，种桑养蚕放牧牲畜的地方不足，就到燕国去养蚕制丝，到鲁国去牧马，最后入贡国家。墨子听说这件事后说："晏子懂得治国之道，景公也知道自己的短处了。"

## 5.5 [115] DUKE JING DISLIKED LONG-STANDING ACQUAINTANCES. YANZI WITHDREW AND THE STATE FELL INTO CHAOS. YANZI WAS SUMMONED BACK.

Duke Jing and Yanzi stood above the Curved Western Pool[1] when Yanzi exclaimed: "As for clothes, there is nothing better than new ones; as for people, there is nothing better than long-standing acquaintances."[2] The Duke said: "As for new clothes, this saying is certainly true; but, as for long-standing acquaintances, they know each other's genuine character too well."[3]

Yanzi returned to his home; he carried and loaded his things and sent a messenger to submit his resignation, with the following words: "I am indeed worn out and incapable; I request not to serve in a position better fit for a man in his prime."

The Duke then ruled the state by himself but was weakened by the Gao and Guo lineages,[4] and great chaos ensued among the people. The Duke was frightened and summoned Yanzi back. The regional princes were intimidated by the Duke's authority, and the Gao and Guo lineages submitted to his rule. The fields were cultivated and wastelands were reclaimed; not enough space was left for rearing silkworms and breeding domestic animals, so silk had to be processed from Yen and horses pastored in Lu. All regional princes paid tribute and appeared for court audiences. When Mozi heard of this, he said: "Yanzi understood the Way; Duke Jing understood the desperate situation."

401

---

1 A detailed description of the structure of the Curved Western Pool and its surroundings is given previously in Item 2.15.

2 This seems to be a paraphrase of a similar proverb in the *Shujing*, 18/18/22, 人惟求旧; 器非求旧.

3 The Duke would apparently discard his "long acquaintance," Yanzi, in favor of new clothes.

4 The Gao 高氏 and Guo 国氏 were two extremely powerful aristocratic lineages in Qi who were related to the ducal house.

## 5.6 [116] 齐饿晏子因路寝之役以振民

齐国闹饥荒，晏子通过建造宫殿的徭役来赈济人民

【原文】

景公之时饥，晏子请为民发粟，公不许，当为路寝之台，晏子令吏重其赁，远其兆，徐其日，而不趋。三年台成而民振，故上悦乎游，民足乎食。君子曰："政则晏子欲发粟与民而已，若使不可得，则依物而偶于政。"

【今译】

景公在位之时有次闹饥荒，晏子请求拿出仓库中的粮食赈济灾民，景公不同意。当时要建造国君宫殿的平台，晏子就命令官吏提高建造所用材料的价格，提高运输的距离，延长修建的时间，而且不加快进度。三年后平台建成而且民众也得到了救济，所以国君开心地游览平台，民众也得到了足够的食物。君子评论说："这件事是晏子想要发放粮食给民众而已，如果办不到，那就通过修建平台来达到这个目标。"

## 5.6 [116] A FAMINE BROKE OUT IN QI. YANZI BROUGHT RELIEF TO THE PEOPLE BY MEANS OF CONSCRIPT LABOR FOR THE CONSTRUCTION OF THE TERRACE OVER THE ROAD BEDCHAMBER.[1]

During Duke Jing's tenure, there was a famine. Yanzi asked that grain be released for distribution amongst the people, but the Duke did not permit it and insisted upon the construction of the terrace over the Road Bedchamber. Hence, Yanzi ordered officials to increase the wages of the workers, hire manpower in large numbers, and to prolong the project and not be rushed. Three years later, the terrace was completed and the people were given relief. As a result, the Duke took pleasure in his excursions and the people had sufficient food. The man of noble character said: "The sole principle of rulership was Yanzi's wish to distribute grain to the people. When this proved unattainable, he conformed to the circumstances and adjusted his own policy to it."

403

---

1  Cf. the somewhat similar item 2.7 [57], from which we learn that Duke Jing refused to terminate the conscript labor for the terrace construction over the Road Bedchamber.

## 5.7 [117] 景公欲堕东门之堤晏子谓不可变古

景公想要毁坏东门的堤坝，晏子说不可以轻易改变原有的做法

**大中华文库**

**【原文】**

　　景公登东门防，民单服然后上，公曰："此大伤牛马蹄矣，夫何不下六尺哉？"晏子对曰："昔者，吾先君桓公，明君也，而管仲，贤相也。夫以贤相佐明君，而东门防全也，古者不为，殆有为也。蚤岁溜水至，入广门，即下六尺耳，乡者防下六尺，则无齐矣。夫古之重变古常，此之谓也。"

**【今译】**

404

　　景公登上国都东门堤防，看到民众穿单衣才能爬上去，就说："这堤防太高会严重损害牛马的蹄子，为什么不降低六尺呢？"晏子回答说："过去我们的先君齐桓公，是圣明的君主，而管仲又是著名的贤臣。在贤明的相国辅佐圣明的国君时，才让东门的堤防修建完善，古时候没有降低堤防的高度，应该是有他们的原因的。早年每次溜水上涨时，进入广门，水位就在堤下六尺，如果我们将堤坝的高度降低六尺，那么就没有齐国了。所谓古代不轻易变动原来的做法，说的就是这个道理。"

# 5.7 [117] DUKE JING WANTED TO LET THE EMBANKMENT OF THE EASTERN GATE FALL. YANZI SAID THAT IT IS NOT PROPER TO CHANGE ANCIENT PRACTICES.

When Duke Jing climbed the levee of the Eastern gate, the people had to dress in unlined clothing to climb with him.

The Duke said: "This steep height is very injurious to the hoofs of horses and cattle; why can't the levee be six feet lower?"

Yanzi answered: "In the past, our former ruler Duke Huan was an enlightened ruler, and Guan Zhong was his worthy prime minister. It took a worthy prime minister assisting an enlightened ruler to bring the levee of the Eastern gate to completion. In all probability, the people of ancient times had a good reason for not making it lower. Years ago, when the water of the Zi[1] River overflowed and entered the one-*li* protective trench,[2] the water level reached just six feet below the top. If at such a point the levee had been six feet lower, the state of Qi would no longer exist. The point is that in ancient times, people regarded the altering of ancient practices with great gravity."

---

1　溜 → 淄 (*YZCQ-ICS*, 42, n. 3).

2　广门 → 广里 (*JS*, 310/5).

## 5.8 [118] 景公怜饥者晏子称治国之本以长其意

景公怜悯饥饿的人，晏子说这是治理国家的根本来助长他的爱心

### 【原文】

景公游于寿宫，睹长年负薪者，而有饥色。公悲之，喟然（叹曰）令吏养之。晏子曰："臣闻之，乐贤而哀不肖，守国之本也。今君爱老，而恩无所不逮，治国之本也。"公笑，有喜色。晏子曰："圣王见贤以乐贤，见不肖以哀不肖。今请求老弱之不养，鳏寡之无室者，论而共秩焉。"公曰："诺。"于是老弱有养，鳏寡有室。

### 【今译】

景公游览寿宫的时候，看到有位老人背着薪柴，面有饥色。景公非常悲伤，长叹一声，命令政府官员来救助他。晏子说："我听说，喜欢贤良的人而怜悯无能之人，是保持国家的根本。现在国君您爱护老人，恩惠没有达不到的地方，这是治理国家的根本啊！"景公笑起来，露出满意的神色。晏子说："圣明的君王见到贤能的人便会开心，见到无能之人就会怜悯他们。现在我请求年老体弱无人赡养的，鳏夫寡妇没有家室的，根据情况公室发粮食。"景公说："好的。"于是年老体弱的人都有人供养，鳏夫寡妇也都有了家室。

## 5.8 [118] DUKE JING FELT COMPASSION TOWARD A VICTIM OF FAMINE. YANZI, IN ORDER TO FURTHER HIS ARGUMENT, DECLARED THAT THIS FEELING IS THE BASIS FOR MAINTAINING GOOD ORDER IN THE STATE.[1]

While Duke Jing was traveling to the Longevity Palace, he saw an old man who looked famished carrying on his back a bundle of fire-wood. The Duke took pity on him and, with a big sigh, ordered the officials to take care of him.

Yanzi said: "I have heard that feeling happiness regarding the worthy and sorrow regarding the unworthy forms the basis for safeguarding the state. Now your affection for the elderly, my Lord, and your bounty that reaches everywhere, are the basis for maintaining good order in the state."

The Duke smiled with a happy expression on his face.

Yanzi continued: "When the Sage-Kings met a worthy person, they rejoiced in his excellent qualities, and when they met an unworthy one, they felt compassion. Now, I request that you seek out the old and the weak who are ill-nourished, and for widows and orphans who have no shelter, and then, after examining their circumstances, provide them with official support."

The Duke said: "Very well."

From this time on, the old and the weak were nourished and the widows and orphans were provided shelter.

407

---

1    Item 5.8 [118] ↔ *Shuoyuan*, 5.12/34/7.

## 5.9 [119] 景公探雀鷇鷇弱反之晏子称长幼以贺

景公在鸟窝中抓雀，幼雀身体瘦弱于是又放了回去，晏子称赞景公能抚育幼小并祝贺

【原文】

景公探雀鷇，鷇弱，反之。晏子闻之，不（待）时而入见（景公）。公汗出惕然，晏子曰："君何为者也？"公曰："吾探雀鷇，鷇弱，故反之。"晏子逡巡北面再拜而贺曰："吾君有圣王之道矣！"公曰："寡人探雀鷇，鷇弱，故反之，其当圣王之道者何也？"晏子对曰："君探雀鷇，鷇弱，反之，是长幼也。吾君仁爱，曾禽兽之加焉，而况于人乎！此圣王之道也。"

【今译】

景公在鸟窝中抓了年幼的雀，幼雀身体还很瘦弱，于是又送回鸟巢。晏子听说了这件事，没有等到该入宫的时间就进宫面见景公了。景公汗流满面露出惊惧的表情，晏子说："国君您在干什么呢？"景公说："我抓幼雀，幼雀体弱，所以我把它送回鸟巢了。"晏子向后退面朝北方，拜了又拜而且祝贺说："我的国君有圣王的治国之道了！"景公说："我抓幼雀，幼雀体弱，所以我把它送回鸟巢，这件事和圣王的治国之道有什么关系呢？"晏子回答说："国君您抓幼雀，幼雀体弱，所以您把它送回了鸟巢，这是爱护幼小的做法。我的国君有仁爱之心，即使是禽兽也会爱护，更何况人呢？这就是圣王的治国之道啊！"

# 5.9 [119] DUKE JING TOOK A FLEDGLING SPARROW FROM ITS NEST; IT WAS WEAK, SO HE RETURNED IT. YANZI CONGRATULATED HIM, PRAISING HIM FOR CARING FOR THE YOUNG.[1]

Duke Jing took a fledgling sparrow from its nest but it was weak, so he returned it. When Yanzi heard of this, he entered for an audience with the Duke at an irregular hour, and the Duke perspired with fear.

Yanzi said: "What have you done?"

The Duke said: "I took a fledgling sparrow from its nest, but it was weak and so I returned it."

Yanzi drew back, walked around until he faced north, bowed twice, and congratulated the Duke, saying: "My Lord possesses the way of the sage-kings."

The Duke said: "I took a fledgling sparrow from its nest but it was weak, and so I returned it. How does this fit the way of the sages?"

Yanzi answered: "You, my Lord, took a fledgling sparrow from its nest; it was weak, and you returned it. This shows caring for the young. If your compassion and humaneness, my Lord, was applied even toward birds and beasts, how much more can you do for people — is this not so? This is the way of the sage-kings."[2]

---

1    Item 5.9 [119] ↔ *Shuoyuan*, 5.10/33/27.

2    The present paragraph replicates the pivotal idea of *Mencius*, 1.7/3-6.

# 5.10 [120] 景公睹乞儿于涂晏子讽公使（養）〔养〕

景公在路边看到乞讨的孩子，晏子进谏让景公收养他

## 【原文】

景公睹婴儿有乞于涂者，公曰："是无归夫！"晏子对曰："君存，何为无归？使吏（養）〔养〕〔之〕，可立而以闻。"

## 【今译】

景公看到有年幼的孩子在路上乞讨，于是说："这个孩子是无家可归了！"晏子回答说："国君您收养他，怎么能说无家可归呢？让官吏抚养他，等孩子长大了再告诉他，这样您的德行就会名扬天下。"

## 5.10 [120] DUKE JING SAW BEGGING CHILDREN IN THE STREETS. YANZI PERSUADED THE DUKE TO HAVE THEM FED.[1]

Duke Jing saw children begging in the streets. The Duke said: "They have no one to turn to — is this not so?"

Yanzi replied: "You, my Lord, exist — why should they have no one to turn to? Order your officials to feed them, and when they will be able to stand on their own, your virtue will be renowned."

---

1   Item 5.10 [120] ↔ *Shuoyuan*, 5.11/34/4.

## 5.11 [121] 景公惭刖跪之辱不朝晏子称直请赏之

景公因为断足看门人的羞辱而惭愧，不参加朝会，晏子解释看门人的正直并请求赏赐他

### 【原文】

景公正昼，被发，乘六马，御妇人以出正闺，刖跪击其马而反之，曰："尔非吾君也！"公惭而不朝。晏子睹裔款而问曰："君何故不朝？"对曰："昔者君正昼，被发，乘六马，御妇人以出正闺，刖跪击其马而反之曰：'尔非吾君也！'公惭而（出）反，不果出，是以不朝。"晏子入见。景公曰："昔者寡人有罪，被发，乘六马，以出正闺，刖跪击马而反之，曰：'尔非吾君也！'寡人以（天）子大夫之赐，得率百姓以

### 【今译】

景公在正午的时候，披散着头发，乘坐六匹马拉的马车，载着妇人想要从宫中的小门出去，（披发、六驾御妇人、出正闺都不合礼制）断足的看门人击打他的马而阻止说："你不是我的国君！"景公非常惭愧并且不参加朝会。晏子看到裔款就问他："国君为什么不参加朝会呢？"裔款回答说："之前国君在正午的时候，披散着头发，乘坐六匹马拉的马车，载着妇人想要从宫中的小门出去，断足的看门人击打他的马阻止他说：'你不是我的国君！'国君惭愧地返回宫中，最后也没出来，所以没有参加朝会。"晏子进入宫中求见景公。景公说："之前我做错了事，披散着头发，乘坐六匹马拉的马车，从宫中的小门出去，断足的看门人击打我的马而阻止我，并说：'你不是我的国君！'我因

## 5.11 [121] DUKE JING DID NOT HOLD AUDIENCE BECAUSE HE WAS AFRAID TO BE HUMILIATED BY A MAN WHO SUFFERED A PENAL LEG-AMPUTATION. YANZI PRAISED THAT MAN'S DIRECT TALK AND REQUESTED PERMISSION TO REWARD HIM. [1]

Once, Duke Jing was riding with his royal consort in a carriage with six horses. It was midday, and he let his hair hang loosely about his shoulders. As they came out the gate of the inner quarters of the palace, a man who had suffered a penal leg-amputation struck the horses and chased them back, saying: "You are not my ruler." The Duke was ashamed and did not hold court.

Yanzi saw Yi Kuan and asked him: "Why doesn't the Duke hold court?"

Yi Kuan replied: "Some time ago it happened that our ruler was riding with his royal consort in a carriage with six horses. It was midday, and he let his hair hang loosely about his shoulders. As they came out the gate of the inner quarters of the palace, a man who had suffered a penal leg-amputation struck the horses and chased them back, saying: 'You are not my ruler.' The Duke returned ashamed and did not go out for a ride. This is why he isn't holding court."

Yanzi entered the court and appeared before the Duke. Duke Jing said to him: "A while back, I committed an offence. I was riding in a carriage with six horses. It was midday, and I let my hair hang loosely about my shoulders. As I came out the gate of the inner quarters of the palace, a man who had suffered a penal leg-amputation struck the horses and chased me back, saying: 'You are not my ruler.' It is by your grace and that of the high officers,' that I am able to lead the people and protect the temple of my

413

---

1    Item 5.11 [121] ↔ *Shuoyuan*, 9.18/72/25.

**【原文】**

守宗庙，今见戮于刖跪，以辱社稷，吾犹可以齐于诸侯乎？”晏子对
曰：“君勿恶焉！臣闻下无直辞，上有隐君，民多讳（曰）言，君有骄
行。古者明君在上，下多直辞；君上好善，民无讳言。今君有失行，
刖跪直辞禁之，是君之福也。故臣来庆。请赏之，以明君之好善；礼
之，以明君之受谏。”公笑曰：“可乎？”晏子曰：“可。”于是令刖跪倍
资无征，时朝无事也。

**【今译】**

为得到周天子和卿大夫的赐予，能够率领百姓来守卫宗庙，现在却被
断足的看门人所羞辱，因此辱没了社稷，我还能与其他诸侯并立吗？”
晏子回答说：“国君您不要憎恨他！我听说作为臣子的人如果没有正直
不阿的言论，那么就会欺瞒的国君；如果民众都有所顾忌而不敢明说，
那么国君就会有骄纵的行为。古时候圣明的君王在位，臣子多有率直
的言论；国君喜欢赞许他人，民众的言论就不会有所欺瞒。现在国君
您有做错的行为，断足的看门人以正直的言论阻止您，是国君您的福
气。所以我来为您庆祝。我请求您赏赐他，来表明您喜欢赞许他人；
用礼节来对待他，来表明您接受别人的劝谏。”景公笑着说："这样做
可以吗？”晏子说："可以。”于是下令给断足的看门人两倍的薪资，
免于征赋不惩罚他，并且随时可以朝见。

ancestors. But now I have been humiliated by a man who suffered a penal leg-amputation and have brought disgrace upon the altars of soil and grain. How can I still be considered an equal to the other regional princes?"

Yanzi replied: "My Lord, don't take this amiss. I have heard that if inferiors cannot talk straightforwardly, then superiors conceal wrongful deeds.[1] If the people conceal much of their actions, the ruler's conduct will become arrogant. In ancient times, when enlightened rulers occupied the highest positions, the inferior could for the most part talk straightforwardly. When the ruler at the top loved the good, then the people had nothing to conceal. Now, your conduct, my Lord, has been flawed, and this man who suffered a penal leg-amputation, with his straightforward words, put an end to it. This is your great fortune, my Lord, and therefore I came here to congratulate you. I request that you reward him, in order to show that an enlightened ruler like yourself loves the good, and that you treat him according to the rites in order to show that an enlightened ruler like yourself can accept remonstrance."

The Duke laughed and said: "Is this proper?"

Yanzi said: "It is."

Thereupon, orders were given to double the wages of the man with the penal leg-amputation and to exempt him from all taxes. Court audiences were held again at the proper times, with no interruptions.

---

1  隐君 → 隐恶 (*YZCQ-ICS*, 43, n. 5).

## 5.12 [122] 景公夜从晏子饮晏子称不敢与

景公晚上想要和晏子一起饮酒，晏子说不敢

### 【原文】

景公饮酒，夜移于晏子家，前驱款门曰："君至！"晏子被玄端，立于门曰："诸侯得微有故乎？国家得微有事乎？君何为非时而夜辱？"公曰："酒醴之味，金石之声，愿与夫子乐之。"晏子对曰："夫布荐席、陈簠簋者，有人，臣不敢与焉。"公曰："移于司马穰苴之家。"前驱款门曰："君至！"穰苴介胄操戟立于门曰："诸侯得微有兵乎？大臣得微有叛者乎？君何为非时而夜辱？"公曰："酒醴之味，金石之声，愿与

### 【今译】

景公喝酒，晚上想要到晏子家中继续，引路的人前去敲门说："国君来了！"晏子穿着礼服，站在门口说："各国诸侯有变故吗？国家有什么大事吗？国君为何在夜间驾临造访呢？"景公说："美味的酒醴，悦耳的音乐，我想要和夫子你一同享受。"晏子回答说："整理坐的垫席，陈列乘酒的礼器，有专门的人负责，我不敢参与。"景公说："转移到司马穰苴家里去。"引路的人前去敲门说："国君来了！"司马穰苴穿上甲胄手持铁戟站在门口说："诸侯各国发兵攻打了吗？国内大臣起兵叛乱了吗？国君为何在夜间驾临造访呢？"景公说："美味的酒醴，悦耳的音乐，我想要和将军你一同享受。"司马穰苴回答说："整理坐的垫席，陈列乘酒的礼器，有专门的人负责，我不敢参与。"景公说：

## 5.12 [122] DUKE JING WENT TO YANZI'S HOUSE AT NIGHT TO DRINK WINE. YANZI DECLARED THAT HE DARE NOT JOIN HIM. [1]

Duke Jing was having a drinking banquet and during the night, he moved the banquet to Yanzi's house. The outrider knocked on Yanzi's gate and announced: "The ruler has arrived."

Yanzi stood at the gate, dressed in a formal black square-cut robe, and said: "Could it be that there are issues concerning the regional princes or affairs concerning the state at this hour? Why did you embarrass me by coming at night, not at a proper time?"

The Duke replied: "I want to share with you, Master, the joy of the taste of wine and sweet liquor, and the sound of bronze and stone instruments."

Yanzi said: "There are other people to spread the mats and to set up the bowls. I dare not join you."

The Duke said: "Then let us move to the house of Marshal Rang Ju."

417

The outrider knocked on Rang Ju's gate and announced: "The ruler has arrived."

Rang Ju stood at the gate in his armor and helmet, holding a halberd, and said: "Could it be that there are military issues concerning the regional princes, or are the high ranking ministers in revolt? Why did you embarrass me by coming at night, not at a proper time?"

The Duke replied: "I want to share with you, Master, the joy of the taste of wine and sweet liquor, and the sound of bronze and stone instruments."

Rang Ju said: "There are other people to spread the mats and to set up the bowls. I dare not join you."

---

1   Item 5.12 [122] ↔ *Shuoyuan*, 9.19/73/6.

**【原文】**

将军〔夫子〕乐之。"穰苴对曰："夫布荐席、陈簠簋者，有人，臣不敢与焉。"公曰："移于梁丘据之家。"前驱款门曰："君至！"梁丘据左操瑟，右挈竽，行歌而（去）〔出〕。公曰："乐哉，今夕吾饮也！微彼二子者，何以治吾国？微此一臣者，何以乐吾身？"君子曰："圣贤之君，皆有益友，无偷乐之臣，景公弗能及，故两用之，仅得不亡。"

**【今译】**

"转移到梁丘据家里去。"引路的人前去敲门说："国君来了！"梁丘据左手拿着瑟，右手拿着竽，唱着歌出来迎接。景公说："今天晚上我喝酒真开心啊！如果没有晏子和司马穰苴这两位先生，如何来治理我的国家？如果没有梁丘据这位臣子，如何能让我高兴？"君子评价说："圣明贤能的君主，都有有益于自己的朋友，没有贪图享乐的臣子，景公达不到这一点，所以两种臣子都任用，只能保持国家不灭亡而已。"

The Duke said: "Then let us move to the house of the Liangqiu Ju."

The outrider knocked on Liangqiu Ju's gate and announced: "The ruler has arrived."

Liangqiu Ju came out from the house singing, a *se*-zither his right hand and a flute in his left hand.

The Duke said: "What joy! This very night I will be drinking. If it were not for these two masters, how could I rule my state? If it were not for this minister, how could I have personal pleasure?"

The man of noble character said: "All the sages and wise rulers have confidants who are useful to them, but they do not have ministers who indulge in pleasures and comfort. Duke Jing was unable to reach this level and so he employed ministers of the two categories and barely managed to escape his demise."

## 5.13 [123] 景公使进食与裘晏子对以社稷臣

景公让晏子呈送食物和皮裘，晏子用自己是治理国家的臣子来回答

**【原文】**

晏子侍于景公，朝寒，公曰："请进暖食。"晏子对曰："婴非君奉馈之臣也，敢辞。"公曰："请进服裘。"对曰："婴非君茵席之臣也，敢辞。"公曰："然夫子之于寡人何为者也？"对曰："婴，社稷之臣也。"公曰："何谓社稷之臣？"对曰："夫社稷之臣，能立社稷，别上下之义，使当其理；制百官之序，使得其宜；作为辞令，可分布于四方。"自是之后，君不以礼，不见晏子。

**【今译】**

晏子侍奉景公，早上起来非常寒冷，景公说："请先生给我送点暖和的食物。"晏子回答说："晏婴不是给国君进奉食物的臣子，我只能冒昧地拒绝。"景公说："请先生给我送来皮袄。"晏子回答说："晏婴不是给国君整理衣物的臣子，我只能冒昧地拒绝。"景公说："那先生您是我的什么臣子呢？"晏子回答说："晏婴是为社稷服务的臣子。"景公说："什么是为社稷服务的臣子呢？"晏子回答说："为社稷服务的臣子，能够建立国家，区别上下级的义务，使他们的行为合理；制定百官的序列，使他们得到合适的地位；编撰文告命令，可以发布到国家四方。"从那以后，国君在不合乎礼节时，不召见晏子。

## 5.13 [123] DUKE JING INSTRUCTED YANZI TO BRING HIM FOOD AND A FUR COAT. YANZI REPLIED THAT HE WAS THE MINISTER OF THE ALTARS OF SOIL AND GRAIN.

Yanzi attended Duke Jing on a cold morning and the Duke said: "Please bring me something warm to eat."

Yanzi replied: "I am not the minister who serves your food. I dare to decline."

Duke Jing said: "Please bring me a fur coat."

Yanzi replied: "I am not the minister who takes care of your cushions and mats. I dare to decline."

Duke Jing said: "In that case, what do you do for me, Master?"

Yanzi replied: "I am the minister of the altars of soil and grain."

Duke Jing said: "What do you mean by a 'minister of the altars of soil and grain'?"

Yanzi replied: "The minister of the altars of soil and grain is able to establish these altars. He distinguishes between the duties allotted to superiors and inferiors and sees to it that all these duties are carried out in accordance with principle. He regulates the order of all the officials and sees to it that everyone occupies the post due him. He writes the orders and instructions so that they will be promulgated everywhere."

From this time on, our Lord met Yanzi in audience only in accordance with the rites.

## 5.14 [124] 晏子饮景公止家老敛欲与民共乐

晏子宴请景公饮酒，制止家臣征敛百姓，想要和人民一起享乐

**【原文】**

晏子饮景公酒，令器必新，家老曰："财不足，请敛于氓。"晏子曰："止！夫乐者，上下同之。故天子与天下，诸侯与境内，（匹）〔自〕〔大〕夫以下各与其僚，无有独乐。今上乐〔其乐〕，下伤其费，是独乐（音）〔者〕也，不可！"

**【今译】**

晏子请公饮酒，吩咐酒器必须使用新的，他的家臣说："没有足够的钱了，请求向百姓征收。"晏子说："不行！欢乐，应该是上级与下级一同享受的事情。所以天子与天下的百姓一起享乐，诸侯王与国内的百姓一同享乐，卿大夫以下的与自己的臣僚一同享乐，没有自己享乐的。现在上级享受他的欢乐，却要百姓破费财物，是自己享乐的行为，不能那样做！"

# 5.14 [124] YANZI HOSTED A DRINKING BANQUET FOR DUKE JING AND STOPPED HIS MAJORDOMO FROM RAISING TAXES. HE WANTED THE DUKE TO SHARE HIS PLEASURE WITH THE PEOPLE.[1]

Yanzi hosted a drinking banquet for Duke Jing, who ordered that all the utensils be new.

Yanzi's majordomo said: "Our means do not suffice for this. Allow me to raise it in taxes from the people."

Yanzi said: "Stop! Pleasure is something that superiors and inferiors share; therefore, the Son of Heaven takes pleasure along with all in the realm, and the regional princes take pleasure along with those within their borders. From the high officers on down, each shares pleasure with his fitting companions; no one takes pleasure alone. But in the present case, a superior delights in his pleasure, while inferiors bear its cost. This is a case of taking pleasure alone — it is not acceptable."

423

---

1 Item 5.14 [124] ↔ *Shuoyuan*, 5.8/33/18. The idea of "sharing enjoyment with others" is expressed strongly in *Mencius*, 1.2/1/11; 2.4/93.

## 5.15 [125] 晏子饮景公酒公呼具火晏子称诗以辞

晏子服侍景公饮酒，景公要求点火照明，晏子用《诗经》中的诗句来推辞

### 【原文】

晏子饮景公酒，日暮，公呼具火，晏子辞曰：《诗》云：'侧弁之俄'，言失德也。'屡舞傞傞'，言失容也。'既醉以酒，既饱以德，既醉而出，并受其福'，宾主之礼也。'醉而不出，是谓伐德'，宾之罪也。婴已卜其日，未卜其夜。"公曰："善。"举酒〔而〕祭之，再拜而出。曰："岂过我哉，吾托国于晏子也。以其家货养寡人，不欲其淫侈也，而况与寡人谋国乎！"

### 【今译】

晏子请景公喝酒，到了晚上，景公要求点火照明，晏子拒绝说："《诗经》说：'喝醉后歪戴着皮帽'，是说失去了德行。'醉酒后舞蹈忘了形象'，是说失去了仪容。'酒已经喝醉了，饭也吃饱了，那么就离开，主人和客人都会获得福祉'，这是宾客和主人之间的礼节。'喝醉了还不离开，就是所谓的损害品德'，这是宾客的错误。晏婴已经选择白天喝酒，并没有选择晚上喝酒。"景公说："好的。"然后举起酒杯表示感谢，拜了两次后起身离开。景公说："难道这样对我过分吗，我已经把国家托付给晏子了啊！晏子用自己家中的财物来招待我，都不想要过于奢华浪费，更何况帮助我治理国家呢！"

## 5.15 [125] YANZI HOSTED A DRINKING BANQUET FOR DUKE JING. THE DUKE REQUESTED TO LITE A FIRE. YANZI DECLINED, CITING THE ODES. [1]

Yanzi hosted a drinking banquet for Duke Jing. When the sun had set, the Duke requested that a fire be lit, but Yanzi declined: "As it says in the *Odes*:

With their tilted caps they sway back; [2]

These words mean to lose virtue;

They keep dancing frantically; [3]

These words mean to lose one's sober countenance. [4]

If, when drunk, they would go out,

They would receive their blessing with all other guests; [5]

These words refer to the rites between guests and hosts;

But if they stayed in, drunk,

This is called destroying virtue; [6]

These words refer to the offences of the guests. By recourse to divination, I have scheduled this banquet for daytime, not for nighttime."

The Duke said: "Approved." Then he took up wine, offered a libation, bowed twice and left, saying: "Surely it was not a mistake on my part to entrust my state to Yanzi. He used his family resources to provide for me and did not want to be extravagantly excessive in doing so; how much more so will he manifest this attitude when planning state affairs with me!"

---

1  Item 5.15 [125] ↔ *Shuoyuan*, 20.19/178/24.

2  *Shijing*, 220/108/16.

3  Ibid.

4  Omit 既醉以酒, 既飽以德 (*JS*, 324/2).

5  *Shijing*, 220/108/17.

6  Ibid.

## 5.16 [126] 晋欲攻齐使人往观晏子以礼侍而折其谋

晋国想要攻打齐国，派人来观察，晏子以礼节招待使者并破坏了他们的谋划

【原文】

晋平公欲伐齐，使范昭往观焉。景公觞之，饮酒酣，范昭曰："请君之弃樽。"〔公曰："酌寡人之樽，进之于客。"〕〔范昭已饮〕，〔晏子曰〕："〔彻樽〕，更之。"觯具矣，范昭佯醉，不说而起舞，谓太师曰："能为我调成周之乐乎？吾为子舞之。"太师曰："冥臣不习。"范昭趋而出。景公谓晏子曰："晋，大国也，使人来将观吾政，今子怒大国之使者，

大中华文库

晏子春秋 第五卷 杂上

【今译】

晋平公想要攻打齐国，就命令范昭为使者到齐国观察。景公置酒招待他，范昭说："我请求使用国君您用过的酒杯。"景公说："把我的杯子倒满酒，献给客人。"范昭喝完酒后，晏子说："把酒杯撤下去，换一个酒杯。"酒具都准备好了，范昭假装喝醉了，不高兴地站起来要跳舞，对齐国乐师长说："你能为我改为成周的音乐吗？我来为你们舞蹈。"乐师长说："我太愚昧了，没有学过。"于是范昭快步离开。景公对晏子说："晋国，是诸侯中的大国，派遣使者来观察我治理的国家，现在你把大国的使者惹怒了，该怎么办呢？"晏子说："范昭平时的行为举止，并不是粗陋不知礼节的，而且他今天是要试探我们君臣的，所以我惹怒了他。"景公对乐师长说："您为何不为客人改为成周的音

## 5.16 [126] THE DUKE OF JIN WANTED TO ATTACK QI. HE SENT AN ENVOY TO ASSESS IT. YANZI ATTENDED HIM ACCORDING TO THE RITES AND THWARTED HIS STRATEGY.[1]

Duke Ping of Jin wanted to attack Qi and sent Fan Zhao[2] to assess it. Duke Jing threw him a drinking party and when they were drunk,[3] Fan Zhao said: "May I ask you to give up your goblet to me?"

The Duke said: "Fill my goblet and give it to our guest."

After Fan Zhao had drunk from it, Yanzi said: "Take the goblet away from Fan Zhao and replace it with another."

Thereupon, a small goblet was provided. Fan Zhao pretended to be drunk, but was displeased. He rose to dance, saying to the Grand Music Master: "Can you play the music of Cheng-zhou?[4] I will perform the dance for you."

The Grand Music Master said: "I, your blind servant,[5] am not versed in it."

Thereupon, Fan Zhao left hurriedly. Duke Jing said to Yanzi: "Jin is a great state. They sent someone to come here and inspect our government, and now you have angered the envoy of that great state. What are we to do?"

Yanzi replied: "Fan Zhao, as an individual, is not a vulgar person who

---

1   5.16 [126] ↔ *Xinxu*, 1.14/4/18; *Hanshi waichuan*, 8.18/61/1.

2   Fan Zhao 范昭 is Shi Jishe 士吉射, a military figure in Jin who led a rebellion with Xun Yin 荀寅 in 497 and ultimately was forced to flee to Qi. See *Zuozhuan*, A11.13.6/427/18.

3   酖 → 醉 (*YZCQ-ICS*, 44, n. 7).

4   Cheng-zhou 成周 was the ancient Western Zhou capital, the place of residence of the Duke of Zhou and King Cheng. Its music, as the Grand Music Master proceeds to explain, should be played only for rulers and not for their representatives.

5   In this era, the musical profession was confined to the blind.

**【原文】**

将奈何？"晏子曰："夫范昭之为人也，非陋而不知礼也，且欲试吾君，臣故绝之也。"景公谓太师（子）〔曰〕："（曰）〔子〕何以不为客调成周之乐乎？"太师对曰："夫成周之乐，天子之乐也，〔若〕调之，必人主舞之。今范昭人臣〔也〕，〔而〕欲舞天子之乐，臣故不为也。"范昭归以报平公曰："齐未可伐也。臣欲试其君，而晏子识之；臣欲犯其（礼）〔乐〕，而太师知之。"仲尼闻之曰："夫不出于樽俎之间，而知〔冲〕千里之外，其晏子之谓也。（可谓折冲矣）！而太师其与焉。"

**【今译】**

乐呢？"乐师长回答说："成周的音乐，是周天子的音乐，如果演奏的话，必须要国君才能舞蹈。现在范昭作为国君的臣子，想要在天子的音乐中舞蹈，所以我不为他演奏。"范昭回到晋国后报告给晋平公说："齐国不能攻打。我想要试探他们君臣，晏婴识破的我的想法；我想要破坏他们的礼仪，齐国的乐师长明白我的目的。"孔子听说这件事，评价说："还没有离开筵席，就能够知道千里之外的事情，说的就是晏子这种人。这都能够被称为克敌取胜啊！而乐师长也参与了这件事。"

is ignorant of the rites. Furthermore, he wanted to put you, my Lord, to the test, and therefore I had to cut his visit short."

Duke Jing said[1] to the Grand Music Master: "Why didn't you play the music of Cheng-zhou for the guest?"

The Grand Music Master replied: "The music of Cheng-zhou is the music of the Son of Heaven; if it is played, a ruler must be present to dance to it. Now, Fan Zhao is a subject, and he wanted to dance to the sound of the music of the Son of Heaven. This is why I refused to play it."

Fan Zhao returned and reported to Duke Ping: "Qi cannot be attacked yet. I wanted to test its ruler, but Yanzi saw through my intention. I wanted to commit an offence against their music, but the Grand Music Master realized my intent."

When Confucius heard about this, he said: "Yanzi is an example of one who does not leave the space between wine goblets and meat chopping boards,[2] and yet defeats[3] an enemy a thousand *li* away. And the Grand Music Master is allied with him."

429

---

1  为 → 谓 (*YZCQ-ICS*, 45, n. 2).

2  I.e., to conduct diplomatic negotiations over wine and meat.

3  知 → 折 (*YZCQ-ICS*, 45, n. 3).

## 5.17 [127] 景公问东门无泽年谷而对以冰晏子请罢伐鲁

景公问东门无泽今年粮食的收成，东门无泽用冰来回答，晏子请求停止征伐鲁国

**【原文】**

景公伐鲁，（传）〔傅〕许，得东门无泽，公问焉："鲁之年谷何如？"对曰："阴（水）〔冰〕（厥）〔凝〕，阳冰厚五寸。"不知，以告晏子。晏子对曰："君子也。问年谷而对以冰，礼也。阴水厥，阳冰厚五寸者，寒温节，节则刑政平，平则上下和，和则年谷熟。年充众和而伐之，臣恐罢民弊兵，不成君之意。请礼鲁以息吾怨，遣其执，以明吾德。"公曰："善。"乃不伐鲁。

**【今译】**

景公要攻打鲁国，快到许的时候，抓到一个叫东门无泽的人。景公问他："鲁国今年的粮食收成怎么样？"东门无泽回答说："阴暗地方的冰像石头一样坚硬，阳光下的冰有五寸厚。"景公不知道什么意思，就告诉了晏子。晏子回答说："东门无泽是一个君子啊！国君询问他今年粮食的收成，他却用冰来回答，这是熟知礼节的行为。阴暗地方的冰像石头一样坚硬，阳光下的冰有五寸厚，说明鲁国的天气非常规律，有规律那么刑罚政令就公平，刑罚政令公平那么上下级之间就和睦，和睦那么今年的粮食收成就很好。在粮食丰收民众和睦的情况下去攻打他，我恐怕会使齐国的军队和民众疲敝，难以达到国君您的目的。我请求国君以礼节来对待鲁国，来消除我们的怨气，遣送我们抓获的人，来表明我们的德行。"景公说："好的。"于是不再攻打鲁国。

## 5.17 [127] DUKE JING ASKED DONGMEN WUZE[1] ABOUT THE ANNUAL HARVEST OF LU. DONGMEN WUZE REPLIED REFERRING TO ICE. YANZI ASKED THE DUKE TO STOP THE ATTACK ON LU.

Duke Jing was in the process of attacking Lu. His army swarmed over the walls of the city of Xu and captured Dongmen Wuze.

The Duke asked him: "How is the annual harvest of Lu?"

Dongmen Wuze replied: "Shaded ice is frozen hard, yet the sunlit ice is five inches thick."

The Duke did not understand this and informed Yanzi. Yanzi replied: "He is a man of noble character. You asked him about the annual harvest and he replied referring to ice; such are the rites. When he said that shaded ice[2] is frozen hard, yet sunlit ice is five inches thick, he meant that cold and heat are correctly balanced; when balanced, punishments and governmental measures are just; when justice exists, then superiors and inferiors are in harmony; when they are harmonious, then the annual harvest is good. I fear that attacking a country that has an abundant harvest and a harmonious population will drain the people and wear out the soldiers, and you will be unable to accomplish your intent. Please deal with Lu according to the rites, in order to assuage their resentment of us. Return their captives in order to publicize our virtue."

The Duke said: "Approved." Consequently, he did not attack Lu.

431

---

1  An unidentified figure.

2  水 → 冰 (*JS*, 333/6).

大中华文库

## 5.18 [128] 景公使晏子予鲁地而鲁使不尽受

景公让晏子赠予鲁国土地，鲁国的使者不全部接受

### 【原文】

景公予鲁君地，山阴数百社，使晏子致之，鲁使子叔昭伯受地，不尽受也。晏子曰："寡君献地，忠廉也，曷为不尽受？"子叔昭伯曰："臣受命于君曰：'诸侯相见，交让，争处其卑，礼之文也；交委多，争受少，行之实也。礼成文于前，行成章于后，交之所以长久也。'且吾闻君子不尽人之欢，不竭人之忠，吾是以不尽受也。"晏子归报公，公喜笑曰："鲁君犹若是乎。"晏子曰："臣闻大国贪于名，小国贪于实，此诸侯之公患也。今鲁处卑而不贪乎尊，辞实而不贪乎多，行廉不为苟

### 【今译】

景公送给鲁国国君土地，是泰山北侧的数百个村社，让晏子作为使者去赠予鲁国，鲁国派子叔昭伯接受土地，但没有全部接受。晏子说："我们的国君赠送土地，是诚心诚意的，你们为什么不全部接受呢？"子叔昭伯说："我接受国君的命令，国君说：'诸侯之间相见，互相谦让，争着处于较低的一方，这是礼仪所规定的；赠予的多，接受的少，这是诸侯交往的实际情况。先依照礼仪的明文规定，后按照诸侯交往的实际惯例，这样交往才能长久。'况且我听说君子不会将他人的好意全部接受了，不会竭尽他人对自己的忠诚，这就是我不全部接受的原因。"晏子回到齐国报告给景公，景公欣喜地笑着说："鲁国的国君原来是这样做的！"晏子说："我听说诸侯中的大国贪图名声，小国贪图实际利益，这是诸侯间的通病。现在鲁国处在地位较低的位置却不贪图尊位，拒绝实际利益而不贪图多得，行为端正不为一时得失，

## 5.18 [128] DUKE JING COMMISSIONED YANZI TO CONCEDE LAND TO LU, BUT THE ENVOY FROM LU DID NOT ACCEPT ALL OF IT.

Duke Jing ceded to the Duke of Lu land that extended several hundred *she*[1] north from Mt. Tai.[2] He commissioned Yanzi to carry this out. Lu sent Zishu Zhaobo[3] to receive the land, but he did not want to accept all of it.

Yanzi said: "My ruler's offer of this land demonstrates his sincere unselfishness; why do you not accept all of it?"

Zishu Zhaobo replied: "I received the following instructions from my Duke: 'When the regional princes meet, they give precedence to each other and compete in taking a low profile. This is the refined form of the rites. If they give numerous presents to each other, all compete in accepting fewer gifts for themselves. This is the essence of their conduct. Rites create refinement at the outset of the meetings, and proper conduct creates this essence[4] afterwards—this is the raison d'être of long-lasting good relations.' Furthermore, I have heard that a man of noble character does not squander pleasures given to him by others, and does not overexploit the loyalty that others grant him.[5] Therefore, I did not accept."

Yanzi returned and reported to the Duke. The Duke laughed joyfully: "Is such a person the ruler of Lu?"

Yanzi said: "I have heard that great states are greedy for fame, while small states are greedy for practical possessions. Such are the common concerns of the regional princes. Now, Lu occupies a low stature yet is

433

---

1 *She* 社, an altar area, consisted of a six-*li* 里 square.

2 "Mt. Tai," following *JS*, 335/1 (盖泰山之阴也).

3 The *JS*, 335/2, suggests that Zishu Zhaobo 子叔昭伯 is Zifu Zhaobo 子服昭伯 who appears in *Zuozhuan*, B10.16.4/365/15.

4 章 → 实 (*JS*, 336/5).

5 An identical statement appears in the *Liji*, 1.32/5/8.

**【原文】**

得，道义不为苟合，不尽人之欢，不竭人之忠，以全其交，君之道义，殊于世俗，国免于公患。"公曰："寡人说鲁君，故予之地，今行果若此，吾将使人贺之。"晏子曰："不！君以欢予之地，而贺其辞，则交不亲，而地不为德矣。"公曰："善。"于是重鲁之币，毋比诸侯，厚其礼，毋比宾客。君子于鲁，而后明行廉辞地之可为重名也。

**【今译】**

遵从道义不附和他国，不将他人好意全部接受，不竭尽他人的忠诚，来保全双方的交往，这是君子交往的方式，与世俗的交往完全不同，才使鲁国免除诸侯共有的祸患。"景公说："我欣赏鲁国的国君，所以赠予他土地，现在他的做法果然是这样，我要派人去赞许他。"晏子说："不行！国君您因为自己的喜好而赠予他土地，而又赞许他能够辞让土地，那样两国的交往就不亲密，赠予他土地也就不彰显德行了。"景公说："好的。"于是增加给鲁国的钱币，使其数量超过其他诸侯的标准，提高对待鲁国的礼仪标准，使其高于其他宾客。在鲁国的君子，在这之后才明白行为端正辞让土地可以提高国家的名望了。

not covetous of honor. It renounces practical possessions and strives for nothing more. Its conduct is honest and it does not act wantonly for gain. It takes on the way of righteousness and does not form wanton unions. It does not squander pleasures given by others, and does not overexploit the loyalty that others grant, and thereby preserves its relationships intact. Since its ruler is led by the way of righteousness — which is different from the prevailing customs of our world — his state was also spared all those common worries."

The Duke said: "I was pleased with the ruler of Lu, and therefore I granted him some of my land. Since the outcome of my actions is such, I will now send him a messenger with presents."

Yanzi said: "Do not! My Lord, by joyfully conceding land to him and then rewarding his rejection of it, you indicate that the relationship between the two of you is not very close, and that the land transfer did not take place for virtuous reasons."

The Duke said: "Well argued." Thereupon, Lu was given a quantity of monetary tributes disproportionate to that given the other regional princes, and people from Lu were treated to lavish rites — more so than all other guests.

If a man of noble character considers this example of Lu, he will ultimately realize how the practice of honesty and the rejection of land can yield great fame.

# 5.19 [129] 景公游纪得金〔壶〕中书晏子因以讽之

景公到纪游玩，获得金壶中的纸张，晏子通过这件事来劝谏

**【原文】**

〔景〕公游于纪，得金〔壶〕，发（其）〔而〕视之，中有丹书，曰："食鱼无反，勿乘驽马。"公曰："善哉！知若言，食鱼无反，则恶其鲋鱶也；勿乘驽马，恶其（耻）〔取〕道不远也。"晏子对曰："不然。食鱼无反，毋尽民力乎！勿乘驽马，则无置不肖于侧乎！"公曰："纪有书，何以亡也？"晏子对曰："有以亡也。婴闻之，君子有道，悬之闾。纪有此言，注之〔壶〕，不亡何待乎！"

**【今译】**

景公到纪游玩，获得了一个金壶，就打开来看，里面有一张用朱砂书写的纸张，写着："吃鱼的时候不要翻过来，不要乘坐劣等的马。"景公说："说的对啊！我知道他的意思，吃鱼的时候不翻过来，是嫌弃鱼腥味；不乘坐劣等马，是嫌弃它走不了多远。"晏子回答说："不是这样。吃鱼的时候不翻过来，是说不要穷尽民力；不乘坐劣等马，是说不要将没有能力的人放在身边。"景公说："纪国有这样的认识，为什么还灭亡了呢？"晏子回答说："亡国是有原因的。我听说，君子掌握了道理，会把它悬挂在乡里的大门之上。纪国有这样的认识，却放在金壶中，不灭亡还能怎么样呢？"

## 5.19 [129] DUKE JING WENT ON A PLEASURE EXCURSION TO THE AREA OF WHAT HAD ONCE BEEN THE STATE OF JI[1] AND RECEIVED AN INSCRIBED GOLDEN WINE POT. YANZI USED THE INSCRIPTION TO ADMONISH THE DUKE.

Duke Jing went on a pleasure excursion to the area of what had once been the state of Ji and received a golden wine pot. When he opened and examined it, he discovered a red inscription within it, which said: "Do not turn over a fish while eating it; do not ride a nag."

The Duke said: "Excellent! I know what it means: one does not turn over a fish while eating it because one will be disgusted by its stench,[2] and one does not ride a nag because one will be upset about not getting far along on the road."

Yanzi said: "Not so. 'Do not turn a fish over while eating it' means that you should not exhaust the strength of the people; 'Do not ride a nag' means that you should not place the unworthy at your side — is it not so?"

The Duke said: "How Ji could have fallen into ruin if such inscriptions existed there?"

Yanzi answered: "Even with such inscriptions, one can be ruined. I have heard that if a man of noble character adheres to the Way, he emblazons it over the main gate of his neighborhood. Yet in Ji, these words were recorded inside a wine pot — surely the wait for its ruin had not been not long."

437

---

1    In 689 BCE Qi conquered Ji 纪, a small vassal state of Lu.

2    The overturned part of a cooked fish, whose upper, spicy half has already been eaten, will be without spice and therefore will give off unpleasant odors.

## 5.20 [130] 景公贤鲁昭公去国而自悔晏子谓无及已

景公称赞鲁昭公逃离国家后悔改，晏子说已经来不及了

【原文】

　　鲁昭公（弃）〔失〕国走齐，（齐）〔景〕公问焉，曰："君何年之少，而弃国之蚤？奚道至于此乎？"昭公对曰："吾少之时，人多爱我者，吾体不能亲；人多谏我者，吾志不能用〔也〕；是（则）〔以〕内无拂而外无辅〔也〕，辅拂无一人，（谄）〔谄〕谀我者甚众。譬之犹秋蓬也，孤其根而美枝叶，秋风一至，根且拔矣。"景公辩其言，以语晏子，曰："使是人反其国，岂不为古之贤君乎？"晏子对曰："不然。夫愚者多悔，不肖者自贤，溺者不问（队）〔坠〕，迷者不问路。溺而后问坠，迷而后问路，譬之犹临难而遽铸兵，噎而遽掘井，虽速亦无及已。"

【今译】

　　鲁昭公失去王位逃到齐国，齐国国君问他说："您这么年轻，为什么这么早就丢失了王位呢？怎么到了这种地步呢？"鲁昭公回答说："我年轻的时候，敬爱我的人很多，我自己不能亲近他们；劝谏我的人也很多，我内心不能接受；因此公室内部没有辅佐外部没有依靠，没有一个人能够辅佐帮助我，阿谀奉承的人特别多。这就好比是秋天的飞蓬一样，它的根茎孤弱而枝叶华茂，秋风吹过来的时候，根就直接被拔起了。"景公分析他的话，并告诉晏子，说："假如让他返回鲁国，难道不能成为古代贤明的君主吗？"晏子回答说："并不能。愚笨的人会经常后悔，没有才能的人觉得自己贤能，溺水的人不去问如何坠入水中，迷路的人不去问路应该怎么走。溺水之后再问如何坠入水中，迷路之后再问路该怎么走，就好比是战争已经到来才紧急铸造武器，吃饭噎住了才赶紧挖井，即使速度很快也赶不上了。"

## 5.20 [130] DUKE JING THOUGHT DUKE ZHAO OF LU, WHO FLED FROM HIS COUNTRY AND HAD REGRETS, WAS A WORTHY RULER. YANZI SAID THESE REGRETS CAME TOO LATE.

Duke Zhao of Lu[1] lost rule of his state and fled to Qi. Duke Jing asked him: "How did a young ruler like yourself abandon his state at such an early stage — what path led you to this?"

Duke Zhao replied: "Many people loved me when I was young, but I could not be close to them on a personal level. Many others remonstrated against me, but I was too ambitious to employ them. Therefore, I had neither straight-speaking advisors within the palace, nor assistance outside the palace — not a single person advised and assisted me in my rule. Numerous people began flattering and slandering me. My fate is comparable to the autumn tumbleweed — beautiful branches and leaves hang off its single root; yet if brushed by the autumn wind, it can easily be uprooted."

Duke Jing analyzed Duke Zhao's words and discussed them with Yanzi, saying: "If I enable this man to return to his state, will he not then become like one of the wise rulers of ancient times?"

Yanzi answered: "Not so. Fools are full of self-regret; the unworthy consider themselves worthy. The drowned do not ask where to fall into the water; the lost do not inquire about the right path. Those who inquire about where to fall into the water after drowning and those who inquire about the right path after being lost are like those who start forging weapons when on the verge of a great calamity or start digging a well while already choking. No matter how much they hurry, in none of these cases will they finish on time."

439

---

1   Duke Zhao of Lu 魯昭公 (541–510 BCE) is the infamously weak ruler of Lu who was driven to exile in 517 BCE and subsequently died there.

## 5.21 [131] 景公使鲁（布）〔有〕事已 仲尼以为知礼

景公让晏子出使鲁国，朝见结束后，仲尼认为他懂得礼节

【原文】

晏子使鲁，仲尼命门（子弟）〔弟子〕往观。子贡反，报曰："孰谓晏子（子）习于礼乎？夫礼曰：'登阶不历，堂上不趋，授玉不跪。'今晏子皆反此，〔孰〕谓晏子习于礼者？"晏子既已有事于鲁君，退见仲尼，仲尼曰："夫礼，登阶不历，堂上不趋，授玉不跪。夫子反此乎？"晏子曰："婴闻两楹之闲，君臣有位焉，君行其一，臣行其二。君之来

【今译】

晏子出使鲁国，孔子命令门内的弟子前往观看。子贡回来后，报告老师说："谁说晏子精通礼仪？周礼规定：'登台阶的时候不能越级，在朝堂上不能快步走，授给玉器不能下跪。'今天晏子的做法都违犯了规定，谁说晏子精通礼仪呢？"晏子朝见鲁国国君的事情已经结束，来拜见孔子，孔子说："根据周礼规定，登台阶的时候不能越级，在朝堂上不能快步走，授给玉器不能下跪。您今天违反了礼仪吗？"晏子说："我听说在宫殿的两堂之间，君臣各有自己的位置，国君走一步，臣子要走两步。国君走来的速度太快了，所以我越级登上台阶快步走

## 5.21 [131] DUKE JING SENT YANZI ON A DIPLOMATIC MISSION TO LU. WHEN THE MISSION WAS COMPLETED, CONFUCIUS THOUGHT YANZI UNDERSTOOD THE RITES.[1]

When Yanzi was sent on a diplomatic mission to Lu, Confucius instructed his disciples to go and observe him. Zigong[2] returned and reported: "Who says that Yanzi is well-versed in the rites? It is said in the rites: 'One should not skip any stairs while climbing to the audience hall; one should not walk hastily while in the hall; one should not kneel while handing over the Jade Emblem.'[3] But now, Yanzi has acted contrary to all these tenets; who says that Yanzi is a person versed in the rites?"

After Yanzi had completed his mission with the ruler of Lu, he withdrew and had an audience with Confucius, who said: "According to the rites, one should not skip any stairs while climbing the audience hall; one should not walk hastily while in the hall; one should not kneel while handing over the Jade Emblem. Have you acted contrary to all these?"

Yanzi said: "I have heard that a ruler and ministers take their place in the audience hall between two pillars. When the ruler takes one step, the minister takes two. The ruler of Lu walked rapidly, so I had to skip some stairs while climbing to the audience hall; in the hall I had to hurry to reach my place in time, and since he leaned over when I handed the jade over to him, I had to kneel down in order to be lower than him. Furthermore, I have heard that in important matters one may not overstep bounds, but in unimportant matters one may do more or less."[4]

441

---

1    Item 5.21 [131] ↔ *Hanshi waichuan*, 4.12/28/26.

2    Zigong 子贡, one of the prominent disciples of Confucius.

3    *Liji*,1.18/3/1.

4    This line echoes a nearly identical statement about "overstepping bounds" as the one rendered in the *Analects*, 19.11/54/30 as, 大德不踰闲, 小德出入可也.

**【原文】**

（邀）〔速〕，是以登阶历、堂上趋以及位也。君授玉卑，故跪以下之。且吾闻之，大者不踰闲，小者出入可也。"晏子出，仲尼送之以宾客之礼，〔反〕，〔命门弟子曰〕："不法之义，维晏子为能行之。"

**【今译】**

到自己的位置上。国君授予玉器的时候弯腰下倾，所以我跪下接受。况且我听说，在礼仪中大的方面不能超过范围，小的地方可以有所改变。"晏子离开时，孔子用主人对待客人的礼仪送别他，回来告诉自己的弟子说："不遵从礼法的规定却合乎礼仪，只有晏子能做到。"

When Yanzi left, Confucius sent him off in accordance with the proper rites for a guest. Then he returned and proclaimed to his disciples: "None but Yanzi who is able to perform unconventional rites."[1]

443

---

1   不计之义 → 不法之礼 (*YZCQ-ICS*, 46, n. 4).

## 5.22 [132] 晏子之鲁进食有豚亡二肩不求其人

晏子来到鲁国，吃饭的时候食物中小猪的两条腿丢失了，晏子不去找偷盗的人

**【原文】**

晏子之鲁，朝食进馈膳，有豚焉。晏子曰："去其二肩。"昼者进膳，则豚肩不具。侍者曰："膳豚肩亡。"晏子曰："释之矣。"侍者曰："我能得其人。"晏子曰："止。吾闻之，量功而不量力，则民尽；藏余不分，则民盗。子教我所以改之，无教我求其人也。"

**【今译】**

晏子来到鲁国，早饭送来的食物，有一只小猪。晏子说："把小猪的两条腿收起来。"午饭送来食物时，已经没有小猪的腿了。侍奉的人说："午饭中小猪的腿找不到了。"晏子说："没有就算了吧。"侍奉的人说："我能找到偷猪腿的人。"晏子说："不用了。我听说，只考虑功绩却不考虑民众的力量，那么民力将被耗尽；把剩余的东西全部积攒起来而不分给别人，那么民众就会偷盗。您应该教导我如何改正自己的过失，不应该教我找到那个偷盗的人。"

## 5.22 [132] YANZI WENT TO LU AND WAS SERVED WITH A SUCKLING PIG WHOSE TWO LEGS WERE MISSING. YANZI DID NOT LOOK FOR THE PERSON WHO STOLE THEM.

When Yanzi went to Lu, he was offered a suckling pig as one of the breakfast dishes. Yanzi said: "Set aside these two front legs for me." At noon, when food was served, the pig's front legs were missing. The servant said: "The legs of the suckling pig are gone."

Yanzi said: "Let it go."

The servant said: "I can catch the person who took them."

Yanzi said: "No! I have heard that if one merely accounts for achievements and pays no heed to efforts, then the people's strength will be exhausted. If the surplus is hidden away without sharing it, the people will steal it. You should have instructed me to change my attitude and not instructed to look for that person."

445

## 5.23 [133] 曾子将行晏子送之而赠以善言

曾子将要离开，晏子送别他并赠予有意义的话

### 【原文】

曾子将行，晏子送之曰："〔婴闻之〕，君子赠人以轩，不若以言。（吾）〔婴〕请以言之，以轩乎？"曾子曰："请以言。"晏子曰："今夫车轮，山之直木也，良匠揉之，其圆中规，虽有槁暴，不复嬴矣，故君子慎隐揉。和氏之璧，井里之困也，良工修之，则为存国之宝，故君子慎所修。今夫兰本，三年而成，湛之苦酒，则君子不近，庶人不佩；

### 【今译】

曾子马上要离开了，晏子送别他的时候说："君子认为送别的时候赠予财物，还不如赠予有意义的话。我想要知道你是希望我赠予有意义的话呢，还是赠予财物？"曾子说："希望你赠予有意义的话。"晏子说："马车的车轮，原本来自山中挺直的木材，技艺高超的工匠将其弯曲制成。它的圆形非常标准，即使风吹日晒，也不再会变直了，所以君子一定要对外界的影响保持慎重。和氏的璧玉，原本只是埋没在民间，技艺高超的工匠修琢了它，就变成了传国的宝物，所以君子一定要重视外界对自己的雕琢。现在的兰本，三年才长成，泡在苦酒中的话，那么君子就不会接近它，普通的民众也不会佩戴它；泡在碎肉

# 5.23 [133] WHEN ZENGZI WAS ABOUT TO TRAVEL, YANZI SENT HIM OFF AND GAVE HIM THE GIFT OF GOOD WORDS.[1]

When Zengzi was about to travel,[2] Yanzi sent him off and said: "I have heard that for a man of noble character to give the gift of words to others is better than giving the gift of material objects.[3] Would you wish me to give you the gift of words or the gift of a material object?"

Zengzi said: "Please, the gift of words."

Yanzi said: "Now, a chariot wheel began as an upright tree trunk on a mountain; when a master carpenter bends it,[4] its roundness coincides with a circle drawn by pair of compasses. Yet even if it dried out completely in the sun, it will not return to its original straightness.[5] Therefore, a man of noble character is extremely cautious with a press-frame. The jade-disk of Mr. He[6] was initially considered a stone that served as a marker of the village; however, after an accomplished craftsman polished it, it became a treasure maintained in the state. Therefore, a man of noble character is extremely cautious with polishing. Now, it takes three years for the root of an orchid to grow fully, but if one steeps the orchid in bitter wine, a man

447

---

1   Item 5.23 [133] ↔ *Shuoyuan*, 17.35/147/15; *Xunzi*, 27/134/1; *Kongzi jiayu* 15.16/31/4.

2   According to the parallel passage in the *Kongzi jiayu* 15.16/31/4, Zengzi arrived in Qi with Confucius and Duke Jing offered to appoint him as Junior Minister. However, he rejected the offer and left.

3   轩 → 财 according to the parallel passages in the *Shuoyuan* and *Kongzi jiayu*.

4   揉 → 煣 (*YZCQ-ICS*, 47, n. 3). Cf. *Xunzi*, 1/1/4.

5   赢 → 挺 (*YZCQ-ICS*, 47, n. 4).

6   The "Jade-disk of Mr. He" is a famous story that appears in many pre-Han sources concerning the suffering of Mr. He, who presented his uncut jade-disk to two kings and each time was accused of fraud and was subjected to amputation. Ultimately, however, his uncut jade-disk was recognized as an invaluable one. See *Han Feizi*, 13/23/6.

**【原文】**

湛之（縻）〔麋〕醢，而贾匹马矣。非兰本美也，所湛然也。愿子之必求所湛。婴闻之，君子居必择（居）〔乡〕，游必就士，择居所以求士，求士所以辟患也。婴闻〔之〕汩常移质，习俗移性，不可不慎也。"

**【今译】**

酱中，那么就能交换一匹马了。这并不是因为兰本本身的品质，是因为浸泡它的东西决定的。希望您一定要找好浸泡的东西。我听说，君子居住的时候一定要选好邻居，交游的时候一定要选择贤能的士人，选择邻居就是为了找到贤能的士人，找寻贤能的士人就是为了避免灾祸。我听说在混浊的空气中会使人变质，一个地方的习俗能改变人的性情，您一定要慎重啊！"

of noble character will not approach it, and a commoner will not wear it on his belt. Yet, if one steeps it in a minced deer paste, one can sell it for the price of a horse. Its value does not depend upon the beauty of the root of the orchid, but on what it is steeped in. I hope that you, Sir, carefully seek to know that into which you will be steeped. I have heard that a man of noble character must choose his place of residence according to the character of the neighborhood and must keep company with officers when travelling. Selecting the right place of residence is the basis for seeking out officers, and seeking out officers is the key to avoiding troubles. I have heard that immersion in habitual behavior alters one's substance, and that habituation to custom alters one's inborn nature — one must indeed be cautious."

449

## 5.24 [134] 晏子之晋睹齐累越石父解左骖赎之与归

晏子来到晋国，见到齐国劳累的越石父，解开左边的马匹将他赎回，与他一起回到齐国

### 【原文】

晏子之晋，至中牟，睹敝冠反裘负刍，息于涂侧者，以为君子也，使人问焉曰："子何为者也？"对曰："我越石父者也。"晏子曰："何为至此？"曰："吾为人臣仆于中牟，见使将归。"晏子曰："何为之仆？"对曰："不免（涷）〔冻〕饿之切吾身，是以为仆也。"晏子曰："为仆几何？"对曰："三年矣。"晏子曰："可得赎乎？"对曰："可。"

### 【今译】

晏子到晋国去，路上经过中牟，看到一个戴着破帽子，反穿皮衣背着牧草的人在道路旁边休息，认为他是一个君子，就派人过去问他说："先生是什么人呢？"回答说："我是越石父。"晏子说："怎么变成这个样子了？"越石父回答说："我是别人的家臣，在中牟做仆从，见到齐国的使者想要回去。"晏子说："怎么沦落到给别人当仆从了呢？"越石父回答说："为了免除寒冷饥饿的痛苦，所以当了别人的仆从。"晏子说："给人当仆从有多久了？"越石父回答说："已经三年了。"晏子说："我能为你赎身吗？"越石父回答说："可以。"于是晏子解开自己马车左边的马赠给越石父赎身，然后载着他一齐回到齐国。等到了晏子的住所，晏子没有告辞就进去了，越石父非常生气要与晏子绝交，晏子派人回答他说："我并没有与您交朋友，您为别人做仆人三年，我只是今天看到您而为您赎身而已，我对您还不够可以吗？您为什么这么急躁地要和我绝交呢？"越石父回答说："我听说，士人在没有碰到懂得自己的人时会隐藏自己，碰到懂得自己的人的时候才展示出来，所以君子不会因为自己的功劳而看轻别人，也不会因为别人的功劳而

# 5.24 [134] WHEN YANZI WENT TO JIN HE SAW YUE SHIFU, A CAPTIVE FROM QI. YANZI UNTIED HIS LEFT HORSE FROM THE CARRIAGE, REDEEMED THE CAPTIVE AND RODE BACK TOGETHER WITH HIM. [1]

When Yanzi went to Jin and reached Zhongmou,[2] he saw a man with a worn-out hat dressed in a fur coat that was turned inside out, carrying fodder on his back, resting at the roadside. Yanzi, recognizing him to be a man of noble character, sent someone to ask him: "Who are you?" The man replied: "I am Yue Shifu."

Yanzi said: "How did you arrive here?"

Yue Shifu replied: "I am a servant of some ministers in Zhongmou. I was sent on errands and I am about to return."

Yanzi said: "How did you become a servant?"

Yue Shifu replied: "I could not evade the effects of freezing and starving on my body, and therefore become a servant."

Yanzi said: "How long have you been a servant?"

Yue Shifu replied: "Three years."

Yanzi said: "Can you be redeemed?"

Yue Shifu replied: "Yes."

Yanzi then untied the left horse from his carriage and used it to redeem[3] Yue Shifu and then rode together with him back to Qi. When they arrived at Yanzi's house, Yanzi entered without taking his leave. Yue Shifu became very angry and wanted to break off the relationship.

Yanzi sent someone to respond on his behalf: "I have not yet established any formal relations with you, Master. You, Master, have been a servant for three years; today I saw you and redeemed you – is my behavior

---

1   Item 5.24 [134] ↔ *Lüshi chunqiu*, 16.2/91/19; *Shiji*, 2134; *Xinxu* 新序, 7.17/39.10.

2   Zhongmou was situated in present-day Tangyin 汤阴 County, in northeast Henan.

3   赠 → 赎 (*YZCQ-ICS*, 74, n. 9).

**【原文】**

遂解左骖以赠之，因载而与之俱归。至舍，不辞而入，越石父怒而请绝，晏子使人应之曰："吾未尝得交夫子也，子为仆三年，吾乃今日睹而赎之，吾于子尚未可乎？子何绝我之暴也？"越石父对之曰："臣闻之，士者诎乎不（知己）〔己知〕〔者〕，而申乎知己〔者〕，故君子不以功轻人之身，不为彼功诎身之理。吾三年为人臣仆，而莫吾知也。今子赎我，吾以子为知我矣；向者子乘，不我辞也，吾以子为忘；今又不辞而入，是与臣我者同矣。我犹且为臣，请鬻于世。"晏子出，见之曰："向者见客之容，而今也见客之意。婴闻之，省行者不引其过，察实者不讥其辞，婴可以辞而无弃乎？婴诚革之。"乃令粪洒改席，尊醮而礼之。越石父曰："吾闻之，至恭不修途，尊礼不受摈。夫子礼之，仆不敢当也。"晏子遂以为上客。君子曰："俗人之有功则德，德则骄。〔今〕晏子有功，免人于厄，而反诎下之，其去俗亦远矣。此全功之道也。"

**【今译】**

委屈自己。我为别人当了三年仆从，他也没有了解我。今天您为我赎身，我以为您是懂得我的人；刚才您乘坐马车的时候，并没有与我说话，我以为您是忘记了；现在您又不告别就进入家门，是和以我为仆从的人一样了。我仍然是仆从，请您把我卖出去吧。"晏子走出来，接见他说："刚才只是见到了你的面容，现在又认知了你的心意。我听说，反省自己行为的人不会再引述他的过错，观察实质的人不会讥讽他人的言辞，我能因为言辞而被不您抛弃吗？我请求改变自己的言行。"于是下令洒扫门庭更设筵席，置酒以礼节来对待他。越石父说："我听说，最恭敬的礼节不需要修整道路，最尊重的礼节不需要亲自接引宾客。您以礼节对待我，我不敢接受。"晏子于是将他当做最高规格的客人。君子评论说："世俗的人一旦有了功劳就会觉得自己有德行，然后就变得骄傲。晏子有功于越石父，让他免于困厄，却反而委屈自己居于他人之下，他的品行与世俗之人相差太多了。这才是获得成功的方法。"

toward you not acceptable to you? Why do you break with me so abruptly?"

Yue Shifu replied: "I have heard that an officer will accept submission from people who do not see him for what he is, but will stand tall against those who do. Therefore, a man of noble character does not belittle others because of his own accomplishments, and does not bend his own principles because of others' accomplishments. I have been a servant to some ministers for three years, and no one appreciated me. Now you have redeemed me, and I assumed that you, Master, saw me for what I was. Previously, when you mounted the carriage, you did not show polite deference to me and I thought that you forgot, but now you entered your house without taking your leave. You are just like those who took me for a servant and, as I am nothing but a servant, I ask to be put up for sale in public."

Yanzi came out to meet Yue Shifu and said: "Previously, I had seen the face of my guest but now I see his mind. I have heard that if one examines one's conduct critically, someone else should not point out his faults; if one has observed the truth, someone else should not mock his words. May I apologize and not be rejected? I would sincerely like to change all this."

Then he ordered the floor swept and the mats changed. He had a banquet prepared in Yue Shifu's honor and treated him according to the rites.

Yue Shifu said: "I have heard: the highest respect does not consist of repairing roads, and honor accorded by the rites is not bestowed by a formal reception. You, master, grant me all these rites; I dare say that I am too unworthy to accept." Yanzi then treated Yue Shifu as an honored guest.

The man of noble character said: "If a commoner accomplishes something, he turns conceited over his virtue and then becomes arrogant. Now Yanzi has an accomplishment: he saved a man from adversity. Yet despite this, he humbled himself before the man. He went far beyond the common practice. This is the way to keep one's accomplishments intact."

453

## 5.25 [135] 晏子之御感妻言而自抑损晏子荐以〔为〕大夫

晏子的马夫因为妻子的话而变得谦逊，晏子推荐他担任大夫

【原文】

子为齐相，出，其御之妻从门间而窥〔其夫〕，其夫为相御，拥大盖，策驷马，意气扬扬，甚自得也。既而归，其妻请去。夫问其故，妻曰："晏子身不满六尺，身相齐国，名显诸侯。今者妾观其出，志念深矣，常有以自下者。今子长八尺，乃为人仆御；然子之意，自以为足，妾是以求去也。"其后，夫自抑损。晏子怪而问之，御以实对，晏子荐以为大夫。

【今译】

晏子担任齐国相国，出门的时候，车夫的妻子从门缝中窥探，她的丈夫担任相国的车夫，车上树立着华丽巨大的伞盖，鞭打着四匹拉车的马，神采飞扬，非常得意。回来以后，他的妻子请求让他不再担任车夫。车夫问她原因，他的妻子说："晏子的身高还不到六尺，却担任齐国的相国，在诸侯中名声显赫。现在我看他出行的时候，自己的志向被隐藏的很深，常常降低自己的身份，甘心居于别人之下。而你身高八尺，才仅仅担任别人的车夫，但看你的神态，自以为满足了，所以我请求你离开。"从那以后，车夫压抑自己谦逊做人。晏子感觉很奇怪就询问他，车夫就将实情告诉晏子，晏子就推荐他担任大夫。

# 5.25 [135] YANZI'S CHARIOTEER WAS MOVED BY HIS WIFE'S WORDS AND HUMBLED HIMSELF. YANZI RECOMMENDED HIM AS A HIGH OFFICER.[1]

Once, when Yanzi served as prime minister in Qi, he set out for a ride. The wife of his charioteer peeked at her husband through a crack in the door and saw how he served as charioteer to the prime minister. He was screened by a large canopy, whipping a team of four horses, displaying a pompous and self-satisfied manner. After he had returned home, his wife asked to leave him. When he asked for her reasons, she answered him: "Yanzi is not even six feet tall,[2] and yet he functions as the prime minister of Qi and his name is renowned among all the regional princes. But today, while watching him set out for a ride, I saw that he was immersed in deep thoughts and all the while he had a diffident manner. Now you are eight feet tall; you serve others as a charioteer and yet your manner suggests that you are self-satisfied. This is why I ask to leave you." From that point on, the man behaved most humbly. Yanzi was surprised at the change and asked him about it, and the charioteer answered him truthfully. Thereupon, Yanzi recommended him as a high officer.

455

---

1   Item 5.25 [135] ↔ *Shiji*, 2135.

2   Since the ancient Chinese foot, *chi* 尺, is said to be about 23 centimeters, according to the present text Yanzi's height would be less than 138 centimeters and his eight-foot charioteer would be 184 centimeters. According to Item 7.1 [171], Yanzi's height was no more than five *chi* (115 centimeters).

## 5.26 [136] 泯子午见晏子晏子恨不尽其意

泯子午拜见晏子，晏子遗憾没有让他尽情表达

【原文】

燕之游士，有泯子午者，南见晏子于齐，言有文章，术有条理，巨可以补国，细可以益晏子者，三百篇。睹晏子，恐慎而不能言。晏子假之以悲色，开之以礼颜，然后能尽其复也。客退，晏子直席而坐，废朝移时。在侧者曰："向者燕客侍，夫子胡为忧也？"晏子曰："燕，万乘之国也，齐，千里之涂也。泯子午以万乘之国为不足说，以千里之涂为不足远，则是千万人之上也。且犹不能殚其言于我，况乎齐人之怀善而死者乎？吾所以不得睹者，岂不多哉？然吾失此，何之有也？"

【今译】

燕国有一位游士，叫作泯子午的，向南来到齐国求见晏子，他的言辞很有文采，理论很有条理，大的方面有益于国家治理，小的方面有益于晏子的，有三百篇文章。但泯子午见到晏子时，因为害怕导致说不出话来。晏子做出和颜悦色的表情，彬彬有礼地开导他，然后才能正常地交流回答。客人离开后，晏子端正地坐了很久，一直没有处理公务。在他旁边的人说："刚才陪伴燕国的客人，您在担忧什么呢？"晏子说："燕国，是拥有万辆战车的大国；到齐国，路途有千里之远。泯子午认为拥有万辆战车的大国不足以游说，认为千里的路途不算遥远，那么他已经超越千万人了。但是仍然不能把想说的话都告诉我，更何况齐国那些胸怀善言而死去的人呢？我没有见到的贤能的人，难道不是有很多吗？然而我失去了这些人，还能拥有什么呢？"

# 5.26 [136] MIN ZIWU¹ MET YANZI, WHO REGRETTED THE FACT THAT MIN ZIWU HAD NOT EXPRESSED HIS THOUGHTS IN FULL.

Min Ziwu, one of the itinerant persuaders in Yan, traveled southward and met Yanzi in Qi. Min Ziwu's words showed great polish; his strategic thinking was well articulated; and his three hundred essays were of potential value on the broadest scale to the state, and on a small scale they were sufficient to benefit Yanzi. When he saw Yanzi, he became frightened and speechless. Yanzi turned to him with a sympathetic countenance and drew him out with a polite bearing, and only afterwards was the guest able to respond to Yanzi in full.

After the guest had withdrawn, Yanzi straightened his mat and sat down, ailing to attend to his court duties for a short time. Someone at his side said to him: "Why have you become depressed, Master, since the guest from Yan was in attendance upon you?"

Yanzi replied: "Yan is a state of ten-thousand chariots, and the distance from there to Qi is a thousand *li*. If it did not suit Min Ziwu to advocate his theories in a state of ten-thousand chariots, and if a distance of a thousand *li* did not dissuade him, then he is superior to the multitudes. Still, it seems that he was not able to fully express himself in front of me. How much more so is the case with the people of Qi who embraced good thoughts and perished? Isn't it because they were so many that I did not get to see them? What merit remains for me² if I have failed in that respect?"

---

1   An unidentified figure.

2   何之有也 → 何功之有也 (*JS*, 361/6).

## 5.27 [137] 晏子乞北郭骚米以养母骚杀身以明晏子之贤

　　晏子赠予北郭骚粮食来养活他的母亲，北郭骚自杀来显示晏子的贤能

### 【原文】

　　齐有北郭骚者，结（果）〔罜〕网，（捆）〔梱〕蒲苇，织履以养其母，犹不足，踵门见晏子曰："窃说先生之义，愿乞所以（養）〔养〕母者。"晏子使人分仓粟府金而遗之，辞金〔而〕受粟。有间，晏子见疑于景公，出奔，过北郭骚之门而辞。北郭骚沐浴而〔出〕见晏子曰："夫子将焉适？"晏子曰："见疑于齐君，将出奔。"北郭骚曰："夫子勉之矣！"晏子上车太息而叹曰："婴之亡岂不宜哉？亦不知士甚矣。"晏

### 【今译】

　　齐国有一个叫北郭骚的人，编织狩猎使用的网，捆绑蒲苇，织草鞋来供养他的母亲，但仍然难以满足开支，于是亲自上门拜访晏子说："我私下听说先生您非常仁义，希望能乞求一些东西来赡养我的母亲。"晏子就命令人分一些仓库里的粮食和金钱给他，北郭骚拒绝金钱而接受了粮食。不久之后，晏子被景公猜疑，决定出逃，经过北郭骚家门的时候进来辞别。北郭骚沐浴洗澡之后见晏子，说："先生您要去哪里？"晏子说："我被齐国国君所猜疑，将要出逃了。"北郭骚说："先生您要保重啊！"晏子登上马车大声叹气说："我逃亡难道不应该吗？我太不了解士人了。"晏子离开后，北郭骚叫来他的朋友告诉他说："我欣赏晏子的仁义，并且曾经乞求过他的财物来奉养我的母亲。我听说，对赡养过自己亲人的人，要帮他抵抗灾难。现在晏子被国君猜疑了，我要用自己的死去证明他的清白。"于是穿戴好衣冠，让他的朋友拿着剑，捧着竹箱跟着他，来到国君的宫廷，请求传令的官员说："晏子是天下

# 5.27 [137] BEIGUO SAO[1] BEGGED[2] YANZI FOR RICE TO SUPPORT HIS MOTHER. HE KILLED HIMSELF IN ORDER TO PUBLICIZE YANZI'S WORTHINESS[3]

A man by the name of Beiguo Sao in Qi tied nets, plaited reeds, and knitted straw sandals in order to support his mother. But as this was insufficient, he went up to the gate of Yanzi's house and said: "I, in all deference, delight in your righteousness and wish to beg you for the means to support my mother."

Yanzi commissioned someone to take a portion of stored grain and some money to give to him. The man refused the money and accepted the grain. After a while, Yanzi was suspected by Duke Jing and had to flee. He passed by the gate of the house of Beiguo Sao to bid him farewell.

Beiguo Sao cleaned himself thoroughly, stepped outside, saw Yanzi and said: "Where do you plan to go, Master?"

Yanzi said: "I am suspected by the ruler of Qi and I have to flee."

Beiguo Sao said: "Better get to it, Master."

Yanzi boarded his carriage, drew a deep sigh and said: "It is surely true to say that my demise is deserved – after all, I utterly failed to take measure of this gentleman."

Yanzi then left, and Beiguo summoned his friend and reported to him about this: "I have taken delight in the righteousness of Yanzi, and I once begged him for the means for my mother's support. I have heard that when someone supports your parents you should bear his misfortunes with your own body. At present, Yanzi is suspected and I intend to sacrifice my life in order to acquit him."

---

1   An unidentified figure.

2   晏子乞北郭骚米 → 北郭骚乞晏子米 (*JS*, 362/1).

3   Item 5.27 [137] ↔ *Lüshi chunqiu*, 12.2/59/1; *Shuoyuan*, 6.20/45/6.

**【原文】**

子行,北〔郭〕子召其友而告之曰:"吾说晏子之义,而尝乞所以(養)〔养〕母者焉。吾闻之,养(其)〔及〕亲者身伉其难。今晏子见疑,吾将以身死白之。"著衣冠,令其友操剑,奉〔笥〕而从,造于君庭,求复者曰:"晏子,天下之贤者也;今去齐国,齐〔国〕必侵矣。方见国之必侵〔也〕,不若(先)死,请以头托白晏子也。"因谓其友曰:"盛吾头于笥中,奉以(退)〔托〕。"(讬)〔退〕而自刭。其友因奉托而谓复者曰:"此北郭子为国故死,吾将为北郭子死。"又退而(又)〔自〕刭。景公闻之,大骇,乘驲而自追晏子,及之国郊,请而反之。晏子不得已而反,闻北郭子之以死白己也,太息而叹曰:"婴之亡,岂不宜哉?亦愈不知士甚矣。"

**【今译】**

有名的贤者,现在离开齐国,齐国一定会被诸侯侵略的。与其看见国家被侵略,还不如死去,请以我的头颅相托来证明晏子的清白。"于是对他的朋友说:"把我的头颅放在竹箱中,奉献给国君作为证明。"然后北郭骚退下自杀了。他的朋友因为北郭骚的嘱托对传令的官员说:"这北郭骚是为国家而死的,我要为北郭骚而死。"也退下自杀了。景公听说这件事后,非常惊讶,乘坐驿站的马车亲自追赶晏子,走到国都的郊区时追上了晏子,请求他返回国都。晏子没有办法就返回了,听说北郭骚为了证明自己的清白而死,大声叹气说:"我逃亡难道不是应该的吗?更加不了解士人了。"

Then he put on a festive garment and a cape and ordered his friend to follow him holding a sword and bearing a bamboo basket. He arrived at the Duke's court and pleaded with the attendant, saying: "Yanzi is the worthiest person of the realm. Now, if he leaves the state of Qi, Qi will certainly be invaded. It would be better to first die rather than witness the certain invasion of our state. With my head as a pledge, I request that Yanzi be acquitted." Then he said to his friend: "Place my head inside this basket and present it as a pledge."

Thereafter, he stepped back and slashed his own throat. His friend then offered the head as a pledge and said to the attendant: "This death of Master Beiguo's is for the sake of the state, and I will die for the sake Master Beiguo." Thereupon he, too, stepped back and slashed his own throat.

When Duke Jing heard of this, he was shocked. He boarded his courier carriage and personally pursued Yanzi. He caught up with him at the outskirts of the capital and asked him to return. Having no alternative, Yanzi returned.

Upon hearing that Master Beiguo died in order to acquit him, Yanzi drew a deep sigh and said: "It is surely true to say that my demise is deserved — after all, I have most utterly failed to take measure of this officer."

## 5.28 [138] 景公欲见高〔纠〕晏子辞以禄仕之臣

景公想见高纠，晏子以高纠是为俸禄而做官的人来推辞

**【原文】**

景公谓晏子曰："吾闻高〔纠〕与夫子游，寡人请见之。"晏子对曰："臣闻之，为地战者，不能成其王；为禄仕者，不能正其君。高〔纠〕与婴为兄弟久矣，未尝干婴之行，〔补婴之阙〕，特禄仕之臣也，何足以补君乎？"

**【今译】**

景公对晏子说："我听说高纠和先生您一起交游，请求能见见他。"晏子回答说："我听说，为了土地而作战的人，不能成就国君的事业；为了俸禄而做官的人，不能匡正他的国君。高纠和我做兄弟已经很久了，从来没有干预过我的行为，批评我的缺点，他只是一个保持俸禄的臣子，对国君您有什么用呢？"

## 5.28 [138] DUKE JING WANTED TO RECEIVE GAO JIU FOR AN AUDIENCE. YANZI REFUSED BECAUSE GAO JIU HELD OFFICE FOR THE SAKE OF EMOLUMENT.[1]

Duke Jing said to Yanzi: "I have heard that you are a close associate of Gao Jiu. I would like to receive him for an audience."

Yanzi replied: "I have heard: 'One who launches war for territorial gain is not capable of fulfilling his reign. One who holds office for the sake of an emolument is not capable of rectifying his ruler.' Gao Jiu and I have been sworn brothers for a long time, but he has never criticized my conduct, nor has he repaired my deficiencies. Rather, he is a subject who aspires to hold office for the sake of emolument; how could he suffice to benefit a ruler?"

---

1    Item 5.28 [138] ↔ *Shuoyuan*, 1.19/5/10.

## 5.29 [139] 高〔纠〕治晏子家不得其俗乃逐之

高纠治理晏子的家，不能按照家法治理，于是晏子驱逐了他

### 【原文】

高〔纠〕事晏子而见逐，高〔纠〕曰："臣事夫子三年，无得，而卒见逐，其说何也？"晏子曰："婴之家俗有三，而子无一焉。"〔纠〕曰："可得闻乎？"晏子曰："婴之家俗，闲处从容不谈议，则疏；出不相扬美，入不相削行，则不与；通国事无论，骄士慢知者，则不朝也。此三者，婴之家俗，今子是无一焉。故婴非特食馈之长也，是以辞。"

### 【今译】

高纠事奉晏子而被驱逐，高纠说："我为先生您做了三年的工作，没有得到任何俸禄爵位，最后还被您驱逐了，这是为什么呢？"晏子说："晏婴的家法有三条，但你一条都没有做到。"高纠说："能说给我听听吗？"晏子说："我的家法，闲暇的时候悠闲地休息而不谈论，就疏远；出去不互相宣扬美德，回来不互相要求德行，就不赞许；国家的大事不去讨论，对贤能的人态度怠慢的，就不与他交往。这三条就是晏婴的家法，现在你一条都没有做到。我并不是专门赠送食物的主人，所以将你辞退。"

# 5.29 [139] GAO JIU ADMINISTERED YANZI'S HOUSE-HOLD. HE DID NOT MAINTAIN THE CUSTOMS OF THE HOUSE. SO YANZI DISMISSED HIM. [1]

Gao Jiu served Yanzi and was dismissed.

Gao Jiu said: "I have served you, my master, three years, and I have nothing to show for it. Ultimately, I was dismissed. How can this be explained?"

Yanzi said: "There are three customs in my household, and you, Sir, possess not a single one of them."

Gao Jiu said: "May I hear about it?"

Yanzi said: "These are my household's customs: I keep my distance from those who spend their time in leisure and indolence, never engaging in critical discussions. I avoid the company of those who do not praise each other's good points publicly and do not sharply criticize each other's conduct in private. I do not summon those who fathom state affairs but avoid discussing them, who treat officers arrogantly and the wise rudely. These three are the customs of my household. Now, you sir, possess not a single one of them. Hence, since I am not the mere head of a household who provides for a livelihood, I dispense with you."

---

1    Item 5.29 [139] ↔ Item 7.23 [193]; *Shuoyuan*, 2.19/17/18.

## 5.30 [140] 晏子居丧逊畣家老仲尼善之

晏子守丧，谦逊地回应家中的管家，仲尼称赞他

【原文】

晏子居晏桓子之丧，粗衰，斩，苴绖带，杖，（管）〔菅〕屦，食粥，居倚庐，寝苫，枕草。其家老曰："非大夫丧父之礼也。"晏子曰："唯卿为大夫。"曾子以闻孔子，孔子曰："晏子可谓能远害矣。不以己之是驳人之非，逊辞以避咎，义也夫！"

【今译】

晏子的父亲晏桓子死去了，晏子为其守丧，穿着粗麻布做的丧服，麻布不缝边，腰间拴着草绳，手里拿着丧杖，脚上穿着草鞋，吃粥，居住在坟墓旁边的草屋中，睡觉的时候盖着草帘子，用野草做枕头。他的大管家说："您这样不是大夫父亲死后所服的礼仪。"晏子说："只有做卿时才是大夫。"曾子把这件事告诉了孔子，孔子说："晏子就是那种能够远离灾害的人啊！他不因为自己的正确去驳斥他人的错误，用谦逊的言辞来避免他人的责难，这是合乎道理的啊！"

## 5.30 [140] YANZI WENT THROUGH A MOURNING AND GAVE A HUMBLE REPLY TO HIS OLD STEWARD. CONFUCIUS PRAISED THIS.[1]

During the period in which Yanzi mourned over Yan Huanzi,[2] he wore unhemmed hemp sackcloth. His head-band and waist-girdle were made of the coarsest hemp, he carried a bamboo stick for a staff, and he wore straw sandals. He ate rice gruel and stayed in the mourning shed that leaned against the house, and he slept on a straw bed and on a grass pillow.[3]

His chief steward said to him: "These are not the rites for a High Officer who is mourning his father."

Yanzi said: "Only eminent ministers are considered High Officers."[4]

Zengzi asked Confucius about this.

Confucius said: "One can say that Yanzi is able to distance himself from harm. He did not use the fact that he was correct to refute the mistakes of others. With humble words, he managed to avoid error; this is an example of righteousness, is it not?"

467

---

1    Item 5.30 [140] ↔ *Zuozhuan*, B9. 19.7/262/17, *Kongcongzi*, 6.1/60/20, *Kongzi jiayu*, 43.16/881.

2    Yan Huanzi 晏桓子 was Yanzi's father.

3    Yanzi's mourning rites follow almost strictly those prescribed by the *Yili*, 11/62/9.

4    *Dafu* 大夫 "High Officer," is a designation of the second highest category of officials below *qing* 卿 "Eminent Minister." The chief steward ignorantly refers to the contemporary tradition at that time, which prescribed lenient mourning rites for the death of the father of a high officer in the state of Qi. Yanzi, who modestly shuns his identity as a high officer in order to save his chief steward the embarrassment of ignorance follows the strict rites of the three-year mourning over the death of one's father prescribed by the *Yili*, 11/62/9. These rites according to *Mencius*, 5.2/25/7, were followed by commoners and emperors alike during the time of the Three Dynasties.

# 第六卷 杂下

## 6.1 [141] 灵公禁妇人为丈夫饰不止晏子请先内勿服

灵公禁止女人穿男人的衣服，难以阻止，晏子请求王宫内先不穿

**【原文】**

灵公好妇人而丈夫饰者，国人尽服之，公使（史）〔吏〕禁之，曰："女子而男子饰者，裂其衣，断其带。"裂衣断带相望，而不止。晏子见，公问曰："寡人使（史）〔吏〕禁女子而男子饰〔者〕，裂断其衣带，相望而不止者何也？"晏子对曰："君使服之于内，而禁之于外，犹悬牛首于门，而卖马肉于（内）〔市〕也。公何以不使内勿服，则外莫敢为也。"公曰："善。"使内勿服，〔不〕逾月，而国莫之服。

**【今译】**

灵公喜欢女人穿戴男人的衣服，因此国都内的女人都穿起男装，灵公下令让官吏禁止这一行为，说："女人穿戴男人衣冠的，撕裂她的衣服，扯断她的腰带。"被撕裂衣服扯断腰带的女人随处可见，但仍然不能阻止这一行为。晏子晋见灵公时，灵公问他说："我让官吏禁止女人穿戴男人的衣冠，撕裂扯断她们的衣服腰带，被惩罚的人到处都是，为什么还是阻止不了这种行为呢？"晏子回答说："国君您让宫内的女人都穿戴男人的衣冠，却禁止宫外的女人穿戴，这就好比在门口悬挂了一个牛的头，却在店里贩卖马的肉一样。您为什么不下令宫内的女人也不穿戴男人衣冠，那么宫外的女人也就不敢穿了。"灵公说："好的。"于是下令宫内女子不得穿戴男人衣冠，过了不到一个月，国都内都没有人穿了。

# Chapter Six    Miscellany — Part B

## 6.1 [141] DUKE LING PROHIBITED WOMEN FROM WEARING MEN'S CLOTHING BUT THE FASHION DID NOT CEASE. YANZI REQUESTED THAT THE DUKE FIRST PROHIBIT THE FASHION IN HIS OWN COURT.[1]

Duke Ling was fond of seeing women wearing men's clothing, and so all the women in the capital dressed themselves in this fashion. The Duke then ordered his officials to issue a prohibition saying: "A woman wearing men's clothing shall have her robe torn at the seam, and her belt cut in two." Thereafter, the number of women with torn robes and cut belts was so great that they could be seen everywhere, yet the style did not end.

When Yanzi came for an audience, the Duke asked him: "I have ordered my officials to issue a prohibition against the style of women wearing men's clothing, and to tear and cut in two their robes and belts. How is it that the number of torn robes and cut belts is so great that are in sight of each other, yet the style has not ended?"

Yanzi replied: "You, my Lord, instigated this fashion inside your own court but you prohibit it outside. It is as if you had hung a cow's head at your gate and sold horse meat in the market. Why don't you prohibit this fashion inside your court? Then no woman would dare wear it outside."

The Duke said: "Well argued." Thereupon, he prohibited this fashion at his court, and less than a month afterwards no woman in the capital dressed herself in that style.

469

---

1    Item 6.1 [141] ↔ *Shuoyuan*, 7.43/ 56/8.

## 6.2 [142] 齐人好毂击晏子绐以不祥而禁之

齐国人喜欢撞击车轮，晏子欺骗他们会招引不祥来禁止

### 【原文】

齐人甚好毂击，相犯以为乐。禁之不止。晏子患之，乃为新车良马，出与人相犯也，曰："毂击者不祥，臣其祭祀不顺，居处不敬乎？"下车（而弃）〔弃而〕去之，然后国人乃不为。故曰："禁之以制，而身不先行，民不能止。故化其心，莫若教也。"

### 【今译】

齐国的民众非常喜欢撞车轮，经常互相冲撞并以此为乐。官府屡次禁止也难以阻止。晏子很忧虑这种情况，于是制作了一辆新车，用骏马拉着，在道路上与别人相撞，然后说："撞击车轮是不吉祥的现象，我是祭祀的时候不够虔诚，还是平时生活不够谦让呢？"下车后抛弃马车而离开，然后国都内的人就不再撞击车轮了。所以说："用法令来强行禁止，而自己不先贯彻实施，民众是不会听从的。因此要改变他们的内心，最好的方法就是教化。"

## 6.2 [142] PEOPLE IN QI WERE FOND OF SIDESWIPING EACH OTHER WITH THEIR CHARIOTS' WHEEL-HUBS. YANZI TRICKED THEM BY SAYING THAT THIS WAS INAUSPICIOUS AND THEREBY STOPPED THE PRACTICE.[1]

People in Qi were extremely fond of sideswiping each other with their chariots' wheel-hubs. They delighted in bumping each other, and the ban that was issued to prohibit this practice was of no avail in stopping it. Yanzi was troubled by this. One day, he drove out in a new chariot with thoroughbred horses, and someone bumped him. He said: "The practice of sideswiping others with wheel-hubs is inauspicious. Was my performance of sacrifices not in accordance with the proper course? Was I irreverent in conducting my private life?" He then stepped down, abandoned the chariot and walked away. Following this incident, no one in the country engaged in this practice again. Therefore, it is said: "If one prohibits something by decree, but does not begin by acting accordingly, then the people cannot be persuaded to desist. Therefore, in transforming hearts, teaching by personal example is best."

---

1    Item 6.2 [142] ↔ *Shuoyuan*, 7.44/56/14.

## 6.3 [143] 景公梦五丈夫称无辜晏子知其冤

景公梦到五个男子诉说自己的无辜，晏子知道他们的冤屈

### 【原文】

景公畋于梧丘，夜犹早，公姑坐睡，而梦有五丈夫北面韦庐，称无罪焉。公觉，召晏子而告其所梦。公曰："我其尝杀不辜，诛无罪邪？"晏子对曰："昔者先君灵公畋，五丈夫罟而骇兽，故杀之，断其头而葬之。命曰'五丈夫之丘'，此其地邪？"公令人掘而求之，则五头同穴而存焉。公曰："嘻！"令吏葬之。国人不知其梦也，曰："君悯白骨，而况于生者乎，不遗余力矣，不释余知矣。"故曰，人君之为善易矣。

### 【今译】

景公在路旁的高坡上打猎，离入夜还早，国君暂且坐着睡着了，然后梦到有五个男子面向北方围绕着他的帐篷，声称自己并没有犯罪。国君醒来后，召见晏子并告诉他梦中的情形。国君说："难道我曾经诛杀过无辜无罪的人吗？"晏子回答说："过去前代国君灵公打猎的时候，有五个男子布网而吓跑了野兽，所以把他们杀了，砍掉他们的头埋葬了，并把埋葬的地方命名为'五丈夫之丘墓'，难道就是这个地方吗？"国君命令人挖地寻找，找到埋葬在同一个墓穴中的五颗人头。景公悲叹道："唉！"下令让官吏把他们重新埋葬了。国都的民众并不知道国君做了梦，说："我们的国君连白骨都会同情，更何况活着的人呢？为了国家我们要竭尽自己的能力，穷尽自己的智慧啊。"所以说，国君做善事是很容易的。

## 6.3 [143] DUKE JING DREAMT OF FIVE STRONG MEN PROCLAIMING THEIR INNOCENCE. YANZI KNEW THAT THEY HAD BEEN SENTENCED UNJUSTLY.[1]

Duke Jing was hunting on a mound that was blocking the road.[2] Early in the night, the Duke fell asleep for a while in a sitting position and dreamt that five strong men presented themselves in his tent, facing north,[3] proclaiming their innocence. The Duke awoke, summoned Yanzi and told him the contents of his dream. The Duke said: "Have I ever executed an innocent person or punished a guiltless one?"

Yanzi replied: "In the past, when our former ruler, Duke Ling, had hunted in this area, there were five strong men who set a trap net, thus frightening the wild animals. Because of this, Duke Ling had them executed, cutting off and burying their heads. This place was called the 'Mound of the Five Men.' Might this be the same place?"

The Duke ordered his men to excavate the place and search for these heads, and the five skulls were all found still together in the same pit. The Duke exclaimed: "Alas!" and he ordered his officials to give them a proper burial. However, as no one in the country knew of his dream, they said: "If our ruler takes pity on dry bones, how much more so will he care for the living? He will spare no effort and will leave no wise counsel unused." Therefore it is said: "How easy is it for a man of noble character to be engaged in good acts."

---

1  Item 6.3 [143] ↔ *Shuoyuan*, 18.30/160/5.

2  The *Erya* 尔雅10/1/9 has 当途 ("blocking the road") for *Wuqiu* 梧丘. Later, *Wuqiu* assumed the name of the mound in which this episode took place. See Xiao Tong 萧统 (501–31), *Wenxuan* 文选, Shanghai: Shanghai guji chubanshe (1986): vol.4, p. 1791.

3  That is, they were facing his royal seat, which faced south traditionally.

## 6.4 [144] 柏常骞禳（鸟）〔枭〕死将为景公请寿晏子识其妄

柏常骞祈祷而鸟死，将要为景公祈祷增加寿命，晏子识别他的虚假

### 【原文】

景公为路寝之台，成，而不踊焉。柏常骞曰："君为台甚急，台成，君何为而不踊焉？"公曰："然，有枭昔者鸣，声无不为也，吾恶之甚，是以不踊焉。"柏常骞曰："臣请禳而去〔之〕。"公曰："何具？"对曰："筑新室，为置白茅〔焉〕。"公使为室，成，置白茅焉。柏常骞夜用事。明日，问公曰："今昔闻鸮声乎？"公曰："一鸣而不复闻。"使人往视之，

### 【今译】

景公要修建宫殿的平台，修建完成后，却不登上平台。柏常骞说："国君您要造平台的时候很着急，现在平台建造完成了，您为什么不登上去呢？"景公说："是这样的，之前有一只猫头鹰在叫，声音非常难听，我非常厌恶它，所以不想登上去。"柏常骞说："我请求为向神灵祈祷让它离开。"景公说："你需要什么东西呢？"柏常骞回答说："修建一间新的房屋，并在里面放入白色的茅草。"景公下令为他修建了房屋，建成后又放进去白色的茅草。柏常骞晚上到里面祈祷。第二天，柏常骞问景公："昨晚听到猫头鹰的叫声了吗？"景公说："叫了一声后就没再听到了。"于是派人前去察看，猫头鹰落在平台的台阶上，两个翅膀张开，趴在地上死去了。景公说："先生你的祈祷都如此灵验的话，也

# 6.4 [144] BOCHANG QIAN[1] CAST OUT AN OWL BY EXORCISM. WHEN THE OWL WAS FOUND DEAD, HE SOUGHT TO PROLONG THE LIFE OF DUKE JING. YANZI REALIZED THAT THIS WAS ABSURD.[2]

Duke Jing built a terrace over the Road Bedchamber, but had not climbed it after completion of its construction. Bochang Qian said: "You have constructed a terrace in extreme haste and now the terrace is completed – why don't you climb up it?"

The Duke said: "You are right, but last night there was a crying owl on the terrace, making all kinds of awful sounds; I was greatly revolted by it and therefore I avoided climbing up the terrace."

Bochang Qian said: "I seek permission to cast out the owl by exorcism."

The Duke said: "What implements do you need?"

Bochang Qian replied: "Build a new house and put some white reeds in it for me."

Thereupon, the Duke's men built the house and put white reeds in it upon its completion.

Bochang Qian performed his sacrifice during the night. The next day he asked the Duke: "Did you hear the cry of the owl last night?"

The Duke said: "One cry and then I heard nothing more." The Duke then ordered someone to go and look for the owl, and it was found lying dead on the ground in front of the flight of steps leading to the throne, with its wings spread out.

The Duke said: "Since you have handled this so brilliantly, can you also prolong my life?"

475

---

1 For Bochang Qian 柏常骞 or 伯常骞 see, Item 1.18 [18].

2 Item 6.4 [144] ↔ *Shuoyuan*, 18.9/152/19; *Huainanzi*, 12/119/1.

**【原文】**

鸮当陛，布翼，伏地而死。公曰："子之道若此其明〔也〕，亦能益寡人之寿乎？"对曰："能。"公曰："能益几何？"对曰："天子九，诸侯七，大夫五。"公曰："子亦有征兆之见乎？"对曰："得寿，地且动。"公喜，令百官趣具禳之所求。柏常骞出，遭晏子于涂，拜马前，辞（骞）曰："〔骞〕为（禳君）〔君禳〕鸮而杀之，君谓骞曰：'子之道若此其明也，亦能益寡人寿乎？'骞曰：'能。'今且大祭，为君请寿，故将往，以

476

**【今译】**

能为我增加寿命吗？"柏常骞回答说："可以。"景公说："能增加多少呢？"柏常骞回答说："天子可以增加九年，诸侯可以增加七年，大夫可以增加五年。"景公说："您也有成功的征兆显现吗？"柏常骞回答说："寿命增加了，大地就会震动。"景公非常高兴，传令百官赶紧准备柏常骞所需要的东西。柏常骞从王宫离开，在路上碰到了晏子，在马前拜见晏子，柏常骞说："我为了消除国君听到的猫头鹰的叫声而杀了它，国君对我说：'先生你的祈祷都如此灵验的话，也能为我增加寿命吗？'我说：'可以。'今天还要举行大祭，为国君请求增加寿命，所以想要前去告诉您。"晏子惊叹地说："是吗？如果能为国君请求增加寿命也很好啊，不过，我听说只有国家的管理和自己的德行顺应神灵的意志，才能够增加寿命，现在仅仅通过祭祀，就能够增加寿命吗？此外，你

Bochang Qian replied: "Yes I can."

The Duke said: "For how long?"

Bochang Qian replied: "Nine years for the Son of Heaven, seven for the regional princes and five for the High Officers."

The Duke said: "Is there a sign that could verify this?"

Bochang Qian replied: "Should I succeed in prolonging your life, the earth will quake."

The Duke was happy and asked all his officials to quickly provide in full whatever Bochang Qian requested.

After Bochang Qian had left, he met Yanzi on the road. Bochang Qian bowed before his horses and said to him: "For our ruler, I have cast out an owl by exorcism and killed it. Our ruler then said to me: 'Since you have handled this so brilliantly, can you also prolong my life?' I replied: 'Yes I can.' Now I am going to perform a grand sacrifice in order to seek long life for our ruler and I was about to let you hear of this."

Yanzi said: "Ah! This is indeed praiseworthy — the ability to seek a prolonged life for our ruler. Nevertheless, I have heard that only by good governance and virtue, and by deferring to the spirits, can one prolong life. Now, how then do you want to prolong life by means of a sacrifice alone? If you succeed, then is there any lucky omen we may see to verify this?"

477

Bochang Qian replied: "Should I succeed in prolonging our ruler's life, the earth will quake."

Yanzi said: "Qian, yesterday I saw that the three Wei stars[1] have declined and the Polestar has vanished. Don't you agree that this is a sign that the earth will quake?"

Bochang Qian lowered his head for a while and then he looked up and said: "Yes."

---

1   According to the *Hanshu*, 1288, the three Wei stars (维星) are the three stars positioned beyond the handle of the Big Dipper.

**【原文】**

（问）〔闻〕。"晏子曰："嘻！亦善〔矣〕。能为君请寿也。虽然，吾闻之，维以政与德而顺乎神，为可以益寿，今徒祭，可以益寿乎？然则福兆有见乎？"对曰："得寿，地将动。"晏子曰："骞，昔吾见维星绝，枢星散，地其动，汝以是乎？"柏常骞俯有间，（抑）〔仰〕而对曰："然。"晏子曰："为之无益，不为无损也。汝薄（柏）〔赋〕〔敛〕，毋费民，且先令君知之。"

**【今译】**

祈福的征兆能显现出来吗？"柏常骞回答说："如果寿命增加了，大地就会震动。"晏子说："柏常骞，晚上我看到维星消失，枢星黯淡，大地将要震动，你是以这个为征兆的吗？"柏常骞弯下腰低下头，过了一会才抬起头来回答说："是的。"晏子说："祭祀这件事做了没什么帮助，不做也没什么损害。你少征收一点税赋，不要让民众破费，而且要先让国君知道这件事。"

Yanzi said: "Taking this course of action is of no benefit; not taking this course of action carries no loss. Lighten the sacrifice-levy; do not strain the people; and, furthermore, let the Duke know of all this."[1]

---

1 The *Shuoyuan* parallel does not have 无 before 令 and reads: 且令君知之 ("and furthermore — let the Duke know of all this."). Had Bochang Qian followed this instruction, he most probably would have been executed by the Duke. This translation therefore follows the *YZCQ* version in which Yanzi manages to both expose Bochang Qian's deception and also keep him alive.

## 6.5 [145] 景公成（赋）〔柏〕寝而师开言室夕晏子辨其所以然

景公新建成柏寝，而师开说房子偏西，晏子解释偏西的原因

### 【原文】

　　景公新成柏寝之台，使师开鼓琴，师开左抚宫，右弹（商）〔商〕，曰："室夕。"公曰："何以知之？"师开对曰："东方之声薄，西方之声扬。"公召大匠曰："〔立〕室何为夕？"大匠曰："立室以宫矩为之。"于是召司空曰："立宫何为夕？"司空曰："立宫以城矩为之。"明日，

### 【今译】

　　景公新建成柏寝台，命令乐师开弹奏古琴，乐师开左手奏宫调，右手弹商调，然后说："房子偏西了。"景公说："你怎么知道的？"乐师开回答说："东方的声音轻柔，西方的声音高扬。"景公召见负责建造的工匠说："你修建的房子为什么偏西呢？"工匠说："房子是以王宫的标准来修建的。"于是景公召见司空说："修建的王宫为什么偏西呢？"司空说："王宫是依照国都的标准修建的。"第二天，晏子朝见景公，景公说："先代国君太公在分封的营丘修建都城，为什么会偏西

## 6.5 [145] WHEN DUKE JING COMPLETED CONSTRUCTION OF THE CYPRESS CHAMBER, MUSIC MASTER KAI DECLARED THAT THE HALL WAS ORIENTED TO THE WEST. YANZI CLARIFIED THE REASON FOR THIS.

Shortly after Duke Jing had the Hall of the Cypress Chamber completed, he ordered Music Master Kai[1] to strum the Qin. Music Master Kai strummed the *gong*-string note with his left hand, with his right hand he plucked the *shang*-string,[2] and then he said: "The hall is oriented to the west."[3]

The Duke said: "How do you know that?"

Music Master Kai replied: "The reverberation coming from the east side of the hall is attenuated and from the west side is intensified."

The Duke summoned the Master Builder and said: "Why did you construct the hall facing the west?"

The Master Builder replied: "In the construction of the hall, we were guided by the patterns of your palace."

The Duke thereupon summoned the Minister of Works and said: "Why did you construct the palace facing the west?"

481

---

1   Court musicians at the time were blind. Therefore, Music Master Kai could discern that the Hall of the Cypress Chamber was oriented to the west only by hearing the reverberation of the sounds, which were based on the orientation of the listening room.

2   The scale of traditional Chinese music has five notes per octave. The notes of this pentatonic scale are called *gong* 宫 ("do"), *shang* 商 ("re"), *jue* 角 ("mi"), *zhi* 徵 ("sol") and *yu* 羽 ("la").

3   The Son of Heaven and the princes of the states performed their royal duties in halls facing to the south. See *Zhouyi* 周易, 67/85/24. Hence, all royal halls should have been constructed on a north-south axis. In declaring that the hall is oriented to the west, Music Master Kai effectively said that the hall did not fulfill the necessary ritual prescription for a royal hall.

## 【原文】

（子朝晏）〔晏子朝〕公，公曰："先君太公以营丘之封立城，曷为夕？"
晏子对曰："古之立国者，南望南斗，北戴枢星，彼安有朝夕哉！然
而以今之夕者，周之建国，国之西方，以尊周也。"公蹴然曰："古之
臣乎！"

## 【今译】

呢？"晏子回答说："古代建立国都的人，南面以南斗为准，北面以枢
星为准，哪里会偏东或者偏西呢？然而现在的都城偏向西方，是周朝
建立的都城在齐国的西方，以此表示对周天子的尊重。"景公恭敬地
说："古时候的臣子才是真正的臣子啊！"

The Minister of Works replied: "In construction of the palace, we were guided by the patterns of the walled capital."

The next day, when Yanzi attended an audience with the Duke, the Duke said: "Why did our former ruler, Duke Tai,[1] with Yingqiu as a fief,[2] constructed the walled capital facing the west?"

Yanzi replied: "When the ancients constructed their capitals, they turned their eyes southwards, towards the South Dipper, while the Polestar of the North Dipper was hanging over them like a cap. How could they have any thought for East or West? Nonetheless, the present orientation of our capital to the west is due to the fact that the Zhou created their realm in the west – our capital is facing the west in honor of the Zhou."[3]

The Duke, with an air of embarrassment, said: "Oh, you are an equal to the ministers of ancient times."

---

1  Duke Tai, the first ruler of Qi, reigned between 1122 and 1078 BCE.

2·  For the events surrounding the founding of the state of Qi in Yingqiu, see, *Shiji*, 1480.

3  The first two capitals, Feng 丰 and Hao 镐, were created by the Zhou and were located in the west, near the present-day city of Xi'an.

大中华文库

## 6.6 [146] 景公病水梦与日斗晏子教占梦者以对

景公患了水肿病，梦到与太阳争斗，晏子教给占卜梦境的人如何回答

### 【原文】

景公病水，卧十数日，夜梦与二日斗〔而〕不胜。晏子朝，公曰："夕者梦与二日斗，而寡人不胜，我其死乎？"晏子对曰："请召占梦者。"出于闺，使人以车迎占梦者。至，曰："曷为见召？"晏子曰："夜者，公梦〔与〕二日（与）（公）斗，不胜。公曰：'寡人死乎？'故请君占梦，是所为也。"占梦者曰："请反（其）〔具〕书。"晏子曰："毋反书。公〔无〕所病，〔病〕者，阴也，日者，阳也。一阴不胜二阳，（故）〔公〕病将已。以是对。"占梦者入，公曰："寡人梦与二日

### 【今译】

景公患了水肿病，躺在床上十几天了，有天夜里梦到与两个太阳争斗，被打败了。晏子朝见的景公，景公说："昨天晚上梦到与两个太阳争斗，没能战胜它们，我是不是要死了？"晏子回答说："请您召见占卜梦境的人。"从殿门出去后，晏子命令人用马车迎接占卜梦境的人。占卜梦境的人来了后，问："为什么召见我呢？"晏子说："昨天晚上，国君梦到有两个太阳和他争斗，并打败了他，国君说：'我是不是要死了？'所以请您帮国君占卜梦境，这就是召见您的原因。"占卜梦境的人说："请让我看看书上的记载。"晏子说："不用看书了。国君所患的疾病，属阴，太阳，属阳。一阴不能战胜二阳，所以国君的病就快要痊愈了。你就这样回答他。"占卜梦境的人进入王宫，景公说：

# 6.6 [146] DUKE JING FELL ILL WITH DROPSY. HE DREAMED THAT HE FOUGHT WITH SUNS. YANZI INSTRUCTED THE DIVINER OF DREAMS HOW TO RESPOND.[1]

Duke Jing fell ill with dropsy and lay sick for more than ten days. He dreamed one night that he was fighting against two suns but could not defeat them. When Yanzi appeared at court for an audience, the Duke said: "Last night I fought with two suns in my dream, but I could not defeat them — am I likely to die?"

Yanzi replied: "Please summon the Diviner of Dreams." He then posted himself in front of the small gate of the palace and sent out people with carriages to escort the Diviner of Dreams in.

The Diviner of Dreams arrived and said: "Why was I summoned?"

Yanzi replied: "Last night, the Duke fought with two suns in his dream, but he could not defeat them. The Duke then asked: 'Am I likely to die?' Therefore, I have requested of our ruler that the Diviner of Dreams be summoned — this is what happened."

The Diviner of Dreams said: "Let me go back to consult my books."

Yanzi said: "You need not go back for your books. The illness of the Duke[2] is *yin*-related and these suns are *yang*-related. One *yin* cannot defeat two *yang* — the Duke's illness will cease. Use this argument when you address the Duke."

The Diviner of Dreams then entered the palace and the Duke said to him: "I have fought with two suns in my dream, but I could not defeat them. Am I likely to die?"

The Diviner of Dreams replied: "Your illness, my Lord, is *yin* and

---

1  Item 6.6 [146] ↔ *Fengsu tongyi* 风俗通义, 9.2/65/19.

2  公无所病, 病者 → 公所病者 (*JS*, 384/11).

**【原文】**

斗而不胜，寡人死乎？”占梦者对曰：“公之所病，阴也，日者，阳也。一阴不胜二阳，公病将已。”居三日，公病大愈，公且赐占梦者。占梦者曰：“此非臣之力〔也〕，晏子教臣也。”公召晏子，且赐之。晏子曰：“占梦者以占之言对，故有益也。使臣〔身〕言之，则不信矣。此占梦之力也，臣无功焉。”公两赐之，曰：“以晏子不夺人之功，以占梦者不蔽人之能。”

**【今译】**

“我梦到与两个太阳争斗而无法战胜它们，我是不是快要死了？”占卜梦境的人回答说：“国君所患的疾病，属阴，太阳，属阳。一阴无法战胜二阳，您的病就快要痊愈了。”过了三天，国君的病痊愈了，景公要赏赐占卜梦境的人。占卜梦境的人说：“这并不是我的功劳，晏子让我这么说的。”景公召见晏子，赏赐了他。晏子说：“占卜梦境的人用占卜的结果来回答，所以才能起到作用。让我来说的话，国君就不会相信了。这是占卜梦境的人的功劳，我没有功劳。”景公赏赐了他们两个人，并说：“赏赐晏子是因为他不抢夺别人的功劳，赏赐占卜梦境的人是因为他不隐瞒别人的才能。”

these suns are *yang*.  One *yin* cannot defeat two *yang*. Your illness, my Duke, will abate."

After three days, the Duke experienced a great recovery from his illness and thereupon was about to reward the Diviner of Dreams, but the Diviner of Dreams said, "Your recovery did not result from my ability — Yanzi instructed me."

The Duke thereupon summoned Yanzi to reward him, but Yanzi said: "My words were beneficial because they came from the Diviner of Dreams. Had I spoken, you would not have believed them. This is due to the ability of the Diviner of Dreams, and it is not my accomplishment."

The Duke rewarded both of them and said: "I rewarded Yanzi because he did not steal someone else's achievement, and I reward the Diviner of Dreams because he did not conceal the skill of another person."

## 6.7 [147] 景公病疡晏子抚而对之乃知群臣之野

景公生病背上生疮，晏子按摩疮伤并对话，景公才知道群臣的粗鄙

### 【原文】

景公病疽在背，高子、国子请。公曰："职当抚疡。"高子进而抚疡，公曰："热乎？"曰："热。""热何如？"曰："如火。""其色何如？"曰："如未热李。""大小何如？"曰："如豆。""堕者何如？"曰："如屦辨。"二子者出，晏子请见。公曰："寡人有病，不能胜衣冠以出见夫子，夫子其辱视寡人乎？"晏子入，呼宰人具盥，御者具巾，刷手温

### 【今译】

景公的背上生了个疮，高子和国子请求接见。景公说："你们的职务要求你们应当为我按摩疮伤。"高子走到景公身边按摩疮伤，景公说："热吗？"高子说："很热。""热得像什么呢？"高子说："热得像火。""它的颜色像什么呢？"高子说："像还没有成熟的李子。""大小像什么呢？"高子说："像碗一样大。""溃烂的地方像什么呢？"高子说："像破烂的鞋子。"高子和国子离开后，晏子请求接见。景公说："我生病了，不能穿衣服出去接见先生您了，能否请您受辱来看看我呢？"晏子进入卧室，呼唤管家准备盥盆，侍臣准备毛巾，洗干净手，将毛

# 6.7 [147] DUKE JING SUFFERED FROM A BOIL. YANZI PALPATED IT AND REPLIED TO THE DUKE'S QUESTIONS. THEN THE DUKE RECOGNIZED THE BOORISHNESS OF HIS MINISTERS.

Duke Jing suffered from an abscess on his back. Gaozi and Guozi[1] asked to take a look at it. The Duke said: "Duty requires that you palpate the boil."

Gaozi entered and palpated the boil. The Duke said: "Does it feel hot?"

Gaozi replied: "It is hot."

The Duke said: "How hot?"

Gaozi replied: "As hot as a fire."

The Duke said: "What color is it?"

Gaozi replied: "As the color of unripe plums."

The Duke said: "How big is it?"

Gaozi replied: "As big as the width of a goblet's rim."

The Duke said: "How deep is it?"

Gaozi replied: "As deep as a crack[2] in a broken sandal."

After the two left, Yanzi asked for an audience. The Duke said: "I suffer from illness and can tolerate neither a gown nor a hat on my body in order to come out for an audience with you, Master. Would you condescend to take a look at me?"

Yanzi entered and loudly instructed the palace steward to fetch a washbasin and the attendant to fetch towels. After he scrubbed his hands and warmed them, he rose from his mat, came near the mat of the Duke and, on his knees, asked to palpate the boil.

489

---

1   Gaozi 高子 and Guozi 国子 are not clearly identified in the relevant sources. They play a similar counterpoint to Yanzi in *Hanshi waichuan,* 10.11/75/1.

2   辨 (*YZCQ-ICS*, 52, n. 3).

**【原文】**

之，发席傅荐，跪请抚疡。公曰："其热何如？"曰："如日。""其色何如？"曰："如苍玉。""大小何如？"曰："如璧。""其堕者何如？"曰："如圭。"晏子出，公曰："吾不见君子，不知野人之（掘）〔拙〕也。"

**【今译】**

巾温热，离开自己的座席来到国君的床边，跪下请求为国君按摩疮伤。景公说："疮伤热得像什么呢？"晏子说："像太阳一样。""它的颜色像什么呢？"晏子说："像青色的玉。""大小像什么呢？"晏子说："像玉璧一样。""溃烂的地方像什么呢？"晏子说："像块圭。"晏子离开后，景公说："我没有见到君子之前，不知道粗野的人的拙劣。"

The Duke said: "How hot is it?"

Yanzi replied: "As hot as the sun."

The Duke said: "What color is it?"

Yanzi replied: "As the color of azure jade."

The Duke said: "How big is it?"

Yanzi replied: "As big as a round jade disk."

The Duke said: "How deep is it?"

Yanzi replied: "As deep as a *gui* jade baton."[1]

After Yanzi had left, the Duke said: "Had I not had an audience with this man of noble character, I would never have recognized the stupidity of the boorish."

491

_____

1   圭 (*YZCQ-ICS*, 52, n. 4).

## 6.8 [148] 晏子使吴吴王命傧者称天子晏子详惑

晏子出使吴国，吴王让接引宾客的人称天子召见，晏子假装疑惑

### 【原文】

晏子使吴，吴王谓行人曰："吾闻晏婴，盖北方〔之〕辩于辞、习于礼者也。"命傧者曰："客见则称天子请见。"明日，晏子有事，行人曰："天子请见。"晏子蹴然。行人又曰："天子请见。"晏子蹵然。又

### 【今译】

晏子出使吴国，吴王夫差对接引宾客的官员说："我听说过晏婴，他是北方言辞善于辩论、对于礼仪非常熟悉的人。"就命令负责迎宾的使者说："宾客来拜见的时候就称天子请入见。"第二天，晏子前来拜见，接引宾客的官员说："天子请您入见。"晏子做出恭敬的姿态。掌管朝觐的官员又说："天子请您入见。"晏子又做出恭敬的姿态。又说：

## 6.8 [148] YANZI WAS SENT ON A DIPLOMATIC MISSION TO WU. THE KING OF WU INSTRUCTED THE OFFICIAL IN CHARGE OF RECEPTION OF ENVOYS TO STATE THAT HE THE KING WAS THE SON OF HEAVEN. YANZI PRETENDED TO HAVE LOST HIS WAY TO THE COURT OF THE KING OF WU.[1]

Yanzi was sent on a diplomatic mission to Wu. The King of Wu said to the Master of Protocol: "I have heard that Yan Ying is a man from the North who is both a master of rhetoric and versed in the rites." He then gave the following instruction to the official in charge of the reception of envoys: "As soon as our guest appears, announce the following: 'The Son of Heaven requests to receive you for an audience.'"

The next day, when Yanzi was paying his courtesy call, the Master of Protocol said: "The Son of Heaven requests to receive you for an audience."

Yanzi frowned.

The Master of Protocol again said: "The Son of Heaven requests to receive you for an audience."

Yanzi frowned.[2]

The Master of Protocol again said: "The Son of Heaven requests to receive you for an audience."

Yanzi frowned[3] for the third time and said: "The ruler of my insignificant city commissioned me to go on a diplomatic mission to the court of the King of Wu. However, being dull-witted, I lost my way and instead I have arrived at the court of the Son of Heaven. Dare I ask where I can find the King of Wu?"

493

---

1   Item 6.8 [148] ↔ *Shuoyuan* 12.12/98/20.

2   蹙 → 蹴 (*YZCQ-ICS*, 52, n. 5).

3   蹙 → 蹴 (*YZCQ-ICS*, 52, n. 6).

**【原文】**

曰："天子请见。"晏子蹴然者三，曰："臣受命弊邑之君，将使于吴王之所，以不敏而迷惑，入于天子之朝，敢问吴王恶乎存？"然后吴王曰："夫差请见。"见之以诸侯之礼。

**【今译】**

"天子请您入见。"晏子第三次做出恭敬的姿态，然后说："我奉我国君的命令，作为使者来到吴王治理的地方，因为愚钝而迷失了方向，来到天子的朝廷，请问吴王在这里吗？"然后吴王说："夫差请您入见。"之后以诸侯之间的礼仪相见。

The King of Wu then said: "Fuchai[1] requests to receive you for an audience." He then conducted the audience with Yanzi in keeping with the rites of a regional prince.

---

1   King Fuchai of Wu 吴王夫差 (r. 495 – 473 BCE).

## 6.9 [149] 晏子使楚楚为小门晏子称使狗国者入狗门

晏子出使楚国，楚国开小门，晏子说出使狗国的人从狗门进入

### 【原文】

晏子使楚，以晏子短，楚人为小门于大门之侧而延晏子。晏子不入，曰："使狗国者，从狗门入；今臣使楚，不当从此门入。"傧者更道从大门入，见楚王。王曰："齐无人耶？〔使子为使〕。"晏子对曰："〔齐之〕临淄三百闾，张袂成（阴）〔帷〕，挥汗成雨，比肩继踵而在，何为无人？"王曰："然则子何为使乎？"晏子对曰："齐命使，各有所主，其贤者使使贤王，不肖者使使不肖王。婴最不肖，故直使楚（矣）〔耳〕。"

### 【今译】

晏子出使楚国，因为晏子的身材比较矮小，楚国人在大门的旁边开了一个小门来迎请晏子。晏子不从小门进，并说："出使狗国的使者，从狗门中进入；现在我出使的是楚国，不应该从这个门进去。"迎接宾客的官员更换道路从大门进入王宫，拜见楚王。楚王说："齐国难道没有人吗？"晏子回答说："齐国国都临淄城有三百闾（二十五家为一闾），展开衣袖可以遮住太阳，挥洒汗水如同下雨，大街上的人肩挨着肩，脚跟着脚，怎么能说没有人呢？"楚王说："那么为什么要让先生作为使者呢？"晏子回答说："齐国任命使者，各国有不同的选择，出使贤能国君的国家就派遣贤能的使者，出使没有能力国君的国家就派遣没有能力的使者。晏婴是齐国最没有能力的人，所以派遣我出使楚国了。"

## 6.9 [149] YANZI WAS SENT ON A DIPLOMATIC MISSION TO CHU. THE PEOPLE OF CHU CONSTRUCTED A SMALL GATE FOR HIM TO ENTER THE CITY. YANZI SAID THAT ENVOYS SENT TO A DOG-STATE ENTER THROUGH DOG GATES.

Yanzi was sent on a diplomatic mission to Chu. As Yanzi was a person of diminutive stature,[1] the people of Chu constructed a small gate beside the big city gate and invited Yanzi to enter the city through it. But Yanzi refused to enter this gate, saying: "One who is sent on a diplomatic mission to a dog-state enters through a dog gate. As I was sent on a diplomatic mission to Chu, it is not appropriate for me to enter the city through this gate."

The official in charge of the reception of envoys changed the route and led Yanzi into the city through the large gate, for an audience with the King of Chu.

The King said: "Are there no men in Qi that they have sent you on this diplomatic mission?"

Yanzi replied: "The capital of Qi, Linzi, has three hundred districts. If the people there opened their sleeves wide they would form tents, and if they shook off their sweat, it would fall as rain. People are living there, shoulder to shoulder and heel to heel. How could there be no men there?"

The King said: "So why then did they send you on this diplomatic mission?"

Yanzi replied: "When Qi commissions its diplomatic envoys, each is selected in accordance with his host. Worthy envoys are sent to worthy kings while unworthy envoys are sent to unworthy kings. Since I am most unworthy, I was sent as an envoy to Chu."

---

1   Yanzi was a person of diminutive stature. His height was less than 138 centimeters. See Item 5.25 [135].

## 6.10 [150] 楚王欲辱晏子指盗者为齐人晏子对以橘

楚王想要羞辱晏子，指着盗贼说是齐国人，晏子用橘子来回答

### 【原文】

晏子将〔使〕楚，楚〔王〕闻之，谓左右曰："晏婴，齐之习辞者也，今方来，吾欲辱之，何以也？"左右对曰："为其来也，臣请缚一人，过王而行，王（者）〔曰〕：'何为者也？'对曰：'齐人也。'王曰：'何坐？'曰：'坐盗。'"〔于是〕晏子至，楚王赐晏子酒，酒酣，吏二缚一人（诣王）〔过王而行〕，王曰："缚者曷为者也？"对曰："齐人也。〔王曰〕：'〔何坐〕？'〔曰〕："坐盗。"王视晏子曰：

### 【今译】

晏子即将到楚国去，楚王听说后，对身边的人说："晏婴，是齐国善于辞令的人，现在他要来楚国，我想羞辱他一番，应该怎么做呢？"身边的人回答说："等到他来的时候，我请求捆着一个人，从国君您面前走过去，国君问：'这是什么人呢？'我回答说：'齐国人。'国君问：'犯了什么罪行？'我回答说：'犯了盗窃的罪。'"晏子来到楚国，楚王赐酒宴给晏子，酒兴正浓之时，两名胥吏捆着一个人来见楚王，楚王说："捆着的是什么人呢？"胥吏回答说："齐国人，犯了偷盗的罪。"楚王看着晏子说："齐国人原来善于偷盗吗？"晏子离开座席回答说："我听说，橘树生长在淮河以南结出的果实就是橘，生长在淮河以北

## 6.10 [150] THE KING OF CHU WANTED TO HUMILIATE YANZI. HE POINTED TO A ROBBER WHO WAS A MAN FROM QI. YANZI REPLIED WITH AN ANALOGY TO ORANGE TREES.[1]

Yanzi was about to go on a diplomatic mission to Chu. When the King of Chu heard of this, he said to his entourage: "Yan Ying is a man from Qi who has mastered the art of rhetoric; he will soon arrive — I would like to humiliate him. How should I do this?"

His entourage said: "Wait until his arrival and then let me bind a man and pass before you, my King — at which moment you should ask: 'Who is that man?' You will then be told that it is a man from Qi; then you should ask: 'Of what crime has he convicted?' and the reply will be: 'He has been convicted of robbery.'"

Thereupon, Yanzi arrived and the King held a banquet in his honor. Then, when they were in their cups, two officials led a bound man before the King. The King said: "Who is this bound man?"

The officials replied: "He is a man from Qi."

The King asked: "Of what crime has he convicted??"

The officials replied: "He has been convicted of robbery."

The King looked at Yanzi and said: "Are people in Qi really prone to robbery?" Yanzi stepped away from his mat and said: "I have heard that when orange trees grow south of the river Huai they produce oranges but if they grow north of the river Huai they produce tangerines. Only their leaves look alike but their fruits taste different. And why is this so? Because the water and soil differ. Now, as long as people are born and raised in Qi they are not robbers, but as soon as they enter Chu they become robbers.

---

1   Item 6.10 [15] ↔ *Hanshi waichuan*, 10.17/76/14.

## 【原文】

"齐人固善盗乎？"晏子避席对曰："婴闻之，橘生淮南则为橘，生于淮北则为枳，叶徒相似，其实味不同。所以然者何？〔其〕水土异也。今民生长于齐不盗，入楚则盗，得无楚之水土使民善盗耶？"王笑曰："圣人非所与熙也，寡人反（耻）〔取〕病焉。"

## 【今译】

结出的果实就是枳，它们只是叶子非常相似，但果实的味道完全不同。这种变化的原因是什么呢？水土不一样而已。现在民众在齐国的时候不偷盗，到了楚国却偷盗，难道不是楚国的水土让民众变得善于偷盗了吗？"楚王笑着说："不能同圣明的人开玩笑，我反而被自己羞辱了。"

Is it not possible that the water and soil of Chu cause people to be prone to robbery?"

The King laughed and said: "The sage is someone you should not trifle with — to the contrary — I have brought disgrace upon myself."

501

## 6.11 [151] 楚王飨晏子进橘置削晏子不剖而食

楚王赐给晏子橘子吃，放了削刀，晏子不剥开就吃了

### 【原文】

景公使晏子于楚，楚王进橘，置削，晏子不剖而并食之。楚（橘）王曰："〔橘〕当去剖。"晏子对曰："臣闻之，赐人主之前者，瓜桃不削，橘柚不剖。今者万乘无教（今）〔令〕，臣故不敢剖；不然，臣非不知也。"

### 【今译】

齐景公让晏子出使楚国，楚王命人进奉橘子，并放置了削刀，晏子没有剥皮就一起吃下去了。楚王说："应该剥开皮再吃。"晏子回答说："我听说，在国君面前接受的赏赐，瓜桃不能用刀切，橘柚不能剥开皮。现在万乘之国的国君没有下令，所以我不敢剥开皮；我不剥皮就吃下去，并不是因为我不知道。"

# 6.11 [151] THE KING OF CHU ENTERTAINED YANZI. HE SERVED HIM A TANGERINE AND PUT A PARING KNIFE BESIDE IT. YANZI ATE IT WITHOUT PEELING IT.[1]

Duke Jing sent Yanzi on a diplomatic mission to Chu. The King of Chu served him a tangerine and placed a paring knife beside it, but Yanzi ate it without peeling it.

The King of Chu said: "You should have cut and peeled the tangerine."

Yanzi replied: "I have heard that if one is in the presence of a ruler who bestowed favor upon him, one should neither cut open melons and peaches nor cut and peel tangerines and pomelos. Now, since I was not instructed by you — a ruler of a state of ten-thousand chariots — to do so, I dared not cut and peel it. Otherwise, I would not have been clueless on how to manage it."

503

---

1  Item 6.11 [151] ↔ *Shuoyuan*, 12.14/.99/1.

## 6.12 [152] 晏子布衣栈车而朝田桓子侍景公饮酒请浮之

　　晏子穿粗布衣服乘坐破旧的马车参加朝会，田桓子服侍景公饮酒，请罚晏子饮酒

### 【原文】

　　景公饮酒，田桓子侍，望见晏子，而复于公曰："请浮晏子。"公曰："何故也？"无宇对曰："晏子衣缁布之衣，麑鹿之裘，栈轸之车，而驾驽马以朝，是隐君之赐也。"公曰："诺。"晏子坐，酌者奉觞〔而〕进之，曰："君命浮子。"晏子曰："何故也？"田桓子曰："君赐之卿位以尊其身，宠之百万以富其家，群臣其爵莫尊于子，禄莫重于子。今子衣缁布之衣，麑鹿之裘，栈轸之车，而驾驽马以朝，〔则是〕（是则）隐君之赐也。故浮子。"晏子避席曰："请饮而后辞乎，其辞而后饮

### 【今译】

　　田桓子侍奉景公饮酒，远远地看到晏子，就向景公说："我请求罚晏子饮酒。"景公说："这是为什么呢？"田桓子回答说："晏子穿着黑布的衣服，披着粗劣的皮裘，乘坐竹木制作的马车，而用劣等马拉着来朝见，这是隐藏国君您对他的赏赐啊！"国君说："好的。"晏子坐下后，倒酒的侍者捧着酒杯给他，并说："国君命令您罚酒。"晏子说："这是为什么呢？"田桓子说："国君赐给您上卿的爵位是为了显示您的尊贵，赏赐您百万的俸禄是为了让您的家室变得富裕，群臣的爵位没有一个比您高的，俸禄没有一个比您更多的。现在您穿着黑布的衣服，披着粗劣的皮裘，乘坐竹木制作的马车，用劣等马拉着来朝见，这是在隐藏国君对您的赏赐。所以要罚您喝酒。"晏子离开自己的座席说："您是要我先饮酒再解释呢，还是先解释再饮酒呢？"景公说："先

# 6.12 [152] YANZI WAS DRESSED IN PLAIN CLOTHES AND DROVE A PLAIN WOOD AND BAMBOO CARRIAGE FOR A COURT AUDIENCE. DUKE JING WAS DRINKING WINE AND TIAN HUANZI[1] WAS IN ATTENDANCE ON HIM. HE REQUESTED THAT YANZI QUAFF A GOBLET AS FORFEIT.[2]

Duke Jing was drinking wine and Tian Huanzi was in attendance on him. When Tian Huanzi saw Yanzi from afar, he turned to the Duke and said: "I request that Yanzi quaff a whole goblet as forfeit."

The Duke said: "For what reason?"

Wuyu replied: "Yanzi is dressed in clothing made of both dark cloth and deer pelts. He drives a plain wood and bamboo carriage and rides a nag to his court audiences. Thereby, he denies the favors you bestow upon him, my Lord."

The Duke said: "I approve."

After Yanzi had sat down, the cup-bearer raised a goblet, offered it to Yanzi and said: "Our Lord orders you to quaff this goblet as forfeit."

Yanzi said: "For what reason?"

Tian Huanzi said: "Our ruler has bestowed upon you the rank of Eminent Minister to honor you; he showered you with his favor in the form of an emolument of a million in order to enrich your family. None of the other ministers holds a more noble rank than you, and no emolument is higher than yours. But now you sir, dress in clothes made of both dark cloth and deer pelts; you drive a plain wood and bamboo carriage, and ride a nag to your court audiences — these actions deny the favors that our ruler

505

---

1  According to the *Shiji*, 1881, Tianhuan Wuyu 田桓无宇, (also Tian Wuyu 田无宇 or Tian Huanzi 田桓子), was a powerful figure in Qi and the son of Tian Wenzi 田文子 who, together with Yanzi, served and remonstrated Duke Zhuang 庄公.

2  Item 6.12 [152] ↔ *Shuoyuan*, 2.14/16/7.

**【原文】**

乎？"公曰："辞然后饮。"晏子曰："君（之赐）〔赐之〕卿位以尊其身，婴非敢为显受也，为行君令也；宠（以）〔之〕百万以富其家，婴非敢为富受也，为通君赐也。臣闻古之贤臣，〔臣〕有受厚赐而不顾其（困）〔国〕族，则过之；临事守职，不胜其任，则过之。君之内隶，臣之父兄，若有离散，在于野鄙〔者〕，此臣之罪也。君之（内）〔外〕隶，臣之所职，若有播（之）〔亡〕，在于四方〔者〕，此臣之罪也。兵革之不完，战车之不修，此臣之罪也。若夫弊车驽马以朝，意者非臣之罪乎？且臣以君之赐，〔臣〕父之党无不乘车者，母之党无不足于衣食者，妻之党无冻馁者，国之闲士待臣而后举火者数百家。如此者，为彰君赐乎，为隐君赐乎？"公曰："善！为我浮无宇也。"

**【今译】**

解释再饮酒。"晏子说："国君您赐给我上卿的爵位来显示我的尊贵，晏婴并不是为了显示自己的尊贵才接受，是为了执行国君的命令；赏赐我百万的俸禄来让我的家室变得富裕，晏婴也并不是为了财富才接受的，是为了展示国君的赏赐。我听说古代的贤臣，有的接受赏赐后却不照顾他的宗族，就要责备他；处理事务担任官职，不能达到应有的标准，就要惩罚他。国君在都城中的人民，是我的父母兄弟，如果有分散到郊外田野中的，这是我的罪过。国君在田野中的人民，是我所掌管的，如果有流亡到其他国家的，也是我的罪过。武器装备不够完善，战车没有修好，这是我的罪过。乘坐劣等马拉着的破车来朝见，这难道是我的罪过吗？况且我因为国君的赏赐，父系的亲属没有不乘坐马车的，母系的亲属没有衣服食物不能满足的，妻子的家族也没有冻伤挨饿的，国都内没有工作等待我的接济才能生火做饭的也有数百家。这样看来，我是为了彰显国君的赏赐呢，还是隐瞒国君的赏赐呢？"景公说："很好。给我罚田桓子饮酒。"

bestows upon you. That is why you have to quaff the goblet as forfeit."

Yanzi stepped away from his mat and said: "May I ask, should I drink first and speak afterwards, or should I speak first and drink afterwards?"

The Duke said: "Speak first and drink afterwards."

Yanzi said: "You, my Lord, bestowed upon me the rank of an Eminent Minister to honor me. I did not dare accept it for the sake of gaining renown but rather for the sake of executing your orders. You showered me with your favor in the form of an emolument of a million in order to enrich my family and I did not dare accept it for the sake of enriching myself but rather for the sake of sharing it with others. I have heard that the worthy rulers of ancient times reprimanded both those who took handsome emoluments without taking care of their clansmen, and those who were not capable of fulfilling their duties in directing affairs and carrying out their tasks. My Lord, if your privy servants or my father or my brother were banished to remote places, I would be guilty of this. If your ministers, my Lord, or those who are my responsibility, were forced to go into exile in every direction, I would be guilty of this. If arms were not completed and war chariots were not kept in repair, I would be guilty of this. But if I come to the audience riding a shabby carriage and a nag, I warrant that I am not guilty? Furthermore, with the favors you have bestowed upon me, my Lord, all relatives on my father's side have carriages to ride in; all relatives on my mother's side have sufficient clothes and food; no relatives on my wife's side starve or suffer cold; and several hundred families of unemployed officers in the state rely on me to cook their meals. Do such actions put on display or conceal your favors, my Lord?"

The Duke said: "Excellent! I command that Wuyu quaff the goblet as forfeit."

## 6.13 [153] 田无宇请求四方之学士晏子谓君子难得

田无宇请征求四方的学士，晏子说君子很难得到

**【原文】**

田桓子见晏子独立于墙阴，曰："子何为独立而不忧？何不求四乡之学士可者而与坐？"晏子曰："共立似君子，出言而非也。婴恶得学士之可者而与之坐？且君子之难得也，若美山然，名山既多矣，松柏既茂矣，望之相相然，尽目力不知厌。而世有所美焉，固欲登彼相相之上，仡仡然不知厌。小人者与此异，若部娄之未登，善，登之无蹊，维有楚棘而已；远望无见也，俛就则伤腰，恶能无独立焉？且人何忧，

**【今译】**

田桓子看到晏子独自站在墙的阴影下，就说："您为什么一个人站着却不忧愁呢？为什么不寻找四方有学识的人一起坐着交谈呢？"晏子说："一起站着的时候看着像君子，一交谈就知道不是了。晏婴难道不愿意找到有学识的人一起坐着交谈吗？况且君子是很难发现的，就像美丽的山峰一样，有名的山峰是很多的，它们的松柏非常茂密，看起来非常高，极尽目力也不觉得累。世人都称赞的名山，大家都愿意登上高高的山顶，即使非常艰难也不知疲倦。小人跟君子是完全不同的，就好像没有登上过的小山丘，看起来很好，攀登的时候没有道路，只有荆棘而已；从远处看不到荆棘，低下身子就会伤害到腰，我怎么

## 6.13 [153] TIAN WUYU ASKED YANZI TO SEEK OUT LEARNED SCHOLARS FROM EVERY QUARTER. YANZI SAID THAT MEN OF NOBLE CHARACTER ARE DIFFICULT TO FIND.

Tian Huanzi saw Yanzi standing by himself in the shade of a wall and said to him: "Sir, why do you stand here by yourself so worry-free? Why don't you seek the company of learned scholars from the four quarters of the realm and congregate with them?

Yanzi said: "When these scholars pose together, they look like men of noble character; but when they speak up—they are not. So where can I find fitting scholars with whom I can congregate? Furthermore, a man of noble character is as difficult to find as a beautiful mountain. There are many famous mountains on which pines and cypresses flourish. From a distance they appear lofty;[1] one could exhaust one's powers of sight and still not be sated. And so, when the people of the world realize their beauty, they feel compelled to climb the lofty peaks[2] with great effort and still they are not sated. With petty people, this is quite different; they are like small hills that look perfectly fine as long as no one climbs them. However, if scaled, they are without paths and have nothing but thistles and thorns. Gazing at them from far distance there is nothing to be seen, but if I deign to draw closer I could be hurt.[3] Why should I then not stand by myself? Furthermore, why should a person have worries? One can live calmly and allow one's thought to look far into the future; the years pass by him like months, his thirst for knowledge is not sated, and he does not feel old-age approaching. Why should one be given to drink?"

---

1  (*YZCQ-ICS*, 54, n. 3).

2  (*YZCQ-ICS*, 54, n. 4).

3  要 → 嬰 (*JS*, 402/9).

**【原文】**

静处远虑，见岁若月，学问不厌，不知老之将至，安用从酒！”田桓子曰："何谓从酒？"晏子曰："无客而饮，谓之从酒。今若子者，昼夜守尊，谓之从酒也。"

**【今译】**

能不一个人站着呢？而且人有什么好担忧的呢，安静地待着思考长远的事情，看淡时间的流逝，学习而不厌烦，不知道寿命就快结束，哪里还需要纵酒呢？"田桓子说："什么是纵酒呢？"晏子说："没有宾客的时候自己喝酒，就被称为纵酒。像你这样的人，日夜都抱着酒杯，就是所谓的纵酒了。"

Tian Huanzi said: "What do you mean by 'given to drink'?"

Yanzi said: "To drink without having guests in the house is what I call 'given to drink.' You, for instance, nurse your wine goblet day and night — this is what I call 'given to drink.'"

## 6.14 [154] 田无宇胜栾氏高氏欲分其家晏子使致之公

田无宇战胜栾氏和高氏，想要瓜分他们的家产，晏子让其将资产献给公室

### 【原文】

栾氏、高氏欲逐田氏、鲍氏，田氏、鲍氏先知而遂攻之。高强曰："先得君，田、鲍安往？"遂〔攻〕虎门。二家召晏子，晏子无所从也。从者曰："何为不助田、鲍？"晏子曰："何善焉，其助之也？""何为不助栾、高？"曰："庸愈于彼乎？"门开，公召而入。栾、高不胜而出，田桓子欲分其家，以告晏子。晏子曰："不可！君不能饬法，而群臣专制，乱之本也。今又欲分其家，利其货，是非制也。子必致之公。且婴闻之，（禁）〔廉〕者，政之本也，让者，德之主也。栾、高不让，

### 【今译】

栾氏、高氏想要驱逐田氏和鲍氏，田氏、鲍氏提前知晓了，于是先出兵攻打他们。高强说："先劫持国君，田氏和鲍氏还能跑到哪里去呢？"于是攻打虎门。两方都拉拢晏子，晏子却不顺从任何一方。随从说："为什么不帮助田氏和鲍氏呢？"晏子说："他们的做法是正确的吗？我帮助他们？""为什么不帮助栾氏和高氏？"晏子说："他们难道比田氏和鲍氏做得更好吗？"宫门打开后，国君征召晏子进入。栾氏、高氏被击败而离开，田桓子想要瓜分了他们的家产，把这个决定告诉了晏子。晏子说："不能这样！国君不能整饬法律，导致群臣专权，这是祸乱发生的根源。现在又想要瓜分他们的家产，贪图他们的财

## 6.14 [154] TIAN WUYU DEFEATED THE FAMILIES OF LUAN AND GAO. HE WANTED TO DIVIDE THEIR FAMILY PROPERTY. YANZI MADE HIM HAND OVER ALL THE PROPERTY TO THE DUKE.[1]

The Luan and Gao lineages wanted to banish the Tian and Bao lineages from Qi. The Tian and Bao lineages realized in advance their intention and attacked them preemptively.

Gao Qiang[2] said: "If we capture the Duke first, where could the Tian and Bao lineages flee to?"

Then they proceeded to attack the Tiger Gate.[3] Both parties wanted to recruit Yanzi to their side, but he joined neither. His followers asked him: "Why don't you lend support to the Tian and Bao families?"

Yanzi replied: "What is so admirable about them that I should lend them my support?"

His followers asked: "So why don't you lend support to the Luan and Gao families?"

Yanzi replied: "Are they any better?"

The gate was opened. The Duke summoned Yanzi and Yanzi entered. The Luan and Gao could not defeat their rivals and were forced to flee. Tian Huanzi wanted to divide their family property and informed Yanzi about this.

Yanzi said: "This is inappropriate. If a ruler is incapable of maintaining legal order and the ministers misappropriate power that becomes the root of havoc. In this case, you wish to divide their family property and derive benefit from their money—this violates the ruling order. You must hand all

---

1  Item 6.14 [154] ↔ *Zuozhuan*, B10·10·2/4.

2  Gao Qiang 高彊 (fl. 540–532), the head of the Gao linage, was ultimately defeated by the Tian and Bao linages and forced to flee to Lu.

3  The "Tiger Gate" led to the Road Bedchamber in the imperial palace.

## 【原文】

以至此祸，可毋慎乎！廉之谓公正，让之谓保德，凡有血气者，皆有争心，怨利生孽，维义〔为〕可以（为）长存。且分争者不胜其祸，辞让者不失其福，子必勿（耻）〔取〕。"桓子曰："善。"尽致之公，而请老于剧。

## 【今译】

货，这是不合乎法律的。您必须要将他们的家产给予公室。况且我听说，廉洁是政治的根本，谦让是美德的主体。栾氏和高氏不谦让，导致遭遇灾祸，难道不应该谨慎吗？廉洁执政才能称为公正，谦让处事才能称为保持品德，凡是有血气的人，都有争斗之心，积蓄财货会引发祸患，只有保持正义才能长久存在。况且争斗不息的人难以承受接连不断的灾祸，推辞谦让的人不会丧失其福祉，您一定不要瓜分他们的家产。"田桓子说："好的。"把栾氏和高氏的家产都交给公室，而且请求回剧城养老。

the property over to the Duke. Moreover, I have heard that integrity is the foundation of good government, and yielding is the core element of virtue. The Luan and Gao lineages did not yield and thereby they encountered this disaster. Can one dare not be cautious in such matters? The meaning of integrity is fairness and uprightness; and the meaning of yielding is preserving virtue. All who have blood and *qi* in their bodies have hostile tendencies. Profit acquired through injustice produces the seeds of disaster, and only righteousness can result in prolonged existence. Furthermore, one who is contentious will not overcome disaster, while one who yields and concedes will not lose good fortune. Sir, you must not seize this property."

Huanzi said: "Approved." Then he handed over all of the property to the Duke and requested to retire and spend his old age in Ju.

515

# 6.15 [155] 子尾疑晏子不受庆氏之邑晏子谓足欲则亡

子尾因为晏子不接受庆氏的封邑而猜疑他，晏子说满足了自己的欲望就要逃亡

## 【原文】

庆氏亡，分其邑，与晏子〔邶〕殿，其鄙（卒）〔六十〕，晏子勿受。子尾曰："富者，人之所欲也，何独弗欲？"晏子对曰："庆氏之邑足欲，故亡。吾邑不足欲也，益之以〔邶〕殿，乃足欲；足欲，亡无（矣日）〔日矣〕。在外不得宰吾一邑，不受〔邶〕殿，非恶富也，恐失富也。且夫富，如布帛之有幅焉，为之制度，使无迁也。夫〔民〕生厚而用利，于是乎正德以幅之，使无黜慢，谓之幅利，利过则为败，吾不敢贪多，所谓幅也。"

## 【今译】

庆氏逃亡后，他的封邑被瓜分了，分给晏子邶殿，有六十个小镇，晏子不接受。子尾说："财富是人们都希望拥有的，为什么只有你不想要呢？"晏子回答说："庆氏的封邑能够满足他的欲望，所以他逃亡了，我的封邑还不能满足我的欲望，如果增加了邶殿，那么就能满足我的欲望了；满足了我的欲望，那么我离逃亡也不远了。逃亡在外的话，连我自己的封邑都难以拥有了，不接受邶殿，不是厌恶财富，是害怕失去财富。况且财富，就像布帛有宽度一样，为它制定好标准，让它不能随意改变。民众一旦生活富足了就会追求利益，于是要制定道德准则来约束他们，让他们不要放肆怠慢，这就是所谓的追求利益的标准，追求利益超过标准就会失败，我不敢贪图太多，这就是所谓的标准。"

## 6.15 [155] ZIWEI[1] WAS BAFFLED BY YANZI'S REFUSAL TO RECEIVE THE CITIES OF THE HEAD OF THE QING LINAGE. YANZI SAID THAT WHAT IS ENOUGH TO GRATIFY DESIRES LEADS TO RUIN.[2]

The head of the Qing linage fled into exile[3] and his cities were divided up. Yanzi was granted Beidian, a district comprised of sixty frontier towns, but he declined to accept it. Ziwei said to him: "Wealth is what people desire—why do you alone lack this desire?"

Yanzi answered: "The cities of the head of the Qing linage were enough to gratify his desire but because of them, he was forced to flee into exile. My cities are not enough to gratify desire. Adding to them the towns of Beidian will be enough to gratify my desire and then, it is only a matter of time before I will be forced to flee into exile and will have not even a single city to rule from afar. My refusal to accept Beidian was not because of any aversion to wealth, but rather because of my fear of losing it. What is more, wealth is comparable to the fixed measurements[4] of width of bolts of cotton and silk. Specific measurements are instituted for them so they cannot vary. If the people's livelihood is ample, and their activities generate profit, in that case, their virtue should be kept in proper measure in order to set limits to avoid become debased and insolent. This is called 'setting limits in striving for profit.' Excessive profit leads to one's downfall. I do not dare to be covetous to excess; this is what is meant by 'setting the limits.'"

517

---

1   Ziwei 子尾, also known as Gongsun Chai 公孙虿 (fl. 545–534), was the head of the Gao linage.

2   Item 6.15 [155] ↔ *Zuozhuan*, B9.28.11.0.0.3.

3   For Qing Feng 庆封, the head of the Qing linage, see Item 3.2 [52].

4   *Fu* (幅 – "measurement") and *fu* (富– "wealth") are homophonous words.

## 6.16 [156] 景公禄晏子平阴与棠邑晏子愿行三言以辞

景公要赐予晏子平阴和棠邑作为俸禄，晏子以希望景公做到三件事来推辞

### 【原文】

景公禄晏子以平阴与棠邑，反市者十一社。晏子辞曰："吾君好治宫室，民之力弊矣；又好盘游玩好，以饬女子，民之财竭矣；又好兴师，民之死近矣。弊其力，竭其财，近其死，下之疾其上甚矣！此婴之所为不敢受也。"公曰："是则可矣。虽然，君子独不欲富与贵乎？"晏子曰："婴闻为人臣者，先君后身；安国而度家，宗君而处身，曷为独不欲富与贵也？"公曰："然则曷以禄夫子？"晏子对曰："君（商）

### 【今译】

景公要赐予晏子平阴和棠邑作为他的俸禄，这里贩卖货物的集市有十一个。晏子推辞说："我的国君喜好修建宫殿，民众已经疲惫了；又喜欢游乐和精美的物品，来取悦王宫内的女子，民众的财产也枯竭了；又崇尚征伐作战，民众的死期不远了。消耗百姓的力量，穷尽百姓的资产，缩短百姓的生命，下层的民众已经非常怨恨统治者了！这是我不敢接受的原因。"国君说："要是这样就算了吧。尽管这样，难道君子都不想要财富和地位吗？"晏子说："我听说作为臣子的人，应该先为国君着想再为自己打算；先使国家安定才能考虑家族，先尊奉

## 6.16 [156] DUKE JING GRANTED PINGYIN AND TANGYI TO YANZI AS AN EMOLUMENT. YANZI DECLINED THE EMOLUMENT, REQUESTING INSTEAD THAT THE DUKE PUT INTO PRACTICE HIS THREE RECOMMENDATIONS.

Duke Jing wanted to give as an emolument to Yanzi the areas of Pingying and Tangyi, in which a population of eleven villages with altars conducted trade.[1] Yanzi declined the offer, saying: "You, my Lord, love to build palaces and residences, thereby exhausting the strength of the people. You also love pleasure trips and beautiful curios, with which you decorate the women in your company — this depletes the property of the people. What is more, you love to initiate military campaigns, which brings the people to the brink of death. When the strength of the people is exhausted, the property of the people is depleted and they are on the brink of death, the hatred of inferiors towards their superiors becomes enormous. This is the reason why I dare not accept."

The Duke said: "What you have said is reasonable; however, why is it that a man of noble character should be a singular exception, free from the desire for wealth and honor?"

Yanzi said: "I have heard that a minister should put his ruler first and his own self last. He secures the state and puts his family in order; he gives honor to his ruler and establishes himself in the world. Why shouldn't he be a singular exception, free of desire for wealth and honor?"

The Duke said: "If so, then how can I reward you with an emolument?"

Yanzi answered: "Develop the trade of fish and salt, and at the customs house and markets have inspections but do not charge duties; collect the

---

1   For a discussion of the meaning of *she* 社 (a village altar), see Allyn W. Rickett, tr. *Guanzi: Political, Economic, and Philosophical Essays from Early China.* Princeton Library of Asian Translations, Princeton (1985): vol. 1, p. 121, n. 36; p. 429, n. 34.

**【原文】**

〔商〕渔盐，关市讥而不征；耕者十（耺）〔取〕一焉；弛刑罚，若死者刑，若刑者罚，若罚者免。若此三言者，婴之禄，君之利也。"公曰："此三言者，寡人无事焉，请以从夫子。"公既行若三言，使人问大国，大国之君曰："齐安矣。"使人问小国，小国之君曰："齐不加我矣。"

**【今译】**

国君再考虑自身，怎么能说不想要财富和地位呢？"国君说："那么应该用什么来做您的俸禄呢？"晏子回答说："您经营渔盐的事务，要严格管理关口市场但不征收关税；耕种土地的人收取十分之一的租税；减轻刑罚，如果要处死的就判处徒刑，如果要判处徒刑的就改为罚财物，如果要判处罚财物的就免除。这三件事，就是我的俸禄，也是符合国君您的利益的。"景公说："这三件事，我都不会阻拦，请按照您的意见办。"景公做了这三件事后，派人向大国询问，大国的国君说："齐国已经安定了。"派人向小国询问，小国的国君说："齐国不会欺凌我国了。"

tithe from the tillers' harvest; and alleviate punishments. You should, for instance, turn death penalties into corporal penalties; corporal penalties into fines; and provide exemptions for fines to be annulled. These three suggestions are my emolument and your benefit, my Lord.

The Duke said: "I have no problem with your suggestions, let me then follow your advice, Master."

After the Duke had carried out Yanzi's three suggestions, he commissioned someone to inquire about their impact in the big states, and the rulers of these states said: "Qi is secured." The Duke also sent people to the small states, and their rulers said: "Qi does not constitute a threat for us."

## 6.17 [157] 梁丘据言晏子食肉不足景公割地将封晏子辞

　　梁丘据说晏子没有足够的肉吃，景公要分封给晏子土地，晏子推辞不受

### 【原文】

　　晏子相齐，三年，政平民说。梁丘据见晏子中食，而肉不足，以告景公。旦日，（割地将）封晏子〔以都昌〕，晏子辞不受，曰：“富而不骄者，未尝闻（者）〔之〕。贫而不恨者，婴是也。所以贫而不恨者，以（若）〔善〕为师也。今封，易婴之师，师已轻，封已重矣，请辞。”

### 【今译】

　　晏子担任齐相三年，政治稳定民众满意。梁丘据看到晏子吃午饭，却没有足够的肉，就把这件事告诉了景公。第二天，景公要把都昌分封给晏子，晏子推辞不接受，说：“拥有财富却不骄横的，我没有听说过。贫穷却不抱怨的，晏婴就是这样的人。之所以能够接受贫穷却不抱怨，是以贫穷作为榜样。现在赐予我封地，改变了我的榜样，榜样被轻视，封地被加重，所以要推辞。”

## 6.17 [157] LIANGQIU JU SAID THAT YANZI WAS NOT EATING ENOUGH MEAT. DUKE JING CEDED TERRITORIES AND WANTED TO GRANT YANZI A FIEFDOM. YANZI DECLINED.

Yanzi served as prime minister in Qi. At the end of three years, the government was just and the people were pleased. Once, Liangqiu Ju saw Yanzi eating common food that did not contain enough meat. He reported this to Duke Jing. The next day, the Duke wanted to grant Duchang to Yanzi as a fiefdom, but Yanzi declined and did not accept it, saying: "I have never heard of anyone who is rich without becoming arrogant. Poor but free of resentment — is my motto.[1] The reason for my being poor but free of resentment is that good conduct serves as my model. If now you grant me a fiefdom, you would force me to replace my model; then my former model would become insignificant and the fief would carry greater weight. That is why, I request to decline."

523

---

1   This statement reads like a condensed paraphrase of the *Analects*, 1.15/2/15.

大中华文库

## 6.18 [158] 景公以晏子食不足致千金而晏子固不受

景公因为晏子食物不充足而给予他千金，但晏子坚决推辞不接受

### 【原文】

晏子方食，景公使使者至。分食食之，使者不饱，晏子亦不饱。使者反，言之公。公曰："嘻！晏子之家，若是其贫也。寡人不知，是寡人之过也。"使吏致千金与市租，请以奉宾客。晏子辞，三（教）〔致〕之，终再拜而辞曰："婴之家不贫。以君之赐，泽覆三族，延及交游，以振百姓，君之赐也厚矣！婴之家不贫也。婴闻之，夫厚取之君，而施之民，是臣代君君民也，忠臣不为也。厚（耴）〔取〕之君，而

### 【今译】

晏子正要吃饭，景公的使者来到他的家。于是晏子将自己的饭食分给使者，使者没有吃饱，晏子也没有吃饱。使者回去后，把这件事告诉了景公。景公说："是吗？晏子的家境，原来这么贫穷。我不知道这个情况，是我的过错。"景公命令胥吏赠予晏子千金和市场的租税，让他用这些财物来供奉宾客。晏子推辞不接受，景公又多次赠予他，最终晏子拜了又拜推辞说："晏婴的家并不贫穷。凭借国君的赏赐，我能够照顾我的父、母、妻三族，能够用来与朋友交游，能够赈济百姓，国君的赏赐已经很优厚了！晏婴的家不贫穷。我听说，如果从国君那里获取很多，然后用于百姓，是臣子替代国君统治百姓了，忠心的臣

## 6.18 [158] DUKE JING THOUGHT THAT YANZI DID NOT EAT ENOUGH FOOD AND SENT HIM A GIFT OF A THOUSAND PIECES OF GOLD. YANZI FIRMLY REFUSED TO ACCEPT.[1]

Once, when Yanzi was having his meal, a messenger sent by Duke Jing arrived. Yanzi divided his meal and invited the messenger to share it with him; thus, neither the messenger nor Yanzi ate their fill. Upon his return, the messenger reported this to the Duke and the Duke said: "Oh, I was not aware that Yanzi's household was as poor as that — this is my fault." Then he sent an official to Yanzi with a gift of a thousand pieces of gold and taxes collected from the markets, and asked him to use the gift to cover guests' expenses, but Yanzi declined.

Three times the gift was offered, until finally, bowing twice, Yanzi declined the gift: "My household is not poor. Your generosity, my Lord, could cover all three lineages of my relatives, could be spread among my friends, and could relieve the common people. My Lord's generosity is extreme. My household is not poor. I have heard that if a minister receives abundant gifts from his ruler and distributes them among the people, he usurps the role of the ruler over the people. A loyal minister would not do this. If a minister receives abundant gifts from his ruler and withholds them from the people, he is a like one who guards wealth in boxes and trunks. A humane person would not do this. If a minister, while advancing in his career, receives gifts from his ruler, and then, in his private life, commits offences against his fellow officers, then when he dies, his wealth is transferred to these officers as if he were just their repository. A wise man would not do this. For me, coarse cloth and a bowlful of food will suffice."[2]

525

---

1 Item 6.18 [158] ↔ *Shuoyuan*, 2.15/16/25.

2 足于中免矣 → 足矣 (*Shuoyuan*, 2.15/16/28). See also, *JS,* 412/14.

## 【原文】

不施于民,是为筐箧之藏也,仁人不为也。进(耴)〔取〕于君,退得罪于士,身死而财迁于他人,是为宰藏也,智者不为也。(十夫)〔夫十〕总之布,一豆之食,足于中免矣。"景公谓晏子曰:"昔吾先君桓公,以书社五百封管仲,不辞而受,子辞之何也?"晏子曰:"婴闻之,圣人千虑,必有一失;愚人千虑,必有一得。意者管仲之失,而婴之得者耶!故再拜而不敢受命。"

## 【今译】

子不会这么做。从国君那里获取很多,却不用于百姓,只是贮藏在自己家中的箱子里,仁义的人不会这么做。先从国君那里接受财物,然后又得罪于士人,自己死后财产转移到他人手中,这是为别人贮藏财富,有智慧的人不会这么做。有质地粗疏的布做衣服,一豆的粮食作为午饭就足够了。"景公对晏子说:"以前我先代的国君齐桓公,曾经以五百社的户籍分封给管仲,管仲没有推辞就接受了,您为何要推辞呢?"晏子说:"我听说,圣贤的人思考千次必然会有一次错误;愚笨的人思考千次必然会有一次是得当的。我想这是管仲错误,晏婴得当的地方吧!所以拜了又拜不敢接受您的赏赐。"

Duke Jing said to Yanzi: "In the past, our former ruler, Duke Huan, granted Guan Zhong five hundred villages with altars as fiefs and he accepted them with no demurral. Why do you decline?"

Yanzi replied: "I have heard that from a many thousand problems, the sage is bound to get one wrong and the fool bound to get one right. In my view, this is a case in which Guan Zhong was wrong and I was right. For this reason, I have bowed twice and have not dared to comply with your command."

# 6.19 [159] 景公以晏子衣食弊薄使田无宇致封邑晏子辞

景公因为晏子衣服食物简陋不足，命令田无宇赐予封邑，晏子推辞

## 【原文】

晏子相齐，衣十升之布，〔食〕脱粟之食、五卵、苔菜而已。左右以告公，公为之封邑，使田无宇致台与无盐。晏子对曰："昔吾先君太公受之营丘，为地五百里，为世国长，自太公至于公之身，有数十公矣。苟能说其君以取邑，不至公之身，趣齐搏以求升土，不得容足而寓焉。婴闻之，臣有德益禄，无德退禄，恶有不肖父为不肖子为封邑以败君之政者乎？"遂不受。

## 【今译】

晏子担任齐相，穿粗布织造的衣服，吃粗糙的饭食，配以盐巴和苔菜而已。周围的人告诉景公，景公要给他划分封邑，命令田无宇将台和无盐赐给晏子。晏子回应说："以前我初代国君太公受封营丘，有五百里的土地，是诸侯国里面最多的了，从太公到国君您，已经经历过数十位国君了。如果只要能取悦国君就可以获得封邑，那么不到您做国君的时候，想到齐国来获得土地的人就连立足存身之地都没有了。我听说，作为臣子如果有德行就增加俸禄，如果没有德行就辞退俸禄，哪有无能的父亲为无能的儿子获取封邑来败坏他国君的政治的呢？"于是不接受封邑。

# 6.19 [159] BECAUSE YANZI'S CLOTHING WAS SHABBY AND HIS FOOD MEAGER, DUKE JING SENT TIAN WUYU TO GRANT HIM FIEF CITIES. YANZI DECLINED.

When Yanzi was prime minister in Qi, he wore clothes made of ten-*sheng* cloth[1] and the food he ate consisted of nothing but unpolished rice, five oval-shaped crystals of salt and sea grass. The Duke's entourage reported this to him. The Duke wanted to grant Yanzi cities as fiefdoms and sent Tian Wuyu to offer him the cities of Tai and Wuyan.

Yanzi said: "In the past, our former ruler, Duke Tai, received his fief in Ying Qiu, an area of five hundred *li*, and he became the head of a state that has been passed on from one generation to another. From the day of Duke Tai down to our present Duke, there have been just over ten Dukes.[2] Yet, if indeed it had been possible to please a ruler by accepting a fief city, our present ruler would never have reached his position at all — everyone would have already rushed to Qi in order to fight over[3] a small piece of land and not even a foot's width of earth would have remained to reside on. I have heard: If a minister has virtues, then his emolument is increased; if he lacks virtues, his emolument is withdrawn from him. Where would you find an unworthy minister who, as a father, granted his unworthy son fief cities and thereby brought his ruler's government into ruin?" Consequently, he did not accept.

529

---

1 One *sheng* consisted of eighty horizontal threads. The protocol required ministers to wear clothes made of fifteen-*sheng*, that is, of twelve-hundred threads. Since Yanzi's clothes were made of only eight-hundred threads, it means that he wore unrefined clothes of a common person.

2 数十 → 十数 (*JS*, 414/6).

3 抟 → 搏 (*YZCQ-ICS*, 56, n. 4).

## 6.20 [160] 田桓子疑晏子何以辞邑晏子答以君子之事也

田桓子质疑晏子为何不接受封邑，晏子用君子的追求来回应他

### 【原文】

景公赐晏子邑，晏子辞。田桓子谓晏子曰："君欢然与子邑，必不受（恨以）〔以恨〕君，何也？"晏子对曰："婴闻之，节受于上者，宠长于君；俭居处者，名广于外。夫长宠广名，君子之事也。婴独庸能已乎？"

### 【今译】

景公赐予晏子封邑，晏子推辞不接受。田桓子对晏子说："国君高高兴兴地赐予您封邑，您坚决不接受，违背了国君的心意，这是为什么？"晏子回答说："我听说，有节制地接受国君封赏的人，能够长期被国君宠任；俭朴地生活的人，他的名声会被外界所传颂。被国君所宠任以及获得名声，才是君子追求的东西。难道只有我不能为了自己这么做吗？"

## 6.20 [160] TIAN HUANZI QUESTIONED YANZI'S MOTIVES IN REFUSING TO RECEIVE A FIEF CITY. YANZI RESPONDED BY REFERRING TO THE DUTY A MAN OF NOBLE CHARACTER.

Duke Jing wanted to grant Yanzi the gift of a fief city, but Yanzi declined. Tian Huanzi said to Yanzi: "Our ruler is happy to give you this city. If you insist on refusing, you will cause our ruler displeasure — why do this?"

Yanzi answered: "I have heard that one who receives from his superior only sparingly will be in his ruler's favor for a long time. One who lives frugally spreads his reputation far and wide. It is the duty of a man of noble character to be in his ruler's favor for a long time and to spread his reputation far and wide. Why should I be the singular exception who puts an end to this practice?"

# 6.21 [161] 景公欲更晏子宅晏子辞以近市得所求讽公省刑

景公想要为晏子更换住宅，晏子以靠近市场可以买到想要的东西而推辞，劝谏景公减省刑罚

## 【原文】

景公欲更晏子之宅，曰："子之宅近市湫隘，嚣尘不可以居，请更诸爽垲者。"晏子辞曰："君之先臣容焉，臣不足以嗣之，于臣侈矣。且小人近市，朝夕得所求，小人之利也。敢烦里旅？"公笑曰："子近市，识贵贱乎？"对曰："既窃利之，敢不识乎？"公曰："何贵何

## 【今译】

景公想要为晏子更换住宅，就说："您的住宅靠近市场，潮湿又狭窄，嘈杂喧嚣尘土飞扬，难以居住，请让我给您换到地势高而干燥的地方吧。"晏子推辞说："您以前的臣子能够居住在这里，我本来没有继承的资格，住在这里对我来说已经很奢侈了。况且我的住宅靠近市场，能够轻易得到想要的东西，这对我来说是有利的事情。怎么还敢劳烦乡里百姓修建房屋呢？"景公笑着说："您住在市场附近，知道东西的贵贱吗？"晏子回答说："既然对我是有利的东西，怎么可能不知道呢？"景公说："什么东西贵，什么东西贱呢？"当时，景公的刑罚

## 6.21 [161] DUKE JING WANTED TO REPLACE YANZI'S RESIDENCE. YANZI DECLINED ON THE GROUNDS THAT HE COULD GET WHATEVER HE NEEDED FROM THE NEARBY MARKET. HE THEN USED VEILED CRITICISM TO REMONSTRATE WITH THE DUKE TO BE MORE SPARING IN CORPORAL PUNISHMENT[1]

Duke Jing wanted to replace Yanzi's residence, saying: "Your residence is situated near the market. It is low-lying and damp, narrow, noisy, and dusty. It is uninhabitable. Permit me to replace it with one that is bright and dry."

Yanzi declined the offer, saying: "My Lord! My father, your previous minister, tolerated living in this residence. I am not worthy to be his successor, and so this residence is in fact an extravagance for me. Besides, your insignificant servant lives close to the market, and I can always get whatever I need, day and night. This is beneficial for your insignificant servant. Would I dare to trouble the people of another neighborhood?"

The Duke laughed and said: "Since you are near the market, you probably know what is expensive and what is cheap — right?"

Yanzi replied: "As I am enjoying this benefit already — how could I presume not to know?"

The Duke said: "Then what is expensive and what is cheap?"

Now at that time, the Duke imposed numerous corporal punishments, and so there were traders who sold shoes catering to those whose toes had been chopped off as a punishment. Therefore, Yanzi replied: "Shoes for people whose toes had been chopped off are expensive while regular shoes are cheap."

---

1  Item 6.21 [161] ↔ *Zuozhuan*, B10.3.3/324/8; *Hanfeizi*, 37/117/26; *Kongcongzi*, 5.3/59/5.

**【原文】**

贱？"是时也，公繁于刑，有鬻踊者。故对曰："踊贵而屦贱。"公愀然改容。公为是省于刑。君子曰："仁人之言，其利博哉！晏子一言，而齐侯省刑。《诗》曰：'君子如祉，乱（无）〔庶〕遄已。'其是之谓乎！"

534

**【今译】**

非常繁重，有在市场上卖假脚的。所以回答说："假脚贵而草鞋贱。"景公的脸色变得悲伤。景公因此减省刑罚。君子评论说："仁义的人说的话，它的作用真的很大。晏子一句话，而让齐国国君减省了刑罚。《诗经》上说：'君子为别人造福，祸乱很快就会消除。'说的就是这种情况吧！"

The Duke was troubled, and his countenance changed. Thereupon, he was more sparing in applying corporal punishments.

The man of noble character said: "The benefit of the words of the humane spreads far and wide. Yanzi made a brief statement and the Lord of Qi became more sparing in applying corporal punishments. As it says in the *Odes*:

If our ruler would grant blessing upon the good,

disorder would quickly cease.[1]

Is this not a precise expression of this point?"

535

---

1   *Shijing*, 198/95/9. The beginning of this ode narrates the complaints that a certain man, who is a victim of slander, has against both Heaven and his ruler. He reflects upon his dire state, saying that if the ruler would deal with his slanderers with "anger" (怒) and with the good, innocent victims with blessings (祉), disorder would cease to exist.

## 6.22 [162] 景公毁晏子邻以益其宅晏子因陈桓子以〔辞〕

景公毁坏晏子邻居的房屋来扩大晏子的住宅，晏子通过陈桓子来拒绝

### 【原文】

晏子使晋，景公更其宅，反则成矣。既拜，乃毁之，而为里室，皆如其旧，则使宅人反之。（且）〔曰〕："谚曰：'非宅是卜，维邻是卜。'二三子先卜邻矣。违卜不祥。君子不犯非礼，小人不犯不祥，古之制也。吾敢违诸乎？"卒复其旧宅。公弗许。因陈桓子以请，乃许之。

### 【今译】

晏子出使晋国，景公重新修建了他的住宅，等他回来的时候已经修好了。晏子拜谢后，就毁坏了新修的住宅，又盖了邻里的房屋，跟原来的样子相同，于是请原来的邻居返回居住。并且说："谚语说：'修建住宅不需要占卜，与谁做邻居才需要占卜。'诸位已经占卜了邻居，违背占卜的结果是不祥的。君子不做不合乎礼节的事情，平民百姓不做不吉祥的事情，这是古代的规矩。我哪里敢违背这些规矩呢？"于是邻居都回到自己原来的住宅居住了。景公不同意。晏子通过陈桓子请求景公，景公才同意。

# 6.22 [162] DUKE JING DEMOLISHED YANZI'S NEIGHBORHOOD IN ORDER TO EXPAND YANZI'S RESIDENCE. YANZI DECLINED, THROUGH THE INTERVENTION OF CHEN HUANZI.[1]

When Yanzi was on a diplomatic mission to Jin, Duke Jing replaced Yanzi's residence and completed the project by the time Yanzi returned. After Yanzi bowed in gratitude, he demolished the new residence and rebuilt the entire neighborhood to its former condition. He then persuaded the old residents to return to their homes, saying: "As the saying goes: 'It is not the site of the house that is divined, it is the neighborhood in particular.' You gentlemen have earlier consulted about this neighborhood through divination; to now flout it would be inauspicious. A man of noble character does not commit acts forbidden by the rites and the petty man does not commit acts that are deemed inauspicious. These are the ancient regulations. How dare I flout them?"

Ultimately, he returned them to their old residences. At first, the Duke was not inclined to allow it, but through the intercession of Chen Huanzi, he gave his permission for their return.

---

1  Item 6.22 [162] ↔ *Zuozhuan*, B10.3.3/324/17.

## 6.23 [163] 景公欲为晏子筑室于宫内晏子称是以远之而辞

景公想要为晏子在王宫内修建房屋，晏子说这是疏远他的做法而推辞

### 【原文】

景公谓晏子曰："寡人欲朝夕见，为夫子筑室于闺内可乎？"晏子对曰："臣闻之，隐而显，近而结，维至贤耳。如臣者，饰其容止，以待承令，犹恐罪戾也，今君近之，是远之也，请辞。"

### 【今译】

景公对晏子说："我想随时都可以见到您，能在王宫内为您修建一间房屋吗？"晏子回答说："我听说，隐居而名声显赫，靠近国君而能收敛，只有最贤能的人可以做到。像我这样的人，专注自己的行为举止，时刻等待国君的命令，还担心因过失而获罪，现在您要亲近我，其实是在疏远我，所以我请求推辞。"

## 6.23 [163] DUKE JING WANTED TO BUILD A HOUSE FOR YANZI INSIDE THE PALACE. YANZI STATED THAT IT WOULD DISTANCE HIM FROM THE RULER, AND DECLINED.

Duke Jing said to Yanzi: "I would like to have audiences with you day and night. Can I build a dwelling for you, Master, within my private quarters?"

Yanzi answered: "I have heard that only the worthiest man resides in the shadows and yet shines, and is constrained within the inner circle of the ruler. In my case, I modify my demeanor and conduct while awaiting your orders, and still I am fearful that I am committing offences. If you, my Lord, now wish to bring me nearer to you, you will grow distant from me. Permit me to decline."

## 6.24 [164] 景公以晏子妻老且恶欲内爱女晏子再拜以辞

景公因为晏子的妻子年老貌丑，想要将自己心爱的女儿嫁给他，晏子拜了又拜推辞了

### 【原文】

景公有爱女，请嫁于晏子，公乃往燕晏子之家，饮酒酣，公见其妻，曰："此子之内子耶？"晏子对曰："然，是也。"公曰："嘻！亦老且恶矣。寡人有女少且姣，请以满夫子之宫。"晏子违席而对曰："乃此则老且恶，婴与之居故矣，故及其少而姣也。且人固以壮托乎老，姣托乎恶，彼尝托，而婴受之矣。君虽有赐，可以使婴倍其托乎？"再拜而辞。

### 【今译】

景公有一个心爱的女儿，想要嫁给晏子，景公于是前往晏子家中赴宴，饮酒到尽兴的时候，景公看到晏子的妻子，然后说："这是先生您的妻子吗？"晏子回答说："是的。"景公说："唉！又老又丑啊！我有一个女儿年轻貌美，把她嫁给你吧。"晏子离开座席回答说："她现在又老又丑，是因为和晏婴在一起居住了很长时间，所以她年轻的时候是很漂亮的。况且人们都将老年托付给壮年，将丑陋来托付给美丽，她曾经将老年托付于我，而我接受了。现在国君虽然有所赐予，但能让我违背她的托付吗？"拜了又拜推辞不接受。

## 6.24 [164] DUKE JING THOUGHT THAT YANZI'S WIFE WAS OLD AND UGLY, AND WANTED HIM TO MARRY HIS FAVORITE DAUGHTER. YANZI BOWED TWICE AND DECLINED.

Duke Jing had a favorite daughter whom he wished to grant to Yanzi in marriage. So, he went to a banquet at Yanzi's house where he drank wine, and after becoming a bit tipsy he glanced at Yanzi's wife and said: "Is this your wife?"

Yanzi replied: "Yes, this is she."

The Duke exclaimed: "Oh! She is old and ugly; I have a daughter who is young and pretty, with whom I would ask you to complete your household, Master."

Yanzi respectfully rose from his mat and replied: "As you can see, she is now indeed old and ugly, for she has lived with me for a very long time. Back then she was young and pretty. What is more, people, when they are young, rely on their youthfulness to provide for them when they become old, and on their beauty to provide for them when they become ugly. She entrusted herself to me and I have accepted it. Now although you want to grant me this favor, my Lord, do you mean to make me betray the trust she bestowed upon me?"

He then bowed twice and declined.

## 6.25 [165] 景公以晏子乘弊车驽马使梁丘据遗之三返不受

景公因为晏子乘坐劣等马拉的破旧马车，命令梁丘据赠予他车马，三次晏子都不接受

**【原文】**

晏子朝，乘弊车，驾驽马。景公见之曰："嘻！夫子之禄寡耶？何乘不（任）〔佼〕之甚也？"晏子对曰："赖君之赐，得以寿三族，及国游士，皆得生焉。臣得暖衣饱食，弊车驽马，以奉其身，于臣足矣。"晏子出，公使梁丘据遗之辂车乘马，三返不受。公不说，趣召晏子。晏子至，公曰："夫子不受，寡人亦不乘。"晏子对曰："君使臣临百官之吏，臣节其衣服饮食之养，以先国之民；然犹恐其侈靡而不顾其行也。今辂车乘马，君乘之上，而臣亦乘之下，民之无义，侈其衣服饮食而不顾其行者，臣无以禁之。"遂让不受。

**【今译】**

晏子参加朝会，乘坐破旧的马车，驾驭劣等的马匹。景公看到后说："唉！先生的俸禄太少了吗？为什么乘坐这么破旧的马车呢？"晏子回答说："凭借国君您的赏赐，我能够照顾父、母、妻三族的生活，国内游学的士人，也都能够生活。我能够吃饱穿暖，以破旧的马车和劣等的马匹来奉养自己，对于我已经足够了。"晏子离开后，国君命令梁丘据赠送给晏子诸侯标准的车马，往返三次晏子都不接受。景公不高兴，派人去征召晏子。晏子来到王宫，景公说："先生不接受我的赠与，那么我也不乘坐了。"晏子回答说："国君您让我统领百官，我节省自己衣服饮食的供应，为国内的官民树立榜样；但仍然害怕他们奢侈靡费而不顾忌自己的行为。现在诸侯标准的车马，国君作为上级乘坐，而我作为臣子也乘坐，民众的行为不讲道义，追求衣服饮食的奢侈而不顾及自己行为的人，我就无法禁止了。"于是辞谢，没有接受。

## 6.25 [165] SINCE YANZI WAS DRIVING A SHABBY CHARIOT HARNESSED TO A NAG, DUKE JING MADE LIANGQIU JU SEND YANZI A PRESENT, WHICH YANZI DECLINED THREE TIMES.[1]

Yanzi rode to a court audience on a shabby chariot harnessed to a nag. When Duke Jing saw this, he said: "Oh, is your emolument so meager? Otherwise, why would you have driven such a worthless chariot?"

Yanzi answered: "Relying on your generosity, my Lord, I am able to support all three lineages of my relatives, while all the peripatetic scholars in our state depend on this for their living as well. As long as I have warm clothes and enough food, this shabby chariot harnessed to a nag will be sufficient to provide for my personal needs."

After Yanzi had left, the Duke ordered Liangqiu Ju to send Yanzi a gift of a royal carriage harnessed to a team of four horses. Three times Yanzi declined the gift and did not accept it.

The Duke was displeased by this and had Yanzi summoned to him forthwith. When Yanzi arrived, the Duke said: "If you do not accept this carriage, Master, I will not travel in a carriage either."

Yanzi replied: "You have commissioned me to supervise the officials of the entire bureaucracy, and have asked them to restrain their expenses for clothing, food and drinks, in order to give priority to the people of Qi.[2] I am afraid, however, that the officials are still wasteful, extravagant, and pay no heed to their conduct. Now if you, my Lord, in your high position, ride a royal carriage harnessed to four horses, and I — as a minister in an inferior position — do likewise, then if the people, who have no innate moral sense, increase their pursuit of excessive clothing, food and drinks, and pay no heed to their conduct, I will have no basis for prohibiting this."

Consequently, Yanzi modestly declined and did not accept.

543

---

1   Item 6.25 [165] ↔ *Shuoyuan*, 2.13/15/29.

2   以先齐国 (*YZCQ-ICS*, 58, n. 5).

## 6.26 [166] 景公睹晏子之食菲薄而嗟其贫晏子称有参士之食

景公看到晏子的饭菜非常差而感叹他的贫穷，晏子说有满足三人的食物

**【原文】**

晏子相景公，食脱粟之食，炙三弋，五卵、苔菜耳矣。公闻之，往燕焉，睹晏子之食也。公曰："嘻！夫子之家如此其贫乎！而寡人不知，寡人之罪也。"晏子对曰："以世之不足也，免粟之食饱，士之一乞也；炙三弋，士之二乞也；五卵，士之三乞也。婴无倍人之行，而有参士之食，君之赐厚矣！婴之家不贫。"再拜而谢。

**【今译】**

晏子做景公的国相，吃仅去掉谷皮的粗粮，烤三只飞鸟，用盐伴着苔菜而已。景公听说后，到晏子家赴宴，看到晏子的饭菜。景公说："唉！先生您家这么贫穷吗？但我却不知道，这是我的过错。"晏子回答说："现在国家的食物还不够，去掉谷皮的粗粮能吃饱，是士人的一种满足；能够烧烤三只飞鸟，是士人的第二种满足；有盐可吃，是士人的第三种满足。晏婴没有成倍于他人的贡献，却能得到满足三人的食物，国君的赏赐已经非常优厚了！晏婴的家室并不贫困。"拜了又拜后谢绝了。

## 6.26 [166] DUKE JING SAW THAT YANZI WAS EATING MEAGER FARE AND SIGHED AT HIS POVERTY. YANZI STATED THAT HIS MEAL COULD FEED THREE OFFICERS.

When Yanzi served Duke Jing as prime minister, he ate nothing but unpolished rice, three roasted small birds, five oval-shaped crystals of salt, and sea grass. The Duke heard of this and went to Yanzi's house during mealtime and saw what Yanzi was eating. The Duke said: "Oh Master, your household is so poor, and I did not know. This is my fault."

Yanzi replied: "In view of the current shortage in the world, one meal of unpolished rice can appease the hunger of one officer, adding three small birds will appease the hunger of two, and adding five oval-shaped crystals of salt will appease the hunger of three. I do not perform the work of two officers and still have food for three. It is due to the abundance of your gifts, my Lord, that my household is not poor." Then he bowed twice and declined.

545

## 6.27 [167] 梁丘据自患不及晏子晏子勉据〔以〕常为常行

梁丘据担心自己难以企及晏子，晏子用持之以恒来勉励他

**【原文】**

梁丘据谓晏子曰："吾至死不及夫子矣！"晏子曰："婴闻之，为者常成，行者常至。婴非有异于人也，常为而不置，常行而不休者，故难及也？"

**【今译】**

梁丘据对晏子说："我到死也赶不上先生您了啊！"晏子说："我听说，只要肯做就能够成功，只要肯走就能到达目的地。晏婴并非与他人有什么不同，只是经常做而不放弃，经常走而不休息，怎么能说难赶上呢？"

## 6.27 [167] LIANGQIU JU WAS TROUBLED THAT HE FELL SHORT OF YANZI. YANZI ENCOURAGED HIM TO ALWAYS TAKE ACTION AND ALWAYS CARRY THINGS THROUGH.

Liangqiu Ju said to Yanzi: "As long as I live I will fall short of you, Master."

Yanzi replied: "I have heard that he who acts unceasingly, always accomplishes, and he who constantly moves forward, always arrives. I am no different from others: I 'unceasingly act' without putting matters aside, and I 'constantly move forward' without taking rest. Why[1] is this so difficult to achieve?"

547

---

1   故 → 胡 (*JS*, 425/1).

# 6.28 [168] 晏子老辞邑景公不许致车一乘而后止

晏子年老了请求退还封邑，景公不同意，退还后赐予了马车一辆才终止

## 【原文】

晏子相景公，老，辞邑。公曰："自吾先君定公至今，用世多矣，齐大夫未有老辞邑者（矣）。今夫子独辞之，是毁国之故，弃寡人也。不可！"晏子对曰："婴闻古之事君者，称身而食；德厚而受禄，德薄则辞禄。德厚受禄，所以明上也；德薄辞禄，可以洁下也。婴老德薄无能，而厚受禄，是掩上之明，污下之行，不可。"公不许，曰："昔吾

## 【今译】

晏子做景公的相国，年老，要求退还封邑。景公说："从我的先君定公到现在，担任官职的人有很多了，齐国的大夫没有因为年老而退还封邑的。现在单单先生您要退还，这是要破坏国家的传统，舍弃我了。不行！"晏子回答说："我听说古代的臣子辅佐国君，衡量自己的能力而接受赏赐；德行深厚的人接受俸禄，德行浅薄的人就辞让俸禄。德才深厚的人接受俸禄，是为了显示国君的英明；德才浅薄的人辞让俸禄，可以使臣下廉洁。晏婴年老德行浅薄也没有能力，却接受丰厚的俸禄，是掩盖国君的英明，污损了臣下的行动。不行！"景公不同意，说："以前我先代的国君齐桓公，有管仲为齐国忧心劳苦，年老之后，桓公赏给他三处住宅，恩泽延续到子孙。现在先生您同样担任我的相国，我想要为您修建三处住宅，恩泽延续到子孙，难道不可以吗？"晏子回答说："以前管子辅佐桓公，桓公的地位高于诸侯，恩德

# 6.28 [168] YANZI GREW OLD AND WANTED TO RESIGN FROM OFFICE AND RETIRE.[1] THE DUKE DID NOT PERMIT IT. YANZI SENT THE DUKE HIS CHARIOT WITH A TEAM OF FOUR HORSES AND TERMINATED HIS APPEARANCE IN COURT AUDIENCES.

Yanzi served Duke Jing as prime minister. When he became old, he wanted to resign his official position and retire. The Duke said: "Since the time of my former ruler, Duke Ding,[2] to this day, many generations have passed.[3] However, it never occurred to the High Officers of Qi to resign their official positions and retire because of old age. If you alone resign your official position and retire, you will violate the precedents of our state and reject me. This is not acceptable."

Yanzi replied: "I have heard that those who served rulers in ancient times earned their keep according to their personal qualifications. If their virtue was substantial, they accepted emoluments, but if their virtue was slight, they declined it. When their virtue was substantial and they accepted emoluments, they put their superiors in good light. When their virtue was slight and they declined emoluments, they could preserve the reputation of their inferiors unsullied. I am old, my virtue is slight, and I have no capabilities. If in spite of all this I receive a substantial emolument, I will only dim the brilliance of my superior and sully the conduct of my inferiors. This is unacceptable."

549

The Duke did not approve and said: "Formerly, our former ruler Duke Huan had Guan Zhong, who compassionately toiled for the state

---

1　辞邑 "Resign an official position and retire," following *Hanyu Da Zidian* 汉语大字典, vol. 11, p. 502.

2　定公 → 丁公 (*JS*, 426/2). Duke Ding reigned in Qi between 1077 and 1051 BCE.

3　用世多 may also mean: "There were many who were in the service of our ducal linage."

## 【原文】

先君桓公，有管仲恤劳齐国，身老，赏之以三归，泽及子孙。今夫子亦相寡人，欲为夫子三归，泽至子孙，岂不可哉？"对曰："昔者管子事桓公，桓公义高诸侯，德备百姓。今婴事君也，国仅齐于诸侯，怨积乎百姓，婴之罪多矣，而君欲赏之，岂以其不肖父（其）〔为〕不肖子厚受赏以伤国民义哉？且夫德薄而禄厚，智悟而家富，是彰污而逆教也，不可。"公不许。晏子出。异日朝，得间而入邑，致车一乘而后止。

## 【今译】

遍及百姓。现在我辅佐国君，齐国仅仅与诸侯地位平等，百姓积怨于心，我的过错太多了，但国君您还要赏赐我，难道能因为无能的父亲而让无能的子孙接受厚赏来破坏国民的大义吗？况且德才浅薄而接受丰厚的俸禄，才智不足而家庭富足，是表彰错误而违背教化，不行！"景公不同意。晏子离开王宫。过了几天朝见景公，得到机会退还了封邑，景公赐予了他一辆马车后才终止。

of Qi. When he became old, Duke Huan awarded him three separated establishments[1] and this beneficence was extended to Guan Zhong's sons and grandsons. Now you, Master, also serve me as prime minister, and it is my wish that you too should have three separate establishments and that this beneficence be extended to your sons and grandsons. How could this not be proper?"

Yanzi replied: "In the past, when Guan Zhong served Duke Huan, the Duke surpassed all the regional princes in righteousness, and his virtue completely affected the people. Now that I am serving you, my Lord, the regional princes consider Qi to be only one state among others, and resentment has accumulated among the people. My guilt is great and still you wish to reward me. How can an unworthy father receive generous rewards for his unworthy sons, without violating the sense of righteousness of the people in our state? What is more, one with slight virtue who receives a high emolument and continues to enrich his family when his mental powers are impaired reveals his defilement and deviates from the moral teaching. This is unacceptable."

The Duke did not permit the resignation and retirement. Yanzi left and, on another day, appeared for court audience. Then, an opportunity arose and he left and entered his fief-city; he sent his Quadriga-Chariot back to the Duke, and terminated his appearances in court audiences.

---

1   For Guanzi's "three separate establishments," "three returning mansions," or "three wives," (三归) see, *Analects*, 3.22/6/20; William H. Nienhauser, Jr., ed. *The Grand Scribe's Records*. Bloomington and Indianapolis: Indiana University Press, (1994) vol. 7, 13, n. 37.

## 6.29 [169] 晏子病将死妻问所欲言云毋变尔俗

晏子生病了就要死去，他的妻子问他还有什么话要说，晏子说不要改变他的家法

【原文】

晏子病将死，其妻曰："夫子无欲言乎？"子曰："吾恐死而俗变，谨视尔家，毋变尔俗也。"

【今译】

晏子生病了就要死去，他的妻子问他："你没有什么话想说吗？"晏子说："我怕我死后家法会改变，你要谨慎地照料这个家，不要改变这家法。"

# 6.29 [169] YANZI WAS ILL AND ABOUT TO DIE. HIS WIFE ASKED HIM WHAT HE WANTED TO SAY. YANZI SAID, DO NOT CHANGE THE HOUSEHOLD CUSTOMS.[1]

When Yanzi was ill and about to die, his wife said to him: "Is it not something you wish to say, Master?"

Yanzi[2] replied: "I am afraid that our household customs will change after I am gone. Carefully look after this household and do not change the customs."

---

1   For Yanzi's three household customs, see Item 5.29 [139].

2   子曰 → 晏子 (*YZCQ-ICS*, 59, n. 1).

# 6.30 [170] 晏子病将死凿楹纳书命子壮而示之

晏子生病了快要死去，凿开厅堂的柱子装进遗言，让孩子长大后再让他看

## 【原文】

晏子病将死，凿楹纳书焉，谓其妻曰："楹语也，子壮而示之。"及壮发书，〔书〕之言曰："布帛不可穷，穷不可饰；牛马不可穷，穷不可服；士不可穷，穷不可任；国不可穷，穷不可窃也。"

## 【今译】

晏子生病了快要死去，凿开厅堂的柱子装进遗言，对他的妻子说："厅堂柱子里的话，等孩子长大了再给他看。"等到孩子长大后打开遗书，书上说："布帛不能缺乏，缺乏了就没有衣服穿；牛马不可以缺乏，缺乏了就无法拉车；士人不可以缺乏，缺乏了就没人可以担任官职；国家不能贫弱，贫弱了就无容身之地。"

# 6.30 [170] YANZI WAS ILL AND WAS ABOUT TO DIE. HE HOLLOWED OUT A HOLE IN A PILLAR AND PUT HIS TESTAMENT IN IT, AND GAVE AN ORDER TO SHOW IT TO HIS SON UPON COMING OF AGE.[1]

When Yanzi was ill and about to die, he hollowed out a hole in a pillar and put his testament in it. He said to his wife: "When our son comes of age, show him the words inside the pillar."

When his son came of age, he opened the last testament and read the following words: "Clothes of cotton and silk should not be over used over used — if they were, it would be impossible to dress up; cattle and horses should not be over used — if they were, it would be impossible to tame; officers should not be over used — if they were, it would be impossible to assign duties; states should not be over used — if they were, it would be impossible to steal."[2]

*555*

---

1   Item 6.30 [170] ↔ *Shuoyuan*, 20.22/179/33.

2   *JS*, 429/8, 窃 → 践. In that case, the ending of this item would read: "States cannot be over used – if they were, it would be impossible to implement anything." I am inclined, however, to accept the bitterly ironic version of this item as the final statement of the *YZCQ*'s Inner Chapters because we can find a similar ironic statement in *Zhuangzi*, 庄子, 10/25/8, which reads: 彼窃钩者诛, 窃国者为诸侯 — "Steal a belt, be punished, steal a state, become a state sovereign." See also *Xunzi* 荀子, 18.2/84/20, 可以有窃国 — "It is possible to take over a state by stealth." In the *Shuoyuan*, 20.22/179/25, however, which records in a parallel passage the final words of Yanzi, we find an alternative, gloomier ending of Yanzi's life saga. Instead of 国不可窃, 穷不可窃也, it reads: 穷乎穷乎穷也 — "Am I over used, am I over used; indeed I am."

# 外　篇

# The Outer Chapters

# 第七卷 重而异者

## 7.1 [171] 景公饮酒命晏子去礼晏子谏

景公饮酒的时候，命令晏子免去礼节，晏子进谏

**【原文】**

景公饮酒数日而乐，（释衣）〔去〕冠〔被裳〕，自鼓〔盆〕（缶）〔甕〕，谓左右曰："仁人亦乐是夫？"梁丘据对曰："仁人之耳目，亦犹人也，夫奚为独不乐此也？"公曰："趣驾迎晏子。"晏子朝〔服〕以至，受觞再拜。公曰："寡人甚乐此乐，欲与夫子共之，请去礼。"晏子对曰："君之言过矣！群臣皆欲去礼以事君，婴恐君（子）之不欲也。今齐国五尺之童子，力皆过婴，又能胜君，然而不敢乱者，畏礼

**【今译】**

景公饮酒好几天，非常高兴，脱去衣服帽子，亲自击缶奏乐，对周围的人说："仁德的人也会因为这些而开心吗？"梁丘据回答说："仁德的人的耳朵和眼睛，也和普通人一样，怎么会只有他们不因此而开心呢？"景公说："赶快驾车去迎接晏子。"晏子身穿朝服来到宫殿，接过酒杯拜了又拜。景公说："我特别喜欢这种快乐，想要和先生您一同享受，请您免去礼节。"晏子回答说："国君的话错了！群臣都想要免去礼节来侍奉国君，我怕就不是国君所希望的了。现在齐国身高五

# Chapter Seven    Repetition Cum Difference

## 7.1 [171] DUKE JING HAD BEEN DRINKING. HE ORDERED YANZI TO DISPENSE WITH THE RITES. YANZI REMONSTRATED.[1]

Duke Jing had been drinking, taking his pleasure for several days. He tossed off his cap, wrapped himself in his skirt, made his own music by drumming on a clay jar, and said to his entourage: "Does the humane person also experience this particular kind of joy?"

Liangqiu Ju replied: "The ears and eyes of the humane person are just like those of men — why exactly would he not experience this particular kind of joy?"

The Duke said: "Make haste, prepare a chariot to go and fetch Yanzi."

Yanzi arrived at the court, dressed as the court protocol demanded. He received the wine cup and bowed twice.

The Duke said: "I am extremely pleased by this amusement and I would like to share it with you, my Master. Please let us dispense with the rites."

Yanzi replied: "My Lord, your words are mistaken. All of your ministers want to dispense with the rites in serving you. You, my Lord, I'm afraid ought not wish for this. At present, all the youngsters in Qi who are taller than five feet are stronger than me, and they can overpower you too, my Lord.[2] However, the reason that they dare not rebel is that they stand in awe of the rites and righteousness. If superiors have no rites, they have no basis by which to command their inferiors. If inferiors have no rites, they

559

---

1    Item 7.1 [171] ↔ Item 1.2 [2]; *Hanshi waichuan*, 9.8/66/20; *Xinxu*, 6.7/33/30.

2    This statement means that Duke Jing, like Yanzi, was a person of diminutive structure, just 115 centimeters in height. According to Item 5.25 [135], Yanzi was quite a bit taller: almost six feet or 138 centimeters tall.

**【原文】**

也。上若无礼，无以使其下；下若无礼，无以事其上。夫麋鹿维无礼，故父子同麀，〔夫〕人之所以（贵以）〔以贵〕禽兽者，以有礼也。婴闻之，人君无礼，无以临其邦；大夫无礼，官吏不恭；父子无礼，其家必凶；兄弟无礼，不能久同。《诗》曰：'人而无礼，胡不遄死。'故礼不

560

**【今译】**

尺的孩童，力量已经超过了晏婴，也超过了国君您，然而却不敢作乱的原因，就是畏惧礼仪啊！国君如果不遵从礼节，就不能管理好臣子；臣子如果不遵从礼节，就无法辅佐国君。麋鹿是不懂得礼节的，所以父子和同一只母鹿交配，而人之所以比禽兽高贵，就是因为人懂得礼节。我听说，国君如果不懂得礼仪，就无法治理他的国家；大夫不懂得礼仪，那么官吏就不会恭敬；父子之间不行用礼节，他们的家庭就必然会遭遇灾祸；兄弟之间不行用礼节，就不能长久居住在一起。《诗经》说：'人如果不讲礼法，还不如早点死去。'所以礼法不能免去。"景公说："我不够聪慧明智，身边的人蛊惑我，才到了这种地步，让我

have no basis by which they can serve their superiors. It is precisely because of the absence of rites among the deer that the buck and its offspring share the same doe. The reason why ordinary people are superior to beasts derives from their possession of the rites. I have heard that if a ruler has no rites, he has nothing by which to govern his state; if high officers have no rites, their underlings and clerks will not respect them; if fathers and sons have no rites, their families will surely be visited by disaster; if elder and younger brothers have no rites, they cannot long abide one another. As it says in the *Odes*:

A man without the rites,

Why should he not die quickly?[1]

Therefore, it is impossible to dispense with the rites."

The Duke said: "I am not quick in understanding, and I lack in goodness. My entourage beguiled me and thus brought me to this state. Let me execute them."

Yanzi said: "Why blame your entourage? If you, my Lord, have no rites, then those who are fond of the rites will leave you and those who have no rites will draw near; if you, my Lord, are fond of the rites, then those who have the rites will draw near and those who have no rites will leave you."

The Duke said: "Well argued. I request to change my clothes, replace my cap and receive more of your instructions."

Yanzi withdrew himself, departed, and stood outside the gate. The Duke ordered people to wet down the floor, sweep it and change the mats. He called for his robe and cap in order to welcome Yanzi. Yanzi entered the gate and after deferring precedence three times, they mounted the staircase. The Duke performed the rite of offering drink three times. Yanzi swirled the wine and tasted the food. He bowed twice, said that he was satiated, and

---

1   *Shijing*, 52/24/9.

**【原文】**

可去也。"公曰:"寡人不敏无良,左右淫蛊寡人,以至于此,请杀之。"晏子曰:"(右左)〔左右〕何罪?君若无礼,则好礼者去,无礼者至;君若好礼,则有礼者至,无礼者去。"公曰:"善。请易衣革冠,更受命。"晏子避走,立乎门外。公令人粪洒改席,召衣冠以迎晏子。晏子入门,三让,升阶,用三献〔礼〕焉;嗽酒尝膳,再拜,告餍而出。公下拜,送之门,反,命撤酒去乐,曰:"吾以彰晏子之教也。"

**大中华文库**

**【今译】**

把他们杀了。"晏子说:"周围的人有什么过错呢?国君如果不遵从礼节,那么遵从礼仪的人就会离开,不遵从礼仪的人就会来到;国君如果遵从礼节,那么遵从礼仪的人就会来到,不遵从礼节的人就会离开。"景公说:"好。请让我换了衣服戴上帽子,再次接受您的教诲。"晏子离开宫殿,站在门外。国君下令打扫宫殿重新布置座席,换上衣服带上帽子来迎接晏子。晏子进入宫殿后,礼让三次,走上台阶,用三次献酒的礼节;晏子饮酒品尝食物后,拜了又拜,表示满足后离开。国君走下台阶回礼,送晏子到门口,回来后,命令撤去酒席和音乐,说:"我这样做来彰显晏子的教导。"

then went out. The Duke bowed, escorted Yanzi to the gate, and returned. He ordered the removal of the drinks and the dismissal of the musicians, saying: "By doing this I demonstrate the moral teaching of Yanzi."

563

# 7.2 [172] 景公置酒泰山四望而泣晏子谏

景公在泰山上摆酒置宴，向四面眺望而哭泣，晏子进谏

## 【原文】

景公置酒于泰山之上，酒酣，公四望其地，喟然叹，泣数行而下，曰："寡人将去此堂堂国者而死乎！"左右佐哀而泣者三人，曰："吾细人也，犹将难死，而况公乎！弃是国也而死，其孰可为乎！"晏子独搏其髀，仰天而大笑曰："乐哉！今日之饮也。"公怫然怒曰："寡人有哀，子独大笑，何也？"晏子对曰："今日见怯君一，谀臣三（人），是以大笑。"公曰："何谓谀怯也？"晏子曰："夫古之有死也，（今）

## 【今译】

景公在泰山上摆酒置宴，喝到兴起的时候，眺望四周他的土地，长叹一声，流下数行眼泪说："我将会离开这个伟大的国家而死去吗！"周围陪伴景公悲伤哭泣的人有三个，并说："我们这种微不足道人，都不愿意接受死亡，何况国君您呢？抛弃这样的国家而死去，怎么能接受呢？"晏子却独自拍着大腿，仰天大笑着说："欢乐啊！今天的酒宴。"景公愤怒地说："我心中悲伤，先生却独自大笑，这是为什么？"晏子回答说："今天见到了一个怯懦的国君，三个阿谀的臣子，所以大笑。"景公说："怯懦和阿谀指的是什么呢？"晏子说："死亡是自古以来的事情，会使后世贤能的人得以成长，没有才能的人得以屈服。如果古代的君王就不会死亡，那么以前我们先代的国君太公到现在还活着，国君您还怎么拥有这个国家并因此哀叹呢？兴盛中藏有衰落，生之后就是死亡，这是天所决定的。万物都有其发展的极限，事情有其变化的规律，这是自古以来的常理。有什么好悲伤的呢？到老了还因

## 7.2 [172] DUKE JING HOSTED A DRINKING BANQUET ON MT. TAI. HE LOOKED AROUND TO THE FOUR DIRECTIONS AND CRIED. YANZI REMONSTRATED.[1]

Duke Jing hosted a drinking banquet on Mt. Tai and became tipsy. He looked around to the four directions and sighed deeply. His tears were streaming down in several rows, and he said: "Am I destined to depart from this magnificent state and die?"

Three among his entourage commiserated tearfully in his sorrow. They said: "We are common people and yet even for us death will be difficult; how much more so will this be in your case, our Lord. To die and leave behind such a state — who could endure this?"

But Yanzi slapped his thigh, raised his eyes to the sky and roared with laughter: "How joyful is the drinking today."

The Duke was annoyed and became angry, saying: "I am sorrowful, and you, for your part, roar with laughter — why?"

Yanzi answered, "Today I saw one cowering ruler and three fawning ministers. This is why I roar with laughter."

The Duke said: "What do you mean by 'cowering' and 'fawning'?"

Yanzi replied: "It is precisely because there was death in ancient times that the worthy in subsequent generations would find respite in it and the unworthy would submit to it. If the ancient kings never experienced death, then from the time of your former ruler Duke Tai[2] until now, they would still be alive. How then could you, my Lord, also have acquired this state and feel sorrow over losing it? Growth is accompanied by decay, life is accompanied by death — these are apportioned by Heaven. Things have a

565

---

1  Item 7.2 [172] ↔ Item 1.17 [17]; Item 1.18 [18].

2  Duke Tai's name was Lü Shang 吕尚. He was an advisor of King Wu 武王 (1169–1116 BCE), who enfeoffed him with the state of Qi. He then reigned there between 1122 and 1078 BCE.

## 【原文】

〔令〕后世贤者得之以息，不肖者得之以伏。若使古之王者毋知有死，自昔先君太公至今尚在，而君亦安得此国而哀之？夫盛之有衰，生之有死，天之分也。物有必至，事有常然，古之道也。曷为可悲？至老尚哀死者，怯也；左右助哀者，谀也。怯谀聚居，是故笑之。"公惭而更辞曰："我非为去国而死哀也。寡人闻之，彗星出，其所向之国君当之，今彗星出而向吾国，我是以悲也。"晏子曰："君之行义回邪，无德于国，穿池沼，则欲其深以广也；为台榭，则欲其高且大也；赋敛如挚夺，诛僇如仇雠。自是观之，茀又将出。（天之变），彗星之出，庸可（悲）〔惧〕乎！"于是公惧，乃归，寘池沼，废台榭，薄赋敛，缓刑罚，三十七日而彗星亡。

## 【今译】

566

为死亡而悲伤，这就是怯懦；身边的人陪着你哀伤，就是阿谀。怯懦和阿谀的人聚到一起，这是我大笑的原因。"国君惭愧地改变自己的话说："我不是因为失去国家死亡而哀伤。我听说，彗星一旦出现，它所指向的国君就要承担它引发的灾难，现在彗星出现并指向我的国家，我是因为这个而悲伤的。"晏子说："国君的行为邪曲不正，对于国家没有恩德，开凿池沼，就想要让它更深更广；修建亭台楼阁，就想要让它更高更大；向百姓征收赋税如同掠夺，诛杀百姓就像对待仇敌。从这些方面来看，彗星还会出现。天象的变化，彗星的出现，还有什么好悲伤的呢？"于是景公非常害怕，回到国都后，填平了池沼，拆除了亭台楼阁，减轻了赋税，减轻了刑罚，三十七天后彗星消失了。

point they must reach; affairs have constancy — from ancient time, this has always been the way. Why should this cause sadness? One who reaches old age and still feels sorrow at the thought of death is a coward; those among his entourage who are facilitating him in his sorrow are sycophants. A coward and sycophants coinciding, that is what caused my laughter."

The Duke was ashamed and changed the course of his words, and said: "I did not feel sorrow because of my departure from this state or because of death. I have heard that when a broom-comet appears, the ruler of the state towards which it is heading will experience a calamity. Now a broom-comet has appeared and it is heading towards our state, therefore I am sad."

Yanzi said, "My lord, your conduct is such that you revert from providing righteousness to wickedness. You have no virtue for the state; when you dredge ponds and lakes, you want them deep and broad; when you construct terraces and pavilions, you want them high and spacious. You tax as if you are robbing, and you execute people as if they are your enemies. From this perspective, a blurred-comet is going to appear as well — yet you are fearful of the appearance of a mere broom-comet?"[1]

At this point, the Duke became fearful. He returned to his palace, filled up[2] the ponds and the lakes, stopped the construction of the terraces and pavilions, limited the collection of taxes and eased punishment, and after thirty-seven days, the broom-comet disappeared.

567

---

1   For the difference between *huixing* 彗星 ("broom comets") and fu 孛 and *bo* 孛 ("bushy", "bristle", "or" "blurred" comets), see Item 1.18 [18], n. 106; 110.

2   寘 → 實 (*YZCQ-ICS*, 61, n. 2).

## 7.3 [173] 景公梦见彗星使人占之晏子谏

景公在梦中出现彗星，令人占卜，晏子进谏

**【原文】**

景公梦见彗星。明日，召晏子而问焉："寡人闻之，有彗星者必有亡国。夜者，寡人梦见彗星，吾欲召（占梦）〔梦者〕者使占之。"晏子对曰："君居处无节，衣服无度，不听正谏，兴事无已，赋敛无厌，使民如将不胜，万民惙怨。（见）茀星又将见梦，奚独彗星乎！"

**【今译】**

景公梦中出现彗星。第二天，景公召见晏子询问说："我听说，有彗星出现的地方一定会亡国。晚上的时候，我梦见彗星，我想召占梦之人让他占卜一下。"晏子回答说："国君您生活开支没有节制，穿衣修饰没有限度，不听从正确的谏言，大兴土木没有限制，征敛赋税没有满足，让民众难以承受，所有的民众都怨恨。见到彗星后又在梦中出现，难道只是彗星吗？"

## 7.3 [173] DUKE JING SAW A BROOM-COMET IN HIS DREAM AND ORDERED THE DIVINER OF DREAMS TO INTERPRET THE OMEN. YANZI REMONSTRATED.[1]

Duke Jing saw a broom-comet in a dream. The next day he summoned Yanzi and asked him about it, saying: "I have heard that when broom-comets appear in dreams, the state will be destroyed. Last night I saw a broom-comet in my dream. I would like to summon the diviner of dreams and order him to interpret the omen."

Yanzi replied: "At your home, my Lord, there is no moderation, and your manner of dress is truly excessive. You do not listen to straightforward remonstrations, you incessantly promote projects, you are never satisfied with the tax revenue, you overwork the people in an unbearable manner, and the multitudes are resentful. A blurred-comet will appear in your dream as well — why only a broom-comet?"

569

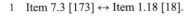

---

1    Item 7.3 [173] ↔ Item 1.18 [18].

## 7.4 [174] 景公问古而无死其乐若何晏子谏

景公询问如果自古以来就没有死亡那么会多么快乐，晏子进谏

### 【原文】

景公饮酒乐，公曰："古而无死，其乐若何？"晏子对曰："古而〔无〕死，则古之乐也，君何得焉？昔爽鸠氏始居此地，季（前）〔蒯〕因之，有逢伯陵（困）〔因〕〔之〕，蒲姑氏因之，而后太公因之。古（君）〔若〕无死，爽鸠氏之乐，非君所愿也。"

大中华文库

### 【今译】

景公饮酒十分欢乐，就说："如果自古就没有死亡，那么该有多么快乐呢？"晏子回答说："如果自古就没有死亡，那么就只有古人的快乐了，国君您能得到什么呢？以前爽鸠氏最开始居住在这个地方，后来季蒯继承了它，之后逢伯陵再继承，蒲姑氏再继承，之后太公才获得这个地方。如果古代君没有死亡，爽鸠氏的快乐，并不是国君您所希望的吧。"

## 7.4 [174] DUKE JING ASKED WHAT KIND OF JOY WOULD EXIST IF THERE HAD BEEN NO DEATH SINCE ANCIENT TIMES. YANZI REMONSTRATED. [1]

Duke Jing was drinking and entertaining himself. He asked: "If there had been no death since ancient times, what kind of joy would there be?"

Yanzi replied, "If there had been no death since ancient times, the ancients would experience joy — but what would you, my Lord, benefit from all this? In the past, the Shuangjiu lineage first settled in this area. The Jize succeeded them — followed by the Youfeng Boling lineage — followed by the Pugu lineage — followed by Duke Tai. If there had been no death since ancient times, the Shuangjiu lineage would experience joy. This is not what you were wishing for, my Lord."

571

---

1   Item 7.4 [174] ↔ Item 1.18 [18].

## 7.5 [175] 景公谓梁丘据与己和晏子谏

景公说梁丘据与自己谐调，晏子进谏

### 【原文】

景公至自畋，晏子侍于遄台，梁丘据造焉。公曰："维据与我和夫！"晏子对曰："据亦同也，焉得为和。"公曰："和与同异乎？"对曰："异。和如羹焉，水火醯醢盐梅，以烹鱼肉，燀之以薪，宰夫和之，齐之以味，济其不及；以洩其（遇）〔过〕，君子食之，以平其心。君臣亦然。君所谓可，而有否焉，臣献其否，以成其可；君所谓否，

### 【今译】

景公打猎回来，晏子在遄台陪侍，梁丘据前来拜见。景公说："只有梁丘据和我谐调啊！"晏子回答说："梁丘据只是和您一样，怎么能说谐调呢。"景公说："谐调和相同有什么不一样吗？"晏子回答说："不一样。谐调就像煲制肉羹，用水、火、肉酱、盐梅来烹调鱼肉，用柴火来烧制，厨师来让它们谐调，使它们的味道一致，补足那些味道达不到的；调整那些味道超过的，君子吃了这样的食物，能够平和其内心。君臣之间也是这样。国君认为可行的，但其中有不可行的，作为臣子的指出不可行的部分，来成就国君认为可行的举措；国君认为不可行的，但其中有可行的，作为臣子的指出可行的部分，来去除国君认为不可行的举措。因此导致政治平稳而没有冲突，民众没有争斗之心。所以《诗经》上说：'也有美味谐调的肉汤，味道合适不咸不淡；作为供奉神灵的贡品没有不满意的，也不会引起人们的争论'。先代的

# 7.5 [175] DUKE JING SAID THAT LIANGQIU JU WAS IN HARMONY WITH HIM. YANZI REMONSTRATED.[1]

Duke Jing returned from hunting and Yanzi attended him at the Chuan Terrace. Liangqiu Ju arrived there.

The Duke said: "Only Ju is in harmony with me!"

Yanzi replied: "Ju is merely in conformity with you; how can this be considered harmony?"

The Duke said: "Is there a difference between harmony and conformity?"

Yanzi replied: "There is a difference. Harmony is like a stew. The cook uses water, fire, vinegar, minced meat sauce, salt and sour plum to cook fish and meat over firewood. The cook harmonizes these ingredients and melds them with different of flavors. He accentuates the delicate and attenuates the excessive. When a man of noble character consumes it, it calms his heart. So it is with rulers and ministers. If the ruler approves a policy that contains unacceptable elements, the minister should point these out in order to make the approved policy successful. Alternatively, if the ruler rejects a policy that contains acceptable elements, the minister should point these out in order to eliminate the unacceptable. In this way, the government is stable, free from offences, and there is no bickering amongst the people.

Therefore, the *Odes* says:

There is also harmoniously seasoned stew;

Well prepared, well proportioned.

We advance silently;

There are no quarrels.[2]

The ancient kings coordinated the five flavors and harmonized the

573

---

1   Item 7.5 [175] ↔ Item 1.18 [18]: *Zuozhuan*, B10.20.8/375/20; B10.26.11/393/15.

2   *Shijing*, 302/156/1.

**【原文】**

而有可焉,臣献其可,以去其否。是以政平而不干,民无争心。故《诗》曰:'亦有和羹,既戒且平;(奏)鬷〔嘏〕无言,时靡有争。'先王之济五味、和五声也,以平其心,成其政也。声亦如味:一气,二体,三类,四物,五声,六律,七音,八风,九歌,以相成也;清浊大小,(矩)〔短〕长疾徐,哀乐刚柔,迟速高下,出入周(流)〔疏〕,以相济也。君子〔听〕之,以平其心,心平德和。故《诗》曰:'德音不瑕'。今据不然,君所谓可,据亦曰可;君所谓否,据亦曰否。若以水济水,谁能食之? 若琴瑟之专一,谁能听之? 同之不可也如是。"公曰:"善。"

**【今译】**

君王调和五味、五声,来平和自己的内心,成就他的政事。声音像味道一样:一气,二体,三类,四物,五声,六律,七音,八风,九歌,来共同组成;声音的清浊、大小、长短、快慢、哀乐、刚柔、高低、出入、密疏,来互相调剂。君子听到这种音乐,可以平和他的内心,内心和平德行才能端正。所以《诗经》说:'成就美好品德的音乐没有瑕疵'。而现在梁丘据并不是这样,国君认为可行的,梁丘据也说可以;国君认为不可行的,梁丘据也说不行。如果用水来调剂水,谁能吃它呢? 如果琴和瑟弹奏同样的调子,谁会喜欢听呢? 事务不能相同就是这个道理。"景公说:"好。"

five sounds, which calmed their hearts and perfected their rule. Sounds and flavors are alike — one breath, two forms,[1] three genres,[2] four objects,[3] five tones,[4] six pitches[5] seven notes,[6] eight winds,[7] nine songs[8] — these complete each other. Pure and turbid, small and big, short and long, fast and slow, sorrowful and joyful, hard and soft, lingering and hurried, high and low, initiation and conclusion, concentrated and diffused – these balance each other. The man of noble character listens to it, and it calms his heart. When the heart is calm, the virtues are harmonized. Therefore, the *Odes* says:

Virtuous tunes feature no dissonant sounds.[9]

But now, this is not the case with Ju. What you, my Lord, approve, Ju also approves; what you, my Lord, reject, Ju also rejects. Who could consume water whose flavor is accentuated with water? If the string instruments of the *qin* and the *se* were to produce a single tone, who could listen to it? Such conformity is intolerable."

The Duke said, "Well argued!"

---

1  I.e., the martial and civil styles of dance.

2  I.e., the three genres of the *Shijing*: "Airs," "Odes" and "Hymns."

3  The four objects are made of the choice materials gathered from the entire kingdom. Cf. *Hanshi waichuan*, 8.26/62/29.

4  The five tones of the pentatonic scale are *gong* 宫 (*do*), *shang* 商 (*re*), *jue* 角 (*mi*), *zhi* 徵 (*sol*) and *yu* 羽 (*la*).

5  For "the six pitches" (六律) that were used for regulating sound, see, Cheng-Yih, Chen, *Early Chinese Work in Natural Science: A Re-Examination of the Physics of Motion, Acoustics, Astronomy, and Scientific Thoughts*. Hong Kong University Press, Hong Kong (1996) 21-22.

6  The seven notes are the five notes of the pentatonic scale plus two half-notes, 变宫 (*fa*) and 变徵 (*ti*).

7  I.e., the winds that blow from all eight directions. For the specific name of each wind in this list see, *Lüshi chunqiu*, 13.1/63/17.

8  The "nine songs" narrate the virtues associated with the "nine accomplishments." See *Zuozhuan*, B6.7.8/135/1.

9  *Shijing*, 160/70/22.

## 7.6 [176] 景公使祝史禳彗星晏子谏

景公命令祝史为彗星祈祷，晏子进谏

### 【原文】

　　齐有彗星，景公使祝禳之。晏子谏曰："无益也，祇（耻）〔取〕诬焉。天道不谄，不贰其命，若之何禳之也！且天之有彗，以除秽也。君无秽德，又何禳焉？若德之秽，禳之何损？《诗》云：'维此文王，小心翼翼，昭事上帝，聿怀多福，厥德不回，以受方国。'君无违德，

### 【今译】

　　齐国有彗星出现，景公命令祝史祈祷消灾。晏子进谏说："没有什么帮助，只是自己欺骗自己。天道不可怀疑，其命数不可改变，像这样的祈祷消灾又有什么用呢！况且天上之所以有彗星存在，就是为了祛除污秽。国君没有污秽的德行，又何必要禳解呢？如果德行有污秽了，那么禳解又有什么帮助呢？《诗经》说：'只有周文王，做事小心谨慎，光明正大地侍奉神明，坚定地相信能够获得福祉，他的德行不违背天道，受到邦国的尊敬。'国君没有违背德行，诸侯国将来盟会，还

## 7.6 [176] DUKE JING ORDERED AN INVOCATOR AND A SCRIBE TO EXORCISE AWAY A BROOM-COMET BY MEANS OF SACRIFICE. YANZI REMONSTRATED.[1]

A broom-comet appeared in the skies of Qi. Duke Jing ordered an invocator to exorcise it away by means of sacrifice.[2] Yanzi remonstrated: "This will be completely useless, it will only generate deception. The way of Heaven cannot be put in doubt — it will not alter its dictates. Hence, what effect would a sacrifice of exorcism have on it? Moreover, the appearance of a broom-comet in the sky signifies the sweeping out of dirt. If your morality, my Lord, is not soiled, why should you still offer a sacrifice to exorcise away the broom-comet? But if it is soiled, what would you diminish by exorcising it away? As it says in the *Odes*:

Now this King Wen,

He was very cautious and reverent;

Enlightened he served God on high,

And then he received many blessings;

His virtue did not deflect allegiance

And thereby he won the allegiance of the states from all quarters.[3]

If you don't defy virtue, states from all directions will come to you; why are you troubled by a broom-comet? As it says in the *Odes*:

If we lack any means of self-examination,

We should look to the rulers of the Xia and the Shang.

Because they wreaked so much havoc

577

---

1　Item 7.6 [176] ↔ Item 1.18 [18]; *Xunxu*, 4.26/23/19; *Zuozhuan*, B 10.26.10/393/8; *Lunheng* 论衡, 17/55/8.

2　The parallel line in item 1.18 [18] reads: 使禳去之.

3　*Shijing*, 236/117/26.

**【原文】**

方国将至，何患于彗？《诗》曰：'我无所监，夏后及（商）〔商〕，用乱之故，民卒流亡。'若德之回乱，民将流亡，祝史之为，无能补也。"公说，乃止。

**【今译】**

担心什么彗星呢？《诗经》说：'我没有什么借鉴的，只有夏桀和商纣，由于政治混乱，最终人民流亡。'如果违背德行，政治混乱，人民将会流亡，祝史的作为，也没有什么帮助了。"景公很高兴，于是停止祈祷。

That their people ultimately drifted away from them.[1]

If virtue is deflected and disordered, people will scatter and disappear and the invocator's and scribe's effort would not be able to remedy the situation."

The Duke was pleased and stopped the sacrifice.

579

---

1   This passage is not found in the extant text of the *Shijing*.

## 7.7 [177] 景公有疾梁丘据裔款请诛祝史晏子谏

景公有疾病，梁丘据和裔款请求诛杀祝史，晏子进谏

### 【原文】

景公疥，遂痁，期而不瘳。诸侯之宾问疾者多在。梁丘据、裔款言于公曰："吾事鬼神丰，于先君有加矣。今君疾病，为诸侯忧，是祝史之罪也。诸侯不知，其谓我不敬，君盍诛于祝固（使）〔史〕嚚以辞宾。"公说，告晏子。晏子对曰："日宋之盟，屈建问范会之德于赵武，赵武曰：'夫子〔之〕家事治，言于晋国，竭情无私，其祝史祭祀，陈言不愧；其家事无（情）〔猜〕，其祝史不祈。'建以语康王，康王曰：

### 【今译】

景公得了疥癣，于是发展为疟疾，一年也没有痊愈。诸侯国派来慰问的使者大都留在齐国。梁丘据、裔款对景公说："我们敬奉鬼神非常丰厚，比先代的国君更加丰厚。现在国君生病了，为各国诸侯王所担忧，这是祝史的过错。诸侯不知道这些，说我们不敬奉鬼神，您为什么不诛杀祝固史嚚来送走诸侯的慰问使者呢。"国君很高兴，告诉了晏子。晏子回答说："以前在宋国会盟时，屈建向赵武询问范会的德行，赵武说：'先生的家庭治理得很好，在晋国发表言论，竭尽自己的心意而不带有个人私念，他的祝、史祭祀鬼神，向鬼神陈述实情而问心无愧；他的家庭中没有猜忌的事情，他的祝、史并不向鬼神祈祷。'屈建把这些话告诉康王，康王说：'神灵和民众都没有怨恨，先生先后辅佐五位国君是合适的，所以能够成为诸侯共主。'"景公说："梁

# 7.7 [177] DUKE JING FELL ILL. LIANGQIU JU AND YI KUAN ASKED PERMISSION TO EXECUTE THE INVOCATOR AND THE SCRIBE. YANZI REMON-STRATED.[1]

Duke Jing suffered from scabies and intermittent fever, from which he did not recover for a whole year. Many guest envoys, sent by the regional princes, came to the court making inquiries about his illness. Liangqiu Ju and Yi Kuan said to the Duke: "Our service to the spirits was more ample than those of our former ruler.[2] But now your illness, our Lord, has become a serious concern for the regional princes. This is the fault of the invocators and the scribes, but the regional princes, who are unaware of this, might think that we were not reverential to the spirits. Why not execute Gu the Invocator and Yin the Scribe, and thereby politely reject these guest envoys?"

The Duke was pleased and transmitted this to Yanzi. Yanzi said: "In the past, at the covenant meeting in Song,[3] Qu Jian asked Zhao Wu about the virtue of Fan Hui.[4] Zhao Wu said: 'The household affairs of master Fan Hui were well ordered; when he spoke in the state of Jin, he exerted himself truthfully without any personal motivation. When his invocators and scribes performed sacrifices, they presented true facts without shame. His household affairs were free of suspicion, and his invocators and scribes did not invoke blessings from the spirits.' Qu Jian then reported this to

581

---

1   Item 7.7 [177] ↔ Item 1.12 [12].

2   The parallel item, 1.12 [12], refers to Duke Huan as the "Former Ruler."

3   For this "covenant meeting," see *Zuozhuan*, B9.27.4/293/4.

4   Fan Hui 范会 or 士会, one of the most meritorious political figures in the state of Jin, who over a period of forty years gloriously served five prominent dukes: Wen 文公 (r. 636–628 BCE); Xiang 襄公 (r. 627–621 BCE); Ling 灵公 (r. 620–607 BCE); Cheng 成公 (r. 606–600 BCE) and Jing 景公 (r. 599–581 BCE).

## 【原文】

'神、人无怨，宜夫子之（先）〔光〕辅五君，以为诸〔侯〕主也。'"公曰："据与款谓寡人能事鬼神，故欲诛于祝、史，子称是语，何故？"对曰："若〔有〕德之君，外内不废，上下无怨，动无违事，其祝、史荐信，无愧心矣。是以鬼神用飨，国受其福，祝、史与焉。其所以蕃

## 【今译】

丘据和裔款说我能够尽心敬奉鬼神，所以想要诛杀祝、史，您却说这些话，为什么呢？"晏子回答说："如果是有德行的国君，宫廷内外都不会废弛，国家上下都不会怨恨，国君的作为没有错误的，它的祝、史向鬼神陈述实情，就会问心无愧。所以鬼神享用祭品，国家受到鬼神的福佑，祝、史也可以分享。他们之所以享受福佑长寿，是因为担任了诚信的国君的使者，对鬼神忠诚信实。如果他们恰好遇到了淫逸的国君，宫廷内外偏颇荒诞，国家上下相互怨恨，国君的作为都是错误的，放纵欲望满足私欲，修建高台开凿深池，奏乐舞蹈，过分消耗民力，掠夺民众的财富，来实现他的错误的行为，不体恤后人，暴虐放纵，肆意进行过度的举措，无所顾忌，不考虑他人的诽谤和怨恨，不害怕鬼神的惩罚，鬼神发怒而百姓痛苦，国君却没有悔改之心。他的

King Kang of Chu,[1] who said in response: 'Since neither spirits nor people bear any resentment against him, it was fitting that he was the master who gloriously assisted five rulers, making them the leaders of the covenant of regional princes.'"

Duke Jing said: "Liangqiu Ju and Yi Kuan expressed their belief in my ability to serve the spirits and they therefore wanted to execute the failed invocator and scribe. What is the purpose of your recounting of this anecdote?"

Yanzi answered: "A virtuous ruler has no negligence within and beyond his court; no resentment exists among superiors nor among inferiors; his initiatives do not violate the prescribed regulations; his invocators and scribes make true statements to the spirits, bearing no feelings of shame in their hearts. For these reasons, the spirits accept the offered sacrifices, and the state, along with the invocators and scribes, all enjoy blessings. The reason they enjoy many blessings and longevity is that the invocators and scribes are envoys of a trustworthy ruler and the words they convey to the spirits are loyal and true. However, in cases in which the invocators and scribes encounter a licentious ruler, then wickedness and bias exist within and beyond his court; resentment and hatred exists among superiors and among inferiors, and the ruler's initiatives are depraved and perverted. Such a ruler indulges in his own desires and satisfies his selfish wishes; his terraces tower above and his ponds are dug deep; musical bells are struck and girls dance. He undercuts the people's strength and appropriates their properties in order to bring his depraved conduct to fruition. He does not show any sign of solicitude for his successors; he is tyrannous, wicked, and indulges his desires. He recklessly conducts improper actions without any remorse. He pays no heed to the slanderous attacks and the loathing the people feel towards him, and he does not fear the spirits. The spirits become

---

1   King Kang of Chu 楚康王 (r. 559–545 BCE).

**【原文】**

（礼）〔祉〕老寿者，为信君使也，其言忠信于鬼神。其适遇淫君，外内颇邪，上下怨疾，动作辟（远）〔违〕，从欲厌私，高台深池，撞钟舞女，斩刈民力，输掠其聚，以成其违，不恤后人，暴虐淫纵，肆行非度，无所还忌，不思谤讟，不惮鬼神，（鬼）神怒民痛，无悛于心。其祝、史荐信，是言罪也；其盖失数美，是矫诬也；进退无辞，则虚

**【今译】**

祝、史沟通鬼神，是说明他的罪过；他们掩盖他的过失而陈述好事，这是狡诈欺骗；罪过和好事都不能陈述，就用空话来取媚鬼神，因此鬼神不享用他国家的祭品而带给它灾祸，祝、史也要承担。他们之所以夭折患病，是因为他们作为暴君的使者，对鬼神说了很多欺骗轻侮的话。"景公说："那该怎么办呢？"晏子说："不能这么做。山林中的木材，衡鹿来守护；湖泽中的芦苇，舟鲛来守护；草野中的柴火，虞候来守护；海中的盐蛤，祈望来守护。居住在乡野边疆的人，到国都来服役；临近国都的关卡，又对民众的财物横征暴敛；世袭的大夫，强行交易民众的财物；发布政令没有准则，征敛赋税没有节制；居住的宫殿经

enraged, the people suffer, and he does not repent in his heart. Should his invocators and scribes make true statements to the spirits, then they would have to recount his crimes; but should they cover up his failures and recount his exquisite merits, then they would be mendacious and cheating. As they cannot say anything about this one way or the other, they utter empty words in order to court favor. These are the reasons why the spirits do not accept the offered sacrifices, and the state, as well as the invocators and scribes, are facing calamity. The reason they die young, lose their senses, suffer the bereavement of orphans, and become ill is that they function as servants to an oppressive ruler, and their words are a profanity against the spirits."

The Duke said: "Then what should be done?"

Yanzi answered: "There is nothing to be done. The timber on your foothills is guarded by your supervisors of forestry, the reeds and the rushes in your lakes by your boathands, fire woods in shallow waters by your monitors, and salts and shells on the seashores by your seafood inspectors. People from remote districts and border regions come to the capital and find themselves in servitude, the checkpoints just outside the capital impose oppressive taxes on private property. The hereditary high officers compel people to sell them their property. Rules are issued without any standards, and taxes are collected out of all proportion. Palaces and mansions are rebuilt on a daily basis, and there is no end to the delight of licentious pleasures. Favored concubines of the palace wantonly rob people in the market, and favored ministers outside the palace issue fabricated orders in the remote border towns. They seek to satisfy their personal desires, and if they fail in achieving this they will take revenge by recrimination. The common people suffer and agonize, and men and women alike utter curses. If the invocator's blessings are beneficial, then curses can also do harm. There is a huge population living in the area that lies to the east of the Liao and She Rivers and to the west of the Gu and You Rivers. And even if your invocators excel in their profession, how can they possibly overcome the

**【原文】**

以成媚，是以鬼神不飨、其国以祸之，祝、史与焉。所以夭昏孤疾者，（其）〔为〕暴君使也，其言僭嫚于鬼神。"公曰："然则若之何？"对曰："不可为也。山林之木，衡鹿守之；泽之（藋）〔萑〕蒲，舟鲛守之；薮之薪〔蒸〕，虞候守之；海之盐蜃，祈望守之。县鄙之人，入从其政；偪（介）〔迩〕之关，暴征其私；承嗣大夫，强易其贿；布常无艺，徵敛无度；宫室日更，淫乐不违；内宠之妾肆夺于市，外宠之臣僭（全）〔令〕于鄙；私欲养求，不给则应。民人苦病，夫妇皆诅。祝有益也，诅（不）〔亦〕有损，聊、摄以东，姑、尤以西，其为人也多矣！虽其善祝，岂能胜亿兆人之诅！君若欲诛于祝、史，修德而后可。"公说，使有司宽政，毁关去禁，薄敛已责，公疾愈。

**【今译】**

常更换，荒淫玩乐不肯离开；宫廷内宠幸的侍妾，肆意地在集市上抢夺，宫廷外宠幸的臣子，在边境上假传政令；为了自己的私欲而肆意要求，不能满足就惩罚他们。百姓因此而痛苦，夫妇都在诅咒。祈祷如果有帮助，那么诅咒也有损害，聊、摄的东面，姑、尤的西面，这样的人有很多啊！虽然他们擅长祈祷，但怎么能胜过亿万人的诅咒呢，国君您如果想因此诛杀祝、史，应该先修行自己的德行才可以。"景公很高兴，命令相关部门放宽政令，毁掉关卡，废除禁令，减轻赋税，免除对公室的逋欠，景公的病很快就痊愈了。

curses of hundreds of millions of people? If you, my Lord, intend to execute the invocator and the scribe, you should first rectify your virtue and then you may proceed in doing that."

The Duke was pleased; then he ordered the officials in charge to be lenient with government oversight, to destroy the tax collection checkpoints, to abolish restrictions on resources, to reduce taxes and to pardon tax debts. Following this, the Duke's illness was cured.

# 7.8 [178] 景公见道殣自惭无德晏子谏

景公看到路旁有饿死的人，惭愧自己没有德行，晏子进谏

大中华文库

## 【原文】

景公赏赐及后宫，文绣被台榭，菽粟食凫雁；出而见殣，谓晏子曰："此何为而死？"晏子对曰："此馁而死。"公曰："嘻！寡人之无德也甚矣。"对曰："君之德著而彰，何为无德也？"景公曰："何谓也？"对曰："君之德及后宫与台榭，君之玩物，衣以文绣；君之凫雁，食以菽粟；君之营内自乐，延及后宫之族，何为其无德〔也〕？顾臣愿有请于君：由君之意，自乐之心，推而与百姓同之，则何殣之有？君不推此，

## 【今译】

景公的赏赐遍及后宫所有的人，用锦绣装饰亭台楼榭，用粮食来喂养鸭鹅；出门时见到饿死的人，对晏子说："这是因为什么而死的？"晏子回答说："因为饥饿而死的。"景公说："唉，我已经无德到这个地步了。"晏子回答说："国君您不仅有德行而且显著，怎么能说无德呢？"景公说："这是怎么说的呢？"晏子回答说："国君的德行遍及后宫和亭台楼榭，国君把玩的物品，都用锦绣来装饰；国君的鸭鹅，都用粮食来喂养；国君经营宫室供自己享乐，还照顾到后宫的人们，怎么能说无德呢？因此我想要向国君请求：按照国君的心意，把自己快乐的想

## 7.8 [178] DUKE JING SAW AN EMACIATED CORPSE ON THE ROAD AND WAS ASHAMED OF HIS OWN LACK OF VIRTUE. YANZI REMONSTRATED.[1]

Duke Jing distributed rewards and gifts throughout his palace, reaching the women of the inner quarters; patterned embroideries were spread across his terraces and pavilions, and his wild geese and ducks were fed with fine beans and millet. Once, when he was out of his palace, he saw an emaciated corpse and asked Yanzi: "What did he die of?"

Yanzi replied: "He died of starvation."

The Duke said: "Oh, my lack of virtue is so great!"

Yanzi replied: "Your virtue, my Lord, is outstanding and glorious — why would you say you have no virtue?"

Duke Jing said: "What do you mean?"

Yanzi answered: "Your virtue reaches throughout the inner quarters of your palace and throughout your terraces and pavilions. Your beautiful curios are covered with patterned embroideries, and your wild geese and ducks are fed with fine beans and millet. Your management within the palace brings you joy, which you extend to all inhabitants of the inner quarters. So how can one say you have no virtue? But, let me make a request, my Lord — if you could extend your own inclinations and joyous heart and share them with the people, then how could there be emaciated corpses? If you, my Lord, do not make these extensions, and if you continue your affairs wantonly within the palace — cherishing your exclusive, selfish favors; collecting properties inequitably; causing beans, grains and bolts of silk to rot in the storehouses; and if your kindness is not dispensed upon the people, and your sense of equity does not apply to the myriad states — then this is what engendered the downfall of King Zhou and King Jie. The ruler's

---

1    Item 7.8 [178] ↔ Item 1.19 [19].

## 【原文】

而苟营内好私，使财货（冲）〔偏〕有所聚，菽粟币帛腐于囷府，惠不遍加于百姓，公心不周乎万国，则桀纣之所以亡也。夫士民之所以叛，由（徧）〔偏〕之也，君如察臣婴之言，推君之盛德，公布之于天下，则汤武可为也。一殣何足恤哉？"

## 【今译】

法推广到百姓身上，那怎么可能有饿死的人呢？国君不推广这种心意，却只是经营王宫满足自己的私欲，使得财物聚集起来，粮食钱币和布帛腐烂在仓库之中，恩惠不能遍及到百姓身上，公心不能遍及诸侯国，这是夏桀和商纣灭亡的原因。士人民众之所以叛乱，就是因为国君的偏心，您如果听从晏婴的话，将您的盛德推及到百姓，公心遍布天下，那么就能够成为商汤、周武王那样的圣君了。何必体恤一个饿死的人呢？"

partiality causes officers and people to rebel. If you, my Lord, examine my words, and extend your abundant virtue and dispense it all over the realm, then you can become like King Tang and King Wu.[1] Why should a single emaciated corpse be sufficient to arouse your pity?"

---

1  The idea of sharing the royal wealth with the people in order to become a "true king" is brilliantly and forcefully presented in *Mencius*, 2.5/9/22.

大中华文库

## 7.9 [179] 景公欲诛断所爱槚者晏子谏

景公想要诛杀折断他喜爱的楸树，晏子进谏

### 【原文】

景公登箐室而望，见人有断雍门之槚者，公令吏拘之，顾谓晏子趣诛之。晏子默然不对。公曰："雍门之槚，寡人所甚爱也，此见断之，故使夫子诛之，〔夫子〕默然而不应，何也？"晏子对曰："婴闻之，古者人君出，则辟道十里，非畏也；冕前有旒，恶多所见也；纩纮珫耳，恶多所闻也；泰带重半钧，舄履倍重，不欲轻也。刑死之罪，日中之朝，君过之，则赦之，婴未尝闻为人君而自坐其民者也。"公曰："赦之，无使夫子复言。"

### 【今译】

景公登上高大的房子而眺望，看到有人折断了雍门的楸树，景公命令胥吏拘捕他，回过头让晏子前去诛杀他。晏子沉默不回答。景公说："雍门的楸树，是我非常喜爱的，现在看到它折断了，所以让先生您诛杀他，您沉默不回答，是为什么呢？"晏子回答说："我听说，古时候国君出行，就要使民众回避十里，并不是畏惧百姓；冠冕前部有旒，是为了避免所见的太多了；王冠纽带垂下的玉石悬挂在耳旁，是为了避免听到的多了；腰带重达半钧，鞋子重达一钧，是不想让其轻巧。被判处死刑的人，在正午进行处决，国君经过时就赦免他，我没有听说过作为百姓的国君而为自己百姓定罪的。"景公说："赦免这个人，不要让先生再说了。"

# 7.9 [179] DUKE JING WANTED TO EXECUTE A MAN WHO CUT DOWN THE CATALPA TREE THAT HE LOVED. YANZI REMONSTRATED.[1]

Duke Jing climbed to the Qing Hall.[2] Peering into the distance, he saw a man chopping down the Catalpa Tree in Yong Gate[3] and ordered officials to arrest him. He looked around towards Yanzi and told him to execute the man at once. Yanzi kept silent and did not respond.

The Duke said: "I am extremely fond of the Catalpa Tree at the Yong Gate. I've just seen a man chopping it down and therefore order you, my Master, to execute him. But you, my Master, kept silent and did not respond — why?"

Yanzi replied: "I've heard that in ancient times, when rulers exited their palaces, the roads were cleared of people for ten *li*. This was not because they were afraid of the people. They had jade strings hanging down from the front of their hats because they disliked to be exposed to excessive seeing; tassels with jade plugs covered their ears because they disliked to be exposed to excessive hearing. Their huge belts were as heavy as half a *jun*[4] and their shoes were double weighted because they did not want to act lightly. Criminals sentenced to capital punishment waited at the execution grounds until midday, but if the ruler would pass by them, he would have pardoned them. I've never heard of a ruler himself sitting in judgment on his own people."

The Duke said: "Pardon the man! Don't let the Master talk to me about it again."

593

---

1  Item 7.9 [179] ↔ Items 2.2 [52]; 2.3 [53].

2  箐室 → 青堂 (*JS*, 453/2).

3  The Yong Gate 雍门, the west gate of Qi capital.

4  A *Jun* 钧 was a unit of weight of approximately 7.4 kilograms.

## 7.10 [180] 景公坐路寝曰谁将有此晏子谏

景公坐在王宫的正殿说谁能拥有这个房屋，晏子进谏

### 【原文】

景公坐于路寝，曰："美哉（其）室，〔其〕（将谁）〔谁将〕有此乎？"晏子对曰："其田氏乎，田无宇为埠矣。"公曰："然则奈何？"晏子对曰："为善者，君上之所劝也，岂可禁哉？夫田氏国门击柝之家，父以托其子，兄以托其弟，于今三世矣。山木如市，不加于山；鱼盐蚌（唇）〔蜃〕，不加于海；民财为之归。今岁凶饥，蒿种茞敛不半，道路有死人。齐旧四量而豆，豆四而区，区四而釜，釜十而钟。田氏

594

### 【今译】

景公坐在正殿中，说："这么壮美的房屋，谁以后会拥有它呢？"晏子回答说："应该是田氏吧，田无宇在修建堤坝。"景公说："那该怎么办呢？"晏子回答说："做善事的人，是国君所勉励的，怎么能禁止呢？田氏是齐国内的大家族，父亲以家业托付给儿子，兄长托付给弟弟，到现在已经三代了。将山上的树木运送到市场，山的负担不会增加；从海中捕捞鱼蚌煮盐，不会增加海洋的负担；民众的财产得以返还。今年齐国大饥荒，种植的粮食收成不到一半，道路上有饿死的人。齐国原有的四种量器，四豆为一区，四区为釜，十釜为钟。田氏的四种量器，都增加了一份。田氏以家内的量器出贷粮食，以齐国公室的

# 7.10 [180] DUKE JING SAT IN THE ROAD BEDCHAMBER AND SAID: "I WONDER WHO WILL OWN THIS?" YANZI REMONSTRATED.[1]

Duke Jing was sitting in the Road Bedchamber and said: "How beautiful is this bedchamber — I wonder who will possess it?"

Yanzi answered: "Perhaps the Tian lineage will possess it, as Tian Wuyu[2] is already building a dam."[3]

The Duke said: "Then what can be done about this?"

Yanzi answered: "Doing good is what rulers encourage the people to do – how could this be stopped? For three consecutive generations, the Tians have been the watchmen of the gate of our capital. From then until now, fathers have entrusted this duty to their sons, and elders to their younger brothers. Their timber brought from the mountains to the markets is no more expensive than in the mountains; their fish, salt, clams, and oysters brought from the sea to the markets is no more expensive than it is by the sea; and so the people's wealth returns to their household. The current year is a disastrous famine year — even the harvests of weeds and wild vegetables are less than half their usual crop; thus, corpses are lying along the roads. Qi has long had four measurement units — *dou*, *qu*, *fu* and *zhong*.[4] Four *dou* equal one *qu*, four *qu* equal one *fu*, ten *fu* equal one *zhong*. The Tians increase these four measurements by one unit each. They give loans according to their own measurements but collect debts according

---

1  Item 7.10 [180] ↔ *Zuozhuan*, B 10.26.11/393/15; *Hanfeizi*, 34/98/22; Item 4.17 [97].

2  Tian Wuyu 田无宇 or Chen Huanzi 陈桓子, the fifth leader of the Tian (Chen) lineage in Qi.

3  I.e., he is already engaged in massive enterprises aimed at preventing harm and benefiting the people.

4  齐旧四量而豆 → 齐旧四量豆区釜钟 (*YZCQ-ICS*, 64, n. 1).

**【原文】**

四量，各加一焉。以家量贷，以公量〔收〕〔之〕，则所以籴百姓之死命者泽矣。今公家骄汏，而田氏慈惠，国泽是将焉归？田氏虽无德而施于民。公厚敛而田氏厚施焉。《诗》曰：'虽无德与汝，式歌且舞。'田氏之施，民歌舞之也，国之归焉，不亦宜乎？"

**【今译】**

量器来收回，就是通过这种方式来买濒死之人的性命。现在齐国的公室骄纵奢侈，而田氏仁慈恩惠，国家还能归谁呢？田氏虽然没有大的恩德却施行于百姓。国君征敛很多而田氏施行的恩惠很多。《诗经》说：'虽然没有恩德于你，也可以一起唱歌跳舞。'田氏施行的恩惠，就是与民众一起唱歌跳舞，国家归属于田氏，不是很合适吗？"

to the public measurements; thus, they give people who were destined to die money to buy grain, and thereby benefit them. Your family, however, is arrogant and wasteful, while the Tians are kind and giving. Therefore, who will the state rally around if not the Tian lineage? Although the Tians have no inherent virtue, they are generous to the people. You collect heavy taxes and the Tians give abundantly. As it says in the *Odes*:

Although I have no virtue to impart upon you,

I will sing and dance. [1]

For the generosity of the Tians, people are singing and dancing. Isn't it fitting that the state rally around them?"

---

1   *Shijing*, 218/107/10.

# 7.11 [181] 景公台成盆成适愿合葬其母晏子谏而许

景公正殿的平台建成，盆成适想要合葬他的母亲，晏子进谏后景公允许

## 【原文】

景公宿于路寝之宫，夜分，闻西方有男子哭者，公悲之。明日朝，问于晏子曰："寡人夜者闻西方有男子哭者，声甚哀，气甚悲，是奚为者也？寡人哀之。"晏子对曰："西郭徒居布衣之士盆成适也。父之孝子，兄之顺弟也。又尝为孔子门人。今其母不幸而死，祔柩未葬，家贫，身老，子（孺），恐力不能合祔，是以悲也。"公曰："子为寡人（吊）〔弔〕之，因问其偏祔何所在？"晏子奉命往（吊）〔弔〕，而问偏之所在。盆成适再拜，稽首而不起，曰："偏祔寄于路寝，得为地下之臣，

## 【今译】

景公晚上住在正殿中，半夜的时候，听到西方有男子哭泣的声音，景公非常悲伤。第二天朝会，景公问晏子说："我晚上听到西方有男子哭泣，声音气息非常悲伤，这是谁呢？我非常可怜他。"晏子回答说："是国都西部闲居的读书人盆成适。他是孝顺父亲的儿子，恭顺兄长的弟弟。还曾经是孔子的弟子。现在他的母亲不幸死去，合葬的棺材还没有下葬，家中非常贫穷，年龄也大了，孩子还幼小，担心自己没有能力给父母合葬，所以非常悲伤。"景公说："请先生为我去他家中吊唁，顺便问他父亲葬在什么地方。"晏子奉景公的命令前往吊唁，并且问他墓葬的地方。盆成适拜了又拜，叩头在地不起身，说："父亲的灵柩葬在王宫正殿，因此得以成为国君地下的臣子，携带书札拿着毛笔，在宫殿右边的台阶下供职，我希望有一天能将母亲送去合葬，但还没有得到

# 7.11 [181] WHEN DUKE JING FINISHED BUILDING A TERRACE, PENCHENG KUO WANTED TO BURY HIS MOTHER TOGETHER WITH HIS FATHER IN THE SAME TOMB. YANZI REMONSTRATED AND THE DUKE GAVE HIS PERMISSION.[1]

Duke Jing spent the night in the Road Bedchamber of his palace. At midnight, he heard the crying voice of a man, coming from the west side. The Duke was moved, saddened by the voice.

On the following day, during a court audience, the Duke asked Yanzi: "Last night, I heard the crying voice of a man, coming from the west. The tone was deeply mournful and the mood extremely sad. Why was he wailing like this? I felt aggrieved for him."

Yanzi replied: "It was Pencheng Kuo, a gentleman of no official status who lives idly at the western outskirts of the capital. He is a filial son to his father and obedient to his elder brother. He was also once a follower of Confucius. Now, unfortunately, his mother has died, and half of her coffin[2] for a joint burial has not yet been entombed. His household is poor; he is old; and his children are very young. He fears he lacks the necessary strength to bury his mother together with his father in the same tomb. That is why he was so stricken by sadness."

The Duke said: "Please convey him my condolences and take the occasion to ask him about the location of the coffin board upon which his deceased father rests."

Yanzi obeyed the Duke's order and proceeded to offer the Duke's condolences to Pencheng Kuo, asking him about the location of his father's coffin board.

599

---

1   Item 7.11 [181] ↔ Item 2.20 [70].

2   I.e., half of a double coffin.

**【原文】**

拥札掺笔，给事宫殿中右陛之下，愿以某日送，未得君之意也。穷困无以图之，布唇枯舌，焦心热中，今君不辱而临之，愿君图之。"晏子曰："然。此人之甚重者也，而恐君不许也。"盆成适蹵然曰："凡在君耳！且臣闻之，越王好勇，其民轻死；楚灵王好细腰，其朝多饿（死）人；子胥忠其君，〔故天下皆愿得以为臣〕；〔曾参、孝己爱其亲〕，故天下皆愿得以为子。今为人子臣，而离散其亲戚，孝乎哉？足以为〔子〕臣乎？若此而得衬，是生臣而安死母也；若此而不得，则臣请挽尸车而寄之于国门外宇溜之下，身不敢饮食，拥辕执辂，木乾鸟栖，袒肉暴骸，以望君憨之。贱臣虽愚，窃意明君哀而不忍也。"晏子入，

**【今译】**

国君的同意。我穷困潦倒难以计划此事，唇干舌枯，心中焦虑烦躁，现在您屈尊来到我的家中，希望您能够帮我做成这件事。"晏子说："好。这是人一生中非常重要的事情，但恐怕国君不会允许。"盆成适突然站起来说："所有的事都靠您了！而且我听说，越王崇尚武勇，他的人民都不怕死亡；楚灵王喜欢细腰的人，宫中许多人因此饿死；伍子胥忠心于他的国君，因此天下都愿意得到他这样的臣子；曾参、孝己孝敬他们的父母，因此天下都愿意得到他们这样的子女。现在我作为子女和臣子，却让自己的双亲分离，这能称为孝吗？还能做人臣子女吗？如果这次能够合葬我的母亲，是让我能够活下去并让我的死去的母亲安定；如果不能合葬，那么我请求拉着装载尸体的车子停靠在国都大门之外屋檐之下，自己不敢饮食，扶靠着马车的辕辂，像干枯的木头一样让鸟儿在身上栖息，袒露自己的肉体形骸，希望能获得国君的怜悯。我虽然愚笨不堪，但私以为圣明的国君会悲伤而不忍心让我这样。"

Pencheng Kuo bowed twice with his forehead touching the ground, and without rising from his mat, said: "My father's coffin board is lodged in the Road Bedchamber, so my father should be considered a minister of the sphere below the ground, holding bamboo slips and gripping writing brushes; administrating affairs beneath the stairs that are located right of the center of the palace. I wish to choose a certain day on which I may conduct the funeral procession, but I still don't have our ruler's consent for this. I am in difficult position, without any means to carry out the matter; my lips are scorched and my tongue tattered; my mind is anxious and I'm burning inside. But now you, Sir, did not consider it a disgrace and honored me with this visit — I wish that you, Sir, carry out the matter."

Yanzi said: "True, this cause is extremely important for people, but I'm afraid that the Duke will not allow it."

Pencheng Kuo was startled and said: "Well, it all depends on you, Sir. What's more, the King of Yue was fond of courage and his people looked lightly upon death; King Ling of Chu was fond of slender waists, so the attendants in his palace starved themselves; Tzuxu was loyal to his ruler, therefore everyone in the realm wanted to recruit people like him to be their ministers; Zengshen and Xiaoji loved their parents, therefore everyone in the realm wanted to have children of a similar kind.[1] Now, if those in a position of a son or a minister separate and scatter their parents and relatives — would they be regarded as a true son or a true minister? Such being the case, if my mother is allowed to be buried together with my father in the same tomb, then it will give me life and give peace to my deceased mother; but if this plan cannot be carried out, then I will pull her hearse outside of our capital gate and park it under its eaves. I myself will not dare to drink or eat; I will hold the hearse's thill and clasp its carriage shaft like a bird perching on a withered branch; I'll bare my flesh and expose my body,

---

1  An identical statement about Zengshen and Xiaoji is found in *Zhanguoce*, 48B/19/20.

**【原文】**

复乎公，公忿然作色而怒曰："子何必患若言而教寡人乎？"晏子对曰："婴闻之，忠不避危，爱无恶言。且婴固以难之矣。今君营处为游观，既夺人有，又禁其葬，非仁也；肆心傲听，不恤民忧，非义也。若何勿听？"因道盆成适之辞。公喟然太息曰："悲乎哉！子勿复言。"乃使男子袒免，女子发笄者以百数，为开凶门，以迎盆成适。适脱衰绖，冠条缨，墨缘，以见乎公。公曰："吾闻之，五子不满隅，一子可满朝，非乃子耶！"盆成适于是临事不敢哭，奉事以礼，毕，出门，然后举声焉。

**【今译】**

晏子回到王宫，回复给景公，景公生气地变了脸色说："您为什么要因为他的话而教导我呢？"晏子回答说："我听说，忠心就不会躲避危险，仁爱就不会有不利的言辞。况且我原本就认为说服您很难。现在国君您建造游乐观赏的地方，不仅夺取了他人的土地，还禁止他们埋葬，这不是仁；只根据自己的心意却不听他人的劝谏，不体恤人民的担忧，这不是义。怎么能不听呢？"因此将盆成适的话告诉了景公。景公长叹一声说："太悲伤了！您别再说了。"于是命令袒露左臂的男子，以麻束发的女子数百人，打开凶门来迎接盆成适。盆成适脱下丧服，戴上有丝带的帽子，涂黑它的边缘，来拜见景公。景公说："我听说，五个人不能充实墙角，一个人可以充满朝堂，这就是说您啊！"盆成适于是在丧事中不敢痛哭，按礼仪的规制举行丧事，结束后，走出宫门，然后才放声大哭。

hoping that our ruler will pity me. Although I, your menial subject, am dim-witted, I humbly harbor the thought that our enlightened ruler will be saddened and unable to bear my suffering."

Yanzi entered for a court audience and reported to the Duke. The Duke flushed with anger and raged: "Why must you be concerned with such words and come instruct me?"

Yanzi replied: "I have heard that a loyal minister should not shun taking risks, and a loving minister should not be averse to speaking out. Furthermore, I was certain from the very beginning that this attitude would create difficulty for you. By now, my Lord, you have already constructed residence quarters for your sight-seeing tours, for which purpose you have seized other people's property, and now you also forbid them to bury their dead — this is inhumane. And to be unscrupulous in your desires, to be too arrogant to pay heed, and not to have pity on the people's suffering — this is unrighteousness. Why do you not pay heed to them?" Hence, he recounted the words pronounced by Pencheng Kuo.

The Duke heaved a heavy sigh and said: "How sad!  Speak no further of this."

603

Thereupon, he sent by the hundreds bareheaded men, with left arms uncovered and women with their hair tied in a white festoon to install a special mourning portal to receive Pencheng Kuo.

Kuo took off his hemp mourning garments and put on a cap with tassels and a gown with black piping at the border of the sleeves and necklines, and came for an audience with the Duke.

The Duke said: "I have heard that sometimes, five sons cannot fill up one corner; sometimes, one son can fill up an entire court. Are you not that son?"

Thereupon, Pencheng Kuo took charge of the funeral and did not dare to weep. He conducted the funeral according to the rites, and upon completion he left through the gate, and then raised his voice and cried.

# 7.12 [182] 景公筑长庲台晏子舞而谏

景公要修筑长庲台，晏子起舞而进谏

## 【原文】

景公筑长庲之台，晏子侍坐。觞三行，晏子起舞曰："岁已暮矣，而禾不获，忽忽矣若之何！岁已寒矣，而役不罢，惙惙矣如之何！"舞三，而涕下沾襟。景公惭焉，为之罢长庲之役。

## 【今译】

景公要修筑长庲台，晏子陪坐在身边。饮酒三次后，晏子起身舞蹈并唱道："到了年终了，但粮食却没有收获，时间都过去了该怎么办啊！到了冬天了，但徭役却没有罢免，心中忧愁该怎么办啊！"舞蹈了三次，眼泪流下沾湿了衣襟。景公非常惭愧，因此停止了修建长庲台的徭役。

## 7.12 [182] DUKE JING WAS CONSTRUCTING THE CHANGLAI TERRACE, YANZI DANCED AND REMONS-TRATED.[1]

When Duke Jing was constructing the Changlai Terrace, Yanzi attended him and sat by him. After three rounds of drinks, Yanzi rose to dance, singing: "It is already the end of the year, yet the crops are still not harvested. I am so lost — what can I do? It is already cold, yet the compulsory labor has not halted. I am so dejected — what can I do?" He danced three times; tears flowed, dampening his lapel. Duke Jing was ashamed, and halted the compulsory labor of constructing the Changlai Terrace.

605

---

1  Item 7.12 [182] ↔ Items 2.5 [55]; 2.6 [56].

## 7.13 [183] 景公使烛邹主鸟而亡之公怒将加诛 晏子谏

景公让烛邹管理鸟却让它们跑掉了，景公生气了想要诛杀他，晏子进谏

### 【原文】

景公好弋，使烛邹主鸟而亡之，公怒，诏吏杀之。晏子曰："烛邹有罪三，请数之以其罪而杀之。"公曰："可。"于是召而数之公前，曰："烛邹！汝为吾君主鸟而亡之，是罪一也；使吾君以鸟之故杀人，是罪二也；使诸侯闻之，以吾君重鸟（以）〔而〕轻士，是罪三也。"（毂）〔数〕烛邹罪已毕，请杀之。公曰："勿杀！寡人闻命矣。"

### 【今译】

景公喜欢射鸟，让烛邹管理鸟雀却让它们跑掉了，景公非常生气，下令胥吏杀掉他。晏子说："烛邹有三项罪名，请让我先历数他的罪名再杀他。"景公说："可以。"于是征召烛邹到国君面前历数他的罪名，说："烛邹！你为我的国君管理鸟雀却让它们跑掉，这是第一项罪名；让我的国君因为鸟雀的原因而杀人，这是第二项罪名；让诸侯听说这件事，认为我的国君重视鸟雀却轻视士人，这是第三项罪名。"历数完烛邹的罪名后，晏子请求杀了他。景公说："不要杀他了！我接受您的教导了。"

## 7.13 [183] DUKE JING APPOINTED ZHU ZOU TO TAKE CHARGE OF HIS BIRDS, BUT ZHU ZOU LOST THEM. THE DUKE WAS ANGRY AND PLANNED TO EXECUTE HIM, YANZI REMONSTRATED.[1]

Duke Jing was fond of shooting arrows at birds. He appointed Zhu Zou to be in charge of the birds, but Zhu Zou let them escape. The Duke was furious, and instructed officials to execute him. Yanzi said: "Zhu Zou has three crimes. Let me list his crimes and then execute him."

The Duke said: "Granted."

Therefore, Yanzi summoned Zhu Zou, and enumerated his crimes in front of the Duke and said: "Zhu Zou, you were appointed to be in charge of the birds for our Lord but you let them escape — this is the first crime. You made our Lord execute people for the sake of birds — this is the second crime. You made the regional princes hear of it and think that our Lord values birds more than officers — this is the third crime. I've completed the list of Zhu Zou's crime, proceed with his execution."

The Duke said, "Cancel the execution! I accept your instruction."

607

---

1   Item 7.13 [183] ↔ Item 1.25 [25].

# 7.14 [184] 景公问治国之患晏子对以佞人谗夫在君侧

　　景公询问治理国家的祸患，晏子用阿谀谄媚的人在国君身边来回答

## 【原文】

　　景公问晏子曰："治国之患亦有常乎？"对曰："佞人谗夫之在君侧者，好恶良臣，而行与小人，此国之（长）〔常〕患也。"公曰："谗佞之人，则诚不善矣；虽然，则奚曾为国常患乎？"晏子曰："君以为耳目而好缪事，则是君之耳目缪也。夫上乱君之耳目，下使群臣皆失其职，岂不诚足患哉！"公曰："如是乎！寡人将去之。"

## 【今译】

　　景公询问晏子说："治理国家的祸患有常见的吗？"晏子回答说："阿谀谄媚的人处在国君的身边，喜欢诽谤贤良的臣子，而品行像小人一样，这是国家常见的祸患。"景公说："阿谀谄媚的人，的确是不好的；虽然如此，他们能称为国家常见的祸患吗？"晏子说："国君以他们为自己的耳目并且喜好与他们谋划国事，那么国君看到的和听到的就会出现错误了。他们向上蒙蔽国君的耳目，向下使群臣难以履行自己的职责，难道还不足以成为祸患吗！"景公说："是这样的啊，我将除去他们。"晏子说："您不能除去他们。"景公很生气变了脸色说："先生您为什么如此小看我！"晏子回答说："我怎么敢如此自大！那些能够被国君所任用的人，才能都不是一般的。他们把大的不忠诚埋藏在心中，必然慎重地将小忠诚表现在表面，来达成他大的不忠诚。在王宫内就

# 7.14 [184] DUKE JING ASKED ABOUT CHIEF CONCERNS IN GOVERNING THE STATE. YANZI ANSWERED THAT THE MAIN RISK IS WHEN SYCOPHANTS AND SLANDERERS ARE AT THE RULER'S SIDE.[1]

Duke Jing asked Yanzi: "Are there permanent chief concerns in governing a state?"

Yanzi answered: "When sycophants and slanderers are by the ruler's side, they are fond of vilifying good ministers, and they act in coalition with petty people. These are the permanent concerns of the state."

The Duke said: "Concerning sycophants and slanderers — these are truly bad; nonetheless, how could they be considered permanent concerns of the state?"

Yanzi said: "When they function as the ruler's ears and eyes, since they are fond of scheming,[2] the ruler's ears and eyes become prone to error. Above, they confuse the ruler's ears and eyes, and below they cause the various ministers to become negligent in their duties. Are all these truly not sufficient to be considered concerns?"

The Duke said: "If so, I will remove them."

Yanzi said: "You are not able to do this, my Lord."

The Duke flushed with anger; he was displeased and said: "How exceedingly little you think of me, my Master!"

Yanzi answered: "How could I dare to be so arrogant?[3] The talents of all those who are in a position to surround you, my Lord, are extraordinary. Those who harbor great insincerity within must be extremely careful about displaying acts of minor sincerity outwardly in order to accomplish their

609

---

1  Item 7.14 [184] ↔ Item 3.9 [59].

2  缪 → 谋 (*YZCQ-ICS*, 65, n. 5).

3  槁 → 骄 (*JS*, 468/10).

**【原文】**

晏子曰："公不能去也。"公忿然作色不说，曰："夫子何（小）〔少〕寡人甚也！"对曰："臣何敢槁也！夫能自周于君者，才能皆非常也。夫藏大不诚于中者，必谨小诚于外，以成其大不诚（于中者），（必谨小诚于外），（以成其大不诚）入则求君之嗜欲能顺之，（公）〔君〕怨良臣，则具其往失而益之，出则行威以（耻）〔取〕富。夫何密近，不为大利变，而务与君至义者也？此难得其知也。"公曰："然则先圣奈何？"对曰："先圣之治也，审见宾客，听治不留，〔患〕（曰）〔日〕不足，群臣皆得毕其诚，谗谀安得容其私！"公曰："然则夫子助寡人止之，寡人亦事勿用。"对曰："谗夫佞人之在君侧者，若社之有鼠也，谚言有之曰：'社鼠不可熏去。'谗佞之人，隐君之威以自守也，是难去焉。"

**【今译】**

探求国君的喜好并且顺从他，国君埋怨贤良的臣子，他们就详细地说明他们以前的过失来增加国君的反感，离开王宫就依仗国君的威权来取得财富。有谁能与国君亲密相处，不因为大的利益而改变，而务必以道义来与国君相处呢？这就很难知道了。"景公说："那么以前的圣君是怎么处理的呢？"晏子回答说："先代的圣君治理国家，认真地接见宾客，处理政事从不滞留，还担心没有处理完，群臣都能竭尽他们的忠诚，怎么能容许阿谀奉承的人谋私心呢！"景公说："那么请先生帮助我除去他们，我也不再任用他们了。"晏子回答说："阿谀奉承的人处在国君的身边，就像神庙中有老鼠一样，有这样的谚语说：'神庙中的老鼠不能用烟熏走。'阿谀谄媚的人，隐藏在国君的威严中保全自己，所以很难除去。"

great insincerity. When they enter your court, they seek out your desires in order to cater to them; if you, my Lord, bear grudges against good ministers, they would list their past mistakes in order to deserve personal benefit; and, when they exit the court, they wield their authority in order to appropriate properties. So who among these is fit to become your intimate aide, without dissimulating their intentions for the sake of huge profit and without focusing on helping you to practice righteousness, my Lord? It is difficult to see through these kinds of people."

The Duke said, "If so, what did the former sages do about that?"

Yanzi answered, "When the former sages governed their states, they carefully investigated their guest envoys; they heard lawsuits and dealt with governmental affairs without delay; they worried only that there were not enough days for their work; and all of the various ministers could act fully on their sincerity. How could there be room for the private interests of flatterers and slanderers?"

The Duke said: "If so, then help me to stop them, my Master, and I will make sure they are unemployed."

Yanzi answered: "When flatterers and sycophants are by the ruler's side, they are like rats living in the altar of soil. There is a proverb that says: 'It is impossible to smoke a rat out of the altar of soil.' The flatterers and sycophants are hiding behind your authority, my Lord, in order to protect themselves; therefore, it is so difficult to get rid of them."

# 7.15 [185] 景公问后世孰将践有齐者晏子对以田氏

景公询问后世谁将占有齐国，晏子用田氏来回答

【原文】

景公与晏子立曲潢之上，望见齐国，问晏子曰："后世孰将践有齐国者乎？"晏子对曰："非贱臣之所敢议也。"公曰："胡必然也？得者无失，则虞、夏常存矣。"晏子对曰："臣闻见（不）足以知之者，智也；先言而后当者，惠也。夫智与惠，君子之事，臣奚足以知之乎！虽然，臣请陈其为政：君强臣弱，政之本也；君唱臣和，教之隆也；刑罚在君，民之纪也。今夫田无宇二世有功于国，而利（耻）〔取〕分寡，公室兼

【今译】

景公和晏子站在潢河弯曲的地方，眺望齐国，询问晏子说："后代谁将占有齐国呢？"晏子回答说："这不是我所敢议论的。"景公说："何必这样呢？如果得到的都不会失去，那么虞、夏就会一直存在了。"晏子回答说："我听说见到的少却知道的多的人，是智；先说而之后能应验的，是慧。智和慧，是君子的事情，我哪里足够知道这些事呢？虽然如此，我请求陈述治理国家的经验：国君势强臣子势弱，是治理国家的根本；国君唱而臣子和，教化就会兴隆；刑罚掌握在国君手中，百姓就会遵从法纪。现在田无宇父子两代有功于国家，而获取的财富又分给贫穷孤寡的人，他兼有公室的利益，专擅国家的权力，君臣的位置颠倒，这样公室能不衰落吗！我听说，臣子富强国君就会灭亡。从这些方面来看，田无宇之后不久，齐国就是田氏的齐国了吧。我已经老了不能再等待国君您以后的事，您去世之后，政权就不会属于公室了。"景公说："那该怎么办呢？"晏子对景公说："只有礼制可以

# 7.15 [185] DUKE JING ASKED WHO WOULD RISE TO POSSESS THE STATE OF QI IN LATER GENERATIONS. YANZI ANSWERED THAT THE TIAN LINEAGE WILL TAKE POSSESSION OF IT.[1]

Duke Jing and Yanzi stood above the Curved Pool[2] and looked at the state of Qi from afar. The Duke asked Yanzi: "Who in later generations would ascend to the throne and take possession of the state of Qi?"

Yanzi answered, "This is not what a humble minister like myself presumes to discuss."

The Duke asked, "Why must you be like this? If those who attain power would never lose it, then the Yu and Xia dynasties would have persisted forever."

Yanzi answered, "I have heard that those for whom a glance is sufficient for gaining knowledge are wise, and those who make predictions that are later proved right are bright. This wisdom and brightness, my Lord, are the affairs of a man of noble character — how could I be sufficient to know them? Nonetheless, permit me to describe the administration of the government affairs. The foundation of government is a strong ruler and weak ministers; the ruler sings and the ministers echo in harmony — this is the pinnacle of moral leadership. Punishments lie in the hands of the ruler —this is the guiding principle of the people. Now, for two generations, Tian Wuyu has serviced our state and his profits have been distributed among the destitute. He took shares of the ducal household, monopolized the political power of the state, and switched the roles of ruler and minister[3] — how could the subsequent decline have been avoided? I've heard that if

613

---

1  Item 7.15 [185] ↔ Items 3.8 [58]; 4.17 [97]; 7.10 [180]; *Zuozhuan*, B 10.26.11/393/15.

2  A detailed description of the structure of the Curved Western Pool and its surrounding is provided previously in Item 2.15 [65].

3  易施 → 移易 (*YZCQ-ICS*, 66, n. 1).

## 【原文】

之，国权专之，君臣易施，而无衰乎！婴闻之，臣富主亡。由是观之，其无宇之后无几，齐国、田氏之国也？婴老不能待公之事，公若即世，（改）〔政〕不在公室。"公曰："然则奈何？"晏子对（其）〔曰〕："维礼可以已之。其在礼也，家施不及国，民不懈，货不移，工贾不变，士不滥，官不（谄）〔谄〕，大夫不〔收〕公利。"公曰："善。今知礼之可以为国也。"对曰："礼之可以为国也久矣，与天地并立。君令臣忠，父慈子孝，兄爱弟敬，夫和妻柔，姑慈妇听，礼之经也。君令而不违（厉），臣忠而不二，父慈而教，子孝而箴，兄爱而友，弟敬而顺，夫和而义，妻柔而贞，姑慈而从，妇听而婉，礼之质也。"公曰："善哉！寡人乃今知礼之尚也。"晏子曰："夫礼，先王之所以临天下也，以为其民，是故尚之。"

## 【今译】

阻止这件事。在礼制的规范中，卿大夫家中的恩惠不能施及到国都，民众不懈怠，财货不转移，工商之人不改变职业，士人不浮泛无实，官员不谄媚，大夫不收取公室的利益。"景公说："好。现在知道礼制可以治理国家了。"晏子回答说："礼制可以治理国家，是由来已久的事了，与天地的产生是同时的。国君圣明臣子忠诚，父亲慈爱子女孝顺，兄弟之间相亲相爱，丈夫温和而正义，妻子柔顺而坚贞，舅姑慈爱而放任，媳妇顺从而温婉，这是礼制的本质。"景公说："好啊！我现在才知道应该尊尚礼制。"晏子说："礼制，是先代君王治理天下的方式，用它来管理百姓，所以尊尚它。"

the minister is rich, then the sovereign is doomed to perish. In light of this, perhaps not long after Tian Wuyu, the state of Qi will become the possession of the Tian lineage. I am old and cannot attend to your affairs, and if you die, my Lord, the government will not be in the hands of your ducal house."

The Duke said, "Then what can be done?"

Yanzi answered, "Only the rites can bring an end to all this. According to the rites, the distribution of gifts from the household of a high officer should not reach to a nationwide scale; the people should not be indolent; prices should not change; artisans and traders should not exchange their occupations; officers should not fail in their official responsibilities; officials should not be flatterers; and high officers should not collect profits that belong to the state."

The Duke said, "Well argued. Now I understand that the rites are something with which I can govern a state."

Yanzi answered, "The rites have long been considered useful in governing a state. They stand alongside Heaven and Earth. Rulers issue orders and ministers faithfully follow; fathers are compassionate and sons are filial; elder brothers love and younger brothers respect; husbands are tender and wives gentle; mothers-in-law are kind and daughters-in-law obedient. These are the principles of the rites. If rulers instruct without breaking the rules, then ministers are loyal without duplicity; if fathers are kind and instructive, then sons are filial and admonished; if elder brothers are loving and befriending, then the younger brothers respect and comply; if husbands are tender and righteous, then their wives are gentle and chaste; if mothers-in-law are kind and soothing, then daughters-in-law pay heed and are submissive. This is the substance of the rites."

The Duke said, "Well argued. Only today have I realized the supreme value of the rites."

Yanzi said, "The rites are that with which the ancient kings ruled the realm and instructed the people. Therefore, they highly valued the rites."

## 7.16 [186] 晏子使吴 吴王问君子之行晏子对以不与乱国俱灭

晏子出使吴国，吴王询问君子的品行，晏子用不与动乱的国家一同灭亡来回答

### 【原文】

晏子聘于吴，吴王问："君子之行何如？"晏子对曰："君顺怀之，政治归之，不怀暴君之禄，不居乱国之位，君子见兆则退，不与乱国俱灭，不与暴君偕亡。"

### 【今译】

晏子出使吴国，吴王询问他："君子的品行是什么样的？"晏子回答说："国君听从就归向他，政事得到治理就归附他，不贪恋暴君的俸禄，不担任动乱国家的官职，君子见到动乱的征兆就离开，不和动乱的国家一起灭亡，不和暴君一起死亡。"

# 7.16 [186] YANZI SERVED AS AN ENVOY TO WU. THE KING OF WU INQUIRED REGARDING THE PROPER CONDUCT OF A MAN OF NOBLE CHARACTER. YANZI ANSWERED THAT A MAN OF NOBLE CHARACTER DOES NOT PERISH TOGETHER WITH A CHAOTIC STATE. [1]

Yanzi was on an official visit to Wu. The King of Wu asked, "What is the proper conduct of a man of noble character?"

Yanzi answered: "If the ruler follows the right principles, the man of noble character will embrace him; if the government of the ruler is well ordered, the man of noble character will attach himself to him. A man of noble character does not cherish emolument given by a cruel ruler; nor does he occupy a position in a chaotic state. He does not cling to the emolument of tyrannical rulers; neither does he assume positions in a chaotic state. At the first sight of such things he retreats; he does not perish together with a chaotic state, nor does he die along with a tyrannical ruler."

617

---

1   7.16 [186] ↔ Item 4.10 [90].

## 7.17 [187] 吴王问齐君僈暴吾子何容焉晏子对以岂能以道食人

吴王问齐君怠慢又暴躁晏子如何能容忍他，晏子回答说怎么能以道义来养活人

### 【原文】

晏子使吴，吴王曰："寡人得寄僻陋蛮夷之乡，希见教君子之行，请私而无为罪。"晏子愀然辟位。吴王曰："吾闻齐君盖贼以僈，野以暴，吾子容焉，何甚也？"晏子遵〔逡巡〕而对曰："臣闻之，微事不通，粗事不能者，必劳；大事不得，小事不为者，必贫；大者不能致人，小者不能至人之门者，必困。此臣之所以仕也。如臣者，岂能以道食人者哉！"晏子出，王笑曰："嗟乎！今日吾讥晏子，（訾）犹裸而〔訾〕高撅者也。"

### 【今译】

晏子出使吴国，吴王说："我生活在这偏僻简陋的蛮夷之地，很少被教导君子的品行，请和您谈论一些私事不要怪罪。"晏子恭敬地站了起来。吴王说："我听说齐国国君残忍而傲慢，粗野而暴虐，您却能容忍他，怎么会有这么大的度量呢？"晏子沉吟了一会回答说："我听说，精细的事情不擅长，粗略的事做不到的人，一定会劳累；大事做不了，小事不想做的人，一定会贫穷；地位高的人不能吸引到人才，地位低的人不能投奔他人，一定会困厄。这是我为什么出仕的原因。像我这样的人，怎么能以道义来养活人呢！"晏子离开后，吴王笑着说："唉！今天我讥笑晏子，就好像自己裸体却责备别人脱衣服啊。"

## 7.17 [187] THE KING OF WU ASKED YANZI HOW HE COULD TOLERATE SERVING THE INSOLENT[1] AND VIOLENT RULER OF QI. YANZI ANSWERED THAT ONE CAN NOT PROVIDE FOOD FOR PEOPLE THROUGH THE PURSUIT OF THE WAY.[2]

Yanzi served as an envoy to Wu. The King of Wu said, "I live in a desolate and barbaric region. I seldom receive instruction in the Ways of a man of noble character, so please do not be offended if I offer here a personal word."

Yanzi winced and stood up from his seat.

The King of Wu said, "I've heard that the ruler of Qi appears to be cruel and arrogant, wild and violent. How can you tolerate this to such an extent?"

Yanzi backed off a few paces and replied: "I've heard that those who cannot fathom subtle affairs and cannot perform crude tasks are sure to toil with their bodies; those who cannot take upon themselves great enterprises and do not occupy themselves with small matters are sure to become poor; those who cannot attract people to serve them in great matters and cannot come to other people's private gates to serve them in small matters are sure to experience difficulties. That is why I took an official position. How could someone like me provide food for people through the pursuit of the Way?"

When Yanzi left, the King of Wu laughed and said, "Alas, my mocking of Yanzi today was similar to a naked person who ridicules someone who has just lifted[3] the edge of his garment."[4]

---

1  傲 → 慢 (*JS*, 475/5).

2  Item 7.17 [187] ↔ Item 4.12 [92]; *Shuoyuan*, 12.13/98/25.

3  撅 → 撅 (*JS*, 475/11).

4  *Mozi*, 12.2 (48)/108/21, reads: 是犹裸谓撅者不恭也 — "This is like someone who was stripped naked saying that the person who has just lifted his garments is not respectful." A similar but much more famous analogy is found in *Mencius*, 1.3/1/24: 五十步笑百步 — "One who retreats fifty paces mocks one who retreats a hundred."

## 7.18 [188] 司马子期问有不干君不恤民取（耻）〔取〕名者乎晏子对以不仁也

司马子期询问士人有不担任官职不体恤人民而获得名望的吗？晏子回答说这是不仁

【原文】

司马子期问晏子曰："士亦有不干君，不恤民，徒居无为而（耻）〔取〕名者乎？"

晏子对曰："婴闻之，能足以（瞻）〔赡〕上益民而不为者，谓之不仁。不仁而（耻）〔取〕名者，婴未得闻之也。"

【今译】

司马子期询问晏子说："士人也有不担任官职，不体恤百姓，什么都不作而取得名望的吗？"晏子回答说："我听说，有能力辅佐国君帮助百姓却不做的人，称为不仁。不仁而获得名望的，我没有听说过。"

# 7.18 [188] MARSHAL ZIQI[1] ASKED IF THERE IS AN OFFICER WHO IS NOT ATTACHED TO A RULER AND DOES NOT TAKE PITY ON THE PEOPLE AND YET WINS FAME. YANZI REPLIED WITH REFERENCE TO THE INHUMANE.

Marshal Ziqi queried Yanzi as follows: "Is there also among the officers one who is not attached to a ruler; who does not take pity on the people; whose life is comfortable with taking no action,[2] yet who wins fame?"

Yanzi answered, "I've heard that if one is sufficiently capable of supporting a ruler and increasing the wealth of the people yet does not do so, such a person is called inhumane. I've never heard about an inhumane person who has won fame."

621

---

1 Marshal Ziqi 司马子期, personal name Jie 结 (d. 479 BCE), was the son of King Ping of Chu 楚平王.

2 This line seems to be implanted here directly from the second chapter of the *Dao De Jing*, 2A/1/11, which reads: 是以声人居无为之事.

## 7.19 [189] 高子问子事灵公庄公景公皆敬子晏子对以一心

高子问晏子辅佐灵公庄公景公，他们都尊敬晏子，晏子用一心来回答

**【原文】**

高子问晏子曰："子事灵公、庄公、景公，皆敬子，三君之心一耶？夫子之心三也？"晏子对曰："善哉！问事君，婴闻一心可以事百君，三心不可以事一君。故三君之心非一〔心〕也，而婴之心非三（必）〔心〕也。且婴之于灵公也，尽复而不能立之政，所谓仅全其四支以从其君者也。及庄公陈武夫，尚勇力，欲辟胜于邪，而婴不能禁，故退而野处。婴闻之，言不用者，不受其禄，不治其事者，不与其难，吾于庄公行之矣。今之君，轻国而重乐，薄于民而厚于养，藉敛过量，使令过任，而婴不能禁，庸知其能全身以事君乎！"

**【今译】**

高子问晏子说："您辅佐灵公、庄公、景公，他们都尊敬您，三位国君的内心都是一样的吗？先生您的内心是有三种吗？"晏子回答说："好啊！问我辅佐国君的事，我听说一心可以辅佐百位国君，三心不可以辅佐一位国君。所以三位国君的内心并不是一样的，而我的内心也不是三种。而且我辅佐灵公，对他的回复都不能被接受，对政事没有帮助，这就是所谓保全自身来跟从国君的人。到庄公时招揽武夫，崇尚勇力，想要以邪道取胜，而我却不能阻止他，所以离开不再担任官职。我听说，言论不能被采纳的人，不接受国君的俸禄，不参与政事治理的人，不和国君一起承受灾难，我对庄公就是这么做的。现在的国君，轻视国家的治理而重视自己享乐，对百姓刻薄而对自己的供养丰厚，征敛赋税超过限度，役使百姓超出民力，但我不能阻止他，怎么知道我能够保全自己来辅佐国君呢！"

## 7.19 [189] GAOZI INQUIRED REGARDING YANZI'S SERVICE TO DUKE LING, DUKE ZHUANG AND DUKE JING, AND THEIR RESPECT FOR HIM. YANZI REPLIED THAT HE HAD SERVED THEM WITH A SINGLE MIND.[1]

Gaozi asked Yanzi: "You, Sir, served Duke Ling, Duke Zhuang and Duke Jing, and they all respected you. Are the minds of these three rulers one and the same, or are you, Master, of three minds?"

Yanzi answered, "Well put. If you ask about serving rulers, I have heard that with a single mind you can serve a hundred rulers, yet with three minds you cannot serve even one ruler. Therefore, the minds of these three rulers were not one and the same; neither am I of three minds. Moreover, in serving Duke Ling, I responded to all his questions in full but I could not establish my own policies. This is what I call, 'to barely keep one's four limbs intact while following a ruler.' Duke Zhuang had an array of bold warriors; he placed great value on courage and strength, and he expected that perversity would defeat evil[2] — I couldn't stop him. Therefore, I withdrew and lived in the countryside. I've heard that when a ruler does not implement one's words, one should not accept his emolument; when a ruler does not permit one to take an active part in the affairs of government, one need not share in the ruler's demise. I followed this practical attitude with Duke Zhuang. My present ruler has little thought for the state and he emphasizes pleasure-seeking. He is stingy towards the people and creates himself vast wealth; his tax collections are excessive and the orders he issues are beyond the people's capability to follow. I cannot stop him. How can I be sure whether I can serve this ruler without incurring personal harm?"

623

---

1  Item 7.19 [189] ↔ Item 4.29 [109]; Item 8.3 [200]; Item 8.4 [201]; *Kongcongzi*, 6.1/62/3.

2  Retain 于 (*SBCK*, VII, 20B1).

## 7.20 [190] 晏子再治东阿上计景公迎贺晏子辞

晏子再次治理东阿，考核的时候景公祝贺他，晏子推辞

【原文】

晏子治东阿，三年，景公召而数之曰："吾以子为可，而使子治东阿，今子治而乱，子退而自察也，寡人将加大诛于子。"晏子对曰："臣请改道易行而治东阿，三年不治，臣请死之。"景公许〔之〕。于是明年上计，景公迎而贺之曰："甚善矣！子之治东阿也。"晏子对曰："前臣之治东阿也，属托不行，货赂不至，陂池之鱼，以利贫民。当此之时，民无饥〔者〕，〔而〕君反以罪臣。今臣后之东阿也，属托行，货赂至，并重赋敛，仓库少内，便事左右，陂池之鱼，入于权（宗）〔家〕。当

【今译】

晏子治理东阿，过了三年，景公召见他而责备说："我觉得先生您可以，而让您去治理东阿，现在您的治理混乱，您辞去官职自我反省吧，我会严厉处罚您。"晏子回答说："我请求更改我的做法而再次治理东阿，如果三年还没有治理好，请您处死我。"景公答应了他的请求。于是第二年考核的时候，景公迎接并祝贺他说："太好了！先生对东阿的治理。"晏子回答说："以前我治理东阿，他人的嘱托请求都不答应，财货贿赂不会送到我这里，池塘中的鱼虾，为贫穷的百姓增加利益。那个时候，民众没有饥饿的，但国君却归罪于我。后来我治

## 7.20 [190] YANZI GOVERNED DONG-E A SECOND TIME AND SUBMITTED ACCOUNTING BOOKS. DUKE JING WELCOMED AND CONGRATULATED HIM, YANZI DECLINED THE HONOR.[1]

After Yanzi had governed Dong-e for three years, Duke Jing summoned and reproved him as follows: "I thought you were capable and appointed you to govern Dong-e. Now you have governed it, yet it is in chaos. You should withdraw and reflect on yourself critically, and I will inflict a grievous punishment upon you."

Yanzi replied: "I request to be allowed to govern Dong-e in a different way, with a change of practices. If good order is not restored within three years, I'll ask to die on account of this."

Duke Jing consented. Thereupon, after a year, the annual assessment was held. Duke Jing welcomed and congratulated Yanzi as follows: "You have governed Dong-e extremely well!"

Yanzi replied: "When I governed Dong-e before, petitions were denied and bribes were not proffered. Fishes in ponds and lakes were used for the benefit of poor people. At that time, there was no hunger among people, yet you, my Lord, to the contrary found fault with me. When subsequently I arrived at Dong-e, petitions were accepted and bribes poured in. Tax collections were onerous, and incomes to the warehouse decreased. I made things very smooth for my entourage, and the fishes in the ponds and lakes went to the powerful families. At present, more than half of the people are hungry, yet you, my Lord, to the contrary welcomed and congratulated me. Foolish as I am, I cannot govern Dong-e again. I beg to resign[2] from this

1 Item 7.20 [190] ↔ Item 5.4 [114].

2 乞骸骨 — begging for one's remains to be buried in one's home town, a metaphoric request to resign from office.

**【原文】**

此之时，饥者过半矣，君乃反迎而贺臣。〔臣〕愚不能复治东阿，愿乞骸骨，避贤者之路。"再拜，便僻。景公乃下席而谢之曰："子强复治东阿，东阿者，子之东阿也，寡人无复与焉。"

**【今译】**

理东阿，答应别人的嘱托请求，财货贿赂都送到我这里，加重赋税的征收，收入粮仓的减少，为身边的人提供便利，池塘中的鱼虾，都进入有权势的家族。这个时候，饥饿的人超过一半了，国君却反过来迎接并祝贺我。我太愚笨不能再治理东阿，请您准许我退休，不要阻挡贤者的道路。"拜了又拜，就要离开。景公于是走下座位而谢罪说："一定要勉强先生您治理东阿，东阿是先生的东阿，我不会再干预了。"

office and yield the way to one more worthy than myself."

He bowed twice and was about to leave. At that point Duke Jing descended from his seat and apologized to him, saying: "Reluctant as you are, return to govern Dong-e, my Master. Dong-e is your Dong-e, I'll not interfere again."

## 7.21 [191] 太卜绐景公能动地晏子知其妄使卜自晓公

太卜欺骗景公说他能使大地震动，晏子知道他的虚假让太卜自己告诉景公

【原文】

景公问太卜曰："汝之道何能？"对曰："臣能动地。"公召晏子而告之，曰："寡人问太卜曰：'汝之道何能？'对曰：'能动地。'地可动乎？"晏子默（默）〔然〕不对，出，见太卜曰："昔吾见钩星在四心之间，地其动乎？"太卜曰："然。"晏子曰："吾言之，恐子死之也；

【今译】

景公问太卜说："您掌握的道有什么用呢？"太卜回答说："我能使大地震动。"景公召见晏子并告诉他，说："我问太卜说：'您掌握的道有什么用？'太卜回答说：'能让大地震动。'大地能震动吗？"晏子沉默不回答，离开王宫后，往见太卜说："晚上我看到钩星在四星宿之间，大地将要震动了吧？"太卜说："是的。"晏子说："我告诉国君，害怕你会被处死了；沉默不回答，害怕国君就会疑惑。你去告诉国君，对于君臣都有好处。忠心于国君的人，难道必须要伤害别人吗！"

# 7.21 [191] THE CHIEF PROGNOSTICATOR CHEATED DUKE JING, SAYING THAT HE COULD MAKE THE EARTH QUAKE, YANZI KNEW THAT THIS WAS PREPOSTEROUS AND MADE THE CHIEF PROGNOSTICATOR EXPLICATE IT TO THE DUKE ON HIS OWN.[1]

Duke Jing asked the Chief Prognosticator: "What can you accomplish with your Way?"

The Chief Prognosticator replied: "I can make the earth quake."

The Duke summoned Yanzi and told him about it: "I've asked the Chief Prognosticator: 'What can you accomplish with your Way?' and he replied: 'I can make the earth quake.' Is it possible to make the earth quake?"

Yanzi kept silent and did not answer. He then left, met the Chief Prognosticator and said to him: "A few nights ago I saw that the Hook Star[2] was between the Fang[3] and Xin constellations—is an earthquake about to strike?"

The Chief Prognosticator said, "Yes."

Yanzi said, "I'm afraid that had I told this to the Duke, you would have lost your life, and had I kept silent, the Duke would have been confused. Go and tell the Duke the truth on your own, so that both ruler and minister will gain. Why should it be necessary for a loyal subject of a ruler to cause harm to others?"

Yanzi left. The Chief Prognosticator rushed to have an audience with the Duke, and said to him: "I am unable to make the earth quake; the earthquake struck of its own accord."

629

---

1   Item 7.21 [191] ↔ Item 6.4 [144]; *Lunheng*, 17/58/1; *Huainanzi*, 12/119/1.

2   The Hook Star (钩星) is one of the aliases of Mercury.

3   四 → 驷 → 房 (*JS*, 481/7).

【原文】

默然不对，恐君之惶也。子言，君臣俱得焉。忠于君者，岂必伤人哉！"晏子出，太卜走入见公，曰："臣非能动地，地固将动也。"陈子阳闻之，曰："晏子默而不对者，不欲太卜之死也；往见太卜者，恐君之惶也。晏子，仁人也，可谓忠上而惠下也。"

【今译】

晏子离开后，太卜前往王宫面见国君，说："我不能让大地震动，大地本来就要震动了。"陈子阳听说这件事，说："晏子沉默不回答，是不想让太卜被处死；前去见太卜，是害怕国君疑惑。晏子是仁义的人，这可以被称为忠心于国君而又惠泽下属了。"

When Chen Ziyang[1] heard of this, he said: "Yanzi kept silent and did not respond because he did not want the Chief Prognosticator to die; and he then met the Chief Prognosticator because he was afraid that the Duke would be confused. Yanzi was a humane person. It may be said that he was loyal to his superior and kind to his inferiors."

631

---

1   A figure not fully identified in the relevant sources.

# 7.22 [192] 有献书谮晏子退耕而国不治复召晏子

有人上书诬陷晏子，晏子辞去官职去耕种而国家难以治理，景公
又召回晏子

## 【原文】

晏子相景公，其论人也，见贤而进之，不同君所欲；见不善则废之，
不辟君所爱；行己而无私，直言而无讳。有纳书者曰："废置不周于君
前，谓之专；出言不讳于君前，谓〔之〕易。专易之行存，则君臣之
道废矣，吾不知晏子之为忠臣也。"公以为然。晏子入朝，公色不说，
故晏子归，备载，使人辞曰："婴故老悖无能，毋敢服壮者事。"辞而
不为臣，退而穷处，东耕海滨，堂下生（黎藿）〔藜藋〕，门外生荆棘。

## 【今译】

晏子辅佐景公，他议论别人，见到贤能的人就推荐他，不与国君
的要求相同；见到做得不好的就罢黜，不避开国君所宠爱的人；立身
行事毫无私心，直言而从不避讳。有上书的人说："选拔黜陟官员不与
国君商议，可以称之为专权；在国君面前说话毫无避讳，可以称之为
轻慢。专权轻慢的行为存在，那么君臣之道就废弛了，我不知道晏子
怎么成为忠臣的。"景公认可他的意见。晏子上朝的时候，景公的脸
色不悦，因此晏子回去后，整理了自己的行李，派人向景公告辞说：
"我已经老得没有能力了，不敢再做壮年人的事了。"告辞后不再担任
景公的臣子，退隐而且过着俭朴的日子，在东方海边耕种土地，院子
中生长着野菜，大门外长出了荆棘。七年后，燕国和鲁国与齐国纷争，

# 7.22 [192] SOMEONE SUBMITTED A LETTER OF SLANDER, YANZI RETIRED TO PLOUGH HIS FIELDS, AND THE STATE WAS IN DISORDER. YANZI WAS SUMMONED AGAIN.[1]

Yanzi served Duke Jing as prime minister. When he evaluated people, upon encountering a worthy person he would promote him with no regard to the ruler's preference; upon encountering a bad person he would reject him, without considering those whom the ruler favored. He was impartial in his conduct; he spoke out straightforwardly and concealed nothing.

Someone submitted a letter to the Duke, saying: "One who rejects and installs people without coordinating these actions in the presence of the ruler is called self-serving; one who speaks out straightforwardly without any inhibitions is called supercilious. When the conduct of self-serving and superciliousness prevail, the way of the ruler and the minister falls into disuse. I don't understand how Yanzi can be regarded as a loyal minister."

The Duke agreed, and so when Yanzi entered for a court audience, the Duke showed his displeasure. Therefore, Yanzi turned away, lined up all his possessions on chariots and sent his resignation with a messenger, saying: "I am old, recalcitrant and incapable, I dare not serve in a position better fit for a man in his prime." He resigned, did not serve as a minister, and retreated to live in dire straits in the East. He farmed on the sea-coast, pigweed and goosefoot grew beneath his home, and thorny scrubs grew outside his gate. Seven years later, a quarrel broke out between Qi and the states of Yan and Lu. People were in turmoil and householders could not make ends meet. The Duke ruled the state by himself, his power was diminished by the other regional princes, and he was undermined by the Gao and Guo lineages. The Duke was frightened and summoned back Yanzi. As soon as Yanzi arrived,

633

---

1   Item 7.22 [192] ↔ Item 5.5 [115].

**【原文】**

七年，燕、鲁分争，百姓惛乱，而家无积。公自治国，权轻诸侯，身弱高、国。公恐，复召晏子。晏子至，公一归七年之禄，而家无藏。晏子立，（侯诸）〔诸侯〕忌其威，高、国服其政，燕、鲁贡职，小国时朝。晏子没而后衰。

**【今译】**

百姓纷乱不安，而国家没有积蓄。景公自己治理国家，地位轻于诸侯，自身势力也不如高、国二家。景公非常担忧，再次召回晏子。晏子来到国都，景公一次归还了他七年的俸禄，晏子家中无余财。晏子治理齐国，诸侯顾忌他的威望，高、国两家服从他的治理，燕国、鲁国向齐国纳贡，小国按时来齐国朝见。晏子死后齐国才衰落。

the Duke gave him the equivalent of seven years' salary, but Yanzi did not retain it for his household. When Yanzi was appointed, the regional princes were cowed by his authority and the Gao and Guo lineages submitted to his rule. The states of Yan and Lu offered their tributes and small states paid court to him regularly. However, after the death of Yanzi, the state declined.

## 7.23 [193] 晏子使高（紥）〔纠〕治家三年而未尝弼过逐之

晏子让高纠管理他的家，三年从未匡正他的过错，晏子驱逐了他

### 【原文】

晏子使高（紥）〔纠〕，三年而辞焉。傧者谏曰："高（紥）〔纠〕之事夫子三年，曾无以爵位，而逐之，敢请其罪。"晏子曰："若夫方立之人，维圣人而已。如婴者，（反）〔仄〕陋之人也。若夫左婴右婴之人不举，（曰）〔四〕维将不正。今此子事吾三年，未尝弼吾过也。吾是以辞之。"

### 【今译】

晏子让高纠治理他的家，过了三年却辞退了他。接引宾客的人进谏说："高纠为先生您做事已经三年了，没有得到任何爵位，现在却驱逐他，我想知道他有什么过错。"晏子说："能够以道立身的人，只有圣人。像我这样的，只是浅陋不堪的人。如果我身边的人不能纠正我的过错，我的道德就将不规范。现在这个人为我做事三年，却从来没有纠正过我的过错。所以我辞退了他。"

# 7.23 [193] YANZI APPOINTED GAO JIU TO ADMINISTER HIS HOUSEHOLD AFFAIRS. FOR THREE YEARS, GAO JIU DID NOT CORRECT YANZI'S ERRORS, SO YANZI DISMISSED HIM.[1]

Yanzi appointed Gao Jiu to administer his household affairs and dismissed him after three years. The officer who attended Yanzi remonstrated him, saying: "Gao Jiu served you master for three years, and you gave him not a single rank or position, and then you dismissed him. I dare to ask what his offence was."

Yanzi replied: "Only the sages take a stand on the basis of principled rules; but someone like myself who is a lowly person — if all those around me do not make my mistakes known to me, then the four cardinal virtues[2] will not be held upright. Now this man served me three years and never corrected any of my errors, therefore I dismissed him."

637

---

1  Item 7.23 [193] ↔ Item 5.29 [139], *Shuoyuan*, 2.19/17/18.

2  The "four cardinal virtues" or the "four guiding principles" are: the Rites 礼; righteousness 义; integrity 廉; and a sense of shame 耻.

## 7.24 [194] 景公称桓公之封管仲益晏子邑辞不受

景公说齐桓公封给管仲封地，要增加晏子的封邑，晏子推辞不接受

### 【原文】

景公谓晏子曰："昔吾先君桓公，予管仲狐与谷，其县十七，著之（干）〔于〕帛，申之以策，通之诸侯，以为其子孙赏邑。寡人不足以辱而先君，今为夫子赏邑，通之子孙。"晏子辞曰："昔圣王论功而赏贤，贤者得之，不肖者失之，御德修礼，无有荒怠。今事君而免于罪者，其子孙奚宜与焉？若为齐国大夫者必有赏邑，则齐君何以共其社稷与诸侯币帛？婴请辞。"遂不受。

### 【今译】

景公对晏子说："以前我先代的国君桓公，封给管仲狐与谷，一共十七个县，标注在布帛上，书写在竹简上，通告于诸侯，并将其作为他子孙的封邑。我不能辱没我先代的国君，现在要赏赐给您封邑，并且可以传承给子孙。"晏子推辞说："以前圣明的君王根据功劳赏赐贤能的人，贤能的人得到赏赐，没有能力的人失去赏赐，增进德行修行礼制，从来没有懈怠。现在辅佐国君而仅能免于罪过，那么赏赐给子孙封邑合适吗？如果担任齐国大夫的都赏赐封邑，那么齐国的国君还有什么能够供奉社稷，给予诸侯币帛的呢？我不敢接受。"于是没有接受。

## 7.24 [194] DUKE JING PRAISED DUKE HUAN FOR GRANTING GUAN ZHONG FIEFDOMS AND WANTED TO INCREASE THE NUMBER OF YANZI'S FIEF-CITIES. YANZI REJECTED THIS AND DID NOT ACCEPT THE OFFER. [1]

Duke Jing said to Yanzi: "In the past, our former ruler Duke Huan gave Guan Zhong Hu and Gu, seventeen districts in total. He wrote it on silk, reconfirmed this on bamboo slips, and informed the regional princes that these districts were granted as fief-cities to Guan Zhong's descendants. I did not have sufficient opportunity to express my unworthy honor to your father, so now I'd like to grant you fief-cities, master, to be handed down to your descendants."

Yanzi declined, saying: "In the past, the sage kings evaluated merits and rewarded the worthy. The worthy received the rewards and the unworthy missed out on them. They took charge of their virtue and perfected their rites without negligence and idleness. Now let us say there is a person who serves the ruler and manages to avoid wrongdoing — how could his descendants deserve to be granted fief-cities? If the High Officers in Qi must be granted fief-cities, then with what will the ruler of Qi offer sacrifice to the altars of soil and grain? And with what would he exchange tributes of money and silks with the regional princes? I request to decline the offer."

Thereupon, he did not accept.

---

1　Item 7.24 [194] ↔ Items 1.12 [12]; 6.19 [159].

# 7.25 [195] 景公使梁丘据致千金之裘晏子固辞不受

景公让梁丘据给晏子价值千金的皮衣，晏子坚决推辞不接受

## 【原文】

景公赐晏子狐（之白）〔白之〕裘，玄豹之茈，其赍千金，使梁丘据致之。晏子辞而不受，三反。公曰："寡人有此二，将欲服之，今夫子不受，寡人不敢服。与其闭藏之，岂如弊之身乎？"晏子曰："君就赐，使婴修百官之政，君服之上，而使婴服之于下，不可以为教。"固辞而不受。

## 【今译】

景公赐给晏子一件白狐皮裘，并用黑色的豹皮装饰，其价值高达千金，让梁丘据送给他。晏子推辞不接受，送了多次都被拒绝。景公说："我有两件这样的皮裘，本来想要穿它，现在先生您不接受，我也不敢穿。与其把它收藏起来，还不如穿在身上呢。"晏子说："国君您赏赐我，并让我主持百官的政事，地位在上的国君穿着他，地位在下的臣子也穿着它，这样就不能教化百官。"坚决推辞而不接受。

## 7.25 [195] DUKE JING SENT LIANGQIU JU TO DELIVER YANZI A PRESENT OF FUR WORTH A THOUSAND PIECES OF GOLD. YANZI FIRMLY DECLINED THE OFFER.

Duke Jing granted Yanzi a gift of a robe of white fox fur. Its lapel was made of a fur of a dark panther, valued at one thousand pieces of gold. He sent Liangqiu Ju to deliver it. Yanzi declined and did not accept the present, sending it back three separate times.

The Duke said, "I have two identical robes like this, and I would like you to wear it. But now Master, if you do not accept it, I would not dare wear it either. Is it not preferable to wear it on one's body than to store it in a closed place?"

Yanzi said: "You, my Lord, have already reworded and appointed me to perfect the governing of the various offices. If you wear it in your high position and compel me to wear it in my low position, this cannot serve as proper moral instructions." He then rejected the gift firmly and did not accept it.

641

## 7.26 [196] 晏子衣鹿裘以朝景公嗟其贫晏子称有饰

晏子穿着鹿裘来朝见景公，景公感叹他贫穷，晏子说已经有装饰了

**【原文】**

晏子相景公，布衣鹿裘以朝。公曰："夫子之家，若此其贫也，是奚衣之恶也！寡人不知，是寡人之罪也。"晏子对曰："婴闻之，盖顾人而后衣食者，不以贪昧为非；盖顾人而后行者，不以邪僻为累。婴不肖，婴之族又不如婴也，待婴以祀其先人者五百家，婴又得布衣鹿裘而朝，于婴不有饰乎！"再拜而辞。

**【今译】**

晏子担任景公的相国，穿着粗布衣服鹿裘来参加朝会。景公说："先生的家这么贫穷，要穿这么简陋的衣服！我不知道，这是我的过错。"晏子回答说："我听说，先看别人然后再选择自己衣服食物的人，不会认为贪昧是错误的；先看别人再决定自己行为的人，不会认为邪僻是有害的。我没有才能，我的族人还比不上我，依靠我来祭祀祖先的人还有五百家之多，我能得到粗布衣服鹿裘来参加朝会，对我来说不就算有装饰了吗！"拜了又拜而辞谢。

## 7.26 [196] YANZI WORE DEER FUR TO A COURT AUDIENCE AND DUKE JING SIGHED FOR HIS POVERTY. YANZI SAID THAT HE HAD DECORATED CLOTHING.

Yanzi served Duke Jing as prime minister. He went to a court audience wearing cotton clothing and deer fur. The Duke said: "Your family, Master, is so poor — this is why you wear such shoddy clothes! I did not realize it. This is my fault."

Yanzi answered: "I've heard that, as a rule, those who observe other people closely first, and only then proceed to select clothing and food for themselves, will not make greediness and blind covetousness their fault; and that, as a rule, those who observe closely other people first, and then proceed in shaping their own conduct, will not make evilness and perversity turn into their fetters. I am unworthy, and still, there is none in my clan who can have a comparable position to me. No less than five hundred families depend on me for their sacrifices to the ancestors. So if I again can come with cotton clothing and deer fur for my court audience, does this mean that I have no decorated clothing?"

He bowed twice and took his leave.

# 7.27 [197] 仲尼称晏子行补三君而不有果君子也

仲尼称晏子用自己的德行补足三位国君的缺点，却不以此为功劳，果真是君子

## 【原文】

仲尼曰："灵公污，晏子事之以整齐；庄公壮，晏子事之以宣武；景公奢，晏子事之以恭俭：君子也！相三君而善不通下，晏子、细人也。"晏子闻之，见仲尼曰："婴闻君子有讥于婴，是以来见。如婴者，岂能以道食人者哉！婴（婴）〔之〕宗族待婴而（祝）〔祀〕其先人者数百家，与齐国之闲士待婴而举火者数百家，臣为此仕者也。如臣者，岂能以道食人者哉！"晏子出，仲尼送之以宾客之礼，再拜其辱。反，命门弟子曰："救民之姓而不夸，行补三君而不有，晏子果君子也。"

## 【今译】

仲尼说："灵公行为放纵，晏子就以条理规范的行为辅佐他；庄公武勇豪壮，晏子就用止戈息武的方式来辅佐他；景公奢侈，晏子就以温恭俭朴的方式来辅佐他；这是君子啊！辅佐三位国君而好的教令不能下达到百姓，晏子是见识浅薄的人。"晏子听说了，前往见仲尼说："我听说君子有责备我的话语，所以来相见。像我这样的人，怎么能以德行来养活他人呢！我的家族依靠我来祭祀祖先的人有数百家，齐国没有官职的士人依靠我来养活的也有数百家，我是为了他们才出仕的。像我这样的人，能凭借自己的德行养活他们吗！"晏子离开，仲尼用宾客的礼节来送别他，两次拜谢他的到访。回来后，对门下的弟子说："救活了百姓的生命而不夸耀，德行补足三位国君的缺点却不以为功，晏子果真是君子啊。"

## 7.27 [197] CONFUCIUS PRAISED YANZI FOR BENEFITING THREE RULERS AND CLAIMING NO NAME FOR HIMSELF. HE CONCLUDED THAT YANZI WAS INDEED A MAN OF NOBLE CHARACTER.[1]

Confucius said: "Duke Ling was corrupt and Yanzi served him with proper order; Duke Zhuang was a man of physical strength and Yanzi served him with moral strength.[2] Duke Jing was extravagant and Yanzi served him with frugality. Yanzi was a man of noble character. However, he was a prime minister to three and his goodness did not reach the lower classes. Thus, Yanzi was a person of limited worth."

Yanzi heard this, and came for an audience with Confucius and said to him: "I've heard that a man of noble character impugned me that is why I came to see you. How can someone like myself provide food for people through the Way alone? There are several hundred families in my clan that depend on me for their offering of sacrifices to the ancestors; they join the several hundred unemployed officers who rely on me for their cooked meals. This is why I took office. How can someone like myself provide food for people through the Way alone?"

When Yanzi left, Confucius sent him off in accordance with the rites of guests and bowed twice in acknowledgment of the undeserved honor bestowed upon him by Yanzi's visit. Then he returned and said to his disciples: "He saved the lives[3] of the people and he was not boastful; with his conduct he benefited three rulers and claimed no name for himself; Yanzi, indeed, was a man of noble character."

645

---

1 Item 7.27 [197] ↔ *Kongcongzi*, 6.1/62/2.

2 The parallel line in the *Kongcongzi* reads: "Duke Zhuang was timid (怯) and Yanzi served him with courage (勇)."

3 姓 → 生 (*JS*, 490/7).

大中华文库

# 第八卷　不合经术者

## 8.1 [198] 仲尼见景公景公欲封之晏子以为不可

仲尼朝见景公，景公想要分封他，晏子认为不可以

### 【原文】

仲尼之齐，见景公，景公说之，欲封之以尔稽，以告晏子。晏子对曰："不可。彼浩裾自顺，不可以教下；好乐绥于民，不可使亲治；立命而建事，不可守职；厚葬破民贫国，久丧（道）〔遁〕哀费日，不可使子民；行之难者在内，而传者无其外，故异于服，勉于容，不可以道众而驯百姓。自大贤之灭，周室之卑也，威仪加多，而民行滋薄；声乐繁充，而世德滋衰。今孔丘盛声乐以侈世，饰弦歌鼓舞以聚徒，繁登降之礼

### 【今译】

仲尼来到齐国，朝见景公，景公非常高兴，想要将尔稽之地分封给他，将这个想法告诉了晏子。晏子回答说："不可以。他傲慢自大，不能教导百姓；对待百姓过于宽缓，不能让他亲自治理百姓；修身养性而厌倦于事，不能恪于职守；主张厚葬破伤民财导致国家贫困，丧礼长久哀悼不止耗费时间，不能让他差遣百姓；德行修养的困难在于内心，而儒者只重视外表的修饰，所以服装奇特，重视举止容貌，这是不能引导和驯化百姓的。自从大贤消失，周王室地位下降，威仪的形制增多，但百姓的品行变得浅薄；声乐繁杂充斥，而世间的德行日益衰微。现在孔丘使声乐盛大导致世风奢侈，以舞蹈礼乐来教育学生，用繁琐的礼仪来确定身份尊卑，细致的礼节来令百姓效仿，他们虽然

# Chapter Eight    Incompatible with Classical Learning

## 8.1 [198] CONFUCIUS MET DUKE JING FOR AN AUDIENCE. DUKE JING WANTED TO CONFER UPON HIM A FIEF BUT YANZI THOUGHT THIS WOULD NOT BE PROPER.[1]

Confucius went to Qi and had an audience with Duke Jing. Duke Jing was delighted with him and wanted to confer upon him a fief in Erji.

Duke Jing reported this to Yanzi, and Yanzi replied: "This would not be proper. This man is arrogant and acts in a complacent manner — he should not be allowed to instruct inferiors. He is fond of music and neglectful[2] of the people — he should not be allowed personal access to government. He relies on fatalism and neglects[3] his duties — he should not be allowed to hold a responsible office. He performs lavish burials, crushes the people, impoverishes the state, prolongs mourning, extends grief and squanders days — he should not be allowed to care for the people. The difficult point of proper conduct is found in the inner part of man, but the Confucians[4] are entranced[5] by the exteriors. Therefore, they make their clothing outlandish and exert themselves over external appearances. They should not be allowed to lead the multitude and guide the people. Ever since the Great Worthies perished and the Zhou household deteriorated, the number of rules of decorum have multiplied and yet proper conduct among people became extremely scarce. Sounds and music filled the air, but virtue greatly declined

647

---

1   Item 8.1 [198] ↔ *Mozi*, 9.6/66/4; *Kongcongzi*, 6.1/60/14.

2   绥 → 缓 (*YZCQ-ICS*, 70/ n. 1).

3   建 → 怠 (*YZCQ-ICS*, 70/ n. 2).

4   传 → 儒 (*YZCQ-ICS*, 70/ n. 5).

5   无 → 妖 (*JS*, 493/12).

**【原文】**

〔以示仪〕，〔务〕趋翔之节以观众，传学不可以仪世，劳思不可〔以〕补民，兼寿不能殚其教，当年不能究其礼，积财不能（瞻）〔赡〕其乐，繁饰邪术以营世君，盛为声乐以淫愚其民。〔其道〕也，不可以示〔世〕；其教也，不可以导民。今欲封之，以移齐国之俗，非所以导众存民也。"
公曰："善。"于是厚其礼而留其〔封〕，敬见不问其道，仲尼乃行。

**【今译】**

博学但不能作为效仿的目标，思虑劳苦却无益于人民，寿命增倍也无法竭尽他的教化，人到壮年也无法学尽他的礼仪，积蓄财富不足以供给礼乐的花费，修饰复杂的邪术来蛊惑国君，用盛大的声乐来使民众愚昧。他治理国家的方式，不可以作为示范；他的教化，不可以引导人民。现在想要分封他，来改变齐国的风俗，这是不能引导和保存民众的方式啊！"景公说："好。"于是增加送给他的礼物而留下了封地，尊敬地接见他而不询问他的治国之道，仲尼于是离开了。

for generations. Now, Confucius fosters sounds and music and thereby leads the world into excesses.[1] He embellishes the music of stringed instruments, dances to the sound of beating drums, and thereby attracts followers. He multiplies the rites of ascending and descending stairs, thereby flaunting his ceremonies. He emphasizes the rules of taking small, speedy steps and flapping sleeves around the court, thereby impressing the multitudes. His broad learning cannot provide a model for the present generation and his burdensome thought cannot provide aid to the people's need. Two combined lifetimes cannot exhaust his teachings, a person in the prime of life cannot delve into his ritual, and an abundance of wealth cannot subsidize his musical performances. With his elaborate ornamentations and perverse techniques, he deludes the rulers of the age. He fosters the production of sounds and music to confound the people. His Way cannot be presented to the present generation and his teachings cannot guide the people. Now you want to confer upon him a fief and thereby transform the customs of Qi. This is not the way to lead the multitudes and preserve the people."

The Duke said: "Well argued." Thereupon, he treated Confucius with lavish rites but withheld the fief; he respectfully met him but did not ask him about his Way; and then Confucius left.

---

1   The parallel line in *Mozi* has 蛊世 ("beguile the world") instead of 侈世 ("gets the world into excesses").

## 8.2 [199] 景公上路寝闻哭声问梁丘据晏子对

景公登上正殿，听到哭声，询问梁丘据，晏子回答

### 【原文】

景公上路寝，闻哭声。曰："吾若闻哭声，何为者也？"梁丘据对曰："鲁孔丘之徒鞠语者也。明于礼乐，审于服丧，其母死，葬埋甚厚，服丧三年，哭泣甚疾。"公曰："岂不可哉！"而色说之。晏子曰："古者圣人，非不知能繁登降之礼，制规矩之节，行表缀之数以教民，以为烦人留日，故制礼不羡于便事；非不知能扬干戚钟鼓竽瑟以劝众也，以为费财留工，故制乐不羡于和民；非不知能累世殚国以奉死，哭泣处

### 【今译】

景公登上王宫的正殿，听到哭泣的声音。说："我好像听到了哭泣的声音，这是谁呢？"梁丘据回答说："这是鲁国孔丘的学生鞠语。他明晓礼乐，熟知丧礼的规制，他的母亲去世了，丧葬的物品非常丰厚，服丧礼三年，哭泣得非常悲痛。"景公说："这是可以的。"而露出赞许的神色。晏子说："以前的圣人，并非不知道能够让区分尊卑的礼节繁复，制定合理的规矩，推行典范的要求来教化民众，但认为繁复的礼节会扰乱人民耗费时间，所以制定礼仪不超过便于行事的范围；并非不知道能够通过礼乐来劝导民众，是认为这样会消耗财力和人力，所以制定礼乐不超出和睦百姓的标准；并非不知道能够数代竭尽国力来祭祀

## 8.2 [199] DUKE JING ASCENDED THE TERRACE OVER THE ROAD BEDCHAMBER AND HEARD THE SOUND OF WEEPING. HE ASKED LIANGQIU JU ABOUT IT AND YANZI REPLIED.[1]

Duke Jing ascended the terrace over the Road Bedchamber and heard the sound of weeping. He said: "It seems I hear a sound of weeping — who is doing this?"

Lianqiu Ju replied: "It is Ju Yu, a follower of Confucius of Lu. He is well versed in rites and music and is careful about observing the mourning practices. When his mother died, the burial was extremely lavish. For three years, this man has been wearing mourning clothes and weeping in severe distress."

The Duke said: "How could this not be proper?" And he seemed pleased with this.

Yanzi said, "In ancient times, it was not that the sages did not know how to instruct the people by means of multiplying the rites of ascending and descending stairs, enforcing strict regulations, and employing surveying techniques. However, they considered all these to be an annoyance to the people and a waste of time. Therefore, the rites that they regulated did not exceed practical matters. It was not that they did not know how to exhort the multitudes by means of flaunting shields and hatchets, bells and drums, pipes and string instruments. However, they considered all these to be frittering away wealth and wasting labor. Therefore, the music that they regulated did not exceed what instilled harmony in the people. It was not that they did not know how to serve the dead by means of exhausting the present generation, depleting the resources of the state, wailing, and living in grief for a prolonged period. However, they refrained from these practices

651

---

1    Item 8.2 [199] ↔ *Kongcongzi*, 6.1/62/12.

**【原文】**

哀以持久也，而不为者，知其无补死者而深害生者，故不以导民。今品人饰礼烦事，羡乐淫民，崇死以害生，三者，圣王之所禁也。贤人不用，德毁俗流，故三邪得行于世。是非贤不肖杂，上妄说邪，故好恶不足以导众。此三者，路世之政，单事之教也。公曷为不察，声受而色说之？"

**【今译】**

死去的人，哭泣悲伤很长时间，之所以不这么做，是知道这对于死去的人没有什么益处而对活着的人有很深的损害，所以不用它来教导人民。现在一些人制定繁复的礼节，崇尚礼乐来教化人民，尊崇死者来伤害生者，这三种做法，是圣明的君王所禁止的。贤能的人得不到任用，德行被破坏，粗鄙的风气盛行，所以这三种不正的做法能够在世上流行。对和错，贤能与无能混杂，国君胡乱喜好邪说，所以他的喜好不足以引导百姓。这三种做法，是败坏政治，损害国事的做法。国君您为什么不认真考虑，听到哭泣的声音还露出赞许的神色呢？"

because they realized they do not give any aid to the dead and are very harmful to the living. Therefore, they did not lead the people in this manner. Today, many ordinary men[1] embellish the rites, make practical undertakings annoying, cherish music and confuse the people. They exalt the dead and thereby harm the living. These three practices are what the sage-kings banned. The worthy are not employed, virtue is destroyed, and vulgar practices spread far and wide. Therefore, the three perversions are gaining currency in our age. Right and wrong, worthiness and unworthiness blend together; superiors become ridiculous and enjoy depravity. And so they are fond of evil and are not worthy of the task of leading the multitudes. These three things mark the government of a declining age and the teachings of tainted[2] affairs. How can you, my Duke, not examine all this carefully and listen to these weeping sounds with evident pleasure?"

653

---

1  Following *Hanyu Da Zidian*, which has 众人; 常人 for 品人.

2  单 → 瘅 (*JS*, 499/11).

## 8.3 [200] 仲尼见景公景公曰先生奚不见寡人宰乎

仲尼朝见景公，景公说先生没有拜见我的宰相吗

**【原文】**

仲尼游齐，见景公。景公曰："先生奚不见寡人宰乎？"仲尼对曰："臣闻晏子事三君而得顺焉，是有三心，所以不见也。"仲尼出，景公以其言告晏子，晏子对曰："不然！〔非〕婴为三心，三君为一心故，三君皆欲其国之安，是以婴得顺也。婴闻之，是而非之，非而是之，犹非也。孔丘必据处此一心矣。"

**【今译】**

仲尼到齐国游学，朝见景公。景公说："先生为何没有拜见我的宰相呢？"仲尼回答说："我听说晏子辅佐三位国君而都顺从他，是有三心，所以我不去拜见他。"仲尼离开后，景公将他的话告诉了晏子，晏子回答说："不对！并不是我有三心，而是三位国君是一心的原因，三位国君都想要让他的国家安定，所以能够顺从我。我听说，把对的说成错的，把错的说成对的，这是不对的。孔丘一定占据了其中的一个。"

## 8.3 [200] CONFUCIUS HAD AN AUDIENCE WITH DUKE JING. THE DUKE SAID: "SIR, WHY DID YOU NOT MEET MY PRIME MINISTER?"[1]

Confucius traveled to Qi and had an audience with Duke Jing. The Duke said: "Sir, why did you not meet with my Prime Minister?"

Confucius replied: "I have heard that Yanzi served three rulers and complied with each one of them. This suggests that he is of three minds and this is why I did not see him."

Confucius left and Duke Jing informed Yanzi about these words.

Yanzi replied: "This is not so! It is not that I am of three minds — I served these rulers because they were of a single mind. The three rulers all wished for their states to be safe — that is why I was able to comply with each one of them. I have heard that when right is considered wrong or when wrong is considered right — it is the same as slander.[2] Confucius could not have escaped one of these two alternatives."[3]

655

---

1  Item 8.3 [200] ↔ Item 8.4 [201]; Item 7.19 [189]; Item 4.29 [109]; *Kongcongzi*, 6.1/62/3.

2  非 → 诽谤 (*JS*, 500/4).

3  孔丘必据处此一心矣 → 孔丘必处此一矣 (*JS*, 500/5). Cf. *Mencius*, 4.3/20/15-16.

## 8.4 [201] 仲尼之齐见景公而不见晏子子贡致问

仲尼来到齐国朝见景公却不见晏子，子贡询问他

### 【原文】

仲尼之齐，见景公而不见晏子。子贡曰："见君不见其从政者，可乎？"仲尼曰："吾闻晏子事三君而顺焉，吾疑其为人。"晏子闻之，曰："婴则齐之世民也，不维其行，不识其过，不能自立也。婴闻之，有幸见爱，无幸见恶，诽谤为类，声响相应，见行而从之者也。婴闻之，以一心事三君者，所以顺焉；以三心事一君者，不顺焉。今未见婴之行，

### 【今译】

仲尼来到齐国，朝见景公而不见晏子。子贡说："朝见国君而不见辅佐他治理国家的人，可以这样吗？"仲尼说："我听说晏子辅佐三位国君而都顺从他，我怀疑他的为人。"晏子听说后，说："我世代是齐国的国民，不保持自己的德行，不知道自己的缺点，就不能自立于齐国。我听说，得到宠幸就会被喜爱，不得幸就会被厌恶，恶意责备别人都是一起的，像声音相互呼应，见到别人这么做就跟着做。我听说，以一心来辅佐三位国君，所以都顺从他；以三心来辅佐一位国君，不会顺从他的。现在没有见到我的行径，就否定国君对我的顺从。我听说，君子独处时面对自己的影子不会惭愧，独自睡觉时不会愧对于自己的灵魂。孔子被人驱逐，自己不认为是耻辱；在陈蔡之间穷困潦倒，

## 8.4 [201] CONFUCIUS WENT TO QI AND HAD AN AUDI-ENCE WITH DUKE JING BUT DID NOT MEET YANZI. ZIGONG POSED A QUESTION.[1]

Confucius went to Qi and met with Duke Jing but he did not meet with Yanzi. Zigong asked, "Is it appropriate to see the ruler but not see those who carry out the affairs of state?"

Confucius replied: "I have heard that Yanzi served three rulers and complied with each one of them. I am suspicious as to what sort of man he is."

Yanzi heard this and said: "Concerning myself, I am a descendant of the people of Qi. Had I not been determined in my actions and not been aware of my errors, I would not have been able to take my place in the world. I have heard that the fortunate are favored and the unfortunate are hated. Slander and praise constitute a class of reverberating echoes to a given sound. When encountering a particular practice, they resonate in response to it. I have heard that one who serves three rulers with a single mind thereby complies with each one of them; however, one who serves one ruler with three minds will not comply with him. Now, Confucius had not yet encountered my behavior and disapproved of me for complying with each one of them. I have heard that standing alone, a man of noble character is not ashamed of his shadow, and sleeping alone he is not ashamed of his soul. Now, when there were people who attempted to make a tree fall on Confucius[2] and when they erased his footprints from the ground,[3] he did

657

---

1   Item 8.4 [201] ↔ Item 8.3 [200]; Item 7.19 [189]; Item 4.29 [109]; *Kongcongzi*, 6.1/62/3.

2   This sentence refers to an attempt on Confucius' life made by Huan Tui 桓魋, the war minister of Song 宋, while Confucius was practicing the rites with his disciples. See *Shiji*, 1921; *Analects*, 7.23/16/21.

3   See *Zhuangzi*, 29/88/1.

## 【原文】

而非其顺也。婴闻之，君子独立不惭于影，独寝不惭于魂。孔子拔树削迹，不自以为辱；穷陈蔡，不自以为约；非人不得其故，是犹泽人之非斤斧，山人之非网罟也。出之其口，不知其困也，始吾望（传）〔儒〕而贵之，今吾望（传）〔儒〕而疑之。"仲尼闻之，曰："语有之：言发于尔，不可止于远也；行存于身，不可掩于众也。吾窃议晏子而不中夫人之过，吾罪几矣！丘闻君子过人以为友，不及人以为师。今丘失言于夫子，〔夫子〕讥之，是吾师也。"因宰我而谢焉，然仲尼见之。

## 【今译】

自己不认为应该节俭；指责别人却不知道事情的原委，这就好像住在水边的人指责斧头，住在山上的人责备网罟一样。轻率地说出这些话，却不知道自己的无知。我一开始见到儒者很尊重他们，现在我看到儒者就会质疑他们。"孔子听说了晏子的话，说："古语说：自己说出的话，不能阻止它传到远处；自己做过的事，不能掩盖不让别人知道。我私下议论晏子却没有说中他的过错，我的过错太大了！我听说君子超过别人就将他作为朋友，赶不上他就将他作为老师。现在我失言于先生，晏子指责我，他是我的老师。"通过宰我向晏子谢罪，然后仲尼拜见了晏子。

not regard this as a personal insult; and when he was destitute in Chen and Cai,[1] he did not regard this as constraining. Criticizing someone without having the relevant facts is similar to a marsh-man criticizing axes and hatchets or a mountain-man criticizing fish nets. When words come out of their mouths, they don't comprehend the others' difficulties. At first, I looked up to the Confucians and respected them but now I look at them skeptically."

Confucius heard this and responded: "There is a proverb that says: 'Words come forth from what is nearby but they cannot be stopped from reaching afar. Actions exist within oneself, but they cannot be hidden from the multitude.' I offered my personal comments about Yanzi but was not precise in weighing his flaws and have almost committed a crime. I have heard that when a man of noble character excels another he befriends the other, but when the other exceeds him, he takes the other as a teacher. Now I spoke improperly about the Master and he reproached this. He is my teacher."

Then, through the good offices of Zaiwo,[2] Confucius apologized to Yanzi and thus met with him.

---

1   For the traumatic experience of the harsh circumstances that Confucius and his disciples had to endure in Chen and Cai see *Analects*, 11/2/26/14; 15/2/42/1; *Shiji*, 1930. See also John Makeham, "Between Chen and Cai: *Zhuangzi* and the *Analects*." In Roger T. Ames, ed. *Wandering at Ease in the* Zhuangzi. SUNY, Albany (1998) 75-100.

2   Zaiwo 宰我, one of Confucius' prominent disciples. For all the disciples and other figures who surrounded Confucius throughout his lifetime, see Bruce E. Brooks and Taeko A. Brooks, *The Original Analects: Sayings of Confucius and His Successors*. Translations from the Asian Classics. New York: Columbia University Press (1998): 272-284.

## 8.5 [202] 景公出田顾问晏子若人之众有孔子乎

景公外出打猎，回头问晏子在众人中能发现孔子吗

**【原文】**

景公出田，寒，故以为浑，犹顾而问晏子曰："若人之众，则有孔子焉乎？"晏子对曰："有孔子焉则无有，若舜焉则婴不识。"公曰："孔子之不逮舜为闲矣，曷为'有孔子焉则无有，若舜焉则婴不识'？"晏子对曰："是乃孔子之所以不逮舜。孔子行一节者也，处民之中，其过之识，况乎处君〔子〕之中乎！舜者（民处）〔处民〕之中，则自齐乎士；处君子之中，则齐乎君子；上与圣人，则固圣人之材也。此乃孔子之所以不逮舜也。"

**【今译】**

景公外出打猎，天气寒冷，所以停下来取暖，还回头问晏子说："如果在人群之中，能分辨出来有没有孔子吗？"晏子回答说："如果人群中有孔子那么我能知道有没有，如果是舜那么我分辨不出来。"景公说："孔子和舜相差得太多了，什么叫作'如果人群中有孔子那么我能知道有没有，如果是舜那么分辨不出来'呢？"晏子回答说："这就是孔子比不上舜的地方了。孔子的行为举止都有一定的规范，处在众人之中，一走动就能分辨出他，更何况处在君子之中呢！而舜处在众人之中，那么行为举止就和众人一样；处在君子之中，就和君子一样；上与圣人一样，他本来就具有圣人的才能。这是孔子比不上舜的地方。"

## 8.5 [202] DUKE JING WENT OUT FOR A HUNT. HE LOOKED BACK AND ASKED YANZI IF A CONFUCIUS MIGHT EXIST IN SUCH A CROWD OF PEOPLE.

Duke Jing went out for a hunt. It was cold, and he had a fire made for warmth, looked back at Yanzi and asked: "Might there be a Confucius among such a crowd of people?"

Yanzi replied: "There is not a Confucius among them; however, if a Shun might be among them, that I do not know."

The Duke said, "Confucius is greatly inferior to Shun, so why do you say: 'There is not a Confucius among them; however, if a Shun might be among them, that I do not know?'"

Yanzi replied: "That is the exact reason why Confucius is inferior to Shun. Confucius is one who acts upon a single discipline. When he dwells among the common people, his errors are recognized — how much more so when he dwells among men of noble character? However, when Shun dwelled among the people, he rendered himself equal to the people;[1] and when he dwelled among men of noble character, he rendered himself equal to them. When he dwelled above, with the sages, then he most certainly was sage-material. This, then, is the reason that Confucius is inferior to Shun."

---

1   士 → 民 (*JS*, 503/5).

## 8.6 [203] 仲尼相鲁景公患之晏子对以勿忧

仲尼担任鲁国的相国，景公非常担忧，晏子回答说不用担忧

**【原文】**

仲尼相鲁，景公患之，谓晏子曰："邻国有圣人，敌国之忧也。今孔子相鲁若何？"晏子对曰："君其勿忧。彼鲁君、弱主也，孔子、圣相也。君不如阴重孔子，设以相齐，孔子强谏而不听，必骄鲁而有齐，君勿纳也。夫绝于鲁，无主于齐，孔子困矣。"居年，孔子去鲁之齐，景公不纳，故困于陈蔡之间。

**【今译】**

仲尼担任鲁国的相国，景公非常担忧，对晏子说："邻国有圣人，这是敌国所担忧的。现在孔子担任鲁国的相国，该怎么办呢？"晏子回答说："国君不需要担忧。鲁国的国君，是权势比较弱的君主，孔子，是贤明的宰相。您不如私下里敬重孔子，许诺他担任齐国的宰相，孔子强力谏诤而鲁国国君不听从，他一定会轻视鲁国而来到齐国，您不要接纳他。已经和鲁国断绝了关系，又不被齐国所任用，孔子就会窘迫了。"过了一年，孔子离开鲁国来到齐国，景公不接纳他，于是就困厄在陈、蔡之间。

## 8.6 [203] WHEN CONFUCIUS WAS PRIME MINISTER IN LU, DUKE JING BECAME WORRIED. YANZI REPLIED THAT THE DUKE SHOULD NOT BE CONCERNED.[1]

When Confucius was prime minister in Lu, Duke Jing became worried and said to Yanzi: "When a neighboring state has a sage, this is a concern for rival states. Now, Confucius is serving as prime minister in Lu, what can be done about it?"

Yanzi replied: "You should not be concerned. This ruler of Lu is a weak sovereign;[2] and Confucius is a sagely prime-minister. Hence, there is nothing better than to work behind the scenes and to strengthen Confucius by promising that you are going to make him the Premier of Qi. Confucius will then do his utmost to remonstrate his ruler, who will not pay heed. Consequently, Confucius will regard Lu with contempt and will come[3] to Qi—but then you, my Lord, should not receive him. At that point, cutting off from Lu and without a supporting sovereign in Qi, Confucius will find himself in a predicament."[4]

After a year, Confucius left Lu and went to Qi, but Duke Jing did not receive him. Therefore, he was placed in a predicament between Chen and Cai.

---

1  Item 8.6 [203] ↔ *Kongcongzi*, 6.1/61/20.

2  The ruler of Lu referred to here is Duke Ding 定公 (r. 509–495 BCE), whom Confucius served as Premier.

3  有 → 适 (*JS*, 504/5).

4  For the details surrounding this event, see, *Shiji,* 1915-1916.

## 8.7 [204] 景公问有臣有兄弟而强足恃乎晏子对不足恃

景公询问有强大的臣子和兄弟能够依靠吗？晏子回答说不能

### 【原文】

景公问晏子曰："有臣而强，足恃乎？"晏子对曰："不足恃。""有兄弟而强，足恃乎？"晏子对曰："不足恃。"公忿然作色曰："吾今有恃乎？"晏子对曰："有臣而强，无甚如汤；有兄弟而强，无甚如桀。汤有弑其君，桀有亡其兄，岂以人为足恃哉，可以无亡也！"

### 【今译】

景公询问晏子说："有强大的臣子，足以依靠吗？"晏子回答说："不足以依靠。""有强大的兄弟，足以依靠吗？"晏子回答说："不足以依靠。"景公生气地变了脸色说："那我还有什么可以依靠的？"晏子回答说："有强大的臣子，也不会超过商汤；有强大的兄弟，也不会超过夏桀。商汤杀死了他的国君，夏桀让他的兄长逃亡，难道以他人作为依靠，可以不灭亡吗？"

## 8.7 [204] DUKE JING ASKED IF ONE CAN RELY ON STRONG MINISTERS AND BROTHERS. YANZI REPLIED THAT THEY CANNOT BE SUFFICIENTLY RELIED UPON.

Duke Jing asked Yanzi, "Can one rely on strong ministers as sufficient?"

Yanzi replied: "They cannot be sufficiently relied upon."

"What about having strong brothers?"

Yanzi replied: "They cannot be sufficiently relied upon."

The Duke flushed with anger and said: "Do I have, at present, anyone to rely upon?"

Yanzi answered: "Among strong ministers, none was ever greater than Tang;[1] among strong brothers, none was ever greater than Jie.[2] However, Tang assassinated his ruler,[3] and Jie eliminated his elder brother. Surely it is not because of the existence of people upon whom you can rely that you will be able to escape demise."

665

---

1   Cheng Tang 成汤, the first king of the Shang 商 (Yin 殷) dynasty (17th–11th cent. BCE).

2   King Jie, the last, tyrannical ruler of the Xia dynasty (17th–15th century BCE). For a vivid description of King Jie's great strength, see, *Huainanzi*, 70/4.

3   This statement conflicts with traditional Chinese historiography, according to which Tang did not kill King Jie but rather forced him into exile.

大中华文库

## 8.8 [205] 景公游牛山少乐请晏子一愿

景公游览牛山，没有什么可娱乐的，请晏子说出一个心愿

### 【原文】

景公游于牛山，少乐，公曰："请晏子一愿。"晏子对曰："不，婴何愿？"公曰："晏子一愿。"对曰："臣愿有君而见畏，有妻而见归，有子而可遗。"公曰："善（晏乎）〔乎〕！〔晏〕子之愿；载一愿。"晏子对曰："臣愿有君而明，有妻而材，家不贫，有良邻。有君而明，日顺婴之行；有妻而材，则使婴不忘；家不贫，则不愠朋友所识；有良邻，则日见君子：婴之愿也。"公曰："善乎！晏子之愿也。"晏子对曰："臣愿有君而可辅，有妻而可去，有子而可怒。"公曰："善乎！晏子之愿也。"

### 【今译】

景公游览牛山，没有什么可以娱乐的，景公说："请晏子说一个自己的愿望。"晏子回答说："不，我能有什么愿望呢？"景公说："您的一个心愿。"回答说："我希望有个可敬畏的国君，归来的家中有个妻子，有个儿子可以留给他财产。"景公说："好啊！晏子的心愿；希望您再说一个。"晏子回答说："我希望有一个圣明的国君，有才干的妻子，家中不贫穷，有好的邻居。有圣明的国君，那么就会顺从我的意见；有才干的妻子，能够让我没有遗漏；家中不贫穷，就不会被朋友所怨恨；有好的邻居，就可以每天见到君子：这是我的心愿。"景公说："好啊！晏子的心愿。"晏子回答说："我希望有国君可以辅佐，有妻子可以离开，有儿子可以对他发怒。"景公说："好啊！晏子的心愿。"

## 8.8 [205] DUKE JING EXPERIENCED LITTLE JOY ON HIS PLEASURE EXCURSION TO MOUNT NIU. HE ASKED YANZI TO MAKE A WISH.

Duke Jing experienced little joy on his pleasure excursion to Mount Niu. He said: "I would like to ask you, Yanzi, to make a wish."

Yanzi replied: "No, what could I possibly wish for?"

The Duke said: "Yanzi — make a wish!"

Yanzi replied: "I wish for a ruler who is held in awe, for a wife who is devoted to me, and for a son to whom I can bequeath my legacy."

The Duke said, "Your wishes, Yanzi, are excellent — make another wish."

Yanzi replied: "I wish for a ruler who is enlightened, for a wife who is capable, for a family that is not poor, and for good neighbors. If my ruler is enlightened, I will adapt to his practices every day; if my wife is talented, I will not become reckless; if my family is not poor, I will not be upset about being recognized by my friends; and if my neighbors are good, I will meet men of noble character every day. These are my wishes."

The Duke said, "Yanzi's wishes are excellent."

Yanzi replied: "I wish for a ruler I could guide, for a wife I could leave when necessary, and for a son I could be angry with, when needed."

The Duke said: "Yanzi's wishes are excellent."

667

## 8.9 [206] 景公为大钟晏子与仲尼柏常骞知将毁

景公制作了大钟，晏子和仲尼、柏常骞知道钟会毁坏

### 【原文】

景公为大钟，将悬之。晏子、仲尼、柏常骞三人朝，俱曰："钟将毁。"冲之，果毁。公召三子而者问之。晏子〔对〕曰："钟大，不祀先君而以燕，非礼，是以曰钟将毁。"仲尼曰："钟大而悬下，冲之其气下回而（下）〔上〕薄，是以曰钟将毁。"柏常骞曰："今庚申，雷日也，音莫胜于雷，是以曰钟将毁也。"

### 【今译】

景公制作了大钟，想要把它悬挂起来。晏子、仲尼、柏常骞三个人参加朝会，都说："钟将会毁坏。"撞钟，果然毁坏了。景公召见他们三个人询问。晏子回答说："钟很大，不用来祭祀先祖而用来演奏燕乐，这是不符合礼节的，所以说钟会毁坏。"仲尼说："钟很大而且悬挂的很低，撞击时气流从下面向上冲击，所以说钟将会毁坏。"柏常骞说："今天是庚申，是打雷的日子，钟声不能超过雷声，所以说钟将会毁坏。"

## 8.9 [206] DUKE JING MADE A HUGE BELL. YANZI, CONFUCIUS AND BOCHANG QIAN PREDICTED THAT THE BELL WOULD BE DESTROYED.

Duke Jing made a huge bell and was going to suspend it. Three men — Yanzi, Confucius and Bochang Qian — came to a court audience, and all of them said: "The bell will be destroyed." Then, when the bell was struck, it was indeed broken. The Duke summoned the three men and inquired about this.

Yanzi replied, "It was a huge bell not used for the sacrifices to the ancestral rulers, but for a banquet. This was contrary to the rites; therefore, I said that the bell would be destroyed."

Confucius said: "The bell was huge and was suspended far too low. When it was struck, the air inside pushed downwards, then reverberated upwards. Therefore, I said that the bell would be destroyed."

Bochang Qian said: "Today is *gengshen* day, a day of thunder. There is no sound as loud as thunder. Therefore, I said that the bell would be destroyed."

## 8.10 [207] 田无宇非晏子有老妻晏子对以去老谓之乱

田无宇责怪晏子有年老的妻子，晏子回答说因为年迈而抛弃她被称为乱

### 【原文】

田无宇见晏子独立于闺内，有妇人出于室者，发班白，衣缁布之衣而无里裘。田无宇讥之曰："出于室（为何）〔何为〕者也？"晏子曰："婴之家也。"无宇曰："位为中卿，〔食〕田七十万，何以老（为妻）〔妻为〕？"对曰："婴闻之，去老者，谓之乱；纳少者，谓之淫。且夫见色而忘义，处富贵而失伦，谓之逆道。婴可以有淫乱之行，不顾于伦，逆古之道乎？"

### 【今译】

田无宇看到晏子独自站立在门内，有一位妇人从屋子里出来，头发斑白，穿着粗布衣服而且里面没有皮裘。田无宇讥讽地问："从屋子里出来的是谁？"晏子说："是我的妻子。"田无宇说："您贵为中卿，田赋收入有七十万，为什么要以年迈的女人做妻子？"晏子回答说："我听说，抛弃年迈的妻子，被称为乱；迎娶年轻的妻子，被称为淫。而且看到美色就忘记道义，身处富贵就丢掉伦常，被称为背离道德。我能有淫乱的行径，不顾及伦常，行背离道德的事吗？"

## 8.10 [207] TIAN WUYU CRITICIZED YANZI FOR HAVING AN OLD WIFE. YANZI REPLIED THAT DISCARDING AN OLD WIFE IS CALLED PROMISCUITY.[1]

Tian Wuyu saw Yanzi standing alone in his private quarters while a woman came out of the private chamber. Her hair was grey and she was wearing dark clothes, without a fur lining.

Mocking her, Tian Wuyu said: "Who is this woman who came out from the room?"

Yanzi said, "She is my wife."

Wuyu said, "You occupy an official position of a middle-ranking minister, and your income is generated from seven hundred thousand fields. Why do you take an old woman for your wife?"

Yanzi replied: "I've heard that discarding an old wife is called promiscuity; taking a young woman instead is called licentiousness. Moreover, when a husband forgets righteousness because of a woman's allure, when he dwells in wealth and honor while abandoning proper relations — this is called going against the Way. How could I have promiscuous and licentious practices, have no consideration for proper relationships, and go against the way of ancient times?"

---

1   Item 8.10 [207] ↔ Item 6.24 [164]; *Hanshi waichuan*, 9.26/76/13.

## 8.11 [208] 工女欲入身于晏子晏子辞不受

工女想要进身做晏子的侍妾，晏子推辞不接受

### 【原文】

有工女托于晏子之家焉者，曰："婢妾，（在）〔东〕廓之野之也。愿得入身，比数于下陈焉。"晏子曰："乃今（日）而后自知吾不肖也！古之为政者，士农工〔商〕异居，男女有别而不通，故士无邪行，女无淫事。今仆托国主民，而女欲仆，仆必色见而行无廉也。"遂不见。

### 【今译】

有工女在晏子的家中干活，说："我是国都东门外乡野中的人。希望能够进身于您家，充当地位低下的婢女。"晏子说："今天我才知道自己没有才能啊！古代治理国家的人，士农工商居住在不同的地方，男女有别互不交往，所以士人没有邪僻的行为，女子没有淫乱的事情。现在国君让我治理国家和民众，而女子想要私自进身于我，我一定是喜爱美色而做没有廉耻事情的人了。"于是拒绝相见。

## 8.11 [208] A CRAFTSMAN'S DAUGHTER WANTED TO OFFER HERSELF TO YANZI. YANZI DECLINED HER OFFER.

A craftsman's daughter asked someone to speak on her behalf to Yanzi's family, saying: "I am a commoner from outside the eastern city wall. I would like to offer myself to you to be regarded as a concubine in your lesser quarters."

Yanzi said, "From now on, I will know that I am unworthy. In ancient times, government performance was such that officers, peasants, craftsmen and tradesmen lived in different neighborhoods; men and women were separated, and there was no contact between them. Therefore, the officers had no immoral practices and the women had no debauched behavior. Now, I am entrusted with the affairs of the state and am in charge of the people, and an amorous woman wants to elope to me — I must have been attracted to woman's allure and practiced dishonesty."

Thereupon, he did not meet with her.

673

## 8.12 [209] 景公欲诛羽人晏子以为法不宜杀

景公要诛杀羽人，晏子认为根据法令不应该杀

【原文】

景公盖姣，有羽人视景公僭者。公谓左右曰："问之，何视寡人之僭也？"羽人对曰："言亦死，而不言亦死，窃姣公也。"公曰："合色寡人也？杀之！"晏子不时而入见曰："盖闻君有所怒羽人。"公曰："然。色寡人，故将杀之。"晏子对曰："婴闻拒欲不道，恶爱不祥，虽使色君，于法不宜杀也。"公曰："恶然乎！若使沐浴，寡人将使抱背。"

大中华文库

【今译】

景公长得很漂亮，有羽人违犯礼节地看景公。景公对身边的人说："问问他，为什么违犯礼节看着我？"羽人回答说："我说是死，不说也是死，我因为景公漂亮才偷看他。"景公说："是贪恋我的容貌吗？杀了他！"晏子还没到朝会时间就入宫拜见景公说："我听说您生了羽人的气。"景公说："是的。他贪恋我的容貌，所以要杀了他。"晏子回答说："我听说拒绝他人的想法不合乎道理，厌恶他人的喜爱不吉祥，羽人虽然贪恋您的容貌，但根据法令不应该杀了他。"景公说："厌恶也要这样做啊！我沐浴的时候，会让他来搓背。"

## 8.12 [209] DUKE JING WANTED TO EXECUTE A PLUME GATHERER. YANZI THOUGHT THAT KILLING THE PLUME GATHERER WOULD BE IMPROPER ACCORDING TO THE LAW.

Duke Jing was most probably beauteous. There was a Plume Gatherer who gave Duke Jing an improper glance. The Duke said to his entourage, "Ask him why he gives me an improper glance?"

The Plume Gatherer replied: "If I tell him, I will die, and if I don't, I will also die — I was stealing a glance of the Duke's beauty."

The Duke said: "Why[1] does he attribute to me a woman's allure? Execute him."

Yanzi entered to conduct an impromptu audience with the Duke, saying: "Surely, I have heard that you, my Lord, are angry with the Plume Gatherer for some reason."

The Duke said, "Right. He attributed to me a woman's allure and therefore I am going to execute him."

Yanzi replied: "I've heard that rejecting desires is not in accordance with the Way, and loathing the affection of others is inauspicious. Even if he attributed to you, my Lord, a woman's allure, executing him would be improper according to the law."

The Duke said, "I'm so disgusted by this — but maybe I should tell him to embrace my back when I take a bath."

675

---

1　合 → 盍 (*JS*, 511/3).

## 8.13 [210] 景公谓晏子东海之中有水而赤晏子详对

景公对晏子说东海中有红色的水，晏子详细地回答

### 【原文】

景公谓晏子曰："东海之中，有水而赤，其中有枣，华而不实，何也？"晏子对曰："昔者秦缪公乘龙舟而理天下，以黄布裹烝枣，至东海而捐其布，彼黄布，故水赤；烝枣，故华而不实。"公曰："吾详问，子何为？"对曰："婴闻之，详问者，亦详对之也。"

### 【今译】

景公对晏子说："东海之中，有红色的水，其中有枣树，开花却不结果，为什么呢？"晏子回答说："以前秦缪公乘坐龙舟治理天下，用黄色的布匹包裹蒸熟的枣，到了东海就将布包扔了进去，黄布被冲坏枣漏出来，所以水是红色的；枣是蒸熟的，所以只开花不结果。"景公说："我问您的问题是假的，您为什么要这样回答？"晏子回答说："我听说，问假问题，就应该用假话来回答。"

## 8.13 [210] DUKE JING TOLD YANZI THAT THERE IS RED WATER IN THE EAST SEA. YANZI FABRICATED A REPLY.

Duke Jing told Yanzi: "There is water in the East Sea that is red. Red jujubes bloom there but bear no fruit — why is this so?"

Yanzi replied: "In the past, Duke Mu of Qin sailed in a dragon boat[1] in order to govern the realm. He wrapped up steamed, red jujubes in a yellow cloth. When he arrived at the East Sea he threw the yellow cloth into the water. The yellow cloth decomposed,[2] the water therefore turned red, and since the red jujubes were steamed, they could bloom but could not bear fruit."

The Duke said, "I faked a question, why did you fabricate an answer?"

Yanzi replied: "I've heard that for those who ask fake questions one should also respond with a fake reply."

677

---

1   Add 舟 after 乘龙 (*JS*, 512/4).

2   彼 → 破 (*JS*, 513/7).

## 8.14 [211] 景公问天下有极大极细晏子对

景公询问天下最大和最小的东西，晏子回答

### 【原文】

景公问晏子曰："天下有极大乎？"晏子对曰："有。〔鹏〕足游浮云，背凌苍天，尾偃天闲，跃啄北海，颈尾咳于天地（乎）！然而潦潦〔乎〕不知六翮之所在。"公曰："天下有极细乎？"晏子对曰："有。东海有（蛊）〔虫〕，巢于蚊睫，再乳再飞，而蚊不为惊。臣婴不知其名，而东海渔者命曰焦冥。"

### 【今译】

678

景公询问晏子说："天下有最大的东西吗？"晏子回答说："有。大鹏鸟在浮云之上飞翔，后背靠近苍天，尾巴延伸到天边，跳起就能够到北海，头和尾巴已经充斥在天地之间了！然而还不知道它巨大翅膀延伸到哪里。"景公说："天下有最小的东西吗？"晏子回答说："有。东海中有一种虫，在蚊子的睫毛上筑巢，在其中孵化再飞走，而蚊子却感觉不到。我不知道它叫什么名字，东海打鱼的人称之为焦冥。"

## 8.14 [211] DUKE JING ASKED IF THERE ARE ENORMOUS AND MINUTE THINGS IN THE WORLD. YANZI REPLIED.[1]

Duke Jing asked Yanzi: "Does something of enormous size exist in the world?"

Yanzi answered, "There is such a thing: the feet of the Peng-bird traverse through the floating clouds; its back reaches up to heaven and its tail flutters down to the horizon. It jumps to the North Sea to peck, while from head[2] to tail it clogs heaven and earth. However, since it is so distant, no one knows where the six outer pinions of its wings are."

The Duke said, "Does something of an extremely minute size exist in the world?"

Yanzi answered, "There is such a thing: an insect in the East Sea. It nests on the eyelash of a mosquito. It gives birth and flies around time and again, but the mosquito is not disturbed. I don't know its name. The fishermen in the East Sea call it Jiaoming."

679

---

1 Item 8.14 [211] ↔ Zhuangzi, 1/1/3; *Liezi* 列子, 5/27/6.
2 Following *Hanyu Da Zidian*, which has 首尾 for 颈尾.

## 8.15 [212] 庄公图莒国人扰（绍）〔绐〕以晏子在乃止

庄公谋取莒城，国都中的人惊扰，知道晏子在国都才停止

### 【原文】

庄公阖门而图莒，国人以为有乱也，皆操长兵而立于〔衢〕间。公召睢休相而问曰：“寡人阖门而图莒，国人以为有乱，皆摽长兵而立于衢间，奈何？”休相对曰：“诚无乱而国以为有，则仁人不存。请（今）〔令〕于国，言晏子之在也。”公曰：“诺。”以令于国：“孰谓国有乱者，晏子在焉。”然后皆散兵而归。君子曰：“夫行不可不务也。晏子存而民心安，此〔非〕一日之所为也，所以见于前信于后者。是以晏子立人臣之位，而安万民之心。”

### 【今译】

庄公关上门来谋取莒城，国都中的人民以为将有动乱，都拿着兵器站立在街道之中。庄公召见睢休相询问说：“我关上门来谋取莒城，国都中的人民以为有动乱，都拿着武器站立在街道之中，怎么办？”休相回答说：“本没有动乱而国都中的人民以为有，是因为仁义的人不在这里。请在国都中下令，说晏子在国都中。”庄公说：“好的。”在国都中下令：谁说国都中将有动乱呢？晏子就在国都之中。然后国都中的人民都放下兵器回家了。君子说：“德行不能不努力培养。晏子在，那么人民心中就安定，这不是一天就能达成的，是因为人民以前了解他才会信任他。所以晏子处于人臣的位置上，才能安定万民的心。”

## 8.15 [212] DUKE ZHUANG MADE PLANS TO ATTACK JU. THE PEOPLE OF THE CAPITAL WERE ANXIOUS AND THE DUKE DECEIVED THEM BY STATING THAT YANZI WAS PRESENT IN THE CAPITAL. THEN THEY CALMED DOWN.

Duke Zhuang, behind closed doors, made plans to attack Ju. The people of the capital thought there was a revolt taking place, so they all took up long weapons and positioned themselves on every lane. The Duke summoned Sui Xiuxiang[1] and asked: "Behind closed doors, I made plans to attack Ju; the people of the capital think that a revolt is taking place, and are all brandishing long weapons and positioning themselves along every lane. What should be done about this?"

Xiuxiang answered: "If truly there is no revolt and nevertheless people in the capital think that there is a revolt, it means that there are no longer any humane people in the capital. Please issue an order in the capital stating that Yanzi is still present in the capital."

The Duke said: "Approved." He issued a command stating: "Who claims that a revolt is taking place? Yanzi is still present here." Then, all of the people scattered their weapons and returned to their homes.[2]

The man of noble character said: "Conduct must be practiced with great care. When Yanzi is present, the hearts of people are pacified. Such a thing is not achieved in a single day. That which has been observed in prior circumstances is subsequently believed by the people. This is why Yanzi held the position of minister and pacified the hearts of all the myriad people."

---

1  An unidentified figure.

2  This episode must have taken place when Yanzi had already resigned from office and lived and farmed on the eastern sea-coast. See Item 5.1 [111].

## 8.16 [213] 晏子死景公驰（哭往）〔往哭〕哀毕而去

晏子去世了，景公赶快前往痛哭哀悼，结束后就离开

**【原文】**

景公游于菑，闻晏子死，公乘侈舆服繁驵驱之。而因为迟，下车而趋；知不若车之遬，则又乘。比至于国者，四下而趋，行哭而往，〔至〕，伏尸而号，曰："子大夫日夜责寡人，不遗尺寸，寡人犹且淫泆而不〔收〕，怨罪重积于百姓。（令）〔今〕天降祸于齐〔国〕，不加于寡人，而加于夫子，齐国之社稷危矣，百姓将谁告夫！"

**【今译】**

景公在菑川游玩，听说晏子去世了，景公乘坐着装饰奢华繁盛的马车前往。景公觉得去的太晚，就下车快走；知道走的不如马车速度快，又乘上马车。等到了国都，已经下车四次快跑了，边跑边哭着前往，到了晏子家中，趴在尸体上号哭着说："先生您日夜责备我，细小的过失也不放过，但我仍旧沉溺玩乐而不收敛，怨恨和责备积蓄在人民心中。现在天降灾祸于齐国，没有降到我的身上，却降到先生的身上，齐国的社稷危险了，百姓以后有事将告诉谁呢！"

## 8.16 [213] YANZI DIED. DUKE JING RUSHED TO YANZI'S HOUSE IN TEARS, AND WHEN MOURNING WAS OVER HE LEFT.[1]

While Duke Jing was on a pleasure excursion to Zi he heard that Yanzi had died. He rushed and mounted his carriage[2] which was harnessed to fine horses, and drove back hastily. The Duke thought the chariot was too slow, so he alighted from the chariot and ran on foot, but once he realized that he could not run as fast as the chariot, he returned and mounted the carriage again. By the time he arrived at the capital, he had alighted from the chariot and run four times. He walked towards Yanzi's house weeping, and then he held the corpse and wailed loudly, saying: "My Master, the High Officer, you criticized me day and night, and didn't yield an inch — yet I'm still licentious and unrestrained, and the people are accumulating a heavy load of complaints and accusations. Now heaven sent down disaster upon the state of Qi — not upon me, but upon the Master. The altars of the soil and grain of the state of Qi are in peril. To whom may the people now appeal?"

---

1   Item 8.16 [213] ↔ *Shuoyuan*, 1.39/9/24; *Hanfeizi*, 32/87/29.

2   公乘侈輿 → 公趨乘輿 (*JS*, 517-518/4).

# 8.17 [214] 晏子死景公哭之称莫复陈告吾过

晏子去世了景公哭着说没有人再说我的过错了

## 【原文】

晏子死，景公操玉加于晏子而哭之，涕沾襟。章子谏曰："非礼也。"公曰："安用礼乎？昔者吾与夫子游于公邑之上，一日而三不听寡人，今其孰能然乎！吾失夫子则亡，何礼之有？"免而哭，哀尽而去。

## 【今译】

晏子去世了，景公拿着玉器放在晏子身上而哭，眼泪沾湿了衣服。章子进谏说："这样是不合乎礼节的。"景公说："现在还用什么礼节呢？以前我和先生一起游览公阜，一天之内三次指出我的过错，现在谁还能这样呢？我失去了先生自己也完了，还讲究什么礼节呢？"摘下帽子服丧礼而痛哭，极尽哀痛后才离开。

## 8.17 [214] YANZI DIED. DUKE JING WEPT AND STATED THAT THERE WOULD NEVER AGAIN BE ONE WHO WOULD POINT OUT HIS FAULTS.

When Yanzi died, Duke Jing took a piece of jade and placed it into his mouth, and then wept over him. Tears soaked his jacket.

Zhangzi[1] remonstrated: "This is contrary to the rites."

The Duke said: "How should we apply the rites? In the past when I travelled with the Master in Gongfu,[2] he used to disagree with me thrice a day.[3] Who is there now who can be like this? Since I lost the Master, I am for naught. What is the point of having the rites?" He took off his hat and wept. Then when the mourning was over, he left.

685

---

1    Zhangzi 章子 is Xianzhang 弦章 of Item 1.4 [4].

2    公邑 → 公阜 (*JS*, 520/4).

3    Cf. Item 1.18 [18].

## 8.18a [215] 晏子没左右谀弦章谏景公赐之鱼

晏子去世后，身边的人都奉承景公，弦章进谏景公赐给他鱼

### 【原文】

晏子没十有七年，景公饮诸大夫酒。公射，出质，堂上唱善，若出一口。公作色太息，播弓矢。弦章入，公曰："章！吾失晏子，未尝闻吾不善。"章曰："臣闻君好臣服，君嗜臣食，尺蠖食黄身黄，食苍身苍，君其食谄人言乎。"公曰："善。"赐弦章鱼五十乘。弦章归，鱼车塞涂。章抚其仆曰："曩之唱善者，皆欲此鱼也。"固辞不受。

### 【今译】

晏子去世十七年后，景公设酒宴请诸大夫。景公射箭，超出了箭靶，殿堂上的人一起称赞，好像出自一个人的口中。景公面带怒色叹了口气，扔掉了弓矢。弦章来到王宫，景公说："弦章！我失去了晏子，就没有再听人说过我的过错了。"弦章说："我听说国君喜欢的衣服臣子就会穿，国君喜欢的食物臣子就会吃，尺蠖吃黄色的树叶就会变成黄色，吃青色的树叶就会变成青色，国君您听了谄媚的话了吧。"景公说："好。"赏赐了弦章五十车鱼。弦章回去后，装鱼的车堵塞了道路。弦章拍着他的仆人说："以前阿谀奉承的人，都是想要这些鱼而已。"坚决推辞不接受。

## 8.18a [215] YANZI PASSED AWAY. THE DUKE'S ENTOURAGE FLATTERED THE DUKE. XIANZHANG REMONSTRATED AND DUKE JING GRANTED HIM FISH.[1]

Seventeen years after Yanzi had died, Duke Jing invited all of the High Officers to drink with him. The Duke shot an arrow and missed the target; "Well done!" exclaimed the entire hall as if from one mouth. The Duke, looking displeased, heaved a deep sigh and dropped his bow and arrow.

Xianzhang then entered. The Duke said: "Zhang, ever since I lost Yanzi, I have not heard about my misdeeds."

Xianzhang replied: "I have heard that what you, my Lord, are fond of, your ministers will wear; and what you relish, your ministers will eat.[2] The inchworm turns yellow when it eats yellow things, and turns black when it eats black things. Perhaps the problem is that you eat the words of ingratiating people?"[3]

The Duke said, "Well argued." He granted Xianzhang fifty carts of fish. Zhang returned home and the fish carts caused a roadblock.

687

Zhang touched his driver's hand and said: "The other day, those who shouted to the king 'well done' all wished for such a gift of fish."

Then he resolutely rejected the gift.[4]

---

1  Item 8.18 [215] ↔ *Shuoyuan*, 1.40/9/29.

2  Cf. *Guanzi*, 1.1/2/18.

3  Add 犹有 after 君其 (*JS*, 523/9).

4  The *Taiping yulan* 太平御览, 人事部, 67, quoted in *YZCQ-ICS*, Item 8.18C, 75/18-20, like the parallel in the *Shuoyuan* item, ends this episode with an intensified nostalgic tone that accentuates the moral heritage that Yanzi had left behind after his death. It reads: "Zhang touched his driver's hand and said: 'In the past, Yanzi rejected rewards in order to rectify his ruler; therefore, no faults were concealed. Now, the various ministers flatter in order to gain profit for themselves. If I accept the fish, it would mean contravening the righteousness of Yanzi and following the desires of the flatterers.' He rejected the fish and did not accept them. A man of noble character said: 'Xianzhang's integrity is Yanzi's heritage.'"

# Personal Name Index

The Personal Name Index lists all the private names that are included in the *YZCQ* whether they refer to identified or unidentified figures. The Chinese characters of the name alone indicate the textual reference in the text. Biographical and other details of the identified figures are given in the relevant note of the first appearance of that figure in the text.

Yanzi [Yan Ying], who plays a role in each and every one of the 215 paragraphs that make up the *YZCQ*, and Duke Jing of Qi who plays a role in 164 of them are not included in the Personal Name Index.

Ai Kong 艾孔. 1.17 [17].

Bao Shu 鲍叔. 4.3 [83].

Beiguo Sao 北郭骚. 5.27 [137].

Bing 禀. 1.5 [5].

Bochang Qian 柏常骞 – 伯常骞. 1.18 [18]; 4.30 [110]; 6.4 [144]; 8.9[206].

Bo Ju 柏遽. 1.5 [5].

Boqin 伯禽. 3.3 [53].

Bo Xi 伯戏. 4.17 [97].

Bushang 卜商. 3.6 [56].

Chen Huanzi 陈桓子. 6.22 [162].

Chen Ziyang 陈子阳. 7.21 [191].

Cheng Fu 成甫. 3.6 [56].

Cheng Tang 汤. 1.1 [1]; 1.22 [22]; 7.8 [178]; 8.7 [204].

Confucius – 孔子 – 仲尼 – 鲁孔丘.

    1.20 [20]; 2.5 [30]; 2.21[46]; 3.6 [56]; 3.30 [80]; 4.29 [109]; 5.16 [126];
    5.21 [131]; 5.30 [140]; 6.6 [146]; 7.11 [181]; 7.27 [197]; 8.1[198];
    8.2 [199]; 8.3 [200]; 8.4 [201]; 8.5 [202]; 8.6 [203]; 8.9 [206].

Cui Zhu 崔杼. 3.1 [51]; 3.2 [52]; 4.12 [92]; 5.1 [111]; 5.2 [112]; 5.3 [113].

Gu Yezi 古冶子. 2.24 [49].

Gongsun Jie 公孙接. 2.24 [49].

Guan Zhong 管仲 – 管子 – 管文仲 – 夷吾 – 仲父. 1.12 [12]; 2.15 [40];
　　2.21 [46]; 3.6 [56]; 3.7 [57]; 4.2 [82]; 5.7 [117]; 6.18 [158]; 6.28
　　[168]; 7.24 [194].

Guozi 国子. 6.7 [147].

Han Zixiu 韩子休. 1.8 [8].

He 和. 5.23 [133].

Hui Qian 会谴. 1.12 [12].

Jibo 其伯. 4.17 [97].

Jici 季次. 3.6 [56].

Ju Yu 鞠语. 8.2 [199].

Kai 开. 6.5 [145].

King Fuchai of Wu 夫差. 6.8 [148].

King Jie of Xia 桀. 1.1 [1]; 1.4 [4]; 1.13 [13]; 1.16 [16]; 2.18 [43];
　　7.8 [178]; 8.7 [204].

King Kang of Chu 楚康王. 7.7 [177].

King Ling of Chu 灵公. 2.7 [32]; 2.8 [33]; 7.11 [181].

King Wu of Zhou 武. 1.1 [1]; 2.19 [44]; 7.8 [178].

King of Yue 越王. 7.11 [181].

King Wen 文王. 2.8 [33]; 3.23 [73]; 4.17 [97]; 7.6 [176].

King Zhou of Shang 纣. 1.1 [1]; 1.4 [4]; 1.6 [6]; 1.13 [13]; 1.16 [16];
　　2.18 [43]; 3.23 [73]; 7.8 [178].

Li 厉. 1.6 [6].

Liangqiu Ju 梁丘据. 1.6 [6]; 1.12 [12]; 1.17 [17]; 1.18 [18]; 2.15 [40];
　　2.20 [45]; 2.22 [45]; 3.26 [76]; 4.29 [109]; 5.12 [122]; 6.17 [157];
　　6.25 [165]; 6.27 [167]; 7.1 [171]; 7.5 [175]; 7.7 [177]; 7.25 [195];
　　8.2 [199].

Min Ziqian 闵子骞. 3.6 [56].

Min Ziwu 泯子午. 5.26 [136].

691

大中华文库

Mozi 墨子. 3.5 [55]; 5.5 [115].

Ning Qi 宁戚. 3.6 [56]; 4.2 [82].

Pencheng Kuo 盆成适. 7.11 [181].

Peng Yuhe 逢于何. 2.20 [45].

Qian 骞. 3.6 [56].

Qing Feng 庆氏– 庆封. 3.2 [52]; 5.3 [53]; 6.15 [155].

Qu Jian 屈建. 7.7 [177].

Rang Ju 穰苴. 5.12 [122].

Shu Diao 竖刁. 1.16 [16]; 2.21 [46].

Shun 舜. 1.25 [25]; 8.5 [202].

Shuxiang 叔向. 4.17 [97]; 4.18 [98]; 4.19 [99]; 4.20 [100]; 4.21 [101]; 4.22 [102]; 4.23 [103]; 4.24 [104]; 4.25 [105]; 4.26 [106]; 4.27 [107].

Sui Xiuxiang 睢休相. 8.15 [212].

Tai Ji 大姬. 4.17 [97].

Taijia 太甲. 1.22 [22].

Tian Huanzi 田桓子. 6.12 [152]; 6.13 [153]; 6.14 [154]; 6.20 [160].

Tian Kaijiang 田开疆. 2.24 [49].

Tian Wuyu 田无宇 – 陈桓子. 3.8 [58]; 6.13 [153]; 6.14 [154]; 6.19 [159]; 7.10 [180]; 7.15 [185]; 8.10 [207].

Tu 荼. 1.11 [11].

Tui Chi 推侈. 1.1 [1].

Tuo 佗. 1.12 [12].

Tzuxu 子胥. 7.11 [181].

Wei 微. 1.14 [14].

Wei Jiong 韦冏. 2.8 [33].

Wu Ding 武丁. 1.22 [22].

Wu Lai 恶来. 1.1 [1].

Xi Peng 隰朋. 3.6 [56].

Xian Ning 弦宁. 3.6 [56].

Xian, prince of Di 翟王子羡. 1.9 [9].

Xianzhang 弦章 – 章子. 1.4 [4]; 8.17 [214]; 8.18a [215].

Xiaoji 孝己. 7.11 [181].

Yan Hui 颜回. 3.6 [56].

Yang Sheng 阳生. 1.11 [11].

Yao 尧. 1.25 [25].

Yan Huanzi 晏桓子. 5.30 [140].

Yi Kuan 裔款. 1.14 [14]; 2.15 [40]; 5.11 [121]; 7.7 [177].

Yi Yin 伊尹. 1.22 [22].

Yin 嚚. 7.7 [177].

Yingqiu 营丘. 6.5 [145]; 6.19 [159].

Yingzi 婴子. 1.9 [9]; 2.21 [46].

Yong 雍. 3.6 [56].

You 幽. 1.6 [6].

Yu 虞. 1.6 [6].

Yu 禹. 2.1 [26].

Yu Sui 虞遂. 4.17 [97].

Yuanxian 原宪. 3.6 [56].

Yue Shifu 越石父. 5.24 [134].

Zaiwo 宰我. 8.4 [201].

Zhao Wu 赵武. 7.7 [177].

Zengshen 曾参. 7.11 [181].

Zengzi 曾子. 4.28 [108]; 5.23 [133]; 5.30 [140].

Zhi Bing 直柄. 4.17 [97].

Zhongyou 仲由. 3.6 [56].

Zhu Zou 烛邹. 7.13 [183].

Zigong 子贡. 5.21 [131]; 8.4 [201].

Ziniu 子牛. 1.23 [23].

Ziqi 子期. 7.17 [188].

Zishu Zhaobo 子叔昭伯. 5.18 [128].

Ziwei 子尾. 6.15 [155].

693

Ziyou 子游. 1.23[23].

Ziyu 子羽. 1.23 [23].

Zuyi 祖乙. 1.22 [22].

# Bibliography

Adelson, Betty M. *The Lives of Dwarfs: Their Journey from Public Curiosity toward Social Liberation.* New Brunswick, N.J.: Rutgers University Press, 2005.

Agassi, Joseph and Abraham Meidan. *Beg to Differ: The Logic of Disputes and Argumentation.* Switzerland: Springer, 2016.

Allan, Sarah. "On the Identity of Shang Di 上帝 and the Origin of the Concept of a Celestial Mandate (*tian ming* 天命)." *Early China* 31 (2007): 1-46.

Ames, Roger T. *Confucian Role Ethics: A Vocabulary.* Honolulu: University of Hawaii Press, 2011.

————., et al., eds. *Interpreting Culture through Translation: A Festschrift For D.C. Lau.* Hong Kong: Chinese University Press, 1991.

————., tr. *The Art of Rulership: A Study of Ancient Chinese Political Thought.* Honolulu: University of Hawaii Press, 1983; rpt., Albany: State University of New York Press, 1994.

————., ed. *Wandering at Ease in the* Zhuangzi. Albany: SUNY, 1998.

Anderson, E.N. *The Food of China.* New Haven and London: Yale University Press, 1988.

Ariel, Yoav. *K'ung-ts'ung-tzu: A Study & Translation of Chapters 15-23 with a Reconstruction of the* Hsiao Erh-ya *Dictionary.* Sinica Leidensia 35. New York: E.J. Brill, 1995.

————. *K'ung-ts'ung-tzu: The K'ung Family Master's Anthology.* Princeton Library of Asian Translations. Princeton, 1989.

Baccini, Giulia. "The Forest of Laughs (*Xiaolin*): Mapping the Offspring of Self-aware Literature in Ancient China." PhD Diss., Universita Ca'Foscari, Venezia, 2011.

Ban Gu 班固. *Hanshu* 汉书. Beijing: Zhonghua shuju, 1962.

695

Beckett, Samuel. *Waiting for Godot*. New York: Grove Press, 1982.

Biderman, Shlomo. Crossing Horizons – World, Self, and Language in Indian and Western Thought. New York: Columbia University Press, 2008.

Blakeley, Barry B. "On the Authenticity and Nature of the *Zuo zhuan* Revisited." *Early China* 29 (2004): 217-67.

Boileau, Gilles. "Wu and Shaman." *Bulletin of the School of Oriental and African Studies,* 65.2 (2002): 350-378.

Bokenkamp, Stephen R. *Ancestors and Anxiety: Daoism and the birth of rebirth in China*. Berkeley: University of California Press, 2007.

Brooks, Taeko A. "Evolution of the Ba 霸 'Hegemon' Theory;" *Warring States Papers*, 1 (2010): 220-26.

Brooks, Bruce E. and Taeko A. Brooks, *The Original Analects: Sayings of Confucius and His Successors*. Translations from the Asian Classics. New York: Columbia University Press, 1998.

Brown, Miranda. *The Politics of Mourning in Early China*. Albany: SUNY, 2007.

Cai, Xiqin 蔡希勤. *Yanzi Says*. Wise Men Talking Series, Beijing: Sinolingua Press, 2012.

Chao, Gongwu 晁公武. *Junzhai dushu zhi* 郡斋读书志. http://ctext.org/wiki.pl?if=gb&res=570208 (2006-2017).

Chen, Ruigeng 陈瑞庚. *Yanzi chunqiu kaobian* 晏子春秋考辨. Taibei: Chang an chu ben she, 1980.

Chen, Tao 陈涛. *Yanzi chun qiu yi zhu* 晏子春秋译注. Beijing: Zhong hua shu ju, 2007.

Chen, Yaowen 陈耀文. *Tian-zhong ji* 天中记. http://ctext.org/wiki.pl?if=gb&res=798023 (2006-2016).

Chen, Yi 陈益. *Yanzi chunqiu xinshi biaodian* 晏子春秋新式标点. Xinwen feng chu ben she 1975.

Chen, Zhensun 陈振孙. *Zhizhai shulu jieti* 直斋书录解题. http://ctext.org/

696

wiki.pl?if=gb&res=717386 (2006-2017).

*Chunqiu Guliangzhuan,* 春秋谷梁传. In Lau, D. C., and Chen Fong Ching, eds. A concordance to the *Chunqiu Guliangzhuan* 谷梁传逐字索引. ICS series, Hong Kong, Commercial Press, 1995.

*Chunqiu Zhuozhuan* 春秋左传. In Lau, D. C., and Chen Fong Ching, eds. A concordance to the *Chunqiu Zhuozhuan* 左传逐字索引. ICS series, Hong Kong, Commercial Press, 1995.

Cook, Scott. "The Changing Role of the Minister in the Warring States: Evidence from the *Yanzi chunqiu* 晏子春秋." In Yuri Pines, *et al.*, eds. *Ideology of Power and Power of Ideology in Early China*. 2015, 181-2010.

Csikszentmihalyi, Mark, and Michael Nylan. "Constructing Lineages and Inventing Traditions through Exemplary Figures in Early China." *T'oung Pao* 89.1-3 (2003): 59-99.

*Dao De Jing* 道德经, in Lau, D. C., and Chen Fong Ching, eds. *A Concordance to the Dao De Jing* 道德经逐字索引. ICS series, Hong Kong, Commercial Press, 1996.

Daor, Dan. "The Yin Wenzi and the Renaissance of Philosophy in Wei-Jin China." PhD diss., University of London, 1974.

Defoort, Carine, and Nicolas Standaert, eds. *The* Mozi *as an Evolving Text: Different Voices in Early Chinese Thought*. Studies in the History of Chinese Texts 4. Leiden and Boston: Brill, 2013.

Deng, Junjie 邓骏捷. *Liu xiang xiao shu kao lun* 刘向校书考论. Beijing: Ren min chu ban she, 2012.

Ding, Sixin. "A Study on the Dating of the *Mozi* Dialogues and the Mohist View of Ghosts and Spirits." *Contemporary Chinese Thought,* vol. 42/4, 2011: 51-53.

Durrant, Stephen. *The Cloudy Mirror: Tension and Conflict in the Writings of Sima Qian*. SUNY Series in Chinese Philosophy and Culture. Albany, 1995.

_____. "Yen tzu ch'un ch'iu." In Loewe, Michael, ed. *Early Chinese Texts: A Bibliographical Guide*. Early China Special Monograph Series 2. Berkeley, 1993, 483-489.

_____, Wai-yee Li, and David Schaberg., trs. *Zuo Tradition* / Zuozhuan 左传: *Commentary on the "Spring and Autumn Annals"*. 3 vols. Classics of Chinese Thought. Seattle: University of Washington Press, 2016.

Eber, Irene, ed. *Confucianism: The Dynamics of Tradition*. New York: Macmillan, 1986.

Epstein, I., ed. *Hebrew-English Edition of the Babylonian Talmud*. London: The Soncino Press, 1986.

Eoyang, Eugene, and Lin Yao-fu, eds. *Translating Chinese Literature*. Bloomington and Indianapolis: Indiana University Press, 1995.

Ezra, Ovadia. *Moral Dilemmas in Real Life* — Current Issues in Applied Ethics. Dordrecht, The Netherlands: Springer, 2006.

*Fa yen* 法言. In Lau, D. C., and Chen Fong Ching, eds. *A Concordance to the Fa yen* 法言逐字索引. ICS series, Hong Kong, Commercial Press, 1995.

Fan, Ye 范晔. *Hou Hanshu* 后汉书. Beijing: Zhonghua shuju, 1973.

Fang, Thomé. *Chinese Philosophy: Its Spirit and Its Development*. Taipei: Linking, 1981.

Feldherr, Andrew, and Grant Hardy, eds. *The Oxford History of Historical Writing*. Vol. 1: *Beginnings to AD 600*. Oxford: Oxford University Press, 2011.

*Fengsu tongyi* 风俗通义 in Lau, D. C., and Chen Fong Ching, eds. *A Concordance to the Fengsu tongyi* 风俗通义逐字索引. ICS series, Hong Kong, Commercial Press, 1996.

Forke, Alfred. Geschichte der Alten Chinesischen Philosophie. Hamburg: L. Friederichsen and Co. (1927), Rep., Cram, De Gruyter & CO (1964): 82-92.

_____. "Yen Ying, Staatsmann und Philosoph, und das Yen-tse tsch'untch'iu." *Asia Major* (first series) Introductory Volume (*Hirth Anniversary Volume*) (1923): 101-144.

Fraser, Chris. *The Philosophy of the* Mozi*: The First Consequentialists.* New York: Columbia University, 2016.

Fu, Junlian. "Chunyu Kun jiqi lunbian ti za fu 淳于髡及其论辩体杂赋." *Qilu xuekan* 齐鲁学刊, 2010; 2, 105-108.

Gao Heng 高亨. "Yanzi chunqiu de xiezuo shidai 晏子春秋的写作时代." In *Wen shi shu lin* 文史述林. Beijing: Zhong hua shu ju: Xin hua shu dian beijing fa xing suo fa xing, 1980, 397-398.

Graham, A. C. *Disputers of the Tao.* La Salle: Open Court, 1989.

*Guoyü* 国语. In Lau, D. C., and Chen Fong Ching, eds. *A Concordance to the Guoyü* 国语逐字索引. ICS series, Hong Kong, Commercial Press, 1996.

Guanzi 管子. In Lau, D. C., and Chen Fong Ching, eds. *A Concordance to the Guanzi* 管子逐字索引. ICS series, Hong Kong, Commercial Press, 1996.

*Gulienüzhuan* 古列女传. In Lau, D. C., and Chen Fong Ching, eds. *A Concordance to the Gulienüzhuan* 古列女传逐字索引. ICS series, Hong Kong, Commercial Press, 1993.

*Hanfeizi* 韩非子. In Lau, D. C., and Chen Fong Ching, eds. *A Concordance to the Hanfeizi* 韩非子逐字索引. ICS series, Hong Kong, Commercial Press, 2000.

*Hanshi waizhuan* 韩诗外传. In Lau, D. C., and Chen Fong Ching, eds. *A Concordance to the Hanshi Waizhuan* (韩诗外传逐字索引). ICS series, Hong

Harbsmeier, Christoph. "Humor in Ancient Chinese Philosophy." *Philosophy East and West,* 39.3 (1989), 289-310.

Healy, Melissa. "Study finds a disputed Shakespeare play bears the master's mark." The LA Times, April 10, 2015.

Henry, Eric. "Anachronisms in *Lüshi chunqiu* and *Shuoyuan*." *Early Medieval China* 9 (2003): 127-38.

_____. "'Junzi yue' versus 'Zhongni yue' in *Zuozhuan*." *Harvard Journal of Asiatic Studies, 59.1*, 1999, 125-61.

Hightower, James Robert. *Han-shih wai-chuan: Han Ying's Illustrations of the Dialectic Application of the Classic of Songs*. Cambridge: Harvard University Press, 1952.

Hinsch, Breth, "The Composition of *Lienüzhuan*: Was Liu Xiang the Author or Editor?" *Asia Major* (third series) 20.1 (2007): 1-23.

Holzer, Rainer. *Yen-tzu und das Yen-tzu ch'un-ch'iu*. Peter Lang, Frankfurt, 1983.

Hsiao, Kung-chuan. *A History of Chinese Political Thought*. Vol. I: *From the Beginnings to the Sixth Century A.D.* Tr. F.W. Mote. Princeton: Princeton Library of Asian Translations, 1979.

Hu, Shi. *The Development of the Logical Method in Ancient China*. Shanghai: The Oriental Book Company, 1921.

*Huainanzi* 淮南子. In Lau, D. C., and Chen Fong Ching, eds. *A Concordance to the Huainanzi* 淮南子逐字索引. ICS series, Hong Kong, Commercial Press, 1992.

Hucker, Charles O. *A Dictionary of Official Titles in Imperial China*. Stanford: Stanford University Press, 1985.

Hunter, Michael. *Confucius beyond the Analects*. Studies in the History of Chinese Texts. Leiden and Boston: Brill, 2017.

Ivanhoe Philip J. Ivanhoe, "Mengzi's Conception of Courage." *Dao* 5.2 (2006): 221-34.

Jiang, Xinyan. "Confucius's View of Courage." *Journal of Chinese Philosophy,* 39.1 (2012): 44-59.

Jing, Julia. *Mysticism and Kingship in China: The Heart of Chinese Wisdom*. Cambridge studies in religious traditions. Cambridge University press, Cambridge, 1997.

700

Johnston, Ian, tr. *Mozi: A Complete Translation*. Hong Kong: Chinese University Press, 2010.

Kao, George. *Chinese Wit & Humor*. Coward-McCann, Inc. New York. 1946.

Kern, Martin. "Excavated Manuscripts and Their Socratic Pleasures: Newly Discovered Challenges in Reading the 'Airs of the States.'" *Asiatische Studien, 61.3* (2007): 775-93.

_____, ed. *Text and Ritual in Early China*. Seattle and London: University of Washington Press, 2005.

Kim, Tae Hyun, and Mark Csikszentmihalyi. "History and Formation of the *Analects*." In Amy Olberding, ed., *Dao Companion to the Analects*. Dao Companions to Chinese Philosophy 4. Dordrecht, Netherlands: Springer, 2013, 21-36.

Kinney, Anne Behnke, tr. *Exemplary Women of Early China: The* Lienü zhuan *of Liu Xiang*. New York: Columbia University Press, 2014.

Knechtges, David R. "Confucius Ridens: Humor in the *Analects*." *Harvard Journal of Asiatic Studies* 50.1 (1990): 131-61.

_____. "Wit, Humor, and Satire in Early Chinese Literature (to A.D.220)." *Monumenta Serica* 29 (1970-71), 79-98.

Knoblock, John, tr. *Xunzi: A Translation and Study of the Complete Works*. 3 vols. Stanford: Stanford University Press, 1988-94.

_____., and Jeffrey Riegel, trs. *The Annals of Lü Buwei: A Complete Translation and Study*. Stanford: Stanford University Press, 2000.

_____., and Jeffrey Riegel, trs. *Mozi* 墨子: *A Study and Translation of the Ethical and Political Writings*. China Research Monograph 68. Berkeley: Institute ofEast Asian Studies, University of California, 2013.

*Kongcongzi* 孔丛子. In Lau, D. C., and Chen Fong Ching, eds. *A Concordance to the Kongcongzi* 孔丛子逐字索引. ICS series, Hong Kong, Commercial Press, 1998.

*Kongzi jiayu* 孔子家语. In Lau, D. C., and Chen Fong Ching, eds. *A Concordance to the Kongzi jiayu* 孔子家语逐字索引. ICS series, Hong Kong, Commercial Press, 1992.

Lau, D. C., tr. *Confucius: The Analects*. 2nd edition. Hong Kong: Chinese University Press, 1992.

————. and Roger T. Ames. *Sun Bin: The Art of Warfare: A Translation of the Classic Chinese Work of Philosophy and Strategy*. Albany: SUNY, 2003.

Legge, James, tr. Ch'u Chai and Winberg Chai, eds. *Li Chi: Book of Rites. An encyclopedia of ancient ceremonial usages, religious creeds, and social institutions*. 2 vols. New Hyde Park, N.Y., University Books, 1967.

————., tr. *The Chinese Classics*, vol. 1, *Confucian Analects, The Great Learning, and the Doctrine of the Mean*. Hong Kong: Mission Press, 1861. 2nd ed. Oxford: Clarendon, 1893. Reprint, Hong Kong: Hong Kong University Press, 1960.

————., trs. *The Chinese Classics*, vol. 2, *The Works of Mencius*. Hong Kong: Mission Press, 1861. 2nd ed. Oxford: Clarendon, 1895. Reprint, Hong Kong: Hong Kong University Press, 1960.

————., tr. *The Chinese Classics*, vol. 3, *The Shoo King, or Book of Historical Documents*. London: Henry Frowde, 1865. 2nd ed. Oxford: Clarendon, 1893–1894. Reprint, Hong Kong: University of Hong Kong Press, 1960.

————., tr. *The Chinese Classics*, vol. 4, The She King. London: Trubner, 1871. Reprint, Hong Kong: Hong Kong University Press, 1960.

————., tr. *The Chinese Classics*, vol. 5, The Ch'un Ts'ew with the Tso Chuen. London: Trubner, 1872. Reprint, Hong Kong: Hong Kong University Press, 1960.

Leslie, Donald [Daniel]. Argument by Contradiction in Pre-Buddhist Chinese Reasoning. Centre of Oriental Studies Occasional Paper 4.

Canberra: Australian National University, 1964.

Li, Cheng 李成, and Chen Anzhe 陈谙哲. "Jian ben Yanzi chunqiu yu chuan shi ben dui du zha ji 简本《晏子春秋》与传世本对读札记." *Journal of Guizhou University for Nationalities*, 2017, 1, 82-92.

Li, Daoyuan 郦道元. *Shuijing zhu* 水经注. http://ctext.org/wiki. pl?if=gb&res=797784 (2006-2017).

Li, Fang 李昉 et al. *Taiping yulan* 太平御览. http://ctext.org/taiping-yulan (2006-2017).

*Liji* 礼记. In Lau, D. C., and Chen Fong Ching, eds. *A Concordance to the Liji* 礼记逐字索引. ICS series, Hong Kong, Commercial Press, 1996.

Li, Shan 李善. *Wenxuan zhu* 文选注. http://ctext.org/wiki. pl?if=gb&res=150222 (2006-2017).

Li, Wanshou 李万寿. *Yanzi chunqiu* yi zhu 晏子春秋译注. Taiwan gu ji chu ben, Taibei, 1996.

Li, Wai-yee. *The Readability of the Past in Early Chinese Historiography*. Harvard East Asian Monographs 253. Cambridge, Mass., 2007.

Lin, Xinxin 林心欣. "Yanzi chunqiu yanjiu 晏子春秋研究." MA thesis, National Sun Yat-Sen University, 2000.

Liu, Shipei 刘师培. *Zuoan ji* 左盦集. http://ctext.org/wiki. pl?if=gb&res=644473&remap=gb (2006-2016).

Liu, Wenbin 刘文斌. *Yanzichunqiu yanjiu shi* 晏子春秋研究史. Beijing: Renmin wenxue chubanshe, 2015.

Liu, Xu 刘昫. *Jiu Tangshu* 旧唐书. Beijing: Zhonghua shuju, 1975.

Loewe, Michael. *Biographical Dictionary of the Qin, Former Han and Xin Periods (221 BC-AD 24)*. Handbuch der Orientalistik IV.16. Leiden: Brill, 2000.

_____. *Chinese Ideas of Life and Death: Faith, Myth and Reason in the Han Period (206 BC-AD 220)*. London: George Allen & Unwin, 1982.

_____., ed. *Early Chinese Texts: A Bibliographical Guide*. Early China Special Monograph Series 2. Berkeley, 1993.

703

Lü, Bin 吕斌. "Chunyu Kun zhu *Yanzi chunqiu* kao 淳于髡著晏子春秋考." *Qilu Xuekan* 齐鲁学刊, (1985; 1): 73-76.

Lu, Shouzhu 卢守助. Yanzi chunqiu yi zhu 晏子春秋译注. Gu ji chu ban she, Shanghai, 2006.

*Lunheng* 论衡. In Lau, D. C., and Chen Fong Ching, eds. *A Concordance to the Lun heng* 论衡逐字索引. ICS series, Hong Kong, Commercial Press, 1996.

*Lunyu* [*The Analects*] 论语. In Lau, D. C., and Chen Fong Ching, eds. *A Concordance to the Lunyu* (论语逐字索引). ICS series, Hong Kong, Commercial Press, 1995.

*Lüshi chunqiu* 吕氏春秋. In Lau, D. C., and Chen Fong Ching, eds. *A Concordance to the Lüshi chunqiu* 吕氏春秋逐字索引. ICS series, Hong Kong, Commercial Press, 1994.

Ma, Zong 马总. *Yilin* 意林. http://ctext.org/yilin/zh (2006-2017).

Major, John S., Sarah Queen, Andrew Meyer, and Harold D. Roth. *The Huainanzi: A Guide to the Theory and Practice of Government in Early Han China*. Translations from the Asian Classics. New York: Columbia University Press, 2010.

Makeham, John. "The Formation of *Lunyu* as a Book." *Monumenta Serica* 44 (1996): 1-24.

_____. *Transmitters and Creators: Chinese Commentators and Commentaries on the* Analects. Harvard East Asian Monographs 228. Cambridge, Mass.: Harvard University Press, 2003.

Munro, Donald J., ed. *Individualism and Holism: Studies in Confucian and Taoist Values*. Michigan Monographs in Chinese Studies 52. Ann Arbor, 1985.

Maspero, Henri. *La Chine antique*. Presses Universitaires de France - PUF; Édition, Nouv. Éd, Paris, 1985.

*Mencius* 孟子. In Lau, D. C., and Chen Fong Ching, eds. *A Concordance to the Mengzi* (孟子逐字索引). ICS series, Hong Kong, Commercial

Press, 1995.

Meyer, Andrew [Seth]. "'The Altars of the Soil and Grain are Closer than Kin' 社稷戚于亲: The Qi 齐 Model of Intellectual Participation and the Jixia 稷下 Patronage Community." *Early China 33*-34 (2010-11): 37-99.

Moloughney, Brian. "History and Biography in Modern China." PhD Diss., Australian National University, 1994.

*Mozi* 墨子. In Lau, D. C., and Chen Fong Ching, eds. *A Concordance to the Mozi* (墨子逐字索引). ICS series, Hong Kong, Commercial Press, 2001.

Munro, Donald J., ed. *Individualism and Holism: Studies in Confucian and Taoist Values*. Michigan Monographs in Chinese Studies 52. Ann Arbor, 1985.

Needham, Joseph. *et al.*, eds. *Science and Civilisation in China*, vol. 3, *Mathematics and the Sciences of the Heavens and the Earth*. Cambridge: Cambridge University Press (1959): 431.

Nienhauser, William H. "Sima Qian and the *Shiji*," in Feldherr and Hardy, vol.1, (2011): 463-483.

_____ Jr., "The Implied Reader and Translation: The *Shih chi* as Example." In Eoyang and Lin, 15-40.

_____ Jr., ed. *The Grand Scribe's Records*. 9 vols. projected. Bloomington and Indianapolis: Indiana University Press, 1994.

Nylan, Michael, tr. *Yang Xiong: Exemplary Figures: Fayan*. Classics of Chinese Thought. Seattle and London: University of Washington Press, 2013.

_____ . "Sima Qian: A True Historian?" *Early China 23*-24 (1998-99): 203-46.

Olberding, Garrett P.S., ed. *Facing the Monarch: Modes of Advice in the Early Chinese Court*. Harvard East Asian Monographs 359. Cambridge, Mass., and London, 2013.

Pan, Zimu 潘自牧 *Jizuan yuanhai* 记纂渊海. http://ctext.org/wiki. pl?if=gb&res=389168 (2006-2016).

Pankenier, David W., *et al. Archaeoastronomy in East Asia: Historical Observational Records of Comets and Meteor Showers from China, Japan, and Korea.* Amherst, N.Y., Cambria, 2008.

Patt-Shamir, Galia. *To broaden the way: a Confucian-Jewish dialogue.* Lanham: Lexington Books, 2006.

Pelliot, Paul. "Un nouveau périodique oriental: *Asia Major*," *T'oung Pao* 22, (1923): 354-5.

Peterson, Willard J., *et al.*, eds. *The Power of Culture: Studies in Chinese Cultural History.* Hong Kong: Chinese University Press, 1994.

Pian, Yuqian 骈宇骞. *Yanzi chunqiu jiaoshi* 晏子春秋校释. Beijing: Shumu wenxian chubanshe, 1988.

_____. *Yinqueshan zhujian Yanzi chunqiu jiaoshi* 银雀山竹简晏子春秋校释. Taipei, Wanjuanlou tushu, 2000.

Pines, Yuri. *Foundations of Confucian Thought: Intellectual Life in the Chunqiu Period, 722-453 B.C.E.* Honolulu: University of Hawaii Press, 2002.

_____. "Friends or Foes: Changing Concepts of Ruler-Minister Relations and the Notion of Loyalty in Pre-Imperial China." *Monumenta Serica* 50 (2002), 35-74.

_____. "From Teachers to Subjects: Ministers Speaking to the Rulers, from Yan Ying 晏婴 to Li Si 李斯." In Garrett P. S. Olberding, ed. *Facing the Monarch*: *Modes of Advice in the Early Chinese Court*, Harvard East Asian Monographs 359, Cambridge, Mass., and London (2013): 70-80.

_____., *et al.*, eds. *Ideology of Power and Power of Ideology in Early China.* Sinica Leidensia 124. Leiden and Boston: Brill, 2015.

_____. "Rethinking the Origins of Chinese Historiography: The *Zuo Zhuan* Revisited" *Journal of Chinese Studies*, The Chinese University of Hong Kong, 49 (2009): 429-442.

Plaks, Andrew, tr. *Ta Hsüeh and Chung Yung (The Highest Order of Cultivation and On the Practice of the Mean).* Harmondsworth: Penguin, 2003.

_____. "*Xin* 心 as the Seat of Emotions in Confucian Self-Cultivation." In Santangelo and Guida, 113-25.

Poo, Mu-chou. *In Search of Personal Welfare: A View of Ancient Chinese Religion.* SUNY Series in Chinese Philosophy and Culture. Albany (1998): 29-30.

_____. "The Use and Abuse of Wine in Ancient China." *Journal of the Economic and Social History of the Orient,* 42.2, 1999.

Rand, Christopher C. *Military Thought in Early China.* Albany: SUNY, 2017.

Rickett, W. Allyn, tr. *Guanzi: Political, Economic, and Philosophical Essays from Early China.* 2 vols. Princeton Library of Asian Translations. Princeton, 1985-98.

Rubin, Vitaly A. *Individual and State in Ancient China: Essays on Four Chinese Philosophers.* Tr. Steven I Levine. New York: Columbia University Press, 1976.

Santangelo, Paolo, and Donatella Guida, eds. Love, Hatred, and Other *Passions: Questions and Themes on Emotions in Chinese Civilization.* Leiden: Brill, 2006.

Sato, Masayuki. *The Confucian Quest for Order: The Origin and Formation of the Political Thought of Xun Zi.* Sinica Leidensia 58. Leiden: Brill, 2003.

Schaberg, David. *A Patterned Past: Form and Thought in Early Chinese Historiography.* Harvard East Asian Monographs 205. Cambridge, Mass., and London, 2001.

_____. "Platitude and Persona: *Junzi* Comments in *Zuozhuan* and Beyond." In Helwig Schmidt-Glintzer, *et al.,* eds. *Historical Truth,*

LIBRARY OF CHINESE CLASSICS

707

*Historical Criticism, and Ideology: Chinese Historiography and Historical Culture from a New Comparative Perspective.* Leiden Studies in Comparative Historiography 1. Leiden and Boston: Brill, (2005): 177-96.

*Shangshu* 尚书. In Lau, D. C., and Chen Fong Ching, eds. *A Concordance to the Shangshu* 尚书逐字索引. ICS series, Hong Kong, Commercial Press, 1995.

Scharfstein, Ben-Ami. *The Dilemma of Context*. New York: New York University Press, 1989.

Schwartz, Benjamin I. *The World of Thought in Ancient China*. Cambridge, Mass., and London: Harvard University Press, Belknap Press, 1985.

*Shijing* 诗经. In Lau, D. C., and Chen Fong Ching, eds. *A Concordance to the Maoshi* 毛诗逐字索引. ICS series, Hong Kong, Commercial Press, 1995.

Shi, Lei 石磊. *Yanzi chunqiu zhuyi* 晏子春秋注译. Haerbin Shi: Heilong Jiang ren min chu ban she, 2003.

Shih, Hsiang-lin. "*Yanzi chunqiu.*" In Knechtges and Chang, eds. *Ancient and Early Medieval Chinese Literature: A Reference Guide*, 1868-1873. Leiden [Netherlands]; Boston: Brill, 2010-2014.

Sima, Qian 司马迁. *Shiji* 史记. Beijing: Zhonghua shuju, 1959.

*Shuoyuan* 说苑. In Lau, D. C., and Chen Fong Ching, eds. *A Concordance to the Shuoyuan* (说苑逐字索引). ICS series, Hong Kong, Commercial Press, 1992.

Sivin, Nathan. "State, Cosmos, and Body in the Last Three Centuries B.C." *Harvard Journal of Asiatic Studies* 55.1 (1995): 5-37.

Smart, R. "How Yanzi Fulfills his Responsibilities as Minister in the Rhetorical Techniques within the *jian* (Remonstrance) of the *Yanzi chun qiu.*" MA Thesis, University of Canterbury, 2008.

Stevenson, Mark and Wu Cuncun, eds. *Homoeroticism in Imperial China: A Sourcebook*. Routledge, New York, 2013.

Sterckx, Roel, ed. *Of Tripod and Palate: Food, Politics, and Religion in Traditional China*. New York: Palgrave Macmillan, 2005.

Sun, Xingyan 孙星衍. *Yanzi chunqiu yinyi* 晏子春秋音义. In *Yanzi Chunqiu* 晏子春秋, *Sibu beiyao* 四部备要, Shangha: Zhonghua shuju, Vol. 53, 1989.

T'ang, Chün-i. "The T'ien Ming (Heavenly Ordinance) in Pre-Ch'in China." *Philosophy East and West* 11 (1961): 195-218; 12 (1962): 29-49.

Tang, Hua 汤化. *Yanzi Chunqiu yi zhu* 晏子春秋译注. Beijing: Zhong hua shu ju, 2011.

Tao, Meisheng 陶梅生. *Xinyi Yanzi chunqiu* 新译晏子春秋. Taibei: San min shu ju gu fen you xian gong si, Min guo, 1998.

Tauber, Zvi. *Heinrich Heine interkulturell gelesen*. Nordhausen: Traugott Bautz, 2006.

Tjan, Tjoe Som, tr. *Po Hu T'ung: The Comprehensive Discussions in the White Tiger Hall*. 2 vols. Sinica Leidensia 6. Leiden: E.J. Brill, 1949-52.

Tu Wei-ming. *Humanity and Self-Cultivation: Essays in Confucian Thought*. Berkeley: Asian Humanities Press, 1979; rpt., Boston: Cheng & Tsui, 1998.

_____. *Way, Learning, and Politics: Essays on the Confucian Intellectual*. SUNY Series in Chinese Philosophy and Culture. Singapore: Institute of East Asian Philosophies, 1989; rpt., Albany, 1993.

Tuo, tuo 脱脱. *Songshi* 宋史. Beijing: Zhonghua shuju, 1977.

Van Der Loon, Piet. "On the Transmission of the *Kuan-tzu*." *T'oung Pao* 41 (1952): 358-393.

Van Els, Paul, and Sarah A. Queen, eds. *Between History and Philosophy: Anecdotes in Early China*. SUNY Series in Chinese Philosophy and Culture. Albany, 2017.

Van Ess, Hans, *et al.*, eds. *Views from Within, Views from Beyond:*

709

*Approaches to the* Shiji *as an Early Work of Historiography*. Lun Wen: Studien zur Geistesgeschichte und Literatur in China 20. Wiesbaden: Harrassowitz, 2015.

————. "Reflections on the Sequence of the First Three Books of the *Mengzi.*" *Journal of Chinese Philosophy* 41.3-4 (2014): 287-306.

Van Norden, Bryan W. "Mencius on Courage." *Midwest Studies in Philosophy* 21 (1997): 237-56;

Waley, Arthur, tr. *The Book of Songs: The Ancient Chinese Classic of Poetry*. Ed. Joseph R. Allen. New York: Grove, 1996 [1937].

Walker, Richard. "Some Notes on the *Yen-tzu ch'un-ch'iu.*" *Journal of the American Oriental Society*, 73.3, (1953): 156-163.

————. *The Multi-State System of Ancient China*. Hamden CT.: Shoe String Press, 1953.

Wang, Gengsheng 王更生. *Xin bian Yanzi chun qiu* 新编晏子春秋. Taibei: Taiwan gu ji chu ban gong si, 2001.

————. *Yanzi chunqiu jin zhu jin yi* 晏子春秋今注今译. Taibei: Shang wu yin shu guan, 1987.

————. *Yanzi chunqiu yanjiu* 晏子春秋研究. Taibei: Wen shi zhe chu ban he, 1976.

Wang, Qinruo 王钦若. *Cefu Yuangui* 册府元龟. http://ctext.org/wiki. pl?if=gb&res=903155 (2006-2017).

Wang, Yaochen 王尧臣. *Chongwen zongmu* 崇文总目. http://ctext.org/ wiki.pl?if=gb&res=285530 (2006-2017).

Wang, Yinglin 王应麟. *Han Yiwenzhi kaozheng* 汉艺文志考证. http://ctext. org/wiki.pl?if=gb&res=816933 (2006-2017).

————. *Yuhai* 玉海. http://ctext.org/wiki.pl?if=gb&res=945969 (2006-2017).

Watson, Burton. *Early Chinese Literature*. New York: Columbia University Press, 1962.

Wei, Zheng 魏征. *Jianlu* 谏录. http://ctext.org/wiki.pl?if=en&res=312766

(2006-2017).

_____. *Qun shu zhi yao* 群书治要. http://ctext.org/qunshu-zhiyao/zh (2006-2017).

Weingarten, Oliver. "Chunyu Kun: Motifs, Narratives, and Personas in Early Chinese Anecdotal Literature." *Journal of the Royal Asiatic Society* 27.3 (2017): 501-521.

_____. "Debates around Jixia: Argument and Intertextuality in Warring States Writings Associated with Qi." *Journal of the American Oriental Society* 135.2 (2015): 283-307.

Wu, Jiulong 吴九龙. *Yinqueshan Han jian shiwen* 银雀山汉简释文. Beijing: Wen wu chu ban she, 1985.

Wu, Shu 吴淑. *Shilei fu zhu* 事类赋注. http://ctext.org/wiki.pl?if=gb&res=101067 (2006-2016).

Wu, Shouyang 吴寿旸. *Bai jing lou cangshu tiba ji* 拜经楼藏书题跋记. http://ctext.org/wiki.pl?if=gb&chapter=105945#晏子春秋 (2006-2017).

Wu, Ze-yu 吴则虞. *Yanzi chunqiu jishi* 晏子春秋集释, 2 vols. Beijing: Zhonghua shuju, 1962.

_____. (*Zeng ding ben*) *Yanzi chunqiu jishi* (增订本) 晏子春秋集释. Beijing: tushuguan chuban, 2011.

Wylie, Alexander. *Notes on Chinese Literature*. Shanghai: Presbyterian Mission Press, 1867.

*Xunzi* 荀子. In Lau, D. C., and Chen Fong Ching, eds. *A Concordance to the Xunzi* (荀子逐字索引). ICS series, Hong Kong, Commercial Press, 1996.

Yan, Lingfeng 严灵峰. *Zhou Qin Han Wei zhuzi zhijian shumu* 周秦汉魏诸子知见书目. Taibei: Zheng zhong shu ju. 1975-1979.

Yang, Li. "The Formation and Circulation of Early Yanzi Lore, Fourth Century B.C. – Third Century A.D." PhD Diss., University of Washington, 2016.

*Yantielun* 盐铁论. In Lau, D. C., and Chen Fong Ching, eds. *A Concordance*

711

to the Yantielun 盐铁论逐字索引. ICS series, Hong Kong, Commercial Press, 1994.

*Yanzi Chunqiu* 晏子春秋. In In Lau, D. C., and Chen Fong Ching, eds. *A Concordance to the Yanzi Chunqiu* 晏春秋逐字索引. ICS series, Hong Kong, Commercial Press, 1994.

*Yanzi Chunqiu* 晏子春秋, *Sibu beiyao* 四部备要. Beijing: Zhong hua shu ju 中华书局, (1989): Vol. 53, 3-49.

*Yanzi Chunqiu* 晏子春秋. Sibu congkan 四部丛刊. http://ctext.org/library. pl?if=gb&res=77386 (2006-2017).

*Yanzi Chunqiu* 晏子春秋. Siku Quanshu 四库全书. http://ctext.org/library. pl?if=gb&file=62378&page=1 (2006-2017).

Yearley, Lee H. *Mencius and Aquinas: Theories of Virtue and Conceptions of Courage.* SUNY Series, Toward a Comparative Philosophy of Religions. Albany: 1990.

*Yili*, 仪礼. In Lau, D. C., and Chen Fong Ching, eds. *A Concordance to the Yili* 仪礼逐字索引. ICS series, Hong Kong, Commercial Press, 1994.

*Yinqueshan Han mu zujian (yi)* 银雀山汉墓竹简 (壹). Beijing: Wenwu chubanshe, 1985.

*Zhan guo ce* 战国策. In Lau, D. C., and Chen Fong Ching, eds. *A Concordance to the Zhan guo ce* 战国策逐字索引. ICS series, Hong Kong, Commercial Press, 1992.

Zhang, Chunyi 张纯一 *Yanzi chunqiu jiaozhu* 晏子春秋校注. In *Xinbian Zhuzi jicheng* 新编诸子集成, Vol. 6. Taibei, Shijie shuju, 1972.

Zhang, Jingxian 张景贤. *Yanzi chunqiu zhuyi* 晏子春秋注译. Zheng zhou: Zhong zhou gu ji chu ban she, 2010.

Zhang, Ping. "Killing Not to Kill — Chosenness in the Stories of *Akedah* and Yu Rang 豫让." *Journal of Chinese Philosophy,* 41.s1 (2014): 669-85.

————., tr. *The Mishnah – Seder Zeraim* 密释纳 —— 种子. Jinan: Shangdong University Press 山东大学出版社, 2011.

Zhang, Shoujie. 张守节. *Shiji zhengyi* 史记正义. http://ctext.org/wiki.
  pl?if=gb&chapter=423039 (2006-2017).

Zhao, Kuifu 赵逵夫. "Yanzichunqiu wei Qiren Chunyu Kun biancheng kao
  晏子春秋为齐人淳于髡编成考."*Guangmingribao* 光明日报, 2005, 1;
  28.

*Zhuangzi* 庄子. In Lau, D. C., and Chen Fong Ching, eds. *A Concordance
  to the Zhuangzi* 庄子逐字索引. ICS series, Hong Kong, Commercial
  Press, 2000.

# Acknowledgements

This book owes its completion to the immense moral and erudite support that I have received from my life-long friends and colleagues, Ben-Ami Scharfstein, Andrew Plaks, Zhang Ping and Ronald Kiener. This group of four *talmidei chachamim* ("wise sages") expended enormous amounts of their time scrutinizing every word in my drafts and steering my translation towards a solid path. Their vast patience, astute textual criticism and inexhaustible insight provided me with unending inspiration and confidence, all of which brought "my" *YZCQ* to fruition.

Yuri Pines meticulously reviewed my introduction and made many helpful comments; Michael Nylan scrutinized several parts of an early version of my translation, correcting errors and suggesting excellent alternatives; Eric Henry and David Schaberg were generous in sharing several chapters of their translations of the *Shuoyuan* and *Zuozhuan* from which I benefited tremendously — my sincere gratitude is extended to all four of them.

My students, Inbal Shamir, Sharon Small and Nadav Yanai regarded my work on the *YZCQ* as their own project, catering to every one of my bibliographical needs. I owe them a debt of gratitude.

I also would like to express thanks to Tracy Liu, Janie Steen, Hephzibah Levin, Wang Liping and Christa Schell, who helped me during various stages of preparation of this book.

I am grateful to the two co-heads of the Confucius Institute at Tel Aviv University, Wu Yang and Asaf Goldschmidt, for introducing my translation of the *YZCQ* to the China Renmin University Press, and to Meng Chao who accepted the book for publication on behalf of Renmin University Press and submitted it for inclusion in the Library of Chinese Classics series. The fact that "my" *YZCQ* is now being published not only in China but also by these two distinguished organizations is fulfillment of a life-long dream.

Special heartfelt thanks are due to Shlomo Biderman, Zvi Tauber, Galia Pat-Shamir, and Abraham Meidan. They were emotionally involved with every stage of this project and provided me not only moral support and intellectual stimulation, but also a profound sense of friendship which fueled my work with a sense of worth.

Alas, my bosom friends, Akiva Baum — Aki, Dan Daor — Dani, Iris Mor — *Mutzkale*, and Ovadia Ezra are no longer with us. I will keep their image in my mind forever.

The close circle of my family tribe: Hagar, Rafi, Yael, Inbal, Naama, Ginat, Chen, Gur, Adam and Idan — now Dr. Idan Ariel — are the air I breathe.

Finally, Raya, this book is now yours.

大中华文库

**图书在版编目（CIP）数据**

晏子春秋：英汉对照 /（以）欧永福（Yoav Ariel）英译、导言、注释；张飘，刘喆今译 . —北京：中国人民大学出版社，2018.9
（大中华文库）

ISBN 978-7-300-26113-3

Ⅰ . ①晏… Ⅱ . ①欧… ②张… ③刘… Ⅲ . ①英语—汉语—对照读物 ②先秦哲学 Ⅳ . ① H319.4：B

中国版本图书馆 CIP 数据核字（2018）第 191046 号

出版策划：刘光宇 黄 婷
责任编辑：王 琼 吴振良

**大中华文库**

**晏子春秋**

[ 以色列 ] 欧永福 导言、注释、翻译
张 飘 刘 喆 今译

© 2018 中国人民大学出版社
**出版发行：**
中国人民大学出版社
（北京中关村大街 31 号）
邮政编码 100080
http://www.crup.com.cn
电话：008610-62511242（总编室）
 008610-62515195（发行公司）
 008610-62514303（版权部）

**印刷：**
涿州市星河印刷有限公司
**开本：**153mm×233mm 1/16 **印张：**52.75
2018 年 10 月第 1 版第 2 次印刷
（汉英）
ISBN 978-7-300-26113-3
（精装）
定价：298.00 元